David Lee Clark

1937

LITERARY OPINION IN AMERICA

LITERARY OPINION
IN AMERICA

Essays Illustrating the Status, Methods,
and Problems of Criticism in the
United States Since the War

EDITED, WITH AN INTRODUCTION BY
MORTON DAUWEN ZABEL

1937

HARPER & BROTHERS
NEW YORK   LONDON

PN771
Z2

FOREWORD

Tʜɪs book offers a selection of fifty American critical essays of the past
twenty years. They appear in an arrangement that attempts to show the
conditions under which critics have written about modern literature, and
the problems they have faced, during a period which, while it has encouraged a vigorous revival of critical activity, has been a time of unusual instability and has provided almost every possible incentive toward
confusing our understanding of what a critic's responsibility must be.
The first section of the volume, "Versions of Tradition and Responsibility," presents a number of statements of critical duty and outlook by
writers who began their activities before 1920 and prepared the situation
in which their followers have worked. The second, "The Individual
Talent," is made up of discussions of writers whose work illustrates in
significant ways the temper and art of the past two decades. The third,
"Prospects and Determinations," gives a group of essays which aim to
define the immediate predicament of creative literature, and the status
and possible advantages at which the critic has arrived after the conflicts
and experiments of the past quarter-century. Here, at whatever hazards,
some effort is made to present the task confronting critics in the coming
decade.

It will be immediately apparent that there is as little community of
method and beliefs among these critics as among the talents they discuss. But they have at least been agreed on the business of discovering
the quality of their subjects, either in terms of the conditions and influences under which these men have written, or through their integrity
and originality as craftsmen. Three possible divisions may be made in
the nature of the essays included here. One portion of them states, from
contrasting positions, principles of critical intelligence and obligation, in
reference both to past traditions and to present and impending creative
problems. A second studies the conditions, personal or social, that have
influenced writing during the past three decades and shaped the character and material of the artist. A third is made up of demonstrations in
critical technique and analyses of esthetic form and style. These have
been allowed a major share of the pages in order to avoid that emphasis
on abstract theory which usually prevents a critic and his reader from
understanding how the ideal qualities of art actually get into the work
of poetry or fiction. It will be noticed that a number of the critics
whose work falls under these headings are themselves creative writers
of distinction. Their presence here is to be emphasized, since the co-

iii

incidence of the creative and the critical talents is a notable feature of
literary activity in recent years. The reference in their discussions to
problems as specifically American as they can be so limited intelligently
is, of course, another factor that has been kept in mind in bringing
coherence into this collection, although it will be at once noticed from
the table of contents that the writers discussed are of no one nationality
and that they include figures who indicate the modern creative problem
in much more than a local or historical sense.

While several critics of the foregoing generation are included by way
of marking a transition toward present-day critical attitudes or for the
anticipations they gave of the difficulties younger writers have faced,
emphasis has been placed on critics whose work has appeared, stated
typical arguments, and exhibited a firmness of opinion or method during the past ten years. This book is not a collaborative project. Its entries support neither a common point of view nor the beliefs and prejudices of the editor. It finds its unity chiefly in a general recognition
among its contributors of what literary quality and distinction are, and
in an approach toward them from recognized requirements of sensitiveness, sympathy, and taste. Its essays have been chosen from American
books and magazines, and in selecting material from the latter it has
been the intention to show the importance of the independent and experimental journals that have been devoted to modern literature in the
United States during the past twenty years. While their work—usually
short-lived in the item but nevertheless continuous in effect—has been
inadequately represented, their titles have been more fully indexed at
the end of the book, where the reader will also find lists of books and
collections of criticism to be consulted in amplifying the study of modern
literature for which, it is hoped, this volume will supply a program and
an incentive.

There are two kinds of anthology which escape the simpler forms of
critical rebuke. One offers an impersonal survey of a field or historical
period, as objective and representative as scholarship and common acceptance can make it. The other develops an editorial argument, a
"criticism by selection," from a specified or emphatically personal point
of view. The present collection enjoys neither of these advantages,
though it has borrowed something from each. It covers a quarter-
century which is still too recent in its experiences and ideas to allow for
historical detachment or agreement. And it has not been the purpose of
the editor to illustrate a special critical thesis. Such specialization has
been the benefit—and the limitation—of three or four recent collections
of American criticism illustrating the impressionist, the humanist, or the
communist arguments. Their profit exists in their singleness and certainty of purpose. The reader is told at the outset what he may expect

to find. Their handicap appears when they show, all too soon, what the reader has no hope of finding, for the more specialized an argument or doctrine is, the more certain it becomes that what will be missing is literary criticism itself. Such books usually end by convincing us that while "the 'greatness' of literature cannot be determined solely by literary standards" (as one distinguished modern critic has recently pointed out) "we must remember that whether it is literature or not can be determined only by literary standards."

In choosing and arranging these fifty critical essays, it has been the purpose to show what such standards count for in America today, how they emerge from the past or develop in the present, and how the recognition of them can come only through responsibility toward criticism as a craft in itself, unconfused by the techniques, sciences, forms of belief, or personal and popularizing motives which are today largely pre-empting its authority. One of the claims of these critics to seriousness comes from their recognition of what these external distractions are, what they arise from in the social and moral adjustments of the age, to what place they must be relegated in the task of esthetic evaluation, and what part they play in deciding the values of literature *after* its existence and quality as literature have first been determined. The only way to rid criticism of its confusions is to show what they are. Their part in shaping the writer or writing under consideration will be an initial problem for the critic who wants to determine their influence on his own thought and to assign it to a proper place in his equipment. In an age like the present, where special doctrines of every type, from moral and psychological to political and social, are arming the believer but weakening the critic, it is necessary to show what a critic may count on to survive in his craft after he has been convinced in his beliefs. Some of the essays in this book are on writers rather than on writing. Several deal with popular ideas or social influences that have affected post-War talents, in contrast to the extreme repudiation of popular compromises asserted by other writers of the period. A few are written from obvious doctrinal positions. These are a necessary part of the book's purpose. They show the role played by literary criticism in what Van Wyck Brooks has defined as a general critical movement in our national life, and it is chiefly through their intelligent sense of that tendency that the serious critics of the United States at any time, but especially during the past twenty-five years, have done much of their most valuable work.

It has been necessary to avoid here two activities that are usually hostile to an active tradition of criticism in America: popular book reviewing and academic scholarship. Their omission has deprived the volume of several distinguished and influential names, but each is provided for elsewhere far too lavishly to require the services of a book like this. The absence of historical and philosophic scholarship is especially regrettable since the genuine part of it is in any age or country a noble achievement, without which the labors of students and critics are easily misspent. But that it is rarely concerned with the existing conditions of creative literature, and that its formulations are seldom tested by the active problems and practices of writers, are disadvantages to which intelligent correctives have barely begun to be applied. The loss of literary journalists and reviewers entails less regret. A number of these have written valuable propaganda for modern books and writers; a few, like H. L. Mencken, have prepared the day for remarkable gains in creative writing itself; others have done work in the Americanization of the literary viewpoint which cannot be discounted in deciding the strength of contemporary art in the United States. But for the most part this activity has nothing to do with criticism. It is an adjunct of the book-trade, of high-pressure literary promotion, of book-clubs, advertising, and the business of exploitation that has gradually deprived the country of its few reputable literary monthlies and reviews. To such service many lively writers have surrendered their talents, but to include them here would be to surrender for this collection the ideal that Henry James imposed on any project which undertakes to consider literature as something more than a commercial commodity: "a plea for Criticism, for Discrimination, for Appreciation on other than infantile lines—as against the so almost universal Anglo-Saxon absence of these things; which tends, in our general trade, it seems to me, to break the heart."

Literary criticism may still be what Poe and Lowell feared of it: the most immature aspect of American literature. If it is, its shortcomings are part of a larger immaturity, that of the critical faculty in American life. (There is no cause here to feel a special affliction in American culture. Coleridge, Hazlitt, Arnold, and Mr. Richards have been baffled by an equal distress and deficiency in their country during the past century. "The so almost universal Anglo-Saxon absence of these things" is not merely a matter of the brevity or provinciality of our literary history.) Opinions on this will differ, but they will hardly disagree on the claim that if there has been a conscious effort toward serious critical responsibility in the United States, it has taken place during the past thirty years, and that what the critic of literature has achieved in that time has been gained under the stimulus of a wider doubt and skepticism in the spheres of social and political thought. Such skepticism has risen at a time when literature itself was enjoying a phenomenal modern revival, a huge public enthusiasm, a popular following outdistancing anything of its kind in the earlier history of the country. These two activities may appear to have operated at odds with one another. Actually it has not been so. The variety and fervor of the one stimulated the factional differences and disputes of the other; while creative artists were producing something to think about, dissect, and evaluate, critics, freed of the provincial clannishness and somnolence of more complacent eras, were sharpening their wits and their tools on the material thus supplied them. The most obvious sign of their awakening came in the succession of critical magazines that have appeared and vanished, but nevertheless formed a channel of expression, between 1912 and the present day. Their styles and personalities have been of all varieties. Some have lived out their short careers as purely personal organs. But they have had the advantage of complete independence from commercial influence and have been devoted to the work of reading books intelligently and judging them with some degree of impartial and technical seriousness. Some of these periodicals—*The Seven Arts, The Dial, Poetry, The Little Review, The Hound and Horn, The Symposium, The American Review, The Southern Review*, as well as the literary departments of weeklies like *The New Republic* and *The Nation*—had no predecessors in the particular work they accomplished for the American reading public. It has been an intention of this book to show the results of their work, to print specimens of the best of it, and to show how they refreshed and stimulated critical thinking at a time when commercial exploitation and the confusions of politics have tended to cancel the gains in critical awareness that were achieved during and just after the War.

The avoidance of partisan extremes has been a more difficult problem. Political bias (literary or otherwise) has grown in recent years largely through the necessities of social belief: often—and healthily—as a corrective to the irresponsibility of the impressionist or "liberal" viewpoints, but equally often as a substitute for the more difficult labor of discriminating and stating the literary values without which no amount of other value can make a piece of writing worth the critic's attention. Several distinguished critics have simplified their problems in this way to such an extent that their services to their own cause (in sanctioning or repudiating whatever fits or disagrees with their doctrines, regardless of the existence of esthetic qualities which are fast becoming one of the few trustworthy indexes to desirable qualities in life and human nature itself) must now be as dubious as their status in the critical field. The writers chosen here to represent such points of views have been included less for their eloquence on behalf of moral or humanitarian truths than because they show some signs of realizing the force of these truths in terms of the only evidence permitted to the critic—that of the literary craft, and of the virtues or deficiencies which alone make such evidence admissible as proof.

At the same time the problems now confronting critics who are also men of convinced beliefs demand attention. They appear especially in the third section of this volume, where some of the social and moral controversies of the past eight years are outlined. Obviously a major issue in the present decade is that of social thought and propaganda in literature. To slight it, even under the conviction that the critic's specific duty begins far behind the political or social argument, would be to misrepresent the situation of the immediate moment. The critics who present that issue are men who see it in its larger setting, and who have not simplified their work or nullified their critical authority by depending on extraneous apologetics or the heated pressure of their cause.

Omissions always irk an anthologist, even when he has no ambition toward impartiality. One of the first to be noticed here is the work of Ezra Pound, whose critical activity, like his creative, has made up in vigor and seminal energy for what it has lacked in finish and analysis, and formed an early spur to more severe discrimination of poetic and fictional qualities among modern writers. Difficulties of copyright have made it impossible to include portions of such books as *Pavannes and Divisions, Instigations,* and *Make It New,* but the reader must supply from these his essays on "Henry James" and "How to Read" which were planned for inclusion in Part I. The study of the American past in its relation to modern writers has been necessarily slighted, and thus the problems suggested by Van Wyck Brooks, H. L. Mencken, and John Crowe Ransom lack the reinforcement of such social or historical studies as those of Lewis Mumford (in *The Golden Day, Herman Melville, The Brown Decades*), Bernard De Voto (in *Mark Twain's America*), and Matthew Josephson (in *Portrait of the Artist as an American*). These books are in any case difficult to represent in short excerpts. Some of the writers who first defined the difficulties of the present generation twenty or more years ago (Randolph Bourne in *The History of a Literary Radical,* Harold E. Stearns in *America and the Young Intellectual*) have given way to critics of more recent appearance or complete development. If there had been a possibility of representing more fully the best in current literary journalism, it would have been chosen from the reviews of Mary M. Colum, Mark Van Doren, T. S. Matthews, Clifton Fadiman, Louis Kronenberger, John Chamberlain, and Peter Monro Jack. A similar curtailment has had to be enforced in the case of several scholarly students of modern literature, particularly T. K. Whipple, F. O. Matthiessen, F. Cudworth Flint, James Burnham, Cleanth Brooks and Joseph Warren Beach. If space had allowed, a fuller representation might also have been given to the controversies which have excited critics in the past three decades: that on realism which engaged the attention of Bourne, Brooks, Mumford, Mencken, and their colleagues of the War years; that on Humanism which culminated at the end of the

Twenties (summarized in two anthologies, *Humanism in America* and *The Critique of Humanism*); and that, more recently, on the issue of Marxist doctrine in literature, which might have been shown by contrasting arguments from Granville Hicks' *The Great Tradition* and James T. Farrell's *A Note on Literary Criticism*. The ideas of these critics are not left unrepresented, however, and the reader must be trusted to use the present essays as indications of the terms and conditions under which such viewpoints have been argued.

The reader or teacher will, in fact, find this book profitable to the degree in which he makes it an opportunity to become a critic himself, to disagree with the critics who speak here, to compare their findings, and to decide how the skill at reading and writing that has brought them into the same company can be achieved—and possibly improved— by studying the problems of modern literature.

Acknowledgments

The editor acknowledges with gratitude the courtesy of the contributors to this volume, whose kind permission to have their work included has made the collection possible. In several cases they have written new essays or made extensive revisions of earlier ones; for this, special thanks are due to Miss Marianne Moore and Miss Louise Bogan, and to Horace Gregory, Philip Blair Rice, Theodore Spencer, William Troy, and Stark Young. The editor is further indebted to T. S. Eliot for permission to include two essays, "Experiment in Criticism" and "Poetry and Propaganda," which have not been collected in his books of prose; they are reprinted here from *The Bookman* of New York because of their value in discussing questions of special significance to American critics during the years covered by this anthology.

For permission to use material from copyrighted volumes, thanks are due to Arrow Editions, New York, for essays by R. P. Blackmur and Yvor Winters; E. P. Dutton and Co., Inc., for an essay by Van Wyck Brooks; Harcourt, Brace and Co., Inc., for essays by Kenneth Burke, T. S. Eliot, and J. E. Spingarn; Houghton Mifflin Company for an essay by Irving Babbitt; Alfred A. Knopf, Inc., for an essay by H. L. Mencken; the Princeton University Press for an essay by Paul Elmer More; and Charles Scribner's Sons for essays by George Santayana, Allen Tate, and Edmund Wilson.

Acknowledgement is also made for material reproduced from magazines: to Seward Collins, editor of *The American Review* and *The Bookman,* for contributions by T. S. Eliot, John Crowe Ransom, George N. Shuster, and Robert Penn Warren; to *The Commonweal* for one essay; to Miss Marianne Moore, the last editor of *The Dial,* for essays by Robert Morss Lovett and Charles K. Trueblood; to Lincoln Kirstein, editor of *The Hound and Horn,* for essays by R. P. Blackmur, Francis Fergusson, Marianne Moore, and Yvor Winters; to *The Nation* for one essay by Newton Arvin and three by Joseph Wood Krutch; to *The New Republic* for essays and reviews by Louise Bogan, Robert Cantwell, Malcolm Cowley, Robert Morss Lovett, and Stark Young; to *The Partisan Review* for an article by Horace Gregory; to *Poetry: A Magazine of Verse* for contributions by Louise Bogan, Marianne Moore, William Phillips and Philip Rahv, and Yvor Winters; to *The Southern Review* for a portion of one essay; and to James Burnham, editor of *The Symposium,* for essays by Robert Cantwell, Philip Blair Rice, and William Troy. Of several other entries earlier versions or serial publication appeared in *The American Review* (Paul Elmer More), *The Bookman* (Kenneth Burke), *The Dial* (Kenneth Burke and George Santayana), *The Forum* (Irving Babbitt), *The Hound and Horn* (Allen Tate), *The Nation* (Allen Tate), *The New Republic* (Edmund Wilson), and *Poetry: A Magazine of Verse* (Allen Tate). More specific acknowledgement to these publications is made in footnotes under the titles of individual essays.

For special favors in connection with the publication of this book the editor is grateful to Horace Gregory, Charles A. Madison, R. P. Blackmur, Van Wyck Brooks, Kenneth Burke, Marianne Moore, Edmund Wilson, George Santayana, and the late Paul Elmer More.

It should be said that while, in spite of the intractable condition of English orthography, an effort has been made in printing this book to standardize the spelling of the original texts, this has not been done with practices of capitalization and punctuation, which are largely a privilege of style. Titles of books or whole works have been set in italics, however; those of short or partial works in quotation marks.

It will also be apparent that these essays are not to be dated by the year in which this book is published. The credit-lines show as closely as possible when they were written. Several of the authors have brought their discussions up to date by revision or have added qualifying notes by way of observing recent aspects of their topics. The value of these discussions lies partly in what they show of critical developments since 1918, and it has not been considered advisable to alter essays that do this to advantage.

CONTENTS

Introduction xv

Part I

VERSIONS OF TRADITION AND RESPONSIBILITY

T. S. ELIOT
Tradition and the Individual Talent 3
Experiment in Criticism 11
Poetry and Propaganda 25

VAN WYCK BROOKS
The Critical Movement in America 39

IRVING BABBITT
The Critic and American Life 50

PAUL ELMER MORE
How to Read "Lycidas" 68

J. E. SPINGARN
The American Critic 83

H. L. MENCKEN
The American Novel 96

JOHN CROWE RANSOM
The Esthetic of Regionalism 106

GEORGE SANTAYANA
Penitent Art 122
Tragic Philosophy 129

Part II

THE INDIVIDUAL TALENT

EDMUND WILSON
James Joyce 145
T. S. Eliot 177

CONTENTS

ALLEN TATE

Hart Crane 206

Ezra Pound 218

MARIANNE MOORE

Henry James as a Characteristic American 225

The Poetry of Wallace Stevens 233

YVOR WINTERS

Traditional Mastery: The Lyrics of Robert Bridges . . 237

Robinson Jeffers 245

CHARLES K. TRUEBLOOD

Emily Dickinson 251

THEODORE SPENCER

The Later Poetry of W. B. Yeats 263

STARK YOUNG

American Drama in Production

I: Mourning Becomes Electra, by Eugene O'Neill . . 278

II: Street Scene, by Elmer Rice 287

III: Winterset, by Maxwell Anderson 292

JOSEPH WOOD KRUTCH

Three Types of American Playwright

I: The Austerity of George Kelly 296

II: The Comic Wisdom of S. N. Behrman . . . 302

III: The Dramatic Variety of Sidney Howard . . . 308

FRANCIS FERGUSSON

Eugene O'Neill 314

ROBERT MORSS LOVETT

Three Phases of Post-War Fiction

I: The Promise of Sherwood Anderson 327

II: An Interpreter of American Life 332

III: Vanity Fair Up-to-Date 336

WILLIAM TROY

Virginia Woolf: The Novel of Sensibility 340

ROBERT PENN WARREN
The Hamlet of Thomas Wolfe 359
T. S. Stribling: A Paragraph in the History of Critical
Realism 372

LOUISE BOGAN
Viola Meynell 390

MORTON DAUWEN ZABEL
Four Poets in America
I: Robinson 397
II: Sandburg's Testament 406
III: Cinema of Hamlet 415
IV: A Literalist of the Imagination 426

GEORGE N. SHUSTER
François Mauriac 437

PHILIP BLAIR RICE
Paul Valéry 455

Part III

PROSPECTS AND DETERMINATIONS

KENNETH BURKE
Psychology and Form 469
Thomas Mann and André Gide 482

MALCOLM COWLEY
John Dos Passos: The Poet and the World 495
Ernest Hemingway: A Farewell to Spain 506

HORACE GREGORY
D. H. Lawrence: The Posthumous Reputation . . . 512
The Proletarian Poet 519

NEWTON ARVIN
Individualism and the American Writer 523

ROBERT CANTWELL
No Landmarks 530
Sinclair Lewis 541

CONTENTS

WILLIAM PHILLIPS and PHILIP RAHV
  Private Experience and Public Philosophy 552

R. P. BLACKMUR
  Notes on E. E. Cummings' Language 558
  A Critic's Job of Work 582

Appendices

I. Recent Works of American Criticism 613

II. Collections of Contemporary American Criticism . . . 619

III. American Magazines Publishing Criticism 621

IV. Notes on Contributors 627

INTRODUCTION

I

THE critic of literature occupies today a position of remarkable and precarious advantages, of a kind almost unknown to his ancestors. He finds himself in an office of far-reaching influence and in command of almost unlimited subject matter and public attention. No special conditions of locality or intellectual climate are needed to make his rank in the community an important one, or his work difficult. He stands among ideas in a state of unrest and causes at crucial odds with one another, all of which pass through his hands in the form of books. His energies are spurred by every possible stimulus from other fields of activity, by the experiments of history and philosophy and the researches of social and psychological science, but when these aids arrive they are likely to prove more confusing than enlightening. He is expected to be almost everything but himself: patriot, moralist, and humanitarian; reformer, revolutionist, and prophet. Where once he was easily accused of "not knowing enough," he is now likely to know too much for his own good about everything but his craft, or about everything that makes his craft a baffling one to master. He has become a recognized arbiter of opinion, but he confronts a public whose needs are as difficult to determine as his means of satisfying them are difficult to reduce to an exact technique of analysis and exposition. His office is so easily and commonly reduced to the cruder uses of journalism and propaganda that it is easy to forget that it can also be one of the most influential in the well-being of society, and one of the few trustworthy indexes we have to the prosperity of intelligence and culture.

This is true in any country, but there are reasons for claiming a special importance for American criticism during the past half-century. It forms the record of a nation's education, of arrival at its spiritual majority and at the responsibility of justifying its claims to an artistic and cultural destiny of its own. This ambition would give dramatic force to any body of writing, and American criticism has become in the hundred years since Poe's and Emerson's day as dramatic in its local and political circumstances, and in its pride of duty and destiny, as any activity of the century. It has found itself divided between the claims of tradition and of an emancipation whose first promise was to simplify those claims or dismiss them altogether. When Whitman wrote his *Democratic Vistas* and the preface to *Leaves of Grass* it was possible to announce that hope in fervent terms, but the day for such confidence is over. Art, for one thing, has refused to be simplified. For another, criticism has been allowed to acquire little complacency. It has found its tools and methods more and more inadequate to the strain laid on them. As soon as a royal road to critical wisdom is pointed out, its path becomes impeded by fresh disputes and obstacles. In the United States this problem is thrown into a relief more difficult to visualize in European countries. For at the same moment that the creative energies of the nation have appeared at their height, the need of a critical discipline has announced itself with vigorous emphasis. The resulting conflict has made of American criticism a battleground of ideals and purposes, as crowded with faction and confusion as any to be seen in the countries of the West.

American criticism has seldom been primarily literary, and only a small part of it is so today. It has been ethical and moral, social and regional, political and religious. The special claims of art have, in fact, been obliged to put up a struggle for recognition. This condition existed in the past as an accepted fact, in spite of the protests of men like Poe, Lowell, and Henry James. But it has been equally present during the past quarter-century, whatever gains in taste and sophistication may be boasted. When there appeared, toward the end of the nineteenth century, a "critical movement in American life," literature played a part in it with manners, morals, and social institutions, but usually a subordinate part. The nation, arriving at a sufficient political isolation and economic independence, began to loosen its protective armor of suspicion and self-esteem, and relaxed its vigilance over the contempt of foreigners and the irreverence of its own satirists. It allowed its "giddy minds" to turn from foreign quarrels and defensives to a healthy doubt about native life and its productions in manners and art. But this change did not come easily or without meeting resistance.

Once such irreverence was frankly considered sacrilegious. The hardpan of American complacency dulled the pick of anyone who tried to break it up. Poe was one of these. His attacks on the crusted dogmatism of his literary overlords and contemporaries crop up everywhere in his essays and reviews. "It is folly to assert, as some at present are fond of asserting, that the Literature of any nation or age was ever injured by plain-speaking on the part of critics. As for American Letters, plain-speaking about *them* is, simply, the one thing needed. They are in a condition of absolute quagmire." He fired his concentrated anger at the immediate tyrants in the field, the "Literati of New York," whose flourishing descendants have testified for the ensuing nine decades to the small effect of his demolitions. Lowell was more decorous in his sense of the same shortcomings; Emerson admitted them to Carlyle; and Hawthorne offered one of his earliest biographers, the youthful Henry James, a special case of the American author who, though acutely conscious of esthetic standards, was doomed to labor on their behalf in an atmosphere from which serious esthetic curiosity was almost totally banished, either by the philosophic ambitions of Boston and Concord or by a fatuous veneration of "the gentleman or the lady who has written a book." In his day an adulation of almost Renaissance-like fervor was accompanied by an artistic stolidity of equal proportions. "If the tone of the American world is in some respects provincial, it is in none more so than in this matter of the exaggerated homage rendered authorship. The gentleman or the lady who has written a book is in many circles the object of an admiration too indiscriminating to operate as an encouragement to good writing." James was writing in the late seventies about conditions half a century earlier, but his remarks are open to more recent application:

There is no reason to suppose that this was less the case fifty years ago; but fifty years ago, greatly more than now, the literary man must have lacked the comfort and inspiration of belonging to a class. The best things come, as a general thing, from the talents that are members of a group; every man works better when he has companions working in the same line, and yielding the stimulus of suggestion, comparison, emulation. Great things of course have been done by solitary workers; but they have usually been done with double the pains they would have cost if they had been produced in more genial circumstances. The solitary worker loses the profit of example and discussion; he is apt to make awkward experiments; he is in the nature of the case more or less of an empiric. The empiric may, as I say, be treated by the world as an expert; but the drawbacks and discomforts of empiricism remain to him, and are in fact increased by the suspicion that is mingled with his gratitude, of a want in the public taste of a sense of the proportion of things.

If this isolation afflicted the American artist it was equally the lot of the honest critic, who lacked even the consolations of hero-worship. He was likely to spend his thrift in wrangling with patriotic citizens and the regimented high-priests of popular journalism, the Griswolds and Bryants of the hour. Melville said, "I feel an exile here," and escaped into the created world of his imagination; Thoreau had the protection of Walden; Hawthorne himself was not prevented from writing his books by the critical poverty around him; and Emily Dickinson had her own way of keeping the "admiring bog" of the inept at a distance. But the critic, with his more practical business to perform, found himself shut out of the inner circles of literary influence. Poe's complaints come to mind again, a modern version of Ben Jonson's in *Timber:*

In a criticism of Bryant I was at some pains in pointing out the distinction between popular "opinion" of the merits of contemporary authors, and that held and expressed of them in private literary society. The former species of "opinion" can be called "opinion" only by courtesy. It is the public's own, just as we consider a book our own when we have bought it. In general, this opinion is adopted from the journals of the day, and I have endeavored to show that the cases are rare indeed in which these journals express any other sentiment about books than such as may be attributed directly or indirectly to the authors of the books. The most "popular," the most "successful" writers among us (for a brief period, at least) are, ninety-nine times out of a hundred, persons of mere address, perseverance, effrontery—in a word, busy-bodies, toadies, quacks. These people easily succeed in *boring* editors (whose attention is too often entirely engrossed by politics or other "business" matter) into the admission of favorable notices written or caused to be written by interested parties—or, at least, into the admission of *some* notice where, under ordinary circumstances, *no* notice would be given at all. In this way ephemeral "reputations" are manufactured which, for the most part, serve all the purposes designated—that is to say, the putting of money into the purse of the quack and the quack's publisher; for there never was a quack who could be brought to comprehend the value of mere fame. Now, men of genius will not resort to these manoeuvres, because genius involves in its very essence a scorn of chicanery; and thus for a time the quacks always get the advantage of them, both in respect to pecuniary profit and what *appears* to be public esteem.

This paradox, of homage for authors serving chiefly to cripple authorship, has always been the invention of journalism, commercial interest, and social coteries. It was never so depressing as in the middle of the nineteenth century, when it offered a special kind of critical confusion to the writers who formed what present-day historians have honored as our literary "golden day." It was a day whose true luminaries were likely to show, either by private seclusion or the sectarianism of groups and farms, the artist's instinctive withdrawal from the indignities of the public literary market or such disgusts as taxed Poe's intelligence in New York. It did the further damage of making critical discrimination appear incompatible with creative achievement at the very moment when such collaboration was necessary to the health of American literature. The mystical imagination of Melville disgusted Henry James, and the prophetic grandiloquence of Whitman appalled the more esthetic poets of his generation. The same division came to exist within the temperaments of individual writers, notably in such ambivalent and contradictory talents as Henry Adams. It created in other writers so open a contempt for American standards in art that they saved themselves by going abroad. The exile from American society had already, in Hawthorne, Thoreau, and Emily Dickinson, taken the form of the recluse. He now became an expatriate. The migrations of Whistler, James, and Hearn provided a model of escape from the practical responsibilities of American literature that remained feasible down to the years of mass exodus to Paris after the World War.

The real task of criticism, however, does not fall on the conscience of the creative writer, even in an age like the present one when the artist and critic often appear in the same person. For a wider reform of the critical intelligence there was required a more thoroughgoing education in literary standards than an artist usually has the patience to give. The success of such a program in America depended on the appearance of men who were willing to make criticism their life-work. Until the last two decades of the nineteenth century no such body of writers came into view. By 1880 and 1890, however, a general sense of this deficiency was apparent. An important labor was waiting to be performed. The skeptical spirit abroad in the land was stimulating and healthy, but it needed translation into positive criteria of value and taste. The hour had arrived for setting up an American school of criticism that would face the ticklish duty of reconciling intelligent artists with their native birthright, and yet of developing in both them and the public sounder principles of appreciation and judgment. When that moment was recognized the contemporary movement in American criticism had its beginnings.

II

Its sponsors had several models of literary purpose to remember from the past. Poe argued equally for the poetic principle in art and for a more complete esthetic education in critics. Emerson examined literature in the empirical spirit of his English contemporaries, Macaulay, Carlyle, and Arnold, for evidences of that "peculiar fruit which each man was created to bear" and which ripens out of his personal hopes and struggles. Lowell had turned toward past masterpieces to find the qualities of moral character and idealism by which the writers around him might be invigorated. Whitman threw on poets his prophecy of the supreme humanitarian destiny of the American nation, and called on critics to instruct and defend the poet blessed with this mission. But these leaders had succeeded neither in founding schools nor in winning followers, and they were too much at odds to arouse concerted action among critics. What was needed was just such action, to co-ordinate dissenting views, instruct a new generation in the traditions of literature, and agree on the means by which the best talents should translate them into timely and active form. There was still missing a vital contact between the abstract standards of culture and the living experience and craftsmanship to which they were now to be applied.

It was one thing to see this program of action. It was another thing to act by it. The critical intelligence was faced not only by the duty of harmonizing tradition with the complexities of modern life, but by the need of an education in esthetic principles that would apply less to the tested achievements of the past than to the books of a new generation. It had to grasp such matters as taste and style in better terms than the outworn usages of academic convention, and it had to acquire enough realism and sophistication to know what they mean in contemporary terms. Critics seeing this responsibility would inevitably turn toward European countries and learn many of their best lessons from older standards, but it was equally important that they should avoid the fallacy of thinking that the mere importation of a foreign example would bring such standards to the United States.

Henry James was the first critic to undertake this task, and saw its difficulties more clearly than any other man of his generation. The fact that he did not remain in America to complete his work is one of the tragedies of our literature—not by any failure of his in greatness, but by ours in sharing his intelligence more fully. As early as the sixties, when he had barely come of age, he was a diligent reviewer of books for *The Nation, The North American Review, The Galaxy,* and other New York journals. He canvassed the taste and sentiments of the Victorian Age—the lady novelists and sentimental poets as soberly as Goethe and Lewes. In another ten years his ground had shifted. He was looking for his bases in art and criticism. He studied Balzac and the realists, Eliot and the moral problem in fiction, George Sand for her imaginative and atmospheric methods, the new French naturalists for their inventories of contemporary society. In ten years more his European education was fairly complete. He had examined the contrasting purposes of the schools of Paris—romantic, symbolist, and realist. He listened to the counsels of Flaubert, Turgeniev, Daudet, and Zola; he wrote his book on Hawthorne and the essays in *French*

Poets and Novelists and *Partial Portraits;* [1] he formed his friendship with Stevenson and arrived at his own creative maturity. He was perhaps the first American man of letters to follow a complete course of literary and critical education, to compare European writers and doctrines, to impose on his own craft and conscience an unprejudiced critical detachment.

He saw the modern creative problem in its two essential aspects: its oppression by social conflict and theories of scientific and moral determinism, and its acute subtilization by the defenses which the esthetic techniques of the modern sensibility had set up against these oppressions. He saw modern criticism confronting the task of reconciling the real and esthetic, human life in "its unprejudiced identity" with the form and laws of art. That task was nowhere more urgent than in America, and during the eighties, when James still had the ambition of becoming the "American Balzac," he formulated his working principles as a critic. His critical doctrine had three clauses. He argued for subtlety and plasticity in the critic's sympathy as a first condition. As a second he demanded a tireless study of the vital experience upon which all art is based and its use as a test of material validity, since for him all art was "in basis moral." And he required finally a knowledge of how the intelligence of the artist stamps this material with its unmistakable impression of form and language, since that imprint constituted for James the "quality of mind" he looked for in any valid work of art.

He held to the mean in both art and criticism. He had an American's natural suspicion of cults and doctrine. He looked upon Gautier's "art for art" as an absurdity and upon naturalism as a "treacherous ideal." To him esthetic quality was as indispensable as realistic documentation, but to insist on one without the other, or on either without the harmonizing presence of a moral conception, was futile. Criticism must begin where a work of imagination begins: with experience tangibly perceived.

To lend himself, to project himself and steep himself, to feel and feel till he understands, and to understand so well that he can say, and to have perception at the pitch of passion and expression as embracing as the air, to be infinitely curious and incorrigibly patient, and yet plastic and inflammable and determinable, patient, stooping to conquer and yet serving to direct—these are fine chances

[1] The titles and dates of books of criticism by the authors discussed in this Introduction will be found listed in the bibliographies at the end of the volume.

for an active mind, chances to add the idea of independent beauty to the conception of success. Just in proportion as he is sentient and restless, just in proportion as he reacts and reciprocates and penetrates, is the critic a valuable instrument.

He thus pled for training in critical sensibility. It alone leads the critic directly into contact with the work of art and with art's own sources. But one must not make the mistake of confusing what James said with what Pater taught in the conclusion to *The Renaissance*. Impressionism was at that time almost as unknown in America as it had been exaggerated in Europe, and it had a service to perform in bringing critics back to an intimate sense of art, but neither James nor his American friends had any intention of subscribing to its methods. They were too thoroughly bred in ethical seriousness. When James declared in *Partial Portraits* that "the deepest quality of a work of art will always be the quality of the mind of the producer," he meant that for both art and criticism "the moral sense and the artistic sense lie very close together." Only their combination will supply the intellect's abstract operations with the vitality of a union that makes such "quality" possible. "The critic's judgment," he repeated, "being in the last analysis an estimate of the artist's quality of mind, is at once moral and esthetic." The persistent linking of these terms runs like a motive through James' essays. To separate the moral and the esthetic is to rob either of its vital complement. Genuine "unity of the mind" exists in such "fusions and interrelations," with "every part of the stuff encircled in every other." That is the secret of esthetic form, a writer's ultimate achievement, just as its elucidation is the secret of the critic's success, his highest rseponsibility. These precepts stayed with James from his critical coming-of-age until he finally assayed his own achievement by their light when writing, a quarter century later, the prefaces for the New York edition of his works.

American literature itself did not long remain, however, the subject-matter of James' critical books. His removal from America after the disillusioning failure of his excursion into social realism in the eighties left the task in the hands of William Dean Howells and William Crary Brownell. In the new program of action Howells took the part of facts, Brownell that of ideals. Howells undertook to explain the foundations of American realism, Brownell the basis of taste and prudence necessary for the existence of cultural and literary achievement. Howells combined a frontier childhood with New England schooling, a study of past masters under the guidance of Lowell, Norton, and Aldrich, with his own zest for art and history during European travels and consulships. But he found his roots in the ambition and rigor of the average American life, and he made the rationalization of its values the task of both his criticism and his novels.

He found two instruments at his service: the esthetics of French naturalism (from whose rawer examples he recoiled, preferring the tempered version of Jane Austen or Tolstoy) and the scientific humanitarianism of the modern sociologists (which he studied not only in Mill, Comte, Spencer, Morris, and Bellamy, but in the social unrest of his middle years, the Pennsylvania coal strikes and Haymarket riots, "the slavery implicated in our liberty"). He defined the principles of this moral realism for critics in his essay of 1894, "Criticism and Fiction." "Realism is nothing more and nothing less than the truthful treatment of material." He repudiated the aristocratic element in romanticism which "seeks to withdraw itself, to stand aloof, to be distinguished and not to be identified." Realism is the particular duty of the artist in the democratic society, for it enables him to feel "in every nerve the equality of things and the unity of men . . . to front the everyday world and catch the charm of its work-worn, care-worn, brave, kindly face." To these doctrines Howells added two riders which locate him infallibly in his generation and define his critical limitations unmistakably. That realism is best which studies the "large cheerful average of health and success and happy life," since "the more smiling aspects of life" are "the more American." And that realism is most successful which rejects the deterministic science of the naturalists in favor of ethical judgment since "morality penetrates all things, it is the soul of all things." Here Howells admitted his patriotic and ethical prejudices as frankly as his followers a quarter-century later. He lacked their basis of special social doctrine, but he stuck to the conviction that unless a critic assumes such prejudices and makes them the source of his judgments, he fails in moral responsibility.

Brownell differed from Howells in many circumstances of temperament and training, but he agreed with him in one fundamental belief: the relation of art to life can be grasped only in terms of a realistic and practical dependence. His manner of demonstrating this principle was as different from Howells' as his sense of the spiritual deficiencies of the American people was different from Howells' firm confidence in their tough and humble integrity. Brownell found his model in Arnold. He too became a priest of the cultural ideal, and he shared Arnold's combination of hope and pessimism in the face of the democratic enlightenment. He too believed literature is a criticism of life, and that criticism in turn "determines the relation of the two, and thus needs as close touch with life as with arts and letters." Yet the critic can do his work effectively only by a knowledge of ideal ends and standards. Standards, indeed, were Brownell's fetish, his touchstone to all worth. "To an intelligence fully and acutely alive, its own time must, I think, be more interesting than any other," he said, but the critic must go on "to discern and characterize the abstract qualities informing the concrete expression of the artist." "It is the *qualities* of the writer, painter, sculptor, and not the *properties* of their production that are his essential concern." Among his *American Prose Masters* he found only Cooper and James free of poverty in these qualities of experience and perception. Hawthorne "neglected imagination"; Emerson's "nature was flooded with light, but it lacked heat"; of Poe it was "impossible to make a great writer . . . because his writings lack the elements not only of great, but real literature. They lack substance." But the critic can also fail if he lacks emotional and esthetic energy. Lowell for all his scholarship "was reflectively indolent." There is, in fact, only one cure for the imaginative poverty and degrading materialism of the times, and that is a cultural ideal. It alone saves the artist from the enervating antagonism of his physical and esthetic faculties.

This solvent Brownell looked for in the sustaining and renewing influence of a firmly ethical civilization. His models for it he found in the "culture" defined by Arnold and in the esthetic achievements of France. He studied *French Traits* with the patient but always half-ironical hope of importing them to the United States. No one but James had his skill in the judicious inspection of such a model, and no one but James had the greater powers of imagination that could show how ineffectual Brownell's fastidious discretion would turn out to be. For forty years he taught his moderate and urbane gospel of discipline, decorum, and intellectual tact. The heresies of "self-expression," naturalism, and impressionism he considered aberrations from a desired norm. He insisted so austerely on this norm, this admirable but ultimately abstract principle, that he lost his hold on the very "substance" he demanded in his prose masters. When he faced the literary productions of the new age around him, or when he attempted to understand tradition as a reality that is valid only by its success in surviving in the present, he proved almost abjectly incompetent. His urgent counsels on taste and sophistication impressed themselves on a few respectful followers but on almost none of the artists and craftsmen he wished to enlighten. Today his precisely phrased and austerely bound books are unread. But excepting only those of James, they provided the most serious formulation of the responsibility that must be exchanged between artist, critic, and public that America had yet seen, and some of their views have never been restated to better effect. They may be recalled some day when another effort at integrating social and esthetic thought comes due. By comparison with the puerilities of academic convention around him (Henry Van Dyke, or Hamilton Wright Mabie with his "White List of Books") he survives with the distinction of sensitive tastes which these prudish culturists never thought it worth their while to envy.

Taste, in those bewildered years of the late Nineteenth Century, was a faculty so threatened by anemia when refined and so exhausted by garish and unprincipled crudity when it was robust, that it is small wonder the word came to be the trade-mark of ludicrous elegance and snobbery among satirists like Mark Twain. James Huneker made something else of it. He was perhaps the first sybarite of the arts in America. His appetite and energy made him a valuable agent in combatting the dead weight of genteel and Puritanic intolerance, the smug cant of "propriety" that acted as a customs barrier to esthetic importations of any kind. Like George Moore and Arthur Symons in England, he was an ambassador of the esthetic movement. He lavished his admiration on almost anything new, exotic, rebellious, and his cascades of lurid publicity swept before the American public the novelties of modern music, drama, painting, fiction, and ballet, not to mention the gastronomic luxuries of every café and hostelry on the continent. He wrote about the arts as he wrote about foods and menus, and before their rich fare professed nothing but an unlimited Epicurean capacity. His writings were the cosmopolite's text books and involved no critical subtleties. They gave a plain man's version of Pater's appetitive ideal and Anatole France's doctrine of esthetic exposure. The critic must aim "to spill his soul," and "humbly to follow and register his emotions aroused by a masterpiece." He spared nothing in the way of epithets, enigmas, and paradoxes when he spilled his soul, and upon the ensuing flood his readers were buffeted by the complete carnival of modern sensuality and insurgence in the arts. The sheer gastronomic pleasure of this feast was crowned by a kind of moral satisfaction in knowing that it was an affront to all the inhibitions and hostilities of the Puritan tradition. There was no need to discriminate special qualities in the items; they had the common quality of scorning the pure and the prurient.

For the sophisticated children of the Gilded Age and for a few more serious apprentices, Huneker was revered as a bringer of gifts. On the popular level his influence was rapid and enormous. Of the critical value of his work little need be added. His foremost disciple has said that for him art was no longer "even by implication a device for improving the mind. It is wholly a magnificent adventure. The notion of it is what Huneker brought into American criticism, and it is for that bringing that he will be remembered." This, spoken in tribute by Mencken, speaks for itself. In any serious sense Huneker did not pretend to write criticism, even in his books on Liszt and Chopin. He wrote esthetic publicity. He brought the fleshpots of modern art into a genteel society, startled the literary conventions out of their frozen molds, shocked the high priests of the Lyceum circuit, inducted a new generation of journalists into a colorful style and extravagant zest for the arts, and introduced an easy brand of impressionism into literary appreciation. He shaped the adolescent phase of a new critical attitude, and as such his labors are preserved in the shelf of books in which his enormous avidity and honest share of sensitive romantic enthusiasm for music, literature, and painting are preserved. He is the child of his period, and to return to his books now, after the sobering events of the last twenty years, is to realize how much of a child he remains. But he may claim a tonic quality: he made American readers more keenly aware of international activities than James managed to do. He probably ruined taste more expertly than James improved it, but he also created an appetite for the arts that had its due effect on the physical health and public prestige of the American artist.

Around the work of James and Brownell, Howells and Huneker, a sizeable critical activity went on between the nineties and 1912, but from it few lasting services may be isolated. Much of this writing came from academic quarters, another share was composed of newspaper reviews, most of which risked little in the way of dispute or defense of new talent, and another part struck out along independent lines which either ended at the impasse of theoretical vagueness or led back to conventional quarters. George Edward Woodberry was one critic who felt dissatisfaction in the stolid confines of the academic world and began to work toward freer purposes. He produces a series of volumes in which the various critical positions were carefully scanned, the work of new critics plotted, and various impending problems suggested; he also said much about the need of a new humanistic and realistic attitude toward values, and in such books as *America in Literature* (1903), *The Torch* (1905), *The Appreciation of Literature* (1910), and *Two Phases of Criticism* (1914) provided the best surveys of the situation and critical methods that existed in those years. But theory took him too far afield, and a lax belle-lettristic idealism removed him too far from the irrepressible forces that were demanding expression. Brander Matthews had less of this, and by combining a shrewd study of European dramatic criticism with a lively attention to the New York stage he lifted the criticism of drama over from the pontifical conservatism of William Winter's era to the brisk journalism soon to come from younger men.

By far the keenest refreshment of esthetic interest to come from academic quarters, however, was supplied by George Santayana. His *Sense of Beauty* in 1896 claimed to be nothing but a new arrangement of "the scattered commonplaces of criticism into a system, under the inspiration of a naturalistic psychology," but the last phrase of this apology explains the great influence the book and its sequels were to have on the study and appreciation of art in the United States. It was the first text-book to refurbish the classical routine of philosophical discourse and add the stimulation of a realistic motive. Santayana set aside the didactic and historical approach to art, and offered the psychological. He presented "esthetic judgments as phenomena of mind and products of mental evolution." He combined his exposition with a vivid sense of his personal appreciation of the arts, and stepped gracefully over the barrier that had immemorially separated the philosophical idealist of the American college from an active grasp of the work of art itself. When he distinguished the three orders of beauty as residing in material, in form, and in expression, he took these criteria out of the dark-chamber of theory and made them applicable to existing masterpieces. And fourteen years later, in *Three Philosophical Poets,* he showed that figures like Lucretius, Dante, and Goethe could be used as opportunities for the collaboration between philosophical and literary criticism which was needed to rescue esthetic teaching from endless and enfeebling conventionality. But the "inspiration of a naturalistic psychology" remained basic to Santayana's activity in this line; it gave him his popularity among realists and psychologists; and it provided a clue to a new line of reaction which was presently to put in an appearance and prepare a heated repudiation of his influence and affiliations. That reaction proceeded cautiously, built its attack conservatively, and took almost a quarter-century before it faced the enemy of naturalism in open battle. In 1904 Paul Elmer More issued the first volume of his *Shelburne Essays* and in 1908 Irving Babbitt began his campaign against romanticism with *Literature and the American College.*

III

The work of these critics who attempted to bridge the distance between nineteenth century habits and the experimental conditions of modern literature now appears, especially when we recall the difficulties of prejudice and conventionality they faced, to gain in courage and distinction. More's phrase in his 1904 volume—"Before we can have an American literature, we must have an American criticism"—is a sufficient warrant of this. But when a new revival of literary activity arrived around 1912 it took, like most cases of insurgence, the immediately preceding generation as its first object of attack. It announced two purposes: the demolition of the genteel tradition and a rediscovery of the American spirit. These served to indict as academic, unrealistic, or corruptive the labors of most of the elder critics still on the scene. Henry James then appeared as a deserter from a sacred trust, a shirker of his duty as an American, tainted by the effete and artificial influences of English society and French theory. Brownell and Woodberry became supreme examples of academic dry rot and polite formulation. Paul Elmer More fell under contempt as a dogged apologist for ethical dogma. Huneker, in spite of his more attractive personality and acceptable epicureanism of taste, was lamed by vulgar estheticism and exhausting garrulity, incapable of getting a close view of the serious duties of the artist, and rendered helpless as a judge of either life or art by his welter of gross and indiscriminate enthusiasms. The young critics who now took the field were of an equally heady breed, but they professed very different purposes. Reality was to provide their basic standard, and the existing life of the United States their chief test of values. In one of his essays Van Wyck Brooks suggested the new attitude toward history: "On Creating a Usable Past." The title of one of his most successful books gave the new criticism its label: *America's Coming of Age*. He and his colleagues corrected More's dictum; they believed that before there could be either an American literature or an American criticism there had to appear a fresh and realistic understanding of what America itself meant. What they produced was accordingly not criticism in any pure or technical sense. It was Americanization.

That it was to be a critical and practical kind of Americanization, escaping the weakness of earlier prophecies and panegyrics, was made clear in another of Brooks' volumes, *Letters and Leadership*. There he took up a clue furnished by John Macy in his *Spirit of American Literature* (1913) and gave it as his conclusion that "our life is, on all its levels, in a state of arrested development, that it has lost, if indeed it has ever possessed, the principle of growth." He credited this adolescence to the commercial and materialistic obsessions of the nation. "We are," he said, "the victims of a systematic process of inverse selection so far as the civilizing elements in the American nature are concerned. Our ancestral faith in the individual and what he is able to accomplish (or in modern parlance, to 'put over') as the measure of all things, has despoiled us of that science, art, philosophy, the self-subordinating service of which is almost the measure of the highest happiness. In consequence of this our natural capacities have been dissipated, they have become egocentric and socially centrifugal and they have hardened and become fixed in the most anomalous form." He sketched a program for the correction of this state of affairs, if only to keep alive "the hope of a 'national culture' to come . . . in order that America may be able in the future to give something to the rest of the world that is better than what the world too generally means by 'Americanism.'" The elder critics whom he condemned as "unpractical" had done little toward this end, chiefly because while "they say that we are emotional . . . what they really object to is that we are emotional at all, the strength of their own case resting wholly on the assumption that literature ought to spring not from the emotions but from the intellect." They had fostered a "fear of experience."

Such, in fact, is the deficiency of personal impulse, of the creative will, in America, so overwhelming is the demand laid upon Americans to serve ulterior and impersonal ends, that it is as if the springs of spiritual action had altogether evaporated. Launched in a society where individuals and their faculties appear only to pass away, almost wholly apart from and without acting upon one another, our writers find themselves enveloped in an impalpable atmosphere that acts as a perpetual dissolvent to the whole field of reality both within and without themselves, an atmosphere that invades every sphere of life and takes its discount from everything that they can do, an atmosphere that prevents the formation of oases of reality in the universal chaos.

In Brooks' program for critics, the new critical realism joined hands with this corrected view of the American ideal. It was immediately taken as a call to action both by the young critical talents of the pre-War years and by a new group of "journals of opinion" which appeared on the scene—*The New Republic, The Masses, The Liberator,* the renovated *Nation,* the more esthetic *Seven Arts,* and later *The Freeman.* These found an almost ideal condition for their activities: the unrest and dislocation of the pre-War years, the excitement and controversy that followed our entry into the conflict, and a flourishing literary revival that brought the work of insurgent poets and novelists to reinforce what the critics hoped to achieve. Dreiser, Sandburg, Masters, Frost, Lindsay, Cather, and Robinson supplied object-lessons for the new critical text. The moment was alive with creative energy and rebellion, with the hope of casting out the venerable American superstitions. These critical journalists were able to boast that they saw the creative problem from the inside. They felt its motives and difficulties with the artist, instead of holding off in suspicion and condescending scorn.

"The older critics," said Randolph Bourne in his *History of a Literary Radical,* "long since disavowed the intention of discriminating among current writers. These men, who had to have an Academy to protect them, lumped the younger writers of verse and prose together as 'anarchic' and 'naturalistic,' and had become, in these latter days, merely peevish and querulous, protesting in favor of standards that no longer represented our best values. Everyone . . . bemoaned the lack of critics, but the older critics seemed to have lost all sense of hospitality and to have become tired and a little spitefully disconsolate, while the newer ones were too intent on their crusades against puritanism and philistinism to have time for a constructive pointing of the way." Bourne had nothing but contempt for academic standardizers or importers of foreign fashions, but he saw the unorthodox belligerents threatened by another danger. He saw, "on the one hand, Mr. Mencken and Mr. Dreiser and their friends, going heavily forth to battle with the Philistines, glorying in pachydermous vulgarisms that hurt the polite and cultivated young men of the old school. And he saw these violent critics, in their rage against Puritanism, becoming themselves moralists, with the same bigotry and tastelessness as their enemies." And continuing:

> The older American critic was mostly interested in getting the proper rank and reverence for what he borrowed. The new critic will take what suits his community of sentiment. He will want to link up not with the foreign canon but with that group which is nearest in spirit with the effort he and his friends are making. The American has to work to interpret and portray the life he knows. He cannot be international in the sense that anything but the life in which he is soaked, with its questions and its colors, can be the material for his art. But he can be international—and must be—in the sense that he works with a certain hopeful vision of a "young world," and with certain ideal values upon which the younger men, stained and revolted by war, in all countries are agreeing.

The "international" element in this program was chiefly an attack on provincialism. It had its earlier sponsors in Henry James and Brownell, its immediate godfather in Huneker, its practical workers in exiles like Ezra Pound and T. S. Eliot. Critics like Spingarn and Santayana had also, for different reasons, advised a familiarity with the critical ideas that were circulating in Europe. For the realists and liberals, however, this plea for an international point of view was incidental, a supplementary means of fighting down the conservatives and "professors." Against such foes any weapon was useful, and European radicalism offered ripe experience in the tactics of battle. Ludwig Lewisohn told the young critics to look toward France, where "their battle was fought and won thirty years ago," or toward Germany, "where the heritage of Goethe's supreme vision made the battle needless." Spingarn pointed toward the books of Croce. France was, as always, held up as a model of unshackled liberalism in art and thought. But the defenders of the "authentic American" had work to do at home which no amount of internationalism and foreign example would make easier.

A great deal of it was negative in character. They attacked prudery, decorum, politeness, and every other evil that might be safely ascribed to the Puritans. But they also wanted to give American writers a genuine confidence in their native materials, a pragmatic and disillusioned approach to the life around them, a standard of honesty, and if possible a critical understanding of their problems. With so many prejudices to correct, it is little wonder that a critical basis for the new realism was never satisfactorily arrived at. The gusto of the "debunking" movement had little patience for that. Brooks and Bourne laid out a program, to which their colleagues, Robert Morss Lovett, Robert Littell, Harriet Monroe, Francis Hackett, Max Eastman, Alfred Kreymborg, Harold E. Stearns, and Lewis Mumford contributed their energies. Among them a dominating voice was heard; the cause found its most entertaining spokesman in H. L. Mencken.

It is easy now, in rereading Mencken's books, to limit his performance to low-comedy journalism. The pages teem with the follies of twenty-five of the oddest years in American history and form a hilarious *Dunciad* of an age. Mencken delivered his barrage against them with the energy of a Swift or Voltaire. War-time jingoism, the Prohibition era, the Monkey Trial in Tennessee, the pieties of the Bible Belt, Coolidge prosperity, and the endless prodigalities of the jazz age, the alfalfa *Gelehrten,* and the *Booboisie* now almost bury the high reputation he once held as a literary influence who made *The Smart Set* and *The American Mercury* serious forces in the lives of important writers. But one fact must be remembered: he aimed less to be a critic than a commissary of literary materials. He ransacked American life to justify writers like Dreiser, Masters, Sandburg, and Lewis, and to show younger writers what the realistic and critical spirit had to work on. He was an evangelist of the vulgar, as much of an artist in his display of its phenomena as many of the novelists he praised, and what Edmund Wilson has recently pointed out must be recalled: that while

Brooks exposed the negative aspects of our literary tradition and urged us to get away from our governesses, Mencken showed the

positive value of our vulgar heritage; and he did more than anyone
else in his field to bring about that "coming of age" for which
Brooks sounded the hour. The publication of Mencken's *Book of
Prefaces* in 1917, with its remarkable essay on Dreiser and its assault
on "Puritanism as a Literary Force," was a cardinal event for the
new American literature. Mencken did not precisely discover Dreiser,
but he was able to focus him clearly for the first time as a figure of
dignity and distinction, because he appreciated and made us taste the
Americanism of Dreiser as Americanism, without attempting to write
him down for not being something other than American. This *positive* treatment of Dreiser—so different from the negative attitude with
which even sympathetic critics had in the past approached American
writers like Mark Twain, was really a weight that tipped the scales.

His test of a book was rough and pragmatic. He mingled his burly
prejudices with an uninhibited impressionism derived from Huneker.
It is not hard to imagine what this procedure amounted to when he
tackled an author beyond his depth or taste—Henry James, Herman
Melville, or any poet of subtle originality. But at another level he
brought an enormous stimulation to the literary scene, and he took
that to be his function as a critic. "The function of a genuine critic of
the arts is to provoke the reaction between the work of art and the spectator. The spectator, untutored, stands unmoved; he sees the work of
art, but it fails to make any intelligible impression on him; if he were
spontaneously sensitive to it, there would be no need for criticism."
The common assumption, that a critic "writes because he is possessed
by a passion to advance the enlightenment, to put down error and
wrong, to disseminate some specific doctrine: psychological, epistemo-
logical, historical, or esthetic" is true "only of bad critics, and its degree
of truth increases in direct ratio to their badness. Criticism at bottom
is indistinguishable from skepticism," and Mencken rejected the arguments for "constructive criticism" as based "upon the same false assumption, that immutable truths exist in the arts, and that the artist will be
improved by being made aware of them. . . . Truth is something that
is believed in completely only by persons who have never tried personally to pursue it to its fastnesses and grab it by the tail. . . . The
true aim of a critic is certainly not to make converts. He must know
that very few of the persons who are susceptible to conversion are worth
converting."

These remarks, scattered throughout his essays, indicate the elements
in his literary outlook: a contempt of popular taste, a suspicion of intellectual and a skepticism of dogmatic attitudes toward art, and an ambition to demolish any tradition that had fostered the delusions of

ethical and ideal theory in literature. Most of that tradition he labeled Puritan, and he translated his contempt of its moral absolutes into a scorn of esthetic absolutes. "The American, save in moments of conscious and swiftly lamented deviltry, casts up all ponderable values, including even the values of beauty, in terms of right and wrong," and the only cure for this habit was to demolish the entire basis of rational and authoritarian judgment. Under tenets like these, it was hardly to be expected that Mencken would bring his literary preferences to the test of analysis or exact discrimination. His usefulness was of a more elementary character. He wrote a history of American manners, howled into perdition the genteel superstitions of culture and dignity, and provided a basis for evaluating the realistic principle in fiction for what it was worth. His own criticism will probably be remembered chiefly for the humor that accompanied its purgative effects.

In Van Wyck Brooks another form of the patriotic motive appeared; it combined affection and skepticism as Mencken's did, but it was tempered to a soberer employment. His early books on the revision of American society—*The Wine of the Puritans* (1909), *America's Coming-of-Age* (1915), and *Letters and Leadership* (1918)—were intended as manifestoes and were accepted as such. Brooks never intended an assult on genuine American loyalties; his reverence for these was profound and sincere, and he did not consider cosmopolitanism a cure-all for cultural ingrowth and provincialism. He proposed first to indict the traitors within the gates, the defilers of the pioneer idealism and all who had nursed along the enfeebling conformism of the academic life. After that he would take his "usable past" and apply its lessons to the unrealized present. In two of his books these purposes were first demonstrated in practical terms—*The Ordeal of Mark Twain* (1920) and *The Pilgrimage of Henry James* (1925). Both these inheritors of the American tradition were depicted as unworthy of its promise—Twain through pessimism and a failure of personal integrity, James through temperamental restlessness and esthetic over-refinement. Brooks set up in his mind that standard of American honesty and fortitude which he has recently described so beautifully in *The Flowering of New England*. In it he found his prescription for the authentic American artist, the source of his usable past and his productive present. Any betrayal of its promise spelled for him the secret failure of the artist.

It is in his book on James that the defects of Brooks' argument appear most strikingly. Starting with his thesis, he broke the body of James to fit it. James' qualities of irony and self-criticism, his subtle pessimism on the condition of English society and French literature, his sense of catastrophe in the European moral order, his skeptical detachment and unforgotten American loyalties are all simplified or neglected in order to push to its logical conclusion the argument that they were ultimately stultified by James' refusal to return to his native shores to live and write. The words and speeches of James' fictions are used to convey his own personal attitude, ostensibly to give an "effect of immediacy" but actually with the result of reading into his personal career a coherent fiction which an exact reading of his letters, the autobiographical books, or the major novels themselves would have rendered impossible. Yet the desired effect was achieved. *The Pilgrimage of Henry James* becomes a parable of the American artist's betrayal of his birthright. The patriotic motive cripples the critical. A valuable project of revision and reclamation falters in the individual test. In the end Brooks was to prove more expert as a historian of the past than as a student of the present. His distinguished talent at length settled down to the labor of writing a literary chronicle of the United States and produced in its first segment, *The Flowering of New England* (1936), a masterpiece of vivid and affectionate reconstruction.

Among Brooks' followers Lewis Mumford became a versatile and energetic leader. He wanted not merely to recover the usable past, but to apply it as speedily as possible to the present distractions of literature. He looked for it in the same quarter—the *Golden Day* of New England culture, and saw modern American wealth as a decline from that ideal. He studied the Utopian symbol as a means of combining its philosophic vitality with the humanitarian vision of Emerson, Whitman, and Melville. He took "Whitman with his cosmic faith" and "Melville in his cosmic defiance" as his prophets and believed that "they will guide us to a splendid future," where the technics of civilization will cease to tyrannize over man and provide instead a richer opportunity for his self-fulfillment. Like many of his contemporaries, Mumford was stronger on the side of indictments than of affirmations. In *Sticks and Stones* (1924) and *The Brown Decades* (1931) he produced two of the best accounts of American art and architecture that have yet been written, and in them shows that the practical arts furnish him with safer examples for speculation than the literary. He has fallen too glibly into the prophet's rôle to be anything but restive and generalizing in his treatment of literary style and craftsmanship. "The social sciences will lie beneath the foundations of the New Jerusalem precisely in the fashion that the physical sciences now underlie the stony exterior of New York" is one of Mumford's observations, and another: "The future of our civilization depends upon our ability to select and control our heritage from the past, to alter our present attitudes and habits, and to project fresh forms into which our energies may be freely poured." The glow here is messianic, the accent Whitman's, the skepticism as facile as the self-assurance is quick, and instead of producing the focus of scrutiny and discrimination where critical values come to a point, Mumford's energies have radiated and explored. He has contributed to the background of esthetic thought more than he has given that thought principles and a discipline to work by.

Under the guidance of these men several things were accomplished. The past was revived in colorful and intimate terms, even though the uses to which it was put were not very intelligently defined, or free of a great deal of the cant about progress, patriotism, and disillusionment that circulated so recklessly in the post-War years. The term "American" was stripped of dogmatic and academic accretions. Large areas of subject-matter formerly considered out of polite artistic bounds were thrown open for conquest by writers. A necessary leaven of plain sense and active speech was added to the fare in which novelists dealt and critics argued. Literature was brought to closer terms with experience and fortified by candor and audacity. It was reduced to those simpler necessities and practices which correct the laxities of academic idealism or esthetic refinement, but which may also put up the deluding appearance of being self-sufficient and in no need of the intellectual benefits of esthetic or philosophic discipline. In fact, this entire activity was so attractive to journalists that it became vulgarized beyond its own intentions. It made the writing of books seem as easy as talking about them. Under its influence American literature was strengthened, but as often reduced to facile and rapid-fire journalism, criticism meanwhile becoming equally loose in its language, haphazard in its terminology, indifferent in analysis, and complacently hostile to anything in the way of intellectual attitudes or esthetic experimentation. The realists and Americanizers nagged pure art and ridiculed its defenders: they encouraged the flight of experimentalists to Paris; they scoffed at originality by calling it "cerebralism"; and they did their part in keeping the literary activity of the twenties on a fairly low and confused level.

However, they flourished in their day. *The Saturday Review of Literature* became one of their strongholds, *The American Mercury* another, and independent or creative journalism was kept at the distance of Greenwich Village (in *The Dial, Others,* and *The Little Review*), Chicago (in *Poetry*), or Europe (in *Secession, Broom,* and *Transition*). Occasionally this vein of American revivalism took on the colors of prophecy, as in Lewisohn's *The Creative Life* and *Expression in America* or in Waldo Frank's *The Re-Discovery of America,* where the "great tradition" became a specter of mystic and international proliferations. Nothing showed better than these heavy-handed conjurings how severely the realistic revival stood in need of critical direction from both social and artistic authorities if it was to be saved from bombast and rhetoric, or from a debasement of the American principle fully as debilitating as the genteel conventions which it had first come to oppose. Such correction began to appear some years after the War, one of the most important manifestations of it being in the form of a regional principle in the study of tradition and art, shown particularly among the group of Southern critics—John Crowe Ransom, Donald Davidson, and Allen Tate—who combined literary study with cultural investigations and who had their first organ in *The Fugitive* of Nashville. Another, from a different quarter, appeared in the form of social criticism of the radical type, of which such writers as Upton Sinclair and V. F. Calverton were pioneer professors, but which was ultimately to develop a method much more formal and extreme (particularly under the tenets of Marxism) than these men had exhibited. In any case, the arrogance and visionary gusto of the realistic movement were its weakest features. They exposed it most readily to critical attack and soon brought it under contempt from several quarters of the literary scene.

IV

One of these was occupied by the students of modern esthetics, who first found their ideas or centered their activities abroad. Paris and London were already before the War the accepted capitals of artistic experimentation, and a revision of esthetic ideas was in progress there far removed from the academic influences and public indifference that made such activity out of place at home. The departure from American shores of Ezra Pound and T. S. Eliot was a hint that their talents were indifferent to the revival of an American ideal or the promotion of new standards of social realism. Their loadstone was neither the real nor the humanitarian, it was art; and they turned toward the schools of Italy, Paris, and pre-War London to learn their lessons and ultimately to become recognized as leaders of the experimental groups that flourished there.

The deficiencies of American criticism in esthetic and technical understanding had long been a by-word. Poe had issued the first indictments on this score, and in the eighteen-forties John Lothrop Motley had published in *The North American Review* a series of essays presenting the man of letters as an artist and pleading, especially in an essay on Balzac, that fiction be respected as an art before it is tested for its ethical and social respectability. These arguments later formed the chief responsibility of Henry James, but before 1900 the instructions of esthetic critics in France, Germany, and England found scant hospitality

in the United States, Huneker's defense of their doctrines being held a
matter of highly questionable taste. Impressionism was as little known
to American critics as to American writers. The Harvard professor,
Lewis E. Gates, was probably its only sympathetic interpreter among
the elect. In his essay on "Impressionism and Appreciation," published
in *Studies and Appreciations* in 1900, he introduced his readers to the
special conditions and mysteries of the esthetic experience. There he
argued that

> The history of literary criticism from Addison's day to our own is,
> if viewed in one way, the history of the ever-increasing refinement
> of the critic's sensorium; it is a growing tendency on the part of the
> critic to value, above all else, his own intimate personal relation to
> this or that piece of literature—a tendency that more and more takes
> the form of prizing the fleeting mood, the passing poignant moment
> of enjoyment in the presence of art, until at last certain modern
> critics refuse, on principle, to feel twice alike about the same poem.

"Impressionism," he said, "justifies itself historically. But more than
this, it justifies itself psychologically; for it recognizes with peculiar
completeness the vitalizing power of literature—its fashion of putting
into play the whole nature of each reader it addresses and its consequent, unlimited, creative energy." Santayana had also aimed to combine the philosophical rationalization of art with modern principles of
inductive psychology in determining the character of esthetic experience, and in counteracting the academic and philosophical influence
with a more practical training in sensibility. In 1910 these influences
were challenged even more defiantly by J. E. Spingarn in a celebrated
lecture on "The New Criticism." This was a manifesto for a completely new program among critics. Under the guidance of Croce he
attempted to import into America an unsparing revision of the critical
motive, described by his term "creative criticism," in which the appreciative faculties of the critic's trained sensibility would serve as a basis
for testing and rationalizing the intuition of the work of art. "The
New Criticism" made a clean sweep of existing conventions:

> We have done with all the old Rules. . . . We have done with the
> *genres,* or literary kinds. . . . We have done with the comic, the
> tragic, the sublime, and an army of vague abstractions of their kind.
> . . . We have done with the theory of style, with metaphor, simile,
> and all the paraphernalia of Graeco-Roman rhetoric. . . . We have
> done with all moral judgment of art as art. . . . We have done with
> the confusion between the drama and the theatre which has per-
> meated dramatic criticism for over half a century. . . . We have

done with technique as separate from art. . . . We have done with
the history and criticism of poetic themes. . . . We have done with
the race, the time, the environment of a poet's work as an element
in Criticism. . . . We have done with the "evolution" of literature.
. . . We have done with the old rupture between genius and taste.

This provided a much-needed ventilation of the critical class-rooms
and it served for a time its purpose in affronting the conservative forces.
Unfortunately Spingarn never demonstrated by inspection and analysis
the technique he desiderated, and his usefulness was confined to stirring up controversy. It was the general limitation of these men that
they had little talent for specific analysis. They taught, corrected, and
debated, but they gave their readers little practical training in literary
methods and craftsmanship.

"Active criticism" of this sort was what Ezra Pound went abroad
to learn when he left America in 1907 and began his thirty-year career
in Italy, England, and France. In the early days of his apprenticeship
he stood for a militantly esthetic standard in literary experimentation,
a rescue of art from formulae and discreet abstraction. He was drawn
toward critics and editors like Henry James, Remy de Gourmont,
W. B. Yeats, T. E. Hulme, and Ford Madox Hueffer, who made
less pretense of organizing a philosophic system out of their tastes and
appreciations than of refreshing and extending these by constant study
of the problems of form and style. He put himself to school, as poet
and critic, among the experimental masters of the past and the non-
conformist teachers of the present. On an eclectic principle he studied
the Latin lyrists, the balladists of Provence and medieval Italy, the
Elizabethan translators and classicists, and the Chinese manuscripts he
inherited from Ernest Fenellosa, all with the same zest as he gave to the
ideas of Gourmont in Paris and Hulme in London. His enthusiasm
was so contagious that he himself was soon a recognized leader in
innovation and critical pedagogy.

From Gourmont he heard those conversations on style and esthetic
form which were expressed in an aphorism that gives focal expression
to the liaison now set up between the impressionistic principle and the
new esthetic formalism: "Ériger en lois ses impressions personnelles,
c'est le grand effort d'un homme s'il est sincère." From Hulme he
took up a protest against the romantic, the sentimental, the formally
vague and subjective, the relative and the abstract, which the author of
the fragmentary *Speculations* offered as his prophecy of a revival of
classic formalism in modern literature. This principle of form, however, had little to do with the revival of the Aristotelian laws. It gained
its chief stimulation from a contemptuous opposition to the degenerate

romanticism of late Victorian and contemporary writers. For that reason it made a necessity of experiment, and Pound's career became a continuous participation in unconventionality—in Imagism, in Vorticism, in the estheteic laboratories of Paris, in Objectivism, in fact in any activity that satisfied his demand for novelty, exploration, and invention. These labors he never gave the appearance of a system—and purposely so, since "systems become tyrannies overnight"; and although in recent years he has worked toward arguments of social and economic reform, his purpose was never primarily moral, except in the sense that esthetic discipline demands an integrity beyond the formality of practical ethics. His book titles indicate his motives: *Instigations, Irritations, How to Read, The A. B. C. of Reading, Make It New.* All of these were written less to persuade than to irritate and thus to *apply* the authority of creative literature itself. When he defines his "categories" of criticism he opposes the ineffectuality of abstract dogma with the dynamic value of the actual literary text. For him there are:

> 1. Criticism by discussion, extending from mere yatter, logic-chopping, and description of tendencies up to the clearly defined record of procedures and an attempt to formulate more or less general principles. . . . 2. Criticism by translation. . . . 3. Criticism by exercise in the style of a given period. . . . 4. Criticism by music, meaning definitely the setting of a poet's words. . . . This is the most intense form of criticism save: 5. Criticism in new composition.

And "Criticism so far as I have discovered has two functions:"

> 1. Theoretically it tries to forerun composition, to serve as gunsight, though there is, I believe, no recorded instance of this foresight having *ever* been of the slightest use save to actual composers. I mean the man who formulates any forward reach of co-ordinating principle is the man who produces the demonstration. . . . 2. Excernment. The general ordering and weeding out of what has actually been performed. The elimination of repetitions. The work analogous to that which a good hanging committee or curator would perform in a National Gallery or in a biological museum; the ordering of knowledge so that the next man (or generation) can most readily find the live part of it, and waste the least possible time among obsolete issues.

Pound brought criticism back to an active study of texts more directly and unequivocally than impressionism ever aimed to do, and with none of the obstruction by scientific methods that I. A. Richards and his disciples have brought about. His arguments have suffered as much as his style from their explosive purposes; so much so, in fact, that where his later books do not sin by endless reiteration of the familiar clichés of his much-boasted impudence, they become an indistinguishable clutter of classifications that do not classify and distinctions that confuse discrimination. But Pound's work, for all its violence, haphazardness, and shock tactics, has had the virtues that go with these deliberate offenses: it has been direct, energetic, experimental, and seminal. It has had a virtue to which academic criticism can rarely pretend: it has been useful to writers. And it is in his rôle as a teacher of writers that Pound's service has been greatest and his importance in the esthetic thought of our times most decided.

T. S. Eliot shares this distinction, but for very different reasons of temperament and presentation. In him contemporary criticism again finds an influence reinforced at every point by poetic practice. It is in his ability to suggest a principle by pointing out an example that his short essays show their vitality. In *The Sacred Wood* of 1920 Eliot began his work by defining the defects in modern critical methods— the historical and deterministic leanings of Sainte-Beuve and Taine, the ethical bias of the American schools (especially in More and Babbitt), the facile suggestibility of the impressionists, the obscuring rhetorical taste of romanticists like Swinburne and Wyndham, the exaggerated common sense of journalists like Charles Whibley. He found instead his first lessons in the books of Gourmont, whom he called "the critical consciousness of a generation." He set out to bridge the gap between impressionism and reason in critical thought, and his critical program was an attempt to educate the exact and conscientious sensibility (which is as basic to all genuine criticism as it is to poetic creation) through discipline in the ideal conditions and formal principles of art, and only then in the ulterior purposes which art may serve. Eliot was temperamentally as much an anti-romantic as Hulme, and yet he knew that the classic discipline cannot be obtained in modern art or thought through academic exhumation. "One must be firmly distrustful of accepting Aristotle in a canonical spirit; this is to lose the whole living force of him." It was for this reason that he took Gourmont as a model: "He combined to a remarkable degree sensitiveness, erudition, sense of fact and sense of history, and generalizing power," and this combination of assets serves Eliot in his definition of "the perfect critic."

He himself found comparison and the exactly discriminating epithet his two most useful tools in determining the quality of a piece of writing. Though his essays are notable for their aphoristic generalizations, he resisted assuming a doctrine or principle without subjecting it to the empirical proof of his text. With this stress on the necessity of exact textual scrutiny he reproved, especially in his earlier essays where he was still more closely concerned with esthetic and less with ethical problems, the tendencies in modern criticism toward historical explanation, biographical irrelevancies, and the deterministic effects of scientific method or sociological theory. The authors around whom he wrote his best criticism—the Elizabethan dramatists, the metaphysical poets, Dante, Donne, Blake, Baudelaire, Valéry, and Pound—gave those essays on style and form a practical virtue which begins to dissipate as Eliot's criticism has become more philosophically ambitious. His belief in the "isolated superiority" of the artist to practical justification has been modified by his desire to bring the literary object into closer relation with its historical tradition, its moral environment, and its wider human conditions: by his wish, in other words, to explain *The Use of Poetry and the Use of Criticism*. But he remains one of the most fructifying elements in contemporary literary thought, as anxious as ever to keep criticism close to its specific duties. In one of his recent essays, on "Experiment in Criticism," he defines the need of a dialectic discipline which will establish the terminology and analytical methods of literary study and thus correct a deficiency in means which still cripples the work of literary students; and in "Religion and Literature," he makes a statement that ought to be as corrective of existing critical confusions as it indicates the line his own critical career has followed: "The 'greatness' of literature cannot be determined solely by literary standards; though we must remember that whether it is literature or not can be determined only by literary standards."

It was on a basis of the disciplines proposed by Pound and Eliot that esthetic criticism was rescued from vague and static generalization and stimulated by contact with the processes of the modern sensibility. That contact was lacking in men like Brownell and More, and its absence produced in their minds and tempers an inflexible decorum that did an even greater injustice to their own refinements and delicacies of taste than it did to the books that fell under their inspection. It was the maintenance of precisely such a contact that now engaged a younger generation of critics. In 1920 *The Dial* was transformed from its senile condition of reactionary conservatism in Chicago to a new life of literary experimentation in New York, and for a decade it was the chief organ of esthetic critics in America, and with *The Criterion* of London provided a standard for the short careers of *The Hound and Horn* and *The Symposium* that followed. Some of its contributors, like Conrad Aiken, Charles Trueblood, and Cuthbert Wright, adhered to the impressionist manner but keyed it to new effects by their verbal and imaginative skill in poetic analysis. The most brilliant descriptive talent of this kind appeared in Marianne Moore, who showed in her essays the same wit in selecting, discriminating, and combining the effects of an esthetic object as she manifested in her poems.

Two other members of *The Dial's* circle carried their study of modern texts to a point of masterly exposition: Kenneth Burke by situating a book in its setting of ideas and moral influences—the "quality of mind" reduced to the basic structure and complexity of the writer's imagination; and Edmund Wilson by producing from the book in hand an illumination of the specific experience and environment that produced it. Burke, in fact, has been distinguished among contemporary American critics by the persistence and alertness of his training in ideas. It has made him less effective than several of his colleagues in handling the literary item; his practical grasp of stylistic and imaginative properties is diverted in such books as *Counter-Statement* (1931) and *Permanence and Change* (1935) by his larger effort to synthesize the esthetic with the moral and psychological functions of modern literature. But he has examined and corrected the terminology of modern criticism and assayed its scientific and psychological resources to better effect than any other American writer.

Edmund Wilson took another direction. He fell heir to the historical method of the nineteenth century French critics of Sainte-Beuve's, Taine's, and Renan's line who looked to literature for evidence of social and moral forces in the age and the men that produced it. But where this procedure has led most modern critics to a deterministic conception of creative talent, and to the even cruder mechanization of art through sociological and political theory, Wilson kept it critically vigorous by his accurate and sensitive reading of the text before him, by an almost unrivaled talent for narrative summary and exposition, and by seeing esthetic and imaginative developments as something far subtler than the personal and social conditions which surround or at times coerce them. Wilson has divided his interest between the realistic attitude and the esthetic, and in his later work, motivated by his recent and highly unorthodox shift to social sympathies, his contact with the realist school has been revived. He has moved far away from the parochial fastidiousness of his fellow-contributors to *The Dial,* and has yet kept at the distance of alert suspicion his later contemporaries of the Marxist school. In *Axel's Castle* (1930) he wrote studies of six modern authors who show the assimilation and extension of French symbolist and esthetic techniques which, for their historical balance and a lively perception of esthetic motives, make that book one of the most enlightening sketches of the modern literary movement that has been produced in any country.

Another contribution to poetic analysis was made by Yvor Winters. He carried into his essays the same scrutiny of verbal and formal structures that has made his verse a valuable indication of changing motives and disciplines during the past fifteen years. His efforts to analyze the form of modern poetry, to define its processes and find a terminology for them, and to rescue it from the disorder and confusion of aimless experimentation, have led him toward more and more con-servative principles, partly influenced by the neo-classical arguments of Irving Babbitt, partly by a personal contempt for the abuses and anti-intellectual tendencies of artistic experiment based on psychic and amoral motives. Recently, in *Primitivism and Decadence* (1936), he reverts to one of the most austere and reproving statements of the classical position that has been written in the present century. A similar sense of traditional disciplines has worked in the criticism of Allen Tate, but with wider cultural references and with more specific appli-cation to the predicament of contemporary society, as measured by the classic standards of Southern life. Here again the obligation of poetic analysis has preceded the responsibility of historical arguments or moral relationships. It is by combining these three issues that he has made his volume of *Reactionary Essays* (1936) an important demonstration of the problems that meet a critic when he attempts to reconcile modern innovation with the formal order implicit in tradition. The special distinction of R. P. Blackmur's criticism, on the other hand, lies in its elucidation of verbal and stylistic properties. No one except William Empson in England has carried this method to greater lengths of meticulous discrimination, and no one in the field of linguistic analysis has shown greater patience or sensitiveness. It is a method particularly dangerous to transfer from the descriptive to the synthetic level, and in *The Double Agent* (1935) Blackmur has not arrived at that co-ordina-tion. But the effort would be worthless without the kind of severe scrutiny of technique he has made, and his criticism remains at its present point of indecision largely because he has realized so fully the complexity of the literary problems which an exact analysis of the text can impose on a critic.

It is in fact the thoroughness of their stylistic investigations, the pene-trating insight of their studies of poetic words, patterns, and structures, that has not only removed the best of these younger esthetic critics from the irresponsible conjurings of the impressionists, but has made them far too conscious of all that is implied and involved in the creative process to bring it into easy alignment with social or moral formulae. In them the impressionist procedure is at once rationalized and corrected, and more utilitarian critical methods are shown up in their routine of in-flexible prejudice and ineptitude.

V

The apparent hostility among the new critical schools after the War was to some extent deceptive. Beneath it there existed a secret treaty among realists and esthetes, a recognition of the common enemy of reaction, and an implicit alliance of the kind one may detect beneath the conflicting appearances of naturalism, impressionism, and symbolism in the French schools of the late nineteenth century. They joined in accepting the heritage of romanticism, however they may have varied in their use of it. They assumed the unity of man and nature on a monistic principle, and the common belief that this unity is to be realized initially through sensory and intuitive agencies. They differed chiefly in their notions of the means—the instruments of esthetic experience and expression—by which the work of art conveys this unity. They were divided as craftsmen and temperaments, but not as believers, and the same may be said of the critics who adhered to them as prophets or defenders.

There was also a general agreement among them concerning the subject matter of art—its freedom from, or its equal value in, moral purpose; and when a sudden display of reaction struck from another quarter, it threw them into an alliance more abrupt and strenuous than their two decades of public success and divergence had prepared them for. For a number of years the enemy was considered cowed, but he was not invisible. Books like *Democracy and Leadership, Rousseau and Romanticism,* and the eleven volumes of *Shelburne Essays* had been appearing for twenty years. Mencken had fulminated against the "gloomy humors" of Paul Elmer More for several decades, and Babbitt had raised the dust of controversy in both academic and public circles. But critics as a whole had relegated such vexations to the dust-bins of the Victorian Age. They were as certain of their emancipation as they were that the day was over for reviving beliefs about the dualism of man and nature, of good and evil, of reason and instinct, and convictions about the distance that lies between the purely natural order of experience and the art which results only when prudence selects, judgment shapes, and the moral will gives ethical value to that experience. Those beliefs were implicit in the American moral tradition and a latent fear of their eruption was implied by Lewisohn's anthology of 1918, *A Book of Modern Criticism,* which came as a warning against the slumbering dragon of reaction, by Spingarn's manifesto of a decade earlier, and by a critical symposium printed in *The New Republic* in 1921 which formed a fresh defense of impressionism and liberal rebellion for the younger critics of the hour.

Meanwhile the reaction was organizing its forces. Its name, "Humanism," had already been accepted from Babbitt's teachings. It had representatives all over the country, chiefly on college faculties; Prosser Hall Frye promoted the cause in Nebraska, Norman Foerster in North Carolina, Robert Shafer in Ohio, a considerable phalanx in the strongholds of New England, and Stuart Sherman in Illinois before he finally confessed himself a renegade from the ranks, became a literary editor in New York, turned liberal, and lost the wit and geniality he had contributed to his first allegiance. The acknowledged leaders of these men remained More and Babbitt, who wrote the program and creed by which all of them, with due allowance for personal errors and deviations, swore.

It was a creed which defined one central enemy, the Romantic Movement; one chief source of grievance, Rousseau; one main purpose, the integration of literary criticism with ethical; and one chief means of deciding the quality of a work of literature, its validity in moral qualities. Inheriting the Puritan austerity of the early American fathers, it had skirted the skepticism of Emerson and his generation in such a way as to remain aloof from committal to religious faith and dogma. It preferred the discipline not of theological beliefs but of the human norm, and it looked for salvation not by sacrificing personal energy in an acceptance of supernatural authority, but by enhancing its sense of human identity through restraint and self-control. Art thus became a means of judging man's nature chiefly in the degree to which it expressed this discipline.

More published his first book of essays in 1904 and there, in an essay on "Criticism," he lamented in nineteenth century critics like Arnold not "any intrinsic want of efficiency in the critical spirit, not . . . any want of moral earnestness," but the fact that "these men were lacking in another direction: they missed a philosophy which could bind together their moral and their esthetic sense, a positive principle besides the negative force of ridicule and irony; and missing this, they left critcism more easily subject to a one-sided and dangerous development" —that which promoted the modern heresies of "naturalism," impressionism, subjectivity, and moral anarchy. For him literary criticism was "the specific exercise of a faculty which works in many directions. All scholars, whether they deal with history or sociology or philosophy or language or, in the narrower use of the lord, literature, are servants of the critical spirit, in so far as they transmit and interpret and mold the sum of experience from man to man and generation to generation."

The humanist ethic gave More his binding principle. At first his sense of art and personality was eager and often penetrating, but as the *Shelburne Essays* mounted, his responsibility to "the sum of experience" subdued it more and more, until finally he turned away from literature and explored the historical background of modern humanism itself, attempting to integrate the Christian ideal with the humanistic principle of Plato and the Greeks.

What he brought to American philosophic and ethical thought was one matter; what he contributed to criticism another. He supplied a model of erudition and high seriousness that admitted no suspicion of purely esthetic or vaguely cultural leanings. But unfortunately this came to shed less and less light on either the contemporary world around him or the literature it produced; it stiffened his sensibilities as well as his integrity; and while he never erred by the blunting pedantry of many of his younger colleagues, his confinement of acceptable art in the tight circle of his moral prejudice caused him to reject the very art that would really have invigorated and humanized his doctrines. He believed that "literature divorced from life is an empty pursuit," but his conceptions of literature's dependence on experience became as arbitrary and as remote from the moral struggles of his contemporaries as his sense of the "meaning of life" stopped short of the understanding that kindles in imagination or language the fire of an overwhelming conviction. His belief that such conviction had failed to appear in modern literature may have been a reflection of its failure in his own thought.

Irving Babbitt was always a keener controversialist than More, and to him fell the more polemical rôle in the Humanist revival that broke out late in the twenties. He was less a critic of books than of ideas, and the ideas he attacked inevitably led him back to the chief source of his vexations, Rousseau. He assayed creative works rarely, but made an exhaustive study of the influences and cultural circumstances that produce them—educational systems, political movements, religious bodies, academic standards, classical traditions, ethical beliefs. The modern condition of these he invariably deplored as anarchic and decadent. He accepted in his early years the classic ideal, and declared himself the enemy of all that opposed it under the romantic canon: democratic individualism, freedom of press and speech, free esthetic experiment, any vestige of the eccentric or idiosyncratic in art or conduct. He formulated the tenets to which the younger Humanists subscribed—the ideals of wholeness, proportion, and the human norm; the constants of tradition as against the limiting "specialism" of the time-spirit; the discipline of reason, of imagination when controlled by reason, and those virtues of restraint and humility which are the final evidence of the ethical dignity of man.

Babbitt's work had its esthetic motive, and his prescription of virtues was intended to apply to criticism their instrument of discipline in the disordered world of modern culture. When he stated his rule for critics he made that clear: the critic must "rate creation with reference to some standard set both above his own temperament and that of the creator. . . . He will begin to have taste only when he refers the creative expression and his impression of it to some standard that is set above both." This is a worthy precept for any kind of rational judgment, and Babbitt had the worthy intention of correcting by it the sterility and solipsism of critical license around him. But the validity of such a rule depends wholly on its grasp of the two terms it employs: the integrity of the "impression" gained from a literary investigation, and the authority of the "standard" to which it is referred. Babbitt's failure in sensibility was extreme: in his last book, *On Being Creative* (1931), he equated modern writers like Dreiser, Joyce, and Dos Passos with no effort at discriminating their qualities, and the standard he defined in Greek and Latin masterpieces proved so inert that he was incapable of sympathizing with, and therefore understanding, any but a few isolated or academic imitations of it in the past eight centuries. Babbitt's distinguished mind was a prey to this mechanistic and pharisaical inflexibility of doctrine, and his critical limitations (as opposed to his scholarly and historical eminence) have been well pointed out recently by a confessed disciple, Yvor Winters: "his analysis of literary principles appears to me to be gravely vitiated by an almost complete ignorance of the manner in which the moral intelligence actually gets into poetry."

The battle over Humanism was unfortunately conducted in a mood too full of heat, rancor, and confusion to represent the issues involved fairly. Thus it appeared as a last stand of the Puritan tradition against the enemies that had multiplied around it. What it might have achieved in correcting the aimlessness and vulgarity of the more irresponsible talents it opposed was as largely nullified by its own intolerance and imperviousness as by the enraged violence of the forces it stirred to attack. There were looseness, irresponsibility, and crudity to reprove, and Humanism has left good effects behind, even though they bear little resemblance to what Babbitt and More demanded. But it never attacked its problems squarely. It aimed to correct and guide the conflicts of the modern consciousness, but it succeeded chiefly in ignoring them; it reduced imaginative and creative processes to a mechanical routine; it missed the wider and profounder sympathy of a genuinely religious spirit and at the same time failed to grasp the struggles of the skeptical spirit in seeking a basis of values in experience. Thus it fell ambiguously between the rigor of realistic induction that has produced the valid thought of naturalist writers, and the genuine metaphysical convictions of Frenchmen like Maurras, Maritain, and

DuBos, whose interpretations of Thomistic esthetic doctrine have thus far encouraged little similar activity in America. The controversy of 1929 and 1930 centered in serious issues, but these were reduced to the obtuse didacticism of the "genteel tradition," the pedantry and intolerance of an academic principle. And when it died down it left the critical situation much as it found it, and another type of moral argument—that of the social critics and proletarian revolutionaries—took up the attack on such irresponsibility as was held to reside in realist and esthetic liberalism. A new alignment of critics soon appeared, one closer to the specific conditions of modern writing and therefore more vigorous in its appeal to the public and in its grasp of the problems of imaginative writers.

VI

It was a more realistic attack that now rose against the free critical traffic of the nineteen-twenties. That decade ended under darker clouds than Humanism had conjured up. When the economic disaster of 1929 struck, it dropped its bolts on one of the most productive literary periods America had seen. The high hopes and privileges of the liberal generation were bent at a blow, and prophets of disaster like Dreiser and Robinson, who had spoken in the hour of general illusion, found a new honor. From Paris the esthetes returned with shorn incomes and roughly opened eyes, finding their historian in Malcolm Cowley, whose *Exile's Return* described their awakening from the "religion of art" to the realities of making a living in a jobless world. The confidences of 1912 or 1918 sank as swiftly as the graph-lines on stock-brokers' charts. The realist and esthetic critics found their claims diminishing under harsh dispute, and deserters from their ranks began to take up the study and defense of economic arguments. Humanism had reacted chiefly against the claims of naturalism, but the awakened sense of social responsibility in reformers took esthetic and liberal doctrines as its chief object of attack. It was by this alignment of creeds that the major critical issues of the nineteen-thirties were defined.

The necessity in criticism of a social principle was not a new argument. Whitman, Howells, and Adams were three of its early prophets, and the liberals of Bourne's generation made it a dominant tenet in their program of critical realism. These pioneers, however, submitted too easily to the malady of the humanitarian ideal to satisfy their inheritors. They accepted the grandeurs of the American future in too mystical a spirit, compromising too easily with the hopes of rugged individualism or democratic culture, and holding aloof from committal to more positive beliefs. These required in their simplest essentials an attack on the capitalistic monopoly and competitive license which Howells, whatever sense he may have had of the ethical defects of American society, considered the proper complement of democratic enterprise. The nineteenth century reformers most acceptable to the American way of life had been acceptable because they left their revolutionary counsels at a mid-point of compromise, and stopped short of imposing the technical and forcible reforms of economic socialism. Some books were written, however, outside the literary field which forecast those reforms in highly trenchant language, and these in time were to influence critics of sociological sympathies more than the manuals of their own craft. The most important of these was Thorstein Veblen's *Theory of the Leisure Class.* More recently American criticism itself had turned toward economic premises: Upton Sinclair published *The Industrial Republic* as early as 1907 and *Mammonart* as late as 1925, and his angle of literary interpretation was turned to more esthetic uses by V. F. Calverton in his "sociological criticism of literature," *The Newer Spirit* (1925) and in *The Liberation of American Literature* (1930). Both these men were urging a need while their recent rivals were still absorbed by now-repudiated liberal or esthetic allegiances. But the shortcomings now commonly charged against them on dialectic grounds were fully as obvious on esthetic grounds when their books were first published. They made literature a function of the social order without having arrived at a realistic articulation of the creative imagination with social necessities, and at the same time without a technique of rationalization which could cope successfully with the subtleties of esthetic, as opposed to economic, experience. Calverton, though he has lately expressed a healthy dislike of the mechanistic routine of the average Marxist interpretation, has himself accepted too smoothly the deterministic procedure of Taine. The result is that his *Liberation of American Literature* is chiefly interesting for the lengths to which it pushes a prejudice and a method.

The social line of criticism since 1930 has profited by a situation much more conducive to serious discipline than existed before. For one thing, controversy is sufficiently active to offset the extravagances of party politics. For another, the defenders of the esthetic approach to literature have bestirred themselves to a more severe line of reasoning in order to match the subtleties of the materialist dialectic, and thus benefited their own cause while challenging the extremes of its opposite. Again, fresh growths of socially motivated literature have revealed the pitfalls of propaganda so obviously as to provide a caution to those critics who have defended this function in art too glibly. And finally, the profound economic distress of the times has aroused a general agreement on the moral ends of literature, spurred a critical examination of them, and established much more forcefully than formerly the necessity of seeing what constitutes the truth and integrity of a work of literature before it can produce its desired effects in social or moral regeneration. Obviously these benefits have been accompanied by corresponding evils. Critical activity has been distracted by false simplifications and partisan bias. Its magazines have substituted personal abuse for sober thinking, and eloquence for logic. There has flourished a loose contempt for whatever is out of momentary fashion and a consequent discarding of many literary works that might enlighten the dispute (or even support the cause of their condemners) to far greater advantage than the shoddy tracts that are often seized upon as profoundly significant. And there has risen so slovenly and uncritical a warfare of terms and premises—debates over the "function" of art, "utility," "ideology," "mass consciousness," "bourgeois" versus "proletarian," and "autonomy" versus "propaganda"—that the mere communication of intelligence about these causes, lacking as it does the very discipline of logic or dialectic that is the boasted advantage of their exponents, has lapsed into dilemma and confusion.

The implications of this problem are too complex to admit of easy statement. But the responsibilities of criticism remain at the same time too emphatic and unmistakable to allow the term to be applied to nine-tenths of what has passed by that title in the journals and newspapers of the past eight years. (This is equally true, however, of other kinds of apologetic; it would be unjust to make the reservation against the social critic any severer than against the common types of religious or political.) Yet the work of a number of writers in this field shows exceptional distinction, either in historical analysis or in a careful discrimination of issues. On the historical side the best statements appear in the last chapter of Wilson's *Axel's Castle,* where the divergence of art and life, pure poetry and social realism, in modern literature is described; in Cowley's *Exile's Return,* where the same division in the lives of present-day artists and critics is defined; and in such literary memoirs as Granville Hicks' *John Reed* or Joseph Freeman's *An American Testament,* which form sequels to the sort of biographical study of literary problems that Bourne wrote in his *Literary Radical.*. The most ambitious attempt to bring the literary history of America into alignment with the Marxist propositions is that of Granville Hicks' *The Great Tradition* (1933), but its coherence of argument and its graphic distinction are soon rendered suspect by the facility with which he accepts or dismisses the writers of American literature according to the degree in which they satisfy his highly simplified and crudely applied proposition on the interdependence of literature and economic law. It is be-

cause of their talent for more closely reasoned and yet more broadly
informed interpretation that the essays of William Phillips and Philip
Rahv are an improvement over those of Hicks, and have become in the
last two or three years, especially through their obvious distress over the
abuses of "leftist" journalism, among the keenest to appear in American
radical journals.   The same distinction applies to the work of Kenneth
Burke since his recent conversion to communist principles.   A valuable
contribution to this controversy came in 1936 from the novelist, James
T. Farrell, in *A Note on Literary Criticism.*   This essay was prompted
by the flagrant lapses in sound appreciation and valid reasoning among
social critics of the past decade.   It formed a reproof to offenders, and
a sketch of highly necessary corrections and qualifications, thus far not
surpassed by the critics to whom it was addressed.   And it further
reminds one that an escape from the mechanistic routine of the average
social criticism is also available in the work of men who know, by their
own practice, the creative task too intimately to permit it to be humbled
by propagandist and utilitarian assignments.   This is the value of the
poetic criticism of Horace Gregory and the discussions of the modern
novel of Robert Cantwell, in both of whom the esthetic insight usually
missing among their fellow-believers is redeemed.

That a firmer activity is in force among these critics may be seen in
the bulletins of the Writers' Congress, in the presence of men like Kenneth Burke, and in such statements as this one by Phillips and Rahv:

> Unfortunately many misguided enthusiasts of revolution, effacing
> their own experience, take for their subject-matter the public philos-
> ophy as such, or attempt to adorn with rhetorical language conven-
> tionalized patterns of feeling and action.   What they don't see is that
> these patterns are, in the final analysis, just as impersonal as the
> philosophy itself. . . . If there is to be an ever-fresh balance between
> the accent of the poet and the attitude he shares with other people,
> he must understand the connection between what is *real* to him as
> an individual and what is *real* to him as a partisan of some given
> philosophy.

And in his introduction to the anthology, *Proletarian Literature in
the United States* (1935), Joseph Freeman, admitting the immaturity of
much of the writing and criticism of his cause, gives another indication
of how much caution and discipline is required there:

> No party resolution, no government decree, can produce art, or
> transform an agitator into a poet.   A party card does not automati-
> cally endow a communist with artistic genius.   Whatever it is that

makes an artist, as distinguished from a scientist or man of action, it is something beyond the power of anyone to produce deliberately. But once the artist is here, once there is the man with the specific sensibility, the mind, the emotions, the images, the gift for language which make the creative writer, he is not a creature in a vacuum.

This may be embarrassingly elementary; it may merely rephrase what James and Eliot long ago learned; but it indicates the corrective impulse at work in the social ranks, and a promise of the serious results their ambition is already fixed on.

VII

Probably no other space of fifty years has seen the conflict of so many critical schools as the half-century which has been sketched here. America has seen something of all of them, from those that look on art as no longer "even by implication a device for improving the mind" to those that recognize neither the artist nor the critic except in the rôle of moralist and reformer. This outline of developments has been short; it has simplified greatly the ideas of the critics it has discussed; it has merely suggested the ordeals of modern life and thought that have made their difficulties great. But it has traced a line of activity that brings us to the situation of the present moment and even if it does little to solve the perplexities of those who go to criticism for guidance and advice, it should show why those perplexities exist; why, indeed, they exist in the mind of the critic himself and give his work its special importance in our time.

The title of critic is no longer allowed to the mere sampler of books, the enthusiast for art, the adventurer among masterpieces. A few men have written beautiful prose in these rôles, but criticism comes much harder than that. It ranks next to art itself in the insight it commands into the intellectual and spiritual problems of an age. It studies the most intense and subtle forms which those problems can assume. Unless the critic ultimately realizes that he is handling such problems in their fullest complexity and meaning, he is not likely to hold the respect of a serious reader, or make a contribution to the intelligence of his contemporaries.

The difficulty with most modern criticism is that it tackles these problems long before it understands what literature makes of them. It looks for them in the shape of systematic arguments, or simple statements of emotion and belief. No definition of poetry or fiction was ever worth listening to that claimed for art no purpose but to serve up the subtleties and ordeals of human experience in such formulated terms. Yet that is what many critics demand of it, and that is why they defeat their purposes and do so little to advance either the true value of art, the intelligence of their readers, or even the causes they claim to defend. And as a result they misapply their energies, and assume that because the air is stirred by conflict and hostility a great deal is being accomplished.

In an elementary sense something is. Contemporary American critics have achieved their first distinction by refusing to be complacent, academic, and easy to accept. These virtues afflicted their calling when Poe, Whitman, and Henry James began to disturb the scene, and whenever they gain the upper hand, criticism falls into pedantry, loses touch with art, and lapses into abstract formulation and inert theory. Occasionally they threaten to return, but that danger is no longer so likely. Another has taken its place: the danger of making criticism as well as art the obvious agent of propaganda. When that purpose succeeds, the critic falls into fully as great an ineffectuality as when he takes on the robes of academic pedantry. He may be serving a nobler cause, but his claim to the critic's title is fully as spurious. He may express a just contempt of academic routine or the irresponsibility of "liberalism" and "impressionism," but he may merely be shirking his own responsibilities when he does so, and is likely to have little of value to say about literature.

We have seen in recent years the shortcomings of so many critical methods that it is not surprising that a general doubt has risen as to whether criticism has any craft or principles of its own. No theory seems to work satisfactorily, and when practical analysis is applied to a piece of writing, it is likely to take the form of verse-tests, vowel and consonant statistics, charts, graphs, and the lumbering machinery of the class-room. To suppose that these of themselves get any closer than abstract dogmas to the workings of the creative imagination is to delay still further the whole appreciation of what criticism must undertake to do. We have had in our time several descriptions of "the perfect critic." If perfection is wanted, one might as well say that a critic must have everything in the way of sensitiveness, perception, and even verbal skill that the artist himself has. But instead of *expressing* his intelligence he explains it; instead of exposing it by the laws of art he defines and examines it by the laws of reason; instead of writing poetry or fiction he decides why others have written them, and how successfully. It is only when he has reached such a decision by the fullest exercise of his sensibility and rational powers that the critic can use his findings for some purpose beyond the specific conditions that art itself imposes. To do this well is work enough for a life-time of patience, sympathy, and curiosity. If the American critic needs any encouragement to undertake it, he may turn to several of his fellow-citizens, Henry James the first among them, who have not only assured him that his work is worth doing, but have done a good deal to show how it can be carried out.

Part I

VERSIONS OF TRADITION AND RESPONSIBILITY

T. S. ELIOT

Tradition and the Individual Talent

In English writing we seldom speak of tradition, though we occasionally apply its name in deploring its absence. We cannot refer to "the tradition" or to "a tradition"; at most, we employ the adjective in saying that the poetry of So-and-so is "traditional," or even "too traditional." Seldom, perhaps, does the word appear except in a phrase of censure. If otherwise, it is vaguely approbative, with the implication, as to the work approved, of some pleasing archaeological reconstruction. You can hardly make the word agreeable to English ears without this comfortable reference to the reassuring science of archaeology.

Certainly the word is not likely to appear in our appreciations of living or dead writers. Every nation, every race, has not only its own creative, but its own critical turn of mind; and is even more oblivious of the shortcomings and limitations of its critical habits than of those of its creative genius. We know, or think we know, from the enormous mass of critical writing that has appeared in the French language the critical method or habit of the French; we only conclude (we are such unconscious people) that the French are "more critical" than we, and sometimes even plume ourselves a little with the fact, as if the French were the less spontaneous. Perhaps they are; but we might remind ourselves that criticism is as inevitable as breathing, and that we should be none the worse for articulating what passes in our minds when we read a book, and feel an emotion about it, for criticising our own minds in their work of criticism. One of the facts that might come to light in this process is our tendency to insist, when we praise a poet, upon those aspects of his work in which he least resembles anyone else.

From *Selected Essays, 1917-32,* by T. S. Eliot. Pp. 3-12. Copyright, 1932. By permission of Harcourt, Brace and Co., Inc. Reprinted from *The Sacred Wood* (1920).

3

In these aspects or parts of his work we pretend to find what is individual, what is the peculiar essence of the man. We dwell with satisfaction upon the poet's difference from his predecessors; we endeavor to find something that can be isolated in order to be enjoyed. Whereas if we approach a poet without this prejudice we shall often find that not only the best, but the most individual parts of his work may be those in which the dead poets, his ancestors, assert their immortality most vigorously. And I do not mean the impressionable period of adolescence, but the period of full maturity.

Yet if the only form of tradition, of handing down, consisted in following the ways of the immediate generation before us in a blind or timid adherence to its successes, "tradition" should positively be discouraged. We have seen many such simple currents soon lost in the sand; and novelty is better than repetition. Tradition is a matter of much wider significance. It cannot be inherited, and if you want it you must obtain it by great labor. It involves, in the first place, the historical sense, which we may call nearly indispensable to anyone who would continue to be a poet beyond his twenty-fifth year; and the historical sense involves a perception, not only of the pastness of the past, but of its presence; the historical sense compels a man to write not only with his own generation in his bones, but with a feeling that the whole of the literature of Europe from Homer and within it the whole of the literature of his own country has a simultaneous existence and composes a simultaneous order. This historical sense, which is a sense of the timeless as well as of the temporal and of the timeless and of the temporal together, is what makes a writer traditional. And it is at the same time what makes a writer most acutely conscious of his place in time, of his own contemporaneity.

No poet, no artist of any art, has his complete meaning alone. His significance, his appreciation is the appreciation of his, relation to the dead poets and artists. You cannot value him alone; you must set him, for contrast and comparison, among the dead. I mean this as a principle of esthetic, not merely historical, criticism. The necessity that he shall conform, that he shall cohere, is not one-sided; what happens when a new work of art is created is some-thing that happens simultaneously to all the works of art which preceded it. The existing monuments form an ideal order among themselves, which is modified by the introduction of the new (the really new) work of art among them. The existing order is com-plete before the new work arrives; for order to exist after the super-vention of novelty, the *whole* existing order must be, if ever so slightly, altered; and so the relations, proportions, values of each work of art toward the whole are readjusted; and this is conform-ity between the old and the new. Whoever has approved this idea of order, of the form of European, of English literature, will not find it preposterous that the past should be altered by the present as much as the present is directed by the past. And the poet who is aware of this will be aware of great difficulties and responsibilities.

In a peculiar sense he will be aware also that he must inevitably be judged by the standards of the past. I say judged, not ampu-tated by them; not judged to be as good as, or worse or better than, the dead; and certainly not judged by the canons of dead critics. It is a judgment, a comparison, in which two things are measured by each other. To conform merely would be for the new work not to conform at all; it would not be new, and would therefore not be a work of art. And we do not quite say that the new is more valuable because it fits in; but its fitting in is a test of its value—a test, it is true, which can only be slowly and cautiously applied, for we are none of us infallible judges of conformity. We say: it ap-pears to conform, and is perhaps individual, or it appears individual and may conform; but we are hardly likely to find that it is the one, and not the other.

To proceed to a more intelligible exposition of the relation of the poet to the past: he can neither take the past as a lump, an indiscriminate bolus, nor can he form himself wholly on one or two private admirations, nor can he form himself wholly upon one preferred period. The first course is inadmissible, the second is an important experience of youth, and the third is a pleasant and highly desirable supplement. The poet must be very conscious of the main current, which does not at all flow invariably through the most distinguished reputations. He must be quite aware of the obvious fact that art never improves, but that the material of art is never quite the same. He must be aware that the mind of Europe—the mind of his own country—a mind which he learns in time to be much more important than his own private mind—is a mind which changes, and that this change is a development that abandons nothing *en route,* which does not superannuate either Shakespeare, or Homer, or the rock drawing of the Magdalenian draughtsman. That this development, refinement perhaps, complication certainly, is not, from the point of view of the artist, any improvement. Perhaps not even an improvement from the point of view of the psychologist or not to the extent which we imagine: perhaps only in the end based upon a complication in economics and machinery. But the difference between the present and the past is that the conscious present is an awareness of the past in a way and to an extent which the past's awareness of itself cannot show.

Someone said: "The dead writers are remote from us because we *know* so much more than they did." Precisely, and they are that which we know.

I am alive to the usual objection to what is clearly part of my program for the *métier* of poetry. The objection is that the doctrine requires a ridiculous amount of erudition (pedantry), a claim which can be rejected by appeal to the lives of poets in any pantheon. It will even be affirmed that much learning deadens or perverts poetic sensibility. While, however, we persist in believing that a poet ought to know as much as will not encroach upon his necessary receptivity and necessary laziness, it is not desirable to confine knowledge to whatever can be put into a useful shape for examinations, drawing-rooms, or the still more pretentious modes of publicity. Some can absorb knowledge, the more tardy must sweat for it. Shakespeare acquired more essential history from Plutarch than most men could from the whole British Museum. What is to be insisted upon is that the poet must develop or procure the consciousness of the past and that he should continue to develop this consciousness throughout his career.

What happens is a continual surrender of himself as he is at the moment to something which is more valuable. The progress of an artist is a continual self-sacrifice, a continual extinction of personality.

There remains to define this process of depersonalization, and its relation to the essence of tradition. It is in this depersonalization that art may be said to approach the condition of science. I shall, therefore, invite you to consider a suggestive analogy, the action which takes place when a bit of finely filiated platinum is introduced into a chamber containing oxygen and sulphur dioxide.

II

Honest criticism and sensitive appreciation is directed not upon the poet but upon the poetry. If we attend to the confused cries of the newspaper critics and the susurrus of popular repetition that follows, we shall hear the names of the poets in great numbers; if we seek not Blue-book knowledge but the enjoyment of poetry, and ask for a poem, we shall seldom find it. I have already tried to point out the importance of the relation of the poem to other poems by other authors, and suggested the conception of poetry as a living whole of all the poetry that has ever been written. The other aspect of this impersonal theory of poetry is the relation of the poem to its author. And I hinted, by an analogy, that the mind of the mature poet differs from that of the immature one not precisely in any valuation of "personality," not being necessarily more interesting, or having "more to say," but rather being a more finely perfected medium in which special or very varied feelings are at liberty to enter into new combinations. The analogy was that of the catalyst. When the two gases previously mentioned are mixed in the presence of a filament of platinum, they formed sulphurous acid. This combination takes place only if the platinum is present; nevertheless the newly formed acid contains no trace of platinum, and the platinum itself is apparently unaffected; has remained inert, neutral, and unchanged. The mind of the poet is the shred of platinum. It may partly or exclusively operate upon the experience of the man himself; but the more perfect the artist, the more completely separate in him will be the man who suffers and the mind which creates; the more perfectly will the mind digest and transmute the passions which are its material.

The experience, you will notice, the elements which enter the presence of the transforming catalyst, are of two kinds: emotions and feelings. The effect of a work of art upon the person who enjoys it is an experience different in kind from any experience not of art. It may be formed out of one emotion, or may be a combination of several; and various feelings, inhering for the writer in particular words or phrases or images, may be added to compose the final result. Or great poetry may be made without the direct use of any emotion whatever: composed out of feelings solely. Canto XV of the *Inferno* (Brunetto Latini) is a working up of the emotion evident in the situation; but the effect, though single as that of any work of art, is obtained by considerable complexity of detail. The last quatrain gives an image, a feeling attaching to an image which "came," which did not develop simply out of what precedes, but which was probably in suspension in the poet's mind until the proper combination arrived for it to add itself to. The poet's mind is, in fact, a receptacle for seizing and storing up numberless feelings, phrases, images, which remain there until all the particles which can unite to form a new compound are present together.

If you compare several representative passages of the greatest poetry you see how great is the variety of types of combination, and also how completely any semi-ethical criterion of "sublimity" misses the mark. For it is not the "greatness," the intensity of the emotions, the components, but the intensity of the artistic process, the pressure, so to speak, under which the fusion takes place, that counts. The episode of Paolo and Francesca employs a definite emotion, but the intensity of the poetry is something quite different from whatever intensity in the supposed experience it may give the impression of. It is no more intense, furthermore, than Canto XXVI, the voyage of Ulysses, which has not the direct dependence upon an emotion. Great variety is possible in the process of transmutation of emotion: the murder of Agamemnon, or the agony of Othello, gives an artistic effect apparently closer to a possible original than the scenes from Dante. In the *Agamemnon,* the artistic emotion approximates to the emotion of an actual spectator; in *Othello* to the emotion of the protagonist himself. But the difference between art and the event is always absolute; the combination which is the murder of Agamemnon is probably as complex as that which is the voyage of Ulysses. In either case there has been a fusion of elements. The ode of Keats contains a number of things which have nothing particular to do with the nightingale, but which the nightingale, partly perhaps because of its attractive name, and partly because of its reputation, served to bring together.

The point of view which I am struggling to attack is perhaps related to the metaphysical theory of the substantial unity of the soul: for my meaning is, that the poet has not a "personality" to express, but a particular medium, which is only a medium, and not a personality, in which impressions and experiences combine in peculiar and unexpected ways. Impressions and experiences which are important for the man may take no place in the poetry, and those which become important in the poetry may play quite a negligible part in the man, the personality.

I will quote a passage which is unfamiliar enough to be regarded with fresh attention in the light—or darkness—of these observations:

And now methinks I could e'en chide myself
For doating on her beauty, though her death
Shall be revenged after no common action.
Does the silkworm expend her yellow labours
For thee? For thee does she undo herself?
Are lordships sold to maintain ladyships
For the poor benefit of a bewildering minute?
Why does yon fellow falsify highways,
And put his life between the judge's lips,
To refine such a thing—keeps horse and men
To beat their valours for her? . . .

In this passage (as is evident if it is taken in its context) there is a combination of positive and negative emotions: an intensely strong attraction toward beauty, and an equally intense fascination by the ugliness which is contrasted with it and which destroys it. This balance of contrasted emotion is in the dramatic situation to which the speech is pertinent, but that situation alone is inadequate to it. This is, so to speak, the structural emotion, provided by the drama. But the whole effect, the dominant tone, is due to the fact that a number of floating feelings having an affinity to this emotion by no means superficially evident have combined with it to give us a new art emotion.

It is not in his personal emotions, the emotions provoked by particular events in his life, that the poet is in any way remarkable or interesting. His particular emotions may be simple, or crude, or flat. The emotion in his poetry will be a very complex thing, but not with the complexity of the emotions of people who have very complex or unusual emotions in life. One error, in fact, of eccentricity in poetry is to seek for new human emotions to express; and in this search for novelty in the wrong place it discovers the perverse. The business of the poet is not to find new emotions, but to use the ordinary ones, and in working them up into poetry, to express feelings which are not in the actual emotions at all. And emotions which he has never experienced will serve his turn as well as those familiar to him. Consequently we must believe that "emotion recollected in tranquillity" is an inexact formula. For it is neither emotion nor recollection, nor, without distortion of meaning, tranquillity. It is a concentration, and a new thing resulting from the concentration, of a very great number of experiences which to the practical and active person would not seem to be experiences at all; it is a concentration which does not happen consciously or of deliberation. These experiences are not "recollected," and they finally unite in an atmosphere which is "tranquil" only in that it is a passive attending upon the event. Of course, this is not quite the whole story. There is a great deal in the writing of poetry which must be conscious and deliberate. In fact, the bad poet is usually unconscious where he ought to be conscious, and conscious where he ought to be unconscious. Both errors tend to make him "personal." Poetry is not a turning loose of emotion, but an escape from emotion; it is not the expression of personality, but an escape from personality. But, of course, only those who have personality and emotions know what it means to want to escape from these things.

III

ὁ δὲ νοῦς ἴσως θειότερόν τι καὶ ἀπαθές ἐστιν.[1]

This essay proposes to halt at the frontier of metaphysics or mysticism, and confine itself to such practical conclusions as can be applied by the responsible person interested in poetry. To divert interest from the poet to the poetry is a laudable aim: for it would conduce to a juster estimation of actual poetry, good and bad. There are many people who appreciate the expression of sincere emotion in verse, and there is a smaller number of people who can appreciate technical excellence. But very few know when there is expression of *significant* emotion, emotion which has its life in the poem, and not in the history of the poet. The emotion of art is impersonal. And the poet cannot reach this impersonality without surrendering himself wholly to the work to be done. And he is not likely to know what is to be done unless he lives in what is not merely the present, but the present moment of the past, unless he is conscious, not of what is dead, but of what is already living.

Experiment in Criticism

THERE is no department of literature in which it is more difficult to establish a distinction between "traditional" and "experimental" work than literary criticism. For here both words may be taken

[1] FREELY translated:
The mind of man can be as inspired as it is apathetic.

From *The Bookman*, LXX, No. 3. November, 1929. Pp. 225-233. Reprinted by permission of author and editor. The essay has not been collected by the author in his books.

in two senses. By traditional criticism we may mean that which follows the same methods, aims at the same ends, and expresses much the same state of mind as the criticism of the preceding generation. Or we may mean something quite different; a criticism which has a definite theory of the meaning and value of the term "tradition," and which may be experimental in reverting to masters who have been forgotten. And as for "experiment" one may mean the more original work of the present generation, or else the work of critics who are pushing into new fields of inquiry, or enlarging the scope of criticism with other kinds of knowledge. To use the word "experimental" in the first sense would be invidious, for it would cover all the critical work of our time which one considers to have merit. For it is obvious that every generation has a new point of view, and is self-conscious in the critic; his work is twofold: to interpret the past to the present, and to judge the present in the light of the past. We have to see literature through our own temperament in order to see it at all, though our vision is always partial and our judgment always prejudiced; no generation, and no individual, can appreciate every dead author and every past period; universal good taste is never realized. In this way, all criticism is experimental, just as the mode of life of every generation is an experiment. It is only in my second sense, therefore, that it is worth while to talk of experimental criticism; only by considering what critics today may be deliberately attempting some kind of critical work which has not been deliberately attempted before.

In order to make clear exactly what there is that is new in contemporary critical writing I shall have to go back a hundred years. We may say, roughly, that modern criticism begins with the work of the French critic Sainte-Beuve, that is to say about the year 1826. Before him, Coleridge had attempted a new type of criticism, a type which is in some respects more allied to what is now called esthetics than to literary criticism. But from the Renaissance through the eighteenth century literary criticism had been confined to two narrow, and closely related, types. One was a type which has always existed and I hope always will, for it can always have very great value; it may be called practical notes on the art of writing by practitioners, parallel to the treatises on painting which have been left us by Leonardo da Vinci and others. Such notes are of greatest value to other artists, particularly when studied in conjunction with the author's own work. Two classical examples in English are the Elizabethan treatises on rhymed and unrhymed verse written by Thomas Campion and Samuel Daniel. The prefaces and essays of Dryden, the prefaces of Corneille, are of the same type but on a larger scale and engage wider issues. But at the same time there is a large body of criticism, a considerable quantity in English and still more in French, written by men who were professionally critics rather than creative writers; the most famous critic of this sort is of course Boileau. This type of critic was primarily the *arbiter of taste,* and his task was to praise and condemn the work of his contemporaries, and especially to lay down the laws of good writing. These laws were supposed to be drawn from the practice, but still more from the theory, of the ancients. Aristotle was highly respected; but in practice this type of criticism was usually far from following the profound insight of Aristotle, and confined itself to translating, imitating, and plagiarizing Horace's *Art of Poetry.* At its best, it confirmed and maintained permanent standards of good writing; at its worst, it was a mere sequence of precepts. In general, French criticism was more theoretic and, as in La Harpe, more desiccated; the normal English type was nearer to plain good sense, as in Johnson's *Lives of the Poets;* though interesting theory, usually on specific literary types such as the drama, is found in authors like Thomas Rymer and Daniel Webb in the seventeenth and eighteenth centuries.

It is worth delaying for a moment to point out one of the qualities of seventeenth- and eighteenth-century literary criticism, which gives it enduring value and at the same time marks it off from more modern criticism. We are apt to think of this older criticism as dry and formal, and as setting up classical molds in which no living literature could be shaped. But we should remember in its favor that this criticism recognized literature as literature, and not another thing. Literature was something distinct from philosophy and psychology and every other study; and its purpose was to give a refined pleasure to persons of sufficient leisure and breeding. If the older critics had not taken for granted that literature was something primarily to be enjoyed, they could not have occupied themselves so sedulously with laying down rules of what was right to enjoy. This seems a very commonplace remark, and no distinction; but if you compare the criticism of those two centuries with that of the nineteenth, you will see that the latter does not take this simple truth wholly for granted. Literature is often treated by the critic rather as a means for eliciting truth or acquiring knowledge. If the critic is of a more philosophic or religious mind, he will look for the expression of philosophic or religious intuition in the work of the author criticised; if he is of a more realistic turn, he will look to literature as material for the discovery of psychological truths, or as documents illustrating social history. Even in the mouths of Walter Pater and his disciples, the phrase "art for art's sake" means something very different from the sense in which literature was literature for literature's sake up to the latter part of the eighteenth century. If you read carefully the famous epilogue to Pater's *Studies in the Renaissance* you will see that "art for art's sake" means nothing less than art as a substitute for everything else, and as a purveyor of emotions and sensations which belong to life rather than to art. To distinguish clearly between these two attitudes, that of art for art's sake and that of the eighteenth century, does require a strong effort of imagination. But the former doctrine would have been unintelligible to the earlier age. For the earlier period, art and literature were not substitutes for religion or philosophy or morals or politics, any more than for dueling or love-making: they were special and limited adornments of life. On each side there is a profit and a loss. We have gained perhaps a deeper insight, now and then; whether we enjoy literature any more keenly than our ancestors I do not know; but I think we should return again and again to the critical writings of the seventeenth and eighteenth centuries, to remind ourselves of that simple truth that literature is primarily literature, a means of refined and intellectual pleasure.

How, we ask immediately, did human beings ever come to abandon so simple and satisfying a limitation of criticism? The change comes about incidentally to a larger change, which may be described as the growth of the historical attitude. But this change —to which I shall return in a moment—is preceded, so far as literary criticism is concerned—by a freakish phenomenon, by a book written by one of the wisest and most foolish men of his time and perhaps the most extraordinary; a book which is itself one of the wisest and silliest, the most exciting and most exasperating book of criticism ever written—the *Biographia Literaria* of Coleridge. There, if you like, was "experiment in criticism," everything in fact except the power of sticking to the point—a power noticeably absent from Coleridge's ill-regulated life. Coleridge was one of the most learned men of his time, and no man of his time had wider interests except Goethe; and one of the first things that strikes us about his book, besides its uncommon diffuseness, is the novel variety of knowledge which he brings to bear on literary criticism. Much of his knowledge, as of the romantic German philosophers, does not seem to us today particularly worth having, but it was held to be valuable then; and we owe to Coleridge as much as to anybody our enjoyment of the doubtful benefits of German Idealism. His book naturally contains specimens of several types of criticism; its impulse, of course, was a defense of the new—or as the newspapers of our time would say, "modernist"—poetry of Wordsworth; and as such belongs to the type of technical notes of a craftsman; but when Coleridge started on anything, it could lead to almost everything else. He had not the historical point of view, but by the catholicity of his literary lore, and his ability for sudden and illuminating comparisons drawn from poetry of different ages and different languages, he anticipated some of the most useful accomplishments of the historical method. But one thing that Coleridge did effect for literary criticism is this. He brought out clearly the relation of literary criticism to that branch of philosophy which has flourished amazingly under the name of esthetics; and, following German writers whom he had studied, he puts the criticism of literature in its place as merely one department of the theoretic study of the Fine Arts in general. His fine discrimination of Fancy and Imagination cannot be held as permanent, for terms and relations change; but it remains one of the important texts for all who would consider the nature of poetic imagination. And he establishes literary criticism as a part of philosophy: or, to put it more moderately, he made it necessary for the "literary critic" to acquaint himself with general philosophy and metaphysics.

Biographia Literaria appeared in 1817; the activities of Charles Augustin Sainte-Beuve may be said to begin about 1826. Coleridge and Sainte-Beuve have very little in common—as little, that is, as two men who were both great critics could have in common. And Sainte-Beuve would not have been a great critic solely on the ground of what is new and experimental in his work. He had a very French intelligence and good taste which enabled him to share the ideals and sympathies of the great French writers of every time; there was much in him of the eighteenth century, a good deal even of the seventeenth. There were many gaps, certainly, in his appreciations, both of his contemporaries and of his predecessors; but he had that essential critical quality of imagination which made it possible for him to grasp literature as a whole. Where he differed from previous French critics was in his implicit conception of literature, not only as a body of writings to be enjoyed, but as a process of change in history, and as a part of the study of history. The notion that literary values are relative to literary periods, that the literature of a period is primarily an expression and a symptom of the time, is so natural to us now that we can hardly detach our minds from it. We can hardly conceive that the degree and kind of self-consciousness which we have could ever not have been. How much criticism of contemporary literature is taken up with discussing whether, and in what degree, this book or novel or poem is expressive of our mentality, of the personality of our age; and how often our critics seemed to be interested rather in inquiring what we (including themselves) are like, than with the book, novel, or poem as a work of art! This is an extreme, but the extreme of a tendency which began, in criticism, a good hundred years ago. Sainte-Beuve was not, like Coleridge, a metaphysician; he is indeed more modern and more skeptical; but he was the first interesting historian in criticism. And it is by no means irrelevant that he began his career with the study of medicine; he is not only an historian but a biologist in criticism.

It is, I think, interesting to turn to some good recent piece of literary criticism, and underline some of the assumptions of knowledge and theory which you would not find in criticism of two hundred years ago. Mr. Herbert Read's lucid little primer, *Phases of English Poetry,* will do for our purpose. On the second page he tells us that his is an inquiry into the evolution of poetry, and speaks presently of English poetry as a "living and developing organism." Even these few words should give a hint of the extent to which the critical apparatus has changed with the general changes in scientific and historical conceptions, when a literary critic can treat his audience to terms like "evolution" and "living organism" with the assurance of their being immediately apprehended. He is taking for granted certain vague but universal biological ideas. A little later he informs us that "the beginning of this study belongs to anthropology." Now, a great deal of work has had to be done by a great many people, and already more or less popularized, before a critic of literature can talk in this way. The work of Bastian, Tylor, Mannhardt, Durkheim, Lévy-Brühl, Frazer, Miss Harrison, and many others has gone before. And a great deal of purely literary investigation has been made too, before anyone can talk of the evolution of poetry. Mr. Read begins by studying the origins of ballad poetry. It would not have been possible for him to do so without a great deal of work done in the later nineteenth century and the early twentieth; for example, by Professor Child of Harvard, Professor Gummere of Haverford, Professor Gaston Paris of the Sorbonne, and Professor W. P. Ker of London. Such studies in ballad poetry, and in all the heretofore unexplored ages of literature, have fostered in us the sense of flux and evolution, the sense of the relation of the poetry of each period to the civilization of the period, and also have tended slightly to level literary values. It was W. P. Ker, who perhaps knew the whole history of European poetry better than any man of his time, who said that in literature there were no Dark Ages. And in the next paragraph to the one which I have just quoted, Mr. Read observes that in theories of the origin of poetry we "go right back to the origin of speech." Even to make so simple a remark as this requires the work of another group of scientists: the philologists. The modern critic must have some acquaintance with them too—with the work of such contemporary philologists as Professor Jespersen of Copenhagen.

There are other branches of knowledge (or at least of science) some acquaintance with which you take for granted in any applicant whom you may employ as literary critic. Especially, of course, psychology, particularly analytical psychology. All of the studies I have mentioned, and more, do themselves touch the edges, and handle some of the problems, of criticism; so conversely the critic is distinguished first by the current notions which he shares with all educated or half-educated persons, such as the notion of evolution, and by the number and variety of sciences of which he has to know a little. And he has to know them, not in order to do their work for them, but to collaborate—and also in order that he may know where to stop. We require much general knowledge in order to see the limits of our particular ignorance.

Now although Sainte-Beuve did not have the equipment which we expect of our contemporaries, he had a great deal of the method, and very typically the state of mind which results from such a method at our stage of history. The awareness of the process of time has obscured the frontiers between literature and everything else. If you read the earlier critics, such as Dryden, you find the problems of literature comparatively simple ones. For Dryden and his contemporaries there were the Greek and Latin classics, a solid block of accepted canon, and there were their contemporaries, that is to say, English literature from Shakespeare and French literature from Malherbe; and they spent a good deal of their time in discussing whether the moderns, as they called themselves, had any literary virtues not surpassed by the ancients. Their estimate of the classics was not complicated by worrying about serpent and mistle-

toe cults, or the finances of the Athenian government. And between the ancients and Shakespeare and Malherbe there was nothing much to think about. They had really a great deal more faith
in themselves than we have. They were certainly not bothered
about "the future." It often seems to me that all our concern of
it, which Mr. Shaw and Mr. Wells used to enjoy, are tokens of a
profound pessimism. We hardly have time to get any fun out of
what is being written now, so concerned are we about the quality
of what may be written fifty years hence. Even Mr. Read's chapter
on "Modern Poetry" seems to be as much engrossed by the puzzle
of what poetry will be as by the puzzle of what it is. This kind
of doubt seems to me to continue the doubt of Sainte-Beuve and
Renan. Sainte-Beuve wrote a book of seven volumes on that remarkable French religious movement of the seventeenth century
known as "Port Royal," and on that remarkable group of religious
people of whom the most famous is Pascal. It is the masterpiece
on that subject. It comes to no conclusion. It ends with the words:
"He who had it most at heart to know his object, whose ambition
was most engaged in seizing it, whose pride was most alert to paint
it—how powerless he feels, and how far beneath his task, on the
day when, seeing it almost finished and the result obtained, he
feels his exaltation sink, feels himself overcome by faintness and
inevitable disgust, and perceives in his turn that he too is only
a fleeting illusion in the midst of the infinite illusory flux!" Sainte-
Beuve was a modern critic for this reason: he was a man of restless
curiosity about life, society, civilization, and all the problems which
the study of history arouses. He studied these things through literature, because that was the center of his interests; and he never
lost his literary sensibility in his investigation of problems reaching
far beyond literature. But he was an historian, a sociologist (in the
best sense of that word) and a moralist. He is a typical modern
critic in that he found himself obliged to brood over the larger
and darker problems which, in the modern world, lie behind the
specific problems of literature.

The criticism of literature has by no means been absorbed in
something else, as alchemy into chemistry. The core of the matter

is still there, though the ramifications are endless, and the task of the critic is indeed hard. But there is still a valid distinction to be drawn between those modern critics who would make literature a substitute for a definite philosophy and theology, and thus promulgate, in an inverted form, the old gospel of art for art's sake, and those who would try to keep the distinctions clear, while admitting that the study of the one leads to the other, and that the possession of clear literary standards must imply the possession of clear moral standards. The various attempts to find the fundamental axioms behind both good literature and good life are among the most interesting "experiments" of criticism in our time.

The most considerable of such attempts so far is that which is known under the name of Humanism, and which owes its origin chiefly to the work of Professor Babbitt of Harvard. Mr. Babbitt, who is one of the most learned men of our time, is to some extent a disciple of Sainte-Beuve. There is no one living who knows more intimately (among many other things) the whole history of literary criticism. In his own writings, criticism of literature has been a means of criticising every aspect of modern society. He is a scholar of classical education, and classical tastes. He is keenly aware of the fact that the weaknesses of modern literature are symptoms of the weaknesses of modern civilization, and he has set himself with immense patience and perseverance to analyze these weaknesses. His conclusions may be read in his two most recent books, *Rousseau and Romanticism,* an account and a theory of the deterioration of taste since the early eighteenth century, and a book of still wider scope, *Democracy and Leadership.* As a moralist and as an Anglo-Saxon, he has on one side more in common with Matthew Arnold than with Sainte-Beuve. The tendency of the "humanist" in France is rather to diagnose, without prescribing a remedy; witness two recent books of brilliant literary and social criticism by M. Julien Benda, *Belphégor* and *La Trahison des clercs;* the Anglo-Saxon finds it intolerable to diagnose a disease without prescribing a remedy. Mr. Babbitt, like Arnold and Sainte-Beuve, finds that the decay of religious dogma has inflicted grave injury on society; like Arnold and Sainte-Beuve, he refuses to accept the remedy of returning to religious dogma; like Arnold and unlike Sainte-Beuve, he proposes another remedy, a theory of positive ethics based on human experiment, on the needs and capacities of the human as human, without reference to revelation or to supernatural authority or aid.

I do not propose, in this brief account, to discuss Mr. Babbitt's positive contribution, or the points at which I agree or disagree. I only want to call attention to a most important movement which is primarily, or in its inception, a movement within literary criticism, and of which a great deal more will be heard. It is significant because it shows that the modern literary critic must be an "experimenter" outside of what you might at first consider his own province; and as evidence that nowadays there is no literary problem which does not lead us irresistibly to larger problems. There is one weakness, or rather danger, of literary criticism which perceives the inevitable continuation of literary questions into general questions, which I might as well point out, because otherwise you will see it for yourselves and attach too much importance to it. The danger is that when a critic has grasped these vital moral problems which rise out of literary criticism, he may lose his detachment and submerge his sensibility. He may become too much a servant of his mind and conscience; he may be too impatient with contemporary literature, having pigeonholed it under one or another of the modern social maladies; and may demand edification at once, when appreciation of genius and accomplishment should come first. When he upholds "classicism" and denounces "romanticism" he is likely to give the impression that we should write like Sophocles or Racine; that everything contemporary is "romantic" and therefore not worth talking about. He makes us suspect that if a truly great, original classical work of imagination were to be written today, no one would like it. There will always be romantic people to admire romantic work; but we wonder whether the classicists would certainly know a classical work when it came. But these qualifications should not lead us to reject the humanist's theories: they should only lead us to apply them for ourselves.

Mr. Ramon Fernandez is a younger critic who has also taken the word humanism for his device, though his humanism, arrived at independently in France, is of a rather different brand from that which has arisen in America. His humanism has this in common: that it is also a development from literary criticism, and that it is also an attempt to arrive at a positive ethics while rejecting any revealed religion or supernatural authority. His first volume of essays, *Messages,* has been translated into English. It is important I think not so much by its achievement—for indeed the author has still a great many tangled knots in his style, which is cumbered by a good deal of philosophical and psychological terminology—as by its new attempt. Mr. Fernandez is less encyclopedic, less concerned with the past. He pores steadily over contemporaries and over the nineteenth century, and is more devoted to the study of special individuals, such as Montaigne, than to the study of the general course of literary history. Like the American humanists, he ponders over "classicism" and "romanticism"; but he wishes to be flexible, and is anxious to distinguish the essentials of classicism (which he finds, for instance, in George Eliot) from its appearances at any particular time. His theory is one which I do not wholly understand, and which has not yet been fully expounded, and probably not yet fully developed: but he illustrates, as clearly as the American humanists, the new experimental method of dealing with literary problems as moral problems, and the attempt to find guidance in conduct out of statement in literature—especially from the great novelists, and particularly, for he is a close student of English literature, from George Eliot and George Meredith. (In any case, his essay on Marcel Proust, the French novelist, in the volume mentioned, is a masterpiece of his particular method.) He is, in general, less the sociologist and more the individual psychologist. And from the best of his essays on novelists one draws this conclusion: that if we should exclude from literary criticism all but purely literary considerations, there would not only be very little to talk about, but actually we should be left without even literary appreciation. This is true of our appreciation of ancient authors but still more obviously of our appreciation of modern authors. For the same expansion of interest which has been imposed upon the modern critic, has been imposed, or at least has been assumed, by the modern imaginative writer. We cannot write a purely literary criticism of George Eliot, for instance, unless it is admittedly a very imperfect criticism: for as the interests of the author were wide, so must be those of the critic.

I have tried to show that the tendency throughout a whole epoch to the present moment has been to widen the scope of criticism and increase the demands made upon the critic. This development might be traced in terms of the development of human self-consciousness, but that is a general philosophical question beyond the margin of this paper. There is along with this expansion a compensating tendency. As the number of sciences multiply, of sciences that is which have a bearing upon criticism, so we ask ourselves first whether there is still any justification for literary criticism at all, or whether we should not merely allow the subject to be absorbed gently into exacter sciences which will each annex some side of criticism. Just as in the history of philosophy, we find many subjects surrendered from time to time by philosophy, now to mathematics and physics, now to biology and psychology; until there seems to be almost nothing left to philosophize about. I think that the answer is clear: that so long as literature is literature, so long will there be a place for criticism of it—for criticism, that is, on the same basis as that on which the literature itself is made. For so long as poetry and fiction and such things are written, its first purpose must always be what it always has been—to give a peculiar kind of pleasure which has something constant in it throughout the ages, however difficult and various our explanations of that pleasure may be. The task of criticism will be, accordingly, not only to expand its borders but to clarify its center, and the insistency of the latter need grows with that of the former. Two hundred years ago, when it was taken for granted that one knew well enough what literature was, and it was not the number of other things which it is always now seeming to be, terms could be used more freely and carelessly without close definition. Now, there is an urgent need for experiment in criticism of a new kind, which will consist largely in a logical and dialectical study of the terms used. My own interest in these problems has been fostered partly by dissatisfaction with the meaning of my own statements in criticism, and partly by dissatisfaction with the terminology of the Humanists. In literary criticism we are constantly using terms which we cannot define, and defining other things by them. We are constantly using terms which have an *in*tension and an *ex*tension which do not quite fit; theoretically they ought to be made to fit; but if they cannot, then some other way must be found of dealing with them so that we may know at every moment what we mean. I will take a very simple example with which I have been dealing myself: the possibility of defining "metaphysical poetry." Here is a term which has a whole history of meanings down to the present time, all of which must be recognized, although it cannot have all of them at once. The term means on the one hand a certain group of English poets in the seventeenth century. On the other hand it must have an intensive meaning, must stand for a peculiar whole of qualities which is exemplified by the several poets. The ordinary critical method would be to define what "metaphysical poetry" means to you in the abstract, fit as many poets to it as well as you can, and reject the rest. Or else, you take the poets who have been held to be "metaphysical," and find out what they have in common. The odd thing is that by doing the sum, so to speak, in two different ways, you get two different results. A larger problem in the same kind of definition is that of "classicism" and "romanticism." Everyone who writes about these two abstractions believes that he knows what the words mean; actually they mean something a little different for each observer, and merely seem to mean the same things. In this way you have material for endless wrangling with no conclusion, which is not satisfactory. Such problems involve, of course, both logic and the theory of knowledge and psychology; there is no one, perhaps, more concerned with them than Mr. I. A. Richards, the author of *Principles of Literary Criticism* and *Practical Criticism*.

There is good cause for believing—apart from the obvious assertion that every generation must criticise for itself—that literary criticism, far from being exhausted, has hardly begun its work. On the other hand, I am more than skeptical of the old superstition that criticism and "creative writing" never flourish in the same age: that is a generalization drawn from a superficial inspection of some past ages. "Creative writing" can look after itself; and certainly it will be none the better for suppressing the critical curiosity. And in any case, the times which we have lived in seem to me, on the false antithesis mentioned, rather "creative" than "critical." (The current superstition that our epoch is Alexandrine, decadent, or "disillusioned" is parallel; there are no "disillusioned ages," only disillusioned individuals; and our time is just as deluded as any other.) The present age has been, rather, uncritical, and partly for economic causes. The "critic" has been chiefly the reviewer, that is to say, the hurried amateur wage-slave. I am aware of the danger that the types of criticism in which I am interested may become too professional and technical. What I hope for is the collaboration of critics of various special training, and perhaps the pooling and sorting of their contributions by men who will be neither specialists nor amateurs.

Poetry and Propaganda

THE text for this paper is taken from Whitehead's *Science and the Modern World,* page 127:

The literature of the nineteenth century, especially its English poetic literature, is a witness to the discord between the esthetic intuitions and the mechanism of science. Shelley brings vividly before us the elusiveness of the eternal objects of sense as they haunt the change which

From *The Bookman,* LXX, No. 6. February, 1930. Pp. 595-602. Reprinted by permission of author and editor. The essay has not been reprinted by the author.

infects underlying organisms. Wordsworth is the poet of nature as being the field of enduring permanences carrying within themselves a message of tremendous significance. The eternal objects are also there for him,

The light that never was, on sea or land.

Both Shelley and Wordsworth emphatically bear witness that nature cannot be divorced from its esthetic values; and that these values arise from the cumulation, in some sense, of the brooding presence of the whole onto its various parts. Thus we gain from the poets the doctrine that a philosophy of nature must concern itself at least with these six notions: change, value, eternal objects, endurance, organism, interfusion.

So far Professor Whitehead. Now I must insist clearly at the beginning that what I have to say has nothing to do with this book as a whole, or with Mr. Whitehead's theory as a whole: I am not here judging or valuing his theory or his method or his results. I am concerned only with this one chapter, which is called "The Romantic Reaction," and only with this one passage in that chapter. And only, therefore, with two specific questions: can poetry be cited to *prove* anything? and to what extent can it even be cited to *illustrate* anything?

It appears to me that Mr. Whitehead is here summoning Shelley and Wordsworth to *prove* something in connection with what he calls a "philosophy of nature"; that is what his words *thus we gain from the poets the doctrine that,* seem to me to mean; even if the author did not mean that, it is at least what many of his readers must have taken it to mean.

When so distinguished a scientist and philosopher makes this use of poetry, a great many people will follow him, in the belief that anyone who can understand symbolic logic must certainly understand anything so simple as poetry. And indeed I must say that in the earlier part of his book Mr. Whitehead does prepare us to consent to any use of literature he may choose to make: his knowledge and appreciation of history and literature are so great, and his summaries and reviews of historical processes and periods so very skillful, his allusions so apt, that we are charmed into assent. Nevertheless, I believe that the passage I have just read is nonsense, and dangerous nonsense at that. Consider first how really remarkable it is that we should

gain from the poets the doctrine that a philosophy of nature must concern itself at least with these six notions: change, value, eternal objects, endurance, organism, interfusion.

There are, to begin with, two steps in Whitehead's legerdemain. He has quoted, and discussed generally, two poets of one period, Shelley and Wordsworth. These two then become "the poets"; would any beginner in scientific inquiry ever exhibit such a perfect example of imperfect induction? And then the poets are said to demonstrate that a philosophy of nature must be concerned at least with the six concepts mentioned.

Let us take the first sentence:

The literature of the nineteenth century, especially its English poetic literature, is a witness to the discord between the esthetic intuitions of mankind and the mechanism of science.

To call the whole of English poetry of the nineteenth century to witness such a generality is certainly rash, and the meaning of the sentence is not clear. It might mean that the great English poets were all *aware* of this discord between intuitions and mechanism. In this form the statement might be true of the author of *In Memoriam*. But how far is it true of Browning or Swinburne, and as far as it may be true how significant is it in their respective views of life? But perhaps Mr. Whitehead means merely that poets, by affirming the reality of values, are denying by implication the sufficiency of a mechanistic philosophy. But in this form the statement is too comprehensive, for it applies to all artists at every time, as they all have affirmed the validity of esthetic intuitions. And in the proposition there are two terms to be examined, "esthetic intuitions," and "the mechanism of science"; and we must then consider in what way there can be any "discord" between terms so disparate.

That poor old creature, "mechanistic philosophy" or "material-ism" has been in our time thoroughly repudiated by its old friends the scientists, and receives no kindness from anyone but a few lib-eral theologians.   It is not of course quite the same thing as "the mechanism of science": the latter is strictly merely the corpus of pre-Einstein and pre-Rutherford physical theory, which has been rejected more or less by physicists on the good ground that it does not account for all the facts—not on the doubtful ground that it offends poetic intuitions.   The mechanism of science is not the same thing as a *philosophy* based on that science, which would assert that physical science would explain the whole universe, and that what would not be explained in this way was unworthy of notice. But in any case, I find myself in the curious position of having to defend the "mechanism of science," which is no friend of mine, against an eminent scientist.

Are we to suppose that a mechanistic philosophy is fundamen-tally antagonistic to the esthetic intuitions of mankind?   That is certainly surprising, as some works of literary art seem to have been built upon it.   The philosophy, such as it is, of Thomas Hardy's novels, seems to be based upon the mechanism of science.   I think it is a very bad philosophy indeed, and I think that Hardy's work would be better for a better philosophy, or none at all; but there it is: has he not exploited determinism to extract his esthetic values from the contemplation of a world in which values do not count? There is a more important poet than Hardy, who is Lucretius.   We cannot deny "esthetic intuitions" to Lucretius.   His world was me-chanical enough, in all conscience; and just because it was, Lu-cretius gets the particular emotional values that he does get.   We may admit therefore a discord between the mechanism of science and *some* esthetic intuitions; but then we shall have to say that *every* philosophy is discordant with *some* intuitions.   The new philosophy of Professor Eddington, for instance, is discordant with some of the intuitions of all Christians except members of the So-ciety of Friends; the philosophy of Dante is not the ideal ground on which to reap the intuitions of Wordsworth.

So far I have not questioned the term "esthetic intuitions"; but this term is beset with ambiguity and vagueness. I suppose that Mr. Whitehead means such intuitions as are more or less common to mankind, but of which the artist is the most sensitive receiver, and without which he would not have the material for great art. But however we define the term, there is a gulf, and I think an impassable one, between the intuitions of poets *as such,* and any particular philosophy, or even any philosophical direction rather than any other. The existence of art certainly implies the reality of values, but that does not take us anywhere, and certainly points to no philosophic theory of value.

If I examined each of the sentences I should quickly grow tedious, so I will pass now to the last of them:

Thus we gain from the poets the doctrine that a philosophy of nature must concern itself at least with these six notions: change, value, eternal objects, endurance, organism, interfusion.

The first question is, if we get all this from the poets, where do the poets get it? Take *change* and *endurance,* for which Mr. Whitehead is so obliged to Shelley. Shelley, I suspect, got them where everybody else has got them in the end—that is, from Plato. The reality of eternal objects sounds to me much more like Plato than a discovery of Shelley, or all the romantic poets together. I do not deny the possibility that Shelley may have had a fresh intuition of these things, but Plato did get there first. And also it is very difficult to spot these intuitions: Shelley must have had an esthetic intuition that there is no God, and that the Christian religion is an odious lie; for he could hardly have reached such passionate conviction on the subject from mere reasoning. (Of course it is possible that he read Rousseau and Voltaire, or even Godwin.) Even if we gain the doctrine in question from *the poets,* we hardly needed to have gone to the poets for that. And in passing, I wonder whether the concept of *organism* is so fundamental to a philosophy of nature as Mr. Whitehead supposes. We may get a better term some day, or we may even return to Aristotle, who knew as much about what this term represents as anybody.

At the very best, Mr. Whitehead is, I think, confusing the *per-*

suasive power of poetry with evidence of truth. He is transferring to poetry, as a scientist, that credulity which previous generations, including some poets, are said to have bestowed upon science.

Professor Whitehead may serve as a warning that a man may be one of the greatest living exponents of formal logic, and yet be quite helpless in a field with which he is not familiar. I should not however have devoted this space merely to the churlish pleasure of attacking a famous man; but because I believe that the theory of poetry implicit in Whitehead's chapter is dangerous, because we could prove by it, choosing our examples judiciously, almost anything we like. I also believe, what is a related point which I cannot deal with here, that Mr. Whitehead errs by his ignorance of theology just as he errs by his not having thought seriously enough about poetry.

Now among those persons who have thought directly about poetry—and indeed some of them are greatly indebted to Mr. Whitehead and Mr. Russell for their logical training—there have arisen lately two interesting views. One is that of Mr. Montgomery Belgion, in one chapter of his recent book *Our Present Philosophy of Life*. His theory is that the *literary* artist—he is not concerned with the other arts—is what he calls an "irresponsible propagandist." That is to say, every writer adopts a view or theory of life; his choice may have been more or less justified or capricious, may be more or less right, may be true or false: it happens to be the view which suits *him;* he makes use of it as material for his literary art. The effect of the work of literary art is always to *persuade* the reader to accept that view or theory. This persuasion is always illicit. That is to say, that the reader is always led to believe something, and that assent is hypnotic—the art of the presentation seduces the reader: even if what he is led to believe is right to believe, the reader has been *mis*lead into believing it. This theory is, as you see, rather depressing, and is remotely similar to that of Plato, who ejected the poets from his ideal republic; but it is neither fantastic nor easy to overthrow.

The other theory is that of Mr. I. A. Richards, as expressed particularly in his recent book *Practical Criticism*. Mr. Richards holds that while it is probably necessary for the poet to believe something, in order to write his poetry—although he inclines to think that a further step will be made when the poet believes nothing—the ideal reader will appreciate the poetry in a state of mind which is not belief, but rather a temporary suspension of disbelief. The one critic would say, you see, that you will value Dante more highly if you are a Catholic; or alternatively, that if you are enchanted by the poetry of Dante you will probably become a Catholic. Mr. Richards would say, I think, that the more you know about what Dante believed or more exactly the more you know about the philosophy of life on which Dante's poem is based—leaving out of account the question of what and how Dante himself believed—the better: but that when you are enjoying Dante's poem to the full as poetry, you cannot be said either to believe, or to doubt, or to disbelieve, its scholastic philosophy. So you *ought* to be able to appreciate, as literature, *all* literature, of whatever place, race or time.

These two theories are not so antithetical as they at first seem. Mr. Belgion is more concerned with what actually does happen; he says that, whether you know it or not, you tend to believe, you are *influenced,* by any author whose form of expression you admire. Mr. Richards is less concerned with the actual than with the ideal reader: he says, in effect, this may happen, but in so far as it does happen your reaction is impure; you *ought not* to be affected in this way: it is possible and it is right to enjoy poetry as poetry, and you merely use in the reading the philosophy of the author; just as the author was using, unconsciously, that philosophy in order to write the poetry.

In a note to a recent essay which I have published on Dante, I made a first attempt to criticise both views, and to find some way of mediation between the truth of both. I am now making a fresh start.

First of all no art, and particularly and especially no literary art, can exist in a vacuum. We are, in practice, creatures of divers interests, and in many of our ordinary interests there is no obvious coherence. Read, for instance, the information given by those personages in *Who's Who* who condescend to fill in that space of the form marked *Recreations.* There is no apparent relation, to fabricate a specimen, between breeding prize Persian cats and racing toy yachts. This is one extreme of the scale. At the other end, we do tend, I am sure, to unify our interests. To suppose that anyone likes only the *best* poetry, and that he likes all of the best poetry equally, and that he likes all of the second-best poetry in a second-best liking, and so on until he destests all of the worst poetry equally, is to suppose a monster. I do not suppose that there ever has been, or ever will be, a critic of any art, whose appreciation was a separate faculty, quite judicious and wholly isolated from his other interests and his private passions: if there was, is or will be, he was, is or will be a bore with nothing at all to say. And yet, on the other hand, there is no worse bore, and no more futile critic, than the one who renounces all objective standards in order to recount his own reactions. "A voyage among masterpieces" is, I believe, the phrase that Anatole France used to describe his own criticism, implying that it was merely an account of his own feelings—yet the phrase itself admits that the masterpieces were there as masterpieces, before the voyage began.

But this apparent paradox—this need of aiming at one thing in order to do another—this apparent gospel of hypocrisy or self-deception, is right, because it is in the nature of the human soul and embodies its need and craving for perfection and unity. We do tend, I think, to organize our tastes in various arts into a whole; we aim in the end at a theory of life, or a view of life, and so far as we are conscious, to terminate our enjoyment of the arts in a philosophy, and our philosophy in a religion—in such a way that the personal to oneself is fused and completed in the impersonal and general, not extinguished, but enriched, expanded, developed, and more itself by becoming more something not itself.

There is, according to my view, not *one,* but a *series,* of appreciators of poetry. One of the errors, I think, of critical theory, is to conceive one hypothetical poet on the one hand, and one hypothetical reader on the other. It is perhaps a less dangerous error than to have no hypotheses at all. My point is that the legitimate motives of the poet, and also the legitimate responses of the reader, vary very widely, but that there is a possible order in the variations. In my series let us put Mr. Belgion at one end of the scale and Mr. Richards at the other. The one extreme is to like poetry merely for what it has to say: that is, to like it merely because it voices our own beliefs or prejudices—which is of course to be quite indifferent to the *poetry* of the poetry. The other extreme is to like the poetry because the poet has manipulated his material into perfect art, which is to be indifferent to the material, and to isolate our enjoyment of poetry from life. The one extreme is not enjoyment of poetry at all, the other is enjoyment of an abstraction which is merely *called* poetry. But between these extremes occurs a continuous range of appreciations, each of which has its limited validity.

The validity of this range of appreciations is confirmed by our examination of the impulses of different poets. We may for convenience contrast three different types. There is the philosophic poet like Lucretius and Dante, who accepts one philosophy of life, so to speak, in advance, and who constructs his poem on one idea. There is the poet like Shakespeare, or possibly Sophocles, who accepts current ideas and makes use of them, but in whose work the question of belief is much more baffling and evasive. There is finally another type, of which we might take Goethe as an example, who neither quite accepts a particular view of the whole, nor merely sees views of life to make poetry out of, but who in himself more or less combines the functions of philosopher and poet—or perhaps Blake; poets who have their own ideas and definitely believe them.

Some poets are of so mixed a type that it is impossible to say how far they write their poetry because of what they believe, and how far they believe a thing merely because they see that they can make poetry out of it. And if I am justified in allowing this range of possible motives to the true poet (and an analogous range to the true reader of poetry) then Mr. Belgion's and Mr. Richards' theories must be considerably modified. For the "irresponsible propaganda" is sometimes less irresponsible, and sometimes less propoganda. Lucretius and Dante, for instance, are what Mr. Belgion would call propagandists, certainly, but they are particularly conscious and responsible ones: you have only to read what Dante says in the *Convivio* and in his letter to Can-Grande to understand what his purpose was.

Milton was also a deliberate propagandist; but here we must allow for another difference. The philosophies of Lucretius and Dante, different as they are from each other, are still potent to influence mankind. I cannot imagine any reader today being affected in his theological views by Milton. The reason is, I think, that Lucretius and Dante are each summing up and restating in great poetry two views which are central to the history of the mind of western man; whereas Milton is merely restating in great poetry a view which was very largely his own invention, or his own concoction, and which represents an eccentric heresy revived in his own mind. In Milton it is much easier to separate the greatness of the poetry from the thought, serious as it is, behind that poetry. Milton, therefore, is much more apprehensible from the Richards point of view; because in reading Milton we are, I think, rapt by the splendid verse without being tempted to believe the philosophy or theology. In considering whether a literary artist is an irresponsible propagandist or not, we have therefore to take into account both varieties of intention, and varieties of effect in time. Milton may, I feel, have had this powerful influence at one time which I feel that Lucretius and Dante can have at any time; but I do not believe that he has it now. And in general, the element of propaganda in the actual effect of any piece of literature upon us will depend either upon the permanence of the doctrine, or upon its nearness to us in time. The effect of a book like *The Way of All Flesh* was, I am sure, for the generation immediately following Butler much what he intended; for the next generation it is not at all the same.

You will infer, perhaps, that we must come to the conclusion that it is impossible to enjoy (or judge) a work of art as such, until sufficient time has elapsed for its doctrines to be quite out of date: so that we merely inspect and accept them, as Mr. Richards would have us do: wait a few hundred years, and we shall know how good any piece of literature is. There are several reasons why this simple solution will not do. One is that when an author is so remote from us, in time or in race, that we know nothing of his material and cannot at all understand his beliefs, we cannot appreciate his work as poetry. To enjoy Homer as poetry, we need a good deal more than Greek vocabulary and Greek accidence and syntax; and the more we saturate ourselves in the life of the ancient Greeks, the more we attempt to recreate imaginatively their world, the better we understand and enjoy the poetry of that world. Another reason is that time, alas, does not necessarily bring detachment. It may merely substitute for a set of prejudices favorable to the poet, another set unfavorable to him. It is interesting to read the comments of Mr. Richards's students, as set forth in *Practical Criticism,* on Donne's great sonnet "At the round world's imagined corners . . ." Some of the misunderstanding is due, I believe, not so much to ignorance of the theology of Donne's time, as to these students' more or less conscious acceptance of another set of beliefs current in our own time.

I have called Lucretius and Dante *responsible propagandists.* But there are some poets whom it is a strain to think of as propagandists at all. Take Shakespeare. He is never, like the former, expounding one definite philosophical system. I am aware that many attempts have been made, and will be made, to expound in clear prose the theory of life which Shakespeare is supposed to have held; and that any number of views of life have been extracted from Shakespeare. I do not say that such attempts are illegitimate or altogether futile; it is a natural tendency to philosophize on Shakespeare just as it is to philosophize on the world itself. Only, the philosophy of Shakespeare is quite a different thing from that of Dante; it really has more in common with, let us say, the philosophy of Beethoven. That is to say, those of us who love Beethoven find in his music something that we call its meaning, though we cannot confine it in words; but it is this meaning which fits it in, somehow, to our whole life; which makes it an emotional exercise and discipline, and not merely an appreciation of virtuosity. Shakespeare does certainly influence us; but as he influences each man according to his own education, temperament and sensibility, and as we have no clue to the relation of his influence upon any one mind with what Shakespeare actually meant, it is almost fantastic to call it propaganda.

When we come to Mr. Whitehead's mentors, Shelley and Wordsworth, the situation is again different. Judging from their effect upon Mr. Whitehead, we should certainly call them irresponsible propagandists. But I suspect that their influence upon such a mind as Mr. Whitehead's is in direct ratio to the vagueness of their ideas, or to the fact that they take certain things for granted, instead of expounding them. The orthodox Christian, for example, is hardly likely to take Dante as proving Christianity; the orthodox materialist is hardly likely to adduce Lucretius as evidence of materialism or atomism. What he will find in Dante or in Lucretius is the *esthetic* sanction: that is, the partial justification of these views of life by the art to which they give rise. And there is no doubt that we are all of us powerfully influenced by the esthetic sanction; and that any way or view of life which gives rise to great art is for us more plausible than one which gives rise to inferior art or to none. And on the other hand I do not believe that a Christian can fully appreciate Buddhist art, or vice versa.

But Mr. Whitehead was not, I suspect, making this use, which I consider legitimate, of the esthetic sanction. You do not get this by going to the poets for maxims or gnomic sayings, or by attributing to them some inspiration as of the Delphic oracle. You can only say: this or that poet had used these ideas to make poetry, and has accordingly shown that these ideas can and do give rise to certain values. These ideas consequently are valid not merely in a theory, but can be integrated into life through art. But in order to do this we are obliged to value first the art of a Shelley or a Wordsworth. How complete, how intelligent, how well understood, is the philosophy used by the poet, how completely does he realize it poetically; where does he get it from, how much of life does it cover? Such questions we must ask first. And what poetry proves about any philosophy is merely its possibility for being lived—for life includes both philosophy and art.

But, we may ask, is the greatness, the comprehensiveness of the philosophy in any actual or theoretical relation to the greatness of the poetry? Actually, we may find a poet giving greater validity to an inferior philosophy, by realizing it more fully and masterfully in literary art, and another employing a better philosophy and realizing it less satisfactorily. Yet we can hardly doubt that the "truest" philosophy is the best material for the greatest poet; so that the poet must be rated in the end both by the philosophy he realizes in poetry and by the fullness and adequacy of the realization. For poetry—here and so far I am in accord with Mr. Richards —is not the assertion that something is true, but the making that truth more fully real to us; it is the creation of a sensuous embodiment. It is the making the Word Flesh, if we remember that for poetry there are various qualities of Word and various qualities of Flesh. Of course, as I said above, for some kinds of poetry it is necessary that the poet himself should believe the philosophy of which he is making use. I do not wish however to overemphasize the importance of the philosophy, or to speak of it as if it was the exclusive material. What we find when we read Lucretius or Dante is that the poet has effected a fusion between that philosophy and his natural feelings, so that the philosophy becomes real, and the feelings become elevated, intensified and dignified.

And we must remember that part of the *use* of poetry for human beings is similar to their use for philosophy. When we study philosophy as a humane discipline we do not do so merely in order to pick out one which we shall adopt as "true," or either to confect a philosophy of our own out of all philosophies. We do so largely for the exercise in assumption or entertaining ideas; for the enlargement and exercise of mind we get by trying to penetrate a man's thought and think it after him, and then passing out of that experience to another. Only by the exercise of understanding without believing, so far as that is possible, can we come in full consciousness to some point where we believe *and* understand. Similarly with the experience of poetry. We aim ideally to come to rest in some poetry which shall realize poetically what we ourselves believe; but we have no contact with poetry unless we can pass in and out freely, among the various worlds of poetic creation. In practice, our literary judgment is always fallible, because we inevitably tend to overestimate a poetry which embodies a view of life which we can understand and which we accept; but we are not really entitled to prize such poetry so highly unless we also make the effort to enter those worlds of poetry in which we are alien. Poetry cannot prove that anything is *true;* it can only create a variety of wholes composed of intellectual and emotional constituents, justifying the emotion by the thought and the thought by the emotion: it proves successively, or fails to prove, that certain worlds of thought and feeling are *possible.* It provides intellectual sanction for feeling, and esthetic sanction for thought.

VAN WYCK BROOKS
The Critical Movement in America

I<small>T</small> was only the other day that America first came in for its effective share of self-criticism. The critical movement in America happened, as it were, overnight; and the critic in this country is still so new a type that we cannot be surprised if he is regarded as an undesirable alien, even a traitor. There is nothing else in all modern history like the unanimity of praise and confidence with which, by its passengers, the American Ship of State was launched and manned. In all our long nineteenth-century past, there was scarcely a breath of dissent, doubt, or censure: the semi-outlaw Whitman's *Democratic Vistas* was almost unique in this regard, for Emerson's and Lowell's strictures were lost in the flood of their social optimism. No wonder we became the most complacent of peoples. No wonder the tide of criticism rose at last.

One thinks of all this as one considers, for instance, such an alien point of reference as John Ruskin. To most of us, no doubt, Ruskin has always seemed a normal and familiar possession. Yet, as one reflects on his career, the thought comes to one's mind: How different this man was from anything the America of his day could have produced! Hear, for example, what Mr. Masefield recently said of him: "Ruskin, looking out upon his native land some eighty years ago, decided that he could not believe in it, that there was nothing spiritual there which he could trust, nor human work being done which he could share." Imagine a nineteenth-century American giving utterance to such a sentiment, the sentiment from which Ruskin's work sprang! Yet this

was surely the animating sentiment of the greatest English literature of the century, even of Charles Dickens: who but Macaulay,
of all the writers of England, was not filled, as regards the future
of his people, with more or less fundamental doubts? And meanwhile the writers of America chanted a unanimous hymn to
progress. They were happy, they were hopeful. They agreed,
or seemed to agree, with the famous utterance of Edward Everett:
"Our government is in its theory perfect, and in its operation it
is perfect also. Thus we have solved the great problem in human
affairs." Was this because the American life of their epoch was
finer and more wholesome than English life? Because it contained a greater spiritual promise? Few in our generation would
affirm this. We know too well how fully justified were most of
the European travelers' reflections on our old social life—which
used to cause such resentment in American breasts: they were
not malignant, those travelers' reflections, any more than the
comments of the European critics and scholars—Ruskin himself,
for instance—who looked upon "Americanism" as a poisonous
growth that might well infect and destroy all civilization. And as
we observe the complacency to which our national optimism gave
birth, we ask ourselves whether this optimism was ever a symptom
of health, whether it was not indeed the symptom of a great evil:
the loss of a clear sense of the true values of life.

It is certain, in any case, that our criticism has suffered from
the obvious necessity or making up for much lost time. We do
not understand criticism, and this is because we have had so
little of it. We have had no candid friends of our own race,
no "national conscience," in short, such as every European people
has had, for England is not unique in this respect: and, consequently, it was difficult a few years ago for most Americans to
question the belief of Mr. Meredith Nicholson, for instance, that
"if there is any manifestation on earth of a divine ordering of
things, it is here in America." This is the sort of belief the
Philistine majority in every country cherishes in its heart; it is
the sort of belief that Matthew Arnold so well described as
"vulgar, and not only vulgar, but retarding," for retarding it

surely is if, in order to go somewhere, to get somewhere, to advance, to develop, we must first have an inner conviction that we have not already arrived. If American life as we know it is indeed a manifestation of a divine ordering of things, there is nothing for us to do but to continue to manifest our divinity. But is our life divine? Is it so much better than the life of England, France, Germany, Russia that the comments of a Ruskin, a Renan, a Nietzsche would have been sheer impertinences on our side of the Atlantic? The prosperous middle class the world over looks upon itself and its own fatness with an overkindly eye; but America is the only modern country where, until recent years, the prosperous middle class has gone unchallenged, where the Philistines have never been aroused to a sense of their limitations. Heine never permitted the Germans to forget how much they had to learn; no one was ever more outspoken than Nietzsche in regard to "what the Germans lack." The French are complacent enough; but Renan never ceased to remind them of their "incurable religious mediocrity," of "the alternations of levity and dullness, of narrow timidity and foolish temerity" which are among the features of the French mind. Arnold, Ruskin, Carlyle, as we know, kept their guns steadily trained on the weaknesses of the English character; and while Ibsen lived how many illusions in regard to their peculiar superiority were the people of Norway suffered to cherish?

Merely to mention these names is to suggest how uniformly our American fur has been rubbed the right way. For while Emerson, Lowell, Whitman deplored the imperfections of our social life, their criticism was neither sustained nor drastic. Emerson was the incarnation of optimism and lived, besides, too much in a timeless world to concern himself with a single phase of history: this was not his rôle. Lowell was so conscious of that "certain condescension in foreigners" that he could not sufficiently draw the veil over the shortcomings of his countrymen. And there was Howells, with his rosy vision of the American scene, all the more delusive because he professed an intransigent realism. There was even Henry James, whom nothing could have induced to live in America: did he not apologize in one of his prefaces for having spoken in terms of disrespect of a certain small city in Massachusetts, adding so much thereby to the ultimate obloquy of those who have since reproached our Gopher Prairies? These men, of course, were not primarily critics, and that is just the point; Thoreau was not primarily a critic; in fact, before the war we had no critics. Those who could not put up with our life in the East quietly went West, and those who could not put up with our life at all quietly went to Europe. No one stood still and spoke out; and after the Civil War, even the voices of the traveling foreigners who told the truth about many of our ways were cloaked and muffled. Everyone waited, waited, by common consent, to see how the great experiment of democracy was going to work out. We had sixty years of grace while the oracles were dumb.

We were, in a word, singularly unconscious. America "just growed"—in the manner of the British Empire perhaps, but certainly in a very different manner from England itself, or France or Germany. It grew by sheer activity, expansion, immigration, without forethought, afterthought, reflection of any kind. That is to say, since no population is ever aware of itself as a population, save perhaps in times of war, it had no governing and directing minority more conscious than the multitude, more conscious of human values, no class of thinkers who, while having no administrative authority, might yet have exercised a real authority over popular opinion, interpreting the movements of society in the light of historical principles, and arousing in those who were intelligent and articulate a just sense of what was really happening. Who knew, for instance, that America was becoming an empire, apprehended this fact in all its implications? America never "meant" to become an empire, and few Americans know, even today, really know, I mean *apprehend,* that America is an empire, with all the paraphernalia of imperialism. This change came automatically, as it were, because, contrary as it plainly was to the professed genius of the Republic, no strong, articulate minority showed the people what was taking place before their eyes.

One has only to compare the feeble protests that arose throughout this country over the annexation of the Philippines with the outburst of resentment and remonstrance, of satire and impassioned poetry, evoked in England by the Boer War, to perceive the difference between a conscious and an unconscious society; and the difference only widens when we remember that imperialism in the England of those days had been for generations a deliberate national policy.

So it was that after the Civil War our social history became an illustration of what might be called a policy of indifference. The individual stood aside and let things take their course. To a large extent, this has been true of our thought from the beginning: whether optimistic, as with Emerson and Whitman, or pessimistic, as with Henry Adams and Mark Twain, it has always tended to be fatalistic. It has assumed, or tended to assume, that things were "coming out all right," because Americans are Americans, or else that things were coming out all wrong, because nothing could stop them from doing so, because human life itself is a mistake, as Mark Twain thought, or because, as Henry Adams thought, evolution is merely a matter of thermodynamics. These attitudes are all fatalistic because they beg the question of human control or deny its possibility; and together they have formed the various strands of a national tradition in which the critical intellect has played scarcely any part whatever. That America must and will be perfect just by being itself, or that America is doomed and damned: these are the two poles between which, even to this day, our public opinion oscillates. The cultivated classes are too often convinced, although they keep their opinion to themselves, that the country is already doomed and damned. The rest are equally sure, not that the country will be, but that the country already is what Mr. Nicholson calls it; and they have plainly arrived at this opinion by lowering their human standards to a point where the great values of life do not exist. Mr. Nicholson, who speaks so complacently of the "divine ordering of things" in America, also says that a "town is better advertised by enlightened sanitary ordinances duly enforced than by the number of its citizens who are acquainted with the writings of Walter Pater. If Main Street knows," he adds, "what America is all about, and bathes itself and is kind and considerate of its neighbors, why not leave the rest on the knees of the gods?" Why, indeed, if we share Mr. Nicholson's indifference to the great human values? "We do not know," he says again, "we do not know but that in some far day a prowling New Zealander, turning up a banjo and a trap-drum amid the ruins of some American college, will account them nobler instruments than the lyre and lute." But why wait for the "ruins" of this American college? The ruins are with us already if we have lost a sense of the distinction between the trap-drum and the lyre and lute.

And the sense of this distinction has been lost, too largely lost, because criticism, in all these years, has failed to keep it alive. Mr. William Allen White has observed that he would like to collect the junior pessimists who are raking America with their criticism and duck them in the town-pump. One readily understands Mr. White's resentment, for he has himself gone through life without once being held up, without once being checked in his rampant career of self-congratulation over the virtues of Kansas. And Mr. White's resentment is widely shared; one constantly hears of apostles of good-Americanism who have "had about enough" of these junior pessimists. And it cannot be denied that for this resentment there exists a certain reason, for few indeed of the pessimists in question are not open to the retort that they are themselves no more essentially civilized than the civilization they attack. We are always well aware of what they hate; we are seldom aware at all of what they love, and only what they love can civilize us. This is true; yet, save for these same vipers, whose critical equipment is, one admits, defective, where else in America can we turn for criticism? The "best" magazines freely open their columns to Mr. Nicholson's and Mr. White's opinions; the "best" people, as we are led to suppose, delight in these opinions. At every adverse comment on our civilization the cry still goes up: But there is so much to be said on the other side! And no one questions this; what one asserts, and asserts, and asserts again, is that there is so much to be said on *this* side. If it were not for these vipers who have risen among us, we should all find ourselves intellectually on the level of the "man in the street" for whom Messrs. Nicholson and White are so proud to speak. The conservative reviews, as one might think, exist for the purpose of combating the radical reviews, giving aid and comfort to that false-Americanism, now dominant through the world, the rise and spread of which was the nightmare of those European critics of the nineteenth century whose standards they profess to uphold.

In short, before the emergence of our critical movement, the clear sense of the great values of life had long been submerged in America. For we are obliged to take Mr. White and Mr. Nicholson at their word and assume that they really do not know the difference between the trap-drum and the lyre and lute, or between the Valley of Democracy anad the Kingdom of Heaven. We are even obliged to take at their word the defenders of some pseudo-American tradition who failed to challenge Edward Bok, for instance, when he adopted the word "Americanization" to describe a career that was throughout devoted, with whatever good intentions, to the vulgarization of American life. And we cannot expect that those who are color-blind to the great values of life, in the name of which criticism speaks, will see anything but animus in this criticism, or regard it as anything but insulting. This indeed would be true if our criticism were ten times more certain of its values than it is: we know that Mr. White would as readily duck a Ruskin as a Mencken. For Americans are not accustomed to plain speaking. We cherish a romantic view of our activities, and an American spade, to most of us, is not a spade at all: it is a sword, an implement of knighthood, and to call it a spade is to challenge our fondest prepossessions. The romantic soul dwells in the region of hyperbole, and its virtues are not the virtues of understatement. This fact explains the apparent censoriousness of much of our recent social criticism. Some of this criticism has really been censorious, it has been so by reaction; but much of it has only appeared censorious. If we had been accustomed to a realistic view of affairs, and a true historic sense of human values, we should have accepted this criticism and even rejoiced in it.

For we know how America appears in the eyes of the world. The Japanese poet, Mr. Yone Noguchi, is the spokesman of contemporary humanity when he describes our country as "floating comfortably on the ocean all by itself, as if a well-fed seal or lazy iceberg." And those who have an interest in America, its true life, its true historic rôle, are aware that such a posture is a perilous posture. No doubt, in the beginning, this uncritical attitude, this attitude of uncriticised faith and hope, contributed much to our dawning civilization. A new country is obliged to affirm its existence, to believe in itself against all comers. If the America of three generations ago had seen itself as Europeans saw it, as its own cultivated minds saw it in the privacy of their souls, it would have lost heart; for with nations as with individuals nothing is more paralyzing than a premature self-consciousness. Our old writers were surely aware of all that was imperfect in our society, but they were aware also that too much cannot be expected of a new country. They saw, moreover, that America was too deeply in the grip of unusual natural forces for criticism to have much effect upon it; for, as Frederick Turner pointed out in his study of *The Frontier in American History,* the development of American civilization in the nineteenth century exhibited a constant return to primitive conditions on a continually advancing frontier-line. Our social development was always beginning again *de novo* on the frontier, and this largely prevented Americans even in the settled areas from retaining a firm hold upon civilized values. And so our old writers, convinced of the futility of criticism, turned their reluctant energies in other directions. Meanwhile, with few exceptions, the immigrants from the Old World belonged to the inarticulate classes; and for them it was enough, or seemed enough, that the New World afforded them opportunities, of an economic sort, which they had not possessed in the Old. We know how these immigrants expressed themselves. Such works as *The Promised Land* and *The Making of an Amer-*

ican contributed immensely to our national self-esteem; and, what is more to the point, in the absence of native spokesmen who might have maintained the sense of human values, they served as the final proof in American eyes that our civilization was superior in all essentials to the civilization of Europe. In this realm, the realm of self-congratulation, it never rains but it pours.

Because of these peculiar circumstances, our social history differs from that of any of the European countries. We have never conceived it as possible to shape our social life. This social life has grown and changed so rapidly, so many racial strains have merged themselves in it, so many territories have opened before it, this life has indeed existed in such a flux that the idea of molding it has scarcely entered our calculations. It was this that prevented for so long the development of criticism in America. We know how quietistic Hawthorne was regarding every prospect of social change: we know his fear, embodied in the character of Hollingsworth, of tampering with "the natural order of things." A similar diffidence inhibited Mark Twain, and surely this was one of the reasons that led Henry Adams to hide his life and restrained him from coming forward as the critic he plainly wished to be. They felt, these gifted men, that the only course for them was to stand aside and watch the American process—some in faith, others in despair, and more and more in despair, as they saw how little the process contemplated of what to them was important for civilization. For they felt that they could never shape the process, or control it in any way. Yet the longer the process continued, the more it became apparent that Americans, in so far as they were Americans who piqued themselves on their "Americanism," were ceasing to desire, were ceasing even to be able to desire, consciously and with their minds and wills, any goals in life except the goals that were placed before them by the world of trade. Yes, even to the point where their perceptions had come to rest on a purely physical plane.

But *autres temps, autres mœurs.* We have nourished ourselves on hope in America, where we should have nourished ourselves on desire. Many have hoped for America, few have desired for America. And desire is the mother of intention. And desire cannot come without criticism. "It is an *idea*," as John Eglinton says, for which we wait. "Without an idea man is frivolous, dissatisfied, despicable. With an idea the long-hoarded initiatives of his nature are liberated, he strains forward to new consummations." Criticism, so silent in the past, is vocal now in America; and why should it be vocal if there were not within it a sudden faith in the ability of Americans to shape their destiny, to mold it and give it form, to ride things as things have ridden them? The division between the two great camps of modern American writers is a division between those who are still satisfied with a national state of adolescence and those who exact of America the traits and responsibilities of maturity; and if the latter appear a little rough and importunate, it is because they are obliged to shake out of a deep sleep a population that should have been kept awake by an unbroken succession of gentle proddings. The recent damming-up of our social energies, through the closing of the frontier at the West and the slackening of immigration at the East, enables us really for the first time to submit to a candid scrutiny our prepossessions in regard to property and every other fundamental issue, to desire a great and beautiful corporate life. How scattered our forces have been! We have taken pleasure, it seems, in making machines of men; and repudiating the vision of a good society, we have not discouraged our finest intellects from giving up society as a bad job and devoting to the material periphery the passion they might have devoted to human beings. Our thought has been centrifugal instead of centripetal; it has gone out to the frame, it has never fixed itself upon the picture.

The great social thinkers, the great critics have given us a sense of society as a whole, and of man as a social animal, capable of molding his environment towards a humane ideal. And Ruskin, as Lawrence Binyon says, might well have taken as his motto the lines of Blake:

I will not cease from mental fight,
Nor shall my sword sleep in my hand,
Till we have built Jerusalem
In England's green and pleasant land.

American criticism, too, is capable of such a vision. But this is certain, American criticism will never attain its object as long as it fails to conceive, as something ever-present in its purview, the "green and pleasant land" it contemplates. The great critics have always convinced the world in spite of the prepossessions of the world; it is their ability to do so that makes these critics great and worthy of attention, for unless they speak with reasonableness and human understanding they confess in their own words that they do not possess that in the name of which they pretend to speak. No doubt, for many years in this country the critics and the unconverted public are destined to wage the blindest kind of warfare; for the critical attitude in our general mind has perished from disuse. But as long as this continues let us remember that our work is only a kind of spadework, which antecedes the real task of criticism. To forget this is to have lost the battle. For Amiel expressed the just motto of critics in those memorable words: "Truth should not merely conquer, it should win."

IRVING BABBITT

The Critic and American Life

A FREQUENT remark of the French about Americans is: "They're children"; which, interpreted, means that from the French point of view Americans are childishly uncritical. The remark is relevant only in so far as it refers to general critical intelligence. In dealing with the special problems of a commercial and industrial society, Americans have shown that they can be abundantly critical. Certain Americans, for example, have developed a critical keenness in estimating the value of stocks and bonds that is nothing short of uncanny.[1] The very persons, however, who are thus keen in some particular field are, when confronted with questions that call for general critical intelligence, often puerile. Yet in an age like the present, which is being subjected to a constant stream of propaganda in everything from the choice of religion to its cigarettes, general critical intelligence would seem desirable.

As a matter of fact, most persons aspire nowadays to be not critical but creative. We have not merely creative poets and novelists, but creative readers and listeners and dancers. Lately a form of creativeness has appeared that may in time swallow up

[1] This was written before the collapse of the great common stock bubble in the autumn of 1929. It then became evident that what the financial leaders of the "Boom" period lacked was not so much expertness in their own field as general critical intelligence—especially some working knowledge of the ways of Nemesis. There were, of course, honorable exceptions. The late Paul M. Warburg showed that he was one of them when he remarked, apropos of the so-called business cycle, that "it is a subject for psychologists rather than for economists." [What is involved] "is the answer to the question: How long—in industry, commerce and finance—does the memory of painful experiences prevent human greed and conceit from regaining control, etc."

From *On Being Creative,* by Irving Babbitt. Pp. 201-234. Houghton Mifflin Co., 1932. Reprinted by permission.

all the others—creative salesmanship. The critic himself has caught the contagion and also aspires to be creative. He is supposed to become so when he receives from the creation of another, conceived as pure temperamental overflow, so vivid an impression that, when passed through his temperament, it issues forth as a new creation. What is eliminated in both critic and creator is any standard that is set above temperament, and that therefore might interfere with their eagerness to get themselves expressed.

This notion of criticism as self-expression is important for our present subject, for it has been adopted by the writer who is, according to the *Encyclopedia Britannica*,[1] "The greatest critical force in America"—Mr. H. L. Mencken. Creative self-expression, as practiced by himself and others, has, according to Mr. Mencken, led to a salutary stirring up of the stagnant pool of American letters: "Today for the first time in years there is strife in American criticism. . . . Heretics lay on boldly and the professors are forced to make some defense. Often going further they attempt counterattacks. Ears are bitten off, noses are bloodied. There are wallops both above and below the belt."

But it may be that criticism is something more than Mr. Mencken would have us believe, more in short than a squabble between Bohemians, each eager to capture the attention of the public for his brand of self-expression. To reduce criticism indeed to the satisfaction of a temperamental urge, to the uttering of one's gustos and disgustos (in Mr. Mencken's case chiefly the latter) is to run counter to the very etymology of the word which implies discrimination and judgment. The best one would anticipate from a writer like Mr. Mencken, possessing an unusual verbal virtuosity and at the same time temperamentally irresponsible, is superior intellectual vaudeville. One must grant him, however, certain genuine critical virtues—for example, a power of shrewd observation within rather narrow limits. Yet the total effect of his writing is nearer to intellectual vaudeville than to serious criticism.

The serious critic is more concerned with achieving a correct

---

[1] Thirteenth edition. In the fourteenth edition we are informed that Mr. Mencken is a satirist rather than a critic.

scale of values and so seeing things proportionately than with self-expression. His essential virtue is poise. The specific benefit he confers is to act as a moderating influence on the opposite insanities between which mankind in the lump is constantly tending to oscillate—oscillations that Luther compares to the reelings of a drunken peasant on horseback. The critic's survey of any particular situation may very well seem satirical. The complaint that Mr. Mencken is too uniformly disgruntled in his survey of the American situation rather misses the point. Behind the pleas for more constructiveness it is usually easy to detect the voice of the booster. A critic who did not get beyond a correct diagnosis of existing evils might be very helpful. If Mr. Mencken has fallen short of being such a diagnostician, the failure is due not to his excess of severity but to his lack of discrimination.

The standards with reference to which men have discriminated in the past have been largely traditional. The outstanding fact of the present period, on the other hand, has been the weakening of traditional standards. An emergency has arisen not unlike that with which Socrates sought to cope in ancient Athens. Anyone who is untraditional and seeks at the same time to be discriminating must almost necessarily own Socrates as his master. As is well known, Socrates above all sought to be discriminating in his use of general terms. Before allowing one's imagination and finally one's conduct to be controlled by a general term, it would seem wise to submit it to a Socratic scrutiny.

It is, therefore, unfortunate that at a time like the present, which plainly calls for a Socrates, we should instead have got a Mencken. One may take as an example of Mr. Mencken's failure to discriminate adequately, his attitude towards the term that for several generations past has been governing the imagination of multitudes—democracy. His view of democracy is simply that of Rousseau turned upside down, and nothing, as has been remarked, resembles a hollow so much as a swelling. A distinction of which he has failed to recognize the importance is that between a direct or unlimited and a constitutional democracy. In the latter we probably have the best thing in the world. The former, on the other hand, as all thinkers of any penetration from Plato and Aristotle down have perceived, leads to the loss of liberty and finally to the rise of some form of despotism. The two conceptions of democracy involve not merely incompatible views of government but ultimately of human nature. The desire of the constitutional democrat for institutions that act as checks on the immediate will of the people implies a similar dualism in the individual— a higher self that acts restrictively on his ordinary and impulsive self. The partisan of unlimited democracy on the other hand is an idealist in the sense the term assumed in connection with the so-called romantic movement. His faith in the people is closely related to the doctrine of natural goodness proclaimed by the sentimentalists of the eighteenth century and itself marking an extreme recoil from the dogmas of total depravity. The doctrine of natural goodness favors the free temperamental expansion that I have already noticed in speaking of the creative critic.

It is of the utmost importance, however, if one is to understand Mr. Mencken, to discriminate between two types of temperamentalist—the soft and sentimental type, who cherishes various "ideals" and the hard, or Nietzschean type, who piques himself on being realistic. As a matter of fact, if one sees in the escape from traditional controls merely an opportunity to live temperamentally, it would seem advantageous to pass promptly from the idealistic to the Nietzschean phase, sparing oneself as many as possible of the intermediary disillusions. It is at all events undeniable that the rise of Menckenism has been marked by a certain collapse of romantic idealism in the political field and elsewhere. The numerous disillusions that have supervened upon the War have provided a favoring atmosphere.

The symptoms of Menckenism are familiar: a certain hardness and smartness and disposition to rail at everything that, rightly or wrongly, is established and respected; a tendency to identify the real with what Mr. Mencken terms "the cold and clammy facts" and to assume that the only alternative to facing these facts is to fade away into sheer romantic unreality. These and similar traits are becoming so widely diffused that, whatever one's opinion of Mr. Mencken as a writer and thinker, one must grant him representativeness. He is a chief prophet at present of those who deem themselves emancipated but who are, according to Mr. Brownell, merely unbuttoned.

The crucial point in any case is one's attitude towards the principle of control. Those who stand for this principle in any form or degree are dismissed by the emancipated as reactionaries or, still graver reproach, as Puritans. Mr. Mencken would have us believe that the historical Puritan was not even sincere in his moral rigorism, but was given to "lamentable transactions with loose women and fiery jugs." This may serve as a sample of the assertions, picturesquely indiscriminate, by which a writer wins immediate notoriety at the expense of his permanent reputation. The facts about the Puritan happen to be complex and need to be dealt with very Socratically. It has been affirmed that the point of view of the Puritan was stoical rather than truly Christian, and the affirmation is not wholly false. The present discussion of the relationship between Puritanism and the rise of capitalism with its glorification of the acquisitive life also has its justification. It is likewise a fact that the Puritan was from the outset unduly concerned with reforming others as well as himself, and this trait relates him to the humanitarian meddler or "wowser" of the present day, who is Mr. Mencken's pet aversion.

Yet it remains true that awe and reverence and humility are Christian virtues and that there was some survival of these virtues in the Puritan. For a representative Puritan like Jonathan Edwards they were inseparable from the illumination of grace, from what he terms a "divine and supernatural light." In the passage from the love and fear of God of an Edwards to the love and service of man professed by the humanitarian, something has plainly dropped out, something that is very near the center. What has tended to disappear is the inner life with the special type of control it imposes. With the decline of this inner control there has been an increasing resort to outer control. Instead of the genuine Puritan we then have the humanitarian legalist who passes innumerable laws for the control of people who refuse to control themselves. The activity of the uplifters is scarcely suggestive of any "divine and supernatural light." Here is a discrimination of the first importance that has been obscured by the muddy thinking of our half-baked intelligentsia. One is thus kept from perceiving the real problem, which is to retain the inner life, even though one refuse to accept the theological nightmare with which the Puritan associated it. More is involved in the failure to solve this problem than the Puritan tradition. It is the failure of our contemporary life in general. Yet, unless some relation is reached by a full and free exercise of the critical spirit, one remains a mere modernist and not a thoroughgoing and complete modern; for the modern spirit and the critical spirit are in their essence one.

What happens, when one sets out to deal with questions of this order without sufficient depth of reflection and critical maturity, may be seen in Mr. Sinclair Lewis's *Elmer Gantry*. He has been lured from art into the writing of a wild diatribe which, considered even as such, is largely beside the mark. If the Protestant Church is at present threatened with bankruptcy, it is not because it has produced an occasional Elmer Gantry. The true reproach it has incurred is that, in its drift toward modernism, it has lost its grip not merely on certain dogmas, but simultaneously on the facts of human nature. It has failed above all to carry over in some modern and critical form the truth of a dogma that unfortunately receives much support from these facts—the dogma of original sin. At first sight Mr. Mencken would appear to have a conviction of evil—when, for example, he reduces democracy in its essential aspect to a "combat between jackals and jackasses"—that establishes at least one bond between him and the austere Christian.

The appearance, however, is deceptive. The Christian is conscious above all of the "old Adam" in himself; hence his humility. The effect of Mr. Mencken's writing, on the other hand, is to produce pride rather than humility, a pride ultimately based on flattery. The reader, especially the young and callow reader, identifies himself imaginatively with Mr. Mencken, and conceives of himself as a sort of morose and sardonic divinity surveying from some superior altitude an immeasurable expanse of "boobs." This attitude will not seem especially novel to anyone who has traced the modern movement. One is reminded in particular of Flaubert, who showed a diligence in collecting bourgeois imbecilities comparable to that displayed by Mr. Mencken in his *Americana*. Flaubert's discovery that one does not add to one's happiness in this way would no doubt be dismissed by Mr. Mencken as irrelevant, for he has told us that he does not believe in happiness. Another discovery of Flaubert's may seem to him more worthy of consideration. "By dint of railing at idiots," Flaubert reports, "one runs the risk of becoming idiotic oneself."

It may be that the only way to escape from the unduly complacent cynicism of Mr. Mencken and his school, is to reaffirm once more the truths of the inner life. In that case it would seem desirable to disengage, so far as possible, the principle of control on which the inner life finally depends from mere creeds and traditions and assert it as a psychological fact; a fact, moreover, that is neither "cold" nor "clammy." The coldness and clamminess of much so-called realism arises from its failure to give this fact due recognition. A chief task, indeed, of the Socratic critic would be to rescue the noble term "realist" from its present degradation. A view of reality that overlooks the element in man that moves in an opposite direction from mere temperament, the specifically human factor, in short, may prove to be singularly one-sided. Is the Puritan, John Milton, when he declares that "he who reigns within himself and rules passions, desires, and fears is more than a king," less real than Mr. Theodore Dreiser when he discourses in his peculiar dialect of "those rearranging chemisms upon which all the morality and immorality of the world is based"?

As a matter of fact, according to the degree and nature of the exercise of the principle of control, one may distinguish two main types of realism which may be denominated respectively religious and humanistic: as the principle of control falls into abeyance, a third type tends to emerge, which may be termed naturalistic realism. That the decline of the traditional controls has been followed by a lapse to the naturalistic level is indubitable. The characteristic evils of the present age arise from unrestraint and violation of the law of measure and not, as our modernists would have us believe, from the tyranny of taboos and traditional inhibitions. The facts cry to heaven. The delicate adjustment that is required between the craving for emancipation and the need of control has been pointed out once for all by Goethe, speaking not as a Puritan, but as a clear-eyed man of the world. Everything, he says, that liberates the spirit without a corresponding growth in self-mastery is pernicious. This one sentence would seem to cover the case of our "flaming youth" rather completely.

The movement in the midst of which we are still living was from its inception unsound in its dealing with the principle of control. It is vain to expect from the dregs of this movement what its "first sprightly running failed to give." Mr. Carl Sandburg speaks of the "marvelous rebellion of man at all signs reading *Keep off*." An objection to this purely insurrectional attitude is that, as a result of its endless iteration during the past century and more, it has come to savor too strongly of what has been called the "humdrum of revolt." A more serious objection to the attitude is that it encourages an unrestricted and merely temperamental liberty which, paradoxically enough, at first sight affords the modern man no avenue of escape from the web that is being woven about him by the scientific determinist.

Realists of the current type are in point of fact intimately allied with the psychologists—glandular, behavioristic, and psychoanalytical—who, whatever their divergences among themselves, unite in their deterministic trend and therefore class fundamentally with both religious and humanistic realists. The proper method of procedure in defending the freedom of the will would seem to insist upon it as a fact of experience, a fact so primary that the position of the determinist involves an evasion of one of the immediate data of consciousness in favor of a metaphysical dream. What is genuinely experimental in naturalistic psychology should of course be received with respect; but the facts of which it takes account in its experiments are unimportant compared with the facts it either neglects or denies. Practically it is running into grotesque extremes of pseudo-science that make it a shining mark for the Socratic critic.

Here at all events is the issue on which all other issues finally hinge; for until the question of moral freedom—the question of whether man is a responsible agent or only the plaything of his impulses and impressions—is decided, nothing is decided; and to decide the question under existing circumstances calls for the keenest critical discrimination. Creation that is not sufficiently supported by such discrimination is likely to prove premature.

One may illustrate from Mr. Dreiser's *American Tragedy,* hailed in certain quarters as the "Mount Everest" of recent fiction. He has succeeded in producing in this work something genuinely harrowing; but one is harrowed to no purpose. One has in more than full measure the tragic qualm but without the final relief and enlargement of spirit that true tragedy succeeds somehow in giving, and that without recourse to explicit moralizing. It is hardly worth while to struggle through eight hundred and more very pedestrian pages to be left at the end with a feeling of sheer oppression. The explanation of this oppression is that Mr. Dreiser does not rise sufficiently above the level of "rearranging chemisms," in other words, of animal behavior. Tragedy may admit fate— Greek tragedy admits it—but not of the naturalistic variety. Confusion on this point may compromise in the long run the reputations of writers more eminent than Mr. Dreiser—for example, of Thomas Hardy. Fatalism of the naturalistic type is responsible in large measure for the atmosphere of futility and frustration that hangs heavily over so much contemporary writing. One finally comes to feel with a recent poet that "dust" is the common source from which

stream

The cricket's cry and Dante's dream.

Anyone who admits reality only in what derives from the dust, whether in a cricket or Dante, must, from the point of view of the religious or the humanistic realist, be prepared to make substantial sacrifices. In the first place, he must sacrifice the depth and subtlety that arise from the recognition in some form of the duality in

man's nature. For the interest that may rise from the portrayal of
the conflict between a law of the spirit and a law of the members,
the inordinate interest in sex for its own sake promoted by most
of the so-called realists is a rather shabby substitute. A merely
naturalistic realism also involves the sacrifice of beauty in almost
any sense of that elusive term. Closely related to this sacrifice is the
sacrifice of delicacy, elevation, and distinction. The very word
realism has come to connote the opposite of these qualities. When
we learn, for example, that someone has written a realistic study
of a great man, we are sure in advance that he has devoted his main
effort to proving that "Plutarch lied." The more the great man is
reduced to the level of commonplace or worse, the more we feel he
has been "humanized."

Mr. Sherwood Anderson has argued ingeniously that, inasmuch
as we ourselves are crude, our literature, if it is not to be unreal
and fictitious, should be crude likewise. But the writer who hopes
to achieve work of importance cannot afford to be too deeply immersed in the atmosphere of the special place and passing moment. Still less can he afford to make us feel, as writers like Mr.
Anderson and Mr. Dreiser and Mr. Sinclair Lewis do, that, if
there were any lack of vulgarity in what they are depicting, they
would be capable of supplying the defect from their own abundance.
More is involved here than the mere loss of distinction. We have
come, indeed, to the supreme sacrifice that every writer must make
who does not transcend a naturalistic realism. He must forego
the hope of the enduring appeal—the hope that every writer worthy
of his salt cherishes in some degree. In the absence of humanistic
or religious standards, he is prone to confound the real with the
welter of the actual, and so to miss the "grandeur of generality."

Certain books in the current mode are so taken up with the
evanescent surfaces of life that they will survive, if at all, not as
literature but as sociological documents. The very language in
which they are written will, in a generation or two, require a glos-
sary. So far from imposing an orderly pattern on the raw material
of experience, they rather emphasize the lack of pattern. The resulting effect, to borrow a phrase from the late Stephen Crane, who

has had a marked influence on the recent movement, is that of a "cluttered incoherency." As an extreme example of this tendency one may cite *Manhattan Transfer,* by John Dos Passos. In the name of reality Mr. Dos Passos has perpetrated a literary nightmare. Such a work would seem to have slight value even as a sociological document; unless, indeed, one is prepared to admit that contemporary Manhattan is inhabited chiefly by epileptic Bohemians.

"It is as much a trade," says La Bruyère, "to make a book as it is to make a clock"; in short, literature is largely a matter of technique. The technique of *Manhattan Transfer* is as dubious as its underlying philosophy. Neither can be justified save on the assumption that the aim of art is to exaggerate the clutter and incoherency of the mundane spectacle instead of eliciting its deeper meaning. Technique counts for even more in poetry than in prose. It would be possible to base on technical grounds alone a valid protest against the present preposterous overestimate of Walt Whitman. Fundamental questions need, in these very untraditional days, to be critically elucidated with a view to right definition if the poet is not to lack technique or still worse, if he is not, like certain recent practitioners of free verse, to be hagridden by a false technique. It evidently concerns both the form and substance of poetry, whether one define it with Aristotle as the portrayal of representative human action, or whether one define it with Mr. Carl Sandburg as a "mystic, sensuous mathematics of fire, smokestacks, waffles, pansies, people, and purple sunsets."

There is no doubt much in America of today that suggests a jazzy impressionism. Still our naturalistic deliquescence has probably not gone so far as one might infer from poetry like that of Mr. Sandburg or fiction like that of Mr. Dos Passos. The public response to some of the realistic novels has been considerable: allowance must be made however for the *succès de scandale,* also for the skill attained by the modern publisher in the art of merchandising. The reputation of certain books one might mention may be regarded as a triumph of "creative" advertising. What has been created is a mirage of masterpieces where no masterpieces are. It is well also to remember in regard to some of the works that have been most discussed that, so far from being an authentic reflection of the American scene, they are rather a belated echo of certain European movements. For it is as certain that in our literary and artistic modes we follow Europe—usually at an interval of from five to forty years—as it is that we lead Europe in our bathtubs and sanitary plumbing. Anyone who resided in Paris in the nineties and later in America, will, as I can testify from personal experience, have the sense of having lived through the same literary fads twice. Mr. Dreiser reminds one of Zola and his school. The technique of Mr. Dos Passos recalls that of the Goncourts. Our experimenters in free verse have followed in the wake not merely of Walt Whitman but of the French symbolists, and so on.

We shall presently begin to hear of certain new developments in French literature and critical thought that point, though indecisively as yet, to a radical departure from what has been the main current since the eighteenth century and in some respects since the Renaissance. It is well that we should become familiar with the writers who reveal in different ways this latest trend—notably with Maritain, Maurras, Lasserre, Seillière, and Benda; for they give evidence of a quality of cerebration that is rare in our own literati. At the same time we should not adopt with our usual docility the total outlook of any of these writers: for no one of them has worked out a point of view exactly adapted to our requirements. In general, it is not fitting that a great nation at the very height of its power should go on indefinitely trailing after Europe. It is time for us to initiate something of our own. This does not mean that we should proceed forthwith to inbreed our own "originality." It means almost the exact opposite. The most original thing one could do nowadays would be to question the whole theory of originality as mere temperamental overflow and self-expression that has prevailed from the "geniuses" of the eighteenth century down to one of our youthful and very minor bards who aspires to "spill his bright illimitable soul."

A genuinely critical survey would make manifest that the unsatisfactoriness of our creative effort is due to a lack of the standards that culture alone can supply. Our cultural crudity and insignificance can be traced in turn to the inadequacy of our education, especially our higher education. Mr. Mencken's attack on the "professors" is therefore largely justified; for if the professors were performing their function properly Mr. Mencken himself would not be possible. One must add in common justice that the professors themselves, or at least some of them, are becoming aware that all is not well with existing conditions. One could not ask anything more perspicacious than the following paragraph from a recent report of Committee G to the American Association of University Professors:

American education has suffered from the domination, conscious or unconscious, direct or indirect, of political and sentimental, as well as educational, theories that are demonstrably false. If the views of some men are to prevail the intellectual life of the country is doomed; everybody except the sheer idiot is to go to college and pursue chiefly sociology, nature study, child study, and community service—and we shall have a society unique only in its mediocrity, ignorance, and vulgarity. It will not do to dismiss lightly even so extreme a view as this; it is too indicative. Such influences are very strong, their pressure is constant; and if education has largely failed in America, it has been due primarily to them.

In short, as a result of the encroachments of an equalitarian democracy, the standards of our higher education have suffered in two distinct particulars: first, as regards the quality of students; second, as regards the quality of the studies these students pursue. The first of these two evils is generally recognized. There is even some prospect of remedial measures. Certain institutions, Harvard, for example, without being as yet severely selective, are becoming more critical of the incompetent student. On the other hand, there seems to be less hope than ever of any righting of the second and more serious evil—the failure to distinguish qualitatively between studies. The main drift is still towards what one may term a blanket degree. (Dartmouth, for example, has just merged its bachelor of arts and bachelor of science.) Yet rather than blur certain distinctions it would have been better, one might suppose, to use up all the letters of the alphabet devising new degrees to meet the real or supposed educational needs of the modern man. To bestow the A.B. degree indiscriminately on a student for whom education has meant primarily a specialization in chemistry and one for whom it has meant primarily an assimilation of the masterpieces of Greek literature is to empty it of any effective meaning. At the present rate, indeed, the time may come when the A.B. degree will not throw much more light on the cultural quality of its recipient than it would if, as has been suggested, it were bestowed on every American child at birth.

It goes without saying that those who have been lowering and confusing educational standards have been profuse in their professions of "service." A critical examination, not merely of American education, but of American life at the present time, will almost necessarily hinge on this term. The attitude of the Socratic critic toward it is not to be confounded with that of Mr. Mencken and the "hardboiled" contingent. "When a gang of real estate agents," says Mr. Mencken, "bond salesmen, and automobile dealers get together to sob for Service, it takes no Freudian to surmise that someone is about to be swindled." But if one entertains doubts about this current American gospel, why waste one's ammunition on any such small fry? Other and more exalted personages than the members of the Rotary Club at Zenith have, in Mr. Mencken's elegant phrase, been "yipping for Service." If one is to deal with this idea of service Socratically, one needs to consider it in relation to the two figures who have rightly been taken to be most representative in our cultural background—Benjamin Franklin and Jonathan Edwards. Franklin's idea of service is already humanitarian. Edwards' idea is still traditionally Christian—service not of man but of God. What Franklin stood for is flourishing prodigiously at the present moment, so much so that he may perhaps be defined in his chief line of influence as the great superrotarian. What Edwards stood for is, on the other hand, largely obsolete or survives only in the form of habits, which, lacking doctrinal support, are steadily declining along with the whole Puritan culture.

Intermediary types are possible. One may in one's character reflect the Puritan background and at the same time in one's idea of service derive rather from Franklin. Precisely that combination is found in the most influential of our recent educational leaders—the late President Eliot. A legitimate admiration for his personal qualities should not interfere with the keenest critical scrutiny of his views about education, for the two things stand in no necessary connection. Practically this means to scrutinize the humanitarian ideal that he probably did more than any other man of his generation to promote. In this respect most of the heads of our institutions of learning have been and still are understudies of President Eliot.

In an address on the occasion of his ninetieth birthday President Eliot warned his hearers against introspection, lest it divert them from a whole-hearted devotion to service. Between this attitude and a religious or humanistic attitude there is a clash of first principles. Both humanism and religion require introspection as a prerequisite of the inner life and its appropriate activity. With the disappearance of this activity what is left is the outer activity of the utilitarian, and this leads straight to the one-sided cult of material efficiency and finally to the standardization that is, according to nearly all foreign critics and many of our own, a chief American danger. We cannot return to the introspection of the Puritan. We shudder at the theology an Edwards would impose as the condition of his "divine and supernatural light." Yet it does not follow, as I have already suggested, that we should reject the inner life along with this theology. One may recognize innumerable advantages in the gospel of service and yet harbor an uneasy suspicion withal that in the passage from the old religion to the modern humanitarian dispensation something vital has disappeared, something from which neither the outer working of the utilitarian nor again the expansive sympathy of the sentimentalist can offer an equivalent.

The problem of the inner life is very much bound up with two other problems that are now pressing for solution in our higher education and have as yet found none: the problem of the specialist and the problem of leisure. The man of leisure is engaged in an inner and specifically human form of activity, a form that is, according to Aristotle, needful if he is to compass the end of ends—his own happiness. The question is whether one should consent like the specialist to forego this activity and to live partially and as a mere instrument for the attainment of some outer end—even though this end be the progress of humanity. We are beginning to hear a great deal nowadays about the "menace" of leisure. It has been estimated that with the prefecting of mechanical devices the man of the future will be able to satisfy his material wants by working not more than four hours a day. It is vain to anticipate that the rank and file will use this release from outer activity intelligently unless the leaders, notably those in high academic station, show the way. The notion of true leisure is the ultimate source of the standards of any education that deserves to be called liberal. When even a few of our college and university presidents show that they are thinking to some purpose on the nature of leisure it will be time enough to talk of "America's coming of age."

As it is, our institutions of learning seem to be becoming more and more hotbeds of "idealism." Their failure, on the whole, to achieve standards as something quite distinct from ideals, on the one hand, and standardization, on the other, may prove a fact of sinister import for the future of American civilization. The warfare that is being waged at the present time by Mr. Sinclair Lewis and others against a standardized Philistinism continues in the main the protest that has been made for several generations past by the temperamentalists, hard or soft, against the mechanizing of life by the utilitarian. This protest has been, and is likely to continue to be, ineffectual. The fruitful opposite of the standardized Philistine is not the Bohemian, nor again the hard temperamentalist or superman, as Mr. Mencken conceives him, but the man of leisure. Leisure involves an inner effort with reference to standards that is opposed to the sheer expansion of temperament, as it is to every other form of sheer expansion.

Perhaps a reason why the standards of the humanist are less popular in this country than the ideals of the humanitarian is that these standards set bounds to the acquisitive life; whereas it seems possible to combine a perfect idealism with an orgy of unrestricted commercialism. It is well for us to try to realize how we appear to others in this matter. Our growing unpopularity abroad is due no doubt in part to envy of our material success, but it also arises from the proneness of the rest of the world to judge us, not by the way we feel about ourselves, but by our actual performance. If we are in our own eyes a nation of idealists, we are, according to a recent French critic, M. André Siegfried,[1] a "nation of Pharisees." The European, M. Siegfried would have us believe, still has a concern for the higher values of civilization, whereas the American is prepared to sacrifice these values ruthlessly to mass production and material efficiency.

It is easy to detect under this assumption the latest form of a "certain condescension in foreigners." The breakdown of cultural standards is European as well as American. It is not clear that M. Siegfried himself has an adequate notion of the form of effort that can alone serve as a counterpoise to the one-sided activity of the utilitarian. At the same time his anatomy of our favorite ideal of service is not without interest. This ideal opposes no effective barrier to our expansiveness. An unchecked expansiveness on the national scale is always imperialistic. Among the ingredients of a possible American imperialism M. Siegfried enumerates the American's "great self-satisfaction, his rather brutal sense of his own interests, and *the consciousness, still more dangerous, of his 'duties' towards humanity.*" M. Siegfried admits however that our imperialism is likely to be of a new and subtle essence, not concerned primarily with territorial aggrandizement.

A proper discussion of M. Siegfried's position as well as of other issues I have been raising would transcend the limits of an essay. My end has been accomplished if I have justified in some measure the statement with which I started as to the importance of cultivating a general critical intelligence. James Russell Lowell's dictum that before having an American literature we must have an American criticism was never truer than it is today. The obvious reply to those who call for more creation and less criticism is that one needs to be critical above all in examining what now passes for creation. A scrutiny of this kind would, I have tried to show, ex-

---

[1] See his volume *Les États-Unis d'aujourd'hui* (1927), translated under the title *America Comes of Age*.

tend beyond the bounds of literature to various aspects of our national life and would converge finally on our higher education.

We cannot afford to accept as substitute for this true criticism the self-expression of Mr. Mencken and his school, unless indeed we are to merit the comment that is, I am told, made on us by the South Americans: "They are not a very serious people!" To be sure, the reader may reflect that I am myself a critic, or a would-be critic. I can only express the hope that, in my magnifying of the critical function, I do not offer too close a parallel to the dancing-master of Molière who averred, it will be remembered, that "all the mistakes of men, the fatal reverses that fill the world's annals, the shortcomings of statesmen, and the blunders of great captains arise from not knowing how to dance."

PAUL ELMER MORE

How to Read "Lycidas"

AFTER passing, as I might say, through the valley of the shadow of death, after months of physical prostration so abject that reading of any sort was beyond the strength of a depleted brain, the poet to whom I turned instinctively with the first renewal of health was Milton. And so I have been reading Milton again and books about him, with the old zest I had as a boy, and with an added joy of almost tremulous excitement such as a miser might feel at the rediscovery of a treasure of gold stolen from him and long buried out of sight. But with this delight have been mingled certain scruples which had troubled me in the old days and for which I had never found quite a satisfactory answer. Again, as many times before, on laying down one of the poems the familiar words of Tennyson would come unbidden to my mind:

> O mighty-mouth'd inventor of harmonies,
> O skill'd to sing of Time or Eternity,
> God-gifted organ-voice of England,
> Milton, a name to resound for ages.

Of the mighty harmonies there would be no doubt; God-gifted voice certainly; organ-voice certainly, for those who have ears to hear. If anyone in English Milton had the divine craft of words, the mastery of sonorous speech. His is not Shakespeare's incalculable gift; it lacks the element of magic that captures us in Shakespeare; it is, or soon after his earliest experiments it was, an art that came by reflection, and as we read him we imagine that we might by equal deliberation attain the same perfection—only we never do attain it. And something of this distinction Milton himself seems to have felt when he wrote of Shakespeare:

From *On Being Human,* by Paul Elmer More. Pp. 184-202. Princeton University Press. Copyright, 1936. Reprinted by permission.

For whil'st to th' shame of slow-endeavoring Art
Thy easie numbers flow.

The same distinction, I think, was present to Irving Babbitt when he spoke, as I have heard him do more than once, of his experience in quoting. It was Babbitt's custom in the first draught of his essays to cite from memory, and then, before printing, to verify the quotation by reference to the text. He would find occasionally that even his retentive memory had slipped and that he had substituted a word of his own for the poet's. And sometimes, he would say, he could not see that the substitution was inferior to the original— except in the case of Shakespeare. He never made a change in Shakespeare's language but some force or charm was lost. That was not so even with Milton. Such a difference exists between the seemingly careless spontaneity and the elaborated art of our two supreme masters of poetical diction; and he would be a rash judge who should say that the advantage was all on one side or the other.

But to return to the question that vexed my mood of acquiescent joy. God-gifted organ-voice Milton possessed in full measure—but "voice of England"? Does he speak for the whole of England, or, that being scarcely possible, does he speak from the heart of England, giving articulate expression to that central quality which has made England what we know and love? And by his influence did he maintain that balance and moderation, that sense of law enveloping the individual, which made of Falkland a true type of the Englishman that was to be? Here the question begins with style, but extends beyond mere style to psychology and to principles of government and life.

Now, if there be any hesitation with me to accept Milton's style as the norm of good English, it is certainly not on the ground of that "dissociation of sensibility" which draws a school of modern critics and poets to repudiate what may be called the Miltonic line of development and to seek their parentage in Shakespeare and Donne and the "Metaphysicals." If I understand what the leader of that Choir means by this rather obscure phrase, it is that Milton by conscious choice and judgment dissociated his mind from one whole range of perceptions, refusing to respond to them emotionally as unrelated to a fixed theory of values, and by the same deliberate act of selection created a more or less artificial language, whereas the poets proceeding from Donne held their sensibility open to any and every perception and employed words to convey the sharp immediate impression of each fact of sense and experience without discrimination. The distinction is valid, and it is interesting; for the "modernist" in poetry it is of vital significance. But I am not sure that the "dissociation of sensibility," so taken, has been the source of dead monotony and of verbal unreality in our literature; and I am sure that if Milton failed in national leadership it was not for this reason. Rather I should say that his influence in this respect has made for sanity and form and for limitations which are characteristically English. Rather I should maintain that Milton's failure, so far as he failed, was owing to something essentially un-English, or only partially English, to something belonging to his individual temperament, which passed into his philosophy of life and diverted the love of liberty, which was the central driving force of all his being, into a morbid and isolating passion. Here too Milton was clear-headed in his application of the law to others, but curiously perverse when his own interests were affected. In the second of the sonnets on the book called *Tetrachordon,* he berates his fellow countrymen as "Owles and Cuckoos, Asses, Apes and Doggs" for the very reason that they have lost the true meaning of liberty, while they

> bawle for freedom in this senceless mood,
> And still revolt when truth would set them free.
> License they mean when they cry libertie;
> For who loves that, must first be wise and good;
> But from that mark, how far they roave we see
> For all this wast of wealth, and loss of blood.

That is sound doctrine, but—alas to say it!—Milton did not see how apt would be the retort, *de te fabula;* how easy the reply: License he meant when he cried liberty.

This book called *Tetrachordon,* written by Milton himself, was the second of his treatises on divorce, and is a bitter invective against those who, by opposing the facile freedom of marital separation, enslave the soul under man-made laws, forgetting that which "makes us holiest and likest to God's immortal image," and, for the law of liberty, setting up "that which makes us most conformable and captive to civil and subordinate precepts: . . . although indeed no ordinance, human or from heaven, can bind against the good of man." By "the good of man," as Mr. Tillyard observes in his comment on the passage, Milton means what elsewhere he calls "nature"—damnable word, I add, into which have been distilled all the fallacies of human wit through thousands of years. If you track the word down through its many ambiguities, you will discover that in the end it signifies that which a man temperamentally and personally desires as distinguished from that which is prescribed for him by human rule or divine precept. So it was that Milton, fretted and humiliated because his wife, finding existence with him intolerable, left him and ran away home—so it was that incontinently he rebelled against the human and divine laws of marriage and wrote his pleas for freedom of divorce as complying with natural law and the good of man. If ever there was a case of liberty becoming license, it was here. However they may have differed in other respects, in this quality Milton resembled Shelley: they both identified what they desired at any moment with the natural good of man; they both made self-righteousness the law of right.

That was the beginning of Milton's public career and of his prose writings, and it was typical of what ensued. If the bishops in any way interfered with his personal idea of worship, then down with episcopacy and away with the Church; if the monarchical form of government hampered his political independence, then down with monarchy and away with the Constitution. There is no more painful reading in English literature than these apologies for free divorce and regicide which occupied the greatest genius of the age between "Lycidas" and *Paradise Lost,* and the style in which they are written is as heavy and un-English as their spirit is perverse. There are purple patches scattered through these treatises, which are all that most readers know of Milton's prose and which would give the impression that he is as magnificent here as in his verse; but if these passages are examined it will be found that, taken apart from their context, they are expressions of a personal ambition, legitimate in itself and magnificent in its devotion to the aim of a poet, while all about them floats and rages a sea of rebellious discontent. I will not endorse Hilaire Belloc's sweeping condemnation of the prose in his study of *Milton,* but as a whole it must be admitted to form a repellent body of reading. Following the ideas of the tractates through the surging verbiage, one is reminded of the monsters in the account of creation, "wallowing unweildie" in

> the vast immeasurable Abyss
> Outrageous as a Sea, dark, wasteful, wilde,
> Up from the bottom turn'd by furious windes.

There is something disconcerting in the spectacle of a supreme artist, as Milton was in his verse, so losing his craftsmanship in another medium; what I would insist on is that the very style of his prose has a close relation to the fact that when he passes from imagination to theory his voice is not that of his people but of an exasperated individual. The seventeenth century, with all its greatness, is an age of frustration, filled with fine promises that, except in the field of science, came to no fruition, replete with noble utterance that somehow failed to convince. In the Church, in the State, in society, the one thing needed and not found was a commanding genius that should have been indeed the voice of England. It is the tragedy of the time that he who had the genius so to speak should have wasted his energies in querulous complaints against what was, and in the future was to show itself, the true spirit of the land. In a word that spirit may be described precisely as liberty, not license, as centrality, not dissent.

But I am not concerned to pass judgment on Milton's character and its effect upon his work as a whole; that is a longer theme than I care now to discuss. What I started out to do was to consider one small piece of his output, the "Lycidas," and to ask myself how it should be read. To this question, at least in its acuter form, I was moved by chancing to take up at the same time Mr. Tillyard's estimation of the poem and Dr. Johnson's. As a whole I should regard Mr. Tillyard's *Milton* as about the best book we have on the man and the poet, a study admirable for its scholarship and discrimination, and particularly notable for its treatment of the philosophical problems raised by *Paradise Lost,* such as Milton's conception of the nature of evil and the cause of man's fall. Now to Mr. Tillyard " 'Lycidas' is the last and greatest English poem of Milton's youth; though shorter, it is greater than *Comus,* written with newly won but complete mastery and expressing a mental experience both valuable and profound." That is a sentiment with which my own reaction is in perfect accord; indeed, I should go further and hold it to be the greatest short poem of any author in English, the very criterion and touchstone of poetical taste.

Yet with that opinion I have felt bound to remember the sweeping condemnation of Johnson, to whom "the diction" of the poem "is harsh, the rhymes uncertain, and the numbers unpleasing." It is without passion and without art. In part no doubt Johnson's lack of appreciation can be set down to his known deficiency in the higher faculty of imagination. His comment on the diction and rhythm does nothing more than indicate a certain insensitiveness to the finer and more delicate effects of poetry in general. But one cannot read the whole essay without perceiving that his hostile criticism of the art of "Lycidas" sprang not so much from his miscomprehension and esthetic obtuseness as from hostility to the poet and to all that Milton as a man stood for. Touching Milton's plea for looser laws of divorce, the neglect of which by the ruling Presbyterians turned him against that sect, Johnson observes, and justly: "He that changes his party by his humor is not more virtuous than he that changes it by his interest; he loves himself rather than truth." As for the political tirades, Johnson in his attack ran true to form: "Milton's republicanism was . . . founded in an envious hatred of greatness, and a sullen desire of independence. . . . He hated monarchs in the State, and prelates in the Church; for he hated all whom he was required to obey. . . . He felt not so much the love of liberty as repugnance to authority." Now for myself I do not like Belloc's summary and contemptuous characterization of Milton as "a man rotten with the two worst vices: falsehood and pride"; for somehow one shrinks from using such language of a very great poet. To Johnson's charge, on the contrary, I can subscribe without reservation (indeed I have already said much the same thing in weaker language), and I do not see how the charge, in substance, can be countered by any impartial student of Milton's life. But to Johnson the faults of the man were ruinous to the earlier work of the poet, and he denounced "Lycidas" because he read into it the author's ecclesiastical and political heresies; whereas I must reject the maker whilst admiring what he has made. And there the difficulty lies—or has lain for me: how can one so combine detestation and love? how can one make so complete a separation between Milton the destroyer of Church and State, and Milton the creative artist? how is one to read "Lycidas"?

That particular difficulty, it will be observed, opens up into one of the major problems of criticism in general: the relation between the content of a poem and the art of a poem independent of its content. In the beginning, when that distinction first presented itself to the Greek mind, it took a very simple form and indeed scarcely provoked any doubt: the *Iliad* and the *Odyssey* were valued theoretically, not for their charm and interest, but because in them the statesman, the soldier, the athlete, the man who desired to live honorably, could find the wisest precepts and the best models. For later times, and for us of the West, the principle involved was formulated by Horace in his famous saying that the most successful poet was he who knew how to mix the *utile* and the *dulce*. What Horace meant by the *dulce* is clear enough; it is just that in a poem which gives pleasure to a reader. And what he meant by the *utile* is equally clear; it is that in a poem from which we draw instruction. So in one of the *Epistles* he tells a friend, held in Rome by the practice of declaiming, no doubt about the schools of philosophy, that he is in the country reading Homer, who is a better teacher than all the philosophers:

> Qui, quid sit pulchrum, quid turpe, quid utile, quid non,
> Plenius ac melius Chrysippo et Crantore dicit.

In exactly that form the question reached the Renaissance critics, with the emphasis still heavily on the *utile*. So Puttenham, to cite a single example, thinks it necessary to preface his treatise on *The Arte of English Poesie* with a long apology, wherein is shown how "poets were the first priests, the first prophets, the first Legislators and politicians in the world," as seen in Homer, Orpheus, Amphion, and the rest. You are back a thousand years and more, and might be reading one of the ancient Greek commentators. But a change came with the advent of the romantic movement. The *utile* and the *dulce* took on a new significance, and the old division was sharpened to something like an absolute contrast between two irreconcilable criteria of excellence. The *utile* was broadened so as to embrace the whole substance of a poem whether instructive or not, its sense or meaning. The *dulce* on the other hand was refined to a conception of pure poetry, the quintessence of art, as a sort of abstract entity which could be felt and judged somehow apart from any articulate thought or story conveyed; indeed the ideal poem would be a succession of beautiful words with no meaning at all.

Such a thesis, baldly stated, is manifestly bare nonsense; but practically the early romantics applied it to criticism by taking "Kubla Khan" as the ideal poem, because, while the content was no more than the shimmering matter of a dream, it reeked of that mysterious entity called pure poetry. And it was not so long ago that the theory flared up again in France under the impulse of the Abbé Brémond's monograph on *La Poésie pure*. The discussion that ensued was confused by the Abbé's association of esthetic rapture with a mystical view of the function of prayer. More illuminating, to me at least, is T. S. Eliot's pursuit and final rejection of the same ideal of absolute poetry. In his earlier essays, particularly those on Seneca, Shakespeare, and Dante, you will see him tentatively using this *ignis fatuus* as the ultimate standard of value. In the first of those studies he ranks Shakespeare and Dante together as the supreme poets of the world, and the two are equally great though the Italian has taken up into the *Commedia* the profoundest wisdom of human experience as expounded in the Thomistic theology, whereas the Englishman has no interpretation of life's riddle beyond the stale platitudes of Seneca. "Perhaps it was Shakespeare's special rôle in history to have effected this peculiar union—perhaps it is a part of his special eminence to have expressed an inferior philosophy in the greatest poetry." It is true that Mr. Eliot has his reservations in supporting this romantic dream of pure poetry, which came to him from certain, as I think unfortunate, associations in the period before he had fully found himself, and which has haunted him all through his years of self-development. It is more important to note that in his latest enunciation he has worked himself quite clear of the disturbing inheritance. There lies before me now his recently published volume of *Essays Ancient and Modern,* and in the opening paragraph of one of the "modern" (that is, hitherto unprinted) essays I am held by this sentence: "The 'greatness' of literature cannot be determined solely by literary standards; though we must remember that whether it is literature or not can be determined only by literary standards." That I take to be a complete truth perfectly formulated; and the whole essay on "Religion and Literature" is a masterly application of this sentence to modern currents in verse and fiction. It is the critic come to full maturity after years of probation.

And so, to apply this canon of taste to "Lycidas," it may be possible for a young man, enamored of the sheer beauty of words and untroubled as yet by the graver issues of life, to enjoy the marvelous art of the poem with no thought of what the poem means if connected with the poet's place in the world of ideas and action. But such a rupture between the form and the substance of literature cannot long be maintained with the ripening of experience. Sooner or later we are bound to make up our account with that law of taste so ably formulated: "The 'greatness' of literature cannot be determined solely by literary standards; though we must remember that whether it is literature or not can be determined only by literary standards." That "Lycidas" is literature, poetry and not mere verse, depends on the language, the images, the form, on that mysterious working of the imagination which we can feel but cannot ultimately analyze or adequately describe; that it is great literature must depend on the junction of such qualities with nobility of content. And such nobility is there, in full measure.

The poem is an elegy prompted by the drowning of a college friend of the author. It has been the complaint of more than one critic that the expression of grief has little of that warmth which might be expected from such a subject. Dr. Johnson can find no "effusion of real passion, for passion runs not after remote allusions and obscure opinions." Against this charge of frigidity Mr. Tillyard contends with great acumen that the true theme of the poem is not the death of Edward King at all, but the possible death of the poet himself. Milton was writing just before he set out on his voyage to Italy, when such an adventure was more or less perilous, and the possibility of shipwreck and drowning might very well have occupied his mind. So taken, the charge of coldness towards a friend might be changed to one of cowardice or egotism. But Milton was no coward and, however he may have shown himself elsewhere, the note of egotism is relieved by the artful, though doubtless unconscious transference of anxiety for himself to sorrow for another. And it was not the mere termination of life that made him anxious, but the fear that his one all-absorbing ambition might so be left unfulfilled. To understand his state of mind and the emotion that was impelling him to write, the elegy should be read in the light of those passages of self-dedication scattered through his prose works. These purple patches laid upon the coarse cloth of controversy are too well-known to need repeating here. The keynote is given by the words inserted in the gross *Apology for Smectymnuus:*

He who would not be frustrate of his hope to write well hereafter in laudable things, ought himself to be a true poem; that is, a composition and pattern of the best and honourablest things; not presuming to sing high praises of heroic men, or famous cities, unless he have in himself the experience and the practice of all that which is praiseworthy.

And joined with this personal ambition was the conviction that no loftier or purer service could be rendered to one's country and to the world than such a work as he was preparing himself to produce.

Under the spell of a great heroic poem the mind of the people would respond in efforts towards great and heroic living. That was Milton's faith. It was the spirit of the reformer engrafted upon the temperament of the artist. In such a profession, wherein personal glory is identified with public welfare, pride with humility, there lurks, let us admit, a subtle danger; to fall short of brilliant success must leave the professor a monument of ridicule, like the mountains in labor that brought forth only a mouse. But, on the other hand, such a purpose, if carried through valiantly to a successful issue, makes the ordinary ambition of the artist and poet to appear in comparison no more than a cheap parade of vanity. And Milton had the courage of conviction and the genius to succeed. In the history of English letters there is nothing like this determination carried through from youth to age except the solemn dedication of Wordsworth to a similar purpose. All this must be read into "Lycidas." Under the pretext of grief for the loss of a comrade in hope the poem is in reality as it were the quintessence of those prose passages through which there speaks a self-confidence as sublime as it was justified.

It is in the light of this life-long ambition that we should read the savage attack on the abuses in Church and State which raises the note of elegy to the "higher mood" of righteous indignation:

> Last came and last did go,
> The Pilot of the *Galilean* lake . . .
> He shook his Miter'd locks, and stern bespake,
> How well could I have spar'd for thee, young swain,
> Anow of such as for their bellies sake,
> Creep and intrude, and climb into the fold? . . .
> But that two-handed engine at the door,
> Stands ready to smite once, and smite no more.

And apart from any theory of episcopacy and royalty the abuses were there and cried out for remedy. Laud knew them as well as did Baxter, Charles as well as Cromwell; but none but Milton possessed the "dread voice" which—alas, but for defects of temper!— might have done so much to set them right.

In this light also we should interpret the allegorical symbolism of the poem:

> The hungry Sheep look up, and are not fed.

To Dr. Johnson all this masquerade of sheep and shepherds is "easy, vulgar, and therefore disgusting," a cheap device of images without passion and without art. Johnson had good reason to be suspicious of a *genre* that has invited so many weak poets to indulge in flim-flam. But he should not have forgotten how all through the Old Testament, from the call that came to Amos, "who was among the herdmen of Tekoa," and all through the New Testament, from the angelic vision that broke upon the shepherds who were "abiding in the field" about Bethlehem to the parable that Jesus spake to his disciples, "I am the good shepherd and know my sheep,"—how all through the Bible this pastoral allegory of the Church runs like the very music of religion.

These were the thoughts that haunted the memory of the poet when he linked himself with his friend as shepherds:

> Together both, ere the high Lawns appear'd
> Under the opening eye-lids of the morn,
> We drove a field.

Together they were practicing their "rural ditties" in preparation for the louder chant that was to stir the nation from its ignoble lethargy, when one of the twain was washed away by the sounding sea, and his voice forever silenced. And what if a like fate awaited the other, who also was about to start on a voyage? "What boots it with incessant care . . . to meditate the thankless Muse," of what avail to "live laborious dayes," when, just as we

> think to burst out into sudden blaze,
> Comes the blind *Fury* with th' abhorred shears,
> And slits the thin spun life?

"But not the praise," he exclaims; the reward and the outcome are not confined to this world nor are they measured by success "on mortal soil," but in heaven before the "witness of all judging *Jove.*" I do not know how others are affected, but I can never peruse the climax of the poem without a thrill such as scarcely any other verses of the language excite.

> Weep no more, woful Shepherds weep no more,
> For *Lycidas* your sorrow is not dead,
> Sunk though he be beneath the watry floor,
> So sinks the day-star in the Ocean bed,
> And yet anon repairs his drooping head,
> And tricks his beams, and with new spangled Ore,
> Flames in the forehead of the morning sky:
> So *Lycidas* sunk low, but mounted high,
> Through the dear might of him that walk'd the waves
> Where other groves, and other streams along,
> With *Nectar* pure his oozy Lock's he laves,
> And hears the unexpressive Nuptiall Song,
> In the blest Kingdoms meek of joy and love.
> There entertain him all the Saints above,
> In solemn troops, and sweet Societies
> That sing, and singing in their glory move,
> And wipe the tears for ever from his eyes.

Milton always rang true when he wrote of the world to come, but never before nor after did he attain quite this elevation, or achieve so realistic an expression of the invisible mysteries wrapt in the future. A few of his contemporaries possessed this power of giving substance to the hopes of eternity—notably Vaughan—but none of them approach the master. And in later times the art was simply lost. Choose the best of the moderns, Newman for instance in *The Dream of Gerontius,* and they will appear cold and unconvincing beside Milton. Nor did any of the great poets of the earlier ages of faith quite equal him in this field. I would not compare the few lines of an elegy with the mighty structure of Dante's *Paradiso,* but for myself at least there is no single incident in Dante's voyage through the celestial spheres that touches me with the shock of actuality like that which I feel when I read "Lycidas." I am not competent to explain by what devices, by what choice of words, Milton obtains his sublime effect. It would be easy of course, if it seemed worth while, to point to the rich manipulation

of vowel sounds in this or that verse, to note the startling obvious-
ness of the allusion to the might of him that walked the waves, but
the final alchemy of art escapes such an analysis; indeed I question
whether any skill of criticism can penetrate to the heart of that
mystery of the word which we call inspiration, and leave at that.
But one phase of Milton's method impresses me: the fact that his
images are borrowed from the simplest commonplaces of faith—
the return of dawn after the sinking of the sun in the ocean stream,
the tears wiped away, the heavenly choiring of the blest. A comparison of Newman's attempt to translate the subtler speculations
of theology into a poetic account of the soul's awakening after death
shows how inevitably right was Milton's choice. There are regions
of spiritual experience where the untutored imagination of the
people goes deeper into reality than all the groping wisdom of
philosophy.

One thing in the end is certain, the "greatness" of "Lycidas" is
determined by an intimate marriage of form and matter, expression and substance. He who would read the poem worthily must
see this, and must be equally sensitive to the delicacy of its art and
to the sublimity of its ideas. This does not mean that he will forget
or slur over the disagreeable traits of the poet's character or the
repulsiveness of his ecclesiastical and political theories. But for our
good fortune what repels us in the man and roused Johnson to a
fury of protest is reserved for his prose and is excluded from his
poetry—not completely indeed, for, not to mention the more out-
rageous sonnets, occasionally the bitterness of his disappointed soul
breaks out in his later works, yet to such an extent that it is not
impossible to keep the poet and the controversialist apart as two
almost separate powers. That divorce has its unhappy aspect; for
one thing it debars Milton, in his total effect, from being accepted
as the voice of England. But it leaves to him the high credit of
having raised in *Paradise Lost,* to the honor of his native land, the
one monumentally successful product of that humanistic culture of
the Renaissance in which originality of genius and faithfulness to
the classical tradition are combined in perfect union. And for
"Lycidas" there is this further apology, that the elegy was composed

before Milton's splendid spirit of liberty was exacerbated by opposition into petulant license, when his personal pride flamed with a yet undiverted zeal to make of his own life a true poem and so to train himself for creating such a work of art as would lift his people from the ugly slough of faction and greed, where they were grovelling, into the finer atmosphere where pure religion and the love of beauty might flourish together.

J. E. SPINGARN
The American Critic

WHEN I wrote the essays which were collected in a volume bearing the subtitle of "Essays on the Unity of Genius and Taste," the pedants and the professors were in the ascendant, and it seemed necessary to emphasize the side of criticism which was then in danger, the side that is closest to the art of the creator. But now the professors have been temporarily routed by the dilettanti, the amateurs, and the journalists, who treat a work of the imagination as if they were describing fireworks or a bullfight (to use a phrase of Zola's about Gautier); and so it is necessary now to insist on the discipline and illumination of knowledge and thought—in other words, to write an "Essay on the Divergence of Criticism and Creation."

American criticism, like that of England, but to an even greater extent, suffers from a want of philosophic insight and precision. It has neither inherited nor created a tradition of esthetic thought. Golden utterances there have been aplenty—utterances wise, or acute, or daring enough to confound those who refuse to recognize the American spirit except where they find a faded moralism—utterances that anticipate the most modern concepts of criticism throughout the world. To this American ancestry of my own thought I "point with pride." How can we forget Jefferson's literary Declaration of Independence, with its contempt for "the artificial canons of criticism" and its insistence that the only test of literary excellence is whether a work gives pleasure and is "animating, interesting, attaching"—even though the idea of pleasure no longer sums up for us the whole spiritual world of art? How can we forget Poe's conception of poetry as "the rhythmical creation of beauty" and of beauty as having "no concern whatever either with Duty or with Truth"; of Emerson's kindred idea that beauty, no less than truth, is "an ultimate end," and his definition of criticism, with its striking challenge, "Here was a new mind, and it was welcome to a new style"? Margaret Fuller believed like Goethe that the best critics "enter into the nature of another being and judge his work by its own law, but having done so, having ascertained his design and the degree of his success in fulfilling it, they do also know how to put this aim in its place and how to judge its relations," and said of Lowell as a poet that "his interest in the moral questions of the day has supplied the want of vitality in himself"; and yet even Lowell, as a critic, has clearly defined "the difference between what appeals to our esthetic or to our moral sense, between what is judged of by our taste or by our conscience." The author of our first formal treatise on esthetics, Moffat's *Introduction to the Study of Aesthetics,* published before the Civil War, and his successor, John Bascom, whose *Aesthetics* was contemporary with the battle of Antietam, write in the same spirit; for the former, "Art, in itself considered, is neither moral nor immoral; it belongs to an entirely separate class of things," while the latter insists that the processes of reasoning and judgment "have no power over Beauty," which is arrived at by the faculty of "internal intuition." Whether these ideas are false or true, one thing is clear: they are thoroughly American, and even though momentarily forgotten, are an integral part of the heritage of American criticism.

If we have forgotten these utterances, it is because they have remained more or less isolated, and their implications but half apprehended; they have never been consolidated into a body of thought or imposed themselves as a state of mind on American critics. For virtually all of us every critical problem is a separate problem, a problem in a philosophic vacuum, and so open for discussion to any astute mind with a taste for letters. Realism, classicism, romanticism, imagism, impressionism, expressionism, and other terms or movements as they spring up, seem ultimate realities instead of matters of very subordinate concern to any philosophy of art—

mere practical programs which bear somewhat the same relation to esthetic truth that the platform of the Republican Party bears to Aristotle's *Politics* or Marx's *Capital*.

As a result, critics are constantly carrying on a guerilla warfare of their own in favor of some vague literary shibboleth or sociological abstraction, and discovering anew the virtues or vices of individuality, modernity, Puritanism, the romantic spirit or the spirit of the Middle West, the traditions of the pioneer, and so on ad infinitum. This holds true of every school of American criticism, "conservative" or "radical"; for nearly all of them a disconnected body of literary theories takes the place of a real philosophy of art. "Find an idea and then write about it" sums up the average American writer's conception of criticism. There are even those who conceive this scattering of casual thoughts as the sole duty of a critic, on the extraordinary assumption that in this dispersion of thought and power the critic is "expressing himself" as an "artist." Now, while the critic must approach a work of literature without preconceived notion of what that individual work should attempt, he cannot criticise it without some understanding of what all literature attempts. The critic without an esthetic is a mariner without chart, compass, or knowledge of navigation; for the question is not where the ship should go or what cargo it should carry, but whether it is going to arrive at any port at all without sinking.

Criticism is essentially an expression of taste, or that faculty of imaginative sympathy by which the reader or spectator is able to relive the vision created by the artist. This is the soil without which it cannot flourish; but it attains its end and becomes criticism in the highest sense only when taste is guided by knowledge and rises to the level of thought, for then, and only then, does the critic give us something that the artist as artist cannot give. Of these three elements, implicit in all real criticism, the professors have made light of taste, and have made thought itself subservient to knowledge, while the dilettanti have considered it possible to dispense with both knowledge and thought. But even dilettante criticism is preferable to the dogmatic and intellectualist criticism of the professors, on the same grounds that Sainte-Beuve is superior to Brunetière, or Hazlitt to Francis Jeffrey; for the dilettante at least meets the mind of the artist on the plane of imagination and taste, while the intellectualist or moralist is precluded by his temperament and his theories from ever understanding the primal thrill and purpose of the creative act.

Back of any philosophy of art there must be a philosophy of life, and all esthetic formulae seem empty unless there is richness of content behind them. To define criticism without defining art, to define art without distinguishing it from philosophy and history, and to make this distinction without some understanding of the meaning of philosophy and history themselves, can only be compared with the mythical tasks of Tantalus. So that the critic, like the poet or the philosopher, has the whole world to range in, and the farther he ranges in it, the better his work will be. Yet this does not mean that criticism, in so far as it remains criticism of the arts of expression, should focus its attention on morals, history, life, instead of on the forms into which the artist transforms them. Art has something else to give us; and to seek moral or economic theories in it is to seek moral or economic theories, but not art. It is true that art is the product of human personality, and that personality has little meaning when divorced from moral personality, that is, from some actual or imaginative sense of moral values; but out of that moral personality must be created an aqueduct or an airplane, a treatise on logic or chemistry, a poem or a picture, and a host of other products whose excellence must be judged by their own standards, without reference to ethics. The personality behind the poem or the picture is merely, as it were, inchoate material and not the new and essential *form* that distinguishes the work of art. Even in the larger sense in which a poem may be said to be moral in so far as it aims at unity and order, at some relation with the whole of life, we may ask whether the esthetic order is identical with the moral order, or whether we have not here two commensurate but not identical planes or aspects of life.

But "to those who cannot understand the voice of Nature or

Poetry, unless it speak in apothegms, and tag each story with a moral," as Margaret Fuller put it nearly eighty years ago, "I have nothing to say." A critic guilty of the incredible assertion that Goethe almost failed of being a great poet merely because he makes Mephistopheles say, "I am the spirit that denies," may be a distinguished moralist, but has completely failed to apprehend the meaning both of criticism and of poetry. The United States is the only civilized country where moral judgment takes precedence over esthetic judgment when face to face with a work of art; France, Germany, and Italy liberated themselves from this faded obsession long ago, except for a few unimportant reactionary cliques; even in England critics of authority hesitate to make moral standards the first and foremost tests of critical judgment. Yet this is precisely what divides the two chief schools of American criticism, the moralists and the anti-moralists, though even among the latter masquerade some whose only quarrel with the moralists is the nature of the moral standards employed. The seeds of a more fruitful tradition had been planted in our earlier criticism, as we have seen, but the seed had been left to wither and bore no ample fruit.

The main forces that have influenced the present clashes in the American attitude toward literature seem to be three. There is first of all the conception of literature as a moral influence, a conception which goes back to the Graeco-Roman rhetoricians and moralists, and after pervading English thought from Sidney to Johnson, finds its last stronghold today among the American descendants of the Puritans. There is, secondly, the Shavian conception of literature as the most effective instrument for the conversion of the world to a new Weltanschauung, to be judged by the novelty and freshness of its ideas, a conception particularly attractive to the school of young reformers, radicals, and intellectuals whose interest in the creative imagination is secondary, and whose training in esthetic thought has been negligible; this is merely an obverse of the Puritan moralism, and is tainted by the same fundamental misconception of the meaning of the creative imagination. And there is finally the conception of literature as an external thing, a complex of rhythms, charm, technical skill, beauty without inner content, or mere theatrical effectiveness, which goes back through the English Nineties to the French Seventies, when the idea of the spiritual autonomy of art—that "beauty is its own excuse for being"—was distorted into the merely mechanical theory of "art for art's sake"; the French have a special talent for narrowing esthetic truths into hard-and-fast formulae, devoid of their original nucleus of philosophic reality, but all the more effective on this account for universal conquest as practical programs.

All three of these conceptions have their element of truth, but all three are inadequate and incomplete. Works of literature, as mere documents, provide important material for history; the winged words of great poets have had a profound moral and social influence; the prophetic quality of the imagination gives its message an explosive force; and the technique of art is part of the material out of which the artist fashions his creations. All this the historian of culture may, indeed must, take into consideration; out of these elements the moralist or the esthete may draw material for his studies; yet to rest the case here is to ignore the essential problem of art. Pity the poor esthete, for whom art, in any of its single outer manifestations, is the whole life of the spirit; pity the poor moralist for whom the life of the spirit in one of its highest moments is cribbed and confined by a narrow theory of the meaning of art and life. It may be difficult to tell which of them misses the most; yet who can doubt that when we meet them in practical life the error of the moralist seems the nobler of the two? And how could it be otherwise?—for it is precisely in the life of action that we seek for the guiding star of moral values, which the esthete attempts to evade in assuming that the ideal freedom of the artist as an artist is one with the practical duty of the artist as a man. But in the ideal world of art moralism must always find itself homeless and dispossessed. The very nature of poetry must forever be a bitter challenge to those who have only this narrow single standard; and there is no other way out except that of Plato, who because of the "immorality" of poetry banishes all poets forever from the ideal Republic. Of all the moralistic critics, Plato is one of the very few who are thoroughly consistent.

The apparent paradox which none of these critics face is that the Weltanschauung of the creative artist, his moral convictions, his views on intellectual, economic, and other subjects, furnish the content of his work and are at the same time the chief obstacles to his artistic achievement. Out of morals or philosophy he has to make, not morals or philosophy, but poetry; for morals and philosophy are only a part, and a small part, of the whole reality which his imagination has to encompass. The man who is overwhelmed with moral theories and convictions would naturally find it easiest to become a moralist, and moralists are prosaic, not poetic. A man who has strong economic convictions would find it easiest to become an economist or economic reformer, and economic theory as well as practice is also the prose of life, not the poetry. A man with a strong philosophic bias would find it easiest to become a pure thinker, and the poet's visionary world topples when laid open to the cold scrutiny of logic. A poet is a human being, and therefore likely to have convictions, prejudices, preconceptions, like other men; but the deeper his interest in them is, the easier it is for him to become a moralist, economist, philosopher, or what not, and the harder (without the divine aid of the Muses) to transcend them and to become a poet.

But if the genius of the poet (and by poet I mean any writer of imaginative literature) is strong enough, it will transcend them, pass over them by the power of the imagination, which leaves them behind without knowing it. It has been well said that morals are one reality, a poem is another reality, and the illusion consists in thinking them one and the same. The poet's conscience as a man may be satisfied by the illusion, but woe to him if it is not an illusion, for that is what we tell him when we say, "He is a moralist, not a poet." Such a man has merely expressed his moral convictions, instead of *leaping over and beyond them* into that world of the imagination where moral ideas must be interpreted from the standpoint of poetry, or the artistic needs of the characters portrayed, and not by the logical or reality value of morals. When we say with Emerson that beauty, like truth, is "an ultimate end," the narrow moralist or the man of practical mind assumes that we are giving advice to the dilettante trifler in verse (who is not an artist at all) instead of attempting to define the essential secret of the art of Aeschylus and Dante, Shakespeare and Goethe, Milton and Racine, and all their high compeers, classic and romantic, in the ancient and modern world. But how can we solve that secret if we see no difference whatever between their art and the thought of a Plato or Spinoza, the moral illumination of an Emerson or Franklin, or the noble exaltation of the Gettysburg Address? The critic who has missed that difference has missed everything. By ignoring one of the vital elements necessary to form a synthesis, he has even missed the power of understanding their essential unity in the life of the spirit.

That is what we mean when we say that this "leaping over" is the test of all art, that it is inherent in the very nature of the creative imagination. It explains a myriad problems. It explains, for example, how Milton the moralist started out to make Satan a demon and how Milton the poet ended by making him a hero; and from this "hymning of the devil" we learn how our moralistic critics cannot understand even a Puritan poet. From another angle, it explains the blindness of the American critic who recently objected to the "loose thinking" of Carl Sandburg's poem, *Smoke and Steel,* in which steel is conceived as made of "smoke and blood," and who propounded this question to the Walrus and the Carpenter: "How can smoke, the lighter refuse of steel, be one of its constituents, and how can the smoke which drifts away from the chimney and the blood which flows in the steelmaker's veins be correlates in their relation to steel?"

Where shall we match this precious gem? Over two centuries ago, Othello's cry after the death of Desdemona,

> O heavy hour,
> Methinks it should now be a huge eclipse
> Of sun and moon!

provoked another intellectualistic critic to inquire whether "the sun and moon can bothe together be so hugely eclipsed in any one heavy hour whatsoever"; but Rymer has been called "the worst critic that ever lived" for applying tests like these to the poetry of Shakespeare. Over a century ago a certain Abbé Morellet, unmoved by the music of Chateaubriand's description of the moon—

She pours forth in the woods this great secret of melancholy which she loves to recount to the old oaks and the ancient shores of the sea—

asked his readers: "How can the melancholy of night be called a secret; and if the moon recounts it, how is it still a secret; and how does she manage to recount it to the old oaks and the ancient shores of the sea rather than to the deep valleys, the mountains, and the rivers?" And so when Macbeth, stung by his agony into immortal eloquence—"tomorrow and tomorrow and tomorrow"— finds time but a petty pace that has lighted fools the way to dusty death, and life itself nothing but a tale

> Told by an idiot, full of sound and fury,
> Signifying nothing,

can we not imagine some of our own professors, for whom Art is but a pretty page serving King Virtue and Queen Truth, crying out in disdain: "And it is this passage, gentlemen, in which a false and immoral conception of life is expounded, that some of the so-called esthetic critics consider the highwater mark of poetry"? Or if we cannot imagine it, it is only because the passage is not by a modern poet without the prestige of Shakespeare's fame.

These are simply exaggerations of the inevitable consequence of subjecting the world of the imagination to the moods and tests of actual life. "Sense, sense, nothing but sense!" cried a great Austrian poet, "as if poetry in contrast with prose were not always a kind of divine nonsense. Every poetic image bears within itself its own certain demonstration that logic is not the arbitress of art." And Alfieri spoke for every poet in the world when he said of himself, "Reasoning and judging are for me only pure and generous forms of feeling." The trained economist, philosopher, or moralist, examining the ideas of a poet, is always likely to say: "These are not clearly thought out or logical ideas; they are just a poet's fancy or inspiration"; and the sneer of the expert may be the final praise of the poet. To give us a vision of reality, and not reality, imagination rather than thought or morals, is the eternal mission of the artist. To forego that vision is to miss one of the highest moments of the life of the spirit. No other experience can serve as a substitute; no life that has not known it can regard itself as completely fulfilled.

These are some of the elementary reasons why those who demand of the poet a definite code of morals or manners, the ready-made standards of any society, however great, that is bounded by space or time—"American ideals," or "Puritanism," or on the other side, "radical ideas"—seem to me to show their incompetence as critics. Life, teeming life, with all its ardors and agonies, is the only limit within which the poet's vision can be cabined and confined; and all we ask of him is that he create a new life in which the imagination can breathe and move as naturally as our practical selves can live in the world of reality. How can we expect illumination from critics who share the "typical American business man's" inherent inability to live in the world of fantasy which the poets have created, without the business man's ability to face the external facts of life and mould them to his will? These men are schoolmasters, pedants, moralists, policemen, but neither critics nor true lovers of the spiritual food that art provides. To the creative writers of America I should give a wholly different message from theirs. I should say to them: "Express what is in you, all that serene or turbulent vision of multitudinous life which is yours by right of imagination, trusting in your own power to achieve discipline and mastery, and leave the theoretical discussion of 'American ideals' to statesmen, historians, and philosophers, with the certainty that if you truly express the vision of your highest self, the statesmen, historians, and philosophers of the future will point to your work as a fine expression of the 'American ideals' you have helped to create. Do not wait for the flux of time to create a society that you can copy, but create your own society;

and if you are a great writer it will be a Great Society, which the world will never cease to live in and to love. For you America must always be not old but new, something unrealised, something to be created and to be given as an incredible gift to a hundred million men. Courage is the birthright of the poet as much as of the soldier or statesman; and courage in trusting your imagination is to you the very breath of life. But mastery of the imagination, and not mere submission to it, must be your goal; for how can the true artist express himself in terms of slavery rather than power? By giving what is best in him to his art, the American artist serves America best."

A profound inner reform is needed in order that the critics of America may prepare themselves adequately to interpret this new literature, to separate the chaff from the wheat, and in so doing to purify and ennoble the taste and enlarge the imaginative sympathies of a whole people.

The first need of American criticism today is education in esthetic thinking. It needs above all the cleansing and stimulating power of an intellectual bath. Only the drenching discipline that comes from mastery of the problems of esthetic thought can train us for the duty of interpreting the American literature of the future. The anarchy of impressionism is a natural reaction against the mechanical theories and jejune text-books of the professors, but it is a temporary haven and not a home. The haphazard empiricism of English criticism and the faded moralism of some of our own will serve us no more. We must desert these muddy waters, and seek purer and deeper streams. For the conception of the critic as censor or as eulogist we must substitute the conception of the critic as esthetic thinker. In a country where philosophers urge men to cease thinking, it may be the task of the critic to revivify and re-organize thought.

The second need of American criticism can be summed up in the word scholarship—that discipline of knowledge which will give us at one and the same time a wider international outlook and a deeper national insight. One will spring from the other, for the timid colonial spirit finds no place in the heart of the citizen of the world; and respect for native talent, born of a surer knowledge, will prevent us alike from overrating its merits and from holding it too cheap. For the lifeless pedantry of the antiquarians, who think that tradition actually lives in monuments, heirlooms, dead ancestors, and printed books, we must substitute the illumination of a humane scholarship, which realizes that learning is but a quest for the larger self and that tradition is a state of the soul. Half-knowledge is either too timid or too cocksure; and only out of the spiritual discipline that is born of intellectual travail and adventure can come a true independence of judgment and taste.

For taste is after all both the point of departure and the goal; and the third and at this moment the greatest need of American criticism is a deeper sensibility, a more complete submission to the imaginative will of the artist, before attempting to rise above it into the realm of judgment. The critic is not a man seated on a block of ice watching a bright fire, or how could he realize the full force of its warmth and power? If there is anything that American life can be said to give least of all, it is training in taste. There is a deadness of artistic feeling, which is sometimes replaced or disguised by a fervor of sociological obsession, but this is no substitute for the faculty of imaginative sympathy which is at the heart of all criticism. By taste, I mean, of course, not the "good taste" of the dilettante or the amateur collector, or taste in its eighteenth-century sense, but that creative moment of the life of the spirit which the artist and the enjoyer of art share alike. For this the ardor of the reformer, the insight of the historian, even the moral passion of the saint is no substitute; for taste, or disciplined esthetic enjoyment, is the only gateway to the critic's judgment, and over it is a flaming signpost, "Critic, abandon all hope when this gate is shut."

This is your task, critics of America—to see that Plato's dream of banishing poets from the ideal Republic does not come true. It is your chief duty, against moralist and hedonist and utilitarian alike, to justify the ways of the artist to Americans. In a land where virtuous platitudes have so often been mistaken for poetry, it is your task to explain the real meaning of the esthetic moment for the higher lives of men. But no one knows better than I that you cannot rest satisfied even with this. For the modern critic has learnt to distinguish clearly between art, philosophy, history, religion, morals, not for the purpose of denying but of establishing their essential unity in the life of the spirit. Those who deny this unity and those who would substitute for it a muddle-headed if well-meaning confusion are alike the Enemy. Though you reject the criticism in which art is forever measured and tested by the moralist's rigid rules and justified by virtues that are not her own, still less can you be satisfied with the criticism in which "ideas" are struck out in random and irresponsible flashes like sparks from the anvil of a gnome. You cannot be satisfied with anything but truth—that whole truth which is life—even in the service of art and beauty.

H. L. MENCKEN
The American Novel

It is an ancient platitude of historical criticism that great wars and their sequelae are inimical to the fine arts, and particularly to the arts of letters. The kernel of truth in it lies in the obvious fact that a people engaged in a bitter struggle for existence have no time for such concerns, which demand not only leisure but also a certain assured feeling of security, well-being and self-sufficiency —in brief, the thing often called aristocratic (or sometimes intellectual) detachment. No man ever wrote good poetry with his wife in parturition in the next room, or the police preparing to raid his house, or his shirt-tail afire. He needs to be comfortable to do it, and if not actually comfortable, then at all events safe. Wars tend to make life uncomfortable and unsafe—but not, it must be observed, inevitably and necessarily, not always and invariably. A bitter and demoralizing struggle goes with wars that are lost, and the same struggle goes with wars that are won only by dint of stupendous and ruinous effort, but it certainly does not go with wars that are won easily. These last do not palsy and asphyxiate the artist, as he is palsied and asphyxiated by cholera morbus, suits for damages or marriage. On the contrary, they pump him full of ozone, and he is never more alive and lively than following them.

I point to a few familiar examples. The Civil War, as everyone knows, bankrupted the South and made life a harsh and bitter struggle for its people, and especially for the gentler and more civilized minority of its people. In consequence, the South became as sterile artistically, after Lee's surrender, as Mexico or Portugal, and even today it lags far behind the North in beautiful letters, and even further behind in music, painting and architecture. But the war, though it went on for four years, strained the resources of the North very little, either in men or in money, and so its conclusion found the Northerners very rich and cocky, and full of a yearning to astonish the world, and that yearning, in a few decades, set up a new and extremely vigorous American literature, created an American architecture of a revolutionary character, and even laid the first courses of American schools of music and painting. Mark Twain, Walt Whitman, Henry James, and William Dean Howells, all of them draft dodgers in the war itself, were in a very real sense products of the war, for they emerged as phenomena of the great outburst of creative energy that followed it, and all of them, including even James, were as thoroughly American as Jay Gould, P. T. Barnum, or Jim Fisk. The stars of the national letters in the years before the war had been Americans only by geographical accident. About Emerson there hung a smell of Königsberg and Weimar; Irving was simply a new York Englishman; Poe was a citizen of No Man's Land; even Hawthorne and Cooper, despite their concern with American themes, showed not the slightest evidence of an American point of view. But Mark Twain, Howells and Whitman belonged to the Republic as palpably as Niagara Falls or Tammany Hall belonged to it, and so did James, though the thought horrified him and we must look at him through his brother William to get the proof. Turn now to Europe. France, harshly used in the war of 1870-71, was sterile for a decade, but the wounds were not deep, and recovery was in full swing by 1880. Germany, injured scarcely at all, produced Nietzsche almost before the troops got home, and was presently offering an asylum and an inspiration to Ibsen, preparing the way for the reform and modernization of the theatre, and making contributions of the utmost value to practically all of the arts and sciences. Spain, after the Armada, gave the world Cervantes and then expired; England produced Shakespeare and founded a literature that is not surpassed in history.

What has thus happened over and over again in the past—

and I might pile up examples for pages—may be in process of repetition today, and under our very noses. All Europe, plainly enough, is in a state of exhaustion and depression, and in no department of human activity is the fact more visible than in that of the arts. Not only are the defeated nations, Russia, Germany, and Austria, producing nothing save a few extravagant eccentricities; there is also a great lowness of spirit in the so-called victorious nations, for their victory was almost as ruinous as defeat. France, as after 1870, is running to a pretentious and artificial morbidity in letters, and marking time in music and painting; Italy is producing little save psychopathological absurdities by such mountebanks as D'Annunzio and Papini; even England shows all the signs of profound fatigue. The great English writers of the age before the war are passing. Meredith is gone; Hardy has put up his shutters; Kipling went to wreck in the war itself; Conrad is dead; Shaw, once so agile and diverting, becomes a seer and prophet. Nor is there any sign of sound progress among the younger men. Arnold Bennett, a star of brilliant promise in 1913, is today a smoking smudge. Wells has ceased to be an artist and become a prophet in the Sunday supplements. Masefield has got no further than he was on August 2, 1914. The rest of the novelists are simply chasing their own tails. The Georgian poets, having emerged gloriously during the war, now disappear behind their manners. Only a few women, led by May Sinclair, and a few iconoclastic young men, led by Aldous Huxley, are still indubitably alive.

It seems to me that, in the face of this dark depression across the water, the literary spectacle on this side takes on an aspect that is extremely reassuring, and even a bit exhilarating. For the first time in history, there begins to show itself the faint shadow of a hope that, if all goes well, leadership in the arts, and especially in all the art of letters, may eventually transfer itself from the eastern shore of the Atlantic to the western shore. Our literature, as I have more than once pointed out in the past, is still oppressed by various heavy handicaps, chiefly resident in the failure of the new aristocracy of money to function as an aristocracy of taste. The artist among us is still a sort of pariah, beset by public contempt on the one hand and by academic enmity on the other; he still lacks the public position that his brothers enjoy in older and more civilized countries. Nevertheless, it must be obvious to everyone that his condition tends to improve materially—that, in our own time, it has improved materially—that though his rewards remain meager, save in mere money, his freedom grows steadily greater. And it must be obvious, too, that he begins to show that that increasing freedom is not wholly wasted upon him—that he knows how to use it, and is disposed to do so with some gusto. What all the younger American writers have in common is a sort of new-found elasticity or goatishness, a somewhat exaggerated sense of aliveness, a glowing delight in the spectacle before them, a vigorous and naïve self-consciousness. The schoolmaster critics belabor them for it, and call it a disrespect for tradition, and try to put it down by denouncing it as due to corrupt foreign influences. But it is really a proof of the rise of nationalism—perhaps of the first dawn of a genuine sense of nationality. No longer imitative and timorous, as most of their predecessors were, these youngsters are attempting a first-hand examination of the national scene, and making an effort to represent it in terms that are wholly American. They are the pioneers of a literature that, whatever its defects in the abstract, will at least be a faithful reflection of the national life, that will be more faithful, indeed, in its defects than in its merits. In England the novel subsides into formulae, the drama is submerged in artificialities, and even poetry, despite occasional revolts, moves toward scholarliness and emptiness. But in America, since the war, all three show the artless and superabundant energy of little children. They lack, only too often, manner and urbanity; it is no wonder that they are often shocking to pedants. But there is the breath of life in them, and that life is far nearer its beginning than its end.

The causes of all this are not far to seek. The American Legion is right: we won the war. It cost us nothing in men; it brought us a huge profit in money; as Europe has gone down, we have gone up. Moreover, it produced a vast discharge of spiritual electricity, otherwise and more injuriously dissipated in the countries more harshly beset. The war was fought ignobly; its first and most obvious effect was to raise up a horde of cads, and set them in authority as spokesmen of the nation. But out of that swinishness there was bound to come reaction, and out of the reaction there was bound to flow a desire to re-examine the whole national pretension—to turn on the light, to reject old formulae, to think things out anew and in terms of reality. Suddenly the old houses of cards came tumbling down, and the professors inhabiting them ran about in their nightshirts, bawling for the police. The war, first and last, produced a great deal more than John Dos Passos' *Three Soldiers*. It also produced Lewis' *Babbitt*, and Cabell's *Jurgen*, and Fergusson's *Capitol Hill*, and O'Neill's *The Emperor Jones*. And, producing them, it ended an epoch of sweetness and light.

II

The young American literatus of today, with publishers ready and eager to give him a hearing, can scarcely imagine the difficulties which beset his predecessor of twenty years ago; he is, indeed, far too little appreciative of the freedom he has, and far too prone to flee from hard work to the solace of the martyr's shroud. When I first began practice as a critic, in 1908, there was yet plenty of excuse for putting it on. It was a time of almost inconceivable complacency and conformity. Hamilton Wright Mabie was still alive and still taken seriously, and all the young pedagogues who aspired to the critical gown imitated him in his watchful stupidity. This camorra had delivered a violent wallop to Theodore Dreiser eight years before, and he was yet suffering from his bruises; it was not until 1911 that he printed *Jennie Gerhardt*. Miss Harriet Monroe and her gang of new poets were still dispersed and inarticulate; Miss Amy Lowell, as yet unaware of Imagism, was writing polite doggerel in the manner of a New England schoolmarm; the reigning dramatists of the nation were Augustus Thomas, David Belasco, and Clyde Fitch; Miss Cather was imitating Mrs. Wharton; Hergesheimer had six years to go before he'd come to *The Lay Anthony;* Cabell was known only as one who provided the text for illustrated gift-books; the American novelists most admired by most publishers, by most readers and by all practicing critics were Richard Harding Davis, Robert W. Chambers, and James Lane Allen. It is hard indeed, in retrospect, to picture those remote days just as they were. They seem almost fabulous. The chief critical organ of the Republic was actually the Literary Supplement of the *New York Times*. *The Dial* was down with diabetes in Chicago; *The Nation* was made dreadful by the gloomy humors of Paul Elmer More; *The Bookman* was even more saccharine and sophomoric than it is today. When the mild and pianissimo revolt of the middle 90's—a feeble echo of the English revolt—had spent itself, the Presbyterians marched in and took possession of the works. Most of the erstwhile revoltés boldly took the veil—notably Hamlin Garland. No novel that told the truth about life as Americans were living it, no poem that departed from the old patterns, no play that had the merest ghost of an idea in it had a chance. When, in 1908, Mrs. Mary Roberts Rinehart printed a conventional mystery story which yet managed to have a trace of sense in it, it caused a sensation. And when, two years later, Dr. William Lyon Phelps printed a book of criticism in which he actually ranked Mark Twain alongside Emerson and Hawthorne, there was as great a stirring beneath the college elms as if a naked fancy woman had run across the campus. If Hergesheimer had come into New York in 1908 with *Cytherea* under his arm, he would have worn out his pantaloons on publishers' benches without getting so much as a polite kick. If Eugene O'Neill had come to Broadway with *The Hairy Ape,* he would have been sent to Edward E. Rose to learn the elements of his trade. The devilish and advanced thing, in those days, was for the fat lady star to give a couple of matinées of Ibsen's *A Doll's House.*

A great many men and a few women addressed themselves to the dispersal of this fog. Some of them were imaginative writers who found it simply impossible to bring themselves within the prevailing rules; some were critics; others were young publishers. As I look back, I can't find any sign of concerted effort; it was, in the main, a case of each on his own. The more contumacious of the younger critics, true enough, tended to rally 'round Huneker, who, as a matter of fact, was very little interested in American letters, and the young novelists had a leader in Dreiser, who, I suspect, was quite unaware of most of them. However, it was probably Dreiser who chiefly gave form to the movement, despite the fact that for eleven long years he was silent. Not only was there a useful rallying-point in the idiotic suppression of *Sister Carrie;* there was also the encouraging fact of the man's massive immovability. Physically and mentally he loomed up like a sort of headland—a great crag of basalt that no conceivable assault seemed able to touch. His predecessor, Frank Norris, was of much softer stuff. Norris, had he lived longer, would have been wooed and ruined, I fear, by the Mabies, Boyntons, and other such Christian critics, as Garland had been wooed and ruined before him. Dreiser, fortunately for American letters, never had to face any such seduction. The critical schoolmarms, young and old, fell upon him with violence the moment he appeared above the horizon of his native steppe, and soon he was the storm center of a battle-royal that lasted nearly twenty years. The man himself was solid, granitic, without nerves. Very little cunning was in him and not much bellicose enterprise, but he showed a truly appalling tenacity. The pedagogues tried to scare him to death, they tried to stampede his partisans and they tried to put him into Coventry and get him forgotten, but they failed every time. The more he was reviled, sneered at, neglected, the more resolutely he stuck to his formula. That formula is now every serious American novelist's formula. They all try to write better than Dreiser, and not a few of them succeed, but they all follow him in his fundamental purpose—to make the novel true. Dreiser added something, and here following him is harder: he tried to make the novel poignant—to add sympathy, feeling, imagination to understanding. It will be a long while before that enterprise is better managed than he managed it in *Jennie Gerhardt.*

Today, it seems to me, the American imaginative writer, whether he be novelist, poet or dramatist, is quite as free as he deserves to be. He is free to depict the life about him precisely as he sees it, and to interpret it in any manner he pleases. The publishers of the land, once so fearful of novelty, are now so hospitable to it that they constantly fail to distinguish the novelty that has hard thought behind it from that which has only some Village mountebank's desire to stagger the wives of Rotarians. Our stage is perhaps the freest in the world—not only to sensations, but also to ideas. Our poets get into print regularly with stuff so bizarre and unearthly that only Christian Scientists can understand it. The extent of this new freedom, indeed, is so great that large numbers of persons appear to be unable to believe in it; they are constantly getting into sweats about the taboos and inhibitions that remain, for example, those nourished by comstockery. But the importance and puissance of comstockery, I believe, is quite as much overestimated as the importance and puissance of the objurgations still hurled at sense and honesty by the provincial professors of American Idealism, the Genius of America, and other such phantasms. The Comstocks, true enough, still raid an occasional book, particularly when their funds are running low and there is need to inflame Christian men, but that their monkeyshines ever actually suppress a book of any consequence I very much doubt. The flood is too vast for them. Chasing a minnow with desperate passion, they let a whole school of whales go by. In any case, they confine their operations to the single field of sex, and it must be plain that it is not in the field of sex that the hottest battles against the old American manner have been fought and won. *Three Soldiers* was far more subversive of that manner than all the stories of sex ever written in America—and yet *Three Soldiers* came out with the imprint of one of the most respectable of American publishers, and was scarcely challenged. *Babbitt* scored a victory that was still easier, and yet more significant, for its target was the double one of American business and American Christianity; it set the whole world to laughing at two things that are far more venerated in the United States than the bodily chastity of women. Nevertheless, *Babbitt* went down so easily that even the alfalfa *Gelehrten* joined in whooping for it, apparently on the theory that praising Lewis would make the young of the national species forget Dreiser. Victimized by their own craft, the *Gelehrten* thus made a foul attack upon their own principles, for if their principles did not stand against just such anarchistic and sacrilegious books, then they were without any sense whatever, as was and is, indeed, the case.

I shall not rehearse the steps in the advance from *Sister Carrie,* suppressed and proscribed, to *Babbitt,* swallowed and hailed. The important thing is that, despite the caterwauling of the Comstocks and the pedagogues, a reasonable freedom for the serious artist now prevails—that publishers stand ready to print him, that critics exist who are competent to recognize him and willing to do battle for him, and that there is a large public eager to read him. What use is he making of his opportunity? Certainly not the worst use possible, but also certainly not the best. He is free, but he is not yet, perhaps, worthy of freedom. He lets the popular magazine, the movie and the cheap-John publisher pull him too hard in one direction; he lets the vagaries of his politics pull him too hard in another. Back in 1908 I predicted the destruction of Upton Sinclair the artist by Upton Sinclair the visionary and reformer. Sinclair's bones now bleach upon the beach. Beside them repose those of many another man and woman of great promise—for example, Winston Churchill. Floyd Dell is on his way—one novel and two doses of Greenwich Village psychology. Hergesheimer writes novelettes for the *Saturday Evening Post.* Willa Cather has won the Pulitzer Prize—a transaction comparable to the election of Charles W. Eliot to the Elks. Masters turns to prose that somehow fails to come off. Dreiser, forgetting his trilogy, experiments rather futilely with the drama, the essay, free verse. Fuller renounces the novel for book reviewing. Tarkington is another Pulitzer prize-man, always on the verge of first-rate work but always falling short by an inch. Many of the White Hopes of ten or fifteen years ago perished in the war, as surely victims of its slaughter as Rupert Brooke or Otto Braun; it is, indeed, curious to note that practically every American author who moaned and sobbed for democracy between the years 1914 and 1919 is now extinct. The rest have gone down the chute of the movies.

But all this, after all, may signify little. The shock troops have been piled up in great masses, but the ground is cleared for those that follow. Well, then, what of the youngsters? Do they show any sign of seizing their chance? The answer is yes and no. On the one hand there is a group which, revolving 'round *The Bookman,* talks a great deal and accomplishes nothing. On the other hand there is a group which, revolving 'round *The Dial* and *The Little Review,* talks even more and does even less. But on the third hand, as it were, there is a group which says little and saws wood. There seems to be little in common between its members, no sign of a formal movement, with its blague and its bombast, but all of them have this in common: that they owe both their opportunity and their method to the revolution that followed *Sister Carrie.* Most of them are from the Middle West, but they are distinct from the Chicago crowd, now degenerated to posturing and worse. They are sophisticated, disillusioned, free from cant, and yet they have imagination. The raucous protests of the evangelists of American Idealism seem to have no more effect upon them than the advances of the Expressionists, Dadaists, and other such café-table prophets. Out of this dispersed and ill-defined group, I believe, something will come. Its members are those who are free from the two great delusions which, from the beginning, have always cursed American letters: the delusion that a work of art is primarily a moral document, that its purpose is to make men better Christians and more docile cannon-fodder, and the delusion that it is an exercise in logic, that its purpose is to prove something. These delusions, lingering beyond their time, are responsible for most of the disasters visible in the national literature today—the disasters of the radicals as well as those of the 100 per cent, dunderheads. The writers of the future, I hope and believe, will carefully avoid both of them.

JOHN CROWE RANSOM
The Esthetic of Regionalism

Dᴜʀɪɴɢ a summer in New Mexico the philosophical regionalist, as he secretly described himself, made two acquisitions: a scene which he witnessed with his own eyes, and a story which he received on good enough authority.

The scene first. The eastbound train out of Albuquerque, climbing into the mountains, winds through dry and scrubby country which has a certain fascination for green visitors from the green regions and looks incapable of supporting human life. This visitor was going to pull down his window shade and try simply to keep cool, when he was surprised by the sight of human habitation after all, and on a rather large scale: a populous Indian pueblo. A second appeared presently, and then another. One displayed a very good church, but all were worth passing that particular day for this reason: it was threshing time. On the outskirts of each town were the threshing-floors, evidently of home-made concrete and belonging each to a family or unit of the tribal economy. On the floors Indians were beating out the grain; on some the work was nearly done, the grain had been separated from the chaff and lay in a golden pile. The threshers were old and young, of both sexes, and beautifully arrayed. They laughed, and must have felt pleased with their deities, because the harvest was a success, and bread was assured them for the winter.

So this was regionalism; flourishing on the meanest capital, surviving stubbornly, and brilliant. In the face of the efforts of the insidious white missions and the aggressive government schools to "enlighten" these Indian people, their culture persists, though for the most part it goes back to the Stone Age, and they live as

From *The American Review*, II, pp. 290-310. January, 1934. Reprinted by permission.

they always have lived. It may be supposed that they find their way of living satisfactory, and are so far from minding it that they prefer it above others, receiving from it the two benefits which a culture can afford. First, the economic benefit; for they live where white men could scarcely live, they have sufficient means, and they are without that special insecurity which white men continually talk about, and which has to do with such mysterious things as the price of wheat; they thresh, bake, and eat their own grain and do not have to suffer if they cannot sell it. And second, a subtler but scarcely less important benefit in that their way of living is pleasant; it "feels" right, it has esthetic quality. As a matter of fact the Indian life in that one animated scene appeared to the philosophical regionalist one to be envied by the pale-faces who rode with him in painful dignity on the steel train, reflecting upon private histories and futures, but neither remembering nor expecting anything so bright and charming as this.

And now the story. For several consecutive years an Indian tribe suffered from even drier seasons than usual and made insufficient crops. Their distress was such that a voice was raised for them in Congress and a sum of something like $20,000 appropriated for their relief. An agent of the Government came out to make the presentation, and sought the chief. To his surprise the chief did not jump for it; he was rather indifferent, but he agreed to call his counselors together and deliberate. He reported later to the agent that the tribe would not accept the white man's money *because it would be bad for the young men.*

The interpretation which a philosophical regionalist might place upon this incident is not the one which would probably occur to the mere moralist or Puritan. It was not because the chief was too proud that he refused the white brother's favors, for he was too courteous not to accept them if they were well meant and if there was no harm in them. But the question was whether it was safe to entrust the young men with spending money, when they had never had much of it, if any, and did not live by money. What would they do with it? The chief knew that, while Indians compose in the mass a strong race, there are always weak-headed Indians, and these would want to take the money and buy white men's goods with it to import into the tribal life and corrupt it. The chief knew at least as much about this as did the philosophical regionalist, and the latter knew, having been instructed by his friends when he was going about making some small purchases of Indian things, that Indians are apt to set an inordinate value upon highly colored articles sold in the white ten-cent stores, which are less than trash when compared with the beautiful ornaments which Indian weavers, potters, and jewelers make; that Indian bucks fancy white men's shirts, which are unworthy of them; and that they are apt to part with anything in order to secure alarm-clocks. The chief must have looked with apprehension upon importations in general, knowing that a culture will decline and fall when the people grow out of liking for their own native products, and he drew the line at alarm-clocks.

He surrendered an economic advantage which entailed an esthetic disadvantage; probably possessing firmly the principle that the esthetic values are as serious as the economic ones, and as governing. Thereupon the philosophical regionalist, seeking to justify the title, regaled himself with certain reflections.

"The Indian of the Southwest is a noble specimen." That is a persistent saying, and every white traveler comes away repeating it—but on what ground? Noble in his hard-headed pride perhaps; and surely every traveler has seen some Indian brave in his gorgeous costume standing on the busy corner of the white city, aloof and disdainful, his arms folded, as if determined to give a public demonstration of his toleration of the whites before they can demonstrate how they tolerate him. Noble with a more positive merit too, for Indians lead a life which has an ancient pattern, and has been perfected a long time, and is conscious of the weight of tradition behind it; compared with which the pattern of life of the white men in that region, parvenus as they are, seems improvised and lacking in dignity. And noble because the Indians make their life precisely what it is, in every particular, whereas life for the white men depends on what they can buy with their money, and they buy from everybody, including the Indian.

The superiority of Indians, by which term the philosophical spectator refers to their obviously fuller enjoyment of life, lies in their regionalism.

Regionalism is as reasonable as non-regionalism, whatever the latter may be called: cosmopolitanism, progressivism, industrialism, free trade, interregionalism, internationalism, eclecticism, liberal education, the federation of the world, or simple rootlessness; so far as the anti-regional philosophy is crystallized in such doctrines. Regionalism is really more reasonable, for it is more natural, and whatever is natural is persistent and must be rationalized.

The reasonableness of regionalism refers first to its economic, and second to its esthetic.

A regional economy is good in the sense that it has always worked and never broken down. That is more than can be said for the modern, or the interregional and industrial economy. Regionalism is not exactly the prevalent economy today; it has no particular status in Adam Smith's approach to economic theory, which contemplates free trade, and which has proved very congenial to the vast expansions of the nineteenth and twentieth centuries; therefore regionalism suffers a disability. Yet just now, by reason of the crash of our non-regional economy, it tends to have its revival. Of the two economies, the regional is the realistic one. The industry is in sight of the natural resources of the region and of its population. The farmers support themselves and support their cities; and the city merchants and manufacturers have their eyes on a local market and are not ambitious to build up trade with the distant regions; perhaps it occurs to them that an interregional or world trade cannot be controlled. The quantity and quality of world trade which a given community carried on even as late as 1900 are probably changed beyond recognition now, for a great variety of reasons, of which some were predictable and others were not; but at any rate a community can be badly hurt by the storm, if it chooses to fish in the ocean. Regionalism offers an economy as safe as it is modest.

Now it must be great fun to produce on a grand scale, so long as there is consumption for what you produce. The philosophical regionalist is quite disposed to grant that, and to concede the importance of the producer's having fun. But too much fun runs to mischief. It is agreed now that producers' fun must be curtailed, and producers regulated, as if they were irresponsible boys, unable to be trusted with their freedom, and with their grandiose concept of trade as something which will always love them and take care of their production. The interregional business men of the future will not look like joyous producers so much as communistic ants and wasps; and as between the economy of big business and interregionalism, with its privations, and the old regional economy in which producers had every reason to be realistic, and could be left to their own discretion, there is indeed some show of reason for the latter.

The esthetic of regionalism is less abstract, and harder to argue. Preferably it is a thing to try, and to feel, and that is what it is actually for some Europeans, and for the Indians of our Southwest. They do not have to formulate the philosophy of regionalism. But unfortunately regionalism for white America is so little an experience that it is often obliged to be a theory.

Coming to the theory, the first thing to observe is that nature itself is intensely localized, or regional; and it is not difficult to imagine that the life people lead in one of the highly differentiated areas of the earth's surface is going to have its differences also. Some persons, with a sociological bias, suppose that the local peculiarities of life and custom, for example in the Southern highlands, are due to the fact that the population is old and deeply inbred, and has developed a kind of set because it has been out of communication with the world. Other persons, who are economists, think at once of the natural resources of the region, and the sort of subsistence it affords to its population, and find there the key to the cultural pattern. Both must be right; regionalism is a compound effect with two causes. But the primary cause is the physical nature of the region. A region which is physically distinct supports an economic unit of society; but its population will have much more of "domestic" trade than of foreign, and it will develop special ways and be confirmed in them.

As the community slowly adapts its life to the geography of the region, a thing happens which is almost miraculous; being no necessity of the economic system, but a work of grace perhaps, a tribute to the goodness of the human heart, and an event of momentous consequence to what we call the genius of human "culture." As the economic patterns become perfected and easy, they cease to be merely economic and become gradually esthetic. They were meant for efficiency, but they survive for enjoyment, and men who were only prosperous become also happy.

The first settlers in a region are occupied with its conquest, and driven by a pure economic motive. Human nature at this stage is chiefly biological, and raw; physical nature, being harried and torn up by violence, looks raw too. But physical nature is perfectly willing to yield to man's solicitations if they are intelligent. Eventually the economic pattern becomes realistic, or nicely adapted to the bounty which nature is prepared in this region to bestow. It is as if man and nature had declared a truce and written a peace; and now nature not only yields up her routine concessions, but luxuriates and displays her charm; and men, secured in their economic tenure, delight in this charm and begin to represent it lovingly in their arts. More accurately, their economic actions become also their arts. It is the birth of natural piety: a transformation which may be ascribed to man's intuitive philosophy; by religious persons, such as Mary Austin, to the operation of transcendental spirit in nature, which is God. It is certainly the best gift that is bestowed upon the human species. The arts make their appearance in some ascending order, perhaps indicated like this: labor, craft, and business insist upon being transacted under patterns which permit the enjoyment of natural background; houses, tools, manufactured things do not seem good enough if they are only effective but must also be ornamental, which in a subtle sense means natural; and the fine arts arise, superficially pure or non-useful, yet faithful to the regional nature and to the economic and moral patterns to which the community is committed. It is in this stage that we delight to find a tribe of Navajos, or some provincial population hidden away in Europe.

For now the expert travelers come through, saying, Here is a region with a regionalism, and this is a characteristic bona fide manifestation of human genius. The region is now "made" in the vulgar sense (useless to a philosophical regionalist) that the curious and eclectic populations of far-away capitals will mark it on their maps, collect its exhibits for their museums, and discuss it in their literary essays. But for the regionalists who live in the region it is made already, because they have taken it into themselves by assimilation.

The regionalists receive the benefit of regionalism, not the distant eclectics; it is they who have the piety, and for whom the objects and activities have their real or pious meaning. This piety is directed first towards the physical region, the nature who has always given them sustenance and now gives them the manifold of her sensibilia. It is also directed towards the historic community which has dwelt in this region all these generations and developed these patterns. It is their region and their community, and their double attachment might well seem too powerful, and too natural, and also too harmless, to excite the wrath of any reputed philosophers; or it may be the envy, if the philosophers are so abstract and intellectual that they have never sufficiently felt such attachments; yet, whatever the motive be, some philosophers do actually represent themselves as aggrieved by it.

Cookery is one of the activities which go by regions. A cookery owes its form partly to the climate and to the natural foods of the region, and partly to the cumulative experimentation of the generations of native cooks; perhaps in equal measure. So with architecture, furniture, the decorative motif of interiors; so with clothing; so with the social pastimes and pageants; so with speech and idiom; and so with literature and other fine arts. Sometimes the tradition seems more the consequence of the region than of the community, or vice versa; but both have played their part; the region first, naturally, because it isolated the community. Critics of the arts, and of *objets d'art,* if they wish to be up to date, must now require themselves both to trace in them an adaptation to a

special variety of physical nature, and also to find the patient historical development of local "schools" which produced them.

In contrast to the regional view that critics have learned to take
of the arts, the broad or eclectic view now seems too fatuous. Eclectic minds are doubtless good for something, but they are very dangerous for the health of the arts. If their interest is in the arts they
would be well advised not to carry their missionary zeal into the
regions, for presently they will extinguish regionalism and have
nothing to average up; then they will be without careers. And
capital cities, which are the fortresses of eclecticism, should hardly
be built and pushed on the assumption that they are to overrun and
standardize all their regions. The city is a dangerous necessity in
regional society. It is useful, and it is even creative in the way of
esthetic forms; for example, the architecture of capitols and land-
scaping of parks, the drama, and the other fine arts; in all of which
it had better condescent to try to catch the genius of the hinterland.
If it invites the patterns from too many regions, in an excess of hospitality, and tries to compose its arts out of perfectly average materials, its esthetic life will become a mere formality and perish of
cold, and then it will be left with a function which is strictly economic and gross. A capital of the world would be an intolerable
city. And lesser cities, with more ambition than piety, which build
grandly but upon indifferent and eclectic foundations, are nearly as
bad. Cities lately are being zoned and planned; but in the planning, if it is not too late, they should aim at the center of the esthetic effect, which is regionalism; at the most, nationalism.

But it takes a long time for regionalism to arrive. It is the work
of many generations, of which the earliest ones must live and die
in war with the region, exploiting it, trying to impose their own
economic wishes upon it, not yet knowing the sort of peace that
would be lasting. What chance have frontiersmen, backwoodsmen,
"colonials," of attaining to the completeness of life? What they
may look forward to principally, if they are lucky, is livelihood.
They bring ways and means which suit their old region but not the
new region. Or they take pains to bring nothing, and to be open-
minded, in order to learn as rapidly as possible; which is not very

rapidly. Wherever the settlement of the New World has been undertaken by Europeans, it might have been promised at once that the new region would hardly become the seat of a culture comparable to that of the parent European region within any period which was not commensurate with some centuries of European history.

This latter proposition seems to the philosophical regionalist binding; on second thought perhaps too binding. It is true that the immemorial Europeans, those with acute perceptions and even those with the best will in the world, have looked repeatedly with honest deprecation upon their brethren, the new settlers in America, Australia, or Argentina, knowing without having to reason about it that a Europe could not be improvised in these remarkable regions even if it could be realized in time. By their look and their tone, if nothing else, they have exhibited "a certain condescension in foreigners" and caused us much concern; we could not help resenting it, nor could they help feeling it. However rich they might believe American life to be materially, they could not yet believe it to be rich spiritually. Very largely they must have been right, and must still be right. Nor is it a great consolation to retort that what we lack in esthetic attitude we make up in economic power, whereas the Europeans in more regions than one seem likely, for one reason or another, to be caught clinging to their attitudes when the economic structure tumbles down and pulls them with it, attitudes and all. If it is not becoming in Europeans to dislike us for our power, it is not becoming in us to wish economic evil upon them in order that their esthetic superiority may be blotted out of our consciousness. Nevertheless, however that may be, it is just possible that we may have made or may be making a better and quicker job of regionalism than the Europeans allow for; than a dogmatic philosophical regionalist allows for. There may be a short cut.

What we have in this country, of course, is not so much a regionalism *de novo* as a transplanted regionalism, if that is possible. The Fathers of the Republic were not savages; or rather, since savages are likely to have a quite flourishing regionalism, they were not strictly business men. They were European regionalists, and they set about to apply to their new regions as much of their European regionalism as was applicable. New England they meant to be a Puritan England, Virginia an Elizabethan and royalist England. If they could not quite transfer their economic techniques, in such matters as building, tilling the soil, travel, and politics, they were more successful in transferring a language and some of the technique of the fine arts; which is as if to say that they had to erect a new house but were able to crown it for the time being with an imported capital. The matter of classical education, for instance, is a foreign matter for modern Europe as well as for ourselves; yet to some extent it has proved negotiable. We can use Greek, if we know it, in forming our poetry and politics, and we certainly have used it in forming our public buildings and our statues. We can also use English, French, Italian, and German models; but not so easily since the rise in us of that proper state of mind attested by our declarations of independence, because we must regard these cultures as competing and correlative ones, not as our archetypes. Now it must be remembered that what is Greek to us was native and nameless to the Greeks themselves, and not the same thing at all; and it enters into our regionalism only as some undigested Egyptian influence may have entered early into theirs. It should be a comfort to us, however, that we scarcely know for certain of any regional culture anywhere that can be called, in strictness, "indigenous." A regional culture ordinarily represents an importation, or series of importations, that has been lived with and adapted for so long that finally it fits, and looks "native." It may be ages before we can assimilate all the foreign modes that now conglomerate in what we call our American culture, and only then will they be really ours. In the meantime they will serve. Some of the regionalism which we have not had time to acquire we can borrow.

By the year 1850 our continental acquisitions were completed, and the settlement of North America, by a stock whose language and inheritance were largely British, was proceeding irregularly westward, region by region, and perhaps working faster with each advance. The momentum behind the advance was great, and the formula of settlement, or at least the formula of open-mindedness, was familiar; these being the conditions, if any, under which such work may be speeded up. The destiny of this enormous area must have seemed to the philosophical regionalists of the period to be roughly definable: to be comfortably occupied by a population which was now distinct, and was distinguished as "American"; but to fall culturally, as it fell physically, into a great number of regions, to which the general pattern of Americanism was to make its adaptations; that is, to develop culturally according to the implications of the political scheme, which was that of sovereign States within a federal Union. Naturally the States east, which were older as compared with the States west, and particularly with those empty areas west whose States were not yet born, were more highly developed; their economies more stable, and their mode of life more esthetic. New England had achieved a rather strong regionalism. The South had done about as well, or if anything better. The peculiar institution of slavery set this general area apart from the rest of the world, gave a spiritual continuity to its many regions, and strengthened them under the reinforcement of "sectionalism," which is regionalism on a somewhat extended scale. But what New England and the South had done the other sections would do; and they might do it more quickly, though no philosophical sectionalist could be sure about that. The future was promising, though the futurist must look a long way ahead. The federal set-up for the development was admirable.

At about this time, however, the American varieties of regionalism, developing healthily, and at their uneven stages of development, came under a powerful destructive influence, and the philosophical historian of their subsequent course must bear witness that they have nearly been destroyed by it. This influence was not the dissension which resulted in the Civil War; that was destructive, but may now be regarded as one of the incidents in its march. It was nothing less than a whole new economy; it was industrialism, or the machine economy. It was European, and mainly English, in origin, and it was to have a baleful effect upon the charming regionalisms of Europe. But it was to be seized upon with

almost mortal infatuation by the Americans; as if they were thinking that if they could not soon equal the Europeans at regionalism,
they could distance them quickly at industrialism, and therefore
they had better make a switch in their objectives.   Only the South
consistently opposed it, and may even now be said temperamentally
to dislike it; yet the South was eventually to finger it too.

The machine economy, carried to the limit with the object of
"maximum efficiency," is the enemy of regionalism.   It always has
been; not only at the present stage of affairs has the issue between
them become really acute, and been raised specifically and publicly
in many places; for example, in Southern communities, now agi-
tated as to their proper alignment between the Southern "tradition"
and the "new" industrialism.   The industrialism is not new, but
the awakening of the Southern communities to its menace is new.

The machine economy was bad enough in coming to America,
where the regionalisms were at many different periods of growth,
but it came to the perfected cultures of Europe with the disruptive
force of a barbarian conquest, turning the clock back, canceling the
gains of many mellowing centuries.   (Such strong terms will apply
of course to those regions which sooner or later allowed the machine economy to take charge of things.)   It is no wonder that a
good many pious European thinkers have been appalled by a sort
of havoc which was much less visible on this side, and which the
pious American thinkers, if any, have therefore been at much less
pains to think about.

The new economy restored to the act of labor the tension from
which it had delivered itself so hardly and so slowly.   It returned
the laboring population, and in some degree the whole business
population, to a strictly economic status; a status with which the
Europeans were fairly unfamiliar, and which their history recorded
only putatively as the possible status of serfs, or the possible status
of the original savages fighting for subsistence; and a status in all
respects more ignominious than that of pioneers and frontiersmen
in America.   For under this economy the laborer is simply preoccupied with tending his abstract machine, and there is no opportunity for esthetic attitudes.   And not much material for them,

either, since it is now more and more the machine which makes the contact with nature and not the man. But most of the machines are concerned with processing the materials taken out of the land, and they are housed in factories, while the factories are housed in cities. Therefore the landed population tends to lose its virtue, and the population as a whole becomes more and more urbanized. Now a city of any sort removes men from direct contact with nature, and cannot quite constitute the staple or normal form of life for the citizens, so that city life is always something less than regional. But the cities of a machine age are peculiarly debased. They spring up almost overnight, a Detroit, an Akron, a Los Angeles. They are without a history, and they are without a region, since the population is imported from any sources whatever; and therefore they are without a character.

So painful a reversion must bear the promise of wonderful compensations, and it does. They define themselves in the new volume and multiplicity of the goods for consumption. But since the necessities of consumption were secured already in sufficient volume and multiplicity (sufficient in Europe, abundant in America) the additional volume and multiplicity must have reference to the luxuries; that is, to the hours of leisure and the pure esthetic enjoyments. Here it must be said that, on the whole, the expectations of the moderns have been cheated. The products of machines may be used, but scarcely enjoyed, since they do not have much esthetic character. Esthetic character does not reside in an object's abstract design but in the sense of its natural and contingent materials, and the esthetic attitude is piety.

The symbol of the esthetic torpor and helplessness of the moderns lies in their money. There was never so much money in the world, never a time when goods and labor were so universally for sale; and never so little affection lavished on the products of region, which is natural enough when they do not have their real or private value for us but only the value which is determined by the universal market. It is the intention of the machine economy to furnish everybody with money, and then with a free market in which all the goods of the world will be purchasable. The consequence is that persons with much money, who set the standards of taste, go out and buy in with it the houses, furniture, vases, educations, lectures and doctrines, foods and drinks, clothes and millineries, of all regions impartially; and people with less money do the same in their degree. To say that is simply to say that the age thinks it has discovered an esthetic principle which is not regionalism.

The philosophical regionalist in conclusion is inclined to exhibit his good faith by professing his concrete or particular regionalism: an Upper South variety, less rich in many respects than the regionalism of Louisiana, which by virtue of its physical nature and its history is most distinct among the Deep South varieties. Traversing by car the east-and-west dimension of Tennessee, and the north-and-south or Delta dimension of Mississippi, he makes his way to Baton Rouge, startled equally by the distinctness and by the unassimilatedness of the regions entered and crossed, finally marveling at the power of that interregional but sympathetic symbol, the South. There is too much economic settlement yet to be done in this section to permit him to point with too much pride, and in fact it would appear that during some large part of the period from 1865 to the present day the settlers have taken a holiday. In the Mississippi Delta he is forced to believe that the progress has been backward, as it has been in those unsouthern regions which have felt the extreme impact of the machine economy: what could be more like the homelessness of men in those regions than the life of this black population on this black land, resembling the life of a camp, forcing from nature an annual tribute of cotton and otherwise scarcely obtaining a single token of her usual favors? But in Louisiana it seems different.

The darkey is one of the bonds that make a South out of all the Southern regions. Another is the climate. The South is a place in which it is generally pleasant to be in the open air, and nature blooms and waxes prodigiously; one of the earth's areas most easily habitable by man, and perhaps, for the morale of the inhabitants, too easily. The large Negro population, the all-the-year farming—was it not inevitable that the South should develop a distinctly agrarian culture, whose farmers would dominate their cities, which could not be expected to be large? If the Southern cities are growing rapidly now it does not in the least reflect the intelligent consent of their hinterlands, which are the real South, but the coming of industrialism, which destroys the native tradition, and calls the traditionalists "reactionary." The South has had a noble tradition, as traditions go in these longitudes. But at the moment it is just coming out of being intimidated by the get-rich-quick element that has concentrated in its cities, and is only beginning to think about reviewing seriously its old tradition with the thought of a proper future.

The regionalism of Louisiana is most important for the South, in its still divided mind. The region is more charming than others naturally, with its live-oaks hung with moss, its sub-tropical flora, its waters, its soft air; and culturally, in the respect of the finish of its old French features, and its domestic architecture, which is not surpassed in the world.

But regionalism has to fight for its life in Baton Rouge, all the same, just as elsewhere. This fact is written where the least philosophical of regionalists may read it: in the stones. First of all, in the new buildings of the State University.[1] The old buildings still stand, or at least the "Barracks" do, in the heart of the city; the others had to go, since the city needed their room, and the University, with four thousand students, needed still more room and larger buildings. The old buildings are simple, genuine, and moving; precisely the sort of thing that would make a European town famous among the tourists. When the much larger plant of the new University was constructed it seems probable that buildings on the order of the Barracks but on the new scale would not have been economical, nor successful; therefore the builders conceived a harmonious plan for the campus in a modified Spanish, and it suits the regional landscape, and is not altogether foreign to the regional history.

But the visiting regionalist in Baton Rouge cannot escape its most

[1] This paper, in substance, was presented as a speech to the Graduate Club of Louisiana State University at Baton Rouge.

famous feature: the State Capitol. It is nearly 500 feet high, bold in design, sumptuous in detail and finish, perfect in appointments, costing doubtless more money than a State Capitol ever did before— and extremely disconcerting to the sense of regional proprieties. It denotes power and opulence, and this is fitting for the architectural symbol of the State of Louisiana. But the manner of the expenditure of the millions of dollars that went into it was peculiarly unimaginative, like the manner in which money is inevitably spent by new men who have made their pile. The State of Louisiana took its bag and went shopping in the biggest market; it came back with New York artists, French and Italian marbles, African mahogany, Vesuvian lava for the paving. The local region appears inconspicuously in some bas-reliefs and statues, and in the alligators, pelicans, magnolias, sugar canes, and cat-tails worked in bronze in the gates and the door-panels. They are so ineffectual against the shameless eclecticism of the whole that the Louisiana State Capitol could almost as easily stand in Topeka or Harrisburg or Sacramento as in Baton Rouge.

The State Capitol is a magnificent indiscretion. But the philosophical regionalist does not therefore despair. For many reasons; and because it occurs to him that the ironic perpetuation of the old Barracks, which stand in strange juxtaposition at the base of the Capitol, may bring to many half-hearted regionalists the understanding that what is called progress is often destruction.

GEORGE SANTAYANA

Penitent Art

Art is like a charming woman who once had her age of innocence in the nursery, when she was beautiful without knowing it, being wholly intent on what she was making or telling or imagining.

Then she has had a season of passion and vanity, when having discovered how beautiful she was, she decked herself out in all possible pomp and finery, invented fashion after fashion to keep admiration alive, and finally began to put on rouge and false hair and too much scent, in the hope of still being a belle at seventy.

But it sometimes happens, during her long decline, that she hears a call to repentance, and thinks of being converted. Naturally, such a fine lady cannot give up her carriage; she is obliged occasionally to entertain her old friends at dinner, and to be seen now and then at the opera. Habit and the commitments she has in the world, where no function is complete without her, are too strong for her to be converted suddenly, or altogether; but henceforth something in her, in her most sensitive and thoughtful hours, upbraids her for the hollowness of her old airs and graces. It is really a sorry business, this perpetual presence of being important and charming and charmed and beautiful.

Art seems to be passing at present through a lenten mood of this sort. Not all art, of course: somebody must still manufacture official statues and family portraits, somebody must design apartment houses, clubs, churches, skyscrapers, and stations. Visible through the academic framework of these inevitable objects, there is often much professional learning and judgment; there is even, sometimes, a glint of poetic life, or a suggestion of exotic beauty. In

From *Obiter Scripta,* by George Santayana. Pp. 151-161. Copyright, 1936, by Charles Scribner's Sons. Reprinted by permission of the author and publishers.

Mr. Sargent's painting, for instance, beneath the photographic standards of the studio, we often catch a satirical intention, or a philosophic idea, or love of the sensuous qualities in the model and in the accessories; a technical echo of Velasquez and Goya, though without plastic vitality or dramatic ease; a sort of Van Dyck, as it were, for the days of Edward VII; the dreadful lapse in refinement not being greater, perhaps, than is requisite for the documentary value of a true mirror of fashion in the later age. Taste of the old honest worldly sort is far from dead; it is found still in milliners and designers of fashionable garments, of furniture and ornaments. All this luxurious traditional art is as far as possible from repentance. Yet as the Magdalene was potentially a saint—perhaps always a saint really—so the most meretricious contrivances in the arts may sometimes include and betray the very principle of redemption, which is love; in this case the love of beauty. For example, here is the Russian ballet, doubling the dose of luxurious stimulation in every direction, erotic, tragic, historical, and decorative; yet see how it glides at times into simplicity, and in spite of all the paraphernalia of expert estheticism, issues in forms of unmistakably penitent art, like pure color and caricature.

I call pure color and caricature penitent art, because it is only disappointment in other directions that drives artists back to these primary effects. By an austere and deliberate abstinence from everything that naturally tempts them, they achieve in this way a certain peace; but they would far rather have found it by genuinely recovering their naïveté. Sensuous splendor and caricature would then have seemed to them not the acme of abstract art, but the obvious truth of things; they would have doted on puppets and pantomime as a child dotes on dolls, without ever noticing how remote they are from reality. In the nineteenth century some romantic artists, poets, and philosophers actually tried being rebaptized, hoping that a fresh dip in the Jordan might rejuvenate them; but it was of no use. The notion of *recovering innocence* is a contradiction in terms; conversion can only initiate a non-natural life of grace; death must intervene before corruption can put on incorruption. That age was accordingly an age of revivals, of antiquaries, nothing in art and religion but retrospective; it was progressive only in things material and in the knowledge of them. Even its philosophical idealism and psychology were meant to be historical and descriptive of facts, literary and egotistical as the view of the facts might be. Romanticism thought it was exquisitely sensitive to the spirit of remote things, but in reality it was sensitive only to material perspectives, to costume and stage-setting; it grew sentimental over legends and ruins, and being moonstruck, thought it was imbibing the spirit of the past. But the past had not been consciously romantic; what the ancients actually thought and felt was understood much better before the nineteenth century than since; for formerly they were regarded simply as men, essentially contemporary—which comes much nearer the truth. Of course, the passion that can drive people to such earnest affectations must be itself genuine. Keats or Ruskin or Oscar Wilde had abundant vitality and expressed, each in his studied archaism, the profound helplessness that beset him; but what was vital in them was some sensuous or moral or revolutionary instinct of their own, such as in Shelley had existed pure; only in them it was contorted by their terrible preoccupation with being early, or rich, or choice. They were hypnotized by dead beauty; and not having invention nor influence enough to remodel their own age, they fled from it to exotic delights, sometimes primitive, sometimes luxurious, sometimes religious, and sometimes all these things at once. Similarly the revivals in architecture and in the minor crafts expressed a genuine love of color, ornament, and beauty; they gave the snobbish middle classes a taste of cheap luxury; they could sip culture in a teacup. Yet the particular fashions revived were unstable; each successive affectation had hardly ceased to seem exquisite when it began to look foolish. Art at best is subject to fashion, because there is a margin of arbitrary variation in its forms, even when their chief lines are determined by their function; but in revived art fashion is all; it is a fancy dress, unsatisfying even in the glamour of the ballroom, which we are positively ashamed to be seen in in the morning.

Fortunately revivals now seem to be over. Ruins and museums

are interesting to the antiquary; they stir the historical imagination, and dazzle us here and there with some ray of living beauty, like that of a jewel; but they cannot supply inspiration. In art, in poetry, unless you become as a little child you cannot enter the kingdom of heaven. Little children is what artists and poets are now striving hard to be; little children who instead of blowing a tin trumpet blow by chance through a whole orchestra, but with the same emotion as the child; or who, instead of daubing a geometrical skeleton with a piece of chalk, can daub a cross-eyed cross-section of the entire spectrum or a compound fracture of a nightmare. Such is Cubism: by no means an inexpert or meaningless thing. Before you can compose a chaos or paint the unnamable, you must train yourself to a severe abstention from all practical habits of perception; you must heroically suppress the understanding. The result, when the penance is genuinely performed, has a very deep and recondite charm; you revert to what the spinal column might feel if it had a separate consciousness, or to what the retina might see if it could be painlessly cut off from the brain; lights, patterns, dynamic suggestions, sights and memories fused together, hypnotic harmonies such as may visit a vegetative or even mineral sensibility; you become a thousand prisms and mirrors reflecting one another. This is one kind of esthetic repentance. Vain, vain, it says to itself, was the attempt to depict or beautify external objects; let material things be what they will; what are they to the artist? Nature has the urgency of life, which art cannot rival; it has the lure, the cruelty, of actual existence, where all is sin and confusion and vanity, a hideous strife of forms devouring one another, in which all are mutilated and doomed. What is that to the spirit? Let it confess its own impotence in that field, and abandon all attempts to observe or preserve what are called *things:* let it devote itself instead to cleansing the inside of the cup, to purifying its sensibility, which is after all what nature plays upon when she seems to us to be beautiful. Perhaps in that way spirit may abstract the gold of beauty and cast the dross away—all that alloy of preoccupation with material forms and external events and moral sentiments and vain animal adventures which has so long distracted the misguided artist, when he could paint the whole world and had lost his own soul. It is always the play of sensibility, and nothing else, that lends interest to external themes; and it was an evil obsession with alien things that dragged sensibility into a slavery to things which stifled and degraded it: *salvation lies in emancipating the medium.*

To renounce representation, or be representative only by accident, is accordingly one sort of penitent art; but there is another sort, more humble and humorous. This second sort makes no attempt to resist the impulse to observe and to express external things. It does not proudly imagine that the medium, which is the human contribution to representation, can be sufficient unto itself. On the contrary, in its sensuous orchestration it is content to be rudimentary, to work in clay or in wood, and to dress in homespun. It is all feeling, all childlike tenderness, all sense of life. Persons and animals fascinate it. At the same time, warned by the fate of explicit poets and realistic painters, it does not attempt, in its portraiture, to give more than a pregnant hint, some large graphic sign, some profound caricature. Don't be rhetorical, it says; don't try to be exhaustive; all that is worth saying can be said in words of one syllable. Look long, and be brief. It is not in their material entirety and detail that things penetrate to the soul, but in their simple large identity, as a child knows his mother, nurse, or dog. Fresh inchoate forms, voices draped in mantles, people the mind, and return to it in dreams. Monsters and dwarfs were the first gods; the half, said a Greek proverb, is better than the whole. The implicit is alone important where life is concerned: nothing is more eloquent than an abstract posture, an immovable single gesture. Let art abandon reproduction and become indication. If it threatens thereby to become caricature, know that profound art can never be anything else. If men, when seen truly, take on the aspect of animals or puppets, it is because they are animals and puppets at bottom. But all caricature need not be unkind; it may be tender, or even sublime. The distortion, the single emphasis, the extreme simplification may reveal a soul which rhetoric and self-love had hidden in a false rationality. The absurd is the naked truth, the pathetic appeal of sheer fact, attempting to come into existence, like a featherless chick peeping out of its eggshell. All this pompous drapery of convention was a disguise; strip it away. Do not make maps of your images; make companions of them, make idols. Be reticent, emphatic, moody, bold; *salvation lies in caricature.*

Accustomed as they are to revivals, some critics have called this form of esthetic penance a revival of savage art; but the mood is reversed. Savages were never rudimentary on purpose; they were not experimenting in the distortion or simplification of forms; much less, of course, did they voluntarily eliminate all representation of objects in order to deepen sensibility for the medium. They simply painted as well as they could. We have got far beyond that. Penitent art, childish as it may seem at times, is a refinement, perhaps an over-refinement; it is not so much crude or incompetent, as ascetic or morbid. It is also sometimes a little vulgar; because one of the forms of caricature and self-revelation is to be brutal, to flaunt what is out of place, what spoils the picture. Tragedy used to be noble; there is a new refinement in seeing how often it is ignoble; there is a second tragedy in that. Perhaps what we regard at first sight as a terrible decline in art may be sometimes the awakening of this sort of self-scorn. See how ugly I am, it cries, how brutish, common, and deformed! There are remains of sculpture and paintings of the late Roman Empire in some respects like our latest experiments. The decorative splendor (which was very marked) is lost; we miss the colored marbles, the gold, the embroideries, the barbaric armor and jewels; but the stunted pathetic human figures remain in crowds. It seems that the spirit had no joy in man any more; it hid him in hieratic garments or pityingly recorded his gregarious misery. He was a corpse laid out in pontifical vestments. We too are dying; but in nature the death of one thing is commonly the birth of another. Instead of decorating a Byzantine sanctuary, our artists do penance in a psychological desert, studying their own sensations, the mysteries of sheer light and sound; and as music was long ago divorced from poetry and instrumental music from singing, so a luxurious but strident art is detaching itself from everything but its won medium. This on the decorative side; in representation the same retrenchment stops at another level. Representation too has a psychological medium; fancy must create the images which the observer or reproducer of things conceives to be their forms. These images are not the forms of things at all; not only is their perspective created by the observer, but their character, when it is truly considered, is amazingly summary, variable, and fantastic—a mere wraith, a mere hint, a mere symbol. What we suppose we see, what we *say* things look like, is rather an inventory, collected in memory and language, of many successive observations; it is discursive study, registered perhaps in discursive painting. But as the total composition never was nor ever could be a living image, so its parts are not images any longer; in being arrested they have acquired new boundaries and lost half their primitive essence. We may paint the things we see, we cannot arrest the images by which we see them; all we can do—if the images and not the things are what interest us—is to paint something that, by some occult trick of optics, may revive the image in some particular; and then, although the picture when studied discursively may not resemble the thing at all, it may bring back to us, as it were by scent, the feeling which the thing originally gave us; and we may say that it has caught the *spirit* of the thing. It is the medium that in such a case animates the object, and seems to obscure it; and this medium which we call sense in so far as things affect us through it, we call spirit in so far as it modifies our view of the things. The more we transform things in seeing them, the more we seem to spiritualize them and turn them into forms of our own sensibility, regarding the living image in us as the dramatic essence of the object. It is the business of science to correct this illusion; but the penitent artist—who has taken refuge in the spirit and is not striving to stretch his apprehension into literal truth, since the effort to depict things discursively has proved a vain and arid ambition—the penitent artist is content with the rhythms, echoes, or rays which things awaken within him; and in proportion as these reverberations are actually renewed, the poem remains a cry, the story a dream, the building a glimpse, the portrait a caricature.

Tragic Philosophy

In comparing a passage from *Macbeth* with one from the *Paradiso,* Mr. T. S. Eliot tells us that poetically the two are equally good, but that the philosophy in Shakespeare is inferior. By what standard, I am tempted to ask, may the poetic value of different types of poetry in different languages be declared equal? By the equal satisfaction, perhaps, that fills the critic's mind? But the total allegiance of a mature person, his total joy in anything, can hardly be independent of his developed conscience and his sense for ultimate realities. He cannot be utterly enchanted by what he feels to be trivial or false. And if he is not utterly enchanted, how should he recognize the presence of the supremely beautiful? Two passages could hardly be pronounced equal in poetic force if the ultimate suggestions of the one were felt to be inferior to those of the other.

Admitting, then, that poetry expressing an inferior philosophy would to that extent be inferior poetry, we may ask this further question: In what respect other than truth may philosophies be called inferior or superior? Perhaps in being more or less poetical or religious, more or less inspired? Sometimes a philosophy may spring up imaginatively, and in that sense may be inspired rather than strictly reasoned or observed, as the myths of Plato are inspired; but nobody would call such inspired philosophy *superior* unless he felt it to spring from the total needs and total wisdom of the heart; and in that case he would certainly believe, or at least hope, that this superior philosophy was true. How then should the poetic expression of this inspired philosophy not be conspicuously superior as poetry, and more utterly enchanting, than the expression of any other philosophy?

Let me postpone generalities, and turn to the passages in question.

Lady Macbeth is dead. Macbeth foresees his own end. All the prophecies flattering his ambition have been fulfilled, and after the mounting horror of his triumph he stands at the brink of ruin. Surveying the whole in a supreme moment, he consents to his destiny.

> Tomorrow, and tomorrow and tomorrow
> Creeps in this petty pace from day to day
> To the last syllable of recorded time;
> And all our yesterdays have lighted fools
> The way to dusty death. Out, out, brief candle!
> Life's but a walking shadow; a poor player
> That struts and frets his hour upon the stage,
> And then is heard no more. It is a tale
> Told by an idiot, full of sound and fury,
> Signifying nothing.

Mr. Eliot says that this philosophy is derived from Seneca; and it is certain that in Seneca's tragedies, if not in his treatises, there is a pomp of diction, a violence of pose, and a suicidal despair not unlike the tone of this passage. But would Seneca ever have said that life signified nothing? It signified for him the universal reign of law, of reason, of the will of God. Fate was inhuman, it was cruel, it excited and crushed every finite wish; yet there was something in man that shared that disdain for humanity, and triumphed in that ruthless march of order and necessity. Something superior, not inferior, Seneca would have said; something that not only raised the mind into sympathy with the truth of nature and the decrees of heaven, but that taught the blackest tragedy to sing in verse. The passions in foreseeing their defeat became prophets,

in remembering it became poets; and they created the noblest
beauties by defying and transcending death.

In Seneca this tragic philosophy, though magnificent, seems
stilted and forced; it struts rhetorically like an army of hoplites
treading down the green earth. He was the last of ancient
tragedians, the most aged and withered in his titantic strength; but
all his predecessors, from Homer down, had proclaimed the same
tragic truths, softened but not concealed by their richer medium.
Some of them, like Virgil, had rendered those truths even more
poignant precisely by being more sensitive to the loveliness of
perishable things. After all, the same inhuman power that crushes
us, breeds us and feeds us; life and death are but two aspects of
the same natural mutation, the same round of seed-time and
harvest. And if all human passions must be fugitive, they need not
all be unamiable: some are merry in their prime, and even smile
at their own fading. An accident of ritual led the ancients to
divide tragedy sharply from comedy; I think it has been a happy
return to nature in modern dramatists and novelists to intermingle
the two. Comic episodes abound in the most tragic experience, if
only we have the wit to see them; and even the tragic parts are
in reality relieved by all sorts of compensations that stimulate our
sense of life and prompt us to high reflection. What greater
pleasure than a tear that pays homage to something beautiful and
deepens the sense of our own profundity?

Not every part of this classic philosophy re-echoes in the pessimism of Macbeth. Shakespeare was not expressing, like Seneca,
a settled doctrine of his own or of his times. Like an honest miscellaneous dramatist, he was putting into the mouths of his different characters the sentiments that, for the moment, were suggested to him by their predicaments. Macbeth, who is superstitious
and undecided, storms excessively when he storms; there is something feverish and wild in his starts of passion, as there is something delicate in his perceptions. Shakespeare could give rein in
such a character to his own subtle fancy in diction and by-play,
as well as in the main to the exaggerated rhetoric proper to a
stage where everybody was expected to declaim, to argue, and to

justify sophistically this or that extravagant impulse. So at this point in Macbeth, where Seneca would have unrolled the high maxims of orthodox Stoicism, Shakespeare gives us the humors of his distracted hero; a hero nonplussed, confounded, stultified in his own eyes, a dying gladiator, a blinded lion at bay. And yet intellectually—and this is the tragedy of it—Macbeth is divinely human, rational enough to pause and survey his own agony, and see how brutish, how insignificant, it is. He sees no escape, no alternative; he cannot rise morally above himself; his philosophy is that there is no philosophy, because, in fact, he is incapable of any.

Shakespeare was a professional actor, a professional dramatist; his greatness lay there, and in the gift of the gab; in that exuberance and joy in language which everybody had in that age, but he supremely. The Renaissance needed no mastering living religion, no mastering living philosophy. Life was gayer without them. Philosophy and religion were at best like travels and wars, matters for the adventurer to plunge into, or for the dramatist to describe; never in England or for Shakespeare central matters even in that capacity, but mere conventions or tricks of fancy or moods in individuals. Even in a Hamlet, a Prospero or a Jacques, in a Henry VI or an Isabella, the poet feels no inner loyalty to the convictions he rehearses; they are like the cap and bells of his fools; and possibly if he had been pressed by some tiresome friend to propound a personal philosophy, he might have found in his irritation nothing else to fall back upon than the animal despair of Macbeth. Fortunately we may presume that burgherly comfort and official orthodoxy saved him from being unreasonably pressed.

That which a mastering living philosophy or religion can be, we may see at once by turning to the passage from Dante. In the lowest circle of Paradise, that of the inconstant moon, dwells the spirit of Piccarda, a lady who, having once been a nun but having been carried off and married by force, when later she became a widow preferred to continue her life in the world rather than return to her convent. Dante asks her if those who dwell in this part of Heaven ever desire to go higher, so as to see more and to love more. And she replies, No: for the essence of religious love is union with the order of creation. Perfect happiness would be impossible, if we were not perfectly happy in what God has given us; and in his will is our peace.

> Frate, la nostra volontà quieta
> . Virtù di carità, che fa volerne
>   Sol quel ch'avemo, e d'altro non ci asseta
> Se disiassimo esser più superne,
>   Foran discordi gli nostri disiri
>   Dal voler di colui che qui ne cerne;
> Che vedrai non capere in questi giri,
>   S'essere in carità è qui necesse,
>   E se la sua natura ben rimiri.
> Anzi è formale ad esto beato esse
>   Tenersi, dentro a la divina voglia,
>   Per ch'una fansi nostre voglie stesse;
> Si che, come noi sem di soglia in soglia
>   Per questo regno, a tutto il regno piace
>   Com' a lo re ch'a suo voler ne invoglia.
> E'n la sua volontade è nostra pace:
>   Ell'è quel mare al qual tutto si move
>   Ciò ch'ella crea e che natura face.
> Chiaro mi fu allor come ogni dove
>   In cielo è paradiso, e sì la grazia
>   Del sommo ben d'un modo non vi piove.[1]

[1] Brother, the quality of love stilleth our will,
    and maketh us long only for what we have,
    and giveth us no other thirst.
Did we desire to be more aloft, our longings
    were discordant from his will who here
    assorteth us,
and for that, thou wilt see, there is no room
    within these circles, if of necessity we have
    our being here in love, and if thou think again
    what is love's nature.
Nay, it is the essence of this blessed being to
    hold ourselves within the divine will, whereby
    our own wills are themselves made one.
So that our being thus, from threshold unto
    threshold throughout the realm, is a joy to all

I questioned at the beginning whether the poetic value of unlike things could be pronounced equal: and if now I compare this whole passage with the passage from Macbeth I find that to my sense they are incommensurable. Both are notable passages, if that is all that was meant; but they belong to different poetic worlds, appealing to and developing different sides of the mind. And there is more than disparity between these two worlds; there is contrariety and hostility between them, in as much as each professes to include and to subordinate the other, and in so doing to annul its tragic dignity and moral finality. For the mood of Macbeth, religion and philosophy are insane vapors; for the mood of Dante, Macbeth is possessed by the devil. There is no possible common ground, no common criterion of truth, and no common criterion even of taste or beauty. We might at best say that both poets succeed in conveying what they wish to convey, and that in that sense their skill is equal: but I hardly think this is true in fact, because in Shakespeare the medium is rich and thick and more important than the idea; whereas in Dante the medium is as unvarying and simple as possible, and meant to be transparent. Even in this choice passage, there are stretches of pure scholastic reasoning, not poetical at all to our sensuous and romantic apprehension; yet the studious and rapt poet feels himself carried on those wings of logic into a paradise of truth, where choir answers choir, and everything is beautiful. A clear and transparent medium is admirable, when we love what we have to say; but when what we have to say is nothing previously definite, expressiveness depends on stirring the waters deeply, suggesting a thousand half-thoughts, and letting the very unutterableness of our passion become manifest in our disjointed words. The medium then becomes domi-

---

the realm as to the king, who draweth our
wills to what he willeth;
and his will is our peace; it is that sea to
which all moves that it createth and that nature maketh.
Clear was it then to me how everywhere in heaven
is Paradise, even though the grace of the chief
Good doth not rain there after one only fashion.

Paradiso, III, 70-90. (Wicksteed's translation)

nant: but can this be called success in expression? It is rather success in making an impression, if the reader is impressed; and this effect seems essentially incomparable with that of pure lucidity and tireless exact versification in one chosen form. To our insecure, distracted, impatient minds, the latter hardly seems poetry.

Voltaire said that Dante's reputation was safe, because nobody read him. Nowadays that is hardly true; all superior persons read him a little or read a great deal about him. He sets tempting problems for professional critics and antiquarians, and he appeals to archaistic taste, that flies for refuge into the fourth dimension, to everything that seems pure and primitive. But as living poetry, as a mold and stimulus for honest feeling, is Dante for us at all comparable to Shakespeare? Shakespeare, in passages such as this from *Macbeth,* is orchestrated. He trills away into fancy: what was daylight a moment ago, suddenly becomes a candle: we are not thinking or reasoning, we are dreaming. He needs but to say "all our yesterdays," and presently the tedium of childhood, the tedium of labor and illness, the vacancy of friendships lost, rise like vague ghosts before us, and fill us with a sense of the unreality of all that once seemed most real. When he mentions "a poor player" we think at once of the poet himself, because our minds are biographical and our sympathies novelesque; we feel the misery and the lurid contrasts of a comedian's life; and the existence that just now seemed merely vain, now seems also tempestuous and bitter. And the rhythms help; the verse struts and bangs, holds our attention suspended, obliges our thoughts to become rhetorical, and brings our declamation round handsomely to a grand finale. We should hardly have found courage in ourselves for so much passion and theatricality; but we bless Shakespeare for enabling us still to indulge in such emotions, and to relieve ourselves of a weight that we hardly knew we were carrying.

Nothing of the sort in the Italian: the simplest language, the humble vernacular, made pungent and to us often obscure only by an excess of concision and familiarity, or by allusions to events then on everybody's tongue. Dante allows his personal fortunes and hatreds to crop out in many places, perhaps quickening the interest of the modern gossip-loving reader. Yet these are incidental indiscretions, which the poet's own conscience might have regarded as blemishes. His work as a whole, and in intention, is that of a consecrated mind. A single thread of thought guides him; the eye is focused on pure truth, on human wills illustrating the divine laws against which they profess to rebel; hell in the heart of earth, and earth enveloped in celestial harmonies. No occasion, as in modern edifying works, to avoid mentioning things unpleasant or to explain them away. Every detail is noted, not bashfully or apologetically but with zest; when anything is wicked, its wickedness is exhibited and proved for our instruction. We learn the scientific complexity of the moral world, all plain facts, demonstrable truths, principles undoubted and certified. Mastered and chastened by this divine dispensation, what need should we feel of verbal opulence or lurid rhetoric? Not one rare epithet, not one poetic plum; instead, a childlike intellectual delight in everything being exact, limpid, and duly named, and dovetailed perfectly into everything else. Each word, each rhyme, files dutifully by in procession, white verses, three abreast, like choristers, holding each his taper and each singing in turn his appointed note. But what sweetness in this endless fugue, what simple exactitude, what devout assurance; and how unanimously these humble voices, often harsh and untutored if taken singly, rise together into a soaring canticle! The poetry, you might say, of industrious children, careful to make no mistake, but having nothing of their own to say, or not daring to say it. And indeed Dante's mind is busy, learned, and intense; exact even in allegory, as in a sort of heraldry; yet this very minuteness and pedantry are the work of love. Never was heart more tender or subtle or passionate; only that its intensity is all turned towards metaphysical joys, and transferred to an inward spiritual heaven.

I doubt whether either the beauty or the weakness of such poetry can be understood without understanding the nature of religion, as neither religious people nor irreligious people are likely to do; not the irreligious, because of insensibility, and not the religious because of delusion. Still, a disinterested student, say of the origins of Christianity, ought to understand. Religion is not essentially a supplement to common knowledge or natural affection on the same level as the latter: it is not essentially a part of rational life, adjusted however gropingly to cosmic or social influences, and expressing them and their effect. Religion is rather a second life, native to the soul, developed there independently of all evidence, like a waking dream: not like dreams coming in sleep and composed largely of distorted waking impressions, but an autonomous other life, such as we have also in music, in games, and in imaginative love. In religion the soul projects out of her own impulses, especially when these are thwarted, the conditions under which she will regard herself as living. If she need salvation, she will posit a savior; if the thought of death offends her, she will posit resurrection or even immortality; if she is troubled at the injustice of fortune, she will posit previous crimes or original sins of her own, to explain her misery. If in general she wishes to impose her will where she is impotent, she will utter that will in prayers or imprecations, and posit an invisible power inclined to listen, and able to help.

Now such an inner fountain of life and thought is evidently akin to poetic inspiration. As in poetry, so in religion, imagination evokes a more or less systematic invisible world in which the passions latent in the soul may work themselves out dramatically. Yet there are differences. The profane poet is by instinct a naturalist. He loves landscape, he loves love, he loves the humor and pathos of earthly existence. But the religious prophet loves none of these things. It is precisely because he does not love them that he cultivates in himself, and summons the world to cultivate, a second more satisfying life, more deeply rooted, as he imagines, in the nature of things. Earthly images therefore interest him only as symbols and metaphors, or as themes for denunciation. He is hardly a poet in the ordinary sense, except in so far as (like Milton, for instance) he may owe a double allegiance, and be a profane poet altogether when he is a poet at all. Religion is often professed and intellectually accepted without ever having flowered in the soul, or being suspected to have any kinship with poetry.

It may have withered into a forced and angry metaphysics or semi-political party doctrine, poetically deplorable.

The opposite is the case in Dante, whose poetry is essentially religious, as his religion is essentially poetical. We are in the presence of an overpowering inspiration, become traditional, become also learned and quasi-scientific, but still kindled by moral passion and fertile in poetic ideas. The Hebrew prophets had begun by denouncing that which was and proclaiming that which should be; but that which should be could evidently never become actual without a miracle and a total revolution in the world; so that prophecy turned to eschatology and to expectation of a Messiah. At this point pagan streams of inspiration began to mingle with the Hebraic stream. Perhaps the Messiah had already come. Perhaps he was to be no conquering monarch, but a god in disguise. Perhaps he had been crucified, as the spirit is always crucified. Perhaps his kingdom was not of this world. Were there not reports that Jesus, who had been crucified, had been seen, risen from the dead? Would he not surely come again with glory in the clouds of heaven? Transfigured by this new spiritual faith, many current legends and maxims were ascribed to Jesus, and beautifully set down in the Gospels. The fathers worked out the theology. The saints repeated the miracles and explored all the phases of ascetic and mystical experience. Nothing remained but for Dante, with exquisite fidelity and minuteness, to paint a total picture of the Christian universe. The whole substance of that universe was poetry; only the details could threaten to become prosaic; but his danger was removed, in the more important places, by Dante's extraordinary sensitiveness. He had had a revelation of his own in childhood, interrupted later by the false glare of the world, but finally restored in the form of religious wisdom and consecration. The fresh dew of poetry and love trembled upon everything. Indeed, for our modern feeling the picture is too imaginative, too visionary, soaked too much in emotion. In spite of the stern historical details, when we rub our eyes and shake off the spell, the whole thing seems childishly unreal. We can understand why Mr. Eliot feels this to be a "superior" philosophy; but how can he fail to see that it is false?

Inspiration has a more intimate value than truth and one more unmistakably felt by a sensitive critic, since inspiration marks a sort of spring-tide in the life of some particular creature, whereas truth impassively maps the steady merciless stretches of creation at large. Inspiration has a kind of truth of its own, truth to the soul; and this sincerity in intuition, however private and special it might be, would never conflict with the truth of things, if inspiration were content to be innocently free and undogmatic, as in music or lyric poetry. The inmost vegetative impulses of life might then come to perfect flower, feeling and celebrating their own reality without pretending to describe or command reality beyond, or giving any hostages to fortune. But unfortunately animals cannot long imitate the lilies of the field. Where life is adventurous, combative and prophetic, inspiration must be so too. Ideas, however spontaneous, will then claim to be knowledge of ulterior facts, and will be in constant danger of being contradicted by the truth. Experience, from being lyrical, will become tragic; for what is tragedy but the conflict between inspiration and truth? From within or, as we may fancy, from above, some passionate hope takes shape in the mind. We fall in love or hear a voice from heaven; new energies seem to leap up within us; a new life begins crowding the old life out, or making it seem dreary or wicked. Even when inspiration is not moral, but merely poetical, it kindles a secret fire and an inner light that put vulgar sunshine to shame. Yet not for long, nor for ever; unless we passionately shut ourselves up in the *camera obscura* of our first inspiration, and fear the darkness of other lights. The more profound and voluminous that first inspiration was, the more complete at last will be our astonishment and despair. We shall cry with *Le Cid*:

> Percé jusque au fond du cœur
> D'une atteinte imprévue aussi bien que mortelle . . .
> Je demeure immobile, et mon âme abattue
> Cède au coup qui me tue.

Tragedy must end in death: for any immortality which the poet or his hero may otherwise believe in is irrelevant to the passion that has absorbed him. That passion, at least, dies, and all he cares for dies with it. The possibility of ulterior lives or alien interests destined in future to agitate the world makes no difference to this drama in this soul; and the mention of those irrelevant sequels to ruin, and to this ruin, and to this tragic acceptance of ruin, would tinkle with a ghastly mockery at this supreme moment, when a man is entering eternity, his measure taken, his heart revealed, and his pride entire.

These considerations may help us to understand why Shakespeare, although Christianity was at hand, and Seneca, although a Platonic philosophy was at hand, based like Christianity on moral inspiration, nevertheless stuck fast in a disillusioned philosophy which Mr. Eliot thinks inferior. They stuck fast in the facts of life. They had to do so, whatever may have been their private religious convictions, because they were dramatists addressing the secular mind and concerned with the earthly career of passionate individuals, of inspired individuals, whose inspirations contradicted the truth and were shattered by it. This defeat, together with a proud and grandiloquent acceptance of it, is final for the tragic poet. His philosophy can build only on such knowledge of the world as the world can give. Even in the seventeenth century, when Christian orthodoxy was most severe, most intellectual, and most dominant, also most courtly and presentable to the worldly mind, Christianity was nevertheless strictly banished from the stage, except in a few expressly religious plays written for young ladies. Both Christian and pagan personages talked and felt throughout like thoroughly unregenerate mortals. To have allowed religion to shift the scenes, override the natural passions of men, and reverse the moral of the story, would have seemed an intolerable anti-climax.

Nor does even Dante, who calls his vision a comedy, really escape this tragic reality. Existence is indeed a comedy, in that it is a series of episodes, each blind and inconclusive, though often merry enough, but all having their justification beyond themselves, in a cosmic music which they help to make without knowing it. Nonetheless, the individual souls in Dante's hell and heaven speak the language of tragedy, either in desperate pride or in devout self-surrender. In either case, in eternity, they have no further hopes, fears, or ambitions. Their lives *there* are simply the full knowledge of what their lives had been *here*. If the *Divine Comedy* had not had in it this sublime note of recollection, if it had attempted to describe new adventures and fanciful Utopias succeeding one another *ad infinitum,* it would not have been divine at all, but only a romantic medley like the second part of *Faust*. In Dante the hurly-burly is rounded out into a moral tale, into a joyful tragedy, with that sense of finality, of eternity, which Christian eschatology had always preserved.

I can think of only one tragedy in which religion might well play a leading part, and that is the tragedy of religion itself. The point would be to show that a second life of pure inspiration, freely bred in the soul out of moral impulses, must sooner or later confront the cold truth. The illusions then surrendered would not lose their poetic value, since their source would remain alive in the soul; and the element of deception involved might disappear insensibly, as it did in paganism, yielding with a good grace to an impartial philosophy. Such a philosophy need not be in the least hostile to inspiration. There is inspiration wherever there is mind. The sensuous images and categories of thought on which common knowledge relies are themselves poetic and wholly original in form, being products of a kind of inspiration in the animal organism. But they are controlled in their significance and application by experiment in the field of action. Higher fictions are more loosely controlled by the experience of the heart. They are less readily revived or communicated. They flare up into passionate prophecies, take themselves for revealed truths, and come more often to a tragic end.

Part II

THE INDIVIDUAL TALENT

EDMUND WILSON

James Joyce

JAMES JOYCE's first work of fiction, the volume of short stories called *Dubliners,* was finished in 1904 and was to have been brought out by a Dublin publisher; but for a combination of reasons, including the supposed impropriety of certain of the stories, the introduction by name of the Dublin shops, restaurants and pubs, and some disrespectful references to Queen Victoria and Edward VII on the part of one of the characters, the Irish publishers could never bring themselves to publish the book until it had first been brought out in England in 1914, ten years after it had been written. *A Portrait of the Artist as a Young Man* was published first in New York in 1916. Neither of these books had much in common with the English fiction then being written: the typical novelists of that time were H. G. Wells and Arnold Bennett, and Joyce was not in the least like either. In their recent literary renaissance the Irish had been closer to the Continent than to London; and James Joyce, like George Moore, was working in the tradition, not of English, but of French fiction. *Dubliners* was French in its objectivity, its sobriety and its irony, at the same time that its paragraphs ran with a music and a grace quite distinct from the taut metallic quality of Maupassant and Flaubert. And *A Portrait of the Artist as a Young Man,* coming at a time when the public was already surfeited with the early histories of sensitive young men—the Edward Ponderevos, the Clayhangers, the Jacob Stahls, the Michael Fanes—not only was able to attract attention, but had the effect of making most of these books look psychologically superficial and artistically shoddy.

Ulysses was published in Paris in 1922. It had originally been

From *Axel's Castle,* by Edmund Wilson. Pp. 191-236. Charles Scribner's Sons. Copyright, 1931. Reprinted by permission of the author and publishers.

conceived as a short story for *Dubliners,* and was to have been
called "Mr. Bloom's Day in Dublin" or something of the sort.
But this idea was afterwards combined with the further history
of Stephen Dedalus, the hero of the autobiographical *Portrait of
the Artist as a Young Man. Ulysses,* however, in its final form
as a volume of seven hundred-odd large pages, took shape as something entirely different from either of Joyce's earlier books, and
it must be approached from a different point of view than as if it
were merely, like the others, a straight work of Naturalistic fiction.

The key to *Ulysses* is in the title—and this key is indispensable
if we are to appreciate the book's real depth and scope. Ulysses,
as he figures in the *Odyssey,* is a sort of type of the average intelligent Greek: among the heroes, he is distinguished for cunning
rather than for exalted wisdom, and for common sense, quickness
and nerve rather than for, say, the passionate bravery of an Achilles
or the steadfastness and stoutness of a Hector. The *Odyssey* exhibits such a man in practically every situation and relation of an
ordinary human life—Ulysses, in the course of his wanderings,
runs the whole gauntlet of temptations and ordeals and through
his wits he survives them all to return at last to his home and
family and to reassert himself there as master. The *Odyssey* thus
provides a classical model for a writer attempting a modern epic
of the ordinary man—and a model particularly attractive to a modern writer by reason of the apparently calculated effectiveness, the
apparent sophistication, of its form. By a device suggestive of
some of the novels of Conrad, Homer has framed the wanderings of Ulysses between an introductory group of books in which
our interest is aroused in the hero before we meet him by
Telemachus' search for his lost father, and a culminating group
of books which present dramatically and on a larger scale the
wanderer's return home.

Now the *Ulysses* of Joyce is a modern *Odyssey,* which follows
closely the classical *Odyssey* in both subject and form; and the significance of the characters and incidents of its ostensibly Naturalistic narrative cannot properly be understood without reference
to the Homeric original. Joyce's Telemachus of the opening books

is Stephen Dedalus—that is, Joyce himself. The Dedaluses, as we
have already learned from *A Portrait of the Artist as a Young Man,*
are a shabby-genteel family of Dubliners. Stephen's father, Simon
Dedalus, has run through a great variety of employments to end
up as nothing in particular, a drinker, a decayed sport, an amateur tenor, a well-known character of the bars. But Stephen has
been given a good education at a Jesuit college, and we have seen
him, at the end of the earlier novel, on the point of leaving for
France to study and write. At the beginning of *Ulysses,* he has
been back in Dublin a year: he had been summoned home from
Paris by a telegram that his mother was dying. And now, a year
after her death, the Dedalus family, already reduced to poverty,
has become completely demoralized and disintegrated. While Stephen's young sisters and brothers have hardly enough to eat, Simon
Dedalus makes the rounds of the pubs. Stephen, who has always
resented his father, feels now that in effect he has none. He is
more isolated in Dublin than ever. He is Telemachus in search
of a Ulysses. His friend, the medical student, Buck Mulligan,
with whom he is living in an old tower on the coast and who
believes himself to share Stephen's artistic tastes and intellectual
interests, really humiliates him by patronizing him and turns to
ridicule his abilities and ambitions. He is Antinous, that boldest
of Penelope's suitors, who, while Ulysses is away, tries to make
himself master of his house and mocks at Telemachus. Stephen
has announced at the end of the earlier book that he is going
forth "to forge in the smithy of my soul the uncreated conscience
of my race"; and now he has returned to Dublin baffled and disinherited—his life with Mulligan is dissolute and unproductive.
Yet as Telemachus finds friends and helpers, so Stephen is reminded by the old woman who brings the milk for breakfast in
the tower of that Ireland whose uncreated conscience it is still his
destiny to forge: "Old and secret . . . maybe a messenger." She
is Athene in the guise of Mentor who provides Telemachus with
his ship; and the memory of Kevin Egan, an Irish exile in Paris, is
the Menelaus who speeds him on his way.

The scene now shifts, as it does in the *Odyssey,* to the lost

Ulysses himself. Joyce's Ulysses is a Dublin Jew, an advertisement canvasser named Bloom. Like Stephen, he dwells among aliens: a Jew and the son of a Hungarian father, he is still more or less of a foreigner among the Irish; and a man of something less than mediocre abilities, but of real sensibility and intelligence, he has little in common with the other inhabitants of the lower middle-class world in which he lives. He has been married for sixteen years to the buxom daughter of an Irish army officer, a professional singer, of prodigious sexual appetite, who has been continually and indiscriminately unfaithful to him. They have had one daughter, who is already growing up and apparently going the way of her mother; and one son, of whom Bloom had hoped that he might resemble, that he might refine upon, himself, but who died eleven days after he was born. Things have never been the same between the Blooms since the death of this son; it is now more than ten years since Bloom has attempted complete intercourse with his wife—it is as if the birth of the sickly Rudy had discouraged him and made him doubt his virility. He is aware that his wife has lovers; but he does not complain or try to interfere—he is even resigned to her accepting money from them. He is a Ulysses with no Telemachus and cut off from his Penelope.

We now follow Bloom's adventures on the day of June 16, 1904 (the whole of *Ulysses* takes place within less than twenty-four hours). Lotus-eaters allure him; he is affrighted by Laestrygonians. He assists at the burial of an Elpenor and descends with him in imagination to the underworld; he suffers from the varying favor of an Aeolus. He escapes by ruse from the ferocity of a Cyclops and he disengages himself through prudence from the maiden charms of a Nausicaa. And he emerges finally a man again from the brothel of a Circe who had transformed him into a swine.

The comings and goings of Stephen during the day are woven in and out among the wanderings of Bloom: the two encounter each other twice but do not recognize each other. Both men, we become aware, are constantly accompanied and oppressed by ideas which they have tried to dismiss from their minds: the family

situation of each really lies back of and explains all that he does
that day. In Stephen's case, it is only a few days from the anni-
versary of his mother's death, and he is haunted by the memory
of it: she had begged him on her deathbed to kneel down and
pray for her soul and, in rebellion against the Catholic education
which had disciplined and maimed his spirit, jealous of the independence he had won and in fear of the past to which he had
returned, he had cruelly refused and had allowed her to die without the comfort of believing that he had repented of his apostasy.
But now that she is dead, this incident tortures him. He has in
the early morning reproached Mulligan—accusing really himself—
for something the latter had said about Stephen's mother at the
time of her death which Stephen had overheard and resented; and,
as he has looked out upon the bright morning sea, the pathos and
horror of her life have become suddenly vivid to him—he has been
dragged back to relive all that she had suffered. Then, "No,
mother!" he has cried out within himself as he thrust her memory
down out of his mind, "let me be and let me live!" But through
his whole bitter and baffled day, it is his helpless feeling of guilt
toward his mother, his hopeless discouragement and disgust with
his father, which govern all his thoughts and movements. When
he teaches school, he brings the class to a close by a hysterical
joke about "the fox burying his grandmother under a hollybush,"
and in a stupid boy who cannot do his sums he can see now only
his own graceless youth which his mother had shielded from the
world. After school, he has gone to walk on the beach and has
contemplated paying a visit to the family of a maternal uncle
whom he despises, as if he could do penance in this fashion for his
hardness to his mother and somehow make it up to her now
by kindness to her wretched relatives; but again the counter-impulse
which had proved too strong on the former occasion comes into
play to block his intention: his mind drifts off to other things and
he walks beyond where he should have turned. The artist still
conflicts with the son—the two are irreconcilable: he sets out to
compose a poem, but the poem itself breaks down and he is left
gazing at a silent homing ship.—Visiting the library later in the

day, he improvises a long, pretentious lecture on the relation of Shakespeare to his father—a lecture which has little to do with Shakespeare, but a good deal to do with Stephen himself.

And as Stephen is ridden by thoughts of his parents, so Bloom is ridden by thoughts of his wife. He has seen Molly at breakfast get a letter which he suspects—and suspects rightly—to be from Blazes Boylan, a flashy buck about town who is managing a concert tour for her and with whom she is having a love affair. All day he has to change the subject when Boylan's name is mentioned—all day he avoids meeting him in the street. In the afternoon, while Bloom is eating at the Ormond Hotel, Boylan comes into the bar, gets a drink and sets off to call on Mrs. Bloom, and when he has gone, Bloom hears the men in the bar talking and laughing about Molly's easy favors. And the conversation, later on in the pub, about Boylan's having won money in a boxing-match—in spite of Bloom's gently insistent efforts to induce the company to talk about tennis—is one of the incidents which give rise to an antagonism between Bloom and the rest of the company and eventually to the quarrel between the Cyclops-Citizen and Bloom. At the end of the Nausicaa episode, the voice of the cuckoo-clock from the priest's house tells Bloom that he is now a cuckold.

In the evening, Bloom goes to a maternity hospital to inquire after the wife of a friend who has been having a hard delivery: there he meets and recognizes Stephen, who is drinking with the medical students. In the *Odyssey,* the final shipwreck of Ulysses and his subsequent misfortunes are the result of the impiety of his companions, who in defiance of all his warnings have killed and eaten the Oxen of the Sun. So Bloom is pained by the impiety of the medical students as they joke obscenely about childbirth and maternity. On the part of Stephen, whose mother died only a year ago, this levity seems especially shocking, but Stephen's very feeling of guilt about her makes him particularly blasphemous and brutal. Yet Bloom has himself in his own way offended against the principle of fertility by his recent prolonged neglect of Molly: the Calypso who has detained him since his shipwreck is

the nymph who hangs in his bedroom and whom he makes
the object of amorous fantasies. It is this sin against fertility
which—at the hour when Mrs. Bloom is entertaining Boylan—
has landed Bloom on the Phaeacian strand indulging in further
erotic daydreams in connection with little Gerty MacDowell, the
Nausicaa of the Dublin beach.

When Mrs. Purefoy's child has finally been born, the party
rushes out to a public house; and, later on—after a drunken altercation between Dedalus and Buck Mulligan at the tram station,
in which Antinous and Telemachus apparently dispute over the
key to the tower and Telemachus goes away homeless—Stephen,
with one of his companions and with Bloom following some distance behind, proceed to a brothel. Both, by this time, are pretty
drunk—though Bloom, with his invincible prudence, is not so
drunk as Stephen. And in their drunkenness, in the sordid gas-
light and to the tune of the mechanical piano of the brothel, their
respective preoccupations emerge fully for the first time since the
morning into their conscious minds: Bloom beholds himself, in a
hideous vision, looking on at Blazes Boylan and Molly, an abject
cuckold, the laughing-stock of the world; and there rises suddenly
in Stephen's imagination the figure of his dead mother come back
from the grave to remind him of her bleak disheartened love and
to implore him to pray for her soul. But again he will not, cannot, acquiesce; in a desperate drunken gesture, intolerably torn
by his conflict of impulses, by his emotions which deadlock each
other, he lifts his stick and smashes the chandelier—then rushes
out into the street, where he gets embroiled with two English
Tommies and knocked down. Bloom has followed and, as he
bends over Stephen, beholds an apparition of his own dead son,
little Rudy, as Bloom would have had him live to be—learned,
cultivated, sensitive, refined: such a youth, in short, as Stephen
Dedalus. Ulysses and Telemachus are united.

Bloom picks Stephen up and takes him first to a coffee-stand,
then home to his own house. He tries to talk to him of the arts
and sciences, of the general ideas which interest him; but Stephen
is morose and exhausted and makes little response. Bloom begs

him to spend the night—to come and live with them, but Stephen declines and presently takes his leave. Bloom goes up, goes to bed with Molly, describes to her his adventures of the day, and soon drops off to sleep.

But Bloom's encounter with Stephen is to affect both Stephen's life and the relations between the Blooms. To have rescued and talked with Stephen has somehow restored Bloom's self-confidence. He has gotten into the habit in the past of cooking breakfast for Molly in the morning and bringing it to her in bed—it is the first thing we have seen him doing at the beginning of the day; but to-night, before he goes to sleep, he gives her to understand that he expects her to get breakfast next morning herself and to bring it up to him. This amazes and disconcerts Mrs. Bloom, and the rest of the book is the record of her meditations as she lies awake thinking over Bloom's homecoming. She has been mystified by his recent behavior, and her attitude toward him now is at first a mixture of jealousy and resentment. She congratulates herself upon the fact that, if Bloom neglects her nowadays, her needs are ably supplied by Blazes Boylan. But as she begins to ruminate on the possibility of Stephen Dedalus's coming to live with them, the idea of Blazes Boylan's coarseness becomes intolerable to her: the thought of Stephen has made her fastidious, and, rapidly becoming very tender about him, she prefigures a relation between them of an ambiguous but intimate character, half-amorous, half-maternal. Yet it is Bloom himself who has primarily been the cause of this revolution in Molly's mind: in telling her about Stephen, he has imposed upon her again his own values; in staying away from the house all day and coming back very late at night, and in asking for his breakfast in bed, he has reasserted his own will. And she goes back in her mind over her experience of Bloom—their courtship, their married life. She remembers how, when she had promised to marry him, it had been his intelligence and his sympathetic nature, that touch of imagination which distinguished him from other men, which had influenced her in his favor—"because he understood or felt what a woman is and I knew I could always get around him"; and on the day when he had first kissed her, he had called her "a flower of the mountain." It is in the mind of his Penelope that this Ulysses has slain the suitors who have been disputing his place.

As for Stephen, unresponsive as he has seemed to Bloom's interest and cordiality, he has at last, none the less, found in Dublin someone sufficiently sympathetic to himself to give him the clew, to supply him with the subject, which will enable him to enter imaginatively—as an artist—into the common life of his race. It is possible that Molly and Bloom, as a result of Bloom's meeting with Stephen, will resume normal marital relations; but it is certain that Stephen, as a result of this meeting, will go away and write *Ulysses*. Buck Mulligan has told us that the young poet says he is going "to write something in ten years": that was in 1904—*Ulysses* is dated at the end as having been begun in 1914.

II

This is the story of *Ulysses* in the light of its Homeric parallel; but to describe the book in such a way gives no idea of what it is really like—of its psychological and technical discoveries or of its magnificent poetry.

Ulysses is, I suppose, the most completely "written" novel since Flaubert. The example of the great prose poet of Naturalism has profoundly influenced Joyce—in his attitude toward the modern bourgeois world and in the contrast implied by the Homeric parallel of *Ulysses* between our own and the ancient world, as well as in an ideal of rigorous objectivity and of adaptation of style to subject—as the influence of that other great Naturalistic poet, Ibsen, is obvious in Joyce's single play, *Exiles*. But Flaubert had, in general, confined himself to fitting the cadence and the phrase precisely to the mood or object described; and even then it was the phrase rather than the cadence, and the object rather than the mood, with which he was occupied—for mood and cadence in Flaubert do not really vary much: he never embodies himself in his characters nor identifies his voice with theirs, and as a result, Flaubert's own characteristic tone of the somber-pompous-ironic becomes, in the long run, a little monotonous. But Joyce has undertaken in *Ulysses* not merely to render, with the last accuracy and beauty, the actual sights and sounds among which his people move, but, showing us the world as his characters perceive it, to find the unique vocabulary and rhythm which will represent the thoughts of each. If Flaubert taught Maupassant to look for the definitive adjectives which would distinguish a given cab-driver from every other cab-driver at the Rouen station, so Joyce has set himself the task of finding the precise dialect which will distinguish the thoughts of a given Dubliner from those of every other Dubliner. Thus the mind of Stephen Dedalus is represented by a weaving of bright poetic images and fragmentary abstractions, of things remembered from books, on a rhythm sober, melancholy and proud; that of Bloom by a rapid staccato notation, prosaic but vivid and alert, jetting out in all directions in little ideas growing out of ideas; the thoughts of Father Conmee, the Rector of the Jesuit college, by a precise prose, perfectly colorless and orderly; those of Gerty-Nausicaa by a combination of school-girl colloquialisms with the jargon of cheap romance; and the ruminations of Mrs. Bloom by a long, unbroken rhythm of brogue, like the swell of some profound sea.

Joyce takes us thus directly into the consciousness of his characters, and in order to do so, he has availed himself of methods of which Flaubert never dreamed—of the methods of Symbolism. He has, in *Ulysses,* exploited together, as no writer had thought to do before, the resources both of Symbolism and of Naturalism. Proust's novel, masterly as it is, does perhaps represent a falling over into decadence of psychological fiction: the subjective element is finally allowed to invade and to deteriorate even those aspects of the story which really ought to be kept strictly objective if one is to believe that it is actually happening. But Joyce's grasp on his objective world never slips: his work is unshakably established on Naturalistic foundations. Where *A la Recherche du Temps Perdu* leaves many things vague—the ages of the characters and sometimes the actual circumstances of their lives, and—what is worse—whether they may not be merely bad dreams that the

hero has had; *Ulysses* has been logically thought out and accurately
documented to the last detail: everything that happens is perfectly
consistent, and we know precisely what the characters wore, how
much they paid for things, where they were at different times of
the day, what popular songs they sang and what events they read
of in the papers, on June 16, 1904. Yet when we are admitted to
the mind of any one of them, we are in a world as complex and
special, a world sometimes as fantastic or obscure, as that of a
Symbolist poet—and a world rendered by similar devices of language. We are more at home in the minds of Joyce's characters
than we are likely to be, except after some study, in the mind of
a Mallarmé or an Eliot, because we know more about the circumstances in which they find themselves; but we are confronted
with the same sort of confusion between emotions, perceptions and
reasonings, and we are likely to be disconcerted by the same sort
of hiatuses of thought, when certain links in the association of
ideas are dropped down into the unconscious mind so that we are
obliged to divine them for ourselves.

But Joyce has carried the methods of Symbolism further than
merely to set a Naturalistic scene and then, in that frame, to represent directly the minds of his different characters in Symbolistic
monologues like *Prufrock* or *L'Après-midi d'un Faune*. And it is
the fact that he has not always stopped here which makes parts of
Ulysses so puzzling when we read them for the first time. So
long as we are dealing with internal monologues in realistic settings, we are dealing with familiar elements merely combined in
a novel way—that is, instead of reading, "Bloom said to himself,
'I might manage to write a story to illustrate some proverb or
other. I could sign it, Mr. and Mrs. L. M. Bloom,'" we read,
"Might manage a sketch. By Mr. and Mrs. L. M. Bloom. Invent
a story for some proverb which?" But as we get further along in
Ulysses, we find the realistic setting oddly distorting itself and
deliquescing, and we are astonished at the introduction of voices
which seem to belong neither to the characters nor to the author.

The point is that of each of his episodes Joyce has tried to make
an independent unit which shall blend the different sets of ele-

ments of each—the minds of the characters, the place where they are, the atmosphere about them, the feeling of the time of day. Joyce had already, in *A Portrait of the Artist,* experimented, as Proust had done, in varying the form and style of the different sections to fit the different ages and phases of his hero—from the infantile fragments of childhood impressions, through the ecstatic revelations and the terrifying nightmares of adolescence, to the self-possessed notations of young manhood. But in *A Portrait of the Artist,* Joyce was presenting everything from the point of view of a single particular character, Dedalus; whereas in *Ulysses* he is occupied with a number of different personalities, of whom Dedalus is no longer the center, and his method, furthermore, of enabling us to live in their world is not always merely a matter of making us shift from the point of view of one to the point of view of another. In order to understand what Joyce is doing here, one must conceive a set of Symbolistic poems, themselves involving characters whose minds are represented Symbolistically, depending not from the sensibility of the poet speaking in his own person, but from the poet's imagination playing a rôle absolutely impersonal and always imposing upon itself all the Naturalistic restrictions in regard to the story it is telling at the same time that it allows itself to exercise all the Symbolistic privileges in regard to the way it tells it. We are not likely to be prepared for this by the early episodes of *Ulysses:* they are as sober and as clear as the morning light of the Irish coast in which they take place: the characters' perceptions of the external world are usually distinct from their thoughts and feelings about them. But in the newspaper office, for the first time, a general atmosphere begins to be created, beyond the specific minds of the characters, by a punctuation of the text with newspaper heads which announce the incidents in the narrative. And in the library scene, which takes place in the early afternoon, the setting and people external to Stephen begin to dissolve in his apprehension of them, heightened and blurred by some drinks at lunch-time and by the intellectual excitement of the conversation amid the dimness and tameness of the library—"Eglintoneyes, quick with pleasure, looked up shy-brightly. Gladly glancing, a merry puritan, through the twisted eglantine." Here, however, we still see all through Stephen's eyes —through the eyes of a single character; but in the scene in the Ormond Hotel, which takes place a couple of hours later—our reveries absorb the world about us progressively as daylight fades and as the impressions of the day accumulate—the sights and sounds and the emotional vibrations and the appetites for food and drink of the late afternoon, the laughter, the gold-and-bronze hair of the barmaids, the jingling of Blazes Boylan's car on his way to visit Molly Bloom, the ringing of the hoofs of the horses of the viceregal cavalcade clanging in through the open window, the ballad sung by Simon Dedalus, the sound of the piano accompaniment and the comfortable supper of Bloom—though they are not all, from beginning to end, perceived by Bloom himself— all mingle quite un-Naturalistically in a harmony of bright sound, ringing color, poignant indistinct feeling and declining light. The scene in the brothel, where it is night and where Dedalus and Bloom are drunk, is like a slowed-up moving-picture, in which the intensified vision of reality is continually lapsing into phan· tasmagoric visions; and the let-down after the excitement of this, the lassitude and staleness of the cabman's shelter where Bloom takes Stephen to get him some coffee, is rendered by a prose as flavorless, as weary and as banal as the incidents which it reports. Joyce has achieved here, by different methods, a relativism like that of Proust: he is reproducing in literature the different aspects, the different proportions and textures, which things and people take on at different times and under different circumstances.

III

I do not think that Joyce has been equally successful with all these technical devices in *Ulysses;* but before it will be possible to discuss them further, we must approach the book from another point of view.

It has always been characteristic of Joyce to neglect action, narrative, drama, of the usual kind, even the direct impact on one another of the characters as we get it in the ordinary novel, for a sort of psychological portraiture. There is tremendous vitality in Joyce, but very little movement. Like Proust, he is symphonic rather than narrative. His fiction has its progressions, its developments, but they are musical rather than dramatic. The most elaborate and interesting piece in *Dubliners*—the story called "The Dead"—is simply a record of the modification brought about during a single evening in the relations of a husband and wife by the man's becoming aware, from the effect produced on the woman by a song which she has heard at a family party, that she has once been loved by another man; *A Portrait of the Artist as a Young Man* is simply a series of pictures of the author at successive stages of his development; the theme of *Exiles* is, like that of "The Dead," the modification in the relations of a husband and wife which follows the reappearance of a man who has been the wife's lover. And *Ulysses* again, for all its vast scale, is simply the story of another small but significant change in the relations of yet another married couple as a result of the impingement on their household of the personality of an only slightly known young man. Most of these stories cover a period of only a few hours, and they are never carried any further. When Joyce has explored one of these situations, when he has established the small gradual readjustment, he has done all that interests him.

All, that is, from the point of view of ordinary incident. But though Joyce almost entirely lacks appetite for violent conflict or vigorous action, his work is prodigiously rich and alive. His force, instead of following a line, expands itself in every dimension (including that of Time) about a single point. The world of *Ulysses* is animated by a complex inexhaustible life: we revisit it as we do a city, where we come more and more to recognize faces, to understand personalities, to grasp relations, currents and interests. Joyce has exercised considerable technical ingenuity in introducing us to the elements of his story in an order which will enable us to find our bearings: yet I doubt whether any human memory is capable, on a first reading, of meeting the demands of *Ulysses*. And when we reread it, we start in at any point, as if it were indeed something solid like a city which actually existed in space and which could be entered from any direction—as Joyce is said, in composing his books, to work on the different parts simultaneously. More than any other work of fiction, unless perhaps the *Comédie Humaine, Ulysses* creates the illusion of a living social organism. We see it only for twenty hours, yet we know its past as well as its present. We possess Dublin, seen, heard, smelt and felt, brooded over, imagined, remembered.

Joyce's handling of this immense material, his method of giving his book a shape, resembles nothing else in modern fiction. The first critics of *Ulysses* mistook the novel for a "slice of life" and objected that it was too fluid or too chaotic. They did not recognize a plot because they could not recognize a progression; and the title told them nothing. They could not even discover a pattern. It is now apparent, however, that *Ulysses* suffers from an excess of design rather than from a lack of it. Joyce has drawn up an outline of his novel, of which he has allowed certain of his commentators to avail themselves, but which he has not allowed them to publish in its entirety (though it is to be presumed that the book on *Ulysses* which Mr. Stuart Gilbert has announced will include all the information contained in it);[1] and from this outline it appears that Joyce has set himself the task of fulfilling the requirements of a most complicated scheme—a scheme which we could scarcely have divined except in its more obvious features. For even if we had known about the Homeric parallel and had identified certain of the correspondences—if we had had no difficulty in recognizing the Cyclops in the ferocious professional Fenian or Circe in the brothel-keeper or Hades in the cemetery—we should never have suspected how closely and how subtly the parallel had been followed—we should never have guessed, for example, that when Bloom passes through the National Library while Stephen is having his discussion with the literary men, he is escaping, on the one hand, a Scylla —that is, Aristotle, the rock of Dogma; and, on the other, a Charybdis—Plato, the whirlpool of Mysticism; nor that, when Stephen

[1] Stuart Gilbert's book *James Joyce's Ulysses* appeared in 1930 (London: Faber & Faber; New York: Alfred A. Knopf).

walks on the seashore, he is re-enacting the combat with Proteus—in this case, primal matter, of whose continual transformations Stephen is reminded by the objects absorbed or washed up by the sea, but whose forms he is able to hold and fix, as the Homeric Proteus was held and vanquished, by power of the words which give him images for them. Nor should we have known that the series of phrases and onomatopoetic syllables placed at the beginning of the Sirens episode—the singing in the Ormond Hotel—and selected from the narrative which follows, are supposed to be musical themes and that the episode itself is a fugue; and though we may have felt the ironic effect of the specimens of inflated Irish journalism introduced at regular intervals in the conversation with the patriot in the pub—we should hardly have understood that these had been produced by a deliberate technique of "gigantism" —for, since the Citizen represents the Cyclops, and since the Cyclops was a giant, he must be rendered formidable by a parade of all the banalities of his patriotic claptrap swollen to gigantic proportions. We should probably never have guessed all this, and we should certainly never have guessed at the ingenuity which Joyce has expended in other ways. Not only, we learn from the outline, is there an elaborate Homeric parallel in *Ulysses,* but there is also an organ of the human body and a human science or art featured in every episode. We look these up, a little incredulously, but there, we find, they all actually are—buried and disguised beneath the realistic surface, but carefully planted, unmistakably dwelt upon. And if we are tipped off, we are able further to discover all sorts of concealed ornaments and emblems: in the chapter of the Lotus-Eaters, for example, countless references to flowers; in the Laestrygonians, to eating; in the Sirens, puns on musical terms; and in Aeolus, the newspaper office, not merely many references to wind but, according to Mr. Gilbert—the art featured in this episode being Rhetoric—some hundred different figures of speech.

Now the Homeric parallel in *Ulysses* is in general pointedly and charmingly carried out and justifies itself: it does help to give the story a universal significance and it enables Joyce to show us in the actions and the relations of his characters meanings which he perhaps could not easily have indicated in any other way—since the characters themselves must be largely unaware of these meanings and since Joyce has adopted the strict objective method, in which the author must not comment on the action. And we may even accept the arts and sciences and the organs of the human body as making the book complete and comprehensive, if a little laboriously systematic—the whole of man's experience in a day. But when we get all these things together and further complicated by the virtuosity of the technical devices, the result is sometimes baffling or confusing. We become aware, as we examine the outline, that when we went through *Ulysses* for the first time, it was these organs and arts and sciences and Homeric correspondences which sometimes so discouraged our interest. We had been climbing over these obstacles without knowing it, in our attempts to follow Dedalus and Bloom. The trouble was that, beyond the ostensible subject and, as it were, beneath the surface of the narrative, too many other subjects and too many different orders of subjects were being proposed to our attention.

It seems to me difficult, then, not to conclude that Joyce elaborated *Ulysses* too much—that he tried to put too many things into it. What is the value of all the references to flowers in the Lotus-Eaters chapter, for example? They do not create in the Dublin streets an atmosphere of lotus-eating—we are merely puzzled, if we have not been told to look for them, as to why Joyce has chosen to have Bloom think and see certain things, of which the final explanation is that they are pretexts for mentioning flowers. And do not the gigantic interpolations of the Cyclops episode defeat their object by making it impossible for us to follow the narrative? The interpolations are funny in themselves, the incident related is a masterpiece of language and humor, the idea of combining them seems happy, yet the effect is mechanical and annoying: in the end we have to read the whole thing through, skipping the interpolations, in order to find out what has happened. The worst example of the capacities for failure of this too synthetic, too systematic, method seems to me the scene in the maternity hospital. I have described above what actually takes place there as I have worked it out, after several readings and in the light of Joyce's outline. The Oxen of the Sun are "Fertility"—the crime committed against them is "Fraud." But, not content with this, Joyce has been at pains to fill the episode with references to real cattle and to include a long conversation about bulls. As for the special technique, it seems to me in this case not to have any real appropriateness to the situation, but to have been dictated by sheer fantastic pedantry: Joyce describes his method here as "embryonic," in conformity to the subject, maternity, and the chapter is written as a series of parodies of English literary styles from the bad Latin of the early chronicles up through Huxley and Carlyle, the development of the language corresponding to the growth of the child in the womb. Now something important takes place in this episode—the meeting between Dedalus and Bloom—and an important point is being made about it. But we miss the point because it is all we can do to follow what is happening at the drinking-party, itself rather a confused affair, through the medium of the language of the *Morte d'Arthur,* the seventeenth-century diaries, the eighteenth-century novels, and a great many other kinds of literature in which we are not prepared at the moment to be interested. If we pay attention to the parodies, we miss the story; and if we try to follow the story, we are unable to appreciate the parodies. The parodies have spoiled the story; and the necessity of telling the story through them has taken most of the life out of the parodies.

Joyce has as little respect as Proust for the capacities of the reader's attention; and one feels, in Joyce's case as in Proust's, that the *longueurs* which break our backs, the mechanical combinations of elements which fail to coalesce, are partly a result of the effort of a supernormally energetic mind to compensate by piling things up for an inability to make them move.

We have now arrived, in the maternity hospital, at the climactic scenes of the story, and Joyce has bogged us as he has never bogged us before. We shall forget the Oxen of the Sun in the wonderful night-town scene which follows it—but we shall be bogged afterwards worse than ever in the interminable let-down of the cabman's shelter and in the scientific question-and-answer chapter

which undertakes to communicate to us through the most opaque
and uninviting medium possible Dedalus's conversation with Bloom.
The night-town episode itself and Mrs. Bloom's soliloquy, which
closes the book, are, of course, among the best things in it—but the
relative proportions of the other three latter chapters and the jarring
effect of the pastiche style sandwiched in with the straight Naturalistic seem to me artistically absolutely indefensible. One can understand that Joyce may have intended the colorless and tiresome episodes to set off the rich and vivid ones, and also that it is of the essence of his point of view to represent the profoundest changes of
our lives as beginning naturally between night and morning without the parties' appreciating their importance at the time; but a hundred and sixty-one more or less deliberately tedious pages are too
heavy a dead weight for even the brilliant flights of the other hundred and ninety-nine pages to carry. Furthermore, Joyce has here
half-buried his story under the virtuosity of his technical devices. It
is almost as if he had elaborated it so much and worked over it so
long that he had forgotten, in the amusement of writing parodies,
the drama which he had originally intended to stage; or as if he
were trying to divert and overwhelm us by irrelevant entertain-
ments and feats in order that we might not be dissatisfied with the
flatness—except for the drunken scene—of Dedalus's final meeting
with Bloom; or even perhaps as if he did not, after all, quite want
us to understand his story, as if he had, not quite conscious of what
he was doing, ended by throwing up between us and it a fortifi-
cation of solemn burlesque prose—as if he were shy and solicitous
about it, and wanted to protect it from us.

IV

Yet even these episodes to which I have objected contribute
something valuable to *Ulysses*. In the chapter of parodies, for example, Joyce seems to be saying to us: "Here are specimens of the
sort of thing that man has written about himself in the past—how
naïve or pretentious they seem! I have broken through these assumptions and pretences and shown you how he must recognize

himself today." And in the question-and-answer chapter, which is written entirely from the conventional point of view of science and where we are supplied with every possible physical, statistical, biographical and astronomical fact about Stephen's visit to Bloom: "This is all that the twentieth-century man thinks he knows about himself and his universe. Yet how mechanical and rigid this reasoning seems when we apply it to Molly and Bloom—how inadequate to explain them!"

For one of the most remarkable features of *Ulysses* is its interest as an investigation into the nature of human consciousness and behavior. Its importance from the point of view of psychology has never, it seems to me, been properly appreciated—though its influence on other books and, in consequence, upon our ideas about ourselves, has already been profound. Joyce has attempted in *Ulysses* to render as exhaustively, as precisely and as directly as it is possible in words to do, what our participation in life is like—or rather, what it seems to us like as from moment to moment we live. In order to make this record complete, he has been obliged to disregard a number of conventions of taste which, especially in English-speaking countries, have in modern times been pretty strictly observed, even by the writers who have aimed to be most scrupulously truthful. Joyce has studied what we are accustomed to consider the dirty, the trivial and the base elements in our lives with the relentlessness of a modern psychologist; and he has also—what the contemporary Naturalist has seldom been poet enough for—done justice to all those elements in our lives which we have been in the habit of describing by such names as love, nobility, truth and beauty. It is curious to reflect that a number of critics—including, curiously enough, Arnold Bennett—should have found Joyce misanthropic. Flaubert is misanthropic, if you like—and in reproducing his technique, Joyce sometimes suggests his acrid tone. But Stephen, Bloom and Mrs. Bloom are certainly not either unamiable or unattractive—and for all their misfortunes and short-comings, they inspire us with considerable respect. Stephen and Bloom are played off a little against the duller and meaner people about them; but even these people can scarcely be said to be treated with bitter-

ness, even when, as in the case of Buck Mulligan or the elder Dedalus, Stephen's feeling about them is bitter. Joyce is remarkable,
rather, for equanimity: in spite of the nervous intensity of *Ulysses,*
there is a real serenity and detachment behind it—we are in the
presence of a mind which has much in common with that of a certain type of philosopher, who in his effort to understand the causes
of things, to interrelate the different elements of the universe, has
reached a point where the ordinary values of good and bad, beautiful and ugly, have been lost in the excellence and beauty of transcendent understanding itself.

I believe that the first readers of *Ulysses* were shocked, not merely
by Joyce's use of certain words ordinarily excluded today from
English literature, but by his way of representing those aspects of
human nature which we tend to consider incongruous as intimately, inextricably mingled. Yet the more we read *Ulysses,* the
more we are convinced of its psychological truth, and the more
we are amazed at Joyce's genius in mastering and in presenting, not through analysis or generalization, but by the complete
recreation of life in the process of being lived, the relations of
human beings to their environment and to each other; the nature
of their perception of what goes on about them and of what goes
on within themselves; and the interdependence of their intellectual,
their physical, their professional and their emotional lives. To have
traced all these interdependences, to have given each of these elements its value, yet never to have lost sight of the moral through
preoccupation with the physical, nor to have forgotten the general
in the particular; to have exhibited ordinary humanity without
either satirizing it or sentimentalizing it—this would already have
been sufficiently remarkable; but to have subdued all this material
to the uses of a supremely finished and disciplined work of art is
a feat which has hardly been equaled in the literature of our time.

In Stephen's diary in *A Portrait of the Artist,* we find this significant entry apropos of a poem by Yeats: "Michael Robartes remembers forgotten beauty and, when his arms wrap her round, he
presses in his arms the loveliness which has long faded from the

world. Not this. Not at all. I desire to press in my arms the loveliness which has not yet come into the world."

And with *Ulysses*, Joyce has brought into literature a new and unknown beauty. Some readers have regretted the extinction in the later Joyce of the charming lyric poet of his two little books of poems and the *fin de siècle* prose writer of the *fin de siècle* phases of *A Portrait of the Artist as a Young Man* (both the prose and verse of the early Joyce showed the influence of Yeats). This poet is still present in *Ulysses:* "Kind air defined the coigns of houses in Kildare Street. No birds. Frail from the housetops two plumes of smoke ascended, pluming, and in a flaw of softness softly were blown." But the conventions of the romantic lyric, of "esthetic" *fin de siècle* prose, even of the esthetic Naturalism of Flaubert, can no longer, for Joyce, be made to accommodate the reality of experience. The diverse elements of experience are perceived in different relations and they must be differently represented. Joyce has found for this new vision a new language, but a language which, instead of diluting or doing violence to his poetic genius, enables it to assimilate more materials, to readjust itself more completely and successfully than that of perhaps any other poet of our age to the new self-consciousness of the modern world. But in achieving this, Joyce has ceased to write verse. I have suggested, in connection with Valéry and Eliot, that verse itself as a literary medium is coming to be used for fewer and fewer and for more and more special purposes, and that it may be destined to fall into disuse. And it seems to me that Joyce's literary development is a striking corroboration of this view. His prose works have an artistic intensity, a definitive beauty of surface and of form, which make him comparable to the great poets rather than to most of the great novelists.

Joyce is indeed really the great poet of a new phase of the human consciousness. Like Proust's or Whitehead's or Einstein's world, Joyce's world is always changing as it is perceived by different observers and by them at different times. It is an organism made up of "events," which may be taken as infinitely inclusive or infinitely small and each of which involves all the others; and each of these events is unique. Such a world cannot be presented in terms of such artificial abstractions as have been conventional in the past: solid institutions, groups, individuals, which play the parts of distinct durable entities—or even of solid psychological factors: dualisms of good and evil, mind and matter, flesh and spirit, instinct and reason; clear conflicts between passion and duty, between conscience and interest. Not that these conceptions are left out of Joyce's world: they are all there in the minds of the characters; and the realities they represent are there, too. But everything is reduced to terms of "events" like those of modern physics and philosophy—events which make up a "continuum," but which may be taken as infinitely small. Joyce has built out of these events a picture, amazingly lifelike and living, of the everyday world we know —and a picture which seems to allow us to see into it, to follow its variations and intricacies, as we have never been able to do before.

Nor are Joyce's characters merely the sum of the particles into which their experience has been dissociated: we come to imagine them as solidly, to feel their personalities as unmistakably, as we do with any characters in fiction; and we realize finally that they are also symbols. Bloom himself is in one of his aspects the typical modern man: Joyce has made him a Jew, one supposes, partly in order that he may be conceived equally well as an inhabitant of any provincial city of the European or Europeanized world. He makes a living by petty business, he leads the ordinary middle-class life— and he holds the conventional enlightened opinions of the time: he believes in science, social reform and internationalism. But Bloom is surpassed and illuminated from above by Stephen, who represents the intellect, the creative imagination; and he is upheld by Mrs. Bloom, who represents the body, the earth. Bloom leaves with us in the long run the impression that he is something both better and worse than either of them; for Stephen sins through pride, the sin of the intellect; and Molly is at the mercy of the flesh; but Bloom, though a less powerful personality than either, has the strength of humility. It is difficult to describe the character of Bloom as Joyce finally makes us feel it: it takes precisely the whole of *Ulysses* to put him before us. It is not merely that Bloom is mediocre, that he is clever, that he is commonplace—that he is comic, that he is pathetic—that he is, as Rebecca West says, a figure of abject "squatting" vulgarity, that he is at moments, as Foster Damon says, the Christ—he is all of these, he is all the possibilities of that ordinary humanity which is somehow not so ordinary after all; and it is the proof of Joyce's greatness that, though we recognize Bloom's perfect truth and typical character, we cannot pigeonhole him in any familiar category, racial, social, moral, literary or even—because he does really have, after all, a good deal in common with the Greek Ulysses—historical.

Both Stephen and Molly are more easily describable because they represent extremes. Both are capable of rising to heights which Bloom can never reach. In Stephen's rhapsody on the seashore, when he first realizes his artist's vocation, in *A Portrait of the Artist as a Young Man,* we have had the ecstasy of the creative mind. In the soliloquy of Mrs. Bloom, Joyce has given us another ecstasy of creation, the rhapsody of the flesh. Stephen's dream was conceived in loneliness, by a drawing apart from his fellows. But Mrs. Bloom is like the earth, which gives the same life to all: she feels a maternal kinship with all living creatures. She pities the "poor donkeys slipping half asleep" in the steep street of Gibraltar, as she does "the sentry in front of the governor's house . . . half roasted" in the sun; and she gives herself to the bootblack at the General Post Office as readily as to Professor Goodwin. But, none the less, she will tend to breed from the highest type of life she knows: she turns to Bloom, and, beyond him, toward Stephen. This gross body, the body of humanity, upon which the whole structure of *Ulysses* rests—still throbbing with so strong a rhythm amid obscenity, commonness and squalor—is laboring to throw up some knowledge and beauty by which it may transcend itself.

These two great flights of the mind carry off all the ignominies and trivialities through which Joyce has made us pass: they seem to me—the soaring silver prose of the one, the deep embedded pulse of the other—among the supreme expressions in literature of the

creative powers of humanity: they are, respectively, the justifications of the woman and the man.

V

Since finishing *Ulysses,* Joyce has been engaged upon another
work, about half of which has been published in the transatlantic
monthly, *Transition.* It is not possible to judge this book properly
in the imperfect form in which it has appeared. It is intended as a
sort of complement to *Ulysses;* Joyce has explained that, as *Ulysses*
deals with the day and with the conscious mind, so his new work
is to deal with the night and with the subconscious. The whole
book is apparently to occupy itself with the single night's sleep of
a single character. Joyce has already exhibited in *Ulysses* a unique
genius for the representation of special psychological states: I know
of nothing else in literature, for example, like the drunken night-
town scene, with its astounding recreation of all the deliriums,
dazes, gibberings, exaltations and hallucinations of drunkenness.
And Joyce's method of rendering the phases of sleep is similar to
his methods in the Circe episode. But he is here attempting something even more difficult, and his way of doing it raises an important question in regard to all Joyce's later work. Joyce, as I have
said, always nowadays represents the consciousness of his characters
directly: but his method of representing consciousness is to let you
overhear his characters talking to themselves. Joyce's people think
and feel exclusively in terms of words, for Joyce himself thinks in
terms of words. This is partly due, no doubt, to his defective eye-
sight, which of late years has become so serious as to make it difficult for him to work. There is an interesting passage in *A Portrait of the Artist* in which Joyce himself discusses this aspect of his
writing:

He drew forth a phrase from his treasure and spoke it softly to
himself:
—A day of dappled seaborne clouds.—
The phrase and the day and the scene harmonized in a chord.
Words. Was it their colors? He allowed them to glow and fade, hue

after hue: sunrise gold, the russet and green of apple orchards, azure of waves, the greyfringed fleece of clouds. No, it was not their colors: it was the poise and balance of the period itself. Did he then love the rhythmic rise and fall of words better than their associations of legend and color? Or was it that, being as weak of sight as he was shy of mind, he drew less pleasure from the reflection of the glowing sensible world through the prism of a language many colored and richly storied than from the contemplation of an inner world of individual emotions mirrored perfectly in a lucid supple periodic prose.

And in *Ulysses* we hear the characters far more plainly than we see them: Joyce supplies us with descriptions of them in sparse, scrupulous phrases, one trait here, another there. But the Dublin of *Ulysses* is a city of voices. Who has a clear idea of how Bloom or Molly Bloom looks?—and should we have a clear idea of Stephen if we had never seen photographs of Joyce? But their eternally soliloquizing voices become our intimate companions and haunt us long afterwards.

Joyce already seems sometimes, in *Ulysses,* to go a little beyond the probabilities in the vocabulary which he allows Bloom to command. When Bloom, in the drunken scene, for example, imagines himself giving birth to "eight male yellow and white children," all "with valuable metallic faces" and each with "his name printed in legible letters on his shirt-front: Nasodoro, Goldfinger, Chrysostomos, Maindorée, Silversmile, Silberselber, Vifargent, Panargyros"— we have difficulty in believing that he would have been learned enough for this. Yet I do not suppose that Joyce means us to think of Bloom as actually formulating these words in his mind: it is the author's way of conveying in words a vision which on the part of Bloom must have been a good deal less distinct, or at least a good deal less literary, than this. Now, in his new book, Joyce has tried to make his hero express directly in words, again, states of mind which do not usually in reality make use of words at all—for the subconscious has no language—the dreaming mind does not usually speak—and when it does, it is more likely to express itself in the looking-glass language of "Jabberwocky" than in anything resembling ordinary speech. Joyce's attempts to write the language of dreams have a good deal in common with those of Lewis Carroll; but the difference between his new novel and the Alice books is that, whereas in the Alice books it is the author who is supposed to be telling in straight English the adventures which his heroine thinks she is having and the literary language peculiar to dreams appears only in a poem which she reads, in Joyce's book he is plunging us directly into the consciousness of the dreamer itself, which is presented, without explanations by the author, entirely in the Jabberwocky language. The book is thus more easily comprehensible to literary people than to people who are not "word-minded," whose minds do not habitually breed words in response to sensations, emotions and thoughts. Yet it is worth making the effort to understand, because what Joyce is trying to do is both artistically and psychologically extremely interesting, and it may be that he will turn out to have written the most remarkable piece of dream-literature in existence.

The best way to understand Joyce's method is to note what goes on in one's own mind when one is just dropping off to sleep. Images—or words, if one thinks in words like Joyce—which were already in the conscious mind will suddenly acquire an ominous significance which has nothing to do with their ordinary functions; some vivid incident which may have taken place just before one went to bed will begin to swell with a meaning, an emotion, which at first we do not recognize because it has come up from the submerged part of the mind and is attempting to pass itself off in the clothes of an immediate experience—because it is dissociated from the situation out of which it originally arose. Or conversely, one may rid oneself of a troublesome abstract idea with which one has been preoccupied by allowing it to transform itself into some innocuous concrete image more easily dismissed from the attention: the page of a philosophical book, for example, where one had been continually stumbling over phrases and terms may vanish on the threshold of sleep in the guise of a spotted man, the spots having substituted themselves for the impenetrable words and phrases. And so the images which our waking mind would keep distinct from one another incongruously mix in our sleep with an effect of perfect

congruity. A single one of Joyce's sentences, therefore, will combine two or three different meanings—two or three different sets
of symbols; a single word may combine two or three. Joyce has
profited, in inventing his dream-language, by Freud's researches
into the principles which govern the language actually spoken in
dreams: certain people, it appears, do make up "portmanteau-
words" in their sleep; but we are not, I take it, to suppose that
Joyce's hero necessarily frames all these sentences to himself. Except
when he dreams he is reading something or carrying on a conversation, the language is merely a literary equivalent for sleeping states
not even articulate in fancy. Nor are we to assume that Joyce's
sleeper is actually master of all the languages or understands all
the allusions of which Joyce makes him avail himself in his dream.
We are now at a level below particularized languages—we are in
the region whence all languages arise and where the impulses to
all acts have their origin.

The hero of the night's sleep in question is, we gather, a man
named H. C. Earwicker, a Norwegian or descendant of Nor-
wegians, living in Dublin. He seems to have attempted a number of occupations—to have been a postman, to have worked in
Guiness's Brewery, to have kept a hotel and a shop. He is married
and has children, but has apparently been carrying on a flirtation
with a girl named Anna Livia. This, along with other lapses from
respectability associated with it in his mind, troubles his conscience
and his repose. We are introduced, at the very beginning, into
Earwicker's drowsing consciousness, and we have to make what we
can of the names, the shapes, and above all, of the voices, which fill
that dim and shifting world—they combine and recombine, they
are always changing into one another—but as we go on, we find the
same themes recurring and we begin to be able to understand
them in relation to one another—we become familiar with the character of Earwicker—we begin to guess at his condition and history.
We identify Maggie and the children, the house in which they live,
the four old men with the donkey, Earwicker's drunken misdemeanors and his fear of being caught by the police, the washer-

women gathering up their washing, Anna Livia on the bank of the Liffey, the Hill of Howth, the tree and the stone. But none of these elements is seen clearly or objectively—they are all aspects, the dramatic projection of aspects, of Earwicker himself: men and women, old and young, stronger and weaker, river and mountain, tree and stone—it is the dreamer who speaks or is spoken to, who sees or is seen, in all of them. The old men come to admire him as he is sleeping on the mountainside, but in a moment it is Earwicker himself who is talking about himself; or he splits up into two personalities, one of whom bullies or accuses the other. He is coming out of a pub into the street with a party of drunken companions, many people are standing about but the revelers do not care how much attention they attract: they egg on one of their number to sing but the song turns out to be a recital of all Earwicker's failures and sins—he has proved himself a fool and a swindler to the derision of all Dublin, his wife is going to read him the Riot Act. Or he sets out very sweetly to explain something by a fable of "the Mookse and the Gripes": the Mookse comes swaggering up to the Gripes, who is hanging on a tree—a sort of altercation takes place, and it turns into rather a painful re-enactment of one of Earwicker's encounters with the police—but dusk falls and the washerwomen come out and carry off the Mookse and the Gripes, who are now merely two pieces of laundry.

One of the most remarkable parts which have so far appeared is the *allegro* conclusion to the first of the four long sections which are to make up the completed work. (Joyce has allowed it to be published separately in a little book called *Anna Livia Plurabelle*.) Here the washerwomen have become identified with the stone and elm on the river bank—we hear them gossiping about Anna Livia, who is both the girl with whom the hero is in love and the river Liffey; and their gossip is the voice of the river itself, light, rapid, incessant, almost metrical, now monotonously running on one note, now impeded and syncopated, but vivaciously, interminably babbling its indistinct rigmarole story, half-unearthly, half-vulgarly human, of a heroine half-legendary, half-real:

Oh tell me all about Anna Livia! I want to hear all about Anna Livia. Well, you know Anna Livia? Yes, of course, we all know Anna Livia. Tell me all. Tell me now. You'll die when you hear. . . . Tell me, tell me, how cam she camlin through all her fellows, the neckar she was, the diveline? Linking one and knocking the next, tapting a flank and tipting a jutty and palling in and pietaring out and clyding by on her eastway. Waiwhou was the first thurever burst? . . . She says herself she hardly knows whuon the annals her graveller was, a dynast of Leinster, a wolf of the sea, or what he did or how blyth she played or how, when, why, where and who offon he jumnpad her. She was just a young thin pale soft shy slim slip of a thing then, sauntering, by silvamoonlake, and he was a heavy trudging lurching lieabroad of a Curraghman, making his hay for whose sun to shine on, as tough as the oaktrees (peats be with them!) used to rustle that time down by the dykes of killing Kildare, that forst-fellfoss with a plash across her. She thought she's sankh neathe the ground with nymphant shame when he gave her the tigris eye!

As darkness falls between stone and elm, the voices grow husky and vague:

And ho! Hey? What all men. Hot? His tittering daughters of Whawk?

Can't hear with the waters of. The chittering waters of. Flittering bats, fieldmice, bawk talk. Ho! Are you not gone ahome? What Tom Malone? Can't hear with bawk of bats, all the liffeying waters of. Ho, talk save us. My foos won't moos. I feel as old as yonder elm. A tale told of Shaun or Shem? All Livia's daughtersons. Dark hawks hear us. Night! Night! My ho head halls. I feel as heavy as yonder stone. Tell me of John or Shaun? Who were Shem and Shaun the living sons or daughters of? Night now! Tell me, tell me, tell me, elm! Night night! Tell me tale of stem or stone. Beside the rivering waters of, hitherandthithering waters of. Night!

Night is just falling in this first section of the book, and the shadow of the past, the memory presumably of the day before, darkens the hero's sleep—the vulgarities of his waking life oppress him and pursue him; but after midnight, as dawn approaches, as he becomes dimly aware of the first light, the dream begins to brighten and to rise unencumbered. If I am not mistaken, the middle-aged Earwicker reverts to the period of his youth, once again he is carefree, attractive, well-liked—his spirit turns refreshed to the new day. Are we to leave him on the verge of waking or are we finally to see the fantasies of the dream closed down into the commonplace fate which we have already been able to divine?

This new production of Joyce's exaggerates the qualities we have noted in *Ulysses*. There is even less action than in *Ulysses*. Joyce has set out with certain definite themes and the themes are evidently all to have their developments, but these developments take a long time. We make progress—we pass from night to morning —and no doubt, when the whole book is before us, we shall see that some sort of psychological drama has been played out in Earwicker's mind—but, as we progress, we go round and round. And whereas in *Ulysses* there is only one parallel, in this new book there are a whole set: Adam and Eve, Tristan and Isolde, Swift and Vanessa, Cain and Abel, Michael and Lucifer, Wellington and Napoleon. The multiplication of references does, to be sure, deepen and extend the significance of Earwicker: he and Anna Livia are the eternal woman and the eternal man, and during the early hours of heaviness and horror of Earwicker's dream, he is an Adam fallen from grace—to be redeemed, Joyce is said to have announced, with the renewal of the morning light. And it would seem that Joyce has provided plausible reasons for the appearance of all these personages in his hero's dream: Napoleon and Wellington have gotten in by way of the Wellington monument in the Phoenix Park, near which one of Earwicker's misdemeanors has been committed; and Michael and Lucifer—it appears from the last installment published, in which Earwicker is partly waked up toward morning by the crying of one of his children—by a picture on the bedroom wall. Yet the effect of the superposition, one upon the other, of such a variety of parallels seems sometimes less to enrich the book than to give it a mere synthetic complication. Joyce is again, we come to the conclusion, trying to do too many things at once. The style he has invented for his purpose works on the principle of a palimpsest: one meaning, one set of images, is written over another. Now we can grasp a certain number of such suggestions simultaneously, but Joyce, with his characteristic disregard for the reader, apparently works over and over his pages, packing in allusions and puns. This appears clearly from the different versions which have been published in various places of the Anna Livia Pluribelle section. (I have given in an appendix three stages of the same passage from this.) Joyce has improved it in making the texture denser, but this enrichment also obscures the main outlines and somewhat oversolidifies and impedes the dim ambiguous fluidity of the dream—especially when it takes the form of introducing in the final version puns on the names of some five hundred rivers. And as soon as we are aware of Joyce himself systematically embroidering on his text, deliberately inventing puzzles, the illusion of the dream is lost.

Yet, on the whole, this illusion is created and kept up with extraordinary success. There is a curious fascination about becoming gradually acquainted with a character whom we know only from the inside and from his dreams. And without the complications of his vocabulary, Joyce would no doubt never be able to paint for us with so sensitive and sure a hand the turbid life of that mental half-world where the unconscious is merged with the conscious—as without his machinery of history and myth, he would not be able to give his subject any poetic freedom of significance beyond the realistic framework which holds it firm. We are to see in H. C. Earwicker Everyman (he imagines his initials standing for Here Comes Everybody). We are to find in his dream all human possibilities—for out of that human nature, that psychological plasm, which swims dark and deep beneath the surface of the meager words, the limited acts, the special mask, of one man's actual daytime career, all history and myth have arisen—victim and conqueror, lover and beloved, childhood and old age—all the forms of human experience. And what humor, what imagination, what poetry, what psychological wisdom, Joyce has put into Earwicker's dream! I have offered the criticisms above only tentatively and without assurance: when we come to think about what we take at first to be the defects in Joyce's work, we find them so closely involved with the depth of his thought and the originality of his conception that we are obliged to grant them a certain necessity. And whatever difficulties we may have with this book in its present fragmentary and incomplete state, I feel confident that, when we read it as a whole, we shall find, not only that it is not unworthy—as the snappers at the heels of genius have been so eager and prompt to assert—of the great master of letters who wrote it, but that he is still at the height of his power.

T. S. Eliot

I HAVE noted the similarity between the English seventeenth-century poets and the French nineteenth-century Symbolists. The poetry of T. S. Eliot has, in our own time, brought together these two traditions, as it is Eliot who, so far as I know, has for the first time called attention to their resemblance. "The form," he says, "in which I began to write, in 1908 or 1909, was directly drawn from the study of Laforgue together with the later Elizabethan drama; and I do not know anyone who started from exactly that point."

I have so far, in discussing the early Symbolists, spoken chiefly of Mallarmé. But T. S. Eliot derived, as he indicates, from a different branch of the Symbolist tradition. In 1873 there had appeared in Paris a book of poems called *Les Amours Jaunes,* by a writer who signed himself Tristan Corbière. *Les Amours Jaunes* was received with complete indifference, and scarcely more than a year after it appeared, the author died of consumption. Only thirty at the time of his death, Tristan Corbière had been an eccentric and very maladjusted man: he was the son of a sea captain who had also written sea stories and he had had an excellent educa-

From *Axel's Castle,* by Edmund Wilson. Pp. 93-131. Charles Scribner's Sons. Copyright, 1931. Reprinted by permission of the author and publishers.

tion, but he chose for himself the life of an outlaw. In Paris, he slept all day and spent the nights in the cafés or at his verses, greeting at dawn the Paris harlots as they emerged from the station house or the hotel with the same half-harsh, half-tender fellow-feeling for the exile from conventional society which, when he was at home in his native Brittany, caused him to flee the house of his family and seek the company of the customs-men and sailors —living skeleton and invalid as he was, performing prodigies of courage and endurance in the navigation of a little cutter which he sailed by preference in the worst possible weather. He made a pose of his unsociability and of what he considered his physical ugliness, at the same time that he undoubtedly suffered over them. Melancholy, with a feverishly active mind, full of groanings and vulgar jokes, he used to amuse himself by going about in convict's clothes and by firing guns and revolvers out the window in protest against the singing of the village choir; and on one occasion, on a visit to Rome, he appeared in the streets in evening dress, with a mitre on his head and two eyes painted on his forehead, leading a pig decorated with ribbons. And Corbière's poetry was a poetry of the outcast: often colloquial and homely, yet with a rhetoric of fantastic slang; often with the manner of slapdash doggerel, yet sure of its own morose artistic effects; full of the parade of romantic personality, yet incessantly humiliating itself with a self-mockery scurrilous and savage, out of which, as Huysmans said, would sometimes rise without warning "a cry of sharp pain like the breaking of a 'cello string"—Corbière's verse brought back into French poetry qualities which had been alien to its spirit since François Villon's day.

So outlandish did Corbière appear even from the point of view of the Romantics that he was dismissed, when he was noticed at all, as not merely unseemly but insane—till Paul Verlaine, in 1883, did him honor in a series of articles *Les Poètes Maudits,* which was one of the important critical events in the development of Symbolism. Verlaine himself, a more accomplished artist, but a less original and interesting personality, had been strongly influenced

by *Les Amours Jaunes*—he seems, indeed, to have caught over
from Corbière, not only certain artistic effects, but even something
of his own poetic personality, his peculiar accent of wistful naïveté:
compare Corbière's "Rondels pour Après" with Verlaine's sonnet
which begins, "L'espoir luit comme un brin de paille dans l'étable";
or "Paria" with "Casper Hauser."

But another French poet, Jules Laforgue, nineteen years younger
than Corbière, had independently developed a tone and technique
—poignant-ironic, grandiose-slangy, scurrilous-naïve—which had
much in common with Corbière's. Laforgue was the son of a
schoolmaster and, for all his nonchalance in handling rudely the
conventions of French poetry, much more a professional man of
letters than Corbière. Laforgue even errs through preciosity in
his fashion; what with Corbière seems a personal and inevitable, if
eccentric, manner of speech, in Laforgue sounds self-conscious and
deliberate, almost sometimes a literary exercise. He was tubercu-
lar, as Corbière was also, and dead at twenty-seven—and his gentle-
ness and sadness are still those of a sick well-cared-for child; his
asperities, his surprising images, his coquetries, his cynicism, and
his impudence, are still those of a clever schoolboy. Laforgue's
friends procured him a post as reader to the Empress Augusta of
Germany; and, falling under the spell of German philosophy, he
brought its jargon into his verse, contributing thereby to Symbolism perhaps the one element of obscurity which it had lacked.

Yet Laforgue is a very fine poet and one of the most remarkable of the Symbolists. He and Corbière had introduced a new
variety of vocabulary and a new flexibility of feeling. With Mallarmé, it may be said that, on the whole, it is the imagery, not
the feeling, which is variable: though sometimes playful, he is
classical in the sense (as Yeats and Valéry are) that he sustains
a certain grandeur of tone. But it is from the conversational-
ironic, rather than from the serious-esthetic, tradition of Symbolism that T. S. Eliot derives. Corbière and Laforgue are almost
everywhere in his early work. The emphatic witty quatrains of
Corbière, with their sudden lapses into tenderness or pathos, are

heard again in the satiric verse of Eliot: a poem like "Mr. Eliot's
Sunday Morning Service" would hardly, one imagines, have been
written without Corbière's "Rapsodie Foraine." And as "Conversation Galante" derives clearly from certain poems in Laforgue's
"Complaintes" and "Imitation de Notre-Dame la Lune," so the
more elaborate "Portrait of a Lady" and "The Love Song of J.
Alfred Prufrock" follow closely the longer poems of Laforgue.
Compare the conclusion of "Prufrock" with the conclusion of the
early version of Laforgue's poem "Légende":

> I grow old . . . I grow old . . .
> I shall wear the bottoms of my trousers rolled.
>
> Shall I part my hair behind?   Do I dare to eat a peach!
> I shall wear white flannel trousers, and walk upon the beach,
> I have heard the mermaids singing, each to each.
>
> I do not think that they will sing to me.
>
> I have seen them riding seaward on the waves
> Combing the white hair of the waves blown back
> When the wind blows the water white and black.
>
> We have lingered in the chambers of the sea
> By sea-girls wreathed with seaweed red and brown
> Till human voices wake us, and we drown.

. . .

> Hier l'orchestre attaqua
> Sa dernière polka
>
> Oh! L'automme, l'automme!
>   Les casinos
>   Qu'on abandonne
> Remisent leurs pianos! . . .

> Phrases, verroteries,
> Caillots de souvenirs.
> Oh! comme elle est maigrie!
> Que vais-je devenir? . . .

Adieu! Les filles d'ifs dans les grisailles
Ont l'air de pleureuses de funerailles
Sous l'autan noir qui veut que tout s'en aille.

Assez, assez,
C'est toi qui as commencé.

Va, ce n'est plus l'odeur de tes fourrures.
Va, vos moindres clins d'yeux sont des parjures.
Tais-toi, avec vous autres rien ne dure.

Tais-toi, tais-toi,
On n'aime qu'une fois . . .

Here it will be seen that Eliot has reproduced Laforgue's irregular metrical scheme almost line for line. Furthermore, the subject of Laforgue's poem—the hesitations and constraints of a man either too timid or too disillusioned to make love to a woman who provokes his ironic pity at the same time that she stirs gusts of stifled emotion—has a strong resemblance to the subjects of "Prufrock" and the "Portrait of a Lady." And in another poem, "La Figlia Che Piange," Eliot has adapted a line of Laforgue's: "Simple et sans foi comme un bonjour"—"Simple and faithless as a smile and shake of the hand." He has even brought over into English some of the unstressed effect of French verse: how different, for example, is the alexandrine of Eliot's just quoted from the classical English alexandrine "which like a wounded snake drags its slow length along" or "with sparkless ashes loads an unlamented urn." (In his exhaustive *Influence du Symbolisme Français sur la Poésie Américaine de 1910 à 1920,* M. René Taupin has shown the influence of Gautier also in Eliot's satiric poems: "The Hippopotamus," it appears, is almost a transcript of a hippopotamus by Gautier, and the "Grishkin is nice" passage in "Whispers of Immortality" repeats a "Carmen est maigre" of Gautier.)

It must not be supposed, however, that Eliot is not original or that he is not the equal of either of his masters. Those longer and more elaborate poems—"Derniers Vers" in the collected edition—which Laforgue was constructing at the time of his death out of more fragmentary and less mature work are certainly his most important performances: through his masterly flexibility of vocabulary and metric, he has here achieved one of the definitive expressions of the pathetic-ironic, worldly-esthetic moods of the *fin de siècle* temperament. Yet, though Eliot has, in certain obvious respects, applied Laforgue's formula so faithfully, he cannot properly be described as an imitator because he is in some ways a superior artist. He is more mature than Laforgue ever was, and his workmanship is perfect in a way that Corbière's and Laforgue's were rarely. T. S. Eliot's peculiar distinction lies, as Clive Bell has said, in his "phrasing." Laforgue's images are often far-fetched and inappropriately grotesque: his sins in this respect are really very closely akin to those of the English metaphysical poets; but Eliot's taste is absolutely sure—his images always precisely right. And the impression that Eliot leaves, even in these earliest poems, is clear, vivid and unforgettable: we do not subordinate him to his Symbolist predecessors any more than, when we find him, as in "Gerontion," writing in the rhythms of late Elizabethan blank-verse, we associate him with Middleton or Webster.

When we come to examine Eliot's themes, we recognize something which we have found already in Laforgue, but which appears in Eliot in a more intense form. One of the principal preoccupations of Flaubert—a great hero of Eliot's, as of Eliot's fellow-poet, Ezra Pound's—had been the inferiority of the present to the past: the Romantics had discovered the possibilities of the historical imagination; with their thirst for boldness, grandeur, and magnificence, they had located these qualities in past epochs—especially the Middle Ages and the Renaissance. And Flaubert, who shared with the Romantics this appetite for the gorgeous and the untamed, but who constrained himself, also, to confront the actual nineteenth-century world, pursued two parallel lines of fiction which lent significance and relief to each other. On the one hand, he reconstructed, in *Salammbô* and in *La Tentation de Saint-Antoine,* the splendid barbarities of the pagan world and the heroic piety of the early Christian; and on the other, he carica-

tured, in *Madame Bovary,* in *L'Education Sentimentale* and in
Bouvard et Pécuchet, the pusillanimity and mediocrity of contemporary bourgeois France. This whole point of view of Flaubert's—
summed up, as it were, in *Trois Contes,* where the three periods
are contrasted in one book—was profoundly to affect modern literature. We shall find it later on in Joyce; but in the meantime we
must note its reappearance in the poetry of Eliot. Eliot, like Flaubert, feels at every turn that human life is now ignoble, sordid or
tame, and he is haunted and tormented by intimations that it has
once been otherwise. In "Burbank with a Baedeker: Bleistein
with a Cigar," the young American tourist in Venice, superseded
in his affair with the Princess Volupine by a vulgar Austrian Jew,
meditates on the clipped wings and pared claws of the Lion of
St. Mark's, the symbol of the old arrogant Venice and of the world
where such a city was possible. In "A Cooking Egg," the poet
demands, after a call upon a very mild, dull spinster: "Where are
the eagles and the trumpets?" and himself returns the saddened
answer: "Buried beneath some snow-deep Alps." In "Lune de
Miel," the Middle Western American travelers, stifled with the
summer heat and devoured by the bedbugs of Ravenna, are contrasted with the noble crumbling beauty of the old Byzantine
church less than a league away, of which they are totally unaware
and to which they have apparently no relation; and in "Mr. Eliot's
Sunday Morning Service," the combined grossness and aridity of
the modern clergymen is contrasted with the pure and fresh religious feeling of a picture of the baptism of Christ by "a painter
of the Umbrian school." In the best and most effective of these
poems, "Sweeney Among the Nightingales," the poet, during a
drowsy, idiotic and mildly sinister scene in some low dive, where
two of the girls are supposed to be plotting against one of the
men, remembers, at the sound of nightingales singing, the murder
of Agamemnon in Aeschylus:

> The host with someone indistinct
> Converses at the door apart,
> The nightingales are singing near
> The Convent of the Sacred Heart,

> And sang within the bloody wood
> When Agamemnon cried aloud,
> And let their liquid siftings fall
> To stain the stiff dishonoured shroud.

The present is more timid than the past: the bourgeois are afraid to let themselves go. The French had been preoccupied with this idea ever since the first days of Romanticism; but Eliot was to deal with the theme from a somewhat different point of view, a point of view characteristically American. For T. S. Eliot, though born in St. Louis, comes from a New England family and was educated at Harvard; and he is in some ways a typical product of our New England civilization. He is distinguished by that combination of practical prudence with moral idealism which shows itself in its later developments as an excessive fastidiousness and scrupulousness. One of the principal subjects of Eliot's poetry is really that regret at situations unexplored, that dark rankling of passions inhibited, which has figured so conspicuously in the work of the American writers of New England and New York from Hawthorne to Edith Wharton. T. S. Eliot, in this respect, has much in common with Henry James. Mr. Prufrock and the poet of the "Portrait of a Lady," with their helpless consciousness of having dared too little, correspond exactly to the middle-aged heroes of *The Ambassadors* and "The Beast in the Jungle," realizing sadly too late in life that they have been living too cautiously and too poorly. The fear of life, in Henry James, is closely bound up with the fear of vulgarity. And Eliot, too, fears vulgarity—which he embodies in the symbolic figure of "Apeneck Sweeney"—at the same time that he is fascinated by it. Yet he chafes at the limitations and pretenses of the culture represented by Boston—a society "quite uncivilized," as he says, "but refined beyond the point of civilization." He has some amusing satiric poems about old New England ladies—in one of which he reflects on his way to the house of his Cousin Harriet, how

> . . . evening quickens faintly in the street,
> Wakening the appetites of life in some
> And to others bringing the *Boston Evening Transcript.*

And the "Portrait of a Lady," whether the scene be laid in Boston
or in London, is essentially a poem of that New England society
"refined beyond the point of civilization": from the Lady, who
serves tea among lighted candles—"an atmosphere of Juliet's tomb"
—with her dampening efforts at flattery and flirtation through the
medium of cultured conversation—her slightly stale and faded gush
about Chopin and her memories of Paris in the spring—the poet
is seized with an impulse to flee:

> I take my hat: how can I make a cowardly amends
> For what she has said to me?
> You will see me any morning in the park
> Reading the comics and the sporting page.
> Particularly I remark
> An English countess goes upon the stage,
> A Greek was murdered at a Polish dance,
> Another bank defaulter has confessed.
> I keep my countenance,
> I remain self-possessed
> Except when a street piano, mechanical and tired,
> Reiterates some worn-out common song
> With the smell of hyacinths across the garden
> Recalling things that other people have desired.

But he is always debating things with his conscience: his incurable
moral solicitude makes him wonder:

> Are these ideas right or wrong?

So Mr. Prufrock in the room where

> . . . women come and go
> Talking of Michelangelo,

wistfully asks himself:

> Shall I say, I have gone at dusk through narrow streets
> And watched the smoke that rises from the pipes
> Of lonely men in shirt-sleeves, leaning out of windows? . . .

And Mr. Prufrock wonders 'also whether he should not put a question to his lady—but he never gets to the point of putting it.

II

But Eliot's most complete expression of this theme of emotional starvation is to be found in the later and longer poem called *The Waste Land* (1922). The Waste Land of the poem is a symbol borrowed from the myth of the Holy Grail: it is a desolate and sterile country ruled by an impotent king, in which not only have the crops ceased to grow and the animals to reproduce, but the very human inhabitants have become incapable of having children. But this sterility we soon identify as the sterility of the Puritan temperament. On the first pages we find again the theme of the girl with the hyacinths (themselves a symbol for the rearisen god of the fertility rites who will save the rainless country from drouth) which has already figured in "La Figlia Che Piange" and "Dans le Restaurant"—a memory which apparently represents for the poet some fulfillment foregone in youth and now agonizingly desired; and in the last pages it is repeated. We recognize throughout *The Waste Land* the peculiar conflicts of the Puritan turned artist: the horror of vulgarity and the shy sympathy with the common life, the ascetic shrinking from sexual experience and the distress at the drying up of the springs of sexual emotion, with the straining after a religious emotion which may be made to take its place.

Yet though Eliot's spiritual and intellectual roots are still more firmly fixed in New England than is, I believe, ordinarily understood, there is in *The Waste Land* a good deal more than the mere gloomy moods of a New Englander regretting an emotionally undernourished youth. The colonization by the Puritans of New England was merely an incident in that rise of the middle class which has brought a commercial-industrial civilization to the European cities as well as to the American ones. T. S. Eliot now lives in London and has become an English citizen; but the desolation, the esthetic and spiritual drouth, of Anglo-Saxon middle-class society oppresses London as well as Boston. The terrible dreariness of the great modern cities is the atmosphere in which *The Waste Land* takes place—amidst this dreariness, brief, vivid images emerge, brief pure moments of feeling are distilled; but all about us we are aware of nameless millions performing barren office routines, wearing down their souls in interminable labors of which the products never bring them profit—people whose pleasures are so sordid and so feeble that they seem almost sadder than their pains. And this Waste Land has another aspect: it is a place not merely of desolation, but of anarchy and doubt. In our post-war world of shattered institutions, strained nerves and bankrupt ideals, life no longer seems serious or coherent—we have no belief in the things we do and consequently we have no heart for them.

The poet of *The Waste Land* is living half the time in the real world of contemporary London and half the time in the haunted wilderness of the medieval legend. The water for which he longs in the twilight desert of his dream is to quench the spiritual thirst which torments him in the London dusk; and as Gerontion, "an old man in a dry month," thought of the young men who had fought in the rain, as Prufrock fancied riding the waves with mermaids and lingering in the chambers of the sea, as Mr. Apollinax has been imagined drawing strength from the deep sea-caves of coral islands—so the poet of *The Waste Land,* making water the symbol of all freedom, all fecundity and flowering of the soul, invokes in desperate need the memory of an April shower of his youth, the song of the hermit thrush with its sound of water dripping and the vision of a drowned Phoenician sailor, sunk beyond "the cry of gulls and the deep sea swell," who has at least died by water, not thirst. The poet, who seems now to be traveling in a country cracked by drouth, can only feverishly dream of these things. One's head may be well stored with literature, but the heroic prelude of the Elizabethans has ironic echoes in modern London streets and modern London drawing-rooms: lines remembered from Shakespeare turn to jazz or refer themselves to the sound of phonographs. And now it is one's personal regrets again—the girl in the hyacinth-garden—"the awful daring of a moment's surrender which an age of prudence can never retract"—the key which turned once, and once only, in the prison of inhibition and isolation. Now he stands on the arid plain again, and the dry-rotted world of London

seems to be crumbling about him—the poem ends in a medley of
quotations from a medley of literatures—like Gérard de Nerval's
"Desdichado," the poet is disinherited; like the author of the *Per-
vigilium Veneris,* he laments that his song is mute and asks when
the spring will come which will set it free like the swallow's; like
Arnaut Daniel, in Dante, as he disappears in the refining fire, he
begs the world to raise a prayer for his torment. "These fragments
I have shored against my ruins."

The Waste Land, in method as well as in mood, has left Laforgue
far behind. Eliot has developed a new technique, at once laconic,
quick, and precise, for representing the transmutations of thought,
the interplay of perception and reflection. Dealing with subjects
complex in the same way as those of Yeats' poem "Among School-
Children" and Valéry's "Cimetière Marin," Eliot has found for
them a different language. As May Sinclair has said of Eliot, his
"trick of cutting his corners and his curves makes him seem
obscure when he is clear as daylight. His thoughts move very
rapidly and by astounding cuts. They move not by logical stages
and majestic roundings of the full literary curve, but as live thoughts
move in live brains." Let us examine, as an illustration, the lovely
nightingale passage from *The Waste Land.* Eliot is describing a
room in London:

> Above the antique mantel was displayed
> As though a window gave upon the sylvan scene
> The change of Philomel, by the barbarous king
> So rudely forced; yet there the nightingale
> Filled all the desert with inviolable voice
> And still she cried, and still the world pursues,
> "Jug Jug" to dirty ears.

That is, the poet sees, above the mantel, a picture of Philomela
changed to a nightingale, and it gives his mind a moment's swift
release. The picture is like a window opening upon Milton's
earthly paradise—the "sylvan scene," as Eliot explains in a note, is
a phrase from "Paradise Lost"—and the poet associates his own
plight in the modern city, in which some "infinitely gentle, in-

finitely suffering thing," to quote one of Eliot's earlier poems, is somehow being done to death, with Philomela, raped and mutilated by Tereus. But in the earthly paradise, there had been a nightingale singing: Philomela had wept her woes in song, though the barbarous king had cut out her tongue—her sweet voice had remained inviolable. And with a sudden change of tense, the poet flashes back from the myth to his present situation:

> And still she *cried,* and still the world *pursues,*
> "Jug Jug" to dirty ears.

The song of birds was represented in old English popular poetry by such outlandish syllables as "Jug Jug"—so Philomela's cry sounds to the vulgar. Eliot has here, in seven lines of extraordinary liquidity and beauty, fused the picture, the passage from Milton and the legend from Ovid, into a single moment of vague poignant longing.

The Waste Land is dedicated to Ezra Pound, to whom Eliot elsewhere acknowledges a debt; and he has here evidently been influenced by Pound's *Cantos. The Waste Land,* like the *Cantos,* is fragmentary in form and packed with literary quotation and allusion. In fact, the passage just discussed above has a resemblance to a passage on the same subject—the Philomela-Procne myth—at the beginning of Pound's Fourth Canto. Eliot and Pound have, in fact, founded a school of poetry which depends on literary quotation and reference to an unprecedented degree. Jules Laforgue had sometimes parodied, in his poems, the great lines of other poets—

> O Nature, donne-moi la force et le courage
> De me croire en âge . . .

And Eliot had, in his early poetry, introduced phrases from Shakespeare and Blake for purposes of ironic effect. He has always, furthermore, been addicted to prefacing his poems with quotations and echoing passages from other poets. But now, in *The Waste Land,* he carries this tendency to what one must suppose its extreme possible limit: here, in a poem of only four hundred and three lines (to which are added, however, seven pages of notes), he manages to include quotations from, allusions to, or imitations of, at least thirty-five different writers (some of them, such as Shakespeare and Dante, laid under contribution several times)—as well as several popular songs; and to introduce passages in six foreign languages, including Sanskrit. And we must also take into consideration that the idea of the literary medley itself seems to have been borrowed from still another writer, Pound. We are always being dismayed, in our general reading, to discover that lines among those which we had believed to represent Eliot's residuum of original invention had been taken over or adapted from other writers (sometimes very unexpected ones: thus, it appears now, from Eliot's essay on Bishop Andrewes, that the first five lines of "The Journey of the Magi," as well as the "word within a word, unable to speak a word" of "Gerontion," had been salvaged from Andrewes's sermons; and the "stiff dishonoured shroud" of "Sweeney Among the Nightingales" seems to be an echo of the "dim dishonoured brow" of Whittier's poem about Daniel Webster). One would be inclined *a priori* to assume that all this load of erudition and literature would be enough to sink any writer, and that such a production as *The Waste Land* must be a work of second-hand inspiration. And it is true that, in reading Eliot and Pound, we are sometimes visited by uneasy recollections of Ausonius, in the fourth century, composing Greek-and-Latin macaronics and piecing together poetic mosaics out of verses from Virgil. Yet Eliot manages to be most effective precisely—in *The Waste Land*—where he might be expected to be least original—he succeeds in conveying his meaning, in communicating his emotion, in spite of all his learned or mysterious allusions, and whether we understand them or not.

In this respect, there is a curious contrast between Eliot and Ezra Pound. Pound's work *has* been partially sunk by its cargo of erudition, whereas Eliot, in ten years' time, has left upon English poetry a mark more unmistakable than that of any other poet writing English. It is, in fact, probably true at the present time that Eliot is being praised too extravagantly and Pound, though he has deeply influenced a few, on the whole unfairly neglected. I should explain Eliot's greater popularity by the fact that, for all his fragmentary method, he possesses a complete literary personality in a way that

Pound, for all his integrity, does not. Ezra Pound, fine poet though he is, does not dominate us like a master imagination—he rather delights us like a miscellaneous collection of admirably chosen works of art. It is true that Pound, in spite of his inveterate translating, is a man of genuine originality—but his heterogeneous shorter poems, and the heterogeneous passages which go to make his longer ones, never seem to come together in a whole—as his general prose writing gives scrappy expression to a variety of ideas, a variety of enthusiasms and prejudices, some ridiculous and some valid, some learned and some half-baked, which, though valuable to his generation as polemic, as propaganda and as illuminating casual criticism, do not establish and develop a distinct reasoned point of view as Eliot's prose-writings do. T. S. Eliot has thought persistently and coherently about the relations between the different phases of human experience, and his passion for proportion and order is reflected in his poems. He is, in his way, a complete man, and if it is true, as I believe, that he has accomplished what he has credited Ezra Pound with accomplishing—if he has brought a new personal rhythm into the language—so that he has been able to lend even to the borrowed rhythms, the quoted words, of his great predecessors a new music and a new meaning—it is this intellectual completeness and soundness which has given his rhythm its special prestige.

Another factor which has probably contributed to Eliot's extraordinary success is the essentially dramatic character of his imagination. We may be puzzled by his continual preoccupation with the possibilities of a modern poetic drama—that is to say, of modern drama in verse. Why, we wonder, should he worry about drama in verse—why, after Ibsen, Hauptmann, Shaw and Chekhov, should he be dissatisfied with plays in prose? We may put it down to an academic assumption that English drama ended when the blank verse of the Elizabethans ran into the sands, until it occurs to us that Eliot himself is really a dramatic poet. Mr. Prufrock and Sweeney are characters as none of the personages of Pound, Valéry or Yeats is—they have become a part of our modern mythology. And most of the best of Eliot's poems are based on unexpected dramatic contrasts: *The Waste Land* especially, I am sure, owes a large part of its power to its dramatic quality, which makes it peculiarly effective read aloud. Eliot has even tried his hand at writing a play,[1] and the two episodes from "Wanna Go Home, Baby" which he has published in *The Criterion* seem rather promising. They are written in a sort of jazz dramatic meter which suggests certain scenes of John Howard Lawson's *Processional;* and there can be no question that the future of drama in verse, if it has any future, lies in some such direction. "We cannot reinstate," Eliot has written, "either blank verse or the heroic couplet. The next form of drama will have to be a verse drama, but in new verse forms. Perhaps the conditions of modern life (think how large a part is now played in our sensory life by the internal combustion engine!) have altered our perception of rhythms. At any rate, the recognized forms of speech-verse are not as efficient as they should be; probably a new form will be devised out of colloquial speech."

In any case, that first handful of Eliot's poems, brought out in the middle of the War (1917) and generally read, if at all, at the time, as some sort of modern *vers de société,* was soon found, as Wyndham Lewis has said, to have had the effect of a little musk that scents up a whole room. And as for *The Waste Land,* it enchanted and devastated a whole generation. Attempts have been made to reproduce it—by Aldington, Nancy Cunard, etc.—at least a dozen times. And as Eliot, lately out of Harvard, assumed the rôle of the middle-aged Prufrock and today, at forty, in one of his latest poems, "The Song of Simeon," speaks in the character of an old man "with eighty years and no tomorrow"—so "Gerontion" and *The Waste Land* have made the young poets old before their time. In London, as in New York, and in the universities both here and in England, they for a time took to inhabiting exclusively barren beaches, cactus-grown deserts, and dusty attics overrun with rats—the only properties they allowed themselves to work with were a few fragments of old shattered glass or a sparse sprinkling of broken bones. They had purged themselves of Masefield as of Shelley for

---

[1] Eliot's further work in drama has since appeared: *The Rock* in 1934 and *Murder in the Cathedral* in 1935.

dry tongues and rheumatic joints. The dry breath of the Waste Land now blighted the most amiable country landscapes; and the sound of jazz, which had formerly seemed jolly, now inspired only horror and despair. But in this case, we may forgive the young for growing prematurely decrepit: where some of even the finest intelligences of the elder generation read *The Waste Land* with blankness or laughter, the young had recognized a poet.

III

As a critic, Eliot occupies today a position of distinction and influence equal in importance to his position as a poet. His writings have been comparatively brief and rare—he has published only four small books of criticism [1]—yet he has probably affected literary opinion, during the period since the War, more profoundly than any other critic writing English. Eliot's prose style has a kind of felicity different from that of his poetic style; it is almost primly precise and sober, yet with a sort of sensitive charm in its austerity—closely reasoned and making its points with the fewest possible words, yet always even, effortless and lucid. In a reaction against the impressionistic criticism which flourished at the end of the century and which has survived into our own time—the sort of criticism which, in dealing with poetry, attempts to reproduce its effect by having recourse to poetic prose—T. S. Eliot has undertaken a kind of scientific study of esthetic values: avoiding impressionistic rhetoric and *a priori* esthetic theories alike, he compares works of literature coolly and tries to distinguish between different orders of artistic effects and the different degrees of satisfaction to be derived from them.

And by this method, Eliot has done more than perhaps any other modern critic to effect a revaluation of English literature. We sometimes follow his literary criticism with the same sort of eagerness and excitement with which we follow a philosophical inquiry. Professor Saintsbury has played in literature much the same sort of

[1] In 1930. Eliot has since issued four further volumes: *The Use of Poetry and the Use of Criticism* (1933), *After Strange Gods* (1934), *Elizabethan Essays* (1934), and *Essays Ancient and Modern* (1936).

rôle that he has played as a connoisseur of wines, that of an agreeable and entertaining guide of excellent taste and enormous experience; Edmund Gosse, often intelligent and courageous in dealing with French or Scandinavian writers, could never quite, when it came to English literature, bring himself to drop his official character of Librarian of the House of Lords—his attitude was always a little that of the Beef Eater in the Tower of London, who assumes the transcendent value of the Crown Jewels which he has been set to guard and does not presume to form a personal opinion as to their taste or their respective merits; and the moral passion of Paul Elmer More has ended by paralyzing his esthetic appreciation. But T. S. Eliot, with an infinitely sensitive apparatus for esthetic appreciation, approaching English literature as an American, with an American's peculiar combination of avidity and detachment and with more than the ordinary English critic's reading in the literatures, ancient and modern, of the Continent, has been able to succeed as few writers have done in the excessively delicate task of estimating English, Irish and American writers in relation to one another, and writers in English in relation to writers on the Continent. The extent of Eliot's influence is amazing: these short essays, sent out without publicity as mere scattered notes on literature, yet sped with so intense a seriousness and weighted with so wide a learning, have not only had the effect of discrediting the academic clichés of the text-books, but are even by way of establishing in the minds of the generation now in college a new set of literary clichés. With the ascendancy of T. E. Eliot, the Elizabethan dramatists have come back into fashion, and the nineteenth-century poets gone out. Milton's poetic reputation has sunk, and Dryden's and Pope's have risen. It is as much as one's life is worth nowadays, among young people, to say an approving word for Shelley or a dubious one about Donne. And as for the enthusiasm for Dante— to paraphrase the man in Hemingway's novel, there's been nothing like it since the Fratellinis!

Eliot's rôle as a literary critic has been very similar to Valéry's in France: indeed, the ideas of the two men and their ways of stating them have corresponded so closely that one guesses they must in-

fluence each other a good deal. Like Valéry, Eliot believes that a
work of art is not an oracular outpouring, but an object which has
been constructed deliberately with the aim of producing a certain
effect. He has brought back to English criticism something of that
trenchant rationalism which he admires in the eighteenth century,
but with a much more catholic appreciation of different styles and
points of view than the eighteenth century allowed. The Romantics, of course, fare badly before this criticism. Vague sentiment
vaguely expressed, rhetorical effusion disguising bad art—these
Eliot's laconic scorn has nipped. For him, Byron is "a disorderly
mind, and an uninteresting one": Keats and Shelley "not nearly
such great poets as they are supposed to be"; whereas the powers
of Dryden are "wider, but no greater than those of Milton." Just
as Valéry lately protested in a lecture that he was unable to understand the well-known lines of Alfred de Musset:

> Les plus désespérés sont les chants les plus beaux,
> Et j'en sais d'immortels qui sont de purs sanglots,

so Eliot, in an essay on Crashaw, has confessed, with a certain
superciliousness, his inability to understand the following stanza
from Shelley's "Skylark":

> Keen as are the arrows
>   Of that silver sphere
> Whose intense lamp narrows
>   In the white dawn clear,
> Until we hardly see—we feel that it is there.

"For the first time, perhaps," says Eliot, "in verse of such eminence,
sound exists without sense."

It will be seen that Eliot differs from Valéry in believing that
poetry should make "sense." And he elsewhere, in his essay on
Dante in *The Sacred Wood,* remonstrates with Valéry for asserting
that philosophy has no place in poetry. Yet Eliot's point of view,
though more intelligently reasoned and expressed, comes down
finally to the same sort of thing as Valéry's and seems to me open
to the same sort of objection. Eliot's conclusion in respect to the

relation of philosophy to poetry is that, though philosophy *has* its place in poetry, it is only as something which we "see" among the other things with which the poet presents us, a set of ideas which penetrate his world, as in the case of the *Divina Commedia:* in the case of such a poet as Lucretius, the philosophy sometimes seems antagonistic to the poetry only because it happens to be a philosophy "not rich enough in feeling . . . incapable of complete expansion into pure vision." Furthermore, "the original form of philosophy cannot be poetic": the poet must use a philosophy already invented by somebody else. Now, though we may admire the justice of Eliot's judgments on the various degrees of artistic success achieved by Dante, Lucretius and others, it becomes plainer and plainer, as time goes on, that the real effect of Eliot's, as of Valéry's, literary criticism, is to impose upon us a conception of poetry as some sort of pure and rare esthetic essence with no relation to any of the practical human uses for which, for some reason never explained, only the technique of prose is appropriate.

Now this point of view, as I have already suggested in writing about Paul Valéry, seems to me absolutely unhistorical—an impossible attempt to make esthetic values independent of all the other values. Who will agree with Eliot, for example, that a poet cannot be an original thinker and that it is not possible for a poet to be a completely successful artist and yet persuade us to accept his ideas at the same time? There is a good deal in Dante's morality which he never got out of the Scholastics, as, for all we know, there may be a good deal in Lucretius which he never got out of Epicurus. When we read Lucretius and Dante, we are affected by them just as we are by prose writers of eloquence and imagination—we are compelled to take their opinions seriously. And as soon as we admit that prose writing may be considered on the same basis with verse, it becomes evident that we cannot, in the case of Plato, discriminate so finely as to the capacity of his philosophy for being "expanded into pure vision" that we are able to put our finger on the point where the novelist or poet stops and the scientist or metaphysician begins; nor, with Blake any more than with Nietzsche and Emerson, distinguish the poet from the aphorist. The truth is, of course, that, in Lucretius' time, verse was used for all sorts of didactic purposes for which we no longer consider it appropriate —they had agricultural poems, astronomical poems, poems of literary criticism. How can the *Georgics,* the *Ars Poetica* and Manilius be dealt with from the point of view of the capacity of their material for being "expanded into pure vision"? To modern readers, the subjects of the *Georgics*—bee-keeping, stock-raising, and so forth— seem unsuitable and sometimes annoying in verse; yet for Virgil's contemporaries, the poem must have been completely successful— as, indeed, granted the subject, it is. Nor does it follow that, because we are coming to use poetry for fewer and fewer literary purposes, our critical taste is becoming more and more refined, so that we are beginning to perceive for the first time the true, pure and exalted function of poetry: that is, simply, as Valéry says, to produce a "state"—as Eliot says, to afford a "superior amusement." It is much more likely that for some reason or other, verse as a technique of literary expression is being abandoned by humanity altogether—perhaps because it is a more primitive, and hence a more barbarous technique than prose. Is it possible to believe, for example, that Eliot's hope of having verse reinstated on the stage— even verse of the new kind which he proposes—is likely ever to be realized?

The tendency to keep verse isolated from prose and to confine it to certain highly specialized functions dates in English at least from the time of Coleridge, when, in spite of the long narrative poems which were fashionable, verse was already beginning to fall into disuse. Coleridge defined a poem as "that species of composition which is opposed to works of science by proposing for its *immediate* object pleasure, not truth; and from all other species (having *this* object in common with it), it is discriminated by proposing to itself such delight from the *whole,* as is compatible with a distinct gratification from each component part." Poe, who had doubtless read Coleridge on the subject, wrote thirty years later that there was no such thing as a long poem, that "no very long poem would ever be popular again," etc. Eliot and Valéry follow Coleridge and Poe in their theory as well as in their verse, and they seem to me to confuse certain questions by talking as if the whole of literature existed simultaneously in a vacuum, as if Homer's and Shakespeare's situations had been the same as Mallarmé's and Laforgue's, as if the latter had been attempting to play the same sort of rôles as the former and could be judged on the same basis. It is inevitable, of course, that we should try to arrive at absolute values through the comparison of the work of different periods—I have just praised Eliot for his success at this—but it seems to me that in this particular matter a good many difficulties would be cleared up if certain literary discussions could be removed from the artificially restricted field of verse—in which it is assumed that nothing is possible or desirable but a quintessential distillation called "poetry," and that that distillation has nothing in common with anything possible to obtain through prose—to the field of literature in general. Has not such a great modern novel as *Madame Bovary,* for example, at least as much in common with Virgil and Dante as with Balzac and Dickens? Is it not comparable from the point of view of intensity, music and perfection of the parts, with the best verse of any period? And we shall consider Joyce in this connection later.

With all gratitude, therefore, for the salutary effect of Eliot's earlier criticism in curbing the carelessness and gush of the aftermath of Romanticism, it seems plain that the anti-Romantic reaction is leading finally into pedantry and into a futile estheticism. "Poetry," Eliot wrote in *The Sacred Wood,* "is not a turning loose of emotion, but an escape from emotion; it is not the expression of personality, but an escape from personality. But, of course, only those who have personality and emotion know what it means to want to escape from them." This was valid, and even noble, in 1920 when *The Sacred Wood* was published; but today, after ten years of depersonalized and over-intellectualized verse, so much of it written in imitation of Eliot, the same sort of thing in the mouths of Eliot's disciples sounds like an excuse for *not* possessing emotion and personality.

Yet, in spite of the weaknesses of Eliot's position as he has sometimes been driven to state it dogmatically, he has himself largely succeeded in escaping the vices which it seems to encourage. The old nineteenth-century criticism of Ruskin, Renan, Taine, Sainte-Beuve, was closely allied to history and novel writing, and was also the vehicle for all sorts of ideas about the purpose and destiny of human life in general. The criticism of our own day examines literature, art, ideas and specimens of human society in the past with a detached scientific interest or a detached esthetic appreciation which seems in either case to lead nowhere. A critic like Herbert Read makes dull discriminations between different kinds of literature; a critic like Albert Thibaudet discovers dull resemblances between the ideas of philosophers and poets; a critic like I. A. Richards writes about poetry from the point of view of a scientist studying the psychological reactions of readers; and such a critic as Clive Bell writes about painting so exclusively and cloyingly from the point of view of the varying degrees of pleasure to be derived from the pictures of different painters that we would willingly have Ruskin and all his sermonizing back. And even Virginia Woolf and Lytton Strachey have this in common with Clive Bell that they seem to feel they have done enough when they have distinguished the kind of pleasure to be derived from one kind of book, the kind of interest to be felt in one kind of personality, from the kind to be found in another. One is supposed to have read everything and enjoyed everything and to understand exactly the reasons for one's enjoyment, but not to enjoy anything excessively nor to raise an issue of one kind of thing against another. Each of the essays of Strachey or Mrs. Woolf, so compact yet so beautifully rounded out, is completely self-contained and does not lead to anything beyond itself; and finally, for all their brilliance, we begin to find them tiresome.

Now there is a good deal in T. S. Eliot of this pedantry and sterility of his age. He is very much given, for example, to becoming involved in literary Houses-that-Jack-Built: "We find this quality occasionally in Wordsworth," he will write, "but it is a quality which Wordsworth shares with Shenstone rather than with Collins and Gray. And for the right sort of enjoyment of Shenstone, we must read his prose as well as his verse. The 'Essays on Men and Manners' are in the tradition of the great French aphorists of the

seventeenth century, and should be read with the full sense of their
relation to Vauvenargues, La Rochefoucauld and (with his wider
range) La Bruyère. We shall do well to read enough of Theophrastus to understand the kind of effect at which La Bruyère aimed.
(Professor Somebody-or-other's book on 'Theophrastus and the
Peripatetics' gives us the clew to the intellectual atmosphere in
which Theophrastus wrote and enables us to gauge the influences
on his work—very different from each other—of Plato and Aristotle.)" At this rate (though I have parodied Eliot), we should
have to read the whole of literature in order to appreciate a single
book, and Eliot fails to supply us with a reason why we should go
to the trouble of doing so. Yet against the background of the criticism of his time, Eliot has stood out unmistakably as a man passionately interested in literature. The real intensity of his enthusiasm makes us forget the primness of his tone; and his occasional
dogmatism is redeemed by his ability to see beyond his own ideas,
his willingness to admit the relative character of his conclusions.

IV

But if Eliot, in spite of the meagreness of his production, has become for his generation a leader, it is also because his career has
been a progress, because he has evidently been on his way somewhere, when many of his contemporaries, more prolific and equally
gifted, have been fixed in their hedonism or despair. The poet of
The Waste Land was too serious to continue with the same com-
placence as some of his contemporaries inhabiting that godforsaken
desert. It was certain he would not stick at that point, and one
watched him to see what he would do.

This destination has now, however, become plain. In the preface
to the new 1928 edition of *The Sacred Wood,* poetry is still regarded
as a "superior amusement," but Eliot reports on his part "an expansion or development of interests." Poetry is now perceived to have
"something to do with morals, and with religion, and even with
politics perhaps, though we cannot say what." In *For Lancelot
Andrewes,* published in the same year, Eliot declares himself a

classicist in literature, an Anglo-Catholic in religion and a royalist in politics, and announces that he has in preparation "three small books" treating to these subjects and to be called respectively "The School of Donne," "The Principles of Modern Heresy," and "The Outline of Royalism." There follows a slender selection of essays, which hint quietly at what may be expected.

We must await the further exposition of Eliot's new body of doctrine before it will be possible to discuss it properly. In the meantime, we can only applaud his desire to formulate a consistent central position, at the same time that we may regret the unpromising character of the ideals and institutions which he invokes. One cannot but recognize in Eliot's recent writings a kind of reactionary point of view which had already been becoming fashionable among certain sorts of literary people—a point of view which has much in common with that of the neo-Thomists in France and that of the Humanists in America. "Unless by civilizations," writes Eliot, "you mean material progress, cleanliness, etc. . . . if you mean a spiritual coördination on a high level, then it is doubtful whether civilization can endure without religion, and religion without a church." Yet you can hardly have an effective church without a cult of Christ as the son of God; and you cannot have such a cult without more willingness to accept the supernatural than most of us today are able to muster. We feel in contemporary writers like Eliot a desire to believe in religious revelation, a belief that it would be a good thing to believe, rather than a genuine belief. The faith of the modern convert seems to burn only with a low blue flame. "Our literature," Eliot has himself recently made a character in a dialogue say, "is a substitute for religion, and so is our religion." From such a faith, uninspired by hope, unequipped with zeal or force, what guidance for the future can we expect?

One cannot, however, doubt the reality of the experience to which Eliot testifies in his recent writings—though it seems to us less an Anglo-Catholic conversion than a reawakening of the New Englander's conscience, of the never quite exorcised conviction of the ineradicable sinfulness of man. Eliot admires Machiavelli because Machiavelli assumes the baseness of human nature as an unalterable fact; and he looks for light to the theologians who offer salvation, not through economic readjustment, political reform, education or biological and psychological study, but solely through "grace." Eliot apparently today regards "Evil" as some sort of ultimate reality, which it is impossible either to correct or to analyze. His moral principles seem to me stronger and more authentic than his religious mysticism—and his relation to the Anglo-Catholic Church appears largely artificial. The English seventeenth-century divines whose poetry and sermons he admires so much, upon whom he seems so much to depend for nourishment, exist in a richer, a more mysterious, a more heavily saturated atmosphere, in which even monumental outlines are blurred; Eliot himself is stiffer and cooler, more intent, more relentless, more clear. He has his own sort of graciousness, but he seems, as the phrase is, a little thin-lipped. His religious tradition has reached him by way of Boston.

In any case, Eliot's new phase of piety has brought with it a new humility. He apologizes in his 1928 preface for the "assumption of pontifical solemnity" which he now detects in *The Sacred Wood,* and his recent little book on Dante (a most admirable introduction) not merely surprises but almost embarrasses us by the modesty with which Eliot professes to desire nothing but to be of use to beginners and to tell us of a few of the beautiful things which he has found in the great poet. I will not say that this humility has enfeebled his poetry. The three devout little poems which he has published as Christmas cards since "The Hollow Men" announced the nadir of the phase of sterility and despair given such effective expression in *The Waste Land,* seem comparatively uninspired; but the long poem or group of poems, *Ash-Wednesday* (1930), which follows a scheme somewhat similar to that of *The Waste Land,* is a not unworthy successor to it.

The poet begins with the confession of his bankruptcy:

> Because I do not hope to turn again
> Because I do not hope
> Because I do not hope to turn
> Desiring this man's gift and that man's scope
> I no longer strive to strive towards such things

(Why should the agèd eagle stretch its wings?)
Why should I mourn
The vanished power of the usual reign? . . .

Because these wings are no longer wings to fly
But merely vans to beat the air
The air which is now thoroughly small and dry
Smaller and dryer than the will
Teach us to care and not to care
Teach us to sit still.

Pray for us sinners now and at the hour of our death
Pray for us now and at the hour of our death.

There follow passages in which the prayer is apparently answered: the poet's contrition and pious resignation are rewarded by a series of visions which first console then lighten his heart. We find an imagery new for Eliot, a symbolism semi-ecclesiastical and not without a Pre-Raphaelite flavor: white leopards, a Lady gowned in white, junipers and yews, "The Rose" and "The Garden," and jeweled unicorns drawing a gilded hearse: these are varied by an interlude which returns to the imagery and mood of *The Waste Land,* and a swirling churning anguished passage which suggests certain things of Gertrude Stein's. At last the themes of the first section recur: the impotent wings of the agèd eagle seem to revive, as,

From the wide window toward the granite shore
The white sails still fly seaward, seaward flying
Unbroken wings.
And the lost heart stiffens and rejoices
In the lost lilac and the lost sea voices
And the weak spirit quickens to rebel
For the bent golden-rod and the lost sea smell
Quickens to recover
The cry of quail and the whirling plover
And the blind eye creates
The empty forms between the ivory gates
And smell renews the salt savour of the sandy earth . . .

The broken prayer, at once childlike and mystically subtle, with which the poem ends seems to imply that the poet has come closer to the strength and revelation he craves: grace is about to descend.

> Blessèd sister, holy mother, spirit of the fountain,
>   spirit of the garden,
> Suffer us not to mock ourselves with falsehood
> Teach us to care and not to care
> Teach us to sit still
> Even among these rocks,
> Our peace in His will
> And even among these rocks
> Sister, mother
> And spirit of the river, spirit of the sea,
> Suffer me not to be separated
>
> And let my cry come unto Thee.

The literary and conventional imagery upon which *Ash-Wednesday* so largely relies and which is less vivid because more artificial than that of Eliot's earlier poems, seems to me a definite feature of inferiority; the "devil of the stairs" and the "shape twisted on the banister," which are in Eliot's familiar and unmistakable personal vein, somehow come off better than the jeweled unicorn, which incongruously suggests Yeats. And I am made a little tired at hearing Eliot, only in his early forties, present himself as an "agèd eagle" who asks why he should make the effort to stretch his wings. Yet *Ash-Wednesday,* though less brilliant and intense than Eliot at his very best, is distinguished by most of the qualities which made his other poems remarkable: the exquisite phrasing in which we feel that every word is in its place and that there is not a word too much; the metrical mastery which catches so naturally, yet with so true a modulation, the faltering accents of the supplicant, blending the cadences of the liturgy with those of perplexed brooding thought; and, above all, that "peculiar honesty" in "exhibiting the essential sickness or strength of the human soul" of which Eliot has written in connection with Blake and which, in his own case, even at the moment when his psychological plight seems most depressing and his ways of rescuing himself from it least sympathetic, still gives him a place among those upon whose words we reflect with most interest and whose tones we remember longest.

ALLEN TATE
Hart Crane

T HE career of Hart Crane will be written by future critics as a chapter in the neo-symbolist movement. A historical view of his poetry at this time would be misleading and incomplete. Like most poets of his age in America, Crane discovered Rimbaud through Eliot and the Imagists; it is certain that long before he had done any of his best work he had come to believe himself the spiritual heir of the French poet. While it is true that he mastered the symbolist use of fused metaphor, it is also true that this is a feature of all poetic language. Whether Crane's style is symbolistic, or should, in many instances like the first six or seven stanzas of "The River," be called Elizabethan, is a question that need not concern us now.

Between *The Bridge* and *Une Saison d'Enfer* there is little essential affinity. Rimbaud achieved "disorder" out of implicit order, after a deliberate cultivation of "derangement," but in our time the disintegration of our intellectual systems is accomplished. With Crane the disorder is original and fundamental. That is the special quality of his mind that belongs peculiarly to our own time. His esthetic problem, however, was more general; it was the historic problem of romanticism.

Harold Hart Crane, one of the great masters of the romantic movement, was born in Garrettsville, Ohio, on July 21, 1899. His birthplace is a small town near Cleveland, in the old Western Reserve, a region which, as distinguished from the lower portions of the state, where people from the southern up-country settled, was populated largely by New England stock. He seems to have

From *Reactionary Essays on Poetry and Ideas,* by Allen Tate. Pp. 26-42. Charles Scribner's Sons. Copyright, 1936. Reprinted by permission of the author and publishers.

known little of his ancestry, but he frequently said that his maternal forebears had given Hartford, Connecticut, its name, and that they went "back to Stratford-on-Avon"—a fiction surely, but one that gave him distinct pleasure. His formal education was slight. After the third year at high school, when he was fifteen, it ended, and he worked in his father's candy factory in Cleveland, where the family had removed in his childhood. He repeatedly told me that money had been set aside for his education at college, but that it had been used for other purposes. With the instinct of genius he read the great poets, but he never acquired an objective mastery of any literature, or even of the history of his country—a defect of considerable interest in a poet whose most ambitious work is an American epic.

In any ordinary sense Crane was not an educated man; in many respects he was an ignorant man. There is already a Crane legend, like the Poe legend—it should be fostered because it will help to make his poetry generally known—and the scholars will decide that it was a pity that so great a talent lacked early advantages. It is probable that he was incapable of the discipline of a formal classical education, and probable too that the eclectic education of his time would have scattered and killed his talent.

His poetry not only has defects of the surface, it has a defect of vision; but its great and peculiar value cannot be separated from its limitations. Its qualities are bound up with a special focus of the intellect and sensibility, and it would be foolish to wish that his mind had been better trained or differently organized.

The story of his suicide is well known. The information that I have seems authentic, but it is incomplete and subject to excessive interpretation. Toward the end of April, 1932, he embarked on the S.S. *Orizaba* bound from Vera Cruz to New York. On the night of April 26 he got into a brawl with some sailors; he was severely beaten and robbed. At noon the next day, the ship being in the Caribbean a few hours out of Havana, he rushed from his stateroom clad in pajamas and overcoat, walked through the smoking-room out onto the deck, and then the length of the ship to the stern. There without hesitation he made a perfect dive into the sea. It is said that a life-preserver was thrown to him; he either did not see it or did not want it. By the time the ship had turned back he had disappeared. Whether he forced himself down —for a moment he was seen swimming—or was seized by a shark, as the captain believed, cannot be known. After a search of thirty-five minutes his body was not found, and the *Orizaba* put back into her course.

In the summer of 1930 he had written to me that he feared his most ambitious work, *The Bridge*, was not quite perfectly "realized," that probably his soundest work was in the shorter pieces of *White Buildings*, but that his mind, being once committed to the larger undertaking, could never return to the lyrical and more limited form. He had an extraordinary insight into the foundations of his work, and I think this judgment of it will not be refuted.

From 1922 to 1928—after that year I saw him and heard from him irregularly until his death—I could observe the development of his style from poem to poem; and his letters—written always in a pure and lucid prose—provide a valuable commentary on his career. This is not the place to bring all this material together for judgment. As I look back upon his work and its relation to the life he lived, a general statement about it comes to my mind that may throw some light on the dissatisfaction that he felt with his career. It will be a judgment on the life and works of a man whom I knew for ten years as a friend.

Suicide was the sole act of will left to him short of a profound alteration of his character. I think the evidence of this is the locked-in sensibility, the insulated egoism, of his poetry—a subject I shall return to. The background of his death was dramatically perfect: a large portion of his finest imagery was of the sea, chiefly the Caribbean:

> O minstrel galleons of Carib fire,
> Bequeath us to no earthly shore until
> Is answered in the vortex of our grave
> The seal's wide spindrift gaze toward paradise.

His verse is full of splendid images of this order, a rich symbolism for an implicit pantheism that, whatever may be its intrinsic merit, he had the courage to vindicate with death in the end.

His pantheism was not passive and contemplative, it arose out of the collision between his own locked-in sensibility, and the ordinary forms of experience. Every poem is a thrust of that sensibility into the world: his defect lay in his inability to face out the moral criticism implied in the failure to impose his will upon experience.

The Bridge is presumably an epic. How early he had conceived the idea of this poem and the leading symbolism, it is difficult to know: certainly as early as February, 1923. Up to that time, with the exception of "For the Marriage of Faustus and Helen" (1922) he had written only short poems, but most of them, "Praise for an Urn," "Black Tambourine," "Paraphrase," and "Emblems of Conduct," are among his finest work. It is a mistake then to suppose that all of *White Buildings* is early experimental writing; a large portion of that volume, and perhaps the least successful part of it, is made up of poems written after *The Bridge* was begun. "Praise for an Urn" was written in the spring of 1922—one of the finest elegies by an American poet—and although his later development gave us a poetry that the period would be much the less rich for not having, he never again had such perfect mastery of his subject—because he never again knew precisely what his subject was.

Readers familiar with "For the Marriage of Faustus and Helen" admire it by passages, but the form of the poem, in its framework of symbol, is an abstraction empty of any knowable experience. It is a conventional revival of the kind of diction that a young poet picks up in his first reading. Crane, I believe, felt that this was so; and he became so dissatisfied not only with the style of the poem, which is heavily influenced by Eliot and Laforgue, but with the "literary" character of the symbolism, that he set about the greater task of writing *The Bridge*. He had looked upon his "Faustus and Helen" as an answer to the cultural pessimism of the school of Eliot, and *The Bridge* was to be an even more complete answer.

There was a fundamental mistake of Crane's diagnosis of Eliot's problem. Eliot's "pessimism" grows out of an awareness of the decay of the individual consciousness and its fixed relations to the world; but Crane thought that it was due to something like pure "orneryness," the unwillingness to "share with us the breath released," the breath being a new kind of freedom that he identified emotionally with the age of the machine. This vagueness of purpose, in spite of the apparently concrete character of the Brooklyn Bridge, which became the symbol of his epic, he never succeeded in correcting. The "bridge" stands for no well-defined experience; it differs from the Helen and Faust symbols only in its unliterary origin. I think Crane was deceived by this difference, and by the fact that Brooklyn Bridge is "modern," and a fine piece of "mechanic." His more ambitious later project permitted him no greater degree of formal structure than the more literary symbolism of his youth.

The fifteen parts of *The Bridge* taken as one poem suffer from the lack of a coherent structure, whether symbolistic or narrative: the coherence of the work consists in the personal quality of the writing—in mood, feeling, and tone. In the best passages Crane has a perfect mastery over the qualities of his style; but it lacks an objective pattern of ideas elaborate enough to carry it through an epic or heroic work. The single symbolistic image, in which the whole poem centers, is at one moment the actual Brooklyn Bridge; at another, it is any bridge or "connection"; at still another, it is a philosophical pun, and becomes the basis of a series of analogies.

In "Cape Hatteras," the aeroplane and Walt Whitman are analogous "bridges" to some transcendental truth. Because the idea is variously metaphor, symbol, and analogy, it tends to make the poem static. The poet takes it up, only to be forced to put it down again *when the poetic image of the moment is exhausted*. The idea does not, in short, fill the poet's mind; it is the starting point for a series of short flights, or inventions connected only in analogy —which explains the merely personal passages, which are obscure, and the lapses into sentimentality. For poetic sentimentality is emotion undisciplined by the structure of events or ideas of which it is ostensibly a part. The idea is not objective and articulate in itself; it lags after the poet's vision; it appears and disappears; and in the intervals Crane improvises, often beautifully, as in the flight of the aeroplane, sometimes badly, as in the passage on Whitman in the same poem.

In the great epic and philosophical works of our tradition, notably the *Divine Comedy,* the intellectual groundwork is not only simple philosophically; we not only know that the subject is personal salvation, just as we know that Crane's is the greatness of America; we are also given the complete articulation of the idea down to the slightest detail, and we are given it objectively apart from anything that the poet is going to say about it. When the poet extends his perception, there is a further extension of the ground-work ready to meet and discipline it, and compel the sensibility of the poet to stick to the subject. It is a game of chess; neither side can move without consulting the other. Crane's difficulty is that of modern poets generally: they play the game with half of the men, the men of sensibility, and because sensibility can make any move, the significance of all moves is obscure.

If we subtract from Crane's idea its periphery of sensation, we have left only the dead abstraction, the Greatness of America, which is capable of elucidation neither on the logical plane nor in the generally accepted idea of America.

The theme of *The Bridge* is, in fact, an emotional simplification of a subject-matter that Crane did not, on the plane of narrative and idea, simplify at all. The poem is emotionally homogeneous and simple—it contains a single purpose; but because it is not struc-turally clarified it is emotionally confused. America stands for a passage into new truths. Is this the meaning of American history? The poet has every right to answer yes, and this he has done. But just what in America or about America stands for this? Which American history? The historical plot of the poem, which is the groundwork on which the symbolic bridge stands, is arbitrary and broken, where the poet would have gained an over-whelming advantage by choosing a single period or episode, a concrete event with all its dramatic causes, and by following it up minutely, and being bound to it. In short, he would have gained an advantage could he have found a subject to stick to.

Does American culture afford such a subject? It probably does not. After the seventeenth century the sophisticated history of the scholars came into fashion; our popular, legendary chronicles come down to us only from the remoter European past. It was a sound impulse on Crane's part to look for an American myth, some simple version of our past that lies near the center of the American consciousness; a heroic tale with just enough symbolism to give his mind both direction and play. The soundness of his purpose is witnessed also by the kind of history in the poem: it is inaccurate, and will not at all satisfy the sticklers for historical fact. It is the history of the motion picture, of naïve patriotism. This is sound; for it ignores the scientific ideal of historical truth-in-itself, and looks for a cultural truth which might win the spontaneous allegiance of the people. It is on such simple integers of truth, not of fact but of religious necessity, that men unite. The American mind was formed by the eighteenth-century Enlightenment, which broke down the European truths, and gave us a temper deeply hostile to the making of new religious truths of our own.

The impulse in *The Bridge* is religious, but the soundness of an impulse is no warrant that it will create a sound art form. The form depends on too many factors beyond the control of the poet. The age is scientific and pseudo-scientific, and our philosophy is John Dewey's instrumentalism. And it is possibly this circumstance that has driven the religious attitude into a corner where it lacks the right instruments for its defense and growth, and where it is in a vast muddle about just what these instruments are. Perhaps this disunity of the intellect is responsible for Crane's unphilosophical belief that the poet, unaided and isolated from the people, can create a myth.

If anthropology has helped to destroy the credibility of the myths, it has shown us how they rise; their growth is mysterious from the people as a whole. It is probable that no one man ever put myth into history. It is still a nice problem among higher critics whether the authors of the Gospels were deliberate myth-makers, or whether their minds were simply constructed that way; but the evidence favors the latter. Crane was a myth-maker, and in an age favorable to myths he would have written a mythical poem in the act of writing an historical one.

It is difficult to agree with those critics who find his epic a single poem, and as such an artistic success. It is a collection of lyrics, the best of which are not surpassed by anything in American literature. The writing is most distinguished when Crane is least philosophical, *when he writes from sensation.* "The River" has some blemishes toward the end, but by and large it is a masterpiece of order and style; it alone is enough to place Crane in the front rank of American poets, living or dead. Equally good, but less ambitious are the "Proem: to Brooklyn Bridge," and "Harbor Dawn," and "The Dance" from the section called "Powhatan's Daughter."

These poems bear only the loosest relation to the symbolic demands of the theme; they contain allusions to the historical pattern or extend the slender structure of analogy running through the poem. They are primarily lyrical, and each has its complete form. The poem "Indiana," written presumably to complete the pattern of "Powhatan's Daughter," does not stand alone, and is one of the most astonishing performances ever made by a poet of Crane's genius. "The Dance" gives us the American background for the coming white man, and "Indiana" carries the stream of history to the pioneer West. It is a nightmare of sentimentality. Crane is at his most "philosophical" in a theme in which he feels no poetic interest whatever.

The structural defect of *The Bridge* is due to this functional contradiction of purpose. In one of his best earlier poems, "The Wine Menagerie," he exclaims: "New Thresholds, new Anatomies!" —new sensation, but he could not subdue the new sensation to a symbolic form.

His pantheism is necessarily a philosophy of sensation without point of view. An epic is a judgment of human action, an implied evaluation of a civilization, a way of life. In *The Bridge* the civilization that contains the subway hell of the section called "The Tunnel" is the same civilization that contains the aeroplane that the poet apostrophizes in "Cape Hatteras": there is no reason why the subway should be a fitter symbol of damnation than the aeroplane: both were produced by the same mentality on the same moral plane. There is a concealed, meaningless analogy between, on the one hand, the height of the plane and the depth of the subway, and, on the other, "higher," and "lower" in the religious sense. At one moment Crane faces his predicament of blindness to any rational order of value, and knows that he is damned; but he cannot face it long, and he tries to rest secure upon the intensity of sensation.

To the vision of the abyss in "The Tunnel," a vision that Dante passed through midway of this mortal life, Crane had no alternative: when it became too harrowing he cried to his Pocahontas, a typically romantic and sentimental symbol:

> Lie to us—dance us back our tribal morn!

It is probably the most perfect word of romanticism in this century. When Crane saw that his leading symbol, the bridge, would not hold all the material of his poem, he could not sustain it ironically, in the classical manner, by probing its defects; nor in the personal sections, like "Quaker Hill," does he include himself in his Leopardian denunciation of life. He is the blameless victim of a world whose impurity violates the moment of intensity, which would otherwise be enduring and perfect. He is betrayed, not by a defect of his own nature, but by the external world; he asks of nature, perfection—requiring only of himself, intensity. The persistent, and persistently defeated pursuit of a natural absolute places Crane at the center of his age.

Alternately he asserts the symbol of the bridge and abandons it, because fundamentally he does not understand it. The idea of bridgeship is an elaborate blur leaving the inner structure of the poem confused.

Yet some of the best poetry of our times is in *The Bridge*. Its inner confusion is a phase of the inner cross-purposes of the time. Crane was one of those men whom every age seems to select as the spokesmen of its spiritual life; they give the age away. The accidental features of their lives, their place in life, their very heredity, seem to fit them for the rôle: even their vices contribute to their preparation. Crane's biographer will have to study the early influences that confirmed him in narcissism, and thus made him typical of the rootless spiritual life of our time. The character formed by those influences represents an immense concentration, and becomes almost a symbol, of American life in this age.

Crane's poetry has incalculable moral value: it reveals our defects in their extremity. I have said that he knew little of the history of his country. It was not a mere defect in education, but a defect, in the spiritual sense, of the modern mind. Professor Charles A. Beard has immense information about American history, but understands almost none of it: Crane lacked the sort of indisputable understanding of his country that a New England farmer has who has never been out of his township. *The Bridge* attempts to include all American life, but it covers the ground with seven-league boots, and like a sightseer, sees nothing. With reference to its leading symbol, it has no subject matter. The poem is the effort of a solipsistic sensibility to locate itself in the external world, to establish points of reference.

It seems to me that by testing out his capacity to construct a great objective piece of work, in which his definition of himself should have been perfectly articulated, he brought his work to an end. I think he knew that the structure of *The Bridge* was finally incoherent, and for that reason—as I have said—he could no longer believe in even his lyrical powers; he could not return to the early work and take it up where he had left off. Far from "refuting" Eliot, his whole career is a vindication of Eliot's major premise—that the integrity of the individual consciousness has broken down. Crane had, in his later work, no individual consciousness: the hard firm style of "Praise for an Urn," which is based upon a clear-cut perception of moral relations, and upon their ultimate inviolability, begins to disappear when the poet goes out into the world and finds that the simplicity of a child's world has no universal sanction. From then on, instead of the effort to define himself in the midst of almost overwhelming complications—a situation that might have produced a tragic poet— he falls back upon the intensity of consciousness, rather than clarity, for his center of vision. And that is romanticism.

His world had no center, and the compensatory action that he took is responsible for the fragmentary quality of his most ambitious work. This action took two forms, the blind assertion of the will, and the blind desire for self-destruction. The poet did not face his first problem, which is to define the limits of his personality and to objectify its moral implications in an appropriate symbolism. Crane could only assert a quality of will against the world, and at each successive failure of the will he turned upon himself. In the failure of understanding—and understanding, for Dante, was a way of love—the romantic modern poet of the age of science attempts to impose his will upon experience and to possess the world.

It is this impulse of the modern period that has given us the greatest romantic poetry: Crane instinctively continued the conception of the will that was the deliberate discovery of Rimbaud. A poetry of the will is a poetry of sensation, for the poet surrenders to his sensations of the object in his effort to identify himself with it, and to own it. Some of Crane's finest lyrics—those written in the period of *The Bridge*—carry the modern impulse as far as you will find it anywhere in the French romantics. "Lachrymae Christi" and "Passage," though on the surface made up of pure images without philosophical meaning of the sort explicit in *The Bridge,* are the lyrical equivalents of the epic: the same kind of sensibility is at work. The implicit grasp of his material that we find in "Praise for an Urn" the poet exchanged for an external, random symbol of which there is no possibility of realization. *The Bridge* is an irrational symbol of the will, of conquest, of blind achievement in space; its obverse is "Passage," whose lack of external symbolism exhibits the poetry of the will on the plane of sensation; and this is the self-destructive return of the will upon itself.

Criticism may well set about isolating the principle upon which Crane's poetry is organized. Powerful verse overwhelms its admirers, and betrays them into more than technical imitation. That is one of the arguments of Platonism against literature; it is the immediate quality of an art rather than its whole significance that sets up schools and traditions. Crane not only ends the romantic era in his own person; he ends it logically and morally. Beyond Crane no future poet can go. (This does not mean that the romantic impulse may not rise and flourish again.) The finest passages in his work are single moments in the stream of sensation; beyond the moment he goes at peril; for outside it there lies the discrepancy between the sensuous fact, the perception, and its organizing symbol—a discrepancy that plunges him into chaos and sentimentality. A true symbol has in it, within the terms of its properties, all the qualities that the artist is able to attribute to it. But the "bridge" is empty and static, it has no inherent content, and the poet's attribution to it of the qualities of his own moral predicament is arbitrary. That explains the fragmentary and often unintelligible framework of the poem. There was neither complete action nor ordered symbolism in terms of which the distinct moments of perception could be clarified.

This was partly the problem of Rimbaud. But Crane's problem was nearer to the problem of Keats, and *The Bridge* is a failure in the sense that *Hyperion* is a failure, and with comparable magnificence. Crane's problem, being farther removed from the epic tradition, was actually more difficult than Keats', and his treatment of it was doubtless the most satisfactory possible in our time. Beyond the quest of pure sensation and its ordering symbolism lies the total destruction of art. By attempting an extreme solution of the romantic problem, Crane proved that it cannot be solved.

Ezra Pound

and as for text we have taken it
from that of Messire Laurentius
and from a codex once of the Lords Malatesta . . .

ONE is not certain who Messire Laurentius was; one is not very certain that it makes no difference. Yet one takes comfort in the vast range of Mr. Pound's obscure learning, which no one man could be expected to know much about. In this great work [1] one is continually uncertain, as to space, time, history. The codex of the Lords Malatesta would be less disconcerting than Laurentius —if we were sure it existed—for more than half of the thirty cantos contain long paraphrases or garbled quotations from the correspondence, public and private, of the Renaissance Italians, chiefly Florentine and Venetian. About a third of the lines are versified documents. Another third are classical allusions, esoteric quotations from the ancients, fragments of the Greek poets with bits of the Romans thrown in; all magnificently written into Mr. Pound's own text. The rest is contemporary—anecdotes, satirical pictures of vulgar Americans, obscene stories, evenings in low Mediterranean dives, and gossip about amazing rogues behind the scenes of European power. The three kinds of material in the cantos are antiquity, the Renaissance, and the modern world. They are combined on no principle that seems in the least consistent to a first

[1] *A Draft of XXX Cantos.* By Ezra Pound. Paris: The Hours Press. New York: Farrar and Rinehart, 1933. *XI New Cantos.* The same, 1935.

From *Reactionary Essays on Poetry and Ideas,* by Allen Tate. Pp. 43-51. Charles Scribner's Sons. Copyright, 1936. Reprinted by permission of the author and publishers.

glance. They appear to be mixed in an incoherent jumble, or to stand up in puzzling contrasts.

This is the poetry which, in early and incomplete editions, has had more influence on us than any other of our times; it has had an immense "underground" reputation. And deservedly. For even the early reader of Mr. Pound could not fail to detect the presence of a new poetic form in the individual cantos, though the full value and intention of this form appears for the first time in the complete work. It is not that there is any explicit feature of the whole design that is not contained in each canto; it is simply that Mr. Pound must be read in bulk; it is only then that the great variety of his style and the apparent incoherence turn into order and form. There is no other poetry like the *Cantos* in English. And there is none quite so simple in form. The form is, in fact, so simple that almost no one has guessed it, and I suppose it will continue to puzzle, perhaps to enrage, our more academic critics for a generation to come. But this form by virtue of its simplicity remains inviolable to critical terms: even now it cannot be technically described.

I begin to talk like Mr. Pound, or rather like the way in which most readers think Mr. Pound writes. The secret of his form is this: conversation. The cantos are talk, talk, talk; not by anyone in particular to anyone else in particular; they are just rambling talk. At least each canto is a cunningly devised imitation of a polite conversation, in which no one presses any subject very far. The length of breath, the span of conversational energy, is the length of canto. The conversationalist pauses; there is just enough left hanging in the air to give him a new start; so that the transitions between the cantos are natural and easy.

Each canto has the broken flow and the somewhat elusive climax of a good monologue: because there is no single speaker, it is a many-voiced monologue. That is the method of the poems—though there is another quality of the form that I must postpone for a moment—and *that is what the poems are about.*

There are, as I have said, three subjects of conversation—ancient times, Renaissance Italy, and the present—but these are not what

the cantos are about. They are not about Italy, nor about Greece,
nor are they about us. They are not about anything. But they
are distinguished poetry. Mr. Pound himself tells us:

> And they want to know what we talked about?
>   *"de litteris et de armis, praestantibus ingeniis,*
> Both of ancient times and our own; books, arms,
> And men of unusual genius
> Both of ancient times and our own, in short the usual subjects
> Of conversation between intelligent men."

II

There is nothing in the cantos more difficult than that. There is
nothing inherently obscure; nothing too profound for any reader
who has enough information to get to the background of all the
allusions in a learned conversation. But there is something that
no reader, short of some years of hard textual study, will understand. This is the very heart of the cantos, the secret of Mr.
Pound's poetic character, which will only gradually emerge from
a detailed analysis of every passage. And this is no more than our
friends are constantly demanding of us; we hear them talk, and
we return to hear them talk, and we return to hear them again,
but we never know what they talk about; we return for that mysterious quality of charm that has no rational meaning that we can
define. It is only after a long time that the order, the direction,
the rhythm of the talker's mind, the logic of his character as distinguished from anything logical he may say—it is a long time
before this begins to take on form for us. So with Mr. Pound's
cantos. It is doubtless easier for us (who are trained in the more
historic brands of poetry) when the poems are about God, Freedom, and Immortality, but there is no reason why poetry should
not be so perplexingly simple as Mr. Pound's, and be about nothing at all.

The ostensible subjects of the cantos—ancient, middle, and modern
times—are only the materials round which Mr. Pound's mind

plays constantly; they are the screen upon which he throws a beautiful, flowing quality of poetic thought. Now in conversation
the memorable quality is a sheer accident of character, and is not
designed; but in the cantos the effect is deliberate, and from the
first canto to the thirtieth the set tone is maintained without a single
lapse.

It is this tone, it is this quality quite simply, which is the meaning of the cantos, and although, as I have said, it is simple
and direct, it is just as hard to pin down, it is as hidden in its
shifting details, as a running, ever-changing conversation. It
cannot be taken out of the text; and yet the special way that Mr.
Pound has of weaving his three materials together, of emphasiz-
ing them, of comparing and contrasting them, gives us a clue to
the leading intention of the poems. I come to that quality of
the form which I postponed.

The easiest interpretation of all poetry is the symbolic method:
there are few poems that cannot be paraphrased into a kind of symbolism, which is usually false, being by no means the chief intention of the poet. It is very probable, therefore, that I am about
to falsify the true simplicity of the cantos into a simplicity that is
merely convenient and spurious. The reader must bear this in
mind, and view the slender symbolism that I am going to read into
the cantos as a critical shorthand, useful perhaps, but which when
used must be dropped.

One of the finest cantos is properly the first. It describes a
voyage:

> And then went down to the ship,
> Set keel to breakers, forth on the godly sea, and
> We set up mast and sail on that swart ship,
> Bore sheep aboard her, and our bodies also
> Heavy with weeping, and winds from sternward
> Bore us out onward with bellying canvas,
> Circe's this craft, the trim-coifed goddess.

They land, having come "to the place aforesaid by Circe"—whatever place it may be—and Tiresias appears, who says:

"Odysseus
Shalt return through spiteful Neptune, over dark seas,
Lose all companions." And then Anticlea came.
Lie quiet Divus. I mean, that is, Andreas Divus,
In officina Wecheli, 1538, out of Homer.
And he sailed, by Sirens and thence outward and away
And unto Circe.

Mr. Pound's world is the scene of a great Odyssey, and everywhere he lands it is the shore of Circe, where men "lose all companions" and are turned into swine. It would not do at all to
push this hint too far, but I will risk one further point: Mr.
Pound is a typically modern, rootless, and internationalized intelligence. In the place of the traditional supernaturalism of the older
and local cultures, he has a cosmopolitan curiosity which seeks out
marvels, which are all equally marvelous, whether it be a Greek
myth or the antics in Europe of a lady from Kansas. He has the
bright, cosmopolitan *savoir faire* which refuses to be "taken in":
he will not believe, being a traditionalist at bottom, that the "perverts, who have set money-lust before the pleasures of the senses,"
are better than swine. And ironically, being modern and a hater
of modernity, he sees all history as deformed by the trim-coifed
goddess.

The cantos are a book of marvels—marvels that he has read
about, or heard of, or seen; there are Greek myths, tales of Italian
feuds, meetings with strange people, rumors of intrigues of state,
memories of remarkable dead friends like T. E. Hulme, comments on philosophical problems, harangues on abuses of the age;
the "usual subjects of conversation between intelligent men."

It is all fragmentary. Now nearly every canto begins with a
bit of heroic antiquity, some myth, or classical quotation, or a
lovely piece of lyrical description in a grand style. It invariably
breaks down. It trails off into a piece of contemporary satire,
or a flat narrative of the rascality of some Italian prince. This
is the special quality of Mr. Pound's form, the essence of his talk,
the direction of these magnificent conversations.

For not once does Mr. Pound give himself up to any single

story or myth. The thin symbolism from the Circe myth is hardly
more than a leading tone, an unconscious prejudice about men
which he is not willing to indicate beyond the barest outline. He
cannot believe in any of them, not even in his own power of
imagining them out to a conclusion. None of his myths is compelling enough to draw out his total intellectual resources; none
goes far enough to become a belief or even a momentary faith.
They remain marvels to be looked at, but they are meaningless,
the wrecks of civilization. His powerful juxtapositions of the
ancient, the Renaissance, and the modern worlds reduce all three
elements to an unhistorical miscellany, timeless and without origin,
and no longer a force in the lives of men.

III

And that is the peculiarly modern quality of Mr. Pound. There
is a certain likeness in this to another book of marvels, those stories
of late antiquity known to us as *The Golden Ass*. The cantos
are a sort of *Golden Ass*. There is a likeness, but there is no
parallel beyond the mere historical one: both books are the production of worlds without convictions and given over to a hard
secular program. Here the similarity ends. For Mr. Pound is
a powerful reactionary, a faithful mind devoted to those ages when
the myths were not merely pretty, but true. And there is a cloud
of melancholy irony hanging over the cantos. He is persuaded
that the myths are only beautiful, and he drops them after a
glimpse, but he is not reconciled to this estheticism: he ironically
puts the myths against the ugly specimens of modern life that
have defeated them. But neither are the specimens of modernity
worthy of the dignity of belief:

> She held that a sonnet was a sonnet
> And ought never to be destroyed
> And had taken a number of courses
> And continued with hope of degrees and
> Ended in a Baptist learnery
>   Somewhere near the Rio Grande.

I am not certain that Mr. Pound will agree with me that he is a traditionalist; nor am I convinced that Mr. Pound, for his part, is certain of anything under heaven but his genius for poetry. He is probably one of two or three living Americans who will be remembered as poets of the first order. Yet there is no reason to infer from that that Mr. Pound, outside his craft, or outside his conversation, knows in the least what he is doing or saying. He is and always has been in a muddle of revolution; and for some appalling reason he identifies his crusade with liberty—liberty of speech, liberty of press, liberty of conduct—in short, liberty. I do not mean to say that either Mr. Pound or his critic knows what liberty is. Nevertheless, Mr. Pound identifies it with civilization and intelligence, of the modern and scientific variety. And yet the ancient cultures, which he so much admires, were, from any modern viewpoint, hatched in barbarism and superstition. One is entitled to the suspicion that Mr. Pound prefers barbarism, and that by taking up the rôle of revolution against it he has bitten off his nose to spite his face. He is the confirmed enemy of provincialism, never suspecting that his favorite, Lorenzo the Magnificent, for example, was provincial to the roots of his hair.

This confusion runs through the cantos, and it makes the irony that I have spoken of to a certain extent unconscious. For as the apostle of humane culture, he constantly discredits it by crying up a rationalistic enlightenment. It would appear from this that his philosophical tact is somewhat feminine, and that, as intelligence, it does not exist. His poetic intelligence is of the finest: and if he doesn't know what liberty is, he understands poetry, and how to write it. This is enough for one man to know. And the thirty *Cantos* are enough to occupy a loving and ceaseless study—say a canto a year for thirty years, all thirty to be read every few weeks just for the tone.

MARIANNE MOORE

Henry James As a Characteristic American

To say that "the superlative American" and the characteristic American are not the same thing perhaps defrauds anticipation, yet one must admit that it is not in the accepted sense that Henry James was a big man and did things in a big way. But he possessed the instinct to amass and reiterate, and is the rediscerned Small Boy who had from the first seen Europe as a verification of what in its native surroundings his "supersensitive nostril" fitfully detected and liked. Often he is those elements in American life —as locality and as character—which he recurrently studied and to which he never tired of assigning a meaning.

Underlying any variant of Americanism in Henry James' work, is the doctrine, embodied as advice to Christopher Newman, "Don't try to be anyone else"; if you triumph, "let it then be all you." The native Madame de Mauves says to Euphemia, "You seem to me so all of a piece that I am afraid that if I advise you, I shall spoil you," and Hawthorne was dear to Henry James because he "proved to what a use American matter could be put by an American hand. . . . An American could be an artist, one of the finest, without 'going outside' about it . . . quite, in fact, as if Hawthorne had become one just by being American enough."

An air of rurality as of Moses Primrose at the fair struck Henry James in his compatriots, and a garment worn in his childhood revealed "that we were somehow queer." Thackeray, he says, "though he laid on my shoulder the hand of benevolence, bent on my native costume the spectacles of wonder." On his return from Europe he marveled at the hats men wore, but it is hard to be certain that the knowledge-seeking American in Europe is quite so

From *The Hound and Horn*, VII, pp. 363-372. April, 1934. Reprinted by permission.

unconsciously a bumpkin as Henry James depicts him. When Newman has said, "I began to earn my living when I was almost a baby," and Madame de Bellegarde says, "You began to earn your living in the cradle?" the retort, "Well, madam, I'm not absolutely convinced I had a cradle," savors of the connoisseur. Since, however, it is over-difficult for Henry James in portrayals of us, not to be portraying himself, there is even in the rendering of the callow American, a sharpness and tightening of the consciousness that threaten the integrity of the immaturity.

"I am not a scoffer," the fellow-countryman says to Theobald, the American painter, and if with Henry James it were a question either of being guarded or ridiculous, he would prefer to seem ridiculous. His respectful humility toward emotion is socially brave, and in diffidence, reserve, and strong feeling, he reminds one of Whittier, another literary bachelor whom the most ardent sadist has not been able to soil. We remember his sense of responsibility for the United States during the World War and that in *Notes of a Son and Brother* he says of the Civil War, "The drama of the War . . . had become a habit for us without ceasing to be a strain. I am sure I thought more things under that head . . . than I thought in all connections together." What is said in the same book of the death of Mary Temple, the cousin who so greatly "had a sense for verity of character and play of life in others," is an instance of reverent, and almost reverend, feeling that would defend him against the charge of lightness in anything, if ever one were inclined to make it. It is not the artist, but the responsibility for living and for family, that wonders here about death and has about "those we have seen beaten, this sense that it was not for nothing they missed the ampler experience . . . since dire as their defeat may have been, we don't see them . . . at peace with victory." Things for Henry James glow, flush, glimmer, vibrate, shine, hum, bristle, reverberate. Joy, bliss, ecstasies, intoxication, a sense of trembling in every limb, the heartshaking first glimpse, a hanging on the prolonged silence of an editor; and as a child at Mr. Burton's small theatre in Chambers Street, his wondering not if the curtain would rise but "if one could exist till then"; the bonfires of his imagination, his pleasure in "the tender sea-green" or "rustling rose-color" of a seriously best dress, are too live to countenance his fear that he was giving us "an inch of canvas and an acre of embroidery."

Idealism which was willing to make sacrifices for its self-preservation, is always an element in the conjuring-wand of Henry James. The fear of profanation is apparent in a remark in connection with the later America, that he felt "like one who has seen a ghost in his safe old house." Of "Independence Hall . . . and its dignity not to be uttered . . . halls and spreading staircase and long-drawn upper gallery . . . one of those rare precincts of the past against which the present has kept beating in vain," he says, "nothing . . . would induce me to revisit . . . the object I so fondly evoke." He would not risk disturbing his recollection of *The Wonder-Book* and *Tanglewood Tales* by reading them over, and Dickens "always remained better than the taste of over-hauling him." The value of the thing is more than the thing. New Hampshire in September was "so delicately Arcadian, like . . . an old legend, an old love-story in fifteen volumes," and "Newport . . . the dainty isle of Aquidneck" and "its perpetually embayed promontories of mossy rock," had "ingenuous old-time distinction . . . too latent and too modest for notation." Exasperated by the later superficiality of New York's determination "to blight the superstition of rest," he terms the Public Libraries "mast-heads on which spent birds sometimes alight in the expanses of ocean" and thought Washington Irving's Sunnyside with its "deep, long lane, winding, embanked, over-arched, such an old-world lane as one scarce ever meets in America . . . easy for everything but rushing about and being rushed at." The "fatal and sacred" enjoyment of England "buried in the soil of our primary culture" leads him to regard London as "the great distributing heart of our traditional life"; to say of Oxford, "no other spot in Europe extorts from our barbarous hearts so passionate an admiration"; and for the two Americans in "hedgy Worcestershire" beneath an "English sky bursting into a storm of light or melting into a drizzle of silver . . . nothing was wanting; the shaggy, mouse-colored donkey, nosing the turf . . . the towering ploughman with his white smock-frock, puckered on chest and back." "We greeted these things," says the narrator, "as children greet the loved pictures in a story-book, lost and mourned and found again . . . a gray, gray tower, a huge black yew, a cluster of village graves, with crooked headstones . . . My companion was overcome. . . . How it makes a Sunday where it stands!"

Henry James' warmth is clearly of our doting native variety. "Europe had been romantic years before, because she was different from America," he says; "wherefore América would now be romantic because she was different from Europe." His imagination had always included Europe; he had not been alienated by travel nor changed by any "love-philtre or fear-philtre" intenser than those he had received in New York, Newport, or our American Cambridge. "Culture, as I hold, is a matter of attitude quite as much as of opportunity," he says in *Notes of a Son and Brother,* and "one's supreme relation, as one had always put it, was one's relation to one's country." In alluding to "our barbarous hearts" he had, of course, no thought of being taken at his word—any more than Mrs. Cleve did when abusing America, and he is delineating grossness in Baron de Mauves who "seemed to regard the New World as a colossal *plaisanterie."* It entertained James to describe Mrs. Gereth as aristocratically British and clannishly dowdy when she went to Church;—as it pleased him to recall "a contemporary cousin" who "was with her stature and shape the finest possible person to carry clothes," and even in the disillusions attendant upon return to this country, he betrays a parentally local satisfaction in the American girl's fitness of costume.

Nationally and internationally "the sensitive citizen," he felt that patriotism was a matter of knowing a country by perceiving the clue. Our understanding of human relations has grown—more perhaps than we realize in the last twenty years; and when Henry James disappoints us, by retaining the Northerner's feeling about the Confederate, we must not make him directly contemporary, any more than we dispute his spelling peanut with a hyphen. He had had no proximity with the South and all that the bother-

taking Henry James needed for doing justice to feeling, was opportunity to feel. "Great things . . . have been done by solitary workers," he says, "but with double the pains they would have cost if
they had been produced in more genial circumstances." Education for him, in a large sense, was conversation. Speaking of
Cambridge, he says,

When the Norton woods, nearby, massed themselves in scarlet and
orange, and when to penetrate and mount a stair and knock at a
door, and enjoying response, then sink into a window-bench and in-
hale at once the vague golden November and the thick suggestion of
the room where nascent "thought" had again and again piped or wailed,
was to taste as I had never done before, the poetry of the prime initiation and of associated growth.

We observe in the memoirs treasured American types: "silent
Vanderpool . . . incorruptibly and exquisitely dumb" was "looked
so as if he came from 'good people' . . . the very finest flower of
shyness . . . a true welter of modesty, not a grain of it anything
stiffer—"; "the ardent and delicate and firm John May"—student
at Harvard; and there was Robert Temple—a cousin "with a mind
almost elegantly impudent . . . as if we had owed him to Thackeray"; and Mary Temple, " 'natural' to an effect of perfect felicity
. . . all straightness and charming tossed head, with long light
and yet almost sliding steps and a large light postponing laugh."
There was a "a widowed grandmother who dispensed an hospitality seemingly as joyless as it was certainly boundless" and
Uncle Albert, a kinsman who was " 'Mr.' to his own wife—
. . . his hair bristling up almost in short-horn fashion at the
sides," with "long, slightly equine countenance, his eyebrows ever
elevated as in the curiosity of alarm."

To say that a child was a student of "history and custom . . .
manners and types" would be saying too much, but to say that
Henry James as a child was "a-throb" with the instinct for meanings, barely suggests that formidable paraphernalia which he was
even then gathering. It is in "the waste of time, of passion, of
curiosity, of contact—that true initiation resides," he said later; and

no scene, strange accent, no adventure—experienced or vicarious—
was irrelevant. The elder Henry James alludes to "the maidenly letters" of Emerson but Emerson in New York was strange and wonderful to Henry James, the child invited "to draw near to him, off
the hearth-rug." He was "an apparition sinuously and elegantly
slim . . . commanding a tone alien to any we heard around about";
and the school-master Louis De Coppet, in "his French treatment of
certain of our native local names, Ohio and Iowa for instance,
which he rendered . . . O-ee-oh and Ee-o-wah . . . opened vistas."
"There hung about the Wards, to my sense, that atmosphere
of apples and nuts . . . and jack-knives and 'squrruls,' of domestic
Bible-reading and attendance at 'evening lecture,' of the fear of
parental discipline and the cultivated art of dodging it, combined
with great personal toughness and hardihood"; and there was
" 'Stiffy' Norcom . . . whom we supposed gorgeous . . . (Divided
I was, I recall, between the dread and the glory of being so greeted,
'Well, Stiffy—!' as a penalty for the least attempt at personal adorn-
ment.)"

"You cannot make a man feel low," his Christopher Newman
says, "unless you can make him feel base," and "a good conscience"
is a pebble with which Henry James is extremely fond of arming his
Davids. Longmore's "truthtelling eyes" are that in him which puzzled and tormented the Baron. "They judged him, they mocked him,
they eluded him, they threatened him, they triumphed over him, they
treated him as no pair of eyes had ever treated him." In every photograph of Henry James that we have, the thing that arrests one is a
kind of terrible truthfulness. We feel also, in the letters and memoirs, that "almost indescribable naturalness" which seemed to him as
behavior, expressive of his Albany relatives; a naturalness which
disappears in the fancy writing of his imitators. If good-nature
and reciprocity are American traits, Henry James was a characteristic American—too much one when he patiently suffered unsuitable persons to write to him, call on him, and give him their
"work." Politeness in him was "more than a form of luxurious
egotism" and is in keeping with the self-effacement of his determination to remain a devotee of devotees to George Eliot "for

his own wanton joy" though unwittingly requested to "take away please, away, away!" two books he had written. Mrs. Greville had lent the books as introductory, previous to her calling with Henry James at the Leweses, but no connection had been noticed between books and visitor. The same characteristic appears in the account of his meeting with Dickens. He speaks of "the extremely hand- some face . . . . which met my dumb homage with a straight in- scrutability. . . . It hadn't been the least important that we should have shaken hands or exchanged platitudes . . . It was as if I had carried off my strange treasure just exactly from under the merciless military eye—placed there on guard of the secret. All of which I recount for illustration of the force of action, unless I call it pas- sion, that may reside in a single pulse of time."

Henry James belonged to "the race which has the credit of know- ing best, at home and abroad, how to make itself comfortable" but there was in him an ascetic strain which causes him to make Longmore think with disgust of the Baron's friend who "filled the air with the odor of heliotrope"; and Eugene Pickering's Ameri- can friend found "something painful in the spectacle of absolute inthralment, even to an excellent cause." Freedom; yes. The con- fidant, in comparing himself compassionately with the Eugene of their schooldays says, "I could go out to play alone, I could button my jacket myself, and sit up till I was sleepy." Yet the I of the original had not "been exposed on breezy uplands under the she- wolf of competition" and there was not about him "the impertinent odor of trade." Some persons have grudged Henry James his free- dom and have called it leisure; but as Theobald, the American painter, said of art, "If we work for ourselves, of course we must hurry. If we work for her, we must often pause." James says of *The Tragic Muse* in a letter, "I took long and patient and care- ful trouble which no creature will recognize"; and we may de- clare of him as he did of John La Farge, "one was . . . never to have seen a subtler mind or a more generously wasteful passion, in other words a sincerer one." Reverting to the past of his own life, he is over-powered by "the personal image unextinct" and says,

"It presents itself, I feel, beyond reason and yet if I turn from it the ease is less."

There was in him "the rapture of observation" but more unequivocally even than that, affection for family and country. "I was to live to go back with wonder and admiration," he says, "to the quantity of secreted thought in our daily medium, the quality of intellectual passion, the force of cogitation and aspiration, as to the explanation both of a thousand surface incoherences and a thousand felt felicities." Family was the setting for his country and the town was all but synonymous with family; as would appear in what is said of "the family-party smallness of old New York, those happy limits that could make us all care . . . for the same thing at once." It "is always a matter of winter twilight, fire-light, lamplight." "We were surely all gentle and generous together, floating in such a clean light social order, sweetly proof against ennui." "The social scheme, as we knew it, was, in its careless charity, worthy of the golden age— . . . the fruits dropped right upon the board to which we flocked together, the least of us and the greatest"; "our parents . . . never caring much for things we couldn't care for and generally holding that what was good to them would be also good for their children." A father is a safe symbol of patriotism when one can remember him as "genially alert and expert"—when " 'human fellowship' " is "the expression that was perhaps oftenest on his lips and his pen." "We need never fear not to be good enough," Henry James says, "if only we were social enough . . . and he recalls his mother as so participatingly unremote that he can say, "I think we almost contested her being separate enough to be proud of ourselves." Love is the thing more written about than anything else, and in the mistaken sense of greed. Henry James seems to have been haunted by awareness that rapacity destroys what it is successful in securing. He feels a need "to see the other side as well as his own, to feel what his adversary feels"; to be an American is not for him "just to glow belligerently with one's country." Some complain of his transferred citizenship as a loss; but when we consider the trend of his fiction and his uncomplacent denouements, we have no tremor about proving him to have been an American. What we scarcely dare ask is, how many Americans are there who can be included with him in his Americanism? Family affection is the fire that burned within him and America was the hearth on which it burned. He thinks of the American as "intrinsically and actively ample, . . . reaching westward, southward, anywhere, everywhere," with a mind "incapable of the shut door in any direction."

The Poetry of Wallace Stevens

For some of us, Wallace Stevens [1] is America's chief conjuror—as bold a virtuoso and one with as cunning a rhetoric as we have produced. He has, naturally, in some quarters been rebuked for his skill; writers cannot excel at their work without being, like the dogs in *Coriolanus,* "as often beat for barking As therefore kept to do so." But for healthy seductiveness, like the patterned correspondences in Handel's Sonata No. 1, he has not been rivaled:

> The body dies; the body's beauty lives.
> So evenings die in their green going,
> A wave, interminably flowing.

His repercussive harmonics, set off by the small compass of the poem, "prove" mathematically to admiration, and suggest a linguist creating several languages within a single language. The plaster temporariness of subterfuge is, he says,

> Like a word in the mind that sticks at artichoke
> And remains inarticulate.

[1] *Harmonium,* by Wallace Stevens. Alfred A. Knopf, 1923. *Ideas of Order,* by Wallace Stevens. Alfred A. Knopf, 1936. *Owl's Clover,* by Wallace Stevens. Alcestis Press, 1936.

From *Poetry: A Magazine of Verse,* XLIX, pp. 268-273. February, 1937. Reprinted by permission.

And besides the multiplying of *h*'s, a characteristically ironic use of scale should be noted, in "Bantams in Pine Woods":

> Chief Iffucan of Azcan in caftan
> Of tan with henna hackles, halt!

The playfulness, that is to say humor, of such rhymings as *egress* and *negress, Scaramouche* and *barouche,* is just right, and by no means a joke; one's sense of humor being a clue to the most serious part of one's nature. But best of all, the bravura. Upon the general marine volume of statement is set a parachute-spinnaker of verbiage which looms out like half a cantaloupe and gives the body of the theme the air of a fabled argosy advancing.

A harmonist need not be proud of dominating us illusorily, by causing a flower in bloom to appear where a moment before there was none; and not infrequently Wallace Stevens' "noble accents and lucid, inescapable rhythms" point to the universal parent, Shakespeare. A novice of verse, required in an examination to attribute to author or century the line, "These choirs of welcome choir for me farewell," might pay Wallace Stevens a high compliment.

> Remember how the crickets came
> Out of their mother grass, like little kin,

has perfectly Shakespeare's miniature effect of innocent sadness, and the consciously pertinaciously following of a word through several lines, as where we see the leaves

> Turning in the wind,
> Turning as the flames
> Turned in the fire,

are cousin to the pun of Elizabethan drama. We feel, in the tentatively detached method of implication, the influence of Plato; and an awareness of if not the influence of T. S. Eliot. Better say that each has influenced the other; with "Sunday Morning" and the Prufrocklike lines in "Le Monocle de Mon Oncle" in mind,

Shall I uncrumple this much crumpled thing?

·   ·   ·   ·   ·

For it has come that thus I greet the spring

and the Peter Quince-like rhythmic contour of T. S. Eliot's "La
Figlia Que Piange." As if it were Antipholus of Ephesus and
Antipholus of Syracuse, each has an almost too acute concept of
"the revenge of music"; a realization that the seducer is the seduced;
and a smiling, strict, Voltaire-like, straight-seeing, self-directed humor which triumphs in its pain. Each is engaged in a similar
though differently expressed search for that which will endure.

We are able here to see the salutary effect of insisting that a piece
of writing please the writer himself before it pleases anyone else;
and how a poet may be a wall of incorruptibleness against any con-
cessive violating of the essential aura of contributory vagueness.
Such tense heights of the romantic are intimated by mere titles, that
one might hesitate to make trial of the content lest it seem bathos,
but Wallace Stevens is a delicate apothecary of savors and precipi-
tates, and no hauteurs are violated. His method of hints and dis-
guises should have Mercury as their patron divinity, for in the guise
of "a dark rabbi," an ogre, a traveler, a comedian, an old woman,
he deceives us as the god misled the aged couple in the myth.

Again, and moreover, to manner and harmonics is added a fine
and exultant grasp of beauty—a veritable refuge of "blessed mornings, meet for the eye of the young alligator"; an equivalence for
jungle beauty, arctic beauty, marine beauty, meridian, hothouse,
consciously urban or unconsciously natural beauty—which might be
alarming were it not for the persistent foil of dissatisfaction with
matter. This frugally unified opulence, epitomized by the "green
vine angering for life"—in *Owl's Clover* by the thought of plun-
dered harassed Africa, "the Greenest Continent" where "memory
moves on leopard's feet"—has been perfected stroke by stroke, since
the period of "the magenta Judas-tree," "the indigo glass in the
grass," "oceans in obsidian," the white of "frogs," of "clays," and in
"withered reeds"; until now, tropic pinks and yellows, avocado and
Kuniyoshi cabouchon emerald-greens, the blent but violent excel-

lence of ailanthus silk-moths and metallic breast-feathers—as open and unpretending as Rousseau's Snake-Charmer and Sleeping Gipsy—combine in an impression of incandescence like that of the night-blooming cereus.

Despite this awareness of the world of sense—which at some points, to a prudish asceticism approximates wickedness—one notices the frequent recurrence of the word heaven. In each clime which the author visits and under each disguise, it is the dilemma of tested hope which confronts him. In *Owl's Clover* "the search for a tranquil belief," and the protest against the actualities of experience, become a protest against the death of world hope; against the unorder and chaos of this "age of concentric mobs." Those who dare to forget that "As the man the state, not as the state the man," who divert "the dream of heaven from heaven to the future, as a god," are indeed the carnivorous owl with African greenness for its repast. The land of "ploughmen, peacocks, doves," of "Leonardo," has been "Combating bushmen for a patch of gourds, Loosing black slaves to make black infantry"; "the widow of Madrid Weeps in Segovia"; in Moscow, in all Europe, "Always everything That is dead except what ought to be"; aeroplanes which counterfeit "the bee's drone" and have the powers of "the scorpion" are our "seraphim." Mr. Stevens' book is the sable requiem for all this. But requiem is not the word when anyone hates lust for power and ignorance of power, as the author of this book does. So long as we are ashamed of the ironic feast, and of our marble victories—horses or men—which will break unless they are first broken by us, there is hope for the world. As R. P. Blackmur has said, "the poems rise in the mind like a tide." They embody hope, that in being frustrated becomes fortitude; and they prove to us that the testament to emotion is not volubility. It is remarkable that a refusal to speak should result in such eloquence and that an implied heaven could be made so definite. Unanimity of word and rhythm has been attained, and we have the seldom exhilaration of knowing that America has in Wallace Stevens at least one artist whom professionalism will never demolish.

YVOR WINTERS

Traditional Mastery: The Lyrics of Robert Bridges

THE latest edition of the lyrics of Bridges [1] represents a selection, sanctioned by himself before his death, and not a complete edition. It omits "Prometheus," "Demeter," "Eros and Psyche," and "The Growth of Love," which were contained in the *Poetical Works* (Oxford, 1914) and contains a very restricted and, but for the omission of the epigram, *Who goes there,* a wholly satisfactory selection from two small volumes published subsequently to the *Poetical Works.* It contains the first fifteen only of the *Later Poems* (*Poetical Works*), omitting the Odes. The omissions represent no serious loss, I suspect, barring the epigram I have already mentioned and a few of the sonnets from *The Growth of Love,* especially number fifty-one, which described so beautifully the poetical quality that Bridges was to realize in his greatest work:

> O my uncared-for songs, what are ye worth,
> That in my secret book with so much care
> I write you, this one here and that one there,
> Marking the time and order of your birth?
> How, with a fancy so unkind to mirth,
> A sense so hard, a style so worn and bare,
> Look ye for any welcome anywhere
> From any shelf or heart-home on the earth?

Bridges' meters have been so often and so fruitlessly discussed that I shall omit entirely to analyze them, though his importance as a subtle and learned renovator of English meters is sufficiently great.

[1] *The Shorter Poems of Robert Bridges.* Oxford University Press. 1931.

From *The Hound and Horn,* V, pp. 321-8. January, 1932. Reprinted by permission. Portions of the material in this and the following essay have been adapted to the discussion of modern poetry in Mr. Winters' recent volume, *Primitivism and Decadence* (Arrow Editions, New York. 1937).

It is my belief that he has been long enough patronized as a sugar-coated pill for those who wish to brush up on their metrics, as a minor manipulator of outworn graces, and that he should be recognized once and for all as the sole English rival of Hardy in nineteenth-century poetry, as in all likelihood, considering his formal versatility, the range of his feeling, and the purity of his diction, a diction so free from any trace of personal idiosyncrasy that a successful imitator of it could never be detected as an imitator but would appear only as that most unlikely of phenomena, a rival, that he should, I say, in all likelihood be recognized as the most valuable model of poetic style to appear in the language since Dryden.

Since Dr. Bridges has never been popular, especially in America, I shall risk a very roughly classified list of the poems on which I base my opinion, all of them to be found in the present collection. Short lyrics, first level: *Wherefore tonight so full of care, The birds that sing on autumn eves, Love not too much, The north wind came up, Why hast thou nothing, The south wind strengthens to a gale, As our car rustled swiftly, How should I be to love unjust, Beautiful must be the mountains, Whither O splendid ship.* Short lyrics, second level: *Clear and gentle stream, The wood is bare, Poor withered rose, O bold majestic downs, Again with pleasant green, Behold! the radiant spring, Perfect little body, My bed and pillow are cold, The hillpines were sighing, April advance in play, The sea keeps not the Sabbath day, Will love again awake.* Longer lyrics at a slow tempo, first level: *Sad sombre place, Joy, sweetest life-born joy, How well my eyes remember the dim path;* second level: *Voyaging northward.* There are in addition two fine epigrams in this volume, *Mazing around my mind,* and *Askest thou of these graves;* there are several fine occasional sonnets at least two of which, *Beloved of all to whom that Muse is dear,* and *Folk alien to the Muse,* would cast no discredit on Milton; there are two admirable didactic poems of some length, *Thou art a poet, Robbie Burns,* and *Je donnerais pour revivre a vingt ans,* of which the second deserves a place very nearly at its author's first level achievement; and there is a formal ode, *Assemble all ye maidens,* no whit inferior, I suspect, to Dryden's "Ode on the death of Mistress Anne Killigrew."

Bridges possessed much more curiosity about the possibilities of various forms than has been shown by most of our modern experimenters. Mr. Pound, Dr. Williams, and Miss Moore, for example, have all worked in a straight line, as if impelled by some more or less fanatical dogma, toward a certain form or tempo, and, having once perfected it, have become slaves to it. Miss Moore, indeed, seems to have exhausted the possibilities of her style and to have abandoned writing; even Mr. Stevens writes, or at least publishes, less and less;[1] and Mr. Pound appears to have entered upon "the old age of a watery realist," indulging in looser and looser repetitions of cadences and mannerisms in Canto after Canto. In fact, some of his recent Cantos are scarcely more coherent than his correspondence. Bridges seems to have been fully aware that a change of tempo involves a complete or nearly complete change in the range of feeling perceived, that it opens up, in other words, a fresh field of subject matter; if one follows his career step by step one finds him taking up one tempo after another, exhausting its possibilities (for himself), and dropping each, once he has thoroughly mastered it and before it has mastered him.

The longer and slower lyrics should be approached only after the shorter have been studied, since in the shorter pieces the diction is more concentrated, less consciously toned down, and the quality of the style is more immediately apparent. I quote three stanzas from a fairly early poem entitled "Dejection":

> Wherefore tonight so full of care,
> My soul, revolving hopeless strife,
> Pointing at hindrance, and the bare
> Painful escapes of fitful life?
>
> Shaping the doom that may befall
> By precedent of terror past:

[1] Since this was written in 1932 Miss Moore and Mr. Stevens have resumed publication and each has issued two new books.

> By love dishonoured, and the call
> Of friendship slighted at the last?
>
> By treasured names, the little store
> That memory out of wreck could save
> Of loving hearts that gone before
> Call their old comrade to the grave?

Compare the above lines to the following, from one of the latest lyrics, "Low Barometer":

> The south-wind strengthens to a gale,
> Across the moon the clouds fly fast,
> The house is smitten as with a flail,
> The chimney shudders to the blast.
>
> On such a night, when air has loosed
> Its guardian grasp on blood and brain,
> Old terrors then of god or ghost
> Creep from their caves to life again. . . .
>
> Unbodied presences, the packed
> Pollution and remorse of Time,
> Slipp'd from oblivion, reenact
> The horrors of unhouseled crime.

The quality of language over the gap of time is constant. In restraint, economy, richness of feeling, in what I should call an extreme generality or universality of import accomplished with no loss in the specification of the perception, these poems and a few others in the volume will stand the most scrutinizing comparison, I believe, with any of Shakespeare's sonnets. No living poet is capable of such masterly writing, and the number of poets dead is very small.

In his longer and more meditative lyrics, Bridges achieved a poetry, the norm of which is scarcely more intense than the norm of distinguished prose, but which, thanks to the quality of its diction, syntax and cadence, never falls short of extreme distinction, and which rises at need and without shock from distinction to extraordinary beauty. Poetry of this sort is not inferior to poetry of the shorter and more lyrical sort, though it may be harder to appreciate and is certainly less popular at the present time. It can handle material impossible in the more specialized lyric: what it loses in concentration, it can regain in subtlety of detail, completeness of description, range of material, and structural elaboration. In "The Summer House on the Mound" (*How well my eyes remember*) Bridges employed the heroic couplet, the form that traditionally seems to lend itself more readily to discursive writing and wide ranges of feeling within a given composition. The poem describes in retrospect the summer house from which the writer as a child was accustomed to watch passing ships at a distance, through a telescope. The house, the mound, and the distant sea are described quietly and precisely; then comes the close-up view of the decks through the telescope:

> There many an hour I have sat to watch; nay, now
> The brazen disk is cold against my brow,
> And in my sight a circle of the sea
> Enlarged to swiftness, where the salt waves flee,
> And ships in stately motion pass so near
> That what I see is speaking to my ear;
> I hear the waves dash and the tackle strain,
> The canvas flap, the rattle of the chain
> That runs out through the hawse, the clank of the winch
> Till half I wonder if they have no care,
> Those sailors, that my glass is brought to bear
> On all their doings, if I vex them not
> On every petty task of their rough lot
> Prying and spying, searching every craft
> From painted truck to gunnel, fore and aft,—
> Thro' idle Sundays as I have watched them lean
> Long hours upon the rail, or neath its screen
> Prone on the deck to lie outstretched at length,
> Sunk in renewal of their wearied strength.

There follows a description of sailing ships, then a description of the first steam dreadnoughts, one of the most magnificent descriptive passages with which I am acquainted and a passage which, despite its grandeur, does not detach itself from its context:

> One noon in March upon that anchoring ground
> Came Napier's fleet unto the Baltic bound:
> Cloudless the sky and calm and blue the sea,
> As round Saint Margaret's cliff mysteriously,
> Those murderous queens walking in Sabbath sleep
> Glided in line upon the windless deep.

Then come an enumeration of some of the ships, a few intimate details of the poet's family and the old age of the Duke of Wellington, and the half-literary, half-colloquial, and superbly handled conclusion:

> But now 'tis other wars and other men;—
> The year that Napier sail'd, my years were ten—
> Yea, and new homes and loves my heart hath found:
> A priest has there usurped the ivied mound,
> The bell that called to horse calls now to prayers,
> And silent nuns tread the familiar stairs.
> Within the peach-clad walls that old outlaw,
> The Roman wolf, scratches with privy paw.

The poem, despite its discursiveness, is flawless in detail and in structure; despite its hovering near the verge of prose, it is never prosy; and despite the wide range of feeling treated, there are no rhetorical gaps. It is a vision of the rising Victorian empire, all the more moving for its immediate familiarity, for its being a vision from a summer house within sight of the Duke of Wellington's castle. This poem alone was sufficient justification of Dr. Bridges' laureateship.

In "Elegy Among the Tombs" (*Sad sombre place*) and "Joy Sweetest Life-born Joy" a longer stanza is employed at a comparably slow tempo, the material being dictated by a somewhat more logical intention. To quote from these poems is even more unfair than to quote from the preceding one; so much depends on the structure, musical and logical, and of the entire piece. Lines that may seem insignificant in a quoted fragment, take on significance in relation to the whole, take on a significance of a sort that can be established only by the greatest stylists, in fact, since it depends upon the subtlest and most minutely controlled of stylistic relationships. These poems, like so many others by their author, may even appear insignificant when read complete for the first or even the fifth time, only to become profoundly moving on the fifteenth or twentieth. Most readers, unfortunately, are nearly always ready to judge as dull that which surpasses them in technical knowledge or in human wisdom to any very great extent; what is not understood seems bad. And Dr. Bridges so far surpasses nearly any of his readers in these respects, is so utterly free of any impure attraction, any undisciplined "personality," that his genius has been ignored more unjustly than that of any other writer since Landor.

In the last two poems mentioned, in "Dejection," and in a good many others, one encounters an attitude that may seem at first glance mere Victorian optimism, and which in a very few pieces ("Fortunatus Nimium," for example) comes near to verging on Victorian optimism, but which is in reality something far more somber and intelligent, a more or less classical resignation, with frequently, as in the professedly optimistic close of "Dejection" and "Elegy Among the Tombs," an undercurrent of calm and carefully restrained bitterness.

Bridges has been so often and so angrily compared to his friend Gerard Hopkins that I may perhaps be pardoned for a word on this subject. Hopkins seems to me to have been a truly great poet, though I cannot carry my enthusiasm as far as do his most violent admirers. The qualities that have won Hopkins almost immediate recognition during the past few years are, I fear, the very reasons for his limitations and his definite inferiority to Bridges. The mere fact that a man is a radical technical innovator does not render him a greater poet than the man who is less an innovator; extreme originality of method almost always involves extreme departure from the norm of experience, involves specialization and limitation of feeling. The greatest technical experimenter in English literature is, I suppose, Milton, and he is muscle-bound by his magnificence and the intricacy of his syntax. When he is not grand, he is grandiloquent; there is no transition between the two in Miltonic blank verse; and he killed English blank verse for two centuries. So with Hopkins: he can express with his violent rhythms an extremely special kind of excitement arising from religious experience, but he can express little else, and even the religious experience is incomplete, for if he does not deal wholly with the resultant excitement, he certainly throws his emphasis very heavily upon it. We are told, for instance, in superbly impassioned verses that the mind has mountains, but the nature of those mountains is never wholly clear. In Bridges the nature of the mountains is absolutely clear—that is, the experience is rendered whole—and the terror of the mountains is not isolated from all other experience but is seen in firm proportion. There is in the metrical experimentation in the present volume of Bridges quite as much originality of thought as in the experiments of Hopkins, coupled with a much more thorough knowledge of English meters and the complexities of feeling involved in their history. Bridges' technique, if the less obviously original of the two, is the more sensitive and the more widely applicable instrument of perception. In saying this, I do not wish it to be thought, let me repeat, that I am blind to the sensitivity or the power of Hopkins, a poet who moves me very deeply.

This limiting effect of the elaborately original may be one reason for the extreme shortness of so many of the most brilliant of contemporary careers: a narrow vein of feeling only can be explored, and once it is finished, the author has got himself so far from a fresh starting point that he lacks either the courage or the vigor to do anything about it; he has systematically deadened himself through specialization. If there is any truth in this supposition, extreme originality of style would appear to be one of the shortest cuts to that condition of atrophy, from which its most fanatical devotees seek, by its means, to escape. On the other hand, traditionalism is not equivalent to dullness; the diction of Bridges is as fresh and living as that of Dr. Williams; his meters allow him greater freedom, or rather greater range; he is in general a more civilized man. It is to be hoped, for the sake of twentieth-century poetry, that he will receive the study which his own poetry merits.

Robinson Jeffers

It is difficult to write of Mr. Jeffers' latest book [1] without discussing his former volumes; after his first collection he deals chiefly with one theme in all of his poems; and all of his works illustrate a single problem, a spiritual malady of considerable significance. Mr. Jeffers is theologically a kind of monist; he envisages, as did Wordsworth, Nature as Deity; but his Nature is the Nature of the physics textbook and not of the rambling botanist —Mr. Jeffers seems to have taken the terminology of modern physics more literally than it is meant by its creators. Nature, or God, is thus a kind of self-sufficient mechanism, of which man is an offshoot, but from which man is cut off by his humanity (just what gave rise to this humanity, which is absolutely severed from all connection with God, is left for others to decide): there is consequently no mode of communication between the consciousness of man and the mode of existence of God; God is praised adequately only by the screaming demons that make up the atom. Man, if he accepts this dilemma as necessary, is able to choose between two modes of action: he may renounce God and rely on his humanity, or he may renounce his humanity and rely on God.

Mr. Jeffers preaches the second choice: union with God, oblivion, the complete extinction of one's humanity, is the only good he is able to discover; and life, as such, is "incest," an insidious and destructive evil. So much, says Mr. Jeffers by implication,

[1] *Dear Judas,* by Robinson Jeffers. New York: Horace Liveright, 1929.

From *Poetry: A Magazine of Verse,* XXXVI, pp. 153-165. February, 1930. Reprinted by permission.

for Greek and Christian ethics. Now the mysticism of, say, San Juan de la Cruz offers at least the semblance of a spiritual, a human, discipline as a preliminary to union with Divinity; but for Mr. Jeffers a simple and mechanical device lies always ready; namely, suicide, a device to which he has not resorted.

In refusing to take this logical step, however, Mr. Jeffers illustrates one of a very interesting series of romantic compromises. The romantic of the ecstatic-pantheist type denies life, yet goes on living; nearly all romantics decry the intellect and philosophy, yet they offer justifications (necessarily foggy and fragmentary) of their attitude; they deride literary "technique" (the mastery of, and development of the sensitivity to, relationships between words, so that these relationships may extend almost illimitably the vocabulary) yet they write (of necessity, carelessly, with small efficiency). Not all romantics are guilty of all of these confusions, nor, doubtless, is Mr. Jeffers; but all of these confusions are essentially romantic—they are very natural developments of moral monism. And Mr. Jeffers, having decried human life as such, and having denied the worth of the rules of the game, endeavors to write narrative and dramatic poems—poems, in other words, dealing with people who are playing the game. Jesus, the hero of *Dear Judas,* speaking apparently for Mr. Jeffers, says that the secret reason for the doctrine of forgiveness is that all men are driven by the mechanism-God to act as they do, that they are entirely helpless; yet he adds in the next breath that this secret must be guarded, for if it were given out, men would run amuck, would get out of hand—*they would begin acting differently.*

The Women at Point Sur is a perfect laboratory of Mr. Jeffers' philosophy. Barclay, an insane divine, preaches Mr. Jeffers' religion, and his disciples, acting upon it, become emotional mechanisms, lewd and twitching conglomerations of plexi, their humanity annulled. Human experience, in these circumstances, having necessarily and according to the doctrine no meaning, there can be and is no necessary sequence of events: every act is equivalent to every other; every act is at the peak of hysteria; most of the incidents could be shuffled around into varying sequences without violating anything save, perhaps, Mr. Jeffers' private sense of their relative intensity. Since the poem is his, of course, such a private sense is legitimate enough; the point is that this is not a narrative, nor a dramatic, but a lyrical criterion. A successful lyrical poem of one hundred and seventy-five pages is unlikely, for the essence of lyrical expression is concentration; but it is at least theoretically possible. The difficulty is that the lyric achieves its effect by the generalization of emotion (that is, by the separation of the emotion from the personal history that gives rise to it in actual concrete experience) and by the concentration of expression. Narrative can survive in a measure without concentration, or intensity of detail, provided the narrative logic is detailed and compelling, as in the case of Balzac, though it is only wise to add that this occurs most often in prose. Now Mr. Jeffers, as I have pointed out, has abandoned narrative logic with the theory of ethics, and he has never achieved, in addition, a close and masterly style. His writing is loose, turgid, and careless; like most anti-intellectualists, he relies on his feelings alone and has no standard of criticism for them outside of themselves. There are occasional good flashes in his poems, and to these I shall return later, but they are very few, are very limited in their range of feeling and in their subject matter, and they are very far between. Mr. Jeffers has no remaining method of sustaining his lyric, then, other than the employment of an accidental (i.e., non-narrative) chain of anecdotes (i.e., details that are lyrically impure); his philosophical doctrine and his artistic dilemma alike decree that these shall be anecdotes of hysteria. By this method Mr. Jeffers continually *lays claim* to a high pitch of emotion which has no narrative support (that is, support of the inevitable accumulation of experience), nor lyrical support (that is, support of the intense perception of pure, or transferable, emotion), which has, in short, no support at all, and which is therefore simply unmastered and self-inflicted hysteria.

Cawdor alone of Mr. Jeffers' poems contains a plot that in its rough outlines might be sound, and *Cawdor* likewise contains his best poetry; the poem as a whole, and in spite of the confused treatment of the woman, is moving, and the lines describing the seals at dawn are fine, as are the two or three last lines of the apotheosis of the eagle. Most of the preceding material in the latter passage, however, like most of the material in the sections that give Mr. Jeffers' notions of the post-mortem experience of man, are turgid, repetitious, arbitrary, and unconvincing. The plot itself is blurred for lack of stylistic finish (that is, for lack of ability on the part of the poet to see every detail of sense and movement incisively down to the last preposition, the last comma, as every detail *is* seen in Racine or Shakespeare); and it remains again a fair question whether a moral monist *can* arrive at any clear conclusions about the values of a course of action, since he denies the existence of any conceivable standard of values within the strict limits of human life as such. In *The Tower Beyond Tragedy* Mr. Jeffers takes a ready-made plot, the Clytemnestra-Orestes situation, which is particularly strong dramatically, because Orestes is forced to choose between two sins, the murder of his mother and the refusal to avenge his father. But at the very last moment, in Mr. Jeffers' version, Orestes is converted to Mr. Jeffers' religion and goes off explaining (to Electra, who has just tried to seduce him) that though men may think he is fleeing before the furies he is really just drifting up to the mountains to meditate on the stars; and the preceding action is, of course, rendered morally and emotionally meaningless.

In the present volume, the title poem, *Dear Judas,* is a kind of dilution of *The Women at Point Sur,* with Jesus as Barclay, and with a less detailed background. Mr. Jeffers' mouthpiece and hero, Jesus, is little short of revolting as he whips reflexively from didactic passion to malice, self-justification, and vengeance. The poem shares the structural principles, or lack of them, of *The Women at Point Sur;* and it has no quotable lines, save, possibly, the last three, which are, however, heavy with dross. *The Loving Shepherdess,* the other long poem of the present volume, deals with a girl who knows herself doomed to die at a certain time in childbirth, and who wanders over the countryside caring for a small and diminishing flock of sheep in an anguish of devotion.

The events here again are anecdotal and reversible, and the emotion is lyrical or nothing. The theme had two possibilities: the poet could have immersed the girl in a dream of approaching death, or he could have immersed her in the sentimental pathos of the immediate situation. There are moments when he seems to be trying for the former effect, but his perceptions are not fine enough and the mass of anecdotal detail is too heavy; the poem succeeds in being no more than a very Wordsworthian embodiment of a kind of maudlin humanitarianism—which is a curious but not an unexpected outcome of Mr. Jeffers' sentimental misanthropy. The heroine is turned cruelly from door to door, and the sheep fall one by one before the reader's eyes, the doors and the sheep constituting the bulk of the anecdotal material; till finally the girl dies in a ditch in an impossible effort to give birth to her child.

The short poems in the book deal with themes that Mr. Jeffers has handled better before. He has written here and there impressive lines descriptive of the sea and its rocks, and of dying birds of prey. "Hurt Hawks II," in the *Cawdor* volume, is the most perfect short poem and is quite fine; there are excellent lines scattered through other pieces. These poems are, however, limited both in paraphrasable content and in experiential implication: they glorify brute nature and annihilation and are numb to the intricacies of human feeling; they share in the latter respect the limitations of all mystical poetry. Mr. Jeffers' insistence on another of his favorite lyrical themes, his own aloofness, is becoming, by dint of repetition, almost embarrassing; one has the constant feeling that he is trying to bully the reader into accepting him at his own evaluation.

Self-repetition has been the inevitable effect of anti-intellectualist doctrine on all of its supporters. If life is valued, explored, subdivided, and defined, poetic themes are infinite in number; if life is denied, the only theme is the rather sterile and monotonous one of the denial. Similarly, those poets who flee from form, which is infinitely variable, since every form is a definite and an individual thing, can achieve only the uniformity of chaos; and those indi-

viduals who endeavor to escape morality, which is personal form
and controlled direction, can, in the very nature of things, achieve
nothing, save the uniformity of mechanism. One might classify
Mr. Jeffers as a "great failure" if one meant by the phrase that
he had wasted unusual talents; but not if one meant that he had
failed in a major effort, for his aims are badly thought-out and
are essentially trivial.

CHARLES K. TRUEBLOOD

Emily Dickinson

In Emily Dickinson there seems to have been much of the visionary; if not in the general understanding of the word, then at least
in the meaning that her imagination inclined to the form of inner
vision rather than inner hearing, or other of the inner analogues
of sense. Her verse-world, so brilliant and so intense, seems yet
in a characteristic way a world of soundless contemplation, of
"quietness distilled," interrupted rarely, and perhaps only on her
own terms, by small low sounds, or those falling gently on the
ear, from far off. Not that she was without images of things vividly heard or felt, but that such images were not so frequent in
comparison to images of things vividly seen, and when they did
occur their vividness was more apt to be achieved by visual rather
than by auditory or other figures; as for example her "blue, uncertain, stumbling buzz" of a fly, or her wind as "tufts of tune,"
or as "caravans of sound." Again, she found, it seemed—for certainly she could communicate—a particular pleasure in vivid stillness, such as the silence of noon on certain summer days, or the
soundless streak of a falling star, or the noiseless brilliance expressed in her conceit of butterflies "leaping off the banks of noon,
plashless as they swim." This distillation of temperament into
vision, this brilliant quiet, might perhaps be more apparent if one
contrasted her poetry with, for instance, the verse-world of Masefield, so thronged with the rich tortuous riot of every sense. Yet
in such contrasts we should be on guard; it is easy to make too
much of a phrase. But if we accept the phrase with enlarging
qualifications, if we understand it as only a hint of characteristics
which may be more than the words can denote, or as a tentative

From *The Dial*, LXXX, pp. 301-311. April, 1926. Reprinted by permission.

bearing taken in surroundings where all is somewhat evanescent and transcending, then it may be of value in pointing at the great delicacy and great force which seemed to coexist in her individuality.

The combination of great delicacy and great force tends, no doubt, to be self-destructive in a serious sense, and we are not without indications that it was so with her. In temperament particularly, delicacy and force might be considered to consist of the same thing, namely, feeling; delicacy relating to the subtlety of the incitement, and force to the depth of the resulting emotion. And that she possessed both such force of heart and such exquisiteness, there is much evidence, subtle as well as obvious. . . . It is evident in that pleasure in contemplation, uninvaded by the disturbing messages of the inferior senses, that delight in brilliant quiet, which has already been noted. It is evident in all that one may suppose as to the explanation of such an attitude, and deduce from the belief that her poetry, like other very original poetry, is the image, not of random thoughts or idle observations, but of fundamental wish, central to mental being. It is most of all obvious in the shrinking and reluctance with which she met the most usual and ordinary, even the most affectionate and tender, of human contacts.

Her shrinking was no gesture. It became an avoidance and a flight. Her involuntary reluctance grew with reiteration into deliberate escape. It passed into gossip, and from gossip into legend, in which it became sufficiently fantastic, one gathers, to furnish reason for an authoritative biography. Turning through this biography, the *Life and Letters*,[1] one has the impression that she fled the world because she felt indeed that it was too much with her. And taking at its face value, as in fact we should, the description therein of her sensibility—from which it appears that the burning of a neighbor's straw shed more played upon her than an earthquake would upon the average person—we may indeed consider that she escaped from circumstance because it too rollingly echoed in her mind. Yet here again we might well be on guard.

[1] *Life and Letters of Emily Dickinson.* Edited by M. D. Bianchi. Illustrated. Houghton Mifflin Company. 1925.

For while we can accept this truth of her as far as it goes, we may find, if we trace the growth of her inwardness both forward and back, that the truth so stated is not quite all the truth. The ivory tower aspect of her seclusions is perfectly intelligible as a refinement upon the general world, as a preservation of treasures of feeling from an excess of irrelevance, as a great factor, no doubt, in contribution to the purity and flowering of her rare poetic instinct. Yet perhaps this seclusiveness was but the outer appearance of an inward bias which not only began much earlier and deeper, but also, in the end, went much farther. Her solitude, one comes to feel, began long before it became obvious, and went much deeper than was ever apparent. And her rare subtle knowledge of the interiors of the spirit, which we now so much remark upon, was perhaps derived from the length, as well as the sadness and the intensity, of her dwelling there.

Her solitude must indeed have dated, in some part, from the time she began to be temperamentally more than a child. It seems reasonable to think it began in her relation to her family, that is, really, her relation to her father; for the family all dwelt, though they seem not to have been aware of it, in the shadow of his personality. He was a man of gentle feeling, great intelligence, but tremendous primness. The last, perhaps, was his marking trait, for the public encomiums of him betray a general impression of immense respectability. As a young man he had signed his kindly, frosty letters to his *fiancée* as her "most ob't servant, Edward Dickinson." And his portrait rather confirms the tale. We see a handsome man of eminent look, but with that perhaps unconscious austerity in lips and brow and carriage of the head, which strikes with awe, not alone the hearts of sinners, but how much more those of the ingenuous and timid. A culprit could, in imagination, feel himself slipping, slipping, hopelessly down the smooth cold sides of that austerity—unless help were vouchsafed from above, as often it was, except in reprehensible cases; yet none would have dared hope for it.

But on the one marked character at the Dickinson hearth, the force of his respectability was imperfectly effective. In Emily there had been early apparent the sparkle of more than ordinary question. It was timid Emily, alone of three hundred girls in the Mt. Holyoke Seminary, who publicly and victoriously defied the regimen of Mary Lyon on the question of whether Christmas day should be spent with fasting and prayer at the seminary, or in celebration at home with one's family. It was Emily, in the seemly Dickinson household, who enjoyed irreverence, and who grew offhand with accepted revelation, and saw in the austerities of the public God merely an infinitude of tedium. It was Emily, only, who could write whimsically to herself, regarding the God of her own solitude:

> I hope the father in the skies
> Will lift his little girl,—
> Old-fashioned, naughty, everything,—
> Over the stile of pearl!

With the growth in force of so much individuality, what of the forebearing, but massive and immovable respectability that was Edward Dickinson? Could he understand a mind that was so like his in some ways, and so different? And what if he could not? Would there be submerged collision? and with what result? Or if there were no collision, what became of the opposition? Force does not evaporate; and as to the growing fact of her force and the established fact of her father's force, or the family force, there could be no doubt.

Adjustment to one's world is generally thought to consist of remaking oneself or of remaking the world. But it seemed that she did neither: she moved to a brilliant and subtle solitude miles within. Without shrinkage, but rather with an increase of her mental and temperamental powers—or perhaps one should say an increase in their effectiveness—a process of withdrawal inward began, which it seemed, never quite ended.

Her interiorization gained impetus from what is usually understood to have been its main cause; this was her encounter with love. It took place in 1853, her twenty-third year. She was, during this year, in Washington and Philadelphia with her father, who at the time was a member of Congress. In Philadelphia she met the man, whose name is not revealed, with whom she fell in love; he was married. When she realized the state of her feeling, she fled back to Amherst, where he followed her. The biography relates that one day

Sister Sue looked up from her sewing to see Lavinia, pallid and breathless from running, who grasped her wrist with hurrying hand, urging "Sue come! That man is here!—Father and Mother are away, and I am afraid Emily will go away with him."

But it does not appear that the contemplated moral succor was required for Emily. The Dickinson generations, it seemed, had already spoken in her blood. She went on with life in her father's house, showing no outward mark of this crisis except an "unexplained picture in a heavy oval frame of gold," hanging on the wall of her room, and an increase of turning from the world, which soon, no doubt, became apparent enough. "To the faithful," she wrote, "absence is condensed presence. To the others—but there are no others."

Now, one would think, she sought the rare inner air of spirit; and it was now, perhaps, as the turmoil of the actual died upon her ear, as she found in some degree the distance, the silence, the light, the "bright detachment" which she sought in anguish, it was now that her poems began, as the private day-book of her heart; for she intended most of them, it seemed, for no other eyes. They mark rememberably the character of her solitude for force and delicacy. Could such tumultuous precision have been achieved otherwise than through her characteristic visionism, so powerful and yet so far from gross? In it only, perhaps, was the full force of a great temperament to find an expression utter and complete, tremendous and yet delicate. Indeed, such burning filigree may mark out for us, as well as anything can, how much more discriminated, how much more useful to the mind and heart, how much greater the world of vision can be than the worlds of the other senses; and how much more we should choose it. if a choice were to be made.

Perhaps it is because this was the direction which her brilliant silent vehemence took; perhaps it is because her retreat inward was to the bright observatories, and not the dark recesses of spirit, that her utterance shows so little of the morbidness which often accompanies the growth inward of mental being. In the deepest mazes of her solitude, it seemed, touch was brilliantly kept with the exteriors of the actual, by the clearest, the finest, and, for her, the most characteristic of the senses. Perhaps the great vitality of the contact by vision is the essence, in part, of her poetic originality. "The eye begins its avarice," she wrote, and the words may have more than their immediate meaning. Her individuality, apparently, made its impress upon her world especially through vision; through vision she exercised her abounding share in that fine lyric tyranny, which makes the poet's whole world the private possession of his personality.

It may have been a phase of this visionism, existing in her love of contrasts, and coupled with an arch humor, which was at the core of her characteristic whimsical charm. It is best seen in a species of inverse hyperbole, a favorite move with her, in which the lion and the lamb are made to lie down together, in which things strange and vast are put in the same figurative company with things homely and small. She likes to speak of "Vesuvius at home," of God as "a noted clergyman," or as "Papa above," of the storm winds as "dogs defeated of a bone," of Eden as "the ancient homestead," or that "old-fashioned house we dwell in every day," of her own being as a tiny craft among "stately sails" oblivious alike of its presence and its absence. These things, possibly, were only whimsicalities, but perhaps they were more too. Since the poet cannot but draw his own likeness, and project the properties of his own feeling into what he describes, was there, in this inverse hyperbole, not only whimsicality, but—what was another phase of her delicacy and her shrinking—an effort to make the gross world less strange and painful by stamping it with the character of her own vision, by figuring it in the terms of her own experience?

It was thus perhaps that she rebuilt her world, of treasured and familiar things, deep within, and distant from fearful circumstance.

Built too, seemingly, of the substance of vision, it was as powerfully yet lightly wrought as she could make it. But the more she
built its loveliness, the more she was contained within it. And
since with so vital a temperament, the creative substance must have
been almost continuously forming, in a sort of reverberation to the
delicate pronouncements of the senses, the progress of her imprison-
ment must indeed have been steady. How keenly she became aware
of these unseen bars is only too evident in her great lyric longings
for escape; and the escape in this instance is a far different thing
from the old escape from circumstance. It is the prison of herself
from which she now wants extrication. One sees it first, perhaps,
in her whimsical longing for namelessness:

> How dreary to be somebody!
> How public, like a frog,
> To tell your name the livelong day
> To an admiring bog!

Or perhaps it first appeared in the wish, implied more than a few
times in her poetry, to be absorbed in a sympathetic force greater
than herself, or great in a different way. And as the inward tendency progresses, one begins to discern its characteristic final forms.
That brilliant inner prison is becoming too confining. From longing for namelessness, one observes the progress to longing for
greater freedom. "What," she wrote,

> What if I file this mortal off,
> See where it hurt me,—that's enough,—
> And wade in liberty?

For that indeed is finally the sole escape for those who are too
much caught in the prisons of themselves.

Strong as was this lyric prison, it was yet based on other things,
outside her personality. It was, in fact, only a slender mansion
in her father's house. And when, in June, 1874, her father suddenly
died, a strange unthought-of night fell indeed on her cherished
"bright detachment." If he had not understood her temperamentally, or perhaps in any way, he had yet never intruded, and he

had shown an immense, if prim tenderness, in which she and the others of his family had long dwelt. How much he must have been in that household we can only imagine, except as we have it vividly said in his daughter's poem:

> We learn in the retreating
> How vast an one
> Was recently among us.
> A perished sun
>
> Endears in the departure
> How doubly more
> Than all the golden presence
> It was before!

And from her manner of speaking in numerous poems of life, death, the grave, and eternity, it seems evident that this loss tore a ghastly breach in her inner citadel. In these poems there is not the old note of longing, which was yet so airy and so alive; there is not the whim in the description of the wind as having "no bone to bind him," which was also her description of her own wish-to-be. This quietism is not so brilliant or so poised for soaring; instead there are deep painful looks at the exteriors of our mortality, in those final moments when the frost is mantling in the clay. Instead, as elsewhere in her poems, in looking forward to the beginning of the bodiless, there is here rather an overmuch of the ending of the body. Instead of the privacy of the breeze there is the privacy of the low dwelling. The idea of escape seems to have been metamorphosed into the idea of refuge, and one cannot be sure but that the note of refuge—in the tomb—was the note on which she ended. It is indeed a possible conclusion to inwardness.

That her exquisite vision should have dwelt so steadfastly, so powerfully, and so often, on the conclusion of our poor clay, is perhaps one of the most formidable of the objections to calling her a mystic, as has been done—loosely, one would think. Would the dead flesh have looked so stricken, if she had not been of "that religion which doubts as fervently as it believes"? Indeed, in calling her a mystic, are we not blurring the outlines of her characteristic effect? Is not to call her a mystic to deny, in a way, her un-equaled general sensitivity? The mystic is but too often polarized by his sustained and indiscriminate ecstasy. But not in all her life was she so polarized. Does not the immense value of her poetry lie in the fact that rather than mysticism it is the rarest of lyric asceticism? Is not that the secret of the strange fine intelligence of the heart, and the comfort that so many have found in her, so many of the stricken? When has stoic's metal been struck to a more exquisite chiming?

II

Consistent with the delicacy and the force of heart which were noticed as so characteristic of her individuality, there appears as perhaps her principal literary quality a certain lyric incisiveness, a bright passionate brevity, a sensitive immediacy of word to thought. In poetry one becomes accustomed to think of incisive-ness as often secured by discreet abrasure; of the brevity in question as a studied brevity, for which the faculties required may be merely intelligence and fine attention; and of immediacy as the product of much choosing. Yet in her case the reverse seems to be true. For her, apparently, to think and write pointedly, briefly, and with the happiest immediacy of word to thought was as natural as to feel powerfully.

There is, in her verse, an obvious absence of studio finish. . . . She was evidently inattentive to the more or less "artistic" arts of metrical and phrasal music, and appears readily capable of letting the verse-scheme of a poem, and even the syntax, stumble or scram-ble, in a curious carelessness of everything but the flash of vision and the gold of phrase. What she says seems always said with the choicest originality, but not always with poetic fluency, or even much attempt at it. And while it perhaps should be remembered in this connection, that most of her poems were written strictly for herself, often probably as the notes of her thoughts, the marginalia in her private book of experience, which she had no idea that others than herself would ever see, it still does not seem certain that the

result would have been widely different had she been writing formally and for publication.

These oddities of structure and finish seem to betray the fact that
a poem of hers is almost wholly first thought and not afterthought.
Compare her work with that of A. E. Housman, who dealt with
many of the same themes, and some of the difference due to afterthought should appear. The verse of Housman, direct and piercing as it is, seems yet to reflect multiplied exclusions, and a final
simplicity that has been minutely wrought. The poems of Emily
Dickinson seem to reflect simply the direct feelings of a profound
heart. They seem less the works of infinitely considered art, in
which the effort has been guided to achievement by a subtly taught
sense of poetic effect, than merely the spontaneous motions of a
rich sensibility phrased with natural immediacy in language, which,
if irregular, is of sparkling definition.

There was, of course, nothing merely wandering about her poetic effort. However wholly from the heart her poems may seem
to come, no one who much reads them can escape the impression
that poetry, in her hands, becomes in good share a mental magic.
Her trenchant measures are as free from the dwelling unction of
the merely sensuous as they are free from the mere piecing out of
insight. The penetrating phrases into which her thought and feeling are sharpened are set down with a close economy that sometimes has the effect of extreme fine dryness. And as significance
is the substance of her force, so her verse follows the forms of wit
as much as the forms of sense. Her poems indeed might be called
epigrams. They might be called conceits, too, being often so whimsical, and so edging on quaintness in their originality; they might
be called conceits, that is, were they less fervently intended. And
whether conceits or epigrams, they seem always at the key of the
often intangible matter, and have not only general pointedness but
specific point.

To the service of her feeling she brought, perhaps as corollary
to her characteristic inner vision, a rare and singular sense of words.
Words, to her, were a festival; and she spent, as the biography
notes, hours with the dictionary. And since there are not many

of her single words that would not have been feasible and usual in ordinary intercourse, we can reasonably imagine that she must have been finding again the vivid, hidden textures in hidden meanings, restoring for herself the lost edges of ordinary expression, searching out the forgotten but astounding faces of customary words. It strikes one too that she had very positively that tremendous command of "things used as words," which, to Emerson, so marked the authentic poet. And to this command, one cannot forbear thinking, her escape from circumstances added, curiously, much strength and nourishing. Is it too much to suppose that when she contracted her existence, she increased in certain ways its depth and height? that when she looked at the things of her lessened life, it was more than before with the remarkable eyes of her imagination? that she then erected the familiar objects in her round of deeper days, with powerful lyric conviction, into symbols of far things? In her verse noon does not always mean merely noon; it seems sometimes to stand for the possibilities of a greater glory. Nor are storms seen from covert merely storms seen from covert; they call up thoughts of the refuge foreverlasting, even if that refuge be only the grave. It is not to be contended, surely, that symbolism achieved through so rich a temperament cannot add a weight to words.

Not only by symbolism, which seems a thing so elemental and so directly of the heart, but by her figures of speech, the products of her sense of similarity, her acute visualizing mentality, did she add strength to her verse. Her characteristic figure, perhaps, was metaphor, and it is apparently in the quality of her metaphor, and in the facts that not only her metaphor, which outstands, but all the smaller parts of her poetic utterance, are made of the same vivid, chiefly visual substance, that her extraordinary poetic distinctiveness lives. Filled with the clearest colors and the most consummate lights, her poetic speech seems alive, to its smallest parts, with its special sparkle. Where is to be found a figurative note like hers in its combination of delicate brilliance and trenchant quaintness, its piquancy and its sincere fervor? It sets a mode in imagination that could found no fashions, for its secret is not detachable. Here, indeed, we are as close as we shall get to the language of her individuality; and here we must rest merely with observing her force of spirit evident in its lightest terms. It recalls again that her poetry was not professional; that it was but a means by which she constructed her "bright detachment," and partly lightened a weight of thinking.

It must also have been, in the same direction, a laying up of the treasures of comprehension, of her deep knowledge of the interiors of the spirit, gained, evidently, with so much anguish. In her poems, said to have been found, for the most part, copied on note-paper, and laid away, tied with ribbon, in little bundles, each of six or eight sheets, one can refresh his feeling and thinking, secure that in what he thus comes back to, he will find no waning of choiceness. This brilliant understanding of the heart and its suffering, this great sensory delicacy, is rare essential wealth, proof against tarnish. It is seldom that one finds surer gold.

THEODORE SPENCER
The Later Poetry of W. B. Yeats

A DISTINGUISHED critic, Mr. Yvor Winters, has recently compared the poetry of W. B. Yeats with the poetry of T. Sturge Moore. His remarks are challenging and need to be discussed. In his opinion, Moore is a greater poet than Yeats; he says that Yeats, at crucial moments, suffers from the "fundamental post-Romantic defect, the abandonment of logic," that Yeats achieves a "factitious coherence," is guilty of intellectual confusion, and is an "unregenerate Romantic." These adverse criticisms sum up very well the case against Yeats as an important poet, and the reason they need to be discussed by anyone concerned with Yeats' poetry is that they have a plausibility which may make them a serious obstacle to a satisfactory judgment of Yeats' position.

There is not much to be said about the first of them. To say that Moore is a better poet than Yeats seems to me meaningless, and I cannot imagine any standards of criticism by which such a statement can be defended. In subtlety of rhythm, in intensity, in richness of verbal association, in force, in everything which implies an original and individual style, the later poems of Yeats are superior to anything by Moore. Compare, for example, the opening lines of Moore's sonnet, "Apuleius Meditates," which Mr. Winters praises very highly, with the opening of Yeats' sonnet on Leda and the Swan. This is Moore:

> An old tale tells how Gorgo's gaze distilled
> Horror to petrify men's mobile limbs:
> Endymion's moonlit beauty never dims,
> Hard-frozen as the fond chaste goddess willed.

From *The Hound and Horn*, VII, pp. 164-175. October, 1933. Reprinted by permission.

And Yeats:

> A sudden blow: the great wings beating still
> Above the staggering girl, her thighs caressed
> By the dark webs, her nape caught in his bill,
> He holds her helpless breast upon his breast.

There is an important distinction illustrated here, a distinction which applies to other poetry than that of Moore and Yeats. It is the distinction between the poetry of revery and the poetry of immediacy. I do not, of course, mean by the poetry of revery poetry which is written necessarily about past events; what I am describing, to put it loosely, is the associative climate into which we feel the poet has moved when he got himself ready for writing, and in which he has remained during the composition of the poem. Even without the revealing phrase "An old tale tells," which begins Moore's sonnet, we know from the rhythm, the fairly obvious and hence unregenerated adjectives, that the subject is being viewed from a distance, that it is not apprehended immediately. The poet and his material have not passed through a period of "intimate welding"; they have been contiguous, not fused. But, "A sudden blow: the great wings beating still": here the poet has put the reader in the midst of the action; the subject is not considered and contemplated from outside; we are convinced that the matter has been so vividly an essential part of the poet's experience, that it becomes, if we are reading with the proper attention, an equally vivid part of the reader's experience too.

The distinction between these two ways of regarding the subject matter of a poem becomes obvious if we think of Wordsworth's famous definition of the origin of poetry. "It takes its origin," he says, "from emotion recollected in tranquillity; the action is contemplated till, by a species of reaction, the tranquillity gradually disappears, and an emotion, kindred to that which was before the subject of contemplation, is gradually produced, and does itself actually exist in the mind." It is the last part of this sentence, the part usually left unquoted, which is important. Without the disappearance of tranquillity no good poem can be written, and the trouble with the kind of poetry I have called the poetry of revery is that when we are reading it we feel the tranquillity is still there; the "emotion which was before the subject of contemplation" has not turned up. It is because we never feel like this about Shakespeare that we consider Shakespeare so great a poet, and it is because we often feel like this about Tennyson, that Tennyson's reputation is dubious.

The difference between immediate poetry and the poetry of revery is a reflection of a difference in poetic temperament, and like all differences in temperament it shows itself in a number of ways. One does not expect that a temperament addicted to revery will seek for startling words or for arrangements of images and thoughts that will surprise the mind. Revery in any form not being a function of the human personality as a whole, its aim, when expressed in poetry, will be to lull rather than excite, to describe, or even lament, as beautifully as possible, rather than to assert or protest. Not that poetry of this kind is without intensity; one has only to think of sections *liv* to *lvi* of *In Memoriam;* but it is not the intensity of immediacy, of anger, or of satire, because it is not an intensity which fully includes the intellect.

Of course the contrast between these two kinds of poetic temperament may be carried too far, and one can waste one's time in putting various poets into the various categories they imply, which is foolish because in many cases it is impossible to draw a satisfactory line between them. The reason I mention the matter at all is that it throws an interesting light on the poetry of Yeats. He is a striking example of a man whose poetic development has been from the one way of writing to the other, of a man who has tried to move from a partial to a complete way of looking at the experience he is putting into words. This change, and the success with which he has brought it about, is one of the reasons why his later poetry is so interesting, and it is one of the facts which justify the assertion that Yeats is the greatest of living English poets.

The point can be made clearer if we compare one of his earlier poems, "The Sad Shepherd," with one written about forty years later, the poem, "Coole Park, 1929," in *Words for Music Perhaps*.[1] "The Sad Shepherd" begins:

> There was a man whom Sorrow named his friend,
> And he, of his high comrade Sorrow dreaming,
> Went walking with slow steps along the gleaming
> And humming sands, where windy surges wend.

There is little, except its rhythm, to recommend that. It is typical writing of an "unregenerate Romantic." The weak personification of Sorrow, the phrase "high comrade" (this emotive use of the adjective "high" is usually suspicious), the inaccuracy and looseness of the rhyme word "wend"—all these make bad writing, for they are the result of soft feeling and of practically no thinking at all. And the poem, with the exception of the closing lines, gets worse as it goes on. It is an excellent example of the poetry of revery at its weakest; of poetry written not with the object imaginatively vivid and sharp before the mind's eye, but written, so to speak, from memory, with the object wrapped in the falsifying haze of illusion, the kind of illusion that flourishes, like algae in a stagnant pool, when the mind is not stirring.

Bad poetry like this can be found in any age, and the kind of mistiness that makes it bad depends on the particular literary conventions of the time. The minor poets of the eighteenth century had a chilly poetic diction which hampered clarity, and the minor poets of the '90's had little clarity because they used a poetic diction which, one is tempted to say, was too warm. Closely connected with this, and in fact inseparable from it, they had a languorous and evasive habit of feeling, which is as dangerous to good writing as it is difficult to get rid of. What makes Yeats so worthy of admiration is that he did get rid of it. He tells us, in his *Autobiographies,* how, by sleeping upon a board (or at least by thinking of sleeping upon a board), by making his rhythms "faint and nervous," by contemplating the Dantesque image, by changing his

---

[1] *Words for Music Perhaps and Other Poems,* by W. B. Yeats. Dublin: Cuala Press. 1932. (In *Collected Poems.* New York: Macmillan Co. 1933.)

subject matter and his vocabulary, he struggled to make his poems bare and clear, and expressive of the whole man. That he has succeeded is one reason why Mr. Winters' comparison of his verse to Sturge Moore's seems to me so imperceptive. His "quarrel with himself," to use his own phrase, has made Yeats a great poet, with a style of communicating his experience which is authentic and individual, whereas the style of Sturge Moore, careful craftsman though he be, never rises above the commonplace.

It is, of course, an over-simplification of the truth to say that Yeats has entirely turned from one way of writing to the other. He has not lost, he has enriched and perfected, the sensitive rhythms which were at the beginning the best thing about his style. What has happened is that Yeats has taught himself to give the exactly right, and hence unsentimentalized, emotional tone to what he wants to say. "I tried," he says in his preface (1925) to the collected edition of his early poems, "after the publication of the *Wanderings of Oisin* to write of nothing but emotion, and in the simplest language, and now I have had to go through it all, cutting out or altering passages that are sentimental from lack of thought." Few poets have had more difficulties to escape from, more veils of unreality to break through—or, to change the metaphor, more intangible vapors to condense into solids—than Yeats. The late Romanticism of the '90's, Irish super-nationalism, the use of occult symbols, reliance upon a private metaphysical system; any one of these might have been the ruin of a lesser talent. But Yeats, in spite of what at times seemed unavoidable disaster, has triumphantly survived. Perhaps a life of action, and the anger it has sometimes generated—anger is an excellent emotion, if aimed at the right things, for a poet to cultivate—has helped to put iron into his style. At any rate, even when writing about the past, Yeats is no longer a poet of revery, in the sense that I have defined. That is the point I want to make by referring to his poem "Coole Park, 1929."

> I meditate upon a swallow's flight,
> Upon an aged woman and her house:
> A sycamore and lime tree lost in night

> Although that western cloud is luminous,
> Great works constructed there in nature's spite
> For scholars and for poets after us,
> Thoughts long knitted into a single thought,
> A dance-like glory that those walls begot.

At first sight this stanza would seem to be an excellent example of revery. The poet is looking back upon the past, the tone is not "active," the rhythm is appropriate for retrospection. But on a more careful reading, it will be seen that every image is at once individually specific and symbolically general in its reference, that no word can be changed except for the worse, and that the climax of the last line is prepared for by the contrasting images and symbols that have gone before. And how admirably the poem continues:

> There Hyde before he had beaten into prose
> The noble blade the Muses buckled on,
> There one that ruffled in a manly pose
> For all his timid heart, there that slow man,
> That meditative man John Synge and those
> Impetuous men Shawe-Taylor and Hugh Lane,
> Found pride established in humility,
> A scene well set and excellent company.
>
> They came like swallows and like swallows went,
> And yet a woman's powerful character
> Could keep a swallow to its first intent;
> And half a dozen in formation there
> That seemed to whirl upon a compass point
> Found certainly upon the dreaming air. . . .

It is tempting to quote the whole poem, but I will leave the last stanza unquoted—though with its swelling rhythm and superb rhetoric it is the finest of all—in hopes that what I have already quoted will send the reader to the book itself.

There are other poems of this kind in *Words for Music Perhaps,* and I should like to call attention particularly to "The Burning Tree" and to "Coole Park and Ballylee, 1932," both written, like

"Coole Park, 1929," in ottava rima, and both containing that re-
verberative haunting quality which Yeats, in such a masterly way,
can give to his rhythms.   Equally striking, and equally masterly,
is the way Yeats uses, in these latest poems, the individual word
to its fullest effect.   He has always been able, as the result of his
control over rhythm, to emphasize any word he pleased, but the
word itself has not always been the final word for its context.
Now, with his more recent intensity of vision, his control of focus,
the individual word has that combination of immediate exactness
with potential expansion which is the mark of great poetry.   Yeats
is particularly successful with adjectives; I can think of few poets
who in this respect are his equals.   Consider, for example, his use
of the word "resinous" in the last line of the following stanza; it
is the end of the final chorus to his play "Resurrection":

> Everything that man esteems
> Endures a moment or a day;
> Love's pleasure drives his love away,
> The painter's brush consumes his dreams;
> The herald's cry, the soldier's tread
> Exhaust his glory and his might:
> Whatever flames upon the night
> Man's own resinous heart has fed.

We have only to compare with this an earlier expression of a
similar idea to see how far Yeats has progressed.   I quote from
"The Happy Shepherd (1889)."

> Nor seeks; for this is also sooth;
> To hunger fiercely after truth,
> Lest all thy toiling only breed
> New dreams, new dreams; there is not truth
> Saving in thine own heart . . .

That is rhythmically effective, but little more; there are too many
unnecessary words ("nor," "also," "only," etc.), and nowhere is
there the concreteness and inevitability of the later poem.

II

The second part of the present volume consists of a number of short poems and songs, many of them built around a figure whom Yeats at first called Cracked Mary, but who now appears as Crazy Jane; an old woman who sings of the wild ineradicable love she had in her youth. I can best give the quality of these poems by quotation.

> I know, although when looks meet
> I tremble to the bone,
> The more I leave the door unlatched
> The sooner love is gone,
> For love is but a skein unwound
> Between the dark and dawn.
>
> A lonely ghost the ghost is
> That to God shall come;
> I, love's skein upon the ground
> My body in the tomb,
> Shall leap into the light lost
> In my mother's womb.
>
> But were I left to lie alone
> In an empty bed—
> The skein so bound us ghost to ghost
> When you turned your head
> Passing on the road that night—
> Mine would walk, being dead.

The technique of this is very interesting. The spondee at the end of the first lines of the first and second stanzas (why does it not occur in the third as well?), the interlocking rhymes, by which the third line of one stanza rhymes with the fifth line of the stanza preceding, the cumulative effect of the triple rhyme, all these form a technical triumph which widens the limits of English poetry.

A further technical device, used very often in these poems, is the refrain, and I should like to examine for a moment the way Yeats handles it, for with its help, he gives a remarkable muscle and pungency to his verse form, and there is much to be learned, by a practicing versifier, from the success of his experiments.

There are, generally speaking, three chief ways in which the refrain has been used by English poets. The first is that found in popular ballads, and to a less extent in Elizabethan songs. Here the effect achieved is rhythmical poignancy and contrast; the repetition of a meaningless phrase, unrelated to the subject of the poem, and balanced in a different rhythm, can first create a kind of rhythmical suspense, and then resolve it:

> There were twa sisters in a bower,
> *Edinburgh, Edinburgh,*
> There were twa sisters in a bower,
> *Sterling for aye;*
> There were twa sisters in a bower,
> There cam a knight to be their wooer,
> *Bonnie St. Johnston stands upon Tay.*

Or it can produce rhythmical variety alone, as in Elizabethan songs:

> Ho ho, ho ho, this world doth pass
> Right merrily, I'll be sworn,
> When many an honest Indian ass
> Goes for a unicorn.
> *Tara-diddle-deino; this is idle feino.*

> Tee-hee, tee-hee, O sweet delight,
> He tickles this age who can
> Call Tullia's ape a marmosite,
> And Leda's goose a swan.
> *Tara-diddle-deino; this is idle feino.*

The second use of the refrain is to bind together and intensify the chief subject-matter of the poem. In the earliest English example, the Anglo-Saxon "Deor's Lament," the repeated words, "That passed over, so may this," by which the poet refers to past calamities in relation to his own, connect the various incidents under one emotional roof, and give unity to what would otherwise be an unrelated series of incidents. Milton, imitating Virgil, uses this device with great success in his "Epitaphium Damonis," where the repetition, at irregular intervals, of the words, "Ite domum impasti, domino iam non vacat, agni," has a singularly haunting effect.

And there is a third, more sophisticated way of using the refrain to be found in the marriage songs of Spenser. Keeping the standard rhythm of the poem, it supplies a background of natural description, and it places the action in a definite environment: "Sweete Themmes! runne softlie, till I end my song." A notable use of this method has been made by Hardy, in a poem called "The Sacrilege," where the refrain descriptive of Nature, "And Dunkery frowned on Exon Moor," changes from gloomy to gay, or rather (characteristically) from gay to gloomy, according to the events in the story.

I make these somewhat pedantic classifications because they throw light on what Yeats has done. He has used the refrain in all three ways, and with each use has broadened its possibilities. We can find the first in "Crazy Jane Reproved," the second in "Crazy Jane on God," and the third in "Three Things." But even more interesting are the poems in which he has used the refrain in two or three ways at the same time.

> Bring me to the blasted oak
> That I, midnight upon the stroke,
> *All find safety in the tomb,*
> May call down curses on his head
> Because of my dear Jack that's dead
> "Cockscomb" was the least he said
> *The solid man and the cockscomb.*

Here we have a combination of the first and second methods: the indirect allusion, *All find safety in the tomb,* grows into a necessary reference; by binding the poem together and giving it rhythmical variety—*The solid man and the cockscomb*—the refrain adds intensity, and the result is that we have, not a single note, as we should have if the refrain were missing, but a chord.

Frequently, as here, Yeats chooses for a refrain some general statement upon which the poem itself is a specific comment. An admirable example is the poem "Crazy Jane Grown Old Looks at the Dancers," where the line, *Love is like the lion's tooth,* repeated at the end of each stanza, is both a statement of a general truth and a representation of the fierceness of the old woman's remembered passion. In fact there is no better example of Yeats' genius than the way in which he chooses his refrains to give this double effect; it was essential to find the right words, and in nearly every poem, Yeats has found them. In his use of this device, as in everything else, we find the later Yeats making his poems a reflection of a complete experience, not of a discrete layer of experience only. Comparison with the earlier poems is again illuminating, and it is interesting to compare a poem called "Running to Paradise (1914)," where the refrain gives merely a rhythmical variety, though it is very effective and surprising, with either of the poems I have just mentioned, where the refrain gives emotional vividness and tautness as well.

In my opinion the finest of all these poems is the one called "I am of Ireland," where the refrain is used more elaborately, with a more subtle rhythmical sway, than anywhere else. In fact it is difficult to tell which is the refrain and which is the chief part of the poem; the refrain is at once a voice and an echo, a question and a reply, and the fusion between the two takes place in that deep part of consciousness, or perhaps unconsciousness, which only true poetry can spring from or can reach. I quote the poem in full, for only by doing so can I hope to explain why I find it so moving.

"I am of Ireland
And the Holy Land of Ireland
And time runs on" cried she,
"Come out of charity
Come dance with me in Ireland."

One man, and one man alone
In that outlandish gear,
One solitary man
Of all that rambled there
Had turned his stately head,

"That is a long way off,
And time runs on," he said
"And the night grows rough."

"I am of Ireland
And the Holy Land of Ireland
And time runs on," cried she.
"Come out of charity
And dance with me in Ireland."

"The fiddlers are all thumbs,
Or the fiddle string accursed,
The drums and the kettle drums
And the trumpets all are burst
And the trombone," cried he,
"The trumpet and trombone,"
And cocked a malicious eye
"But time runs on, runs on."

"I am of Ireland
And the Holy Land of Ireland
And time runs on," cried she.
"Come out of charity
And dance with me in Ireland."

III

I have written at some length about the technique of Yeats'
poetry because a deep respect for Yeats as a craftsman is necessary
to a proper understanding of his work. But his craftsmanship
would hardly be worth mentioning if it were an end in itself;
what is significant about these later poems is that the substitution,
to use Yeats' own description, of "sound for sense and ornament
for thought," which was the fault of his early style, has given place
to vigor and toughness, to a style where thought is substance and
not accident, and which is able to communicate, in an entirely individual way, important emotions. It remains to enquire what
these are.

About ten years ago, it appeared likely that Yeats was in danger

of losing himself in a tangle of occult metaphysics; he published
a book on the subject called *A Vision,* "which book," to use
Chaucer's words,

> Spak muchel of the operaciouns
> Touchynge the eighte and twenty mansiouns
> That longen to the moone, and swich folye
> As in oure dayes is nat worth a flye,

and he wrote several poems which depended, if they were to be
understood, on a fable connected with the philosophy described in
this volume. And though Yeats has since remarked (1929) that
nearly all of *A Vision* "fills me with shame," he also attributes to
the experience behind it the fact that his poetry has gained in "self-
possession and power."

This is doubtless true, and it is therefore unfair to apply
Chaucer's words too literally to *A Vision.* At the present time a
poet must take what external aid he can find to plan the structure
and symbolism of his poetry; but if he is a good poet the mechanics will obviously be more helpful to him than to the reader, and
most of the time they will be out of sight. This is what occurs in
Yeats' later poems; specific references to the philosophy of *A Vision*
are very scarce, only an occasional metaphor is derived from it, and
the subject matter of the poems is not a private world of dreams,
as the most acute of contemporary English critics once feared it
would be, but the subject matter of all great poetry.

That, to be sure, is a very loose statement, for the subject matter
of great poetry is a difficult and complex thing to define. But if
one were pressed for a definition, the reply would be, I believe,
that at the bottom of all great poetry, as at the bottom of all human
experience, lies the problem of the relation between the transient
and the permanent, expressed in innumerable ways, and regarded
from innumerable angles. In mystical poetry, such as Dante's, the
permanent is found and described as the center of experience, for
it is the object of both emotion and thought; in Shelley's poetry
it is sought for by the mind, but found only temporarily, for it is
discovered by the emotions alone; while in Shakespeare, though

the sense of permanence is nearly always somewhere in the background, it is change, not permanence, the Many, not the One, that is emphasized, and passion, as in *Lear,* can play itself out in the dark. Today, as has been frequently said ("What are all those fish that lie gasping on the strand?"), the flux itself seems the only thing that does not change, and to seek a pattern of permanence elsewhere appears an impossible task. *A Vision* is such an attempt, and the apparent intractability of its philosophy for poetry is significant. Yet without such an attempt Yeats' later poetry would lose its richness and its "power." The philosophy may not be acceptable to others, but to Yeats it represents a sense of values which recognizes the importance of the permanent, and without such recognition all statements about life, whether in poetry or prose, are shallow.

The chief subject matter of these poems is the passing of youth into age, of passion into death.

> Earth in beauty dressed
> Awaits returning spring.
> All true love must die,
> Alter at the best
> Into some lesser thing.
> Prove that I lie.
>
> Such bodies lovers have,
> Such exacting breath
> That they touch or sigh.
> Every touch they give
> Love is nearer death.
> Prove that I lie.

It is a poetry of change, striving for stability, for transmutation into "monuments of unaging intellect." And though both the ephemeral and the lasting are continually brought to our attention, it is the passing of the ephemeral that remains most vivid to us. One might expect, as a result, that the prevailing tone would be one of pathos, but this is not true; the emotions here expressed

go deeper than pathos, and slight as these poems are, they leave
in the mind an impression of tragedy.

I trust that I have said enough to show that I consider Yeats'
poetry to have more than a contemporary value. It does not, as
Mr. Winters says it does, abandon logic; it springs from a deeper
well than mere logic ever swam in, and its coherence is far from
"factitious." Even if we may sometimes feel that an individual
poem is not entirely successful, the great majority of these poems
do not grow commonplace with familiarity, nor are they easily
forgotten. On the contrary they sing into the memory, and we feel,
after contemplating them, that Yeats did himself no more than
justice when he once wrote:

> There's not a fool can call me friend,
> And I shall sup at journey's end
> With Landor and with Donne.

STARK YOUNG
American Drama in Production

I: MOURNING BECOMES ELECTRA, *by Eugene O'Neill* [1]

To hear the bare story, shortly told, of this new O'Neill play, with all its crimes and murders, may easily bring a flouting smile or recall Mrs. Malaprop's announcement of Sir Lucius' and Bob Acres' duel: "So, so, here's fine work, here's fine suicide, parricide, and simulation going on in the fields!" The same thing could be said of *Hamlet* or *King Lear* or *Oedipus King,* of course, but this is sure to be the line the jibes will take from such of the play's critics as are unfriendly or impatient or incapable. As to the length of the event, the actual performance at the Guild could be considerably shortened by going faster in many places; the length of the play itself is for the most part organic with both its meaning and its effect. As to the depressing effects of the play, we will come to that later.

The title, as we see, intends to dispose at the start of the relation of *Mourning Becomes Electra* to the Greek drama. The story of the house of Atreus was set down by Homer, Pindar, Aeschylus, Sophocles, Euripides and diverse Greek writers whose works are not extant. From this house shadowed by an ancient curse, Agamemnon, brother of Menelaus, goes forth to the war at Troy. His wife Clytaemnestra, the sister of Helen, during her husband's absence takes for her paramour Aegisthos and shares the govern-

---

[1] *Mourning Becomes Electra,* a trilogy: *Homecoming, The Hunted, The Haunted,* by Eugene O'Neill. Guild Theatre, New York City. October 26, 1931.

From *The New Republic,* LXVIII, pp. 352-355. November 11, 1931. Reprinted by permission.

ment of Argos with him. In due time Agamemnon, having at the god's behest sacrificed his daughter Iphigenia and bringing with him Cassandra, Priam's daughter, returns, and is murdered by Clytaemnestra and her lover. Electra, his daughter, is shamed and degraded and prays for the return of her brother Orestes, long ago sent out of the country by his mother and now become a man. Orestes returns, kills Clytaemnestra and Aegisthos. He is pursued by the Erinnyes, and only after wandering and agony and a vindication of himself before the tribunal of Athena's Areopagos is he cleansed of his sin.

Mourning Becomes Electra begins with the mother and daughter, Christine and Lavinia, waiting, there in this house of the Mannons, the return of Ezra Mannon from the war, which with Lee's surrender is almost over. A thread of romance is introduced between, on the one side, Hazel and Peter, a brother and sister, and, on the other, the son, Orin, and Lavinia. Meanwhile Captain Brant comes to call; he pays a certain court to Lavinia, and she, acting on a cue from the hired man, who has been on the place these sixty years, traps him into admitting that he is the son of one of the Mannons who had seduced a Canadian maid-servant and been driven from home by his father, Lavinia's grandfather. She has all her data straight now. She has suspected her mother, followed her to New York, where Christine has pretended to go because of her own father's illness but has in fact been meeting Adam Brant. Lavinia has written her father and her brother, hinting at the town gossip about her mother. We learn that Captain Brant had returned to avenge his mother but instead had fallen passionately in love with Christine, who loves him as passionately as she hates her husband. From this point the play moves on, with the father's hatred of the son, who returns it, the son's adoration of his mother, the daughter's and the mother's antagonism, the daughter's and the father's devotion, to Christine's murder of her husband with the poison sent by Brant and substituted for the medicine prescribed against his heart trouble. Part One of the play ends here. Orin returns, after an illness from a wound in the head. Christine tries to protect herself in her son's mind against the plots of Lavinia. Lavinia, in the room where her father's body lies, convinces Orin with the facts; they trail Christine to Brant's ship, where she has gone to warn him against Orin. Orin shoots Brant. Christine next day kills herself. Brother and sister take a long voyage to China, stop at the southern isles, come home again. Substitutions have taken place, Lavinia has grown like her mother, Orin more like his father. Meanwhile his old affair with Hazel, encouraged at last by Lavinia, who now wants to marry Peter, is canceled; he finds himself making an incestuous proposal to Lavinia and is repulsed by her. He shoots himself. In the end Lavinia, speaking words of love to Peter, finds Adam's name on her lips. She breaks with Peter, orders the blinds of her house nailed shut, and goes into the house, to live there till her death. Justice has been done, the Mannon dead will be there and she will be there.

So bare an account serves the plot a little, but can give scant indication of the direct speeches and actions heavily charged with the burden and meaning of the scenes; nor does it convey the power and direct arrangement of some of them, that, for example, of the brother anad sister at Brant's cabin, where the mere visual elements convey as much as the words. The chanty with which this scene opens, the song and the singer's drunkenness, the lonely ship in the dusk, establishing as it does the mood of longing, futility, land chains and the sea's invitation and memory, is a fine idea and greatly enriches the scene's texture, though the performance did not fully establish the current or motive.

It will be obvious that the American dramatist, as the Greek did, used a well-known outline which he could fill in to his purpose. Obviously, too, Ezra Mannon is Agamemnon, Captain Brant Aegisthos, Christine Clytaemnestra, Lavinia Electra, and Orin Orestes. But to dismiss the matter by saying that Mr. O'Neill has merely repeated the classic story in modern terms is off the track. Let it go at that and you will miss even the really classic elements in the play and get only the Greek side of it that is self-evident and that would be easy for any dramatist.

The story itself follows the Greek plays up to the middle of the third division of the play, and here the incest motive, the death of Orin and the transference of the whole situation and dramatic conclusion to the sister depart from Aeschylus, Sophocles and Euripides. The blood motive in the lover, Adam Brant's relation to the family, is an addition. The old hired man, the confidant, parallels to some extent a Greek device, familiar to us, however, in countless plays. The townspeople and workmen are now and again a kind of chorus. Many of the shadings and themes are from the older plays; for an example, the servant's line in Aeschylus,

I see the dead are killing one who lives

which underlies one of the new play's main themes. The death of the lover, as in Aeschylus and Euripides, not as in Sophocles, comes before that of the mother, which throws the stress where the O'Neill play needs it. The division of the play into three parts is of course like the trilogy of the Greek dramatists. On the other hand, the dividing line is much less distinct in *Mourning Becomes Electra;* the final curtain of the first part, for example, falls, it is true, on Mannon's death, as in Aeschylus it does on Agamemnon's, but there is not the same effect of totality because of the stress put on Lavinia; in *Agamemnon* Electra does not even appear.

The magnificent theme that there is something in the dead that we cannot placate falsely is in the Greek plays and in the O'Neill play. The end of the play is by imaginative insight Greek in spirit: Lavinia goes into the house, the blinds are closed forever, the stage is silent, the door shut, the exaltation is there, the completion, the tragic certainty. Finally, the peculiar kind of suspense employed in the play is Greek. The playwright has learned the adult suspense of the classics as compared with the adolescent sense of it, hit off happily enough at times, that reigns in the romantic drama of the North. Classic suspense does not depend on a mere crude strain, wondering how things will turn out, however entertaining and often dramatic that effect may be. The classic suspense has even a biological defense: you know that in life you will come to death, but just how the course of all your living will shade and fulfill itself you do not know, and you are borne up by an animal will to survive, a passionate participation, an absorbed contemplation of the course, till the last moment completes itself. In the classic form where the outcome is already known, lies the highest order of suspense. Knowing how things will end, you are left free to watch what qualities and what light will appear in their progression toward their due and necessary finish. You hang on what development, what procession exactly of logic, ecstasy or fate, will ensue with them, what threads of beautiful or dark will come into their human fabric.

It is interesting in our confused and feministic epoch that this new employment of the theme gives the play to Electra. Nowhere in Greek does this happen. From Sophocles there survives what must be only a section of a trilogy, the *Electra;* and though so much of the torment and waiting has been hers, Electra is at the end let off with a betrothal to Orestes' faithful Horatio, Pylades, and the forebodings and remorse rise in Orestes only, who has struck the death blow on his mother. In Euripides' *Electra* the conclusion is the forebodings of Orestes and the marriage of Electra to Pylades; in his *Orestes* Electra cleaves to her brother, who is in a violent neurotic sickness, quite modernly indicated; they are both in danger from the State for their action, and the whole situation is solved with a trivial and silly dénouement, gods from the machine, killings and abductions, wholly undramatic and redeemed, in so far as it is redeemed, only by Euripides' dialectic and poetic glamor. In Aeschylus, Electra appears only in the middle of the trilogy; the central hero is the royal line, Agamemnon and Orestes.

Along with these more accessible and manifest likes and dislikes, there are numerous points about Mr. O'Neill's play that so far at least as the Greek original goes, are variations or additions. The most brilliant of these is the incest motive, coming toward the last of the play. (We must recall Shelley's remark that of all tragic motives incest is the most powerful, since it brings the passions most violently into play.) For Orestes the gray forms at the back, invisible at first to all but himself, are the Erinnyes, the Furies who will avenge the crime he has committed within his own blood. They are the daughters of night, and when they have been appeased, their other selves, the Eumenides, the Gentle Ones, will pass by and leave him peace. For Orin Mannon there comes the sudden form of his desire: incest: the realization and admission of what it has all been about all along, his feelings toward his father, toward his mother, toward Brant, toward Lavinia. This recognition of his obsession is his avenging Erinnyes. The mother in *Mourning Becomes Electra* is not killed by her son but takes her own life; his essential murder of his mother turns in his mind with a terror more modern but no less destroying; his mind storms with the Furies—"thoughts that accuse each other," as Cicero, writing in the sophistication of four centuries later, defined them. In such details alone might rest the argument that Eugene O'Neill, placing a Greek theme in the middle of the last century, has written the most modern of all his plays.

It is not wholly the Guild's fault if there is no overwhelming performance in *Mourning Becomes Electra*. The casting of such a play is very difficult, and doubly so in the absence of any training in our theatre that would prepare actors for the requirements of such parts. The best performances came in the scenes between the mother and son, where Mme. Nazimova's sense of theatre and her fluid response combined with Mr. Earle Larimore's simple and right attack on his part, were truly convincing, and in the scene between husband and wife, where Mr. Lee Baker gave a wholly right impersonation and the exact dramatic value for the play. Mr. Erskin Sanford turns out admirably in two character parts, the village doctor and the old workman who takes a bet on braving the ghost in the house. Miss Alice Brady had the rôle of all rôles in the play most difficult. Her performance of this modern Electra was sincere, and was sustained at times not only by a sort of tour-de-force achievement, but with real physical power, voice and all. In a few scenes she was pathetic as well, clear and moving, and her beauty most impressive. No doubt there was some instruction from the author himself as to keeping the face like a mask, rigid and motionless, as if fate itself were living there in

this passionate and resolute being. As for the Greek of that intention, we must recall that in the Attic theatre the mask for
Electra was very likely one of tortured lines, that the Greek
theatre changed masks if need be from one scene to another, and
that the Greek actor in the part could avail himself of gesture,
dance movement, and a thorough training in voice, meter, speech,
and singing. Realistically—that is to say in life—such rigidity
never occurs except as a sign of disease. Esthetically it belongs only
in the midst of a general stylistic whole, as in the Greek drama
or the Chinese theatre that Mei Lan-fang brought to us. Technically it is immensely difficult, and derives not from an actual
rigidity at all. Rigidity, masklike to the utmost, if you will, is a
form of rhythm, as silence exists with a rhythm, when perceptible.
It is unfair to bring so great an artist as Mei Lan-fang into the
argument, but he gave us the whole model for such a problem in
acting—the eyes constantly moving, the head imperceptibly in
motion, supported by a complete and often almost invisible rhythm
of the body, the emotions precise and compelling because of their
very abstraction. Miss Brady's performance had several unforgettable moments. On the whole it moved gravely and in a manner
remarkably well sustained just below the surface of the motives
set for her by the dramatist; but her performance by failing both
the darkness and the exaltation of the part often made only op-
pressive and unvaried what should have been burning and un-
conquerably alive and dominating. When we come right down
to it, however, the best acting in the play is Mr. Earle Larimore's.
In all his scenes up to the very last part, where he mouths too
much and makes faces instead of a more intense concentration
on his effects, he comes off first. In the scenes with his mother
especially, he surpassed everybody else in the company; he conveyed
to us the dramatist's meanings completely, without implying that
the character himself was conscious of them; and by a certain emotional humility before the moment in which he shared, he came
out securely right.

Out of Mr. Robert Edmond Jones' curtain and four settings,
the rooms and the ship seem to me adequate without any haunt-

ing of the imagination, the front of the house dramatically right
save for the lighting toward the rear, unnecessarily cruel to the
actors. Mr. Philip Moeller's directing was admirable all through
for its taste and evenness, its clear movement and fine placing of
the scene. Its one fault was its tempo. There can be no doubt
that Mr. O'Neill's play suffers greatly and will be accused of pretentiousness where it is wholly sincere and direct, in the first section especially, by the slowness with which the speeches are taken.
Very often the effect is only that of a bourgeois respect for something to be taken as important. If it is the Greek spirit that is
sought, the answer is that the Greek reading of lines was certainly
formal but not necessarily slow; the chances are, in fact, that in the
Greek theatre the cues were taken closely in order to keep the
music going. And the Greeks had the advantage of music, dancing, and a great declamatory style, the lack of which will have to
be balanced by anything rather than this obvious spacing and
pausing and trend toward monotone, a great deal of which anyway proceeds only from a theoretical stage New England.

The two gifts that Eugene O'Neill up to now has displayed are
for feeling and for dramatic image. His plays have often conveyed
a poignancy that is unique in the modern drama, you felt that
whatever was put down was at the dramatist's own expense, he
paid out of himself as he went. His great theatre gift has been
in the creation of images that speak for themselves, such for instance as the tittering of the Great Khan's ladies-in-waiting at the
western Marco Polo, the dynamo in the play by the same name,
and many another, images so vivid that their mere repetition in
people's talk makes the play sound better and more complete than
it ever was. Sometimes this dramatic image spreads to the scope
of a dramatic pattern that is the whole sum of the play. This
happened not in more recent and elaborate plays, such as *Strange
Interlude,* but in at least two of the earlier, *The Emperor Jones*
and *The Hairy Ape,* where the whole plot was like an expanded
sentence. In *Mourning Becomes Electra* Mr. O'Neill comes now
into the full stretch of clear narrative design. He discovers that

in expressive pattern lies the possibility of all that parallels life, a form on which fall infinite shadings and details, as the light with its inexhaustible nuances and elements appears on a wall. He has come to what is so rare in Northern art, an understanding of repetition and variation on the same design, as contrasted with matter that is less deep or subtle, though expressed with lively surprise, variety or novelty. It is a new and definite state in his development.

None of the old tagging appears in this play, no scientific terms that can be mistaken for psychological finalities. The feeling of Orin toward his father, for example, or of the daughter toward him, is not labeled. They are motives contrived to speak for themselves, and no specious explanation appears to be offered. The lapses in taste, as regards the writing itself, the trite jargon or the pushing of a situation to an obvious extreme, have vanished. The interest in shocking the bourgeois, not always lacking hitherto, has matured into the desire only to put in the truth. On the other hand the feeling remains. If not always as lyric as before, it has spread out into a more impersonal and distributed but no less passionate element in the play. The novelties and causes, masks, labor, sex, and asides, devices, are not in evidence, or rather have moved inward whatever there was in them beyond sheer theatrical effectiveness. Through most of its length the play moves steadily. The uncertainty in progression, comparative only, appears in the final scenes. This is a modern difficulty, due to the fact that the matter turns inward, where the Greeks, in contrast, had the advantage of robust and sure outward symbols, tribunals, ceremonial, processions, and the forms of music and dance.

As to the depressing element of *Mourning Becomes Electra,* I have only to say that this play seems to me above anything else exhilarating. I trust I will not be thought pedantic when I say that what depresses me in the theatre is when the author dabbles in what is deep, enters where he has no right to be, and is glib about what he does not even taste the savor of. I need take no example, the stage is full of such. In *Mourning Becomes Electra* the end is fulfilled; Lavinia follows her direction, the completion of herself and her own inevitable satisfaction are seen. It may be that here life, as the Greek proverb said, wails as to a tomb. There may be other ways to manage, Rotarian healthy thoughts, exercise, good sense, saving the situation, leaving us more cheerful, marching on; but what of that? it is another situation that would be saved. There is a line of Leopardi's where he speaks of "my delight and my Erinnyes"; and once, thinking of the eternal silence, he hears the wind among the trees and goes comparing the infinite silence to that voice, and remembers the eternal, and the dead seasons, and the present and living, and the sound of it, *e il suon di lei*. In this immensity his thought drowns, and shipwreck is sweet to him in such a sea. When the play ended, and the last Mannon was gone into the house, the door shut, I felt in a full, lovely sense that the Erinnyes were appeased, and that the Eumenides, the Gentle Ones, passed over the stage.

II: STREET SCENE, *by Elmer Rice* [1]

In a dry season, when so many theatres are closed and not a few managers have given up the game for the nonce and gone off to sunny beaches and Hollywood, Mr. Elmer Rice's *Street Scene* has come to many people as a treat, an excellent play, a worthy entertainment; and there is no need to throw any blight over the flower of their enthusiasm. In the realm of the blind, following the Spanish proverb, let the one-eyed be king; we may cheer *Street Scene* and wish it well.

In a setting by Mr. Jo Mielziner, cleverly realistic without being foolishly so and photographic without idle intrusions of dusty neighborhood detail from Ninth Avenue, where the play is laid, we see the story unwind itself entertainingly, with an amiable pace

[1] *Street Scene,* by Elmer Rice.   The Playhouse Theater, New York City. January 10, 1929.

From *The New Republic*, LVII, pp. 296-298.   January 30, 1929.   Reprinted by permission.

and plenty of time for the talk of the apartment house people as they go in and out, with engaging colors drawn from the contact of diverse nationalities, Jews, Germans, Irish, Italians and 100 per cent Americans, and with a due complaisance and tidy willingness to please. There is a genuinely expert economy in the way in which the life of the Maurrant family is conveyed to us, and an economy of means that is even finer in the portrait of the wife's career, this doomed Anna Maurrant, whose husband is brutal and indifferent in his treatment of her, is given to drink, is full of principles and ideas of what a family should be and what his own has got to be, he'll see to that.

The inmates of the apartment house, then, go in and out, linger about the doorstep in the stifling summer heat, sit at their windows, gossip of their children and each other, of the little husband on the third floor who acts as if he were having the baby instead of his thin little wife, of the Hildebrand family whose head has disappeared and who are about to be dispossessed. And through the whole texture of conversation they weave the thread of this pale woman's tragedy on the second floor, the visits of the milk collector that they have all observed, the spreading scandal about Mrs. Maurrant. Idly and emptily they are doing her to death, but it is all a part of the day's chatter and the neighborhood news. We see Rose, her daughter, and the married suitor, who wants to take her from the job in his office and set her up in an apartment and a place on the stage; we see Maurrant himself, a member of the stage-hands' union, a drinker, sullen and bullying. Meanwhile, Mrs. Jones has something to say about everything, takes her husband, George, to task, and her dog, Queenie, to walk, and professes complete ease of mind about her children, one of whom is a hulking thug and the other almost a tart.

From that on, the play takes its course, clearly foreseen. The baby is born upstairs, Mrs. Maurrant tends the mother all night, she is even more brutally treated by her suspicious husband; he says he is going out of town with a show, her daughter is at the funeral of a member of the firm she works for, and Mrs. Maurrant asks the milk collector—cleverly portrayed by the author as by no means attractive and so more indicative of the woman's despair—to come up to her rooms. The husband returns, kills the lover, and mortally wounds the wife, and after a long search is caught by the police. Rose, his daughter, refuses the attentions of the married suitor, and at the last does not accept the love of the Jewish student; she goes away for her own life, with her own ideas about one's dependence on something within oneself and reflections on the history of her father and mother in the light of that theory.

All this time, as a kind of matrix for the story, people have been passing, an ingenious assemblage of types and interests, curiosities of the town, vignettes of Manhattan, incidents of a day, and so on and so on, rendered with an amiable and accurate diversity that carries matters pleasantly along. And in the apartment house itself the well-edited sayings of the different persons and races accompany this drab pageantry and sweet genre.

Mr. Rice's directing is good. Among the many players necessary for this *monde* of the West Side, Miss Mary Servoss, as the tragic central figure of the woman who is killed, gives a performance that is always convincing, and that, while she is on the stage, lifts the scenes to something like pathos and point. Miss Erin O'Brien Moore, as her daughter, Rose, has to surmount many platitudinous approaches to the character, and speeches that are without imagination or reality, but plays well; she presents a young image that our eyes easily believe in, and a sincere and simple rendering of the character, so far as is possible with the lines. She illustrates, however, one melancholy point that may as well be aired now as any other time, and this is in the matter of clothes. In play after play on Broadway, where there is a young creature whose muted life is in some factory, slum or dingy, tragic neighborhood, we see these young ladies whose rôles are leading ones—the other players may be as mussy as you like and as photographic as the actor or the author chooses—walking about in their trim little frocks and perfect shoes, simple but smartly turned out, and, however modest, taking no chances at lessening the drawing power of their pretty looks. American girls, however poor, may have, if you like, a trick of looking smart, what with the sales and all, but there is a *chic* higher up and more costly that fools nobody with pretenses of humility, and it is the pale cast of this thought that makes so absurd the picture of these leading young ladies in drab plays; and makes us ponder the problem of sincerity in art. Miss Beulah Bondi's Mrs. Jones is excellent playing.

So much for *Street Scene,* then, which on one plane of consideration is pleasantly entertaining. On another plane, where you take the play seriously and where you ask yourself whether for an instant you have believed in any single bit of it, either as art, with its sting of surprise and creation, or as life, with its reality, *Street Scene* is only rubbish, or very close to rubbish. For me, who was not bored with it as an evening's theatre, it is something less than rubbish, theatrical rubbish, in that curious, baffling way that the stage provides. The presence of living beings in the rôles engages us, and gives a certain plausibility to whatever takes place, and a certain actuality to any character whatever. But is it possible that anyone who could understand the values of the first act of *Anna Christie,* for example, or a play of Chekhov's, could fail to see that the last act in *Street Scene*—to take the most evident letdown—is empty and made up? The girl has found her mother shot, seen blood, at the hospital she has seen her mother die without speaking, she has seen her father caught and torn and bleeding, the Jewish boy, who loves her so much, offers to leave everything and go away with her, and she stands there making a little speech about dependence on one's self, and so on and so on, while nurses with perambulators have appeared and various persons come prowling around at the scene of a murder, and the obvious life goes on, amusing remarks from odd characters, and the rest of it—obliging journalism in sum. It must be a very elementary principle that the essential idea of a work of art goes through it, and that the themes and conceptions to be expressed must lie inherently in the substance of it, and that they are to be expressed in creation, not in superimposed sentiments.

Must we gloomily conclude that what most human beings like

in the theatre is a farrago of living matter with the sting taken out of it? If this Anna Maurrant's life and death really bit into us, cost us something, instead of providing a mere thrill and the comfort of pseudo-thought afterward, would we not wreck the stage for rage when we see how little this matter has stung the dramatist? One of the ways we know a work of art is by the cost of its unity in kind, in the same way that the soul within him, determining his form as he comes into the world, prevents a man's having the bulk, strength and peace of an elephant. One of the ways we can tell an artist is by the extent to which reality puts the fear of God into him; a painter of no worth will paint you anything from Napoleon crossing the Alps to an old mill in Vermont, but a real painter trembles before the mere character of human hands and the problem of their conversion into the unity that is his style. Is it any wonder that Ingres, in his despair at the success of the second-rate, threatened to paint an Allegory of Mediocrities?

On a milder level of discourse, we may say that the acting in *Street Scene* furnishes a good instance of one of the problems in the art. For the most part the company at the Playhouse is made up of people who fit the characters ready-made. An Italian plays an Italian, a Jewess a Jewess, and so on, though the roster of names is mostly shining Anglo-Saxon—but that is nothing new in the theatre. In the hurry and pressure of things there is little time to discover or train actors, perhaps, and perhaps the need for actuality in this particular piece led the casting toward these ready-made types. The result is that there is a good deal of entertainment in *Street Scene* that comes from watching these actual people as we might see them on Ninth Avenue, but very little interest in watching them as actors. They are mostly neither bad nor good. Their looks are better than their acting, and they seem better than what they say. As a minor by-product of the perplexity induced by such a situation, I have no idea whether the player written down as Mr. James M. Qualen, whose janitor, Olsen, seems to me the best performance of the evening, is only a Nordic of that ilk, chosen for his type, or a capital actor.

III: WINTERSET, *by Maxwell Anderson*[1]

I had intended from the start to see Mr. Maxwell Anderson's *Winterset* again; and a second visit, as was always manifest, merely enlarges the first impression. The purpose of a work of art is to arouse our response to its content; the ideal means employed will be that which will bring forth the fullest of responses. In the case of *Winterset* the means is, of course, a poetic medium of expression. But there is also a list of characters unusually clear and firm in their outline, and raised far beyond the limits of our familiar stage. These varieties of character are further intensified, each in itself, so that they strike one against another at a high level, or on an intense plane. All these people are seen in a tremendous —and genuinely created—perspective: the judge haunted by a sentence he passed, the son of the victim haunted by his father's innocence, and divers others driven forward by forces within the years. This uncommonly strong element of perspective in the play relates it further, in some elusive sense, to the poetic medium. The alternating resistance and advance of metrical form appears doubly right in the conveyance of this check and impulse, memory and passion, fateful past and power of life, that the characters' lives proceed upon.

Discussion of the use of poetry in drama will always be likely to end in confusion. To some persons the mere term implies the great and deep, to others the soft and pretty. To some—this notion is more nearly ineradicable—great intellectual conceptions appear in prose; we go to poetry for a beautiful and moving expression of concepts already known to us. This is but partially true. The successful poetic expression of a concept is likely to be the first complete expression of it, since in such a case the con-

---

[1] *Winterset,* by Maxwell Anderson.   Martin Beck Theatre, New York City. September 25, 1935.

From *The New Republic,* LXXXIV, p. 365.   November 6, 1935.   Reprinted by permission.

cept in full is expressed in terms of the complete human being
and the human being in terms of the concept. One of the great
descriptions of poetry is Dante's saying that poetry is the loving
use of wisdom. In praising the poetic style we must not say that
our present American drama may be too austere or stark. The
proper word is barren (or arid, or merely journalistic).

It gets nowhere to say, as Mr. Richard Watts, Jr., did in the
Herald Tribune of a fortnight back, that "the state of dramatic
poetry being what it is, the playwright who relies on the quality
of his conception rather than on the turn of his phrases is most
likely to qualify as a master of a great lyric mood." Conception is
inseparable from expression. The playwright who relied on the
turn of a phrase, except in so far as that phrase is organic and
necessary to the conception, writes not only bad drama, he writes
bad poetry. The defects in *Winterset,* in the last act especially,
are not due to the fact that the poetic form is being employed,
but rather to the fact that the poetry is bad, bad either *per se* or
bad in relation to the scene—it comes to the same thing.

Mr. Watts says also that "recognized lyric forms are clearly
no more adapted to the use of drama these days than they are
to other types of current narrative and, since they were originally
devised for other days, it is not easy to employ their archaic mannerisms in the service of authentic and convincing dramatic speech."
You may almost as well say recognized human forms are with difficulty suited to acting. A poet-playwright will, naturally, in so
far as he is successful, use only such poetic forms as express his
content. But much of any content belongs to centuries, not
decades. And recognized lyric forms do not necessarily imply
archaic mannerisms.

"The last fifteen minutes of the play strike me as dull and unfortunate, chiefly because Mr. Anderson appears to be presenting
a defeatist argument on behalf of the beauties of compromise in
modern life, and although that message of his may have its practical virtues it does not exactly express a poetic subject." For
my part, I thought merely that Mr. Anderson got himself rather
far afield with some handsome semi-Irish-poetical, often extraneous

and willful, lines and cadences, and thus crippled the effect. At any rate, it is true that there is no such thing as a non-poetic subject. The possibilities, near and far, of any subject will depend on the artist undertaking it. "I fear," says Mr. Watts, of the last quarter-hour, "that the slightly muddy confusion of the play's ideas may hurt the poetic drama in so far as it suggests that lyricism and hard-headed contemplation have difficulty in getting along together in the theatre." Suggesting difficulty in art hurts nothing; it intimidates fools; it raises the level of the enterprise.

Whatever confusion there may be does not arise from lyricism and contemplation finding it hard to get along together in the theatre; the confusion arises from the writing not having absorbed or expressed the thought with completeness sufficient to include the writer's full self, brain, emotions, and so on. As a matter of fact, all theatrical expression of thought includes immediately a certain lyricism. Contemplation in itself—if there be such a thing —will not project itself into the audience. Nor will the audience contemplate what it can acquire no feeling for.

Speaking practically, on our American theatre's behalf, the greatest compliment we could pay a poetic play is to say it does no harm to poetic drama's chances. In spite of its defects, and in spite of the threats in the last act to do so, *Winterset* does not harm the cause of poetic drama. In its best moments we are aware of the poetic medium only as a matter of heightened respiration on our part. The lines hint of intensified feeling and thought, and of words with all the emphasis of passionate life repeated. At its worst we have only verses that are sucking a sugar-teat in the Muses' nursery. In such of Mr. Anderson's verse the images appear to be a hangover of the period when Stephen Phillips' cadences were petals of blown roses on the grass. In such cases, Mr. Anderson, both as poet and playwright, needs to get away, not so much from traditional forms in poetry as from a merely traditional use of them regardless of their content.

It is true, of course, that on Broadway one must be completely successful, tossing off with facility what the greatest artists might retreat from in despair. *Winterset* is fair enough melodrama at bottom, which is saying a good deal. Why should we expect, also, that a playwright should, almost single-handed, produce a completely successful poetic drama? I should rather say that *Winterset* is not only and easily the most important play of this season, but also the most notable effort in the poetic dramatic medium that up to now we have had in the American theatre.

JOSEPH WOOD KRUTCH
Three Types of American Playwright

I: THE AUSTERITY OF GEORGE KELLY

GEORGE KELLY is something of an anomaly in the contemporary theatre. Two of his plays have enjoyed phenomenal runs on Broadway and one of the two won the Pulitzer prize besides. Yet neither of these is as characteristic of the author as others less successful, and it would not be rash to wager that neither is as close to Mr. Kelly's own heart as one or two which the public has classed as failures. Both of his "hits"—*The Show Off* and *Craig's Wife*—richly deserved their popularity. Both were soundly constructed and both were based upon shrewd and honest observation, but each had, in addition, the advantage of belonging to a familiar and popular genre. The first, with a blustering Babbitt for a hero, was a recognizable addition to the growing literature of native satire. The second, which drew at full length the portrait of a hard woman in whom the virtue of being a good housekeeper had become a vice, was typically "modern" in a slightly different way. It illustrated admirably that tendency to "transvaluate values" which Ibsen had introduced into the theatre and which, in a somewhat popularized form, one will discover in such typical plays of the recent past as *The Silver Cord* and *Rain*. No wonder that Mr. Kelly was set down as a dramatist working in a current tradition and sufficiently of Broadway to find ready acceptance. No wonder, also, that his public was somewhat *froissé* by the increasing bitterness of *Daisy Mayme* or that it should have been frankly bewildered by the almost mystical tone of *Behold*

From *The Nation*, CXXXVII, pp. 240-2. August 30, 1933. Reprinted with the permission of the author.

the Bridegroom. Mr. Kelly refused to stay put and was determined to accentuate those aspects of his attitude which were the least familiar and the least acceptable to his audience. He was saying with a calm and cold emphasis: "Make no mistake. I am not of Broadway."

With his latest work in mind it is easy to look back over the earlier plays and to catch in their text ominous hints of this more stern and acrid tone. Even in *The Show Off* there are moments when a certain unexpected bitterness rises momentarily to the surface, as when, for example, the harassed mother hears the remark that her daughter must lie on the bed she has made and replies quite simply: "It's often not the people who make the beds who have to lie on them. It's someone else." A few moments later the observation has been forgotten in the flow of pure fun, but for an instant there has found expression something in the author which would be cynicism if it were not too sternly moralistic to be quite that. Indeed, the whole character of this mother adds to the play an element quite foreign to its dominant tone, for she is a sort of chorus supplying disillusioned comment, prophesying woe, and refusing to enter fully into the easy joy of the rest when good fortune solves all their difficulties.

Even more significant is the one-act play, *Smarty's Party,* written long before, during the five years when Mr. Kelly was appearing in vaudeville in playlets of his own composition. Here the story is that of a vulgar adventuress who entangles a young man supposed to be very wealthy, who comes to his supposed mother to enjoy her moment of triumph, and who then is crushed with the information that her victim is not really that woman's son at all. Here Mr. Kelly first delineates with cruel expertness the vulgarity of the adventuress and then, with a kind of savage delight, destroys her utterly. Thus the pattern of the play is exactly the same as the pattern of *Craig's Wife,* where another evil woman is analyzed at full length before the author, with an almost sadistic fury, plunges her into a special circle of hell so arranged that her vice will constitute the means by which she is tortured. The heroine of *Smarty's Party* wanted money and got poverty; Craig's wife loved her home so much that she found herself homeless at last.

One cannot help observing that Mr. Kelly's three most bitterly excoriated characters—namely, the two just mentioned and one to be discussed later—are all women. There is in him, therefore, a strain of what one is tempted to call misogyny, but it is not certain that the term would be exactly accurate. He does not seem to be saying that women as a sex are worse than men. He is only saying instead, "Lilies that fester smell far worse than weeds," and the key to his temperament is a particular kind of austerity which goes commonly under the name of puritanism. Vulgarity offends him, not only esthetically but morally as well, and the kind of meanness which he sees most commonly in men and women strikes him always as a sort of vulgarity of the soul. He despises it with a certain cold fury, and his desire is the puritanical desire to see a crushing justice meted out to it. Others may feel that to understand all is to pardon all, but to the puritan that saying is incomprehensible nonsense. To understand all is to hate all— if that "all" be hateful. Each of his most striking heroine-victims is understood with a cruel clarity, but none is pardoned and none, be it noted also, is reformed and then rewarded. All three are cast out instead into outer—and utter—darkness.

It was *Craig's Wife* produced in October, 1925, which won the Pulitzer prize. The next year Kelly produced without great success another acrid study of family life called *Daisy Mayme,* but it is *Behold the Bridegroom* (1928) which represents Mr. Kelly's most determined and most nearly successful effort to break completely away from the themes and methods of the contemporary stage in order to give full expression to his underlying attitude.

All of Mr. Kelly's other plays are richly overlaid with local color. The immediate effectiveness of all depends in large part upon skillful mimicry and upon the literal realism with which he pictures middle-class American life. Here, however, he departs from his accustomed milieu. Manners are more elegant, characters more self-consciously analytic, and the whole style is more formally literary. But the effect is only to disengage more completely the essential moral problem and to make the discussion of it quite clearly the only *raison d'être* of the play. Again the hero—if she can be called that—is a woman, but this time her sin is that vulgarity which results from the indulgence of a too facile and too shallow emotional nature. She is smart, sophisticated, and charming. She has moved gracefully from one love affair to another and thinks that she has demonstrated by her success how completely the intelligence may dispense with those simple rules of puritan morality which are never far from Mr. Kelly's mind. But the moment comes when she realizes that she really loves for the first time in her life. And her creator seizes the opportunity to destroy her as he had destroyed Craig's wife. She looks into the bridegroom's eyes, reads there his contempt, and then dies, not so much because of that contempt as because she has realized at last her own emptiness.

Probably most persons were made a little uncomfortable by the mercilessness with which justice was visited upon Mr. Kelly's earlier heroines. Some have even suggested that a more knowing playwright would not have pushed retribution so far as to swing the sympathy of the audience round in the direction of its victim. But it is no mere dramaturgic mistake which is responsible for Mr. Kelly's relentlessness either in the case of *Craig's Wife* or in the case of *Behold the Bridegroom*. He must have known very well that the public would not judge the heroine of the latter play so harshly as he did, that there is, as a matter of fact, no sin which this public is more ready to forgive—in fiction at least—than the sin of light love. Indeed, the romantic-sentimental tradition makes it almost the necessary prelude to a grand passion. But Mr. Kelly would not compromise here with his puritan conscience or make any effort to hide his contempt for contemporary morality. His heroine had wasted her capacities on cheap loves, she was not ready when the bridegroom came, and she had forfeited all right to the thing whose value she had come to understand only when it was too late. Hence she awakes, not to be saved, but only in order that she may realize what she has lost. Only thus can the puritan sense of justice be served, for the damned must be given one glimpse of paradise before they are plunged into hell forever.

No other play by Mr. Kelly—indeed, few contemporary plays by any author whatsoever—has, in certain respects, a finer literary quality than this one has. There is a passionate sincerity in the conception and a beautiful clarity in the dialogue which raise it far above the level of merely successful dramatic writing. The author seems to be struggling to free himself from the limitations of mere naturalism, and very nearly succeeds, by his passion and his coherence, in raising it to the level of quasi-poetic tragedy. Yet the fact remains that the play was commercially a failure and, what is more important, that all the respect which one feels for it does not prevent certain objections from arising in the mind of either the spectator or the reader.

One is, to put it briefly, neither quite convinced nor quite sure that one ought to be. "Men have died from time to time and worms have eaten them, but not for love." This we have upon the authority of one of Shakespeare's heroines, and it may be urged against the conclusion which Mr. Kelly has given to his play, but the most serious of my doubts are not of this naturalistic kind. I can accept the physical features of his conclusion and I can respect the moral sincerity which has enabled him to develop an almost pietistic thesis without falling into mere priggishness on the one hand or into rant on the other, but I honestly doubt that nature is constructed upon any plan so in accord with a puritan sense of moral fitness. Perhaps a spoiled and empty woman should die of self-contempt when she sees herself; perhaps she should feel herself forever unworthy of love if she chances at last to meet it; but I doubt that she would actually feel so or that there is anything to be gained by trying to make her. We forgive ourselves more easily and it is as well that we should. Artists and moralists both love to contemplate the irreparable—it helps the one to be dramatic and it helps the other to satisfy his sense of justice. But nature is more compliant. Time cannot be called back, and what has been physically destroyed cannot be found again, but nothing else is irretrievably lost and there are no sins that ought not and cannot be forgiven.

Mr. Kelly has been silent since he produced *Maggie the Magnificent* in November, 1929.[1] In this latest of his plays he returned to the middle-class milieu and the more realistic manner. But here again he is concerned with integrity of character as it is brought out in the contrast between the disorderly soul of an uncultivated mother and the efficient determination of a daughter who lifts herself by her own efforts above the vulgarity amidst which she grew up. But Mr. Kelly seems incapable of making either men or women as likable as they ought to be. There is in the characters whom he admires something stiff and prim and priggish which chills the beholder and seems to suggest that the author hates what is cheap and common with such an all-absorbing fury that he has become incapable of exercising his critical judgment upon anyone who escapes the one vice he cannot forgive. The "bridegroom" in the previous play was not intended to be repellently self-righteous, but there was a suggestion of repellent self-righteousness in him. Similarly, the Maggie of this piece is actually a good deal less than magnificent. She is neat, orderly, assured, decent, and correct, but only Mr. Kelly would admire her with warmth. We are expected to feel in her an austere nobility, but we actually feel a kind of spinsterish frigidity, and we cannot rejoice as we should in her triumph because we cannot sympathize warmly enough with her essentially negative aspirations.

This suggests, I think, the key to the mystery surrounding the fact that Mr. Kelly's most characteristic and most seriously meant plays do not quite achieve the success that they seem at times about to reach. There is a touch of coldness in his nature, a certain stubborn negativeness in his moral attitude, which lays a blight upon his plays. Essentially they are rather dour and frost-bitten, rather bleak at the very moments when a grave beauty ought to emerge. He wants, like Milton, to express the grandeur of puritanism, but he is somehow earthbound and cannot entirely escape from a certain unlovely rigidity. There is too much realism, too much prose, where a kind of ecstasy is called for. When a puritan is also a poet,

[1] A new play, *Reflected Glory,* was produced in 1936.

the result can be magnificent, but Mr. Kelly is not quite poet enough. He commands respect but he cannot quite inspire a genuine enthusiasm.

II: THE COMIC WISDOM OF S. N. BEHRMAN

When the Theatre Guild produced *The Second Man* in the fall of 1928 S. N. Behrman was totally unknown. Since then he has written only two other plays which achieved an outstanding success, but there is no American dramatist who has more clearly defined or more convincingly defended an individual and specific talent. It is, as we shall see, difficult to discover in the rather commonplace incidents of his career any explanation of the fact that the whole cast of his mind should be as different as it is from that of any of his fellows, but from the very beginning it was evident that he had accepted and assimilated the Comic Spirit so successfully that he could write with a consistent clarity of thought and feeling unrivaled on our stage. With us farce, burlesque, sentimental romance, and even satire are common enough. They are, as a matter of fact, natural expressions of that superficial tendency toward irreverence which overlays the fundamental earnestness of the American character. Embarrassed by deep feeling or true comedy, we take refuge in the horse-play of farce or the ambiguities of "sophisticated" romance, where the most skittish of characters generally end by rediscovering a sentimentalized version of the eternal verities. But the remarkable thing about Mr. Behrman is the unerring way in which his mind cut through the inconsistency of these compromises, the clarity with which he realized that we must ultimately make our choice between judging men by their heroism or judging them by their intelligence, and the unfailing articulateness with which he defends his determination to choose the second alternative.

Several other American playwrights have hesitated upon the

From *The Nation*, CXXXVII, pp. 74-6. July 19, 1933. Reprinted with the author's permission.

brink of the decision. One or two of them—Sidney Howard and Robert Sherwood, for instance—have written individual plays which all but defined their attitude and, indeed, Edwin Justin Mayer's almost unknown *Children of Darkness* is a masterpiece which may some day be rediscovered. But Mr. Behrman alone has been clear, persistent, and undeviating; he alone has emerged from the group by virtue of a surprising intellectual quality. One might have predicted him a generation hence. One might have foreseen that a definition as clear as his was bound to emerge and that some-one in America would be bound to write comedy in the classical tradition—for the simple reason that such comedy is the inevitable product of a certain stage in the development of any nation's civilization. But the amazing thing was his sudden, unexpected emergency from obscurity with both attitude and technical skill fully formed.

The public was given no opportunity to discover Mr. Behrman until he had completely discovered himself, and *The Second Man* was not only a mature play—quite as good as anything he has written since—but actually a comedy about Comedy and therefore, by implication, the announcement of a program. All its accidental qualities were, of course, those common to nearly every work which even approaches the type of which it represents the fully developed form. The locale was luxurious, the people privileged enough to spend most of their time adjusting amorous or other complications, and the conversation sparkling with wit. But the theme was the Comic Spirit itself and the hero a man forced to make that decision between the heroic and the merely intelligent which must be made before comedy really begins.

Like Mr. Behrman himself, his hero belongs to a society which still pretends rather unsuccessfully to affirm its faith in moral ideals. Romantic love, for example, is still theoretically so tremendous a thing that no man or woman worthy of the name would hesitate to give up everything else in its favor. Life, below even the frivolous surface of fashionable existence, is supposed to be real and supposed to be earnest. But our hero—a second-rate story writer—has brains enough to know, not only that his stories are second-rate, but also that he does not really believe what he is supposed to believe. He can strike the heroic attitude, but the steam is not really there. A "second man" inside himself whispers the counsel of prudence and common sense, tells him that he does not really prefer love to comfort, or exaltation to pleasure. The only integrity he has is the only one which is necessary to a comic hero—the one which makes it impossible for him either to be a conscious hypocrite on the one hand or, on the other, so to befuddle himself with sentiment as to conceal from even his own mind the fact that he is making one choice while pretending to make the other.

In terms of action the result is that he sends packing the determined flapper who wants to marry him and returns to the wealthy mistress who can support him in the luxury to which he has been accustomed. "I suppose it's dreadful to take money from a woman. But why it's worse than taking it from a man I don't know. Do you?" Incidentally, and in the course of this action, the result is also to develop with bold clarity the whole philosophy of a hero who has surrendered the effort to be heroic and is ready to explain without equivocation why such as he must take themselves and the world as they find them without either trying to pretend that they are different or trying to make them so. The originality of the whole—so far as our particular stage is concerned—consists just in the fact that the play neither shirks the logic of its own conclusions nor presents itself as a simple "shocker" but remains essentially "serious" in the sense that it accepts and defends the premises of all pure comedy. "Life is a tragedy to those who feel and a comedy to those who think." Follow the emotions and you may reach ecstasy; but if you cannot do that, then listen to the dictates of common sense and there is a very good chance that you will be comfortable—even, God willing, witty besides.

Mr. Behrman has concealed from the public the inner history of his development and has not, so far as I am aware, told us even what literary influences helped him upon the way to his exceptional maturity, or enabled him to reach so quickly the core of a problem towards which most of our dramatic writers are still only feeling their way. The records say that he was born in Worcester, Massachusetts, and that, as a stage-struck youth, he managed to get as far as Fourteenth Street, New York, by appearing as an actor in a vaudeville skit which he himself had written. Then he attended Clark University and enrolled in Professor Baker's famous course at Harvard. But since then the outward events of his career have been much like those in the careers of half the men connected with the New York theatre. For a period he worked on the *Times* and for a period he acted as a theatrical press-agent—being connected in that capacity with the resounding success of *Broadway*. Since his first play he has spent a good deal of time in Hollywood and he ought, it would seem, to share the weaknesses as well as the strengths of the typical Broadway group into which he seems so obviously to fit. But by now it is evident that *The Second Man* was no accident. He shows no tendency to become submerged in the common tradition, to write merely in the current manner. Instead, each of his succeeding plays has been quite obviously the product of the same talent and the same integral attitude.

It is true that once—in the comedy-drama *Meteor*—he fumbled the intended effect for the very reason that he had, apparently, not thought the situation through to the point where it could be stated in purely intellectual terms. This history of a rebellious and disorganized genius seen through the eyes of a bewildered but admiring acquaintance is not pure comedy because it is suffused with a sense of wonder, because its subject is a mystery, whereas comedy, almost by definition, admits no mysteries and adopts *nil admirari* as its motto. But since that time Mr. Behrman has not faltered. He made a delightful play out of the delightful English *conte Serena Blandish* and then, in *Brief Moment* and *Biography,* he extended his demonstration of the comic solution to the problem of civilized living.[1]

Each of these plays—and especially the last—enjoyed a considerable run. At least *Biography,* moreover, was generally recognized by critics as one of the outstanding plays of the season. And yet neither, I think, was taken unreservedly to its bosom by the general

[1] Mr. Behrman's latest plays are *Rain from Heaven* (1934) and *End of Summer* (1935).

public or given quite the wholehearted approval accorded to certain other plays less relentlessly consistent in tone. The comic attitude —like any other consistent attitude—cannot be undeviatingly maintained without involving a certain austerity. The moment inevitably comes when it would be easier to relax for a moment the critical intelligence and to pluck some pleasant flower of sentiment or—in other words—to pretend that some compromise is possible between the romantic hero and the comic one. But Mr. Behrman never allows himself to be betrayed by any such weakness and he pays the penalty of seeming a little dry and hard to those pseudo-sophisticates who adore the tear behind the smile because they insist upon eating their cake and having it too. Just as they giggle when they find themselves unable to sustain the level of O'Neill's exaltation—unable, that is to say, to accept the logic of his demand that life be consistently interpreted in terms of the highest feeling possible to it—so, too, they are almost equally though less consciously baffled by Behrman's persistent anti-heroicism. Comedy and tragedy alike are essentially aristocratic; only the forms in between are thoroughly popular.

Brief Moment is concerned with a very rich, intelligent, and disillusioned young man who marries a cabaret singer because he fancies her somehow "elemental," and then discovers that she is all too capable of becoming a very convincing imitation of the women of his own class—not only by adopting all their manners, but by developing a genuine enthusiasm for all the manifestations of fashionable pseudo-culture. One of its points, therefore, is that those "simple souls" which sometimes fascinate the too complicated are really less "beyond" than simply not yet "up to" the follies from which they seem so refreshingly free; but the real theme of the play is larger. Its hero is an inhabitant of that Wasteland described in so many contemporary poems and novels. He is the heir of all our culture, the end product of education and privilege, eclectically familiar with so many enthusiasms and faiths that there is none to which he can give a real allegiance. But instead of gesturing magniloquently in the void, instead of trying, like most of his prototypes in contemporary literature, to turn his predicament into tragedy despite the obvious absence of the necessary tragic exaltation, he is content, first to analyze the situation intellectually and then to compensate for the absence of ecstasy by the cultivation of that grace and wit which no one can be too sophisticated to achieve.

Biography is again the vehicle for a comment made by the Comic Spirit upon one of the predicaments of contemporary life. Its heroine is a mediocre portrait painter with a genius for comely living. Her dilemma arises out of the apparent necessity of choosing between two men—the one a likable but abandoned opportunist in public life, the other a fanatical revolutionary idealist. Her solution is ultimately to choose neither, and the play is essentially her defense of her right to be a spectator and to cultivate the spectator's virtue—a detached tolerance. The revolutionist says everything which can be said against her attitude. He denounces it as, at bottom, only a compound of indolence and cowardice which parades as a superiority when it is really responsible for the continuance of all the injustices of the world which the intelligent profess themselves too "wise" to correct. But the heroine sticks to her contention that a contemplative, understanding neutrality is "right" for her. She may be wholly ineffectual. The world's work may be done by persons less reasonable and less amiable than she. But wit and tolerance are forms of beauty and, as such, their own excuse for being.

Mr. Behrman's plays are obviously "artificial"—both in the sense that they deal with an artificial and privileged section of society and in the sense that the characters themselves are less real persons than idealized embodiments of intelligence and wit. No person was ever so triple-plated with the armor of comic intelligence as his hero; no society ever existed in which all problems were solved—as in his plays they are—when good sense had analyzed them. Just as the tragic writer endows all his characters with his own gift of poetry, so Mr. Behrman endows all his with his own gift for the phrase which lays bare to the mind a meaning which emotion has been unable to disentangle. No drawing room ever existed in which people talked so well or acted so sensibly at last, but this idealization is the final business of comedy. It first deflates man's aspirations and pretensions, accepting the inevitable failure of his attempt to live by his passions or up to his enthusiasms. But when it has done this, it demonstrates what is still left to him —his intelligence, his wit, his tolerance, and his grace—and then, finally, it imagines with what charm he could live if he were freed, not merely from the stern necessities of the struggle for physical existence, but also from the perverse and unexpected quixoticisms of his heart.

III: THE DRAMATIC VARIETY OF SIDNEY HOWARD

The theatrical season which began in the fall of 1924 was made remarkable by the appearance of two very original plays from the pens of little-known playwrights. The first was *What Price Glory?* by the Messrs. Anderson and Stallings, the other *They Knew What They Wanted,* by Sidney Howard. In many respects the two were different enough, but they were commonly mentioned together for the very good reason that they were the first thoroughly successful efforts to express in dramatic form a realistic attitude marked by certain novel features. All three of the authors were fresh from their experiences in the Great War, and the fact may very well have had something to do with the tone of the plays, but the best way to describe them would be, perhaps, to say that both were essentially serious without being in the slightest degree "highbrow."

This in itself was a kind of novelty. The "new American drama" written by the "experimental playwrights" who had grown up around the Provincetown Playhouse and the Washington Square Company had been very self-conscious and very much under foreign influences. Sometimes it tended to be a kind of neo-Ibsen problem play, sometimes it was "arty" in much less substantial

From *The Nation,* CXXXVII, pp. 294-5. September 13, 1933. Reprinted with the author's permission.

ways, but it was very much inclined to think of itself as a thing apart, as the product of a "movement" if not actually of a cult. Mr. Howard, on the other hand, had somehow managed to escape from all that. The Theatre Guild produced his play for a general public which found it highly acceptable, and one way to define the fact that he was a new kind of "new playwright" would be to say that he was writing for the commercial theatre. But to say that is to imply something much more important than the fact itself. It is to imply that he had thoroughly assimilated the attitude of the generation which had been busy rebelling against the long lingering Victorianism of our theatre, and that, without arguing or explaining, he could assume it as the point of view from which men and women were to be presented. The "new drama" had lost its self-conscious newness. It was taking itself and asking that it be taken as a matter of course.

Underlying the play was a moral attitude which a Victorian would certainly have found incomprehensible and which an anti-Victorian would certainly have made it his chief business to expound. The heroine is the mother of an illegitimate child conceived on the eve of her marriage to a kindly old man whom she does not love; the hero is this kindly old man, who discovers the wrong which has been done him but who ends by accepting the child because a child was what he really wanted. What an opportunity—entirely neglected by Mr. Howard—to expound a paradoxical morality, to define Love, to explain the Case for the Unmarried Mother, and, in general, *épater les bourgeois!* But the explanation supplied by Mr. Howard for these events is not intellectual at all. They become understandable and acceptable purely in terms of the characters; convincing and satisfactory as a series of concrete situations which work themselves out in that way. The play, in other words, is not a play about ideas but a play about men and women, and the same may be said of all its author's best work. Behind that work may of necessity lie a point of view and a philosophy; but the concrete situation and the concrete persons who find themselves in it always come first. They are not invented to illustrate a thesis. The thesis, if any, is dis-

covered by the audience—and I suspect by the author as well—
by contemplating them.

They Knew What They Wanted was Mr. Howard's third play.
He had come from California and the University of California
to spend one year in Professor Baker's class. After that he had
served in the ambulance corps on the western front during the early
days of the war and as a captain in the flying service after the United
States became involved. He had also collaborated on a book of
reporting, *The Labor Spy,* and produced *Swords* (1922) and *Bewitched* (1924)—the latter in collaboration with Edward Sheldon.
The first of these plays was a romantic melodrama with more
than a suggestion of pastiche; the second a romance rather poetic
than realistic. Both achieved a certain *succès d'estime* without at-
tracting any large audience, and both were apprentice work for
a man who found himself as a dramatist in *They Knew What
They Wanted.*

Since the latter was produced—and won the Pulitzer prize—
Mr. Howard has had nine plays on Broadway. The themes of
the nine show a variety which would probably be impossible for
a playwright who did not, like him, find his inspiration in the
concrete situation, and they have met a variety of fates—ranging
all the way from flat failure like that which attended *Half Gods*
to the triumphant success won by *Ned McCobb's Daughter* (1926),
The Silver Cord (1926), and *The Late Christopher Bean* (1932).
In the meanwhile he has also found time for a very successful
career as a writer in Hollywood, and, as an active member of
the Willard Straight Post of the American Legion, to help that
post be a thorn in the side of the national organization.

All this suggests the energy and vigor which are so characteristic of his work. Being enthusiastic and impulsive rather than
primarily reflective, he is both prolific and not the best judge of
his own work. Indeed, the public has been more right than
he, and his finest plays since his first success have been the other
successes, *Ned McCobb's Daughter, The Silver Cord,* and *The
Late Christopher Bean.* Moreover, each is, despite the variety
of moods and materials, like *They Knew What They Wanted* in

that the author has devoted himself in each to the task of presenting concrete situations and concrete characters. He has, to be sure, a conspicuous gift for achieving a clear, straightforward dramatic construction; he has also been lucky in having a series of excellent actors—Pauline Lord, Richard Bennett, Alfred Lunt, Laura Hope Crewes, and Walter Connolly—for his best pieces. But essentially their effectiveness has been due to the fact that they were less comments on contemporary life than presentations of it. One never knows what Mr. Howard is going to say. With him, one sometimes feels, a conviction is an enthusiasm and, like any other enthusiasm, likely to disappear as soon as it has emerged. But one is always sure that the situations will be dramatic, the characters vivid, and the motives understandable.

The Silver Cord is the only one of his plays which develops in accordance with a rationalistic formula. It deals quite explicitly with a mother complex, and the most dogmatic Freudian would find nothing to disagree with. Yet Mr. Howard is known to have quarreled violently with the Theatre Guild because its directors insisted upon discussing it in Freudian terms, and the fact is significant of his temperamental antipathy to intellectual formulas, of his impatience with anybody's ideas even though they happen to be also his own. Last year he was one of those writers who signed the manifesto in favor of William Z. Foster. Put that fact alongside the further facts that he rushed into the war as soon as possible and then, once it was over, helped organize the obstreperous Willard Straight Post of the American Legion. Together they give you the picture of a man who loves a row, or, rather, who loves a joyous participation in dramatic events. That also is the man who writes the plays. In them the clash of creeds and temperaments interests him for its own sake. He can take sides enthusiastically but he can also change them. He is, whether he knows it or not, pretty certain to be on the side most likely to precipitate a dramatic crisis and pretty likely, in his plays, to see to it that one takes place. Being also a man of intelligence, his attitude is usually intelligible and his crisis significant. But it is the happening which interests him and the happening which interests his audience.

Under the circumstances it would obviously be useless to inquire what his leading ideas are. He is not, like Mr. Kelly, primarily a moralist. Neither is he, like Mr. O'Neill, a writer of tragedy, nor, like Mr. Behrman, a consistent writer of comedy. He can expound Freudianism in *The Silver Cord,* approach tragedy in *They Knew What They Wanted,* declaim rather intemperately in *Half Gods,* and achieve a serene comedy in *The Late Christopher Bean.* But none is more characteristic of him than the rest. Neither is there anything common to them all except the vigor of the characterization plus a certain robust delight in the conflict for its own sake. Their unity, therefore, is only the unity of a temperament, and the only way to describe what kind of plays Mr. Howard writes is to describe what sort of man he reveals himself to be.

To witness one of his plays is to experience the same sort of exhilarating pleasure that one gets from the society of an active man with quick and vigorous perceptions. One is plunged at once into a series of happenings and made to share the wholehearted interest of a writer who throws himself into everything with an unreserved enthusiasm. The characters are observed with extraordinary intentness and set down in sharp bold strokes. Something of the author's own decisiveness is communicated to them, and the dialogue has something of the crisp clarity of his own speech. Subtlety of a kind is by no means absent and poetry of a kind is also present. But the subtlety does not exhibit itself as hair-splitting and the poetry is neither rhapsodical nor dreamy. The men and women are plain people with their feet on the ground; the scene, some very definite corner of our particular America. Obviously Mr. Howard hates any sort of artistic pretentiousness as much as he hates intellectual dogmas. He is determined to exercise his subtlety in the accurate observation of familiar things, to find his poetry in the loves and hates of people who may be distinguished by the strength and the clarity of their passions but who remain, nevertheless, essentially familiar types.

His is, therefore, a daylight world, in which common sense is still the standard by which everything is judged. An epigram may flash forth here and there, but in no other way does he ever permit himself to approach a conventionally literary style. There are no Orphic utterances, no purple patches, no evocation of what the more esoteric devotees of the drama call "moods." Nothing ever eludes the spectator, nothing ever seems vaguely to mean more than it says. But what it does unmistakably say is enough for anyone capable of sharing Mr. Howard's very active pleasure in straightforward passions and straightforward events. His plays are not highbrow plays because their author is not a highbrow, and they teach no doctrine because he is not a doctrinaire. Essentially tough-minded, he is interested in facts and out of them he builds his plays. It is for that reason, no doubt, that the captain of aviation never wrote a patriotic play nor the supporter of Mr. Foster a communistic one. He took part in a war and some day he may, conceivably, help along a revolution. But it would be safe to wager that he will never either preach loyalty to the flag or write a treatise on dialectic materialism.

Writers who are intelligent without being "intellectual," and artistic without being in any sense "arty," frequently get from critics somewhat less consideration than they deserve. They are too clear to require explaining and too popular to need defense. Your critic, accordingly, all too frequently prefers to discourse at more length upon the merits of those persons whose excellences are less evident. But the fact remains that Mr. Howard's plays are among the best ever written in America. They have, in addition, probably had more influence upon dramatic writing than can ever be directly measured. Mr. Howard stands very near to the head of the list of those who rescued the popular drama from that sentimentality which for some reason continued to be considered indispensable there long after it had disappeared from most serious writing in other forms.

FRANCIS FERGUSSON
Eugene O'Neill

AFTER Eugene O'Neill had spent several years traveling about the country with his father, James O'Neill, who was playing in *The Count of Monte Cristo,* and a few more bumming all over the world, he fell ill; and while recovering in a sanatorium, decided he wanted to write plays. His first plays, written while he was studying under Profeessor Baker at Harvard, and working with the young Provincetown Playhouse, are the product of his romantic youth and a desire to write for the stage. They are not complicated by the anxiety about his own soul which gets in his way later, and, more clearly than his later work, they show the real nature of his vocation to the stage. The first published volume, *Thirst,* is now repudiated. Mr. Barrett Clark, whose book on O'Neill contains all the available information about his life and the origins of his plays, says that the plays collected under this title are similar to those in the earliest preserved collection, *Moon of the Caribbees,* though cruder.

The first thing that strikes one on reading the latter collection is the over-emphatic language. The characters, usually the crew of a tramp steamer, communicate almost entirely in profanity. Mr. Clark, who once made the crossing on a cattle-boat, testifies that the dialogue is not inaccurate; but the more educated people in the later plays, while not so profane, also seem to be laboring to express the inexpressible, and achieving a similar flatness. I conclude that the fault is with the dramatist rather than with his material. This conclusion is borne out by the fact that, except in the "atmospheric" play, *Moon of the Caribbees,* the author remains on a level with his characters. We are required to accept

From *The Hound and Horn,* III, pp. 145-60. January, 1930. Reprinted by permission.

people with ineffable sorrows or longings as carrying the main burden of the play. And the plots and situations are built on a similar assumption of a vast emotion which cannot be put into words.

I understand that O'Neill has never liked *In the Zone;* but it seems to differ from the other plays in the volume we are discussing, chiefly in having a neater and more self-conscious technique. It may be that O'Neill thinks that this interferes with its sincerity; or it may be that I do him an injustice. The crew of a tramp steamer crossing the submarine-infested zone, is nervously on the watch for spies. What a spy would be doing there is never satisfactorily explained. This does not prevent the men, in search of a scapegoat, from suspecting Smitty. This character is a recurrent figure in the early plays: a melancholy and solitary hobo "of the higher type." Someone discovers him reading a batch of letters one night; they tie him up in spite of his screams, and investigate. But instead of the telegrams from the Kaiser which they expected, they find letters from Smitty's lady-love, who rejected him years ago because he drank. One dried rose falls to the floor. At this sudden revelation of hidden sorrow the rough sailors, whose hearts are really of gold, are abashed and conscience-stricken.

This plot, which, however absurd it may sound in the telling never fails to move an audience, is really as helplessly bombastic as the language; a language of childish superlatives which are always trying to imply more than they succeed in stating. I take it that the essence of melodrama is to accept emotions uncritically; which, in the writing, amounts to assuming or suggesting emotions that are never realized either in language or action. Melodrama in this sense is a constant quality in O'Neill's work. It disfigures his middle period, when his feeling for a character is out of all proportion to that character's importance to the play, as well as his later period, when his attempt to deal with his own unattached emotion takes the unhappy form of a passion for some large idea. In fact it seems that O'Neill typically resorts to the stage, not to represent emotions through which he has already passed; which have been criticised and digested, and so may be arranged in patterns to form works of art: he resorts to the stage to convey a protest, the *first* cry of the wounded human being. His fundamental feeling for the stage, so clearly shown in these first plays, is not that of the artist, but of the melodramatist: the seeker after sensational effect.

Nevertheless, his naïve belief in emotion is related to a priceless quality, which one may call the histrionic sincerity, the essence of mummery. Every dramatist as well as every actor depends for his power over his audience on his own belief in what he is trying to put on the stage, whether it be an emotion, a character, or a situation. An audience is extremely malleable. It may be swayed by suggestion, hypnotized by the concentration of the stage figure. This complete concentration, which would be wrecked by a wakeful critical faculty or a touch of humor at the wrong time, O'Neill possesses in a very high degree. It is the secret of his success; and when it is joined to an interest in a character, it produces his best scenes.

II

After O'Neill had exhausted the vein of mood and atmosphere derived from his early experiences of bumming, he ceased to write melodrama for its own sake, and developed an interest in people he had known or heard about. His next plays begin with an interest in a character or characters. O'Neill thus explains the origin of *Beyond the Horizon,* the earliest play of this type to be preserved: "I think the real life experience from which the idea of *Beyond the Horizon* sprang was this: On the British tramp steamer on which I made a voyage as ordinary seaman, Buenos Aires to New York, there was a Norwegian A. B. and we became quite good friends. The great sorrow and mistake of his life, he used to grumble, was that as a boy he had left the small paternal farm to run away to sea. He had been at sea twenty years, and had never gone home once in that time. . . . Yet he cursed the sea and the life it had led him—affectionately. . . . I thought, 'What if he had stayed on the farm, with his instincts? What would have

happened?' . . . And from that point I started to think of a
more intellectual, civilized type . . . a man who would have my
Norwegian's inborn craving for the sea's unrest, only in him it
would be diluted into a vague, intangible wanderlust. . . . He would
throw away his instinctive dream and accept the thraldom of the
farm for—why, for almost any nice, little poetical craving—the
romance of sex, say." Though we do not have O'Neill's account
of the origins of most of his plays, I should say, from internal
evidences, that *Gold, Anna Christie, Diff'rent, All God's Chillun
Got Wings,* and perhaps *Desire Under the Elms,* started from a
similar interest in a character, which was sometimes real, sometimes partly or entirely imaginary. I shall look at *All God's Chillun* as typical of this group. It shows his most characteristic failings as well as some of his very best results.

The first scene shows Ella, a white girl, and Jim, a sensitive
little negro boy, having a childish love affair in their native slum.
This scene, unnecessary for the main theme of the play, is typical
of O'Neill. Its only possible relevance is as psychological and
sociological background, for the important information is dupli-
cated later. I shall have more to say later about O'Neill's use
of this type of realism. Meanwhile observe that the realism of
the dialogue and the natural history of the stage full of children
(which, I may say, is extremely difficult to do practically), are
complicated by a kind of symbolism or super-realism of the set.
The scene is a street-corner, one street being full of black faces
and negro tunes, the other street full of white faces and their
tunes. Aside from the sloppiness of leaving so much to the carpenter and the régisseur (which I shall also mention later), it may
be doubted whether realism with a superimposed symbolism of
this kind is ever a success. Even Ibsen, with his Wild Ducks and
his sea-ladies, has the greatest difficulty in making it seem anything but artificial, and Mr. O'Neill hasn't a tenth of his skill.

Ella falls in with tough companions and gradually degenerates,
while Jim painfully acquires education and starts to study Law.
Ella, disillusioned with her own kind, marries Jim in a moment
of depression, as the only "white" man she knows. There is a

good "symbolistic" scene showing the newly married couple emerging from the church between rows of hostile faces, white on one side and black on the other. And then the real drama begins: the struggle in Jim between his love for Ella and his ambition to succeed in the world; the struggle in Ella between her love for Jim and her hatred of him as the cause of her exile from her own people. The point of conflict is Jim's career: for his self-respect he needs to become a lawyer, while Ella, who has never really accepted Jim as her husband, needs to preserve her spiritual ascendancy by preventing him from passing his examinations. Tied together by their love and by their solitude, they alternately take refuge in each other's arms and fight for mastery or vengeance. The scenes throughout this middle part of the play, in spite of their inadequate language, are deeply convincing. But at the end they both give up: Jim agrees to play a little boy to Ella's little girl. In effect, they cease to strive for an adult relation of husband and wife and accept a childish one.

Now if the previous scenes mean anything, this conclusion marks a degeneration on both their parts. But O'Neill, under the necessity of ending his play, asks us to accept it as a hard won *Verklärung*:

Jim—Forgive me, God—and make me worthy! . . . Let this fire of burning suffering purify me of selfishness and make me worthy of the child you send me for the woman you take away!

Ella—Honey, Honey, I'll play right up to the gates of heaven with you!

What is the reason for this extraordinary failure of O'Neill's to master his material? Between the untidy and unnecessary first scene and the bathetic and evasive finale, there are several scenes of really tragic significance. Beginning with a person, and proceeding with that complete concentration on the stage figure which I described above, O'Neill sometimes sees his people so deeply that they acquire overtones of universal import. One may sometimes feel Jim and Ella, through their excellent concreteness, as every pair of exiles in love, and their story as realizing certain profound truths about the relation between a man, his work, and his wife. But these jewels are so rare, and are imbedded in such a disheartening matrix of psychology, bathos, and cheap symbolism that they seem not only accidental but misunderstood when they appear. And the end finally persuades one that the author wrought better than he knew. He turns away from his tragic vision, and all is lost.

But did he ever have a tragic vision? The finale, so wrong for the middle scenes, is not inconsistent with the characters. The reason it jars is that it belies the point of view from which their struggles were seen as having a dignity and a significance beyond themselves. It might be appropriate in some terrible comedy, but the characters are not seen as in any sense comic figures. In fact, they are not seen "as" anything: if they at times reveal heights and depths, that is an accident, for O'Neill's relation to them is personal. They are for him friends and enemies, other individuals in an anarchical universe, not parts of any larger vision. He is prepared to echo their cry, "Can such things be?" It is all very well for a character in a play to demonstrate this emotion, but when an author shows it it means that he has not digested his material to the point where it becomes suitable for a work of art. Interested in his people's psychology, yes: hence the filling in of naturalistic background in scene 1; but interested in the esthetic value of their dignity, no: and hence no possible ending for their story. O'Neill is right when he says, "Life doesn't end, one experience is but the birth of another. Violent death is seldom the solution of anything, in life or in fiction. It is too often a makeshift device. . . ." Life doesn't end, but a work of art does; a work of art is a bounded whole, and O'Neill's unsatisfying endings are a proof that his interest in his people is not the disinterested and final one of the artist, but the developing and tentative one of a man among men.

But O'Neill's power of convincing an audience is vastly aided by the fact that his belief in his characters is so purely naturalistic. Where there is no publicly established convention, the only way to make a character acceptable is to establish him naturalistically.

An audience will believe in a character who used to play on a certain street-corner in Harlem, and whose father was in the coal business, but it will not believe in one who can only be identified by the qualities of his soul, and toward whom it is invited to adopt no personal attitude. The limitations of this type of realism have been admirably studied by Virginia Woolf, in her essay, *Mr. Bennett and Mrs. Brown*. It has this inestimable advantage of being publicly understood, but the most that can be said for it as an art form is that it may, as in this play of O'Neill's, lead to the accidental discovery of a few muddy diamonds. O'Neill himself has never been satisfied with it; he has never called himself a realist: we have seen that even in these plays of his middle period he resorts to symbolism. And finally he abandons his interest in character altogether and attempts to enunciate general ideas.

III

Beginning perhaps with *The Hairy Ape,* and continuing through *The Fountain, The Great God Brown, Marco Millions, Lazarus Laughed,* and *Dynamo,* Mr. O'Neill's character studies are interspersed with, and finally superseded by, plays in which the author shows no interest in the concrete, and assumes the rôle of prophet. It is as though he had ceased to interrogate his acquaintances about which course he is to expect of "Life," and had begun to interrogate Nietzsche and other nineteenth-century philosophers. About the prophecies themselves Mr. Clark says the last word: "If O'Neill were a genuinely original thinker, or even a brilliant spokesman for the ideas of a brilliant thinker, we might argue as to whether we should be the losers if he were to give up writing plays altogether, but his ideas as contributions to contemporary thought are negligible; they are at best slightly varied forms of what we have all been reading during the past decade or so." Lazarus' Nietzschean exclamation is typical: "Men are also unimportant! . . . Man remains! Man slowly arises from the past of the race of men that was his tomb of death! For Man death is not! Man, Son of God's Laughter, is!" O'Neill is not a thinker, and we need not attempt to investigate his thought any further. It is true that Lazarus sounds a little like O'Neill's own fundamental cry, that "life goes on"—implying, perhaps, some confusion between pessimism and the unhappy ending, which would affect his ability to write plays; moreover, it is doubtful whether Lazarus' generalized and rather hysterical optimism could ever be realized in live characters; but the question which concerns us more nearly, in our attempt to understand O'Neill as a playwright, is not so much the quality of the thought as the relation between the thought, the author, and the play.

O'Neill, we find, is more interested in affirming his ideas than in representing the experience in which they are implied. The example of Elizabethan drama seems to prove that an unsatisfying philosophy may underlie a great play. But there the play is the thing, and the philosophy may at most be deduced from it as from a direct experience of life. In *Lazarus Laughed,* on the other hand, there is little or no play at all, for Caligula, the anti-Lazarus, is no more credible than Lazarus himself, and their conflicts fail entirely to move us. The burden of the play is carried by two elements: by Lazarus' philosophical arias, and by spectacular effects of crowd movements and colored lights. About the first of these, enough has been said. With regard to the element of spectacle, Reinhardt has shown us what can be achieved in this line, especially in his production of Büchner's *Danton*. Gordon Craig has hailed these departures as first steps toward a new form, his hypothetical "pure art of the theatre." As a form, it is related to the seventeenth-century masque, and the modern revue. It seems to mean a dissolution of the classic partnership of actor and author, to which we owe most great drama, in favor of a third figure, the régisseur. A good régisseur may of course get artistically satisfying effects with well-trained crowds and carefully calculated light and sound effects with well-trained crowds and carefully calculated light and wound effects—too often at the author's expense. When an author resorts to it, it usually means that he has ceased to be interested in mastering the medium of the stage. This is certainly true in *Lazarus Laughed:* the stage becomes

O'Neill's lifeless megaphone. Nothing stands between the audience and O'Neill, shouting his views. For his relation to his ideas, in these prophetic plays, is the same as his relation to his characters in his middle period: they are emotionally significant to him, they play a part in his equilibrium as a man. Attaining no vision outside himself, his plays remain attached to him by his eternal immaturity.

We are not surprised to find, therefore, that his audience is often more interested in the author than in his play: "It is salvation the agnostic playwright is seeking. One might trace his life like one of those dry southwestern roads where the Penitente Brothers have laid down the dead man they are carrying. O'Neill's plays are crosses. Follow the road he travels and you will often hear the sound of flagellation. Look and you will often see that the whip is brought down by a tormented soul on his own back. But flowers grow on this desert track, and the mountains and the sunset lie *Beyond the Horizon*. The very imperfection which connects the author with his play also connects the author with his audience. The one quality which his admirers agree in stressing is his sincerity. We have seen that he believes in his own mood in his early plays, and in the personal reality of his characters in his middle period, while in his latest plays he is in earnest in asserting some Nietzschean war-cry. As a person, he is sincerely interested in figuring out his life, and perhaps in attaining a stable point of view—though unconsciously. He has in fact never attained it. He has managed to recognize his emotional demands, but he has not reached the further heroism of accepting what becomes to them: of describing them with reference to some independent reality. He has a sense of human needs, but none of human destiny. He offers us the act of seeking, but no disinterested contemplation; himself, therefore, rather than his work. Only the dead cease to change; but by discipline it is sometimes possible to produce a work complete and independent of the suffering individual. O'Neill's failings may all be ascribed to the fact that he has never found any such discipline.

IV

I do not intend, in this essay, to enquire directly to what extent O'Neill's failure to find a discipline through which to realize his talent is due to his own shortcomings, and to what extent to "conditions" beyond his control. A slight acquaintance with modern drama since Ibsen shows one how difficult it is to write plays of artistic as distinguished from sentimental or sociological interest. But to tackle the general question of O'Neill as a modern dramatist —and an American—would involve questions which I am not competent to treat. It seems more profitable to compare briefly O'Neill's career with those of two other American playwrights, George Kelly and E. E. Cummings, who followed very different paths to the stage, in the hope that some sense of O'Neill's place in the contemporary scene may emerge by implication.

O'Neill began to work about the time of the 1912 Renaissance. He belongs with Mencken, Sherwood Anderson, and Theodore Dreiser (who was in advance of his time). This was the generation that raised the hue and cry about Puritanism. They were, as a group, impatient of tradition and convention, and their great discovery was their emotional needs. They were more interested in a man's emotions than in a map of them; therefore, more interested in the man than his work. Most of them wrote fiction —a genre which is much better suited to this temperament than the stage; but they also gave birth to the Little Theater, and O'Neill, whose first plays were produced by the Provincetown, is in many ways a Little Theater product. This movement seems never to have had anything more positive than a dissatisfaction with Broadway, and an ambition. It was a revolt against narrow commercialism; it asserted that the theatre was an art; but, having no standards and no technique, it remained somewhat ineffectual in its new freedom.

George Kelly on the other hand is a product of the commercial, which is also the professional stage. He began as a vaudeville actor and presently he was writing his own skits. He stood behind the scenes with a stop-watch, and if the audience did not laugh soon enough, he rewrote the act. From vaudeville he graduated to the three-act comedy, and finally to the drama. His experience proves that a certain sense of craftsmanship is not incompatible with Broadway, rare though it is there: having set himself the comparatively modest problem of making the *Honnête* Babbitts laugh, he was rewarded by the natural discipline which an actual audience and a particular stage can give. Assuming the viewpoint of "common sense" where O'Neill urges some large idea; accepting the realistic set and the realistic dialogue which he found publicly established, where O'Neill was always making strange demands on the carpenter and the electrician, Kelly's work was that of the artist: to master and refine a given medium to the point where it can be made to realize his vision. While O'Neill's freedom has resulted in a complete loss of bearings, so that he has of late almost ceased to be a dramatist, Kelly has bequeathed us several comedies which are complete, and refer to nothing outside themselves. If they are rather trivial, and if there are signs that his home-folks, having moved to more expensive suburbs and learned to drink gin, are no longer to be satisfied with his neat little interiors, the fault is not with his method, which was after all the method of Shakespeare and Molière. Kelly seems to have encountered the limitations of the theatre as it exists with us here and now. It is doubtful whether a method, which depends upon an acceptance of the existing theatre, would ever prove the solution for a man of O'Neill's potential dimensions.

If the Little Theater, in its revolt against commercialism, forfeited incidentally the discipline of the craftsman which a Kelly could work out for himself on Broadway, it never showed the slightest tendency to develop its own standards and its own conventions. A play with a "kick" has remained its ideal. We have seen that the personality of the author or the agony of some unassimilated "character" can satisfy its cravings for drama better than a formal and autonomous play.

E. E. Cummings, however, was a poet before he tried to write for the stage. That is to say, he had trained himself—with what success I shall not attempt to say: his method rather than his results concern us here—to see his material as an artist. His play, *Him,* is evidently more "autobiographical" than any of O'Neill's and yet the characters at least of Him and Me are acceptable as parts of the pattern of the play without reference to the author. Without trying to judge the merit of the play as a whole, I should say that the scenes between Him and Me have all the qualities we have failed to find in O'Neill's work. The characters, the rhythm, and the sense of the stage are all of a piece, whereas in O'Neill's plays we find realistic dialogue, symbolistic settings, and characters which are unamenable to any pattern or underlying rhythm. In a real writer for the stage, language, character, and the sound and movement of the stage, spring from the same root conception. A Molière dialogue implies the stage empty save for a few spectators, a little furniture, and the actors; it implies a rhythm derived from the pantomime of the "Commedia dell'Arte," and a certain relation between actor and audience. A Cummings dialogue implies a brief light interval between "blackouts," a certain rhythm derived from the vaudeville act, and an audience which good-humoredly challenges the performer to "put his stuff across." Cummings' work, in fact, has style. His solitary discipline has enabled him to work in stage terms, disinterestedly, and with a mastery which O'Neill, for all his experience, has never attained.

But Cummings, unlike Kelly, is an artist of the theatre without either theatre or audience. I have said that his style was derived from vaudeville, but no vaudeville actor could manage a speech of Him's and no vaudeville audience could understand his play. In spite of his very authentic feeling for the stage, and in spite of his ingenious and courageous effort to dramatize his very lack of connection with a live stage and audience (so neatly of a piece with the "stunt" feeling of his vaudeville style), Cummings' first play remains mere closet drama. It was in fact produced at O'Neill's native theatre; but the Provincetown's crowd of Greenwich Villagers, just the thing to relish a revival of *In the Zone* and *Moon of the Caribbees,* were at a loss to deal with Him. Cummings does not belong at the Provincetown. So far he does

not seem to belong anywhere. But O'Neill indubitably belongs
at the Provincetown, at the Guild, in the suburbs of London, in
Berlin, and in Little Theaters all over the English-speaking world.
The man O'Neill is very close to a vast audience.

ROBERT MORSS LOVETT

Three Phases of Post-War Fiction

I: THE PROMISE OF SHERWOOD ANDERSON

Sherwood Anderson's published work is strikingly alike in substance; it is amazingly uneven in execution; but it is animated
by a singular unity of intention. It is all a persistent effort to
come to close grips with life, to master it, to force it to give up
its secret. It suggests a wrestling match in which the challenger
is thrown again and again, and yet each time comes back with
thews and sinews braced and muscles hardened to try another fall.
In his persistence Mr. Anderson is like Jacob with the angel,
crying through the night, "I will not let thee go except thou bless
me." And like Jacob he waits until the breaking of day to triumph: "I have seen God face to face."

Let it be said at once that the morning is not yet. Mr. Anderson has not completely subdued his material to form, has not
thoroughly penetrated it with interpretation. It remains recal-
citrant and opaque. But as his work has progressed he has shown
constantly a firmer grasp on his problem, a more complete conception of the difficulties of approach, and the resources and limitations of his art. In this respect there is something final about
The Triumph of the Egg.[1] It by no means represents the attainment of the goal, but it marks a definite accomplishment beyond
which the method he has tested may carry him on the next dash,
but which remains for the time being a sort of "farthest north."

[1] *The Triumph of the Egg*, by Sherwood Anderson. New York: B. W.
Huebsch, Inc. 1921.

From *The Dial*, LXXII, pp. 79-83. January, 1922. Reprinted by permission.

It is natural to speak of Sherwood Anderson's work in metaphors of physical achievement, for his struggle is first of all an athletic one with the crude stuff of life in a material world. Five years or more ago a former editor of *The Dial* persuaded him to set down his thoughts about American literature in a paper called "An Apology for Crudity," in the light of which his fiction should be read.

For a long time I have believed that crudity is an inevitable quality in the production of a really significant present-day American literature. How indeed is one to escape the obvious fact that there is as yet no native subtlety of thought or living among us? And if we are a crude and childlike people how can our literature hope to escape the influence of that fact? Why indeed should we want it to escape? . . .

We talk of writers of the old world and the beauty and subtlety of the work they do. Below me the roaring city lies like a great animal on the prairies, but we do not run out to the prairies. We stay in our rooms and talk. . . .

I know we shall never have an American literature until we return to faith in ourselves, and to the facing of our limitations. We must in some way become in ourselves more like our fellows, more simple and real.

This is Mr. Anderson's creed. He has tried always to work under its sanctions. He has made it his first object to see American life as it is, without illusion. It is a grim spectacle, and he confesses his inability to see it beautifully.

As a people we have given ourselves to industrialism, and industrialism is not lovely. If any man can find beauty in an American factory town I wish he would show me the way. For myself, I cannot find it. To me, and I am living in industrial life, the whole thing is as ugly as modern war.

But this reality has interest. We are a crude people, but not dull. In some strange way the human forms which this life assumes have a grotesque quality which makes them as fascinating as gargoyles. Over and over again Mr. Anderson has drawn them for us—in Windy McPherson, in Smoky Pete, in Melville Stoner. And the reality tempts always with a demand for interpretation: What is the meaning of it? The answer Mr. Anderson seeks from the starting point of the people to whom the reality belongs. Instead of using it in illustration of themes already conventionalized in old world literature, he tries to let it develop according to its own pattern. Instead of imposing upon it an interpretation from old world philosophy he tries to draw from it its own meaning.

It is true that Mr. Anderson has been influenced by the technical experiments of his predecessors, but in so far as he has yielded to them he has failed. His first novel, *Windy McPherson's Son,* begins with a transcript from middle-Western life so faithful that it seems autobiographic; but having established a complete groundwork of reality the author in an endeavor to maintain interest or to disengage significance has recourse to the romantic formula. The point is clearly perceptible at which his fact passes over into fiction. In *Marching Men* the substance of the book is undubitably experience, but the material is subordinated to a thesis which is more than a part of the psychology of the hero. *Poor White* is the best of the three novels. Here the realism in which Mr. Anderson works so confidently is raised to significance by a symbolism which is so immediate in its process that it seems unpremeditated and unconscious. But the large sweep and scope of the story somehow carry it beyond the author's control. Somewhere he loses his grasp on the meaning of events, the clue to their interpretation, and presents them with an emphasis which is misplaced, and with a conclusion which is mechanical and arbitrary. *Winesburg, Ohio* revealed Mr. Anderson's true vehicle in the short story. As Mr. Garland's *Main Travelled Roads* represented the early practice of realism, so *Winesburg, Ohio* will be cited as the embodiment of the severity and simplification of its later mode. The stories reveal by flashes the life, the activity, the character of the little mid-Western town as completely as the persistent glare of Mr. Sinclair Lewis's searchlight upon Gopher Prairie. *The Triumph of the Egg* has, through greater diversity of material and wider variety of method and style, the same compelling unity, a unity not geographical, but cosmic.

Of the stories which compose this last volume it is not necessary to speak in detail. They fall together as if by predetermined arrangement, and answer to each other like the movements of a *symphonie pathetique*. They combine to give a single reading of life, a sense of its immense burdens, its pains, its dreariness, its futile aspiration, its despair. Sometimes the theme is expressed in farce, the failure of a trick, as in "The Egg"; sometimes in grim comedy as in "War"; again in tragedy as in "Brothers." Sometimes it sounds in the thin treble of childhood as in "I Want to Know Why"; sometimes in the cracking voice of old age as in "Senility." And this hopelessness is not an interpretation playfully or desperately imposed on the phenomena of life from without by thought or reason; it springs implicitly from within; it is of the essence of being. It is pervading and penetrating, overwhelming and unescapable. It is as if, to use Cardinal Newman's words, man were implicated from birth in some "vast aboriginal calamity"; only instead of placing the fall of man historically in the Garden of Eden Mr. Anderson traces it biologically to the egg.

It is characteristic of Sherwood Anderson's art that, instead of seeking escape from life and forgetfulness of it, he grapples with it in an effort to set the tortured spirit free from its servitude to matter. *The Triumph of the Egg* represents to the full that contest with elemental things which leads one to speak of him in terms befitting the wrestler or explorer. And of this struggle of art with nature he is entirely conscious. It gives the headnote to the volume in verses which under still another figure express so perfectly Mr. Anderson's theory of the function of art towards its material that to quote them makes further exposition superfluous.

Tales are people who sit on the doorstep of the house of my mind.
It is cold outside and they sit waiting.
I look out at a window.

> The tales have cold hands,
> Their hands are freezing.

A short thickly-built tale arises and threshes his arms about.
His nose is red and he has two gold teeth.

There is an old female tale sitting hunched up in a cloak.

Many tales come to sit for a few moments on the doorstep and then
go away.
It is too cold for them outside.

The street before the door of the house of my mind is filled with tales.
They murmur and cry out, they are dying of cold and hunger.

I am a helpless man—my hands tremble.
I should be sitting on a bench like a tailor.
I should be weaving warm cloth out of the threads of thought.
The tales should be clothed.
They are freezing on the doorstep of the house of my mind.

I am a helpless man—my hands tremble.
I feel in the darkness but cannot find the doorknob.
I look out at a window.
Many tales are dying in the street before the house of my mind.

The futility of art is a part of the futility of life. It is a theme
personal to the artist: and in Mr. Anderson's case it is the source
of that lyric strain which recurs like a thread of wistful beauty
throughout his book. The first sketch, "The Dumb Man," defines with uncanny precision the artist's dilemma in the face of
his wavering, elusive, baffling subject matter—and his exasperating impotence. The last paragraph of "Brothers" is a lyric cry
of the artist's soul. "The Man with the Trumpet" hurls in strident
notes the defiance of the artist to his public. All this Sherwood
Anderson does as a thoroughly self-conscious as well as conscientious worker in literature. He will make no compromises with life
and no false claims for himself. He has done with illusions. He
has put behind him the conventional armor of fiction. He engages
in his struggle naked and empty-handed. And in spite of the
melancholy scene in which he finds himself, in spite of the darkness in which he gropes and the dimly discerned horrors which he
grasps, he preserves in his enterprise the faith of the artist, the soul

of a poet. It is in this evidence of a true vocation that one finds in largest measure the promise of Sherwood Anderson.

II: AN INTERPRETER OF AMERICAN LIFE

Mr. Sinclair Lewis, like Mr. H. L. Mencken, is a paradox in the United States of today. A leading trait of the American people is a youthful self-consciousness amounting to an inferiority complex, which makes us impatient of all criticism. Everything which we have done is right because we did it. All our wars were just; all our statesmen are pure; all our business is honest. Ours is the land of liberty, of tolerance, of opportunity, of righteousness. Our favorite prophets are the sayers of smooth things in Zion, those who speak comfortably to Jerusalem of her ideals and performances— Wilson, Harding, Coolidge. And yet by some sort of saving grace, in the midst of this complacency appear Mr. Lewis and Mr. Mencken, to tear the hoods and sheets off our moral and civic Ku Klux Klan, to show the cringing forms and the false, cowardly, cruel faces beneath the mask—and Mr. Mencken and Mr. Lewis as critic and novelist are, in this day and generation, the most read and considered interpreters of American life. They are constantly telling truths about their country for which less fortunate devils are being hounded out of pulpits and college chairs, losing business and social standing, and occasionally suffering physical punishment at the hands of court or clan, and yet they flourish like two green bay trees.

One explanation of this phenomenon is to be found in the fact that both Mr. Mencken and Mr. Lewis write the American language. It is a natural impulse when one hears one's own tongue in the midst of foreign speech—and most of his literature is foreign to the ordinary sensual American—to turn and listen, even if the meaning is unpleasant. And a second explanation lies in the fact

From *The Dial*, LXXXVI, pp. 515-518. June, 1925. Reprinted by permission.

that both Mr. Mencken and Mr. Lewis are good-natured and affable. They find the spectacle one tending to amusement rather than indignation. Humor is the form in which the American takes his cathartic—the Biglow Papers, Josh Billings, Artemus Ward, and Mark Twain, for examples. Even so there is still an unexplainable residuum, especially in the case of Mr. Lewis who is undoubtedly long and, in the opinion of many readers whose devotion is the more remarkable, dull. If Mr. Lewis attracts his great audience by the sense of reality which his pages convey, and the careless humor of his approach, he holds it by a sense of the importance of what he has to say.

In *Main Street* Mr. Lewis employed the inclusive formula of the naturalists, setting down as much of the visual and audible stuff of life in Gopher Prairie as his vehicle could carry, the motive power being furnished by the ambitions of Carol Kennicott, wife of the local physician. In *Babbitt* he adopted a much more rapid and impressionistic method. The life of Zenith is merely the background for the hero, who in his egregious vulgarity and pitiful self-conceit, is accepted everywhere along with General Dawes as the typical American business man, booster, and patrioteer. If *Main Street* looks back to Zola, *Babbitt* is in the more humorous, highly colored, exaggerated manner of Daudet. George F. Babbitt is an American Tartarin. In *Arrowsmith*,[1] Mr. Lewis returns to his earlier method. There is much of life as it is lived in a Mid-Western university town, a Dakota village, an Iowa city, and finally in New York; but the background is chiefly occupational as in the classics of the Rougon-Macquart series. Martin Arrowsmith is a physician and a medical scientist, and the experience of his disillusionment with that high calling is the core of the book. We first meet Arrowsmith as a medical student at the University of Winnemac; he gives up his scientific passion for a wife and general practice in the village of Wheatsylvania; he is stirred by the pretentious program of public health, and becomes assistant and finally suc-

[1] *Arrowsmith,* by Sinclair Lewis. New York: Harcourt, Brace and Company. 1925.

cessor to Dr. Pickerbaugh, Director of Public Health of Nautilus, Iowa. Driven forth by a citizenry justly indignant at his interference with business as usual, he turns to the McGurk Institute for medical research in New York. After fighting the bubonic plague in one of the lesser Antilles where his wife, Leora, dies, he returns to find the disinterested pursuit of truth as remote to the patrons and directors of McGurk as to the politicians of Nautilus, and takes refuge in a sort of hermitage of research among the Vermont hills.

In all this there is something of the conscientious thoroughness of Zola. Mr. Lewis is determined to leave no stone of the medical edifice unturned, and under each he finds human nature in reptilian form. Indeed, to reach the fraud of the commercial drug firm he is obliged to cut loose from the hero and follow the story of his teacher, Professor Gottlieb, on his way from Winnemac to McGurk. Undoubtedly in this occupational interest we miss something of the regional unity of *Main Street* and *Babbitt*. We do not know Mohalis, Wheatsylvania, and Nautilus as we do Gopher Prairie and Zenith. Toward the end of the book the social background of New York is hardly realized at all, and this is the chief reason why its entrance into Arrowsmith's life with his second marriage seems mere fiction. The essential truth of Arrowsmith's experience as medical student, country doctor, and director of public health, no physician will question. Even the preposterous Pickerbaugh, Director of Public Health of Nautilus, Iowa, is plausible enough to readers in New York and Chicago. Pickerbaugh revives the exuberant caricature of Babbitt. Besides his titular office he is "founder of the first Rotary Club in Iowa; superintendent of the Jonathan Edwards Congregational Sunday School of Nautilus; president of the Moccasin Ski and Hiking Club, of the West Side Bowling Club, and the 1912 Bull Moose and Roosevelt Club; organizer and cheer-leader of a Joint Picnic of the Woodmen, Moose, Elks, Masons, Oddfellows, Turnverein, Knights of Columbus, B'nai B'rith, and the Y.M.C.A.; and winner of the prizes both for reciting the largest number of biblical texts and for dancing the best Irish jig at the

Harvest Moon Soirée of the Jonathan Edwards Bible Class for the Grown-ups," and author of such rhyming roads to health as

> Boil the milk bottles, or by gum
> You better buy your ticket to Kingdom Come.

All this is in Mr. Lewis's best vein. When he conducts Arrowsmith to the McGurk laboratory we feel that he is on less firm ground. Here he is indebted to Dr. Paul H. De Kruif for the inside stuff. The bacteriological detail is, of course, sound. Never before in fiction has the psychology of the scientist, the passion for research, been rendered with such penetration and justice. When, however, Arrowsmith in fighting the plague in St. Hubert is bidden by his scientific conscience to divide the population into two parts, one half to be inoculated with his phage, the other half to be refused in order absolutely to control the results of the experiment, we have either an example of scientific fanaticism or a piece of pure fiction. The phenomena of the plague have been sufficiently observed to make it practically certain that, if all who were inoculated under favorable circumstances survived, the remedy had been found—and probably half the population would have resisted inoculation anyway. This air of unreality hangs over the latter part of the book as Mr. Lewis becomes more absorbed in his purpose. Leora's death, from smoking in the laboratory a half-finished cigarette on which a maid had spilt a test-tube of germs, at the time when Martin is caressing another woman, is necessary to Mr. Lewis's program. This other woman, Joyce Lanyon, the symbol of the intrusion of the social world into the privacies of science, would be obnoxious were she not quite inconceivable. We suspect her, along with Capitola McGurk, Rippleton Holabird, and other inmates of the McGurk Institute, of being aimed at the people who have been annoying Dr. De Kruif. As such they do not reach their mark.

Arrowsmith is an important step in the campaign to de-bamboozle the American public and relieve its institutions of bunk. Mr. Lewis has attacked this old enemy in one of its highest places. In all phases of medicine—education, private and public practice, and finally research—he has revealed its pretensions and exposed its perpetrators. If he has sacrificed the reality of fiction, it is in the interest of the reality of a public cause which gives largeness of view and significance to *Arrowsmith*.

III: VANITY FAIR UP-TO-DATE

Eighty years ago Thackeray looked out upon the London life which Mr. Huxley sees today, and gave his report of it in *Vanity Fair*.

There is a great quantity of eating and drinking, making love and jilting, laughing and the contrary, smoking, cheating, fighting, dancing and fiddling: there are bullies pushing about, men ogling the women, knaves picking pockets, policemen on the lookout, quacks (other quacks, plague take them!) bawling in front of their booths, and yokels looking up at tinselled dancers and poor old rouged tumblers, while the light-fingered folk are operating on their pockets behind. Yes, this Vanity Fair is not a moral place certainly, nor a merry one, though very noisy.

It is easy to note the differences between Thackeray's *Vanity Fair* and Mr. Huxley's.[1] In the latter there is still eating in Soho, but the drinks are mixed. There is smoking, but the ladies do most of it. Dancing and fiddling have become jazz. Crime is more sophisticated. The police are still "on the lookout," but the protection of vested interests has been reinforced by a great fascist organization of the Brotherhood of British Freemen. The bucks do more than ogle the women; and what Thackeray prudishly called "making love and jilting," has become very specifically fornication and perversity.

Point Counter Point is the modern *Vanity Fair*, and Mr. Huxley is the Thackeray *de nos jours*. Both are fundamentally satirists,

[1] *Point Counter Point*, by Aldous Huxley. New York: Doubleday, Doran and Company. 1928.

From *The New Republic*, LVII, pp. 75-6. December 5, 1928. Reprinted by permission.

and play with their characters in a spirit of mockery. Thackeray usually checked the impulse this side of caricature while Mr. Huxley lets it run. Major Pendennis is more real than life itself, while Mr. Huxley's old men, John Bidlake and Sidney Quarles, are considerably less so. Similarly Thackeray's Becky Sharp, the *arriviste,* is a finished portrait, while Mr. Huxley's Lady Edward Tantamount, who has arrived, is a poster lady. And in Burlap, Mr. Huxley has stood too near his model and set down something in malice. Both Thackeray and Mr. Huxley are masters of worldly wisdom. They know a great many things about a great many people, but Mr. Huxley is freer to communicate his knowledge. The peculiar attraction which a woman of doubtful reputation has for men, observed by Thackeray, is explained by his successor. "A bad reputation in a woman allures like the signs of heat in a bitch. Ill fame announces accessibility."

To neither author is *Vanity Fair* a moral place. Thackeray had, indeed, an honest code of Christian virtues, but he saw their inapplicability to the society wherein he lived. Indeed, the same charge that is made against Mr. Huxley was leveled at Thackeray, that he presented an ambiguous moral world. In both, virtues have always the defects of excess. Thackeray drew in Amelia Sedley an admirable little woman, whose love, first for her husband and afterwards for her son, defeats its object and becomes a bore. Mr. Huxley, in Marjorie Carling, pictures a woman who has sacrificed everything for her lover, and though she sees the fatal result, she cannot restrain herself from trading on her love and her dependence. Both show a kind of cynicism in marking down the virtues on the moral bargain counter. Thackeray applies the great Victorian test of a renunciation in Fanny Bolton, who nurses Pendennis in his illness, only to be trampled on by the virtuous ladies of his family; and gives him up not to die a nun but to find consolation in the arms of Samuel Huxter. Mr. Huxley saves Elinor Quarles from giving herself to a lover, only through the accident of the illness of her little son, but her virtue does not give life to the boy. And the same accident, by making Elinor miss her appointment, brings Everard Webley, the fascist leader, to his death—but the assassination is not a splendid revolutionary crime, but a mere murder for thrills.

Mr. Huxley, like Thackeray, is fond of having a novelist within his novel. From Philip Quarles' notes upon fiction we can understand his author's attitude toward his form.

The musicalization of fiction. Not in the symbolist way, but subordinating sense to sound. But on a large scale, in the construction. . . . The modulations, not merely from one key to another, but from mood to mood. A theme is stated, then developed, pushed out of shape, imperceptibly deformed, until, though still recognizably the same, it has become quite different. . . . Get this into a novel. How? The abrupt transitions are easy enough. All you need is a sufficiency of characters, and parallel, contrapuntal plots. While Jones is murdering a wife, Smith is wheeling a perambulator in the park. You alternate the themes. More interesting, the modulations and variations are more difficult. A novelist modulates by reduplicating situations and characters. He shows several people falling in love, or dying, or praying in different ways—dissimilars solving the same problem. Or, *vice versa,* similar people confronted with dissimilar problems. . . . Another way: The novelist can assume the god-like creative privilege and simply elect to consider the events of the story in their various aspects—emotional, scientific, economic, religious, metaphysical, etc. He will modulate from one to the other—as, from the esthetic to the physico-chemical aspect of things, from the religious to the physiological or financial. But perhaps this is a too tyrannical imposition of the author's will. Some people would think so. But need the author be so retiring? I think we're a bit too squeamish about these personal appearances nowadays.

There is a Thackerayan touch in the style of this (see Smith and Jones and their respective pastimes), and it is a fair description of Thackeray's structure. He would not, indeed, have thought of himself as "modulating from theme to theme," but this is in fact what he does, not as a musician but as a conversationalist. His *Vanity Fair* has been described as a long essay, animated by word pictures or occasional dramatic scenes. Both novelists present a vast inchoate world of events and opinions morally unorganized and socially corrupt. Thackeray, it is true, takes full advantage of his

license to appear as showman, a liberty for which Mr. Huxley wistfully pleads but forgoes.

It might have been said in its own day that Thackeray's *Vanity
Fair* was the richest novel in substance and the most comprehensive
that had appeared in English. The same thing might be said today
of *Point Counter Point*. It is rich in the experience of many characters, completely understood if not always completely realized. It is
rich (and here it passes beyond *Vanity Fair*) in the intellectual
background furnished by science in two forms, the mechanics of
life and knowledge of its biological and social processes, and by the
arts, painting, music, poetry as well as the *ars amatoria*. It is rich
in speculative ideas and points of view. Mr. Huxley has given a
synthesis of modern culture, and has made it, if not always its
exponents, alive. The reader is constantly surprised by the scope of
his knowledge and the depth of his understanding, by the keenness of his intuitions and the soundness of his logic. Throughout
the wide range and variation of scale and color and mood, in his
rendering of action and thought, elevated or vulgar, tragic or obscene, he maintains a largeness of comprehension and a fine equilibrium of feeling that justifies the term, human comedy.

But the English tradition demands a comedian to give relief to
his puppets of human futility. This Thackeray understood when
he made himself the showman of *Vanity Fair*. This Mr. Huxley
understands when he makes Philip Quarles defend the personal
appearance of the novelist, but is too self-conscious, in the presence
of masterpieces of detachment, to play the part himself. Deprived
of this, *Point Counter Point* seems hard, relentless. Yet we must
remember that to Thackeray's contemporaries *Vanity Fair* seemed
a cruel exposure of mankind, and what impressed them in its
author was his cynicism, not his pity. Every age tends to see itself
in the cold light of the evening of the world, after the golden morning and the silver afternoon. Perhaps to the next century Mr.
Huxley's Georgian London will seem sweet and mellow and
inviting.

WILLIAM TROY

Virginia Woolf: The Novel of Sensibility

Life is not a series of gig-lamps symmetrically arranged; but *a luminous halo, a semi-transparent envelope* surrounding us from the beginning of consciousness to the end.

Nor only in rhythm and tone but also in the imponderable vagueness of its diction this statement has a familiar ring to the modern ear. The phrases in italics alone are sufficient to suggest its proper order and place in contemporary thought. For if this is not the exact voice of Henri Bergson, it is at least a very successful imitation. Dropped so casually by Mrs. Woolf in the course of a dissertation on the art of fiction, such a statement really implies an acceptance of a whole theory of metaphysics. Behind it lies all that resistance to the naturalistic formula, all that enthusiastic surrender to the world of flux and individual intuition, which has constituted the influence of Bergson on the art and literature of the past thirty years. Whether Mrs. Woolf was affected by this influence directly, or through the medium of Proust or some other secondary source, is not very important. The evidence is clear enough in her work that the fundamental view of reality on which it is based derives from what was the most popular ideology of her generation. What is so often regarded as unique in her fiction is actually less the result of an individual attitude than of the dominant metaphysical bias of a whole generation.

For members of that generation concerned with fiction the philosophy of flux and intuition offered a relief from the cumbersome

From *The Symposium*, III, pp. 53-63 and 153-166. January and April, 1932. Reprinted by permission.

technique and mechanical pattern of naturalism. (Against even such mild adherents to the doctrine as Wells and Bennett Mrs. Woolf raised the attack in *Mr. Bennett and Mrs. Brown*.) Moreover, the new philosophy opened up sources of interest for the novel which allowed it to dispense with whatever values such writers as George Eliot and Henry James had depended on in a still remoter period. Like naturalism, it brought with it its own version of an esthetic; it supplied a medium which involved no values other than the primary one of self-expression. Of course one cannot wholly ignore the helpful co-operation of psychoanalysis. But to distinguish between the metaphysical and the psychological origins of the new techniques is not a profitable task. It is not difficult to understand how the subjective novel could have derived its assumptions from the one field, its method from the other. And the fusion between them had been completed by the time Mrs. Woolf published her little pamphlet. Everybody, in Rebecca West's phrase, was "doing" a novel in the period immediately following the World War. Everybody, that is to say, was writing a quasi-poetic rendition of his sensibility in a form which it was agreed should be called the novel.

Possessing a mind schooled in abstract theory, especially alert to the intellectual novelties of her own time, Mrs. Woolf was naturally attracted by a method which in addition to being contemporary offered so much to the speculative mind. But the deeper causes of the attraction, it is now evident, were embedded in Mrs. Woolf's own temperament of sensibility. The subjective mode is the only mode especially designed for temperaments immersed in their own sensibility, obsessed with its movements and vacillations, fascinated by its instability. It was the only mode possible for someone like Proust; it was alone capable of projecting the sensibility which because it has remained so uniform throughout her work we may be permitted to call Mrs. Woolf's own. Here it happens to be Bernard, in *The Waves,* speaking:

A space was cleared in my mind. I saw through the thick leaves of habit. Leaning over the gate I regretted so much litter, so much unaccomplishment and separation, for one cannot cross London to see a friend, life being so full of engagements; nor take ship to India and see a naked man spearing fish in blue water. I said life had been imperfect, an unfinished phrase. It had been impossible for me, taking snuff as I do from any bagman met in a train, to keep coherency—that sense of the generations, of women carrying red pitchers to the Nile, of the nightingale who sings among conquests and migrations . . .

But this might be almost any one of Mrs. Woolf's characters; and from such a passage we can appreciate how perfectly the subjective or "confessional" method is adapted to the particular sensibility reflected throughout her work.

And if we require in turn some explanation for this hieratic cultivation of the sensibility, we need only examine for a moment the nature and quality of the experience represented by most of her characters. From *The Voyage Out* to *The Waves* Mrs. Woolf has written almost exclusively about one class of people, almost one might say one type of individual, and that a class or type whose experience is largely vicarious, whose contacts with actuality have been for one or another reason incomplete, unsatisfactory, or inhibited. Made up of poets, metaphysicians, botanists, water-colorists, the world of Mrs. Woolf is a kind of superior Bohemia, as acutely refined and aristocratic in its way as the world of Henry James, except that its inhabitants concentrate on their sensations and impressions rather than on their problems of conduct. (Such problems, of course, do not even exist for them since they rarely allow themselves even the possibility of action.) Life for these people, therefore, is painful less for what it has done to them than for what their excessive sensitivity causes them to make of it. Almost every one of them is the victim of some vast and inarticulate fixation: Mrs. Dalloway on Peter Walsh, Lily Briscoe in *To the Lighthouse* on Mrs. Ramsay, everyone in *The Waves* on Percival. All of them, like Neville in the last-named book, are listening for "that wild hunting-song, Percival's music." For all of them what Percival represents is something lost or denied, something which must remain forever outside the intense circle of their own renunciation. No consolation is left them but solitude, a timeless solitude in which to descend to a kind of self-induced Nirvana. "Heaven be praised for solitude!" cries Bernard toward the close of *The Waves.* "Heaven be praised for solitude that has removed the pressure of the eye, the solicitation of the body, and all need of lies and phrases." Through solitude these people are able to relieve themselves with finality from the responsibilities of living, they are able to complete their divorce from reality even to the extent of escaping the burden of personality. Nothing in Mrs. Woolf's work serves as a better revelation of her characters as a whole than these ruminations of Mrs. Ramsay in *To the Lighthouse:*

> To be silent; to be alone. All the being and the doing, expansive, glittering, vocal, evaporated; and one shrunk, with a sense of solemnity, to being oneself, a wedge-shaped core of darkness . . . When life sank down for a moment, *the range of experience seemed limitless.* . . . Losing personality, one lost the fret, the hurry, the stir; and there rose to her lips always some exclamation of triumph over life when things came together in this peace, this rest, this eternity . . .

What Mrs. Ramsay really means to say is that when life sinks down in this manner the range of *implicit* experience is limitless. Once one has abandoned the effort to act upon reality, either with the will or the intellect, the mind is permitted to wander in freedom through the stored treasures of its memories and impressions, following no course but that of fancy or simple association, murmuring Pillicock sat on Pillicock's Hill or Come away, come away, Death, "mingling poetry and nonsense, floating in the stream." But experience in this sense is something quite different from experience in the sense in which it is ordinarily understood in referring to people in life or in books. It does not involve that active impact of character upon reality which provides the objective materials of experience in both literature and life. And if it leads to its own peculiar triumphs, it does so only through a dread of being and doing, an abdication of personality and a shrinking into the solitary darkness.

Because of this self-imposed limitation of their experience, therefore, the characters of Mrs. Woolf are unable to *function* anywhere but on the single plane of the sensibility. On this plane alone is enacted whatever movement, drama, or tragedy occurs in her works. The movement of course is centrifugal, the drama unrealized, the tragedy hushed. The only truly dramatic moments in these novels are significantly enough precisely those in which the characters seem now and again to catch a single brief glimpse of that imposing world of fact which they have forsworn. The scenes we remember best are those like the one in *Mrs. Dalloway* in which the heroine, bright, excited and happy among the guests at her party, is brought suddenly face to face with the fact of death. Or like the extremely moving one at the end of *To the Lighthouse* in which Lily Briscoe at last breaks into tears and cries aloud the hallowed name of Mrs. Ramsay. In such scenes Mrs. Woolf is excellent; no living novelist can translate these nuances of perception in quite the same way; and their effect in her work is of an occasional transitory rift in that diaphanous "envelope" with which she surrounds her characters from beginning to end.

II

For the novelist of sensibility the most embarrassing of all problems, of course, has been the problem of form. From Richardson to Mrs. Woolf it has been the problem of how to reconcile something that is immeasurable, which is what experience as *feeling* very soon becomes, with something that is measured and defined, which has remained perhaps our most elementary conception of art. In the eighteenth century the impulse toward reconciliation was undoubtedly less acute than it has become today: Richardson and Sterne were working in a medium which did not yet make serious pretensions to being opposed to poetry and drama as a distinct art form. There was not yet a Flaubert or a Tolstoy, a Turgenev or a Henry James. Feeling was enough; and feeling was allowed to expand in volumes whose uncontrollable bulk was an eloquent demonstration of its immeasurability. But when at the turn of the present century, under distinguished philosophical auspices, feeling was restored to the novel, when the sensibility finally triumphed over the floundering nineteenth-century Reason, no such artistic insouciance was possible for anyone at all conscious of the literary tradition. In Proust we see the attempt to achieve form on a large scale through the substitution of a purely metaphysical system for the various collapsing frameworks of values—religious, ethical, and scientific—on which the fiction of the nineteenth century had depended. In Joyce it is through a substitution of quite a different kind, that of a particular myth from the remote literary past, that the effort is made to endow the treasures of the sensibility with something like the *integritas* of the classical estheticians. And in the case of Mrs. Woolf, who is in this respect representative of most of the followers of these two great contemporary exemplars, the pursuit of an adequate form has been a strenuous one from first to last.

In her earliest two books, to be sure, this strain is not too clearly apparent. But *The Voyage Out,* although an interesting novel in many respects, is notably deficient in what we usually designate as narrative appeal. In retrospect the excellence of the dialogue, the skill with social comedy, the objective portraiture of character—all traditional elements which Mrs. Woolf has since chosen to discard—seem remarkable. But already one can observe a failure or reluctance to project character through a progressive representation of motives, which provides the structure in such a novelist as Jane Austen, for example, whom Mrs. Woolf happens to resemble most in this novel. For an ordered pattern of action unfolding in time Mrs. Woolf substitutes a kind of spatial unity (the setting is a yacht at sea and later a Portuguese hotel), a *cadre,* so to speak, within which everything—characters, scenes and ideas—tends to remain fixed and self-contained. This would be an altogether true description if it were not for the promise of some larger development in the love affair that emerges at the end. But even here, in Mrs. Woolf's first novel, no fulfillment is allowed; death is invoked; death supplies a termination which might not otherwise be reached since none is inherent in the plan. *Night and Day* is an effort to write a novel on a thoroughly conventional model, and the result is so uncertain that we can understand the rather sudden turning to a newer method. It is as if Mrs. Woolf had persuaded herself by these experiments (how consciously we may judge from her essay *Mr. Bennett and Mrs. Brown*) that her view of personality did not at all coincide with the formal requirements of the conventional novel. Of course she was not alone in this discovery for there already existed the rudiments of a new tradition, whose main tendency was to dispense with form for the sake of an intensive exploitation of method.

Despite the number of artists in every field who assume that an innovation in method entails a corresponding achievement in form, method cannot be regarded as quite the same thing as form. For the novelist all that we can mean by method is embraced in the familiar phrase "the point of view." As his object is character his only method can be that by which he endeavors to attain to a complete grasp and understanding of that object. "Method" in fiction narrows down to nothing more or less than the selection of a point of view from which character may be studied and presented. The drastic shift in the point of view for which Henry James prepared English fiction has undeniably resulted in many noticeable effects in its form or structure. But it is not yet possible to declare that it has resulted in any *new* form. Dorothy Richardson, in the opening volume of *Pilgrimage,* was among the first to apply this new method but in none of the volumes which followed has she allied it to anything like a consistent form. What Mrs. Woolf absorbed from Miss Richardson, from May Sinclair and from James Joyce, all of whom had advanced its use before 1918, was therefore only method, and not form. In the collection of sketches called *Monday or Tuesday* Mrs. Woolf definitely announced her affiliation with the new tradition. But such pieces as "Kew Gardens" and "The Mark on the Wall" were so slight in scope that they could make their appeal (like the essays of Lamb, for example) without the aid of any formal order or plan. Not until *Jacob's Room* does Mrs. Woolf attempt to use the method at any length, and in this book, with which her larger reputation began, we can first perceive the nature of the problem suggested by her work.

In one sense, the structure of *Jacob's Room* is that of the simplest form known to story-telling—the chronicle. From its intense pages one is able to detach a bare continuity of events: Jacob goes to the seashore, to Cambridge, to Greece, to the War. But what his creator is manifestly concerned with is not the relation of these events to his character, but their relation to his sensibility. The latter is projected through a poetic rendering of the dreams, desires, fantasies and enthusiasms which pass through his brain. The rendering is poetic because it is managed entirely by images, certain of which are recurrent throughout—the sheep's jaw with yellow teeth, "the moors and Byron," Greece. The theme also would seem to be a kind of poetic contrast between the outward passage of events and the permanence of a certain set of images in the mind. It happens that there is enough progression of outward events to give the book about as much movement as any other biographical (or autobiographical) chronicle. But one cannot point to any similar movement, any principle of progressive unity in the revelation of all that implicit life of the hero which makes up the substance of the book. As a sensibility Jacob remains the same throughout; he reacts in an identical fashion to the successive phenomena of his experience. Since he reacts only through his sensibility, since he does not act directly upon experience, he fails to "develop," in the sense in which characters in fiction usually develop. Instead of acting, he responds, and when death puts an end to his response, the book also comes to an end. "What am I to do with these?" his mother asks at the close, holding up an old pair of shoes, and this bit of romantic pathos is all the significance which his rich accumulation of dreams and suffering is made to assume in our minds.

In *Mrs. Dalloway* there is a much more deliberate use of recurrent images to identify the consciousness of each of the characters. The effort is not toward an integration of these images, for that would amount to something which is opposed to Mrs. Woolf's whole view of personality. It is toward no more than the emphasis of a certain rhythm in consciousness, which is obviously intended to supply a corresponding rhythm to the book as a whole. Moreover, in this work use is made for the first time of an enlarged image, a symbol that is fixed, constant and wholly outside the time-world of the characters. The symbol of Big Ben, since it sets the contrast between physical time and the measureless duration of the characters' inner life, serves as a sort of standard or center of reference. But neither of these devices, it should be realized, has anything directly to do with the organization of character: rhythm, the rhythm of images in the consciousness, is not the same thing as an order of the personality; the symbol of Big Ben is no real center because it exists outside the characters, is set up in contrast with them. By means of these devices carried over from lyric poetry, a kind of unity is achieved which is merely superficial or decorative, corresponding to no fundamental organization of the experience.

In her next book, however, Mrs. Woolf goes much further toward a fusion of character and design. *To the Lighthouse,* which is probably her finest performance in every respect, owes its success not least to the completeness with which the symbol chosen is identified with the will of every one of the characters. The lighthouse is the common point toward which all their desires are oriented; it is an object of attainment or fulfillment which gives direction to the movements of their thought and sensibility; and since it is thus associated with them it gives a valid unity to the whole work. Moreover, alone among Mrs. Woolf's works, *To the Lighthouse* has for its subject an action, a single definite action, *"going* to the lighthouse," which places it clearly in the realm of narrative. In fact, as narrative, it may be even more precisely classified as an *incident.* The sole objection that might be raised on esthetic grounds is whether Mrs. Woolf's method has not perhaps caused her to extend her development beyond the inherent potentialities of this form. The question is whether such a narrow structure can support the weight of the material and the stress of its treatment. More relevant to the present question, however, is the consideration that so much of the success of the book rests on the unusually happy choice of symbol, one that is very specially adapted to the theme, and not likely to be used soon again. Not many more such symbols occur to the imagination.

Certainly Mrs. Woolf does not make use of the same kind of symbol in her next novel; for in *The Waves* she returns to the devices of rhythm and symbolical contrast on which she depended in her earlier books. (*Orlando* is not a novel, but a "biography," and has only to follow a simple chronological order. Whatever hilarious variations its author plays on the traditional concept of time do not affect her adherence to this simple order.) In *The Waves* Mrs. Woolf again presents her characters through the rhythm of images in the brain, again bases her structure on a contrast between these and a permanent symbol of the objective world. There is, first of all, the image or set of images which serves as a *motif* for each of the characters: for Louis, a chained beast stamping on the shore, for Bernard, the willow tree by the river; for Neville, "that wild hunting-song, Percival's music." And also there is the cumulative image of each of their lives taken as a whole set in a parallel relationship to the movements of the sea.

Such a parallel, of course, is not an unfamiliar one. "Dwellers by the sea cannot fail to be impressed by the sight of its ceaseless ebb and flow," remarks Frazer in *The Golden Bough,* "and are apt . . . to trace a subtle relation, a secret harmony, between its tides and the life of man." What is unique is Mrs. Woolf's effort to expand what is usually no more than an intuition, a single association, a lyrical utterance to the dimensions of a novel. In one sense this is accomplished by a kind of multiplication: we are given six lyric poets instead of the usual one. For what Mrs. Woolf offers is a rendering of the subjective response to reality of six different people at successive stages in their lives. We are presented to them in childhood, adolescence, youth, early and late middle-age. *"The waves broke on the shore"* is the last line in the book, and from this we are probably to assume that at the close they are all dead. Such a scheme has the order of a chronicle, of a group of parallel biographies, but Mrs. Woolf is much more ambitious. Each period in her characters' lives corresponds to a particular movement of the sea; the current of their lives at the end is likened to its "incessant rise and fall and rise and fall again." In addition, the different periods correspond to the changing position of the sun in the sky on a single day, suggesting a vision of human lives *sub specie aeternitatis*. (The ancillary images of birds, flowers and wind intensify the same effect.) The theme is best summed up by one of the characters in a long monologue at the end: "Let us again pretend that life is a solid substance, shaped like a globe, which we turn about in our fingers. Let us pretend that we can make out a plain and logical story, so that when one matter is despatched—love for instance—we go on, in an orderly manner to the next. I was saying there was a willow tree. Its shower of falling branches, its creased and crooked bark had the effect of what remains outside our illusions yet cannot stay them, is changed by them for the moment, yet shows through stable, still, with a sternness that our lives lack. Hence the comment it makes; the standard it supplies, the reason why, as we flow and change, it seems to measure." In conception and form, in method and style, this book is the most poetic which Mrs. Woolf has yet written. It represents the extreme culmination of the method to which she has applied herself exclusively since *Monday or Tuesday*. It is significant because it forces the question whether the form in which for her that method has resulted is not essentially opposed to the conditions of narrative art.

For this form is unmistakably that of the extended or elaborated lyric; and criticism of these novels gets down ultimately to the question with what impunity one can confuse the traditional means of one literary form with the traditional means of another. This is no place to undertake another discussion of the difference between poetry and prose—or, more particularly, the difference between the lyrical and the narrative. It is a difference which we immediately recognize, and which criticism has always rightly recognized, even when it has not been altogether certain of its explanations. The least sensible of these explanations has undoubtedly been that which would make us believe that the difference between them is *qualitative*—that poetry deals with different things from prose, with the implication that the things of poetry are of a higher order than those of prose. This is a snobbery which, fortunately in one sense, has been pretty well removed in our time, although unfortunately in another it has led to a different kind of confusion. And this is the confusion which consists in removing any *formal* distinctions between the two modes.

The objection to the lyrical method in narrative is that it renders impossible the peculiar kind of interest which the latter is designed to supply. By the lyrical method is meant the substitution of a group of symbols for the orderly working-out of a motive or a set of motives which has constituted the immemorial pattern of narrative art. Perhaps the simplest definition of symbols is that they are things used to stand for other things; and undoubtedly the most part of such a definition is the word "stand." Whatever operations of the imagination have gone on to produce them, symbols themselves become fixed, constant, and static. They may be considered as the end-results of the effort of the imagination to fix itself somewhere in space. The symbol may be considered as something *spatial*. Symbols are thus ordinarily used in lyric poetry, where the effort is to fix ideas, sentiments, or emotions. By themselves, of course, symbols in poetry are no more than so many detached, isolated and unrelated points in space. When projected separately, as in the poetry of the Imagist school, or in too great confusion, as in much contemporary poetry, they do not possess any necessary meaning or value to the intelligence: the worlds that they indicate are either too small or too large to live in. Moreover, whether separate or integrated into a total vision symbols are capable of being grasped, like any other objects of space, by a single and instantaneous effort of perception. The interval of time between their presentation and our response to them is ideally no longer than the time required for our reading of a poem. Even when their presentation is like a gradual exfoliation, as in certain poems by Donne and Baudelaire, for example, that time is never allowed to be too greatly prolonged. We do not require Poe's axiom that all lyrics must be brief to understand why they must be so. The symbols on which they are constructed can be perceived in a moment of time.

When narrative based itself on a simple chronological record of action, it was assured of a certain degree of interest. When, later, it based itself on an arrangement of action which corresponded to an orderly view of life or reality, it attained to the very high interest of a work of art. As long as it based itself firmly on action according to one pattern or another, it was certain of some degree of interest. To understand the nature of the satisfaction which we seem to take in the representation of reality in a temporal order we should have to know more about certain primitive elements of our psychology than science has yet been able to discover. It is enough to recognize that whatever the reasons this satisfaction is rooted in our sense of *time*. It is enough to realize that this is the basis of the appeal which narrative has made through the whole history of fiction, from the earliest fables of the race to the most complex "constructions" of Henry James. For this reason, for example, description has always occupied a most uncertain place in fiction. Description, which deals with things rather than events, interposes a space-world in the march of that time-world which is the subject of fiction. For this reason the use of poetic symbols in fiction, as in all Mrs. Woolf's work since *Monday or Tuesday,* seems to be in direct contradiction to the foundations of our response to that form.

III

Because it is in an almost continuous state of moral and intellectual relaxation that Mrs. Woolf's characters draw out their existence, they can be projected only through a more or less direct transcription of their consciousness. Such a qualification is necessary, however, for the method here is rarely if ever as direct as that of Joyce or his followers. Between the consciousness and the rendition of it there is nearly always interposed a highly artificial literary style. This style remains practically uniform for all the characters; it is at once individual and traditional. The effect of its elegant diction and elaborately turned periods is to make one feel at times as if these sad and lonely people were partly compensated for the vacuity of their lives by the gift of casting even their most random thoughts in the best literary tradition. For some of them, like Bernard in *The Waves* (or is it the author herself speaking?), language is more than a compensation; it has an absolute value in itself: "A good phrase, however, seems to me to have an independent existence." Others may go to religion, to art, to friendship, but Mrs. Woolf's people more often than not go "to seek among phrases and fragments something unbroken." It is as if they seek to net the world of time and change with a phrase, to retrieve the chaos with words. For this reason the presentation of character by Mrs. Woolf gets down finally to a problem of style, to the most beautiful arrangement of beautiful words and phrases.

Here also Mrs. Woolf is pre-eminently the poet; for as an unwillingness to use motives and actions led to her substitution of poetic symbols in their stead so is she also compelled to use a metaphorical rather than a narrative style. In this practice of course she is not without precedent; other novelists have relied on metaphor to secure their finest effects of communication. But while such effects are ordinarily used to heighten the narrative, they are never extended to the point where they assume an independent interest. In Mrs. Woolf's books metaphorical writing is not occasional but predominant; from the beginning it has subordinated every other kind; and it was inevitable that it should one day be segmented into the purely descriptive prose-poems of *The Waves*.

No sooner is the essentially poetic character of this writing admitted than one is confronted with the whole host of problems associated with the general problem of imagery in poetry. It happens, however, that the peculiar use of imagery in Mrs. Woolf's prose suggests among other things a particular distinction, and one which has not been often enough made, although it was recognized by both Coleridge and Baudelaire, a distinction between two kinds of sensibility.

Of the two kinds of sensibility that we can identify in examining works of poetry the first would seem to be incapable of receiving impressions except through the prism of an already acquired set of language symbols. It is as if poets with this type of sensibility are uncontrollably *determined* in the kind of response they can make to reality. And because they are so determined in their initial response they are determined also in their manner of expression. The original language-symbols, acquired through culture, training, or unconscious immersion in some tradition, are infinitely perpetuated in their writing. At its worst such writing is anemic and invertebrate, like the minor verse of any period or like the earlier work of many excellent poets. In such verse the language gives the effect of having occasioned the feeling more often than the feeling the language. At its most sophisticated, however, this verse is capable of achieving a certain superficial quality of distinction all its own. It is a quality of distinction undoubtedly made possible by the reduced effort to discover precise images to convey very definite and particular sensations or emotions. It may consist in the pure musicalization of language through the draining of all specific content from the imagery that we find in Mallarmé or (on a lower plane) in Swinburne. Or it may consist in that plastic manipulation of surfaces which is another department of the interesting verse of any period. The effect in either case is the same, that of a resuscitation rather than a re-creation of language.

The other type of sensibility, of course, is in the habit of receiving direct impressions, of forming images which possess the freshness, uniqueness, and body of the original object. It has the faculty of creating new language-symbols to convey what it has perceived or, as sometimes happens, of re-creating traditional symbols with enough force to make them serve again. (For used symbols are capable of being recharged, so to speak, under the pressure of the new emotion they are called upon to convey.) Only when the original perception is solid and clear is it able to crystallize into images capable of transmitting emotion; and only when the emotion is adequate are these images capable of creating or re-creating language. The difference is between language which is made its own object and language which is made to realize emotion by evoking particular objects of concrete experience. It is the difference between writing which secures a certain effectiveness through being recognizable in a particular tradition and writing which is an exact verbal equivalent for a precise emotion or set of emotions. It is the difference, among the writers of our time, between Conrad Aiken and T. S. Eliot, or between Thornton Wilder and Ernest Hemingway. And in the most characteristic lines of the best writers of any time it is this latter kind of sensibility that we can see at work. We see it in Antony's rebuke to Cleopatra:

> I found you as a morsel, cold upon
> Dead Caesar's trencher

or in Baudelaire's

> J'ai cherché dans l'amour un sommeil oublieux;
> Mais l'amour n'est pour moi qu'un matelas d'aiguilles

or in Yeats'

> I pace upon the battlements and stare
> On the foundations of a house, or where
> Tree, like a sooty finger, starts from the earth.

In prose fiction, when the language approaches the precision and density of poetry, it is a result of the same necessity on the part of author or character, under stress of exceptional feeling, to seize upon his experience for the particular image or images necessary to express his state. The only difference is that the images of fiction are likely to be less remote, less "difficult" perhaps, than those of poetry. And the reason of course is that the images are likely to arise out of the immediate background of the novel. No better example of this can be offered than in the speech in *Wuthering Heights* in which Catherine, in her delirium, shakes the feathers out of her pillow:

That's a turkey's . . . and this is a wild duck's; and this is a pigeon's. Ah, they put pigeons' feathers in the pillows—no wonder I couldn't die! . . . And here is a moor-cock's; and this—I should know it among a thousand—it's a lapwing's. Bonny bird; wheeling over our heads in the middle of the moor. It wanted to get to its nest, for the clouds had touched the swells, and it felt rain coming.

In Mrs. Woolf's novels, as replete with imagery as they are, the effect is never quite the same as in this passage from Emily Brontë. The images that pass through in her characters' minds are rarely seized from any *particular* background of concrete experience. There are few of them which we have not encountered somewhere before. They belong not so much to the particular character as to the general tradition of literature. The effect is of an insidious infiltration of tradition into the sensibility. And this effect is the same whether it is a straight description by the author, as in *To the Lighthouse:*

The autumn trees, ravaged as they are, take on the flash of tattered flags kindling in the gloom of cool cathedral caves where gold letters on marble pages describe death in battle and how bones bleach and burn far away on Indian sands. The autumn trees gleam in the yellow moonlight, in the light of harvest moons, the light which mellows the energy of labour, and smooths the stubble, and brings the wave lapping blue to the shore.

or a presentation of mood, as in *Mrs. Dalloway:*

Fear no more, says the heart. Fear no more, says the heart, committing its burden to some sea, which sighs collectively for all sorrows, and renews, begins, collects, lets fall. And the body alone listens to the passing bee; the wave breaking; the dog barking, far away barking and barking.

or a translation of ecstasy, as in *The Waves:*

Now tonight, my body rises tier upon tier like some cool temple whose floor is strewn with carpets and murmurs rise and the altars stand smoking; but up above, here in my serene head, come only fine gusts of melody, waves of incense, while the lost dove wails, and the banners tremble above tombs, and the dark airs of midnight shake trees outside the open windows.

From such examples it should be apparent to what extent the sensibility here is haunted by the word-symbols of the past. The consciousness of each of these characters is a Sargasso Sea of words, phrases, broken relics of poetry and song. The phrases which rise to the surface are like bright shells resonant with the accumulated echoes of their past histories. Some of them have the familiar charm of cherished heirlooms; only a few retain completely whatever power to stir the imagination they may once have had. Almost all of them depend for their effect on their associations to the cultivated mind rather than on their ability to evoke the fullness and immediacy of concrete experience. And the reason of course is that there is insufficient experience of this sort anywhere reflected in the course of Mrs. Woolf's work.

It is also clear in such passages how Mrs. Woolf has come more and more to cultivate language for its own sake, to seek in phrases some "independent existence" which will give them an absolute beauty in themselves. But detached from experience as they are they attain to no more substantial beauty than that of a charming virtuosity of style. It is not the beauty but the cleverness of Mrs. Woolf's writing which is responsible for the final effect on the reader. "No woman before Virginia Woolf has used our language with such easy authority," wrote the late Sara Teasdale. Indeed few writers of either sex have written English with the same mastery of traditional resources, the same calculated effectiveness, the same facility. And when this facile traditionalism is allied with an appropriate subject, as in a frank burlesque like *Orlando,* the result is truly brilliant. It is only when it is used as the vehicle for significant serious thoughts and emotions, as in the larger portion of Mrs. Woolf's work, that its charm seems false, its authority invalid, and its beauty sterile.

It is only fair to point out what would seem to be a sincere self-questioning in the long monologue at the end of *The Waves.* Bernard, the inveterate phrasemonger, recalling the scene in which he and his friends first heard of Percival's death, remembers that they had compared him to a lily. "So the sincerity of the moment passed," Bernard cries, "so it had become symbolical; and that I could not stand. Let us commit any blasphemy of laughter and criticism rather than exude this lily-sweet glue; and cover him over with phrases." Perhaps it is too much to read into this lapse into sincerity on the part of a single character a confession of dissatisfaction by the author with the kind of language that she has been using all along in her work. But while such an interpretation may be too eager there is at least the implication that she is aware that reality when it is encountered is something far too important to be covered over with beautiful phrases. The vague hope is thrown out that in her later work she may finally be tempted to give us Percival himself, that she may spare him from death and allow him a more solid existence than he ever enjoyed in the minds and memories of his friends.

But no sooner is this idea expressed than one is reminded of the profound changes that would have to happen in Mrs. Woolf's whole metaphysical outlook before any such hope could be realized. For every element of her work that we have considered—her form, her method of characterization, her style even—is affected by the same fundamental view of personality at its root. These elements of form and of style can hardly be expected to change as long as the view which determines them remains unchanged. And nothing in Mrs. Woolf's recent work, it must be admitted, justifies the belief that this view is likely to be changed in the near future.

ROBERT PENN WARREN
The Hamlet of Thomas Wolfe

Tʜᴏᴍᴀs Wᴏʟꜰᴇ owns an enormous talent; and chooses to exercise
it on an enormous scale. This talent was recognized promptly
enough several years ago when his first novel, *Look Homeward,
Angel,* came from the press to overwhelm a high percentage of the
critics and, in turn, a high percentage of the cash customers. Nor
was this sensational success for a first novel undeserved, even if the
book was not, as Hugh Walpole suggested, as "near perfect as a
novel can be." Now Mr. Wolfe's second novel, *Of Time and the
River,*[1] appears, and the enthusiasm of the reception of the first will
probably be repeated; though, I venture to predict, on a scale
scarcely so magnificent. That remains to be seen; but it may not
be too early to attempt a definition of the special excellence and
the special limitations of the enormous talent that has produced two
big books and threatens to produce others in the near future.

If Mr. Wolfe's talent is enormous, his energies are more enormous, and fortunately so. A big book is forbidding, but, at the
same time, it carries a challenge in its very pretension. It seems
to say, "This is a serious project and demands serious attention from
serious minds." There is, of course, a snobbery of the three-decker.
Mr. Wolfe is prolific. His publishers assure the public that he has
written in the neighborhood of two million words. In his scheme
of six novels two are now published (*Look Homeward, Angel,*
1884-1920, and *Of Time and the River,* 1920-1925); two more are
already written (*The October Fair,* 1925-1928, and *The Hills Be-*

[1] *Of Time and the River,* by Thomas Wolfe. Charles Scribner's Sons,
1935.

From *The American Review,* V, pp. 191-208. September, 1935. Reprinted
by permission.

yond Pentland, 1838-1926); and two more are projected (*The Death of the Enemy,* 1928-1933, and *Pacific End,* 1791-1884). Presumably, the novels unpublished and unwritten will extend forward and backward the ramifications of the fortunes of the Gant and Pentland families.

Look Homeward, Angel and the present volume are essentially two parts of an autobiography; the pretense of fiction is so thin and slovenly that Mr. Wolfe in referring to the hero writes indifferently "Eugene Gant" or "I" and "me." There may be many modifications, omissions, and additions in character and event, but the impulse and material are fundamentally personal. The story begins in *Look Homeward, Angel* in the latter part of the nineteenth century with the arrival of Gant, the father of the hero, in Altamont, in the State of Catawba, which is Asheville, North Carolina. It continues with the marriage to Eliza Pentland, the birth of the various children, the debaucheries and repentance of old Gant, the growth of the village into a flourishing resort, the profitable real-estate speculations of Eliza, her boarding house, the education of Eugene Gant in Altamont and at the State University, the collapse of old Gant's health, and the departure of Eugene for Harvard. *Of Time and the River* resumes on the station platform as Eugene leaves for Harvard, sees him through three years there in the drama school under "Professor Thatcher," presents in full horror of detail the death of old Gant from cancer of the prostate, treats the period in New York when Eugene teaches the Jews in a college there, and takes the hero to Europe, where he reads, writes, and dissipates tremendously. He is left at the point of embarking for America. During this time he is serving his apprenticeship as a writer and trying to come to terms with his own spirit and with America. So much for the bare materials of the two books.

The root of Mr. Wolfe's talent is his ability at portraiture. The figures of Eliza Gant and old Gant, of Ben and Helen, in *Look Homeward, Angel,* are permanent properties of the reader's imagination. Mr. Wolfe has managed to convey the great central vitality of the old man, for whom fires would roar up the chimney and plants would grow, who stormed into his house in the evening laden with food, and whose quality is perpetually heroic, mythical, and symbolic. It is the same with Eliza with her flair for business, her almost animal stupidity, her great, but sometimes aimless, energies, her almost sardonic and defensive love for her son, whom she does not understand, her avarice and her sporadic squandering of money. These two figures dominate both books; even after old Gant is dead the force of his personality, or rather the force of the symbol into which that personality has been elevated, is an active agent, and a point of reference for interpretation.

These two characters, and Ben and Helen in a lesser degree, are triumphs of poetic conception. The uncle in *Of Time and the River,* Bascomb Pentland, exhibits likewise some of the family lineaments, the family vitality, and something of the symbolic aspect of the other characters; but the method of presentation is more conventional and straightforward, and the result more static and anecdotal.

Mr. Wolfe's method in presenting these characters, and the special quality of symbol he manages to derive from them, is subject to certain special qualifications. Obviously it would not serve as a routine process for the treatment of character, at least not on the scale on which it is here rendered. The reader of a novel demands something more realistic, less lyrical; he demands an interplay of characters on another and more specific level, a method less dependent on the direct intrusion of the novelist's personal sensibility. As I have said, the figures of the Gant family are powerful and overwhelming as symbols, as an emotional focus for the novel, and as a point of reference. But the method collapses completely when applied to Starwick, a character of equal importance in Mr. Wolfe's scheme.

We amass a great fund of information concerning Francis Starwick. He was born in a town in the Middle West and early rebelled against the crudities and ugliness of his background. At Harvard he assists Professor Thatcher in the drama school and leads the life of a mannered and affected esthete, foppish in dress, artificial in speech, over-sensitive and sometimes cruel. He becomes the best friend of Eugene at Harvard. Later he appears in Europe in company with two young women of Boston families, somewhat older than he, who are in love with him and who are willing to pay, with their reputations and their purses, for the pleasure of his conversation. With these three Eugene enters a period of debauchery in Paris. Finally he discovers that Starwick is homosexual, and in his indefinable resentment beats him into unconsciousness.

But this body of information is not all that the writer intends. F. Scott Fitzgerald and Ernest Hemingway have been able to use effectively such characters as Starwick and to extract their meaning, because as novelists they were willing to work strictly in terms of character. But in *Of Time and the River* the writer is forever straining to convince the reader of some value in Starwick that is not perceptible, that the writer himself cannot define; he tries, since he is writing an autobiography, to make Starwick a symbol, a kind of *alter ego,* for a certain period of his own experience. The strain is tremendous; and without conviction. The writing about Starwick, as the climax of the relationship approaches, sinks into a slush of poetical bathos and juvenility. And here is the scene of parting:

". . . you had a place in my life that no one else has ever had."

"And what was that?" said Starwick.

"I think it was that you were young—my own age—and that you were my friend. Last night after—after that thing happened," he went on, his own face flushing with the pain of the memory, "I thought back over all the time since I have known you. And for the first time I realized that you were the first and only person of my own age that I could call my friend. You were my one true friend—the one I always turned to, believed in with unquestioning devotion. You were the only real friend that I ever had. Now something else has happened. You have taken from me something that I wanted, you have taken it without knowing that you took it, and it will always be like this. You were my brother and my friend—"

"And now?" said Starwick quietly.

"You are my mortal enemy. Goodbye."

"Goodbye, Eugene," said Starwick sadly. "But let me tell you this before I go. Whatever it was I took from you, it was something that I did not want or wish to take. And I would give it back again if I could."

"Oh, fortunate and favored Starwick," the other jeered. "To be so rich—to have such gifts and not to know he has them—to be forever victorious, and to be so meek and mild."

"And I will tell you this as well," Starwick continued. "Whatever anguish and suffering this mad hunger, this impossible desire, has caused you, however fortunate or favored you may think I am, I would give my whole life if I could change places with you for an hour—know for an hour an atom of your anguish and your hunger and your hope. . . . Oh, to feel so, suffer so, and live so!—however mistaken you may be! . . . To have come young, lusty, and living into this world. . . . not to have come, like me, still-born from your mother's womb—never to know the dead heart and the passionless passion—the cold brain and the cold hopelessness of hope—to be wild, mad, furious, and tormented—but to have belief, to live in anguish, but to live—and not to die." . . . He turned and opened the door. "I would give all I have and all you think I have, for just one hour of it. You call me fortunate and happy. You are the most fortunate and happy man I ever knew. Goodbye, Eugene."

"Goodbye, Frank. Goodbye, my enemy."

"And goodbye, my friend," said Starwick. He went out, and the door closed behind him.

The dialogue, the very rhythms of the sentences, and the scene itself, scream the unreality.

The potency of the figures from the family and the failure with Starwick may derive from the autobiographical nature of Mr. Wolfe's work. Eliza and old Gant come from a more primary level of experience, figures of motherhood and fatherhood that gradually, as the book progresses, assume a wider significance and become at the same time a reference for the hero's personal experience. And the author, knowing them first on that level, has a way of knowing them more intimately and profoundly as people than he ever knows Starwick. Starwick is more artificial, because he is at the same time a social symbol and a symbol for a purely private confusion the roots of which are never clear.

Most of the other characters are treated directly. Mr. Wolfe has an appetite for people and occasionally a faculty of very acute perception. The portrait of Abe Jones, the Jewish student at the college in New York, and those of the people at the Coulson household in Oxford, are evidence enough of this capacity. But his method, or rather methods, of presentation are various and not unvaryingly successful. There are long stretches of stenographic dialogue that has little focus, or no focus whatsoever; for instance, the first part of the conversation of the business men in the Pullman in Book I, of the residents of the hotel in Book IV, of the artistic hangers-on at the Cambridge tea parties, or even of Eugene and his companions in the Paris cafés. Some of this reporting is very scrupulous, and good as reporting, but in its mass, its aimlessness, and its lack of direction it is frequently dull; the momentary interest of recognition is not enough to sustain it, and it bears no precise relation to the intention of the novel. It is conversation for conversation's sake, a loquacity and documentation that testifies to the author's talent but not to his intelligence as an artist. Generally this type of presentation is imitative of Sinclair Lewis' realistic dialogue, but it lacks the meticulous, cautious, and selective quality of the best of Lewis, the controlled malice; it is too random, and in an incidental sense, too heavily pointed.

Further, there are tremendous masses of description and characters. Mr. Wolfe has the habit of developing his own *clichés* for description of character, and of then exhibiting them at irregular intervals. It is as if he realized the bulk of the novel and the difficulty a reader might experience in recognizing a character on reappearance, and so determined to prevent this, if possible, by repetition and insistence. For instance, Starwick and Ann, one of the young women from Boston who is in love with Starwick, have a complete set of tags and labels that are affixed to them time after time during the novel. Mr. Wolfe underrates the memory of the reader; or this may be but another instance of the lack of control that impairs his work.

Only in the section dealing with the Coulson episode does Mr. Wolfe seem to have all his resources for character presentation under control. The men who room in the house, the jaunty Captain Nicholl with his blasted arm and the other two young men from the motor-car factory—these with the Coulsons themselves are very precise to the imagination, and are sketched in with an economy usually foreign to Mr. Wolfe. The Coulson girl, accepting the mysterious ruin that presides over the household, is best drawn and dominates the group. Here Mr. Wolfe has managed to convey an atmosphere and to convince the reader of the reality of his characters without any of his habitual exaggerations of method and style. This section, with slight alterations, originally appeared as a short story; it possesses what is rare enough in *Of Time and the River,* a constant focus.

I have remarked that some of Mr. Wolfe's material is not subordinated to the intention of the book. What is his intention? On what is the mass of material focused? What is to give it form? His novels are obviously autobiographical. This means that the binding factor should be, at least in part, the personality of the narrator, or since Mr. Wolfe adopts a disguise, of the hero, Eugene Gant. The two books are, in short, an account of the development of a sensibility; obviously something more is intended than the looseness and irresponsibility of pure memoirs or observations. The work demands comparison with such things as Joyce's *Portrait of the Artist as a Young Man* or Lawrence's *Sons and Lovers;* it may even demand comparison with proper autobiographies such as Rousseau's *Confessions* or *The Education of Henry Adams.* But the comparison with these books is not to the advantage of Mr. Wolfe's performance. It has not the artistry of the first two, the constant and dramatic relation of incident to a developing consciousness of the world, nor has it the historical importance of the third, or the philosophical and intellectual interest of the last.

The hero of *Look Homeward, Angel,* though a child and

adolescent, is essentially more interesting than the Eugene of *Of Time and the River*. He is more comprehensible, because there is a real (and necessarily conventional) pattern to his developing awareness of the world around him. Further, the life of the Gant household, and even of the community, is patterned with a certain amount of strictness in relation to Eugene: the impress of the vast vitality of old Gant, the lack of understanding on the part of the mother and the perpetual emotional drag of resentment and affection she exerts on her son, the quarrels with Steve, the confusion and pathos of the sexual experiences, the profound attachment between Ben and Eugene, and the climactic and daring scene with Ben's spirit. There is a progress toward maturity, a fairly precise psychological interest. The novel contains much pure baggage and much material that is out of tone, usually in the form of an ironic commentary that violates the point of view; but the book is more of a unit, and is, for that reason perhaps, more exciting and forceful.

In *Of Time and the River* as Eugene in his Pullman rides at night across Virginia, going "northward, worldward, towards the secret borders of Virginia, towards the great world cities of his hope, the fable of his childhood legendry," the following passage is interpolated:

Who has seen fury riding in the mountains? Who has known fury striding in the storm? Who has been mad with fury in his youth, given no rest or peace or certitude by fury, driven on across the earth by fury, until the great vine of his heart was broke, the sinews wrenched, the little tenement of bone, blood, marrow, brain, and feeling in which great fury raged, was twisted, wrung, depleted, worn out, and exhausted by the fury which it could not lose or put away? Who has known fury, how it came?

How have we breathed him, drunk him, eaten fury to the core, until we have him in us now and cannot lose him anywhere we go? It is a strange and subtle worm that will . . .

Now this furious Eugene is scarcely made so comprehensible. The reader amasses a large body of facts about him, as about Starwick, but with something of the same result. He knows that Eugene is big; that he is a creature of enormous appetites of which he is rather proud; that he has the habit of walking much at night; that he is fascinated by the health and urbanity of his friend Joel and by the personality of Starwick; that he ceases to like Shelley after spending an afternoon in a jail cell; that he reads 20,000 books in ten years; that he is obsessed by the idea of devouring all of life. Then, the reader knows the facts of Eugene's comings and goings, and knows the people he meets and what they say. But the Eugene susceptible to such definition is not the hero of the book, or at least does not function adequately as such. The hero is really that nameless fury that drives Eugene. The book is an effort to name that fury, and perhaps by naming it, to tame it. But the fury goes unnamed and untamed. Since the book is formless otherwise, only a proper emotional reference to such a center could give it form. Instead, at the center there is this chaos that steams and bubbles in rhetoric and apocalyptic apostrophe, sometimes grand and sometimes febrile and empty; the center is a maelstrom, perhaps artificially generated at times; and the other, tangible items are the flotsam and jetsam and dead wood spewed up, iridescent or soggy as the case may be.

It may be objected that other works of literary art, and very great ones at that, have heroes who defy definition and who are merely centers of "fury." For instance, there is Hamlet, or Lear. But a difference may be observed. Those characters may defy the attempt at central definition, but the play hangs together in each case as a structure without such definition; that is, there has been no confusion between the sensibility that produced a play, as an object of art, and the sensibility of a hero in a play. (And the mere fact that *Hamlet* and *Lear* employ verse as a vehicle adds further to the impression of discipline, focus, and control.)

There are two other factors in the character of Eugene that may deserve mention. The hero feels a sense of destiny and direction, the sense of being "chosen" in the midst of a world of defeated, aimless, snobbish, vulgar, depleted, or suicidal people. (This is, apparently, the source of much of the interpolated irony in both books, an irony almost regularly derivative and mechanical.)   In real life this conviction of a high calling may be enough to make a "hero" feel that life does have form and meaning; but the mere fact that a hero in a novel professes the high calling and is contrasted in his social contacts with an inferior breed does not, in itself, give the novel form and meaning. The transference of the matter from the actuality of life to the actuality of art cannot be accomplished so easily. Second, at the very end of the novel Eugene, about to embark for America, sees a woman who, according to the somewhat extended lyrical epilogue, makes him "lose" self and so be "found":

After all the blind, tormented wanderings of youth, that woman would become his heart's centre and the target of his life, the image of immortal one-ness that again collected him to one, and hurled the whole collected passion, power, and might of his one life into the blazing certitude, the immortal governance and unity, of love.

Certainly this is what we call fine writing; it may or may not be good writing. And probably, falling in love may make a man "find himself"; but this epilogue scarcely makes the novel find itself.

It is possible sometimes that a novel possessing no structure in the ordinary sense of the word, or not properly dominated by its hero's personality or fortunes, may be given a focus by the concrete incorporation of an idea, or related ideas. Now, *Of Time and the River* has such a leading idea, but an idea insufficient in its operation. The leading symbol of the father, old Gant, gradually assumes another aspect, not purely personal; he becomes, in other words, a kind of symbol of the fatherland, the source, the land of violence, drunkenness, fecundity, beauty, and vigor on which the hero occasionally reflects during his wanderings and to which in the end he returns. But this symbol is not the total expression of the idea, which is worked out more explicitly and at length. There are long series of cinematic flashes of "phases of American life": locomotive drivers, gangsters, pioneers, little towns with the squares deserted at night, evangelists, housewives, rich and suicidal young men, whores on subways, drunk college boys. Or there are more lyrical passages, less effective in pictorial detail, such as the following:

It was the wild, sweet, casual, savage, and incredibly lovely earth of America, and of the wilderness, and it haunted them like legends, and pierced them like a sword, and filled them with a wild and swelling prescience of joy that was like sorrow and delight.

This kind of material alternates with the more sedate or realistic progress of the chronicle, a kind of running commentary of patriotic mysticism on the more tangible events and perceptions. For Mr. Wolfe has the mysticism of the American idea that we find in Whitman, Sandburg, Masters, Crane, and Benét, or more recently and frivolously, in Coffin and Paul Engle. He pants for the Word, the union that will clarify all the disparate and confused elements which he enumerates and many of which fill him with revulsion and disgust. He, apparently, has experienced the visionary moment he proclaims, but, like other mystics, he suffers some difficulty when he attempts to prepare it for the consumption of ordinary citizens of the Republic. He must wreak some indignity on the chastity of the vision. This indignity is speech: but he burns, perversely, to speak.

The other promulgators of the American vision have been poets. Mr. Wolfe, in addition to being a poet in instinct, is, as well, the owner on a large scale of many of the gifts of the novelist. He attempts to bolster, or as it were to prove, the mystical and poetic vision by fusing it with a body of everyday experience of which the novelist ordinarily treats. But there is scarcely a fusion or a correlation; rather, an oscillation. On the tangible side, the hero flees from America, where his somewhat quivering sensibilities are frequently tortured, and goes to Europe; in the end, worn out by drinking and late hours, disgusted with his friends, unacquainted with the English or the French, and suffering homesickness, he returns to America. But Mr. Wolfe, more than most novelists, is concerned with the intangible; not so much with the psychological process and interrelation as with the visionary "truth."

The other poets, at least Whitman and Crane, have a certain advantage over the poet in Mr. Wolfe. They overtly consented to be poets; Mr. Wolfe has not consented. Therefore their vision is purer, the illusion of communication (*illusion,* for it is doubtful that they have really communicated the central vision) is more readily palatable, because they never made a serious pretense of proving it autobiographically or otherwise; they were content with the hortatory moment, the fleeting symbol, and the affirmation. (Mr. Benét, of course, did attempt in *John Brown's Body* such a validation, but with a degree of success that does not demand comment here.) It may simply be that the poets were content to be lyric poets, and therefore could more readily attempt the discipline of selection and concentration; in those respects, even Whitman shows more of an instinct for form than does Mr. Wolfe. Mr. Wolfe is astonishingly diffuse, astonishingly loose in his rhetoric— qualities that, for the moment, may provoke more praise than blame. That rhetoric is sometimes grand, but probably more often tedious and tinged with hysteria. Because he is officially writing prose and not poetry he has no caution of the *clichés* of phrase or rhythm, and no compunction about pilfering from other poets. His vocabulary itself is worth comment. If the reader will inspect the few passages quoted in the course of this essay he will observe a constant quality of strain, a fancy for the violent word or phrase (but often conventionally poetic as well as violent): "wild, sweet, casual, savage . . . ," "haunted them like legends," "no rest or peace or certitude of fury," "target of his life," "blazing certitude, the immortal governance and unity, of love." Mr. Wolfe often shows very powerfully the poetic instinct, and the praise given by a number of critics to his "sensuousness" and "gusto" is not without justification in the fact; but even more often his prose simply shows the poetic instinct unbuckled on a kind of week-end debauch. He sometimes wants it both ways: the structural irresponsibility of prose and the emotional intensity of poetry. He may overlook the fact that the intensity is rarely to be achieved without a certain rigor in selection and structure.

Further, Mr. Wolfe, we understand from blurbs and reviewers, is attempting a kind of prose epic. American literature has produced one, *Moby Dick*. There is much in common between *Moby Dick* and *Of Time and the River,* but there is one major difference. Melville had a powerful fable, a myth of human destiny, which saved his work from the centrifugal impulses of his genius, and which gave it structure and climax. Its dignity is inherent in the fable itself. No such dignity is inherent in Mr. Wolfe's scheme, if it can properly be termed a scheme. The nearest approach to it is in the character of old Gant, but that is scarcely adequate. And Mr. Wolfe has not been able to compensate for the lack of a fable by all his well-directed and misdirected attempts to endow his subject with a proper dignity, by all his rhetorical insistence, all the clarity and justice of his incidental poetic perceptions, all the hysteria or magnificent hypnosis.

Probably all of these defects, or most of them, are inherent in the autobiographical impulse when the writer attempts to make this special application of it. In the first place, all the impurities and baggage in the book must strike the author as of peculiar and necessary value because they were observed or actually occurred. But he is not writing a strict autobiography in which all observations or experiences, however vague, might conceivably find a justification. He is trying, and this in the second place, to erect the autobiographical material into an epical and symbolic importance, to make of it a fable, a "Legend of Man's Hunger in his Youth." This much is definitely declared by the sub-title.

Mr. Wolfe promises to write some historical novels, and they may well be crucial in the definition of his genius, because he may be required to re-order the use of his powers. What, thus far, he has produced are fine fragments, several brilliant pieces of portraiture, and many sharp observations on men and nature: in other words, these books are really voluminous notes from which a fine novel, or several fine novels, might be written. If he never writes these novels, it may yet be that his books will retain a value as documents of some historical importance and as confused records of an unusual personality. Meanwhile, despite his admirable energies and his powerful literary endowments, his work illustrates once more the limitations, perhaps the necessary limitations, of an attempt to exploit directly and naïvely the personal experience and the self-defined personality in art.

And meanwhile it may be well to recollect that Shakespeare merely wrote *Hamlet;* he was *not* Hamlet.

T. S. Stribling: A Paragraph in the History of Critical Realism

THE novels of T. S. Stribling have been rewarded by some critical enthusiasm, a considerable cash-money popularity and the official accolade of a Pulitzer prize. All of this is, as it were, within the bounds of conceivable justice: Stribling's work is the product of a good many years of conscientious industry, and of an eye that can unerringly mark the fashions as they fly. Stribling has never been the first by whom the new was tried; he has nothing of the experimenter in his literary constitution. Nor is he the last, precisely, to lay the old aside; some novelists still engage themselves in critico-realistic presentations of the American village or the American peasant, while Stribling has taken his paraphernalia of realism and followed certain adventurous souls into the spacious vistas of American history. Stribling is primarily interesting as the index of a fashion which he has flattered with sober conscience and profound unoriginality.

Stribling's novels will appear in the history of our literature as a paragraph in the development, or conceivably the decline, of what is generally called critical realism in fiction. This is not the mere realism of device, the sort of realism one speaks of in the *Ancient Mariner* or in the novels of Thomas Hardy. It is, instead, an extension of the naturalistic premise: the naturalistic novelist took

From *The American Review,* II, pp. 463-486. February, 1934. Reprinted by permission.

science as the source of his method and his philosophy. His method was, professedly, objective and transcriptive; he was concerned with fact, not value. Motivation of human conduct was to be understood in terms of biology, bio-chemistry, and such. These pretensions received their most substantial criticism some forty years ago from Ferdinand Brunetière, a criticism less trenchantly readapted by Stuart P. Sherman from an attack on Zola to an attack on Dreiser.

As the naturalistic novel, in one sense, is based on a science, biology, so the realistic novel that we now know is based on a pseudo-science, sociology. The realistic novelist, like the sociologist, professes a scientific objectivity in dealing with his materials, that is, in making his surveys. What this objectivity amounts to is no more than the objectivity of the naturalistic writer. It provides the same "truth," if "truth" at all, by the same process of elimination and focus, a process which, indeed, is necessarily common to all fiction. But by differences in nature of origin the realistic and naturalistic novels differ in one fundamental respect. The biologist, the anatomist, when about his professional business, is, as far as is humanly possible, a mere observer, albeit an observer in terms of hypothesis; he never offers a project to rationalize the human figure by endowing it with three legs instead of the traditional two. Nor is he even a physician, a mender of broken-down two-legged figures. The sociologist, on the other hand, is engaged in a study which, finally, must involve values of a kind, and which, therefore, has a prescriptive, as well as descriptive, aspect. The matter may simply rest on this: the distinction between the theoretical and applied branches of a science, biology say, is more clearly marked than that between the theoretical and applied branches of the pseudo-science, sociology. But a further consideration may appear: the biologist cannot yet by taking thought add the Biblical cubit to his stature, he cannot change, can only mend, a body by the application of his knowledge, while the perpetual mutations of social orders perpetually seduce the sociologist from description and prediction to the more arrogant prescription. Sociology lends itself, even assuming the objectivity of its surveys, to the projects of reform; if it were otherwise, the sociologist were not more, but less, man. It is reasonable that, in view of its origin, the realistic novel is never purely realistic; it is critical, which generally means satiric and propagandist as well.

And so it is with the novels of Stribling.

There are two primary issues which appear in the study of a novelist of the order of Stribling. First, what is the actual content of his criticism; that is, what things in society does he dislike, and to what set of ideas do these dislikes refer? Second, what is the effect of this preoccupation on his work as an art form? From a given novel or given episode the two issues may be dissected out, in most cases, only by a certain exercise of violence. But the very crudity of much of Stribling's work, especially in the novels before *The Forge,* makes the task less arduous. And the various elements in a novel like *Teeftallow* are so rudely assimilated that the mayhem of abstraction rests lightly on the esthetic conscience.

The critical premises of Stribling's early and recent work are identical. He has developed in narrative expertness (his mechanical ingenuity has always been considerable), but his point of view has remained unchanged; he has only transferred his method from the contemporary to the historical scene, following what in most current examples of the type is but a fashionable device to heighten the critical importance of a work by making it parade as historical explanation of a contemporary social situation. As such, his historical novels are but an extension of the sociological principle of his previous work.

The critical realist, ordinarily, is sparing of a forthright exposition of constructive ideas in his work; and as a novelist rightly so. But his work is very fruitful of his distastes. And his distastes lend the work its special aura, or in less expert instances, its special mannerisms. They are a clue to the novelist's principles, which may, or may not, according to his powers, be orderly, consistent, and intelligent.

I shall sample some of Stribling's distastes.

In *Teeftallow* the hill boy comes to Irontown to work on the railroad construction gang, and attends for the first time a drinking and gambling party in the woods:

Some of the nearer stragglers whistled discreetly at the two youths, and Zed answered them. Three men came up; one had a bottle. He passed it round with "Have a jolt." "Take a kick." "Bail her out." As each man drank he wiped the mouth of the bottle carefully on his shirt-sleeve and returned it to the owner. There was a certain ritualism about it which impressed Abner as being urbane and cultured. These Irontown men certainly had a polish one didn't find in the hills.

This passage, chosen at random, is a fair example of the sort of thing Stribling dislikes, and of his method in dealing with it. He is not content to describe the drinking manners of the men and the effect on the boy; he must describe them in terms, *culture* and *urbanity,* which are foreign to the boy's way of thinking, and which provide the irony and the criticism. He must cast the scene against a drawing-room background. Such irony, characteristic of all the books before *The Forge,* is too easy; and it may be vulgar.

That agreeable drawing-room, with its culture and urbanity, is never far from Stribling's consciousness; and the theme of his treatment of manners is that it is very far away from the Tennessee and Alabama back country. In *Bright Metal* the Christian Workers enjoy their social hour:

There was something agreeable, almost romantic, to the Christian Workers to have the piano rattling or a song going while they conversed in undertones. It gave them an impression of culture, and of refined drawing-rooms. They were lifted momentarily out of their humdrum lives by what they fancied was in imitation of fine society and wealth. Whereas if they simply sat in silence and listened, they became bored and yawned covertly, and had to blink their eyes to keep from going to sleep.

Or again, from *Teeftallow:*

The dining-room of the Scovell House was dark and smelly as if air and sunlight were luxuries hardly to be arrived at in the country. The table linen was dirty and torn; the silver plating was worn off the spoons; the coffee cost thirty cents a pound. Yet Abner could never enter the dining-room of the Scovell House without a certain embarrassment at the magnificence of its service.

Stribling, in presenting Abner and the Scovell House, has leagued himself and the reader together in a common acquaintance with the decorous and sanitary luxury of expensive hotels. In more complicated fashion he employs the same effect:

Not a person was on the streets. The village was at supper. The village devoted this single moment of the day when all the filth of its streets and all the moral crudities and pettinesses of its life were forgiven in the solemn absolution of sunset; it devoted that single moment to eating. What cared the village for this pageantry of the west? Of what moment to them was this tender forgiving hour; they who had nothing to be forgiven? Let them eat hot bread in mean rooms beneath the lithographs of dead fish, let them talk of the last scandal, or simply eat in silence. That miracle of jade and turquoise fades slowly into the sea-blue depth of night, but what have they to do with that?

The implication of this passage, which, incidentally, is a fair example of Stribling in purple and poetic mood, is twofold. What offends him is not so much the lack of spiritual sympathy between man and nature as the "mean rooms" and the "lithographs of dead fish." If the furnishings were more expensive and decorous, he, apparently, could more easily condone the failure to appreciate the spiritual value of the "pageantry of the west." And further, the implication is that in other places, in large cities, people postpone the dinner hour in order to receive the "solemn absolution of sunset." The point is this: as a criticism of humanity in general, too busy about gratifying its practical appetites, or too weary from so doing, to take what compensation nature affords, Stribling's passage might be just, or partially just; but the trouble with it is that a commentary on human nature in general is paraded as a special piece of social criticism referring to a special locality. The lithographs and the hot bread are the special elements; these special items of realistic perception are treated as symbols for the general proposition, that is, as supplying the machinery of conviction for readers who, since they do not eat hot bread under lithographs of dead fish, feel themselves to be morally and esthetically superior. Irontown has simply stood whipping-boy for the world.

In large part Stribling's criticism savors of the easy hick-baiting of a dead decade. It is dated. For him almost any young white man who does not live in a large city is a "hobbledehoy." No decency of spirit is possible in a house without modern plumbing. All lives lived in sections he deals with are "humdrum" or "monotonous." This sort of thing defines the pervasive tone of his work; by cumulative effect in any of the novels it defines the author's, and possibly the reader's, set toward the material. Thus far it is a snobbery based on radio and nationally advertised mouthwashes. Further, a man like Stribling would, in all probability, find the society of Florence, Alabama, in the sixties and seventies or the society of Lane County, Tennessee, in the 1920's an inappropriate *milieu* for the proper exercise of his education, manners, and talents. Let that be granted, if desired. But it scarcely requires some half-dozen novels to establish the fact; and such preoccupation does not, to employ a phrase once popular among hick-baiters, seem adult.

Stribling does not confine himself to such peripheral items, but has treated, likewise, certain more fundamental social ideas. *Teeftallow* is dedicated to the "hill theocracy," and devoted to the study of the social effects of religion, a theme which also appears in *Bright Metal* and *Birthright*. Religion, for him, is "greasy." And according to *Birthright, Teeftallow,* and *Bright Metal,* it is impossible for a person to be devout without, at the same time, being a fool or a knave, usually in his novels the latter. The banker in *Birthright,* under the excitement of evangelical piety, swindles the mulatto Peter out of a hundred dollars, which is immediately put in an envelope and addressed to a missionary in the Sudan. The banker in *Teeftallow* is the pillar of piety in Irontown, but (or rather, *therefore*) is introduced to the reader in the act of mulcting the ignorant hill boy Teeftallow out of his unsuspected inheritance. Agatha, the New York actress who has married into a Lane County family, when reminded of her husband's fundamental indifference to things religious, thinks: "If Pom hadn't been reared down here, he would be a normal man." As far as one can judge from the material at hand, that is Stribling's doctrine: religion is abnormal. It is also necessarily associated with dishonesty and cruelty, swindling, slander, lynching; on the evidence of *Teeftallow,* the only citizen of Lane County who is capable of unselfishness or idealism is the village atheist.

It remains an open question whether Stribling is ready to apply this description to all religion whatsoever, or whether he reserves it for Lane County fundamentalism. It will, probably, not long remain an open question; for, according to information furnished by the publishers, Stribling's forthcoming *Unfinished Cathedral,* the final member of his trilogy, presents the triumph of modernism in Florence, Alabama, a triumph concretely realized in the non-denominational cathedral which, appropriately, is financed by Colonel Vaiden's somewhat ill-gotten gains. And even Stribling, I suppose, will find it difficult to avoid the conclusion, from this arrangement, that his Southern back country is at last becoming enlightened according to the pattern of American liberal thought, the general pattern from which his previous criticisms are directed.

The conservative sexual morality of Lane County has received some comment. Agatha, the New York actress who has rather illogically married into the community, is riding with a poor neighbor boy whose face reminds her of Pan:

Agatha sensed the discomfort she had wrought in him by this casual mention of bearing children. And his discomfort annoyed her somehow. Why could he not look upon reproduction as a simple biological fact? To be embarrassed at an allusion to it. "In reality," thought Agatha, "to be embarrassed is as distressing as to be salacious about it." She felt sorry for Risdale. She felt someone ought to give the youth a saner view of life.

Which, within a hundred pages or so, she proceeds to do. She brings this enlightenment to Lane County by committing adultery with the youth. But since the act is treated by Stribling in a rare access of romantic charm; since an heirloom lace night-dress is loaned by the boy's mother for the unsuspected occasion; and since the boy himself is connected, if rather remotely, with a cultured land-owning family of Tidewater, Maryland, the act is beyond application of Stribling's critico-realistic method. It is disinfected, and rendered less worthy of comment than the boy's gauche wink while introducing Agatha to Mr. Napoleon Suggs.

Stribling's method of dealing with the race question in the South, another issue that absorbs a considerable amount of his energy, is compact of equal realism. His method is to bring into collision a noble Negro, or rather a mixed-breed, and a white society considerably less than noble. Peter of *Birthright,* and Toussaint and Gracie of *The Forge* and *The Store,* are examples. Through the eyes of Peter, a graduate of Harvard who has come home to found a school, the oppressions, stupidities, and brutalities of the white community are presented: Peter is swindled in buying land for his school, loses the confidence of the Negroes themselves as a result, and, in the end, only marries the wife he desires after she has been blackmailed into becoming the mistress of her white employer. Peter's moral and intellectual superiority is constantly held in contrast to the society about him. The only other educated man in the community, the old aristocrat who, presumably, is Peter's own father, is the intellectual foil for Peter's emancipation, since in the old man's library there are no books that indicate a respect for Darwinism. Peter finally gives up the unequal struggle, beaten by the prejudice of the whites and the inertia and fatalism of the Negroes, and goes North to seek his and Cissie's personal salvation; he goes North where he would soon be "moving briskly, talking to wide-awake men to whom a slightly unusual English word would not form a stumbling block to conversation," where he and his wife could "lead authentic lives."

What is the reference of Stribling's method to actuality? Is it sound sociology? In one respect I have already hinted that it is not. For instance, it is probably bad sociology to assume that religion is necessarily connected with moral depravity. But it is in attempts at social comparison that Stribling's sociology is at its worst, that is, when the snobbery of mouthwash is transferred into the field of ideas. The principle of comparison Stribling uses is to bring the Peter Siner of *Birthright,* the Ditmas of *Teeftallow,* or the Gracie and Toussaint of *The Store* into conflict with the Southern society of his novels. These heroes and heroines are either Yankees or Negroes. They would be, as persons, exceptional in any society: they are not representative by reason of education or individual quality.

Stribling, if pressed, would probably admit this; but he is perpetually tempted in the transaction of his business as a novelist to give another implication in his comparisons between the white and Negro races or between North and South. Ditmas, the Yankee engineer of *Teeftallow,* is astonished at what Stribling calls the "narrow Hebraism" of the village. "What do you Northern folks discuss, what do you think about?" inquires the village atheist, the only citizen of Lane County whom Stribling has ever endowed with any intellectual appetite except the boy of *Bright Metal.* And Ditmas replies: "Well, when you leave out business, we [*i.e.,* Northern society as a whole] are occupied with sports, fiction, drama, science, philosophy, and such things." But a similar effect may be accomplished less barefacedly by mere variation in tone, by treating the chosen characters with a sympathy denied the more average human beings who are selected to represent Southern white society. This is the more subtle device employed in a novel like *The Store* in handling the race question: Toussaint, for instance, is the only man who possesses a true pride and strength of character. Stribling consistently attempts to enlist sympathy for the special individual who happens to oppose the society he treats; and such sympathy, by the tone of the writing, is transferred to a general proposition. He has never, in the whole course of his work, brought into comparison a Peter Siner with an educated white youth; a Southern business man like Colonel Vaiden with a Northern business man; a Toussaint with a white man of equal character; a Southern Methodist with a Boston Catholic. He has never been interested in the dramatic possibilities of a superior Southern white man brought into conflict with his native environment, a theme which Faulkner has used in *Sanctuary* and Caroline Gordon in *Penhally*. This is simply one piece of evidence that Stribling is not primarily interested in the personal and dramatic at all; his imagination is only concerned with a documentation of his thesis.

In the treatment of his favorite critical themes in the two historical novels, *The Forge* and *The Store,* Stribling exhibits another characteristic which impairs, even more than mere prejudice, the value of his sociological observations. His historical sense is deficient. The injustices of the social and economic arrangements of the South, the "narrowness" of its life, are interpreted as a sort of intrinsic brutality, a brutality mystically inherent in the Southern white man and special to him. *The Forge* begins just at the outbreak of the Civil War, the topic which involves most of the author's energies throughout the book. The nature of the system of life which preceded the war is never touched more than casually; consequently a reader of *The Forge* would scarcely understand the issues of the struggle. One character, apparently a spokesman for Stribling, refers to the conflict as one between two opposing forms of wealth, or two forms of capitalism. And even less would a reader understand from *The Store* the complexity of the problems which confronted the South after the Civil War: the problem of labor, the problem of franchise, the problem of race. The fact that these problems have not been solved is accounted for, in implication at least, by a basic stupidity or brutality. And certainly Stribling is unaware of the possibility that the social structure he seems to abhor is to be understood, to a degree, only as a result of the commercialized liberalism and uninformed idealism which directed the consolidation of the conquest of the South in the years immediately following the Civil War. He is trapped in the same sort of paradox as Sinclair Lewis, his master. Lewis satirized small-town life, provincial life; at least that is what he thought he was doing. But an analysis of Gopher Prairie shows that most of the things that distressed Lewis there are largely the result of the attempt on the part of Gopher Prairie to imitate the big city. Gopher Prairie is the kind of village that can be expected in a country where Chicago and New York are the great cities. What

Stribling is attacking is merely the frailty of human nature; but when his attack takes more specific terms its final object, though many times removed, is only the victorious liberalism of the Sixties and the several following decades.

It is probably too much to expect that Stribling should understand this. His thinking stems too directly from that same tradition. If he lacks the historical sense, it is because American liberalism has, in general, lacked the historical sense. If he is a hick-baiter, and sometimes a snob, it is because American liberalism and its more unphilosophical varieties has made such possible. The natural opposition to the liberal movement comes from the conservative country; therefore when the liberal loses his temper hick-baiting is his ordinary recourse. Liberalism flourished as the corollary to our great era of commercial expansion; therefore when the liberal loses his manners his ordinary recourse is snobbery.

Stribling has indicated much abuse and narrowness in Southern society that is indefensible. That is obvious. But there have been three defects in his surveys. He has been consciously or unconsciously disingenuous in his social comparisons. He has been too absolute in his definition of Southern character. He has failed to understand the historical context of the incidents he cites, and consequently has failed to give any final meaning to his criticism. The criticism remains as a sort of exhibit of chaotic observations, keen enough in detail, but incoherent. The state of mind from which the books are written remains a strange compound of hick-baiting, snobbery, and humanitarianism: in a word, disordered liberalism. But that was the state of mind fashionable in the decade when Stribling developed his literary powers.

But there is another, and more important, question: what is the effect of Stribling's preoccupation on his novels as novels?

His novels, even the most recent ones and the most expert, show a quality which is fairly common to writers who are propagandists, that is, who keep their critical doctrines, as doctrines, in the foreground of the reader's consciousness. This quality is a detachment from the material. It is not the sort of detachment found in a story like Ivan Bunin's *Gentleman from San Francisco*, where the rigidly maintained point of view provides an inflection of noble irony to the simple account of the death of a vulgar tourist in Sicily. Nor is it mere dramatic objectivity. It is something else: the propagandist, finally, is never quite close to his material because he is infatuated with some system of abstractions and fears that, if he gets too close to his material, the cherished "truths" may be absorbed in the complexity of its being. His interest in the special persons and the special incidents of his stories is essentially an interest in illustration.

In the books before *The Forge* this detachment is most obvious, for it appears as a commentary that keeps pace with the narrative. The business of this commentary, as Stribling apparently conceives it, is to generalize the particular aspect of character or particular incident and affirm it as a trait of the class he happens to be dealing with at the time. Instances of this mannerism are almost innumerable. An incident may be introduced purely as illustration: "As an example of the progress of a lawsuit as a source of news, here is one of the rumors that went the rounds." With such an introduction, the reader's set toward the forthcoming event is fixed; his interest is to be one of social analysis, pure and simple, the interest in character drained away, even the brute interest in the event deadened. Commonly, Stribling is not so obviously inept as in the instance just quoted, but his commentary always provides the same inflection. The most immediate evil of this method is the constant violation of point of view and a constant interruption of the pace of his narrative. The first two quotations in this essay are excellent examples in so far as examples can be given in little.

Other evils, which impinge less immediately on the reader, are more fundamental. I have said that Stribling is most ingenious in the working out of plot. He is able, especially in *The Store* and *The Forge,* to contrive a plot which involves a great number of actors in several series of co-ordinate incidents. But this ingenuity is, in a sense, wasted. It is wasted because the ingenuity too frequently remains ingenuity: it is applied to the business of illustrating his general propositions. In *Birthright* the mulatto Peter Siner must be brought into contact with as many Southern types as possible; he is the focus of the social survey Stribling is making. And so with Agatha Pomeroy of *Bright Metal,* or Abner of *Teeftallow.* This is the object of plot.

The nature of plot, however, can only be called arbitrary in terms of its relation to character. It is conceivable, for instance, that a Negro graduate of Harvard might decide one fine morning to call on all the business men of Hooker's Bend, Tennessee, and give them a lecture on racial amity and higher wages for cooks, basing his claims on sound economic doctrine and a Christlike vision. But when Peter Siner does this it is a fairly transparent device on the part of Stribling to bring into debate the enlightened with the traditionally Southern view on Negro labor. Peter Siner, as a human being, is as wooden as a post and perfectly irrelevant to the debate. The fact that he wonders how Jesus felt before his first sermon in Nazareth scarcely humanizes the incident; that wonderment itself is too obviously a play for sympathy by the author. The rape of Gracie by Miltiades Vaiden in *The Forge* is equally arbitrary and unmotivated, or unmotivated except on Stribling's assumption that every Southern white man is prepared to assault any Negro woman at the drop of a hat. The fact that in reality such things have occurred with more or less frequency is without bearing on the special case. Stribling's obligation as a novelist is to make the act plausible in its special context; but this is the very thing he does not even trouble to attempt, for he is so easy in his basic assumption that he dismisses any psychological concern. The psychology is that of a novel like *The Clansman,* a work which Stribling, presumably, would not admire.

Character, like plot, is treated with an illustrative bias. In *The Forge* and *The Store,* which set out to give a picture of Southern life for several generations, the characters are selected to illustrate certain preconceived types: Lacefield, the aristocrat; Cady, the share-cropper; Handback, a deacon in the Methodist Church who keeps a Negro mistress and who bleeds the Negro croppers; O'Shawn, the Governor, a windbag politician. Stribling's ingenious sense of plot construction, and his very characters themselves, often appear somewhat artificial, simply because the characters bear too clearly the mark of their conception. They retain the taint of illustration; they are too mathematically exact, and, in consequence, predictable. Lacefield, for instance, is straight out of all the second-rate romantic fiction about the Southern planter; he is in the book simply to express certain sentiments with which Stribling has a sociological concern. Cady is straight out of all the second-rate realistic fiction about the Southern cropper or "poor-white"; he appears in *The Store* simply to serve as a foil for Toussaint's manhood and to illustrate the hatred and brutality of his class—a class that inspires Stribling with unusual rancor—toward the recently emancipated Negroes. These characters do not remind one of life, but of that other fiction. (A mere detail in this failure in reality of the portraits is Stribling's failure of visual imagination. He is no master of that physical detail, often logically irrelevant, that can focus a scene—a detail like the master of the *Patna* scratching his belly in the lantern light as he leans to look at the chart in *Lord Jim.*) The point is that Stribling has been too much occupied with the business of illustration to observe his material in other terms, to give it that loving attention for its own sake that would mean the breath of life in its nostrils. Or perhaps he has been too much occupied with increasing the scope of his work, enlarging his canvas, to suffer the essential concentration. And in fiction the multiplicity of example proves nothing.

Occasionally Stribling is betrayed into a moment of irrelevance when he neglects his ordinary preoccupation, and when, just for those moments, he is an artist. In *The Forge* old Mrs. Vaiden comes suddenly alive for the reader when the daughter-in-law Rose sees her taking an afternoon nap on a pallet on the floor and experiences a wave of tenderness at the smallness, the childlikeness, of the old woman. This is one of the moments. Another, in *The Store,* is when the ghost of the suicide Handback appears to his mulatto mistress in the kitchen. On such occasions Stribling's principle of composition disappears, lost in the too momentary vitality of his characters.

In general, from all of Stribling's novels, but two characters emerge with any final claim on the imagination: Gracie, and

Miltiades Vaiden. But this claim is not consistent. In *The Forge* the presentation of both is marred by Stribling's usual deficiencies, and even in *The Store* something of the allegorical order still clings to the Colonel, especially in the long record of his business dealings. The interest provoked by that chronicle is essentially an interest in pure intrigue or an interest in what it all means as a social proposition. The Colonel resorts to an extra-legal justice to establish the fortune wherewith to imitate the splendors of the defunct order which, as a young man, he had witnessed but not participated in. In this rôle he is not compelling, but the more private aspects of his life, his relations to Ponny or his twenty-year courtship of Drusilla Lacefield, in so far as these aspects can be disengaged from his prevailing ambition, show that Stribling has a positive capacity for the creation of character. In *The Store* the handling of the Colonel's character is relatively free from those blemishes of the arbitrary, such as the rape of Gracie, or perhaps the marriage to Ponny, which appear in *The Forge*. Probably the finest bit in *The Store* is the scene when the Colonel arrives just too late to save from lynching the boy who Gracie has just told him is his own son and whose death he has partially caused. But even here Stribling somewhat impairs his very subtle treatment of the Colonel by his mechanical irony. Gracie and the Colonel have just reached the body that dangles from a tree in the square:

> She reached frantically toward the faces around her.
> "Gimme a knife! Gimme a knife! Oh Lordy! Lordy! Gimme a knife!"
> Two open knives clattered on the brick pavement in the little ring around the trees.
> Gracie caught up one and began slashing the rope. It was tough. She haggled and haggled with the dull knife. At last a strand held it. Another stroke cut it apart. Toussaint collapsed. His mother, trying to hold him up, fell with him.
> A dozen drunken voices in the mob broke into laughter at the downfall of the negro mother and her dead son.

The last sentence shifts the total emphasis of the scene from the Colonel and Gracie, from the human and individual content, to

Stribling's general proposition. The mark of Stribling's success is that the effect of the incident has survived even his ineptitude.

But to return to the general effect of all this on Stribling's art: propagandist art is necessarily incomplete. It is incomplete because the emotional reference, and in fact all reference except for matters of technique, is external. Character appears as a long-hand for a social proposition. Event appears as a sort of allegory, a morality play of "social forces." The whole is a documentation in dramatic form of a social proposition which, presumably, the author wants to see realized in actuality. Propagandist art is never pure propaganda in the first place, for something other than a social conscience forces the choice of the art form, but the purity in this respect depends on the degree in which the author desires to see the practical triumph of his critical ideas and obtrudes that desire. In so far as this aim is possessed, and is obtruded, the work is scientific: it appeals to the scientist, the economist, the sociologist in us, and makes us say, we ought to do something about this. Grant that it may be an abuse we ought to do something about. The response, nevertheless, is not the response evoked by a first-rate novel, play, or poem.

The point, I think, may come clear if Stribling's work is compared with that of certain other novelists who have treated the same material; for instance, William Faulkner. Take the "poor whites" of Faulkner's *As I Lay Dying* as compared with those of *Teeftallow* or *The Store*. As a citizen, in his practical and public rôle, Faulkner may want to see a broadened way of life possible for the back-country people of Mississippi; but he is too much of an artist to commit himself to the easy satire of the reformer or esthete. And it is doubtful that Faulkner, the citizen, approves of Pop Eye, the gangster, or of Temple Drake; but his distaste as a citizen is not the theme of *Sanctuary*. And when the mother in *The Sound and the Fury* rebukes her child for using a nickname, saying nicknames are common, the effect is not a piece of satire on her pretensions, but something more immediate, human, and profound; it is perhaps a pathos at this clinging to a symbol of gentility and self-respect in the midst of decay, and if the scene is complicated with irony it is an irony that the symbol should, after all, be so futile and so stupid.

Light in August employs all the material familiar in Stribling's work, race prejudice, class prejudice, sectional prejudice, and violence, but with a far different effect. Christmas, the white Negro of *Light in August,* unlike Toussaint of *The Store,* is caught in an insoluble problem that can only end in tragedy; it is a problem so fundamental that he cannot evade it, no matter what he does or where he goes. The implication in *The Store* is that if Toussaint could go North, and get an education, and pass as white, and, as Gracie wishes, have a white wife, his problem would be solved. But Christmas does pass as white, even in the South, and does go North, and does have, not one, but many white women; but these things are ultimately irrelevant to the circumstance of his life. Even if he were rich and successful, his character being given, they would remain irrelevant. The death of Christmas has some tragic dignity; the lynching of Toussaint is a mere butchery, or on another view, a competent piece of legerdemain to point a moral if not adorn a tale.

The primary difference, a difference perhaps more of intention than of achievement, between the work of Stribling and that of Faulkner seems to be this: the drama that engrosses Stribling is a drama of external circumstance, a conflict drawn in the purely practical world; the drama that engrosses Faulkner concerns a state of being, a conflict involving, to some degree at least, the spiritual integrity of a character. It is this quality of Faulkner's work that has provoked such a remark as the following from a review by Morris Schappes:

But despite his [Faulkner's] apparent unconsciousness of the complex background that would permit us to understand fully the merely personal situations he explores—a background that would reveal the multiple social relations among the old landed "aristocracy," the newer industrialists, the small peasant farmers, the share cropper, the proletariat of textile and steel mill, the Negro farmer and worker—we still find some meaning in the very surface tension of his world.

It is a question as to which drama, that of Stribling or that of Faulkner, is a "surface tension." The answer may be as simple as this: social constructions and social propositions can only be endowed with value in terms of the individual experience. If that is an answer, obvious as it is, then it is the drama of Stribling, not that of Faulkner, which is concerned with surface tension. And it may well be, in the end, that the work of Faulkner, rather than that of Stribling, is of the order that can give social conscience a meaning.

But the difference may be stated as it relates to method. With Stribling, as I have said, a novel is a device for communication, that is, a device for illustration. The author "intellectualizes" his perceptions so that their vitality is forfeited. The work approaches allegory. But Faulkner, and a considerable group of the younger Southern novelists, are more conservative; they conceive of the novel as *itself* the communication. They are interested in putting, so far as their powers permit, the question about the destiny of certain obscure individuals, their characters, so that the question will remain alive. Perhaps the questions, or some of them, are unanswerable. But that sort of passionate, yet disinterested and patient, contemplation is, presumably, the business of an art, even the art of the novelist. It is a contemplation rooted in the poetic attitude.

But to the critical realist poetry, like religion, would be, I take it, somewhat "greasy."

LOUISE BOGAN
Viola Meynell

Viola Meynell's work lies open to that risk of excellence in a limited field: it can pass under the careless reader's eye as unremarkable. The cool style can be overlooked, because of its very evenness of structure; the characters, built up with the most circumspect observation and detail, may appear colorless to the attention which expects the at once brilliant and carelessly pointed-up stock "humors" which, almost invariably, move through modern fiction.

Since 1913, American publishers have brought out six books by Miss Meynell, yet her work is almost unknown here. *Young Mrs. Cruse,* a volume of short stories published in 1925, gained her some critical praise and a careless comparison to Katherine Mansfield, whose method and point of view hers do not in the slightest degree resemble. She is, rather, sister both to Jane Austen and to Turgenev. She has the early nineteenth-century qualities of classicism, just barely touched and brightened by a kind of light-hearted, lyrical romanticism, that both these writers share.

In *Young Mrs. Cruse,* the form of Miss Meynell's stories is not the swift, skillful *conte.* Her figures never appear to be thrown off by chance from a mind working at brilliant but distorting speed. She has, rather, a patient vision that constructs from partial aspects, themselves in no way remarkable, her characters and their scene. Every moment is clean and credited, as if she knew these people, not only in the brief moments of her story, but quite surely at all other moments of their lives.

The effect of much modern writing depends upon a heightening

From *The Saturday Review of Literature,* I, p. 703, April 25, 1925; *The New Republic,* XXXI, pp. 151-2, June 27, 1928; *Poetry: A Magazine of Verse,* XL, pp. 226-229, June, 1932. Reprinted in this revision by permission.

of, rather than a direction in, emphasis. The characters are caught into the action by some tangential spurt of fancy which wastes the emotional content, so that they appear breathless and spent. Miss Meynell, in these stories, gauges her work more carefully. The situation is often presented below its own level. Yet the result of this understatement is the spectacle of a grief too grievous, and of ecstasy become burdensome. Her men and girls actually embody the young passion for which requitement or loss is absolute.

This art is built straight upon reality, and it is only when reality is observed with precision that perception not usually given the physical eye seems to be involved. Miss Meynell is capable like Turgenev of noting such a detail as when a man walks toward one, under the shadow of trees, shadow flows up over him; when he walks away, shadow flows down. And she notices the gestures, the inflections, the turns in manner and speech by which people betray themselves. She tracks down the strong hypocrises of the human heart, which hide it even from itself, and bases, with the least effort needed, upon reality, the mind's illogical associations between unrelated things.

The stories "The Letter," and "Pastoral," in *Young Mrs. Cruse,* are moved by the rise and change of emotion. The young farm girl in trouble hears night and day from her parents the fact that she must write to her lover. But when it is written the letter does not speak of the bitter reasons she has so often heard. The girl in "Pastoral," stricken quite helpless with grief over a faithless lover, marries a busy farm-owner, the first man who appears after her tragedy. She is beginning to come alive in her new bustling surroundings, to see a world somewhat freed from apathy and despair, when her first lover returns. She yields to the thought of going away with him automatically, without any consciousness of guilt. Yet as she goes about with her husband on his errands along country roads, she begins to protect herself against the realization of his future betrayal and loneliness. By the plans she makes for his life after she will be with him no longer she keeps herself, up to the last moment, from the knowledge that she will not go away.

The stories throughout are weighted with small but moving observations. Miss Meynell knows the exact light of the turning seasons: the feeling of late autumn afternoons, of early winter mornings: "the day began in the quiet dark night." The pregnant girl for whom the countryside, once flat to her quick feet, suddenly becomes full of gradients that take the breath; the lovers who meet secretly at night in the fields and lie quietly to escape notice while all the time they remain there a dog barks "at the utmost note of fury and danger"—these become more real than pages thick with rhetorical blood and tears.

In her novel, *A Girl Adoring,* published in 1928, she again succeeds with the kind of task for which her talent is best suited; she has disposed with intelligent gravity one figure after another about the girl at the heart of the book, a girl taken by "the sweetness and terror" of first love. Her other novels, always elaborating two themes—the inescapable power of human beauty over everything it touches, and the ravaging torture inherent in early and untutored love—have in the same way circled about such a girl. Her heroines are childish, unworldly women struck by a passion which troubles and unnerves them; conventional girls startled by a single emotion as relentless in their hearts as the drive of purpose in the will, or by two conflicting desires that go on at the same time, not defeating each other, but rather aiding and enriching the nature that bears them, up to the moment when they must break apart for one to live at all. It is a difficult task to accomplish this analysis of a gentle mind shocked and torn by a force and agony with which it is unable to cope. Miss Meynell always manages to bring such situations to life, with an art so quiet that it is but slowly recognized as also vigorous and startling.

This is the story of *A Girl Adoring* in the flat.—Clair Vandeleyden lives with her brother, Morely, and his wife, Laura, in the country, where Morely cultivates his own land. She has a sister, Gilda, who, after a disastrous love-affair that continues for years, has married a man in public life and lives in London in the great world of fashion and affairs. Clair looks forward with a

girl's eagerness to visiting Gilda; in the hour before her departure she meets Richard Hague, a man who has recently bought a
neighboring farm. The spell of London is broken; her visit becomes a long period of waiting until she can go back. When she
does return, the interest and passion she and Hague begin to
feel for one another is cut across by the hungry, beautiful, listless
person of Louise, a guest in Morely's house, who fastens her attentions upon Hague. Clair withdraws into her unhappiness;
Hague's obstinacy keeps him from following her, until her suffering breaks his will as it has broken hers.

From the first moment the characters are set apart completely
from any company of named masks. Gilda is given first. "The
passion that sapped the youth of this unfortunate girl was one of
those guilty loves that anguish turns into more of a misfortune
than a sin. Hardly a moralist who knew of her affair would have
thought it necessary to pause and point out what heavy retribution would in justice be her lot—the punishment was too obvious.
By the time her history with her lover had transformed her from
a triumphant girl into a worn and exhausted woman, she had entered into that category of sufferers where saints and sinners are
very much alike." Then there is Morely, the self-indulgent, the
slave of moderation, at once kind and begrudging, who works
hard with a fine show of disinclination, whose heavy moods Clair
tries to lighten for his wife, until she finds that Laura has made
her own automatic adjustment to their weight. There is also
Hague, whose stubbornness is the other side of his love. "From
the moment she did not want him, he no longer wanted her. His
command of himself was something more than the control of the
outward signs that would have betrayed his loss; it was something
between himself and himself. He was not the sort of man whose
pride makes him wary that he may betray by a look or a word.
He gave her up farther back than that, at the source of all looks
and words." And Louise, who lives most in her beauty reflected
in other people's behavior—"her conversation, what there is of it,
is just as attractive as she happens to look while she speaks." And,
finally, there is Clair, humbly helping to burn tussocks of grass

in Hague's water-meadows, or heading his sheep down a road in the darkness, keeping her misery so safely in her mind that it shows only as an accent to lesser miseries, as when she takes it as a personal affront that a fire has not been lighted in a cold room. These people have been imagined, have been observed at their source, behind "all looks and words."

Without the benefit of any enlarged reasons that borrow terms from science or speculation, Miss Meynell works straight through the relations of her characters to each other and to their scene. No fantastic arrangement of motive and emotion balances upon a guessed-at factual underpinning; no wooden props shore up the action. Her people act logically within the bounds set for them because their creator has observed the reason for those limits and has gauged their truth through both her heart and mind. And because she works in little, with no pretense of covering the length and breadth of human experience in a tragic stride, the major notes struck out of her small scheme sound with an added emphasis. And her prose style, which has rejected every effect of distorting rhetoric, and at times seems to move only because her characters move within it, helps her to exceed ready-made explanations of conduct and appearance. Her manner has the same rectitude and clarity as the thought that sets it free.

The numbered group of first-rate women novelists have always realized the dramatic uses of a walled-in stage. Miss Meynell, in her earlier novels—*Modern Lovers, Narcissus, Columbine,* and *Second Marriage*—tells always the simplest story: beyond the fields and houses she has chosen, and the men and women within their confines, she does not hear the world or its echoes. Thus circumscribed, despair and delight can rise to their full. Many times, things seen or heard are presented so intensely that it seems that other senses are erased, and one sense is used for all the others, as though a deaf person were seeing, or a blind person heard. "The pianist was a woman. Her hands and arms, bare to the elbow, were more part of the piano than of herself. In the division of those two, she and her piano, her arms and hands would have gone with the ivory mechanical keyboard." Objects are shown as a child sees them, broken off for a moment from their environment, and printed with a sudden piercing distinction. Miss Meynell knows exactly how small impermanent effects of horror and nostalgia arise, such as the emotion of a traveler, eager to get on with his journey, who leaves a hotel room repudiating it thoroughly, "not yielding it one last consideration as he throws the torn scraps of a letter on the floor," not understanding how he could have been glad to enter it. The humble glance of shame that can be love's proudest look; the ugly feeling that a self-conscious smile makes about the mouth; "the kind of kiss that showed just better spirits, not more love"; those feelings of clouded expectation, of the thing desired kept out of the thought by an act of the will, of the tortuous being self-deceived, the timid spirit which betrays what it most believes—these gain from Miss Meynell an explicitness and tragedy but seldom accorded them.

The daughter of a famous mother, Miss Meynell has always made the quietest claims for her poetic gifts. She has published two books of poetry (*Verses,* 1919, and *The Frozen Ocean,* 1932). In her poetry, even more than in her novels, it is possible to define the quality which has set her apart, yet which has failed, in this period, to bring her the appreciation which she deserves. She is, unlike Virginia Woolf, to whom the word has sometimes been applied, a contemplative. Her cast of mind derives from the most authentic but, modernly, the most neglected field wherein women have exercised their emotional and intellectual capacities. Her poems, like her novels, are frugal in form, undisturbed by rhetoric, candid as thoughtful speech. She has inherited her mother's lucid mysticism, but escapes the faintly dry touch of literary air which Alice Meynell absorbed from the late nineteenth century. Her simplicity, her candor, reveal emotions brightly alive and clearly felt under delicate restraint, emotion that is itself form: the kernel which builds outward from inner intensity every lyric capable of touching the heart and mind. Several of her poems state a girl's romantic passion with the simplicity that has been rare in women's poetry since Christina Rossetti. Others, notably "Jonah and the Whale" and "The Frozen Ocean," manage one conceit with a sure feeling for implication akin to Herbert's or Vaughan's. "The July Gale" illustrates Miss Meynell's perfect veracity of sight, her vivid apprehension of reality, and her power to unite details by the slightest means into poetic fusion.

> This wind goes where no other wind has been,
> Hidden things it finds no other winds have seen.
>
> It shakes the short stiff quills on the bird's breast,
> As if in long loose plumes the bird were dressed.
>
> Through close-cropped turf the windy waves are borne,
> As if along a field of waving corn.
>
> It moves rough stones across the road, as light
> As if they were dead autumn leaves in flight.
>
> And oh, the very earth is undone now,
> And trembles like a stricken winter bough!

Compared to more ambitious novelists, to poets whose powers range more freely, more casually, Miss Meynell must appear limited. But within her limits she exhibits perfect clairvoyance; she can be appreciated by those who prefer the author of *Fathers and Sons* to the author of, say, *War and Peace*. If she lacks scope and power, she also lacks cruelty, pretentiousness, obtuseness and falsification of values. And although the figures in her novels ask nothing of us but recognition, they receive from us, as we receive from them, the delighted memory of all we know without having learned: our double vision, not often claimed or called to mind.

MORTON DAUWEN ZABEL

Four Poets in America

I: ROBINSON

In the poems of his greatest strength—"Eros Turannos," "Cassandra," "Flammonde," "The Book of Annandale," "The Mill," "Rahel to Varnhagen," *The Man Who Died Twice,* five or six sonnets—Edwin Arlington Robinson stands secure among the small company of distinguished minds and resolute artists which the nineteenth-century tradition produced in America. In his lesser work may be found temporization, unwarranted detail of argument, feeble rhythm, and even nondescript statement, but never a trace of the besetting sins of second-rate verse in our day: trumpery emotion, facile journalism in style, coarse personal exploitation, and unabashed incompetence in forming judgments. At one hand Robinson risked condemnation for a virtue that easily becomes a poetic vice—reticence. At the other he courted the fatigue of popular interest by writing far beyond the point where the patience of hasty reviewers and the réclame of propagandists stop. He grew beyond that "creative majority" that ends the careers of most poets in their middle twenties. His successive volumes came to take on the character of an annual literary event. *Matthias at the Door* (1931), *The Glory of the Nightingales* (1930), and *Cavander's House* (1929) were further variants of the drama of self-determination and moral salvation earlier disclosed in "Annandale," "Atherton's Gambit," "Flammonde," *The Man Who Died Twice,* and *Captain Craig. Tristram,* a phenomenal

From *The Commonweal,* XVII, pp. 436-438. February 15, 1933; and *Poetry: A Magazine of Verse,* XLVI, pp. 157-162. June, 1935. Reprinted by permission.

public success of 1927, belongs to the group of Arthurian redactions which admit only fortuitous disclosures of Robinson's personal intelligence and vigor. Their vogue, as much as their derivative nature, has cheapened for many what was in the original merely a baffled portraiture. Unfortunately, these paraphrases, despite their firm direction and disciplined sentiment, have become Robinson's readiest card for publicity. The revisionist motive ascribed to them, as well as a "psychology" modernly superior to Tennyson's, has resulted in a regrettable dislocation of emphasis in his work. Fragmentary in their excellence, these poems remain pendants to a focal, contemporary, and ultimately American achievement. Any historian must recognize its solidity; it has already frustrated the tests of popularity and boredom, and established its permanent character. Within Robinson's poetry exists at once the living ore of a native tradition and the heat of personal conscience. Both combined to fire the crystal of a strong and lucid vision, wherein the issue of creative effort in America finds a focus.

He never compromised for the applause granted his contemporaries. For the people who call his work dull, John Drinkwater, in an essay published in 1922 in *The Yale Review,* may be considered a suitable spokesman. In every age the poet of mature volume must fight his battle, if not before he achieves his own success (as in the case of Browning, Baudelaire, and Hardy), then after. Herbert Read has debated the relevance of the long poem to modern life. The facile mediocrity of Noyes, Masters, and Masefield have seriously discouraged the general and even the critical reader from adequate attention to a *Testament of Beauty,* an *Ecliptic,* or *XXX Cantos* when they come his way. Moreover, the naphtha-flare charm of the currently applauded lyric writers seldom settles down to the constant flame that feeds on a profound spiritual nourishment. The modern anthology (in any age) is populated by adolescents and over-night successes; their worth is topical and their reputations gusty. In this circle Robinson never found a place. His earlier poems were modest, unhurried, and prophetic. His later books made equally little effort to share in

literary fashion, and possessed whatever modernity was credited
to them through the skillful strategy of seeming to ignore all the
arts of being timely, alert, and keen to the opportunism of reputation.

To arrive at this stage of unfashionable and impersonal fame
among his contemporaries means several things in a poet. He
has found refuge from the immediate event that taxes his experience; he has achieved a style that misses the tone of ephemeral
favor and "progress"; and he has met the demands of that historical sense necessary to "any poet if he is to survive as a writer
beyond his twenty-fifth year."

It is convenient to label Robinson's confrontation of modern
distress and perplexity as stoic. This is no attitude suddenly
adopted by conversion or necessity at a crisis in his career. It was
implicit in his earliest publications. The frankly advertised sobriety
and inscrutability of most contemporary stoicism makes it one of
the most deceptive of intellectual positions. It becomes in some
hands a refuge of the bewildered who lack Aiken's or MacLeish's
inclination to pathos, or Eliot's to historical irony. Elsewhere it is
a counsel of desperation of another order: the lugubrious and
heavily paraded manner that seeks to hide a disproportionate self-
esteem. In a certain type of disappointed mind, honor licked to
its kennel foments a conceit that despises reproof, a viewpoint
wholly egocentric, and a literary style warped and defeated by
the resulting spiritual doggedness. Since the term stoic, in these
current usages, has little historical meaning, it is well to note also
how inappropriate a garment it is for defeatism and soured intelligence. Stoic dignity and authority issue only from an assumption of some constant, if ineluctable, authority and direction in
the universe. By submitting to this control, man ennobles his agnos-
ticism through humility and patience. From the principle of
willed design which he admits in creation, he derives his confidence
in order and acquires his private mode of discipline.

> Shall we, because Eternity records
> Too vast an answer for the time-born words
> We spell, whereof so many are dead that once

In our capricious lexicons
Were so alive and final, hear no more
The Word itself? . . .

It goes without saying that stoicism is as easily parodied as mysticism, sentiment, or piety. Enough examples of such parody are available in recent verse. True stoicism, like genuine piety, drives to the root of character, and is likely to test the integrity of character as ruthlessly as any discipline available to modern man. But like the poetic discipline itself, its first requirement is character in its professor. Without that basis, the stoic, whatever his pretensions to self-discipline and integrity, is one of the most pathetic of shams. This basis is nowhere so starkly laid bare, and so rigorously proved, as in the poetic discipline. The more external and political demands of life, as Coleridge remarked in his *Aids to Reflection,* offer comparatively slight consolation to stoicism and the private authority of will in the modern world.

Robinson's example is one of the few that makes the designation *stoic* worth envying or exploiting. From the outset of his career, he lacked the querulous and commiserating tone perfected by his Victorian ancestors. He was, temperamentally, removed from such defenses as Laforgue's irony or Rimbaud's denunciatory violence. The symbolist influence and all it involved did not touch him. Search for a provenience might suggest an alliance between Emerson's libertarian doubt and Emily Dickinson's firm and ruthless inquisition of the spirit, but this would force an issue as improbable (although singularly as appropriate) as that from Donne's falling star and the mandrake root. Robinson is no fatal or exotic child of misalliance. He saw from the start the gravity of his problem, but neither the direction of American culture nor the ruses of literary method helped him solve it. He chose the hard and solitary path of personal probity. In the phrase favorably applied to him from the title of one of his best books, he is a man against the sky, one who has faced the infinite with exceptional self-reliance, and even with skepticism of his New England heritage. His curiosity escapes the facile reach of Emerson's sanguine disillusionment, just as it avoided such physical clues as guided Hopkins in his research of conscience. The firm grip of a problem exceptional in Emerson's verse is customary in Robinson's. His heroes, from Annandale to Hector Kane, from Crabbe and Hood in the tribute sonnets to Toussaint L'Ouverture, are men of scruple, but not of heroism inflated by scruple. Kane is an honest empiricist to his death:

> "Nothing was ever true for me
> Until I found it so," said he;
> "So time for me has always been
> Four letters of a word."

And he shares with Robinson a motive less easily demonstrated in Robinson's verse than in that of Emily Dickinson or in the prose of Melville: the ruthless notation of the experience which conditions and shapes knowledge. That notation in Miss Dickinson produced a verse rich in explorative imagery. It equipped her with a symbolism never mechanistic, yet productive of concept and proof beyond those achieved by the symbolist method in France. It has brought her work finally to share with that of a few contemporaries the distinction that comes of the severest logic in observation, with its resulting vigor of reference and inference.

Robinson's method doubtless limited his contemporary appeal. Its abstractness removed him from the favor of those poets whose language is closer to the symbolist tradition—the sensory language of image and metaphor. The more popular, and often mistaken, aspects of Miss Dickinson's revival is based almost wholly on this element in her work. The latter-day Imagists subscribed to the discipline of this method, even though no party affiliations were necessary for that discipline to flourish in the best work of Pound, Eliot, Stevens, Williams, Louise Bogan, and Marianne Moore. These poets submit to no community of method, yet it is the immediacy of poetic experience suggested by their styles that makes them vivid and forceful. Robinson's substance is not sensation but intuition; his method is not metaphorical but syllogistic; his material is not that of analogy and allegory but of abstract formulation. Thus his typical poem does not strike out for concrete substance in external reality; it drives toward the center of moral consciousness for its certainty, even when the process involves an exploration that leaves sensory logic and the external world behind for the sphere of pure notion. His salvation lies in his never forgetting that the search is a moral test, not an intellectual exercise. At his best, its reality is never lost, and the responsibility of arriving at decisions is never denied. There is no hint of the facile and evasive casuistry of modern dialectic. Robinson is not the most eloquent logician; temporization has vitiated more than one passage in his work, just as it has undermined the quality of his blank verse. But his work never suggests, like Valéry's, the exercise of a purely esthetic logic, or the avoidance of actual moral committal. If abstraction results, it is not geometrical, but in the firmest sense ethical.

Robinson's outward indifference both to his early hardship and to his later success was, first of all, his way of being a poet; he left no other record of his genius, in prose or action. But it was something more. It was his way of defining and surviving a point of view that belongs peculiarly to the half-century of American history that shaped his mature thought and his twenty books of verse. Born in 1869, he reached his twenties by the time the United States entered its full era of pride and commercial splendor; he was approaching fifty when the bursting prowess of 1917 announced the country in its new rôle of world-savior; death overtook him on April 5, 1935, when the outlook of both hemispheres—already darkened by the doubts of economic and political desperation—had reached a new crisis of profound pessimism. Robinson had learned how to offer resistance both to the fulsome glitter of material progress and to the fatalism of defeated hopes. His early struggles as a poet were largely ignored by an age of inflated "culture" that respected few men of sober judgment; it was an age which, at best, stopped its fears with the messianic eloquence of yea-sayers and prophets of utopian prosperity. He could in turn afford to ignore the fame that arrived so profusely during his last twenty years. The vantage-point Robinson occupied was maintained by the help of a diffident personality, but this was bred by two factors that reach beyond the limits of temperament. One was his inheritance of the taciturn rigors of New England pragmatism—a legacy whose sterility he could recognize even though he affirmed it in some of his last poems; the other was his dogged resistance to any form of illusion in his thought. The first of these factors is hard to dissociate from his Maine birth and childhood; the other is difficult to credit to anything but his revulsion from the gilded pretensions surrounding his manhood. He had the good fortune to resist any temptation toward public oratory even in pre-War years when that method was the one guaranty of success for an American writer. The retreat drove him toward a discipline of infinitely greater advantage to him as a poet: the discipline of facts and of critical thought—of facts judged at close hand instead of approached through abstract theory, of ideas scanned and appraised, instead of felt by means of the deceptive emotional apparatus in vogue in the Nineties. Robinson possessed at the outset the grip on reality which a poet like Yeats has come into only after many years of struggle and intellectual exploration; his work shows none of the phenomena of growth that makes Yeats' career so dramatic; and if he never achieved what Yeats has finally mastered in the way of personal eloquence and symbolic richness of style, it is because, by an initial impulse, he rejected the pathways of sensation, trance, and illusion that may lead, by chance or accident or by some special form of imaginative mastery, to a clear and final resolution about man and his destiny.

Robinson's Maine days provided him—out of an environment as unpromising as any section of America could offer—with more than a natural and involuntary grip on human ordeal: with characters to illustrate failure and obscure victory in that struggle. These are the men of his native American drama—Captain Craig, Luke Havergal, Aaron Stark, Bewick Finzer, Richard Cory, Flammonde, Miniver Cheevy, John Gorham, Fernando Nash, Roman Bartholow—a gallery in whom are embodied the puritan tradition in its dark days of spiritual dispossession, and a skeptical courage

which saw no substitute for that tradition in the coming age of
commercial optimism. Misers and profiteers like Finzer and Stark
lean toward the shadow as fatally as glittering husks of popular
heroism like Richard Cory. The blighting touch of moral presumption is on all of them, while madmen, imbeciles, and hermits
alone appear to have worked out a saving irony. But Robinson
is saved from the dogged fatalism of *Spoon River* by the same
force that deprived him of the subtle spiritual victories granted to
Henry James. His faith, being stoic, was unprepared for more
exacting demands on intellectual responsibility; but this was a
stoicism that came at an hour of bewildered confidences and betrayed trusts, an hour that needed (and perhaps permitted) only
that kind of critical reaction which remains sealed and safe in
the private integrity of the individual. It was the hour of "skeptical faith," and faith that shatters as soon as it becomes public.
Outward shows were the surest ways of losing even such strength
as a disillusioned stoicism affords. But Robinson's long line of
defeated men are testimony to the fact that he hoped his inward
discipline would prepare a new kind of leadership. When he
turned away from the typical American life of "Tilbury Town"
or from its analogies in Arthurian legend, he could seize on a
hardier and more active kind of doctrine. He saw the need of
a more vigorous corrective to the facile casuistry of popular rationalism. He celebrated the "sure strength" of George Crabbe's consecrated "flicker"; "the racked and shrieking hideousness of Truth"
in Zola; the Shakespeare who knew "too much of what the world
had hushed in others"; Rembrandt, who scorned "the taste of
death in life"; the sense of "undeceiving fate" in Lincoln. Robinson did not make these men into *personae* of himself; they remain as objective as the duties which he employed them to illustrate. By that acceptance of the "Titan" with the quietist, the
"Forger" with the "Watcher," he saves his irony from irresponsibility, and his grim detachment from the grief of suicide.

Robinson's art, at its best, derives from his sense of the plainest
use of speech. Even his lyrics are written in a taciturn English
that lies between the purely logical and the obviously colloquial

style. His lyric perceptions, like his human values, are rooted in the known and the possible—the capacities of man which survive even in his sorriest condition of stultification and confusion. He never allowed his tragic sense to carry him toward the impotent Promethean rhetoric of Jeffers. It is these firm roots, not only in experience but in language, that bind Robinson so certainly to his moment in modern history—to its economic and social conditions, its moral conflict, its political crisis and immense human claims. He is a realist not only in conscience but in style and diction; in *milieu* as much as in imagery; and this gives him his license to explore the problems of abstract casuistry and moral contradiction which he filed down into that style of attenuated rumination, impassioned hair-splitting, and bleak aphorism which will always remain unmistakably his own. He wrote searching judgments not only on tragedies of love, jealousy, and envy, but on the crimes of imperialism, the folly of the Eighteenth Amendment, and the toppling recklessness of industrial inflation. The gray monotone of his collected works is deceptive, for within it may be discovered both the sweep and anger of righteous denunciation, and the suddenly lavish beauty of such lines as the endings of "Eros Turannos" and "The Sheaves."

He was a poet without school or cenacle; he was fundamentally as inimitable as unapproachable; and his bleaker or more repetitious volumes might almost be interpreted as warning to the public to expect from him none of the innovation or sensationalism that makes literary creeds, movements, and manifestoes. For this he was scorned by youthful insurgents, and apparently by most of the greater names that rival his in recent literature. His influence was more subtle. He brought form and toughness of language into modern verse long before most of his contemporaries, and he corrected by modest example a slow drift toward slovenly habits and facile impressionism in poetic thought. His equipment, technical and verbal, needed only the enriching substance of a more positive and committal belief; like Conrad's, his strength and brilliance are darkened by the touch of negation. But of him, as of Conrad, it may be said that whatever his contemporaries have achieved in art, either by novelty of means or by insurrection of ideas, has been done better because of his cleansing influence, and his model of honesty that no experimental or revolutionary activity can ignore. This was the particular and limited honor of Robinson and the courageous men of his generation. In this satisfaction he ended his work, and left American literature richer for a quality it had never known before in a form so complete or in an art so firm.

II: SANDBURG'S TESTAMENT

The hardest part of being a pioneer comes in remaining a contemporary. This is particularly true in modern poetry, where the average life of a "generation" is five years and where the trailblazing novelty of the pioneers of twenty-five years ago was so exaggerated by public clamor that within a short time they became as much victimized by critical suspicion and boredom as they had once been by the swollen claims of admiring patriots. To pick up any history or anthology of contemporary verse is to be depressed by the high rate of mortality among poetic reputations. No aid is lacking—from group politics and cut-throat rivalries to high-pressure salesmanship and journalistic inflation—in speeding the declines already promised by the ephemeral nature of the average literary beliefs and styles. It would hardly have needed the further discouragement of rapidly shifting critical standards or headlong changes in social and political life to turn the optimism of the American revivalists of 1912 into the despair or silence which many of them found to be the only answer to the contempt directed against them by the rising talents of the post-War years.

We know how few poets of the pre-War revival survived this state of affairs. Several did it in spite of persisting in their original aims; more did it by agile changes of face through the rise

From *Poetry: A Magazine of Verse*, XLIX, pp. 33-45. October, 1936. Reprinted by permission.

and fall of new tastes or styles. The first of these forms of survival carries one risk and the second another. One poet becomes
more and more personal in his ways, skeptical in his view of the
tumult and disorder around him, and so retreats into his own
sphere of private irony or eccentricity; this accounts for the predicament of Robinson or Frost. The other remains young at whatever cost of sober judgment or certain craft, mixes in movements
and experiments, and becomes more and more difficult to connect
with any kind of esthetic or philosophic stability. He keeps his
freshness alive, but becomes too mercurial for believers in real
values; his energy keeps him on the stretch but exhausts the
confidence of his followers; and so he arrives at the ambiguous
authority of Ezra Pound. In this age of high-pressure literary
promotion and easy public credulity, nothing seems easier for an
author than to win a hearing—and nothing harder than to keep it.

Carl Sandburg's new book, *The People, Yes,* is impressive at
first sight because in it he speaks with exactly the same voice he
used in the *Chicago Poems* of 1914 and yet succeeds in making it
as eloquent as any American poem of 1936. He risks two extreme
hazards of the contemporary writer. He writes on the social
problem, and he writes in popular language. It will be suggested
immediately that he has simplified them primarily by stopping
short of his full responsibilities as a poet. To this one must agree
at once that hardly a fifth of this volume is classifiable by any
definition as poetry, although any definition of poetry must include the purpose and imagination that run through its pages,
even when they contain nothing but inventories of popular speech
or long lists of trades and slogans. But no American poet now
living could publish with the same authority and completeness a
survey of the specifically American issue in twentieth-century poetry
—how it has emerged and developed, how it diverges from foreign influence and contacts, and what it may expect, in extension
or solution, from the coming talents of the humanitarian front.
This long document of 286 pages is not only a guide-book on
American themes; it is a manual of words and phrases, episodes
and characters, conflicts and forces, and in addition it contains

a demonstration of how the social idealism of American poetry may be successfully domesticated in the immediate future.

But its first interest comes from the fact that here Sandburg has summarized his purposes of a quarter-century and handed them as a testament to his inheritors. The book forms a remarkable unity with its predecessors. It is true that such consistency has deprived his work of exact points of interest or decision. His poems as they have appeared in his five volumes have progressively canceled their predecessors, repeating their themes and dulling their emphasis. Yet Sandburg is one of the few native poets of whom it may be said, with all respect to the priority of Whitman, that he has written no verse, good or bad, but his own. He has sacrificed to his own single-voiced personality—as candidly as Frost or Robinson, but without their irony or close-lipped pessimism—whatever variety or progress might have made him a more forceful character among post-War writers and readers. In this first book since *Good Morning, America* eight years ago he shows a purpose not only more serious than it has ever been before, but a talent tuned to uses and broken to duties which many members of the present generation of humanitarian poets, whatever their superior sophistication or craftsmanship, have hardly begun to understand.

In poetry or prose dealing with human causes it is usually a rule that there are no substitutes for thorough practical acquaintance with the matter in hand. Here brilliant technical advantages may display what they are intended to disguise—the writer's failure in immediate knowledge of his materials, or his substitution of journalism or second-hand study for it. Dos Passos' recent novels have given a new weight to the name and labor of Dreiser, and the younger proletarian poets who far outstrip Sandburg in metrical skill or formal rigor—in other words, as artists—throw into fresh relief the ruggedness of his achievement. They show him, by the glibness of their arguments or the abstract condition of their beliefs, to be deeply bred and matured in a cause of which they usually have a keen but merely juvenile understanding, or more often only an academic acquaintance. In other words, Sandburg triumphs on all the scores in which experience counts: in his use of speech and lingoes, in the range and authenticity of his folklore, in the scope of his social familiarity, in the reach of his memory, and in the size and variety of the history he has made of the whole age of industrial labor in America during the past half-century. Compared with these resources the younger talents offer a meager fare. Their phrases are thin and their colloquialisms synthetic, their data specialized and experiences green, their references as often warped as enriched by literary derivation, and the structure of their poems is held up by rhetoric or the false props of borrowed arguments.

On these grounds *The People, Yes* escapes criticism, even when it does so by casting esthetic claims to the winds. It is a vast retrospect of life and labor in America that suggests an obvious comparison—*Leaves of Grass*. It is prefaced by a poem that announces the casual and miscellaneous nature of its scheme:

> Being several stories and psalms nobody
> would want to laugh at
>
> interspersed with memoranda variations
> worth a second look
>
> along with sayings and yarns traveling on
> grief and laughter. . . .

It opens with a spectacle of the "Howdeehow powpow," which is the American nation in its immense dimensions and disorder—a "Tower of Babel job" which now stands

> as a skull and a ghost,
> a memorandum hardly begun,
> swaying and sagging in tall hostile winds,
> held up by slow friendly winds—

and so proceeds through 107 sections that alternate, on no apparent principle of contrast or structure, between personal episodes and mass movements, local anecdotes and epic generalities, lists of scenes, trades, occupations, and causes, passages of vague symbolic imagery, long catalogues of popular phrases, catchwords, clichés, and proverbs, and intervals of gnomic lyricism. Nothing has apparently been left out, but everything that Sandburg has put into his earlier poems is here again, particularly from previous surveys like "Many Hats" and *Good Morning, America.* The prevailing quality of style is "tough and mystical." It derives from the dogged patience of common humanity in being outwitted by keener brains and criminal exploiters, the pathetic endurance of the underdog who waits grimly for the reprisals of time. This style derives from Whitman only in structure. It has as little to do with his rhetorical strain or oracular grandiloquence as it has with Whitman's final lyric and choral mastery. It has even little of the belabored hardboiledness of Hemingway, Dos Passos, or Phelps Putnam. It comes with the laconic ease of talk on streets and farms, from section-gangs, night shifts, pick-and-shovel outfits, and hobo campfires, Union Square soapboxes and grocery-store rag-chewing. From these sources Sandburg has compiled a catalogue of American lore that must astonish anyone. Where he gets it all is beyond telling. Whether all of it is equally authentic or not is beyond present calculation. But it rings true to the American ear far beyond the language of the average "regional" novel or proletarian poem, and one has only to compare any random sample of it with the slang parts of Pound's *Cantos* or MacLeish's *Frescoes* to realize that one is the pure article and the other something like a parody heard from the stage of the London Colosseum.

In other words, Sandburg looks after his facts first, and waits for argument to follow from them. He is empirical in the rough native tradition. If he hears the jeer that "the people is a myth, an abstraction," he asks, "What myth would you put in place of the people? And what abstraction would you exchange for this one?" If the cause of social justice has any validity for reformers or poets it must come not from the mind but from "the bowels of that mystic behemoth, the people." The difference between Whitman and Sandburg is primarily a difference between a visionary imagination and a realistic one, between a prophet who deals in the racial and social aspects of humanitarianism and a historian who handles the specific facts of industrial life and labor. Whitman, given his sympathies and cause and with his greater imaginative vision, might have written his book without any immediate contact with its materials, whereas Sandburg, so denied, could have written none of his. The two poets join only at the point which is their common weakness: in the rhapsodic cries and flights that are the diffused and prevalent bane of the one and the merely incidental weakness of the other. Sandburg is saved from this pretension by his plain verbal sanity. He does not discard the lyric imagination; it filters through his pages and produces many short passages of characteristic fancy:

> Alive yet the spillover of last night's moonrise
>   brought returns of peculiar cash
>   a cash of thin air alive yet.

But it is seldom allowed to develop into vague apostrophe or inflated allegory, any more than his language is allowed to use the pompous phrases, French or Latin counterfeit, and hollow pedantry of Whitman's style. In the same way his general tendency is to avoid those vague specters of human ordeal that make up the panoramic symbolism of Perse's *Anabase,* Aragon's *Front Rouge,* or MacLeish's *Conquistador,* and when such effects do appear they immediately strike the eye with their uneasy falseness, as in parts 29 and 107, to select two examples from opposite ends of the poem. Three lines are enough to show how Sandburg on occasion veers into a pompous phraseology from which his cruder humors must rescue him:

> While the rootholds of the earth nourish the majestic people
> And the new generations with names never heard of
> Plow deep in broken drums and shoot craps for old crowns,

but one also runs into longer passages that come with particular inconclusiveness in the book's last pages, when something more than immortal truisms is wanted for force of thought or art, however such temporizations may agree with the skepticism of history:

> The people will live on.
> The learning and blundering people will live on.
> They will be tricked and sold and again sold
> And go back to the nourishing earth for rootholds,
> The people so peculiar in renewal and comeback,
> You can't laugh off their capacity to take it.
> The mammoth rests between his cyclonic dramas.

This kind of writing, coming on top of passages of the most brisk and vivid realism, rings with a special shallowness; another poet, stronger in rhetorical powers or symbolic skill, might make poetry of it, but where the general spirit of the poem casts suspicion on matter or ideas untested by hard fact, these references to dreams and mammoths, "cyclonic dramas," "the strength of the winds" and the "constellations of universal law," or to the people as

> a polychrome,
> a spectrum and a prism
> held in a moving monolith,
> a console organ of changing themes,
> a clavilux of color poems
> wherein the sea offers fog
> and the fog moves off in rain
> and the labrador sunset shortens
> to a nocturne of clear stars
> serene over the shot spray
> of northern lights—

show up as evasions of what either social necessity or poetic strength requires.

In other words, Sandburg, taken in the mass and for the general effect of his detail, is a master without rivals, a poetic realist of great range and authority, a folklorist in the best tradition, and easily the finest reporter of contemporary life that the modern poetic revival has produced, as comparison with Masters, Lindsay, Frost, or their younger successors will show. But taken in the specific poem or argument he offers as unsatisfactory a case to social critics as to literary. He eludes argument and dependability; he seems in the end evasive of responsibility; and his loyal purposes and honesty come to much less than they should. His immense knowledge of human ills and fortunes is too immense; it immerses and engulfs him; he is pulled by so many claims on sympathy and forbearance that nothing survives the prodigious outlay of tolerance and compassion but his inexhaustible supply of pure human nature. His feeling for the masses marching in the darkness with their great bundle of grief is tempered by ironic pathos for the millionaire suicide of Rochester or Marshall Field who left $25,000 for the upkeep of his grave. The farcical delusions of the rich are balanced against the tragic palliatives by which the poor are duped; the meat of privilege and the poison of oppression become mixed up because both destroy their eaters; moral platitudes are canceled by a wise-crack; and finally the only conclusion permitted him is a tough confidence in the abstract will of the people to save themselves. The answer to the whole urgent problem of human salvation is thrown back on "the folded and quiet yesterdays, put down in the book of the past," or thrown forward by the unanswered question, "Where do we go from here? Where to? What next?" or allowed to hang between unresolved opposites: "The people, yes, out of what is their change from chaos to order and chaos again?"

Obviously these are among the most difficult questions in the world to answer, but neither a poet nor a reformer would ask them if he had no answer to offer. As its title indicates, *The People, Yes* is written as a great affirmation of man's strength and value, but the practical regeneration of the human lot promised throughout the record finally hangs suspended in the void of love and patience. We knew it all before, even if not in this vivid and familiar language, and we are left wanting to know more. No doubt the avoidance of formulated solutions is dictated as much by common sense as by the plain facts of history, but one expects more than common sense or plain facts from a poet or a philosopher. It soon follows that if Sandburg had worked harder at his social or moral philosophy, he would have been a greater poet. In a book of this kind the test of poetic form is almost beside the point; it would apply in so small a fraction of the content. Yet as soon as one understands what it takes to achieve real form in the construction of language, one sees what it takes to arrive at that form through the structure and integration of thought. If one's thought remains undecided among the evidence at hand, inconclusively empirical or superior to proof, it is likely that the force and authority of the verse will remain scattered and confused among its details, words, and phrases, however abundant and authentic these may be. Sandburg's poetic instrument is exactly fitted to his purposes; it simply happens that those purposes are too vaguely poetic to make the instrument become anything more than the loose, amorphous, copious, semi-prose medium that it still remains after twenty-five years of use. And one may suppose that if he had exerted more labor on the task of filing and concentrating his verse, giving one phrase or anecdote the pith now thinned out over twenty, he would have arrived at something more fixed and specific in his social beliefs. The beliefs might be arbitrary in form; they might not conclude in what communist critics will logically demand and fail to get in the last ten pages of this book; but they would give a coherence and structure to his faith in mankind that would count for more than that faith in its present all-inclusive and unresolved condition. Sandburg himself implies that facts of this kind are beyond such arbitrary mastery:

> these lead to no easy pleasant conversation
> they fall into a dusty disordered poetry.

And his practical conclusions suggest a similar contempt for the formulations of economic socialism. "Always the storm of propaganda blows"; "yet the sleepers toss in sleep and an end comes of sleep and the sleepers wake." But between these prophecies we get the skepticism of an ironic intelligence which knows so much that it no longer trusts itself: "Who knows the answers, the cold inviolable truth?" "What does justice say?" "Where to? What next?" The potentialities of an epic judgment lie in Sandburg's materials, but he has not realized them. It is doubtful if any poet writing on the premises of Whitman could, since that tradition represents an immense exploration and discovery of poetic resources, but not their proof and mastery as poetry. Hart Crane wrote himself down as a disciple of Whitman, but his verse shows how great a poetic rigor he exerted over his materials, and how far he advanced the cause of American poetry by bringing it to terms with the moral and intellectual conflicts inherent in a genuinely poetic vision. The model of *The Bridge* now appears to be a difficult and confusing one for present poets to follow; the formal structure is too derivative and intricate, the style too complex, and the whole poem strives toward those evils of rhetoric and allegory which seem to be the surest way of producing artificial and didactic verse at the present moment. But if Crane's formal vision were combined with Sandburg's exact realism and thorough mastery of detail, it would be hard to find a more profitable combination for study by the rising poet of humanitarian ambitions. Something of that same merging of talents would have produced in these two poets themselves a richer and firmer art. Sandburg's book lacks exactly what makes Crane's a distinguished achievement, including its failure in a major purpose. Where it succeeds it does so in a way that is Sandburg's personal triumph, and gives him a distinction great enough among the men of his time to ensure him a high place among his fellows in oppression and hope.

III: CINEMA OF HAMLET

"My development as a poet is of no interest to me," says Archibald MacLeish in the preface to his *Poems, 1924-1933*, "and of even less, I should suppose, to anyone else." What his statement lacks in candor it makes up in optimism. For this collection of his best work in ten years shows that like any serious and respectable poet, he has been interested to the point of painful obsession in his

From *Poetry: A Magazine of Verse*, XLIV, pp. 150-158. June, 1934; and *The Southern Review*, II, pp. 177-180. Summer, 1936. Reprinted by permission.

"development." Self-knowledge (if not self-reverence and self-control) has been his involuntary goad in all the work he can now "read without embarrassment," whether disguised by literary anthropology in *The Hamlet*, by American nostalgia in *New Found Land*, by romantic heroism in *Conquistador*, or, in "Cinema of a Man," by post-war miasmas of exile and bewilderment, the poet plodding through simple sentences and assorted geography with "Ernest" ("they are drunk their mouths are hard they say *qué cosa* They say the cruel words they hurt each other") toward the oblivion of racial orphanage and the Nirvana of dead time.

To such an exhibition the public can hardly be expected to remain indifferent, particularly when Mr. MacLeish's plea for indifference is offset by his recent labors as scourge and fury among literary critics and Marxists. Adding to this the fact that he has written a portion of fine verse, and given himself more systematically than most of his contemporaries to the ordeal of his craft and personal predicament, one is obliged to consider the present "Foreword" as another installment of his rather evasive prose work, of his Challenge to the Age whose energies might better go into his poetry, since both History and Controversy, outside his verse, have left him somewhat the worse for his struggles with them.

Those struggles, however, underlie both his poetic "embarrassment" and his claim to dignity. They are a clue to his value as a contemporary. They are the result of several typical experiences: his obligation to forge a spiritual doctrine in the absence of both inherited belief and social necessity, his acceptance of an esthetic method before he had either moral or doctrinal matter to justify it, and notably his enlistment (widely advertised in his books) as a Paris exile some ten years ago and the consequent pathos of distance and sentiment that has troubled his ultimate conflict with America.

One of the oddest aberrations in our cultural history was the great exodus to France of 1918-1929, when literature, to be written, had to be written in Paris. Those were the days when American art moved from the Middle West to the Left Bank; when farm-hands hurried from Ohio and Wisconsin to get in on the Dada movement; when Gertrude Stein brandished the torch that lately sputtered in the grasp of Amy Lowell; when Kiki was the toast of Rotonde and Coupole; when "Ernest" proudly wheeled his well-filled go-cart among the occult biologic growths of the Dôme of an evening to partake of a whiskey and parental pride; when *transition* was young, nothing was sacred, and money was cheap; when whole generations got lost and Jimmie the Barman was accumulating his heady memoirs. These have recently been published, it happens, with an introduction by Mr. Hemingway, valedictorian of the movement: *"This Must Be the Place": Memoirs of Montparnasse,* by Jimmie the Barman. One fruitful passage suggests admirably the spirit of that heroic decade:

> Walking ahead of me was Flossie, both of us on our way to The Dingo. As she came abreast of the bar entrance, a handsome Rolls-Royce drove up to the curb and from it stepped two lavishly dressed ladies. They looked at The Dingo questioningly. They peered into the windows. Flossie, seeing them, looked her contempt. As she passed into the bar she tossed a single phrase over her shoulder: "You bitch!" Whereupon the lady so addressed nudged her companion anxiously. "Come on, Helen," she said, "this must be the place!"

Under much the same inspiration our writers decided that Paris must be the place to produce novels and poetry. This was the setting which Mr. MacLeish, after academic beginnings, war-service, and law-work, chose for his poetic discipline, and its spell upon him, to boast or exorcise, has been his chief spiritual problem ever since.

In those days his idea of poetry was almost purely esthetic. He argued for "mere poetry, poetry made out of poetry, poetry without sex, smirks, or graces, poetry without the sentimentality which passes among us for ironic, poetry without tags of wit." In view of the twin threats of propaganda and vulgarization which, then as now, aim to dispossess poetry of its essential purposes, his stand was a worthy one. Its weakness lay merely in what it denied in his own character, and what serious decisions, of inheritance and moral responsibility, it left him unprepared for. For these decisions the writers of the desultory Twenties substituted two literary methods: the elegiac and the hard-boiled. They were combined in *The Sun Also Rises, Trinc,* and *The Hamlet.* "Make us tough and mystical," said Phelps Putnam, and MacLeish:

> O play the strong boy with the rest of them!
> Be hard-boiled! Be bitter; Face the brassy
> Broad indecent fact and with ironical
> Contemptuous understanding take the world's
> Scut in your hands and name it! Name its name!

This was the *pis aller* of Montparnasse and Minetta Lane, a new version of the fustian desperations of Montmartre and Shropshire. Beyond those despairs lay the dignity of the Stoic tradition, and since hard-boiledness is a strenuous way to keep up one's belief in the deflation of all values but the physical and the esthetic, heroic pathos was substituted in the form of bull-fighters, drunkards, Spanish imperialists, or mere silent men lying flat on the ground, listening to the pulse of centuries, or marking the universal sunlight in its blind measurement of man's insignificant hours. From such impersonal fortitude MacLeish shaped his first serious conceptions of art and human idealism.

From the start his technical labor had been sensitive and sincere; but both sensibility and sincerity come to their supreme test in the solution of an inner, specifically personal problem. To externalize them in the interests of a general depersonalization of the human consciousness is to strike at their very life. This may be done by social propagandists in the cause of public reform or revolution. Or it may be done, as he has done it, in the interests of a more abstract sense of universals, the poet sinking his moral personality in the total consciousness of humanity, and in what is conceived to lie behind it—the unconscious life of nature and the universe. It is notable that after 1923 MacLeish's poetic masters were men who aided him toward this gradual surrender of private intelligence: poets who, like Frazer's anthropology (which he followed

Eliot in using for the symbolism of *The Pot of Earth*), relieved his private agony by opening up prospects of great involuntary human struggles, prospects of man in his most impersonal condition of consciousness against a background of racial transitions and wide-flung geographic movements. Here he could escape the threat of futility by submitting himself and mankind to an unfathomable universal will.

It is no longer A Man against the stars. It is Mankind: that which has happened always to all men, not the particular incidents of particular lives. The common, simple, earth-riding ways of hands and feet and flesh against the enormous mysteries of sun and moon, of time, of disappearance-and-their-place-knowing-them-no-more. The salt-sweating, robust, passionate, and at the last death-devoured lives of all men always. Man in the invisible sea of time that drowns him. . . .

The poets who helped him to this submission were the Cendrars of *Transsibérien* and *Kodak documentaire,* Apollinaire in *Alcools* and *Calligrammes,* and chief of all Perse with *Anabase.* To these Eliot, with "Gerontion," added the appropriate tone of ironic elegy, and Pound, with the earlier *Cantos,* the proper method of historical imagination. The result was the work of MacLeish's early maturity, the lyrics in which he caught pathos before it suffered distension and critical inversion, poems that celebrate with great verbal beauty a surrender to the mystery of existence and the processes of physical anonymity. This was *Le Secret Humain,* and it was the consolation of his *Hamlet:*

> We know what our fathers were but not who we are
> For the names change and the thorns grow over the houses.
> We recognize ourselves by a wrong laugh;
> By a trick we have of resembling something. Otherwise
> There are strange words and a face in a mirror.
>   We know
> Something we have forgotten too that comforts us.

It found its finest form in "You Andrew Marvell," its humorous expression in "Mother Goose's Garland," "Immortal Helix," and "The End of the World," its ironic function in "Tourist Death,"

and in "Einstein" an attempt to harmonize with the abstract ulti-
mates of science:

> He can count
> Ocean in atoms and weigh out the air
> In multiples of one and subdivide
> Light to its numbers.
> If they will not speak
> Let them be silent in their particles.
> Let them be dead and he will lie among
> Their dust and cipher them—undo the signs
> Of their unreal identities and free
> The pure and single factor of all sums—
> Solves them to unity.

Unfortunately MacLeish soon permitted his compliance in this
"pure and single factor of all sums" to undermine the personal resistance upon which such surrender, stoic or otherwise, counts for
salvation. "Men" brought the idea to the brink of parody, and
Conquistador allowed the lavish beauty of its materials to become
vitiated by the huge distension and dilution of an epic scale un-
supported by adequate epic motivation. Moreover, the surrender
of real certitude and "intellectualism" communicates itself to style.
MacLeish's earlier style grew into an astonishing beauty that contradicted the prejudice of anyone who knew the contemporary
sources from which it derived. His real task was to preserve its
integrity. But his progress in anti-intellectual humility meant also
a progress in stylistic self-effacement. This is apparent not only
in the disorganization, the overplayed repetitions, and the symbolic
vagueness of *Conquistador,* but in the progressive tyranny of his
models. Worthy models are the right of every worthy poet; but
in *Conquistador* the exhausted echo of the "old man" theme of
"Gerontion," and the overplayed effect of historic rumination borrowed from the *Cantos,* showed clearly that the models had deadened an ambitious creative purpose. And when, in the *Frescoes
for Mr. Rockefeller's City,* we find a device of the *Cantos* baldly
reproduced:

To Thos. Jefferson Esq. his obd't serv't
M. Lewis: captain: detached:

Sir. . . .

we are led to wonder why Mr. MacLeish, who likes "that clean
sharp stroke which is heard when the axe goes into living wood"
should be so indifferent when he hears the axe sink into Ezra
Pound's neck. "Critics moved by a love of poetry," he says, should

point out the excellence of the work, the way in which, with honesty
and self-respect, the man handles a long and eloquent line, a firm
and vivid phrase and a vocabulary not filched from the thesaurus—

or, presumably, from his fellow-poets. Implicitly he demands that
the absence of these poetic virtues be similarly pointed out. A poet
who aims at them resolutely need waste no petulance on critics who
are trying to rescue poetry from the vulgarity of "couturier criticism" or "The Literature Business" which he himself has deplored.
  MacLeish's irresolution has been emphasized by the serious direction which his work of the past five years has taken. Physical
stoicism and obsession by time had come to him too easily; they
began to stir uneasy scruples in his thought. To feel, "face downward in the sun . . . how swift how secretly The shadow of the
night comes on" was a beatitude disturbed by a sensation that is
likely to disrupt the stoic peace of soul:

> These alternate nights and days, these seasons
> Somehow fail to convince me. It seems
> I have the sense of infinity!

Infinity, paradoxically, is likely to drive a man back to the local
and specific accidents of his own life and self. MacLeish, in European expatriation, was troubled by his duty and birth-right: "It
is a strange thing to be an American." Returning to America, he
was plunged into the crisis of the depression years. To him this
crisis could not be relieved by the technical or forcible reforms of
economic socialism. It was a crisis between the fundamental pioneer idealism of "The Farm" or the selfless heroism of *Conquistador,* and the industrial greed he denounced in "1933" or the revo-

lutionary violence satirized in the *Frescoes*. But between these antitheses his judgment clung to abstract canons of honor—canons which risk committal to neither a positive moral dogmatism nor to a practical social risk. He invoked "Time which survives the generations" when he argued on economics, and "disinterestedness" when he defined the poet:

> It is also strictly forbidden to mix in maneuvers:
> Those that infringe are inflated with praise on the plazas—
> Their bones are resultantly afterwards found under newspapers.
>
> .   .   .   .
>
> There is nothing worse for our trade than to be in style:
>
> .   .   .   .
>
> Neither his class nor his kind nor his trade may come near
> him. . . .

Or, more explicitly:

The intuitions of the poet are valid and may be accepted only because his loyalty is to his art, because his sole test of the acceptability of a word or a phrase or a poem is the test of his art and not the test of his politics or his social indignation. This is not to say that the true poet is without prejudice. He has of course the prejudices of his blood, his countryside, his education, if you will, his "class." But . . . there remain certain individuals who believe that the first and inescapable obligation of the poet is his obligation to his art; who believe that the fact that the practice of his art is difficult in no way releases him from that obligation; who believe that the desertion of his art for any reason, even the noblest, even the most humane, is nevertheless desertion.

This is nobly expressed and it involves an inevitable esthetic loyalty, but MacLeish's practice shows too clearly how for him art, like human stoicism, became an evasion of the specific responsibility to which the poet, no less than the humble honest man, is committed. Poetry, like the moral life, is an art of concrete conditions whose style and strength are realized when conceptual or ethical abstraction is tested by vital experience. It is as easy to fail in that test through an exclusive esthetic idealism as through the simplifying aims of propaganda. Like Jeffers and Lawrence in their different ways, MacLeish brought a keen sense of experience to an abstract vagueness of use. Such a sense need not be degraded to uses a poet cannot admit or acknowledge, but "self-respect," "firmness," and "vividness" stem from positive determination, from the isolation and not the loss of self. Such identity is expressed and *realized* in art, but it is not initially determined there, and it requires such a determination to produce the real Hamlet instead of a cinema of Hamlet. It starts in the personal, intellectual, and social circumstances of which MacLeish tried so long to dispossess himself. Where he succeeded, his work dwindled toward apathy and diffusion. Where he failed, his work found an authority and beauty upon whose final triumph depends whatever soundness of poetic character he may develop for himself. It was inevitable that he should make, in coming to terms with that failure, some effort toward a correction of his habits of resignation and esthetic scorn, and that correction involved, between his *Frescoes* of 1932 and his *Public Speech* of 1936, an admitted reversal of his attitude toward the moral problem offered by the social distress around him.

Public Speech is, as its title implies, a reproof to the hostility he once directed against "the social cant" in contemporary poetry. It carries him beyond the verse-play *Panic* in his compromise with the forces on the literary left. For five years he made himself useful to these critics (particularly in the *Frescoes*) as a prime object for proletarian abhorrence. But apparently his radical critics were right in scoffing at the false hopes he once claimed for art, for science, and for the refuges of historical and racial memory. MacLeish turned from them more abjectly dispossessed than ever, and with the added distress of finding his conscience stricken by what had happened to society in the meantime. He made a truce with his enemies more smoothly than he perhaps expected. His earlier attempts to lose himself in abstract human suffering or even among the interstellar spaces now proved to be a good preparation for joining in the class struggle. His favorite virtue, humility, eased him over the transition, and his favorite tones of elegiac grief, once so appropriate to writing epitaphs on his buried life, now lent themselves to celebrating the death-pangs of caste and capitalism.

In *Public Speech* he offers his past experience in spiritual suffering
as a guidance "to those who say Comrade":

> The brotherhood is not by the blood certainly
> But neither are men brothers by speech—by saying so:
> Men are brothers by life lived and are hurt for it:
>
> Hunger and hurt are the great begetters of brotherhood:
> Humiliation has gotten much love:
> Danger I say is the nobler father and mother.
>
> Those are as brothers whose bodies have shared fear
> Or shared harm or shared hurt or indignity.
> Why are the old soldiers brothers and nearest?

As such a veteran he enlists, retaining the Gerontion-Teresias robes
he wore so fondly in the past. In a poem which he calls a note
on Arnold's "Dover Beach" he renounces his former alliance with
the philosophers of exile and escape:

> After forty a man's a fool to wait in the
> Sea's face for the full force and the roaring of
> Surf to come over him: droves of careening water.
> .   .   .   .
> Speaking alone for myself it's the steep hill and the
> Toppling lift of the young men I am toward now—
> Waiting for that as the wave for the next wave.
> Let them go over us all I say with the thunder of
> What's to be next in the world.

Thus he turns his face from the disenchanted past to the hopeful
future. It will be noticed that he does so without loss of his meek
tones or the dying fall of his cadences as they swoon gently toward
their recessed rhymes and feminine endings.

It may be suspected, after his former retreats into the regions of
memory and history, that the class struggle holds out one more
refuge for that moral evasion which his style has come to suggest.
In about half these new poems he continues the vein of bewilderment and dispossession so wearisomely stressed in *New Found
Land* and *Conquistador*. The theme of the book, "Love that hard-

ens into hate," seems a rather facile derivation from a famous doctrine of Yeats. But to those who have respected MacLeish's real quality in earlier works, it is encouraging to see this (particularly the satiric vigor of *Streets of the Moon*) reappear on several pages. It shows in "The German Girls" and "Speech to the Detractors" and in three divisions of the closing poem, "The Woman on the Stair." These have the somber pathos of his best lyrics. There is still an easy-going reiteration of the themes of love and sacrifice, but love here rises above the laxity of a racial abstraction and becomes once more the responsible emotion it should be. By this time, of course, one must be resigned or nothing to MacLeish's style as a patent derivation from Pound and Eliot. "The Woman on the Stair" descends straight from "La Figlia che Piange," recasting that poem's tragedy into such phrases as "her serious mouth nor pitiful hair/Nor his mouth mortal with the murderous need." But in these cases the derivation does not enfeeble its sources, and often arrives at a very moving beauty. There are also signs that this congenital habit of understudy is being invigorated through several stylists not consulted in MacLeish's earlier studies. His poem to Phelps Putnam improves that poet's rugged movement by a rhythm that clearly refers to Hopkins:

> Christ but this earth goes over to the squall of time!
> Hi but she heels to it—rail down: ribs down: rolling
> Dakotas under her hull! And the night climbing
> Sucking the green from the ferns by these Berkshire boulders!

In a style that has grown toward the mesmerizing sameness of MacLeish's epics and elegies, such echoes of more robust writers come as a decided stimulus. He is still willing to descend to a kind of silly affectedness in his manner; it comes out at its worst in the subtitle of "Words to be Spoken," in the theme-song repetitions of "Pole Star for this Year," and on the appalling dedication-page of *Panic*. But serious craftsmanship and a sense of practical ordeal will make his new alliance with poets of the social struggle a matter of mutual benefit. His latest poems may seem a rather obvious way of inviting the indulgence of the uncon verted, but they are a signal of profitable intentions. Public speech is exactly what his poems have needed as a corrective of their fatigue and self-commiseration. When a poet arrives at the limits of esthetic experience or an impasse of spiritual emptiness, a turn toward external objects may come as a new lease on life. And it is by a renewal of the positive virtues that made his first successful poems so remarkable that he may achieve the work his admirers, and the defenders of American poetry, must hope he will write.

IV: A LITERALIST OF THE IMAGINATION

Marianne Moore's poetry demands gratitude, but to express it by referring to the qualities for which her work has usually been ignored or disputed may seem more a matter of convenience than of good grace. She is a poet about whom praise and blame are not wholly at odds; her detractors and admirers see fairly eye to eye. What irritates the hostile reader exhilarates the admiring, and in the case of a poet so prominent among "difficult" writers, it is pleasant to have no doubt about what is up for reference. Miss Moore's meanings may be mistaken, but not her character. Compared with her, many of her contemporaries become chameleons of evasive and convenient color. She stays fixed under scrutiny and refuses to pose as an illusionist. From the beginning she has protected herself by working out her poetic problems before allowing her poems to be printed; she has had no need to practice the subterfuges of less vigilant writers—the changes of face, manner, and other sleights of hand demanded by public success or moral insecurity. The external traits of her latest poems are those of her earliest: a dispassionate accuracy of detail, literalness of manner, indifference to the standardized feelings and forms of verse,

From *The New Republic*, LXXXIII, p. 370. August 7, 1935; and *Poetry: A Magazine of Verse*, XLVII, pp. 326-336. March, 1936. Reprinted by permission.

and an admission that virtually any subject-matter or reference is fully as appropriate to poetry as to prose. It would not require the addition of eccentric titling, typography, and rhyming to give the suspicious their argument or the irritated a voice.

Her *Observations* of 1924 were rightly named. Among modern poets she is exceptional for a detachment that lifts personal enthusiasm above private uses. She observes, but her eye shows neither the innocence nor the wile of showmanship that obstructs the vision of her contemporaries. It is a vision as complex as it is candid, and as easily mistaken. She would not have survived the decade of post-war innovations if her stylistic novelty rested on nothing but the strained intellection, the forced sophistication, for which it is commonly dismissed. She is a complicated poet, but one suspects that her finished poem is far simpler than the experience from which it sprang. The process that complicates it is not one of artificial refraction. It is Miss Moore's way of piercing— with the aid of humor, obliquity, and an instinctive compassion— through the pretense, erudition, and false emotion that encrust the essential meaning in the life around her.

She may be writing about marriage and poetry with the evasive casuistry of "culture"; or about art and statecraft in the polysyllabic rhetoric of senators and undergraduates; or about animals with the passionless accuracy of a treatise or text-book. Her style combines the frigid objectivity of the laboratory with the zeal of naïve discovery; it mixes the statistics of newspapers with the casual hints and cross-references of a mind constructed like a card catalogue. This is not a perversity of erudition, nor of ironic parody. It is a picture of the problem of the modern intelligence. Irony and curiosity are means towards Miss Moore's intense discriminations, but her purpose is essentially plain and carries the pathos of a passionate sincerity. When asked, in a recent questionnaire, what distinguishes her, she answered: "Nothing; unless it is an exaggerated tendency to visualize; and on encountering manifestations of life—insects, lower animals, or human beings—to wonder if they are happy, and what will become of them."

But her problem is not simple, and grants her neither the charm nor the success of conventional poetry. Hers is no book of neat lyric masterpieces. She is not satisfied to search out the law or purpose beneath the swarming phenomena around her; she feels it in the words she uses. Her language reveals, beneath its calculated technicalities and pastiche, the shock of concealed rhymes and harmonies. Her sentences, whether colloquial or rhetorical, move with a rhythm nerved by humor and "elegance." Her care for meaning makes her break a phrase, or even a word, to bring to the surface a suppressed quality—an embedded assonance, cadence, or tone of thought. Hers is a poetry of superimposed meanings, and her object is to lift the layers of convention, habit, prejudice, and jargon that mask the essential and irreducible truth. She is neither facile nor insincere enough to pretend that these impediments do not exist. In facing them she has not only defined, with the minuteness of an exorbitant sensitiveness, the ordeal of the contemporary conscience; she has energized, by the agility of her imagination, the language in which she works.

In the *Selected Poems* Miss Moore has omitted several short poems which a discussion might conveniently use as "beginnings." Simple aphorisms like "To an Intra-mural Rat" and "To a Prize Bird," and examples of imagism like "To a Chameleon" and "A Talisman," are not reprinted, although Mr. Eliot has fitly quoted the last-named in his preface. These slighter works served their purpose in *Observations,* in 1924, but they would not be out of place here also. Even a brief epigram on Shaw like "To a Prize Bird" escaped the risk of cleverness; it contained three metaphors of exact wit; and one is inclined to guess that it has now been omitted as much because Miss Moore has modified her opinion of Shaw during the past fifteen years as because she finds the style of the poem less than wholly her own. Similarly "A Talisman" departed from the conventional symbolism of the Imagists by not allowing its image to act beyond its powers: the figure of the seagull is developed through a severely spare stanzaic form, it is brought to terms with the formal attitude described by such a structure, and it still retains the impersonality required of true imagism. Of her new poems only one shows Miss Moore working in this simplified manner—"No Swan So Fine." The others exhibit a method much more elaborate than in any of the individual items of *Observations* with the possible exception of "An Octopus" and "Marriage," the second of which still remains her one extended venture in the field of human phenomena where obliquity of treatment is offset by the authority and convention of practical judgment. Only "The Hero" re-enters that province, but it does so with a stricter detachment, and with less assistance from the irony and erudition of quoted texts.

Her special world reappears: the world of lesser life—plant, animal, and mineral—which she scrutinizes unsparingly and translates into a major reality through a sympathy that surpasses mere pathos in becoming intellectual; but it is now far more extensive. This comes not merely by selecting from nature objects of a more formidable character—formidable in their complexity like the Plumet Basilisk or the Frigate Pelican, their wiry delicacy like the Jerboa, their massive subtlety like the Buffalo, or in their sumptuous elegance like *Camellia Sabina* and the porcelain nectarines. All these suggest a greater complexity of attention; they have encouraged a corresponding elaboration of form which marks the one notable advance made by the *Selected Poems* over Miss Moore's two previous books. Her idea of the stanza was already established there, but it had not reached such massive effects of verbal interplay and structure as in seven of the later poems. Along with this there has developed a greater luxuriance of detail, austere annotation having given way to a freer imaginative fascination. The cat, fish, and snake have been supplanted by creatures of a subtler and more exotic existence, and from this one may infer a similar elaboration in the mind that has observed and conferred on them, with unfaltering deftness, the form and scale of its ideas. Where Miss Moore once defined the fish's life of fluid and evasive grace, the cat's imperturbable self-sufficiency, and unity made absolute in the snake, she now analyzes the life of miraculous co-ordination ("The Frigate Pelican"), of impenetrable purposes ("The Plumet Basilisk"), of exquisite nervous vitality ("The Jerboa"), of masked and submissive wit ("The Buffalo"). Her animals have grown in meaning as well as in size and mechanism; they may be considered enlargements of the original vision; but they show the same rigor in definition and sympathy, the same scruple in activity and feature. The swan moves with its "gondoliering legs"; the jerboa with its "three-cornered smooth-working Chippendale claws . . . makes fern-seed foot-prints with kangaroo speed"; the lizard "smites the water, and runs on it—a thing difficult for fingered feet"; the pelican "rapidly cruising or lying on the air . . . realizes Rasselas' friend's project of wings uniting levity with strength"; the Indian buffalo wields "those two horns which, when a tiger coughs, are lowered fiercely and convert the fur to harmless rubbish."

Attributes like these are found among the animals and human beings of literature only when the physical reality of the creature has become so passionately accepted and comprehended that its external appearance, noted with the laconic felicity of science, is indistinguishable from its spirit, and all the banalities of allegory can be discarded. At that level the imagination seizes attributes and makes them act in place of the false sentimental values upon which man's observation of nature usually thrives. In her poem on "Poetry" Miss Moore improves Yeats' characterization of Blake by insisting that poets must be "literalists of the imagination"; they must see the visible at that focus of intelligence where sight and concept coincide, and where it becomes transformed into the pure and total realism of ideas. By this realism, the imagination permits ideas to claim energy from what is usually denied them—the vital nature that exists and suffers, and which alone can give poetic validity to the abstract or permit the abstract intelligence to enhance experience. Blake had such a notion of poetry in mind when he stated his theory of visions: "I question not my corporeal or vegetative eye any more than I would question a window concerning a sight; I look through it and not with it." And he reminds us especially of Miss Moore's rapt gaze at birds:

> How do you know but every bird that cuts the airy way
> Is an immense world of delight, closed by your senses five?

Miss Moore means this when she holds that poetry stands "above insolence and triviality and can present for inspection, imaginary gardens with real toads in them"; that it combines "the raw material . . . in all its rawness and that which is on the other hand genuine." Her literalness of manner should not remain a source of confusion after one has read the works in which her poetics is made fairly explicit—"Poetry," "When I Buy Pictures," "Critics and Connoisseurs," and "Picking and Choosing." If that manner seems ambiguous, it is because she considers poetic truth in opposite terms from those commonly accepted by lovers of the lyric. For her the spirit gives light, but not until the letter gives it first. If the letter is lifeless until the spirit enters it, without it the spirit is equally wasted: it has no body to animate and no clay in which to breathe. She stands poles removed from the poets of disembodied emotion, of Love, Honor, Hope, Desire, and Passion in capitalized abstraction. She does not write in the large and easy generality of sentiment or sensation. She has written about animals without dramatizing her pity, about wedlock without mentioning love, about America with none of the usages of patriotism, and about death without parading awe or reverence. But it would be difficult to name four poems more poignant in their sense of these emotions, or more accurate in justifying them, than "The Buffalo," "Marriage," "England," and "A Grave."

It is not the intention of any of these poems to free the reader from effort, but it is remarkable that difficulty diminishes statement by statement if the poems are read in that order. It is only when read through the translating medium of the whole poetic attitude and form (as they must be ultimately, since they are poems), or under the inhibition of prejudices and conventions about these, that Miss Moore's meaning itself can be, in the initial stages of one's appreciation, an obstruction. Her poems are complex both in origin and in process, and they will remain so finally, thus resembling all poetry of considerable weight; but their first complexity lies in the way they have avoided using the simplifications of the lyric tradition—its language, form, and rhythms. When they present a thought, they do so in terms of all the accidents, analogies, and inhibitory influences that went into its formulation; thus they preserve, along with the clarifying idea, a critical sense of how these accidents and impurities condition the use of the contemporary intelligence. It is, in fact, her recognition and use of such impediments to direct lyric clairvoyance that enables Miss Moore to combine the functions of critic and poet in one performance, and to preserve, along with the passion and penetration of her emotions, her modernity of appeal. One aspect of this is her use of the erudite style—the tone of wordy decorum and learnedness which probably wins her the harshest reproach. This has become her natural manner, but one is never left without hints of its sources; the rhetorical decorum of the past (Bacon, Burke, Richard Baxter) and the literary casuistry of the present (James, Yeats, Pound) combine with ironic overtones derived from the naïveté, pretentiousness, or candor of scientific treatises, orations, "business documents and school books," and intimate conversation. The interpenetration of these tones is not left entirely to the reader's guess-work. Miss Moore's "Notes" at the back of her volumes are a consolation and a stimulus. It is because they give just enough hint of the clues she has used in tracing out a conception or a truth that they spur the reader to analysis, without drugging him by explanation. In this they exceed the notes to *The Waste Land*. It is both amusing and provoking to know that the poem "New York" was given substance through an article on albino deer in *Field and Stream,* that "Novices" drew hints from Gordon's *Poets of the Old Testament,* Forsyth's *Christ on Parnassus,* Landor, and the *Illustrated London News,* that the biological subjects are reinforced by the treatises of R. L. Ditmars, W. P. Pycraft, and Alphonse de Candolle, that "No Swan So Fine" combines a remark from the *New York Times* with "a pair of Louis XV candelabra with Dresden figures of swans belonging to Lord Balfour," and that Peter is a "cat owned by Miss Magdalen Hueber and Miss Maria Weniger." Beyond or below this information and the tentacular curiosity it sets growing, lies a basis of moral and intellectual absolutes—the truth; but Miss Moore has no intention of reducing her grasp of this truth to impotence by abstracting it from the details and confusion with which experience happened to surround it. To do so would not only be an act of unscrupulous evasion; it would not be poetry.

It is profitable to make an attempt at separating in such verse the simpler components that make it up—its basic information, the inference made from it, and the conviction or judgment finally established; and to see in these a possible correspondence with the three stylistic elements that immediately arrest the reader—imagery, syntax (with its diction and rhetorical tone), and the final form (stanzaic or otherwise) of the complete poem. These pages are particularly safe against studious demolition of this kind. "The Fish" is one of Miss Moore's most brilliant and condensed achievements. The poem is first a matter of acute observation: "the crow-blue mussel-shells," one of which "keeps opening and shutting itself like an injured fan," "ink bespattered jelly-fish," "crabs like green lilies." These reach a second existence—become mobile without ceasing to be objects of exact and literal statement—when arranged into sentences; and anyone who finds the poem obscure as a whole will be shocked to find how straightforward it becomes (at least through the first five stanzas) when considered in its normal syntax:

The fish wade through black jade. Of the crow-blue mussel-shells, one keeps adjusting the ash-heaps; opening and shutting itself like an injured fan. . . . The water drives a wedge of iron through the iron edge of the cliff; whereupon the stars, pink rice-grains, ink-bespattered jelly-fish, crabs like green lilies, and submarine toadstools, slide each on the other. . . .

But one immediately sees what this sequence of statements has produced in the details: a sense of impersonal scrutiny that minimizes the exotic character of the original images, and at the same time an austere alignment that heightens and perfects it. Then, imposed on these statements, comes the shaping poetic form of the stanzas, with their regularly varying line-lengths and suddenly discovered rhymes; the physical and emotional impact of the whole experience is confessed; observation and statement have abruptly advanced into the brilliance and intensity of a poetic vision.

THE FISH

wade
through black jade
    Of the crow-blue mussel-shells, one keeps
    adjusting the ash-heaps;
        opening and shutting itself like

an
injured fan.
    The barnacles which encrust the side
    of the wave, cannot hide
        there for the submerged shafts of the

sun
split like spun
    glass, move themselves with spotlight swiftness
    into the crevices
        in and out, illuminating

the
turquoise sea
    of bodies. . . .

Whether this process was gradual in the poet, or immediate and involuntary, is beside the point; the reader has, if he is serious, a reverence in his destruction, and a duty in his analysis. He sees the three simplest elements in the work; he notices its double structure, syntactical and stanzaic; and by realizing the interdependence of the two he approaches Miss Moore's method. He begins to see that ambiguity has not only advanced from imagery and syntax to the form of the stanzas themselves, but that it is deliberate and functional. It continues to be so in other poems. In "England" there is an intended duplicity of meaning both in the formal organization of the thought and in the contrasts by which it is developed. In "Those Various Scalpels" a criticism of feminine vanity is made by means of romantic comparisons, and by exaggerating the intended effect of jewels, clothes, and cosmetics until they react upon themselves and become their own criticism. In "A Grave" "the disturbing vastness of ocean" is made fatal and sublime by the calm and contradictory lucidity with which its trivial incidents are observed:

men lower nets, unconscious of the fact that they are desecrating a
    grave,
and row quickly away—the blades of the oars
moving together like the feet of water-spiders as if there were no such
    thing as death.
The wrinkles progress upon themselves in a phalanx—beautiful under
    networks of foam,
and fade breathlessly while the sea rustles in and out of the sea-
    weed. . . .

Confronting Miss Moore's poems, in other words, calls for a renovation not only of the attention, but of one's habits, definitions, and prejudices; and of what these have done to one's understanding of the words, rhythms, and sentences of poetry. Here, as Mr. Eliot says, "an original sensibility and alert intelligence and deep feeling have been engaged in maintaining the life of the English language," but to any self-improving reader it is also valuable to discover that such external discouragements as novelty, eccentricity, and intellectual irony can be justified by a scrupulous poetic purpose; they cease to appear as irritants or as abuses of originality, and become agents of a new vitality in the reader himself. If there is presumption in these poems, it is the presumption of a sincere and ruthless insight; if there are limitations—and there obviously and deliberately are—they are those of a contented but passionate humility. I think these virtues must be admitted by anyone; only then will qualifying criticisms be in order. When Miss Moore instructs herself on art she also instructs her reader:

Too stern an intellectual emphasis upon this quality or that detracts
    from one's enjoyment.

It must not wish to disarm anything; nor may the approved triumph
   easily be honored—
that which is great because something else is small.
It comes to this: of whatever sort it is,
it must be "lit with piercing glances into the life of things";
it must acknowledge the spiritual forces which have made it.

GEORGE N. SHUSTER

François Mauriac

THE moralist is never refuted by his unpopularity. And mankind, which is always in rebellion against the prophets, nevertheless ends by applauding them heartily. These simple truths have been known for centuries, but it has been to a considerable extent the business of contemporary literature to demonstrate them. Sundry hundreds of novelists have regretted that Balzac-people continue to live in the world and even supervise its affairs. A consciousness of misdirection and moral delinquency is, indeed, so widespread that from a distance the collective voice of humanity must sound like a unanimous anathema. If even so the moralist is derided and the preacher scorned, it is because we have so generally lost all hope of integrity. Balzac-people seem the best the race is entitled to expect. And few of our contemporaries will affirm that the craving for wholeness is more than a delusion. Possibly this attitude is the most serious and important bequest of the war.

This last can be seen visibly exerting an influence if we reduce the problem to its most primitive constituent, the conflict between spirit and flesh. A thousand war-time matters intensified consciousness of just this battle: the brutalities of camp life, the acute yearning for sex union under circumstances which rendered it brief and lawless, the sharpened awareness of death at a moment when the bliss of existence had been immeasurably heightened, the discovery of delirium simultaneous with a new discovery of God. It will forever remain impossible to describe all this as it actually was. One still very interesting commentary on it is the stream of virtually forgotten fiction which immediately followed the war. We

From *The Bookman*, LXXII, pp. 466-475. January, 1931. Reprinted by permission.

read it in Mr. Wells's perplexedly heretical *Mr. Britling Sees It Through* and in M. Henri Bordeaux's perplexedly Catholic *Résurrection de la chair*. At all events, a tremendous desire for purity, for a victory over sex, coincided with what seemed to be new discoveries concerning its invincibility. There had existed no little evidence for the strength of lust, but the theories of Freud and the novels of such men as James Joyce and Marcel Proust simply bowled over every survivor from Queen Victoria's age. If we have any saints they do not, I think, waste much time trying to confute Freud or Proust. They recognize in both ingenious if unusually myopic reasoners on an ancient theme.

But what is the position of the saint in the matter? Or, more generally, where is the ethical ideal? These queries have inaugurated the most significant discussion in modern letters—that inquiry into the aspirations and limitations of the personality which has led to probably unequaled errors and certainly to unprecedented psychological knowledge. When one remembers that English fiction prospered during more than two centuries by reason of seventeenth-century analysis of character, our own literature seems assured of a rich future. But what we know must be gathered round some feasible interpretation of how to act. Accordingly the debate eventually settles down to an inquiry into the just cultivation of the self. In French letters the great protagonists have been Maurice Barrès and André Gide; and I hold that anyone who examines their affirmations with some care will have the clue to what is central in the present-day literature of France. Such an examination cannot, of course, be attempted here. We shall merely risk the generalization that whereas Barrès attempted a synthesis of the fundamental, unifying "drifts" which underlie personality through surrender to the will, Gide suggests that the artist will profit by a certain formula of inaction, of resistance to the will.

II

Though what has been said may serve to introduce François Mauriac, who seems to me the most significant among the younger

French novelists, it is far from being enough to account for him adequately. His novels divide themselves into two groups, one of which (in earlier time) is illustrated by *L'Enfant chargé de chaînes,* and the other of which (published, for the most part, in the series which Bernard Grasset issued as *Cahiers verts*) probably reaches two contrasted climaxes in *Le Baiser au lépreux* and *Destins.* Along with this more or less genuinely objective writing there has gone —like the systole and diastole of one personality—a constant effort at self-explication. It is significant that one finds this relatively calm in *La Vie et la mort d'un poète,* and quite turbulent in *Dieu et Mammon.*[1] A glance at these five books may serve to give an impression of the major points of Mauriac's spiritual compass.

Jean-Paul, in the first book, is a young man deeply branded a Catholic, and marked with the curse which makes one see the universe as either beautiful or ugly. A curious habit of introspection, in which tendencies formed by priest educators blend with not a little sensualism, governs his relations with his father, with his fiancée (poor Marthe, despite the beauty of her hair, sighed uncommonly long for love), and with the world at large. But if our hero's self interests him more than all else in the world, it also arouses his dismay and contempt. He is *l'enfant chargé de chaînes*—a boy the complexity of whose ties to art, pleasure, religion and family entangles him in a web. From his point of view, action is at once the desired goal and the form of human incompetence which lends itself best to satire. Through the medium of his hero, Mauriac douses with irony both the artistic impulses to which youngsters of that time (1913—but of all times as well) loved to succumb, and the plans of moral reform which the ardent supporters of Marc Sagnier (Catholic, democrat, and pacifist) considered the spiritual pinnacle of their age. More fundamentally, however, the novel deals with one kind of conversion. After having tried the sowing of wild oats in a timid way, Jean-Paul remembers that he cannot help being orthodox. He

---

[1] M. Mauriac's celebrated recent novel, *Le Nœud de Vipères* (*Viper's Tangle*), of 1932, had not appeared when this essay was written. It would fit in the second of the two groups defined above and in manner develops from *Destins* and *Dieu et Mammon.*

musters enough courage to profess adherence also to the family and to life. But this conversion cannot be a complete *volte face*. Marthe, on her wedding day, is described as foreseeing "the multiplication of caresses—and the serenity of silent pardons."

If the value of this novel lies almost wholly in the sincerity with which it interprets adolescence, it is nevertheless stimulating primarily because it is a "religious" novel. Not, of course, an edifying treatise or a plea for some moral principle, but rather a measure of truth regarding an average spiritual life in a given era. *Le Baiser au lépreux* retains the same outlook in an entirely different human climate. Jean Péloueyre, deformed of body but nobly sane, if somewhat emancipated, of soul, finds to his astonishment that he may marry Naomi d'Artialh, most beautiful and virtuous of the village maids. But the wife cannot surmount her loathing for the body of her husband. They are fastened to each other like two dead worlds, and the friction is pain. Jean does not struggle to ward off disease and death; Naomi tries desperately to barricade her heart against another man's love. But when her hunchback mate has succumbed, she finds that "her fidelity to the dead man was to be her humble glory." The soul achieves its triumph, somber and melancholy though it be, over the flesh.

By way of vengeance, the flesh is bitterly victorious in *Destins*. In no other of Mauriac's books are the normalities of religious life so completely laid bare to the scalpel. Perhaps the critics had angered an author so conscious of the gulf which must forever lie between the hereditary child of the Church and the ardent *converti;* or perhaps Gide may have been right when he said that in this book Mauriac had approached, curiously and ironically, the border which no Christian dare cross in his quest for images interpretive of life. At all events the novel, which leaves the strange impression of having been etched with a red-hot literary needle, is a summary of what Elizabeth Gormac and young Robert Lagave have wrested from life. He is a dissolute incarnation of youth's pagan beauty (it might almost be asserted that he is hardly anything more), whose friends are roués or worse, whose death is a tragic and unholy accident, but who wears bravely the spicy laurel

of a faun. And Elizabeth Gormac? Though she had her properties and an eminently satisfactory son who was both a priest and
a missionary, the one thing which prevented her "being one of
those corpses that are carried down the stream of life" was a
sudden, secret but violent love for Robert, whom she had known
as a little boy carrying his wet bathing suit in his hand and about
whose sins she cherished no illusions.

Turn now to the other side of Mauriac. *La Vie et la mort d'un
poète* is an exquisite, touching memoir of André Lafon, one of
many sacrifices to the war. Though the book is honest in its
endeavor to describe the meek genius, the self-effacing grandeur,
of a deeply Christian poet, it is none the less a reflection of its
author's own thought. Lafon had failed as a novelist, despite one
notable success, because of his "resolution in advance to do good,"
and a "certain literature that edifies" is untrue to life. Though it
would be necessary, for the good of feeble souls, to invent
astringent censors if these did not exist, "to paint the man of
today in all his misery is to uncover the abyss created, in the
modern world, by the absence of God." Mauriac believes that,
had he been a priestly counselor, he would have said to Lafon:
"A good tree cannot bring forth evil fruit." Let him work for
his own interior perfection until such time as he senses himself
"solidly established in God." But in Lafon there had stirred the
thirst for purity which is, perhaps, the premonition of elected souls.
In modern literature we honor those who "had no career, who
retained a tragic sense of life." And the little book closes with
praise for Barrès and Pascal.

By comparison *Dieu et Mammon* is a summary of the spiritual
journey undertaken after 1924. It is a tangled, a difficult but a
progressive book (1929). Literature is an author's surrender to
his public. And now, in view of the dissolution of the old Christian realization of truth, "there are as many verities as there are
individuals." What has the author found in himself "since he
began to know himself?" This is the modern query, and an
author can, these days, hardly avoid an exposition of himself.
Mauriac professes to be a Catholic because, in the sense employed

by Pascal, he was born one. "I belong to the race of those who, born in the Catholic faith, have known, ever since the age of maturity was approaching, that they could never escape from this faith, that it was not in their power to leave it or return to it after a period of absence." And the difficulty? "Now I imagined that Christianity was the only thing with which the world was concerned, and again I felt that I was a prisoner inside a little Mediterranean sect. But it was necessary to live somehow; I had to find my way at any cost; and so I remember with what ardor I set about, at the age of sixteen, proving to myself the truth of a religion to which I knew myself bound for all eternity."

In the spirit of this faith, God is seen as He from whom there is no escape—who will perforce sublimate even human love by making it affection for Himself. And in the fever of literary effort one is conscious of the flight from Him, no less than of "the atrocious ill-will" of fellow Christians, to whom the apparent non-utility of art is beyond understanding. There follows a subtle but strong defense of the artist's faith. "A man is born the victim of his cross." Hence sin becomes the sole issue; and in the words of Péguy, "the sinner and the saint are the two equally essential parts of the mechanism of Christianity." One may be one or the other, but once inside the mechanism choice is imperative. "The sinner cannot escape the mark of his offence. The author cannot dodge responsibility." But that author is none the less destined to write, to affect the largest number possible. And if the novel is "nothing if it is not a study of man," the question whether a writer ought "to alter the object of his study and falsify the life he observes in order that no soul may be disturbed" becomes acute. Complicated though the drama of the Christian novelist may be, the recipe is, ultimately, "Purify the source!"

III

Such, imperfectly codified, are the essential traits of Mauriac's career. The course is a development, both in more or less subconscious artistry and in critical reflection, but it is even more the natural graph of a state of mind. For Mauriac (and of course for so many of his contemporaries) life is not so much a moral and metaphysical opportunity as a moral and metaphysical problem. He is bound hand and foot to the great French mystics and preachers—Pascal, Bossuet, Lacordaire—but he is a little disdainful of the intelligence. Faith is, for him, not something into which one can be argued. It is a form of living, almost a social stamp, with which one's soul is branded. Yet because it is so, man's drama becomes many times as intense as it might otherwise be. For a man of this temper, flouting a moral mandate is something entirely different from disregarding a "law of nature" or formally ignoring a statute. It is a violation of the harmony in one's own self. But these violations are fatally easy. They continually scourge the soul with its own shame. Indeed, Mauriac may sometimes be fairly accused of setting the forces of good and evil on a plane too nearly that of equality. A tendency to Manicheism is, no doubt, present, assuming that this be interpreted now as excessive pessimistic humiliation of the species.

It is curious to note how persistently this inclination to the views of the Jansenists has appeared in modern French letters. When the Anglo-Saxon is a puritan, he is a self-righteous person, whose crimes, like Bunyan's, lie in the past; but when a Frenchman is a puritan, he is ceaselessly maddened by his unworthiness. This point of view is not so reprehensible as we sometimes think it (unless diseased it is really a kind of tropical religious inquietude), and in art it affords an interesting contemporary advantage. One of Mauriac's recent critical essays ("Le Roman") discusses the fact that fiction writing is improverished by the modern man's failure to attribute fundamental importance to sin. Surrenders to the flesh, illicit armours, are mere incidents, and so life becomes just a chronicle and not the drama which stirred even the author of *Madame Bovary*. Now precisely because he does attribute so much grandeur to the service of God, and so much significance to moral evil, the Christian of Mauriac's temper may legitimately feel that he offers to literature a form of intense activity, moving and mysterious as no mere chronicle can be. It is, of course, easy to object that the adventure of goodness in personal experience is just as important, and that in it—even if there be no more than a mere surmisal of God—greater things are revealed than in the drama of sin. That has immemorially been the English point of view. But it is not the French point of view, and Mauriac is, despite his culture, one of the most indigenous, one of the least cosmopolitan, among living writers in France.

This last fact becomes more apparent when one considers the social outlook of these novels. Mauriac has dashed off one book and several essays to explain the circumstances under which he grew to maturity. Bordeaux, city of bourgeois families who are often land-owners and vintners, occupies in his work much the same place that is granted to Lorraine in the books of Barrès. Yet this attachment, which implies that all fresh experience reposes upon an underlying stratum of souvenir, is by no means entirely affectionate. "I have always contrasted Bordeaux with the Provence, in order to expose its nakedness," Mauriac declares, "and nevertheless I love it—which is to say, I love myself." Then there is also the rural scene. "The country places where I lived as a child and to which I still return regularly embodied," he tells us, "the two essential aspects of the Girondin country—heaths and vineyards. These I may describe as being as different as Italy and Norway could be, but in the region which knows them both my peasant race, which has never moved, plunges down its deep roots." Add to this an unswerving Catholic entourage in the old "country style"—relatives, even a brother, in the priesthood; fidelity at prayer; an indefinable, earnest scrupulousness of demeanor; education in select but strict religious institutions; and a definite orientation towards life as something for which one is perilously responsible.

All this, in France, cannot be separated from class consciousness, and Emanuel Berl seems correct in saying that Mauriac writes (as it were) inside a social prison. That is not a fault but a destiny. It explains, however, why the canvas of these novels is seldom larger than the problem which obsesses them all, and which is invariably the experience of a family. Curiously, Mauriac's story is never that of an individual soul, a human pair, a crowd. The stage is always an interior flanked by four walls, where all the normal personages from grandparent to child in the cradle move in the glare from the hearth. In *L'Enfant chargé de chaînes,* Jean-Paul is both irritated and encompassed by family ties. Thérèse Desqueyroux is the victim of her domestic life. And if Dr. Cler-reseux, the paterfamilias of *Le Désert de l'amour,* is converted in the end to conjugal bliss it is only because senility and defeat have worn him down. Mauriac is afflicted with nostalgia for all those things which lie beyond the veranda, but once out there he succumbs to the fundamental human malady—homesickness. Few men have agreed more fervently with Pascal that all human woe is the result of not being able to sit tranquilly in a room—and none has been more ruthlessly tormented with a desire to get out. Mauriac is he whom Barrès proposed as a model; but he is always the one whom Gide finds in the crowd of listeners.

Let us admit frankly that Mauriac is drawn to the "things of this world" for the same reasons that so much affect the post-war generation—the charm of all that is sensual, color and symmetry and youthful flesh. He can caress these things with as much zest as the Renaissance poets, perhaps; but he can also phrase his renouncement of them in terms not of pure spiritual sacrifice, but in the language of a man who has discerned the absence of satisfaction in them, the penalty which beauty exacts, the lassitude of desire fulfilled. When Mauriac's theme is lust his men and women are no healthy animals, brotheling like pagans, but creatures tormented even as were Paolo and Francesca in the inferno of their discontent, seeking sweetness under the blows of a scourge. He can set before you the mysterious throes of adolescence curious of passion, but he cannot imagine them akin to happiness. One's chief regret is that happiness does not exist in Mauriac's world. Joy—even the most legitimate joy—is always discounted because of the high tariff exacted for it. He himself, as well as others, accounted for this by assuming a tendency to Manicheism and Jansenism, regarding which something has been said. Perhaps it is really the fault of Mauriac's race, inured to spiritual and physical thrift. Croesus trembled when the gods showered him with their bounty. A certain kind of Frenchman—who, alas, does not figure prominently in Anglo-Saxon impressions of the land of Gaul—shudders when Dame Fortune leaves a Christmas gift.

If we follow Mauriac's work to the present, it may be helpful to bear in mind the interpretive data thus summarized. The work of the earlier period might be entitled Studies in Esthetic Adolescence. Its value lies first in its description of a state of mind which existed in France prior to the war (when the movement of return to the Christian faith among young men was really begun), and in the poetic evocation of the troubles incident to crossing the threshold into life. A significant illustration of the first is to be found in the place occupied by Marc Sagnier and his *Sillon* democrats in French Catholic activity after 1900. These, anxious to establish a Christian social order on the basis of modern thinking and political practice, were governed by the "moral primate" expounded by followers of the Abbé Lacordaire. The Vatican discerned excesses in this crusade, which ran afoul of traditionalism in France, and it was soon explicitly condemned. But among the young men there were many whom Sagnier's formulas did not satisfy. On the one hand were those too definitely fixed in their *cadres* ever to be yanked loose by crusading expeditions (and among them was Mauriac); on the other hand were those who sought a more rigid, more reactionary formula (and among these were the early adherents to *l'Action française*). Much of Mauriac's early writing implies his attitude toward this development. First came two volumes of poems—*Les Mains jointes* and *Adieux à l'adolescence* —characterized by a languorous beauty of phrase, an excessively romantic melancholy, and a discernment of nature not dissimilar to what one finds in Francis Jammes, the Basque poet.

The earlier novels, interspersed with essays and short stories, followed almost immediately. *La Robe prétexte* was, I believe, favorably reviewed in France and England as a work of great promise. For us of today it seems to stand apart from the rest of its author's achievement, not merely because, narrated in the first person, it undoubtedly incorporates autobiographical material, but also because it voluntarily affects naïveté. As a portrait of Bordelaise family life, it is not a little malicious. The boy hero exists because Mauriac, naturally addicted to the use of memory, is reliving his boyhood days. Later he would make the *souvenir* an integral part of his artistic method. For the moment, it is indulged in for its own sake—perhaps because this variety of literature was then popular everywhere.

La Chair et le sang is a more troubled and inchoate novel. Claude Favereau, peasant lad who has abandoned the idea of studying for the priesthood because of an all too sensuous nature, and Edward Dupont-Gunthier, cynical son of a parvenu and amateur in all the pleasures, are poles in a drama of two families. Claude is circumscribed, safeguarded perhaps, by his always rudimentary environment; Edward's career is feverish, with an assemblage of intrigues which has led a French critic (Paul Archambault) to term the whole "like an unhealthy place where sickly lilies are wilting." And if, in the end, virtue is frugally rewarded and vice condemned with pathos, the story remains a more than relatively unconvincing attempt to interpret the sting of the flesh. *Préséances* is a better, though still more acrid, book. The love of Augustin, a boy upon whom has been set the seal of election, for Florence, capricious and heartless daughter of a provincial bourgeois family that wishes to rise in the world, is wrecked by the girl's calm vote for a life of wealth and pleasure. But though the baseness of her marriage and subsequent amours is reflected in the steady deterioration of her soul, a dream of perfection subsists, twined round the memory of Augustin. When she finally squanders that, too, tragedy is the only conceivable end. *Préséances* hardly exists for its own sake. It is an almost venomous critique of a mundane bourgeoisie, the vices of which are scathingly symbolized.

If in these first books unity is attained through a blending of symbolism and realistic observation, the author himself is always firmly conscious of the duality of good and evil, of flesh and spirit, of aspiration and failure, which seems to rule life. The post-war novels attain to a new and firmer unity of construction, but the philosophic duality is still more strongly emphasized. We have already noticed *Le Baiser au lépreux,* in which the symbol is so convincingly real and the narrative so classically direct that one is reminded of the grandeur of antique tragedy for all the modernity of its feeling. *Le Fleuve de feu* is a somber tale of a war-time love which plunges Gisèle de Plailly, victim of a frighteningly narrow family circle, into a career of passion from which she emerges finally into repentance with something of the despair which might stir in an animal hounded into a cave toward which the enemy may yet find his way. Here is, frankly, a narrative of a world without light, based on Mauriac's formula: "To describe the man of today in all his misery is to uncover the abyss which the absence of God has made to gape in our world."

Genitrix is perhaps the most impressive book in the whole list, not only because it is written with unforgettable vigor but also because the theme is the essence of all that (to date at least) Mauriac has had to say. Despite appearances, he is neither fond of the subject of illicit love nor interested in the duel between the sexes. In the first place his method does not favor the "psychology of the crisis" (in Bourget's sense), but exactly the opposite—the discovery, in the tapestry woven by long time, of the net in which the human victim is caught. Passion is only one of the forms that net may take. In *Genitrix* it is the most revered, the most sacred of all affections—mother love—which entangles. Fernand Cazenave is bound hand and foot to his mother, relentless tyrant who is in turn the victim of her own morbidly constricted temperament. In the old house to which visitors no longer come, they watch Fernand's young wife die of loneliness and hatred of her mother-in-law. He is not in the least cruel, but only slow, stupid, powerless to escape the tentacles of his mother. And once he has lost the wife he had proved unable to love, a fierce passion for her leads him to live only in the memory of her, so that Madame Cazenave is beaten and famished. The final pages, showing Fernand alone in the old house, are horrible. If there are many other pages in literature which describe so perfectly what it means to exist without love, I do not know them.

Written in a single jet and with a dictional density of rare perfection, *Genitrix* nevertheless succeeds in conveying with marvelous skill the slow creep of time. I cannot help thinking that, from this point of view, it is a more remarkable achievement than any book of Proust's. For while that novelist can convey the sense of the interminable by being himself interminable, Mauriac's treatment of the problem frequently reminds one of the evocative genius of Shakespeare himself. But the majesty, the wholeheartedness, of the great dramatist are missing. *Genitrix* is the story of a cage—of human life conceived of as a cage.

The cage is likewise the central concern of *Thérèse Desqueyroux* and *Le Désert de l'amour*. In the first book, the unfortunate heroine, having neither faith nor happiness, beats against the walls of her insipid family life until a way of escape suddenly seems to present itself. But the attempt to murder her husband leads to no release, but instead to a still more maddening incarceration with "people." The second novel comes near to being Mauriac's best approach to the analysis of passion. Yet we race here on no flood of feeling toward a romantic or tragic end. Raymond Courrèges, enamored of the strange woman whose position in the world gives the lie to her professed spiritual aspirations, is chained to a kind of sadistic hate once she has refused his advances. It is, in its way, a shrewd, true, observant book. But one might well have asked of Mauriac: Where in this world you describe are the mercy and the lure of Christ?

He had, however, not yet finished with his terrible problem. The short tales unified by the title *Trois Récits* indicate, indeed, that Mauriac's tendency to compress duration into an *aperçu* was driving him strangely near the form which Poe had chosen to set forth much the same sort of thing (though Mauriac is not in the least like Poe), but the matter dealt with is still the familiar substance of his novels. In one tale, for instance, the hero walks the treadmill of passion, though the professionalized state of his personality renders him utterly incapable of passion. Every reader might well wonder if his author considers love at all possible or permissible, or the ideal in any manner compatible with the real.

Mauriac soon replied in *Souffrances du chrétien,* a famous essay which restated the old problem in the most acute form. Christ would have all of man; the fundamental evil, therefore, is concupiscence. Yet human nature is so constituted that, excepting for the greatest saints, there is no escape from desire, against which even the sturdiest arguments cannot prevail. Here Mauriac reaches the last stage of his method of playing the points of view of Barrès and Gide against each other. To the first it is granted that the resolve to follow the Saviour is the fundamental, inescapable business of man; but with the second it is argued that man cannot pursue this business without ceasing to be human. The sharpness with which the dilemma is stated may be unreasonable, but it is contemporary.

Mauriac, however, now suddenly recovered from concentrating upon the world of his time to consider those aspects of life which are timeless and serene. In *Bonheur du chrétien* there is joyful recognition—possibly achieved at the cost of some effort—of that happiness accorded to those who shoulder the light burden. And the very fine and thoughtful preface to *Trois Récits* ends with these words: "'The Man Who Strove Toward Inspiration Through Humiliation,' the most attractive story in the present collection which might well have borne this title suggested by a phrase of Pascal, the author has not written—and is, indeed, not yet worthy to have written." Still more pertinent are the later sections of *Dieu et Mammon,* shot through with self-criticism of the most perceptive kind. That Christianity here wells up so clear and strong after an adventure in actuality may well be accepted as a testimonial of its virility. Not that Mauriac had ever ceased to be a creature of his faith. But his route was perilous. The literature of men like Paul Claudel and Jacques Maritain is a literature which knows the world but not men. Its source is a mystic choice—individual, elect. It resembles Saint Paul rather than Saint Vincent de Paul. Mauriac's writing is the novelist's peculiar and hazardous art. I know of no saints who could be entrusted with it excepting Augustine—or Magdalen.

IV

View him as you will, Mauriac is an artist. That can only mean an individual, with the gifts and weaknesses of an individual. There has been a social architecture, a more or less socialized poetry. Both Amiens and Dante have a vast, densely populated background. But no such thing as a social fiction can exist, and for two reasons. First, the novel demands an act of creation. An author must give birth to his characters, and set them to living in such surroundings as he can provide for them. Secondly, the art of fiction is—regardless of appearances—a lyric art. It must have a pattern, but even more it must have a passion. Dickens and Hardy, England's greatest, possibly, struggle for composition and style, succeeding only rarely. But they abide because they have been able to give their writing a meaning, sometimes termed a life. I think Mauriac is of their company. None of his characters seems a whole. They are less obviously caricatures than Dickens's; they happen to be presented with greater skill. But I submit that Madame Cazenave haunts one's memory for essentially the same reason that Gradgrind does.

Let us carry the comparison, odious though it be, a little farther. Dickens was obsessed by a vision of charity and a dream of what it might accomplish. This was not a solitary sentiment, a kind of forlorn hope, but the basic emotion of the Victorian time, when the great modern effort to relieve the plight of the industrialized poor was begun. In other words: Dickens was not a "novelist with a purpose" but a vital artist who had got hold of the most virile emotion of his era. You can discern the difference when you think of Godwin. Here was a man whose writing was, no doubt, better than Dickens's, and whose artistic gift was worth noticing. But Godwin had got hold of an emotion, an idea, which seemed silly to the majority of his contemporaries and which seems even sillier now. He may have reaped harvests of ecstasy from his notions of education and reform, but normal England was first startled and then bored. The decline of Mr. Kipling's popularity probably has its origins in the same cause.

In Mauriac's case, the problem which engrossed his attention may fairly be termed absorbingly interesting. How shall the individual realize his individuality? Must one go whole hog with Nietzsche, venturing beyond good and evil to a new territory occupied exclusively by oneself enthroned? Or can one hover between good and evil, with the majority—between yearning for the strength of nobleness, integrity, sacrifice, and concession to manifold license? Or shall one say that the law of Yahweh and Christ is the priceless recipe for triumph over the world? We may talk of Greece, the Orient and Bolshevism. But the most revolutionary, the most explosive, queries of the age are those named above. That they have been put and answered in conflicting fashions is a fact which constitutes the basic challenge to the modern social system. For this has not relished such questions. It has had a conventional idealism, which one may find in Tennyson; a conventional morality, admirably summarized by Judge Gary; and a conventional religion accountable for the present weakness of the churches. When the individual decided to become unconventional, he was really a Lenin in petto.

Mauriac asks all the questions. His novels are an inquiry into the reasonableness, the validity of them all. I do not see how this investigation could have been valuable if it had not been sincere, but there can be no doubt that Mauriac placed his own response in the test tube. And none of the experiments to which it was there submitted was anything like so critical as the resolve to set it over against the life of the time. To compare an intransigent faith with the assent modern paganism gives to the rule of pleasure is to assume a risk—but it is a risk thousands have taken, either unconsciously or advisedly. In a little book published immediately after the war and entitled *De quelques Cœurs inquiets,* Mauriac offered "short essays in religious psychology" with the object of proving that "it is necessary that the veteran soldiers of our spiritual family should astonish the world by the alliance within themselves of the Christian virtues and those human endowments which stamp them chiefs of the temporal order, organizers of the material world." But after that he came back to the perplexing question: what is the temporal order, what is the material world? And if his books sometimes reply with willfully conjured darkness, if his diagnosis occasionally seems to omit the will-to-improve almost entirely, they nevertheless remain rich in perspicacity, charity and humility.

There is no doubt that Mauriac has more than once brushed with his contemporaries, particularly his Catholic contemporaries, over the question of art. If to some the frankness of *La Fleuve de feu* was disconcerting, to others the metaphysical incompleteness of Mauriac's world seemed obvious and deplorable. It seems to me that Ramon Fernandez is right when he points to the circumstance that Mauriac's novels are "saturated with sensations," most of them odors and sounds rather than visual images, which form a natural frame inside which the personages seem to us "familiar." This is to be accounted for, however, not through an esthetic theory but by Mauriac's ability to steep himself in family life. If we attend to the matter a little, we see that domesticity is only rarely a matter of the eyes. A wife seldom pauses to think of how her husband "looks," and a parsonage is seldom arranged with a view to providing interior decorators with photographs. But you can always tell a parsonage by its odors, and intimacy between husband and wife becomes an affair of listening for footsteps, of vocal intonations and in unhappier moments of smells and gestures. I feel that no other novelist has employed this kind of thing so understandingly as Mauriac.

How all this everyday sensory material affects the spirit is a subject about which much could be written. Here is the universe which truly hems us in, which tempts us with both its voluptuous and its acrimonious suggestions, and which constantly testifies to our bondage. One whose spirit is not without a puritanical strain will, when sensitive, experience all with added keenness. And for Mauriac the odor of a body wet with rain may reveal the extent to which one is chained to the earth, incapable of ascent. Whatever one may allege against it in detail, this is a French and Chris-

tian realism, a French and Christian homeliness. The soul of the
West has never trusted in abstractions or even in conventionality.
But it has believed in a nobler world—in greater human possibilities—than Mauriac has hitherto been willing to consider.
Doubtless there has been a little of Spengler, of the romantic discouraged, in us all since the War. Now our novelist himself has
voted for greater confidence. What that shall bring remains to be
seen.

PHILIP BLAIR RICE
Paul Valéry

M. PAUL VALÉRY has declared from time to time that his poetry is only an exercise. Perhaps this is but mock humility: in any case, his readers refuse to believe that verse so lovely as much of his can fail to be worth while for itself alone. Certainly no other poet enjoys an equal esteem in France today, and it was as a practitioner of *Poésie Pure* that he was elected to the French Academy, through the able publicity work of the Abbé Brémond. M. Valéry, furthermore, is one of the few poets of his nation who have been widely read abroad; floods of essays on his poetic technique have appeared in many languages.

But for once let us take the man at his word. He has versified only intermittently. He does not seem to care whether anyone reads his poetry or not: his volumes are issued in limited editions, which sell at four times their marked price as soon as they appear. This may be, as M. Souday suggests, merely "une espéce de coquetterie, de manège habile pour se faire desirer." Nevertheless it is difficult to read Valéry's works or to hear him speak without believing in his sincerity. Both his verse and his prose have centered around certain problems which for long periods of time have become so absorbing that he has given up poetical composition entirely. If his poetry is only an exercise, an exercise for what?

Before he was twenty, under Mallarmé's influence the poet began to write Symbolist verse, which appeared in the reviews of the cult. Then in 1894, at the age of twenty-three, Valéry was asked to do an essay on Leonardo. Ever since, he has been in quest of something, and the germs of that quest are to be found in the early *Introduction à la Méthode de Léonard de Vinci*. Valéry saw in

From *The Symposium*, I, pp. 206-220. April, 1930. Reprinted by permission.

Leonardo, so he later wrote, the "principal character of that *Comédie Intellectuelle* which has not hitherto found its poet, and which would be, to my taste, still more precious than the *Comédie Humaine,* and even than the *Divine Comedy.*" The object of this study he stated as follows: "I felt that this master of his means, this possessor of design, of images, of calculation, had found the central attitude starting from which the undertakings of knowledge and the operations of art are equally possible, and a happy reciprocity between analysis and acts is singularly probable."

With Leonardo, then, the accepted example of the universal man, did Valéry's search begin. The universal man, he indicates, is not necessarily a jack-of-all-trades. In the first place, he is universal not in the sense of one who is able to do a little of everything but of one who attains to a balance of his faculties. This mental proportion enabled Leonardo, in both his art and his science, to discover universal laws. The secret of this man of the Renaissance lay in his ability to find relations between "things whose law of continuity escapes us." His method was what Valéry calls "construction," a word used "to designate more emphatically the problem of human intervention in the things of the world and to direct the reader's mind toward the logic of the subject, a material suggestion."

Valéry takes up Leonardo's paintings and his architectural and engineering works, showing that his hero sought objective standards for their construction. These standards are found in the geometrical aspects of composition, in the dictates of perspective and in Leonardo's fancy that "the air is filled with an infinite number of straight and radiating lines, intersecting and interweaving without ever borrowing each other's paths, and they represent for each object the true form of its explanation (or its essence)."

As the fine arts go farther from architecture, the more intractable "human element" becomes of increasing importance, and it is necessary to find a non-mathematical objectivity in valuing the work of art. For literature this is difficult and Valéry does little but adduce Poe's theory that the poem must be made not for the poet's own good pleasure, but according to psychological laws by which it will realize a common state in those who read it, even if the readers be taken as a choice few with a similar foundation of culture. "The function of the poet is not to be inspired himself, but to create inspiration in his readers," as M. Valéry later phrased it.

Universality, or objectivity, therefore, requires a discounting of the artist's personal eccentricities. Here Valéry breaks with the main Romantic tradition, which coddled the artist with the notion that all he had to do was to develop his individuality and let it drip over on paper or canvas. Valéry is struggling to escape from the subjectivism which infected the art and thought of the nineteenth century: "Our personality is only a *thing,* mutable and accidental. . . . All criticism is dominated by the superannuated principle that the man is the *cause* of the work—as the criminal in the eyes of the law is the cause of the crime. They are rather the effect!" Or again: "An artist pays for every genuine discovery with a decrease in the importance of his 'ego.' A *person* loses something of himself for everything beautiful he has created." The superior man, he reminds us, is never an "original," and the history of his life is wholly inadequate to explain his works.

If the works are so important, why did Leonardo leave so much unfinished? Valéry implies that even works are incidental to the great artist. "To live, and even to live well, is only a means for him. . . . To act is only an exercise. To love—I don't know if he can." All are subsidiary to the attainment of true universality, which is at the same time to achieve consciousness of self. What self is it that Valéry is trying to know? Not the individual self, the personality, certainly. The superior man, he believes, moves toward a state of pure consciousness, or the pure ego (*le moi pur*), which is identical with the knowledge of universal laws and relations. Rather than Hegelian, it is Spinozistic: Valéry arrives at something very like Spinoza's Intellectual Love of God. This conclusion, it should be remarked, was at most only implicit in the early *Introduction,* for it is first given full statement in the "Note and Digression" which he wrote as a preface to that essay in 1919.

We may, then, find it fruitful to approach Valéry's life work by taking it as the quest for universality. His success may be judged accordingly. From the beginning we find him torn by two seductions which perhaps are irreconcilable. He is lured by action—by the fulfillment and human balance achieved in shaping matter into some concrete embodiment of universal laws which have been discovered by the artist. On the other hand, the discovery of these laws itself seems at times to be the ultimate fulfillment. After long and vigorous travail, "pure consciousness"—this clear flash of a universal law from the hidden bosom of reality—brings an exaltation to which the making of any individual thing, however splendid, seems an anticlimax.

Which then, if either, is the universal man: the builder or the pure spirit? Our author vacillates.

II

In *Monsieur Teste,* which followed soon after the *Introduction,* Valéry swung toward asceticism. M. Teste, this extraordinary bourgeois, this impeccably precise talker, who does not even read, who merely observes and reflects, has attained a perfect working of the intellect. Everything about him—his voice, his bearing, his manner of eating, his absence of gesture—shows the complete abnegation of individuality. His room is the Platonic idea of a room: it contains nothing which bears the stamp of a personality; the chairs, the bed, the table, are as "general" as could be imagined. He spends his hours in contemplating such subjects as the nature of time and consciousness, and in finding the exact word to express his observations. That M. Teste left a deep impression on Valéry is obvious when one hears him speak: the lecture, no matter what the subject, flows with the lucidity and the seeming inevitability of a geometrical theorem.

M. Teste has achieved the "obstinate rigor," the *netteté désespérée* of Leonardo. But he is not the universal man in the sense of the builder. He does not act at all! Furthermore—but this is to raise another point—emotion and certain kinds of sensibility in him are starved by the intellect, the faculty of concepts, as they would not be in a mind that used all its functions. As a counterpoise to

M. Teste, who has been called the *animus,* Valéry creates Mme. Teste, the *anima.* She says of her husband: "Quand il me revient de la profondeur! . . . Il retombe sur moi comme si j'étais la terre même!"

Yet the attractiveness of M. Teste for Valéry proved irresistible. For twenty years he gave himself to the exact disciplines. He studied the foundations of geometry, the nature of time, attention, formal logic, physiology. A few of the notes that Valéry took during his long reclusion have lately trickled into the magazines. More in the fashion of Pascal than of a systematic philosopher, they are inflections upon the personality, its metamorphoses, and its self-abnegating labor of creation.

At the end of this period Valéry, like André Gide, wished to pay "a last debt to the past." He planned to write *La Jeune Parque* in his earlier Symbolist manner. But his prepossession grew upon him. The poem is a long paean of the young Fate awakening to self-consciousness. Then came a scattering of essays and eventually another book of poems, *Charmes.* Among the most important of these works are the charming dialogues, *L'Âme et la Danse,* and *Eupalinos ou l'Architecte.* In the former, Socrates and his companions watch a ballet, giving the most exquisite description of it, and philosophizing upon its significance. Socrates finally decides that the dance does not represent a story, or an emotion such as love, but "the pure act of metamorphoses," "love as well as the sea, and life itself and thoughts." The dancer escapes entirely from her personality to become this pure act. When she comes out of her trance she says:

Asile, asile, ô mon asile, ô Tourbillon!—J'ésais en toi, ô mouvement, en dehors de toutes choses.

After twenty years of silence the poet has proceeded from analysis to act, and he celebrates in this song of triumph. But further reflection, in *Eupalinos,* somewhat dampens his joy. The shades of Socrates and Phaedrus are discoursing in the dim Elysian fields. Their talk gradually shifts to the nature of beauty. Phaedrus quotes his friend, Eupalinos the architect, as saying that there are "buildings which sing"; these are the temples which are built for sheer beauty of form. A factory, on the other hand, talks; it is constructed for utility only. Music and architecture are held to be the supreme arts because of their "purity." Painting, for example, can never escape altogether into a world of its own. It must cover a given surface, and it cannot wholly avoid representing objects or persons. But a melody or a temple feigns to be nothing but itself; it expresses pure relations which have no necessary reference to any other created thing. Thus it attains a sort of universality, in that it is not bound to take any of the individual conformations in which the Demiurge left the world.

Architecture and music, then, have pure beauty. But another advantage is imputed to architecture which makes it superior to music—its "solidity or duration." Duration is inappropriate here, in one meaning of the word: Many of Socrates' sayings, for example, have endured, while the temples of Eupalinos are in ruins. And it is probable that Bach's music will be played long after the Mestrovic chapel in Cavtat will have been destroyed by shells. A temple, like a statue or a painting, can have more duration than a piece of music only by the fact that it exists continuously through time, while the music—though it may "subsist," or float in the realm of essence forever—is embodied but intermittently, that is, when it is played. Why one type of duration should be more sublime than the other is a question. Valéry's rather curious preference for architecture might be taken as a gesture of courtesy—he wrote *Eupalinos* for an architectural magazine—but the psychological explanation would perhaps be more just. After his long period of inactivity . . .

tant d'étrange
Oisivité; mais pleine de pouvoir . . .

Valéry had come to glorify action in its most materialistic sense, the shaping of good solid earth and stone. At the end of the dialogue, Socrates, the mere talker, concluding that his life in the other world was misspent, evokes and praises anti-Socrates, the builder.

In the same way, doubtless, Valéry has found even his versifying unsatisfactory. A poet has something of the pure spirit's pitiful ineptitude. He performs overt actions, indeed, but to one enamored of "pure beauty," how unsatisfying are these scrawls and scratchings with a pencil! Affairs are even worse if the poet's handwriting is bad; he has not even the minor satisfaction of seeing his thoughts embodied in beautiful curves and flourishes. He yearns for the sculptor's chisel, test-tubes, the piano, brush, and canvas; any apparatus by which he could manipulate matter would give him release. And the ultimate product, a book, is but a receptacle for symbols, which as such are nothing to the senses: they speak to the mind in its terrible remoteness and isolation.

Yet the poet, and even the philosopher, is by Valéry's definition somewhat of a builder: "The builder whom I now conjure up finds before him, as chaos and primitive matter, precisely the order of the world that the Demiurge drew from the disorder of the beginning. Nature is formed and its elements are separated; but something compels him to consider this work as incomplete, and needing to be reworked and again put in motion, in order that it may be satisfying more specifically to mankind. Man begins his activity precisely at the point where the god left off." Valéry brought together images and ideas to combine them in a form which the Demiurge—Nature and mankind before him, that is—had never created; Socrates found universal laws about the human mind, the State, and logical reality, which until then had dwelt in limbo. And if the Athenians had only listened to him, perhaps his ideas, too, would have been embodied—not, it is true, in temples, but in human beings living beautifully and intelligently. The architect has no exclusive claim to be the Demiurge's successor.

III

The other question raised in the dialogue, that of the "purity" of the arts, is more important to the subject of the universal man. It was put rather well by Kant in the *Critique of Judgment,* when he made his distinction between free or pure beauty, and dependent beauty. Enjoyment of a flower or an arabesque, he says, presupposes no concept of what the object ought to be, whereas enjoyment of dependent beauty, such as that of a man or a horse (Kant even includes buildings—"be it church, palace, arsenal, or summerhouse") "presupposes a concept of what the thing is to be, and consequently a concept of its perfection." Even Valéry's favorites, music and architecture, are not simon-pure arts. Music, for example, is not a mere pattern of sounds. It produces what may be called an emotional tone in the listener, or, more accurately, a developed emotional experience. To state the matter simply, and rather crudely, in Bach this emotional experience may be one of grandeur; in Mozart, of dignified joy or sadness; in Berlioz or Liszt, of fake heroism or barbaric disorder. The quality of the emotion communicated—to take the emotion alone—is one criterion for judging the worth of the music; and this emotion is akin to the emotions which enter into the rest of life. Likewise, it would be a very limited view of architecture that did not take into account its function, which in the case of the Greek temple involves the congruity of its meaning with that of the Olympian religion.

Valéry applied his esthetic ideas to his own art in the doctrine of *Poésie Pure,* which he derived, or thought he derived, from Poe through Baudelaire. What Poe was getting at in *The Poetic Principle,* the essay to which Valéry refers, and which Baudelaire plagiarized, may be summed up as follows: First, he tried to find the psychological laws governing the effect of the poem on the reader. In this he did not go much farther than to insist that a poem should not be too long to be read in a half-hour or an hour, because the poetic exaltation cannot be maintained for more than that span of time, and the unity of the effect is destroyed if the poem cannot be finished in one reading. Second, he objected to the didacticism of such moralists as Longfellow, on the basis of the old division of mental faculties into pure intellect, taste, and moral sense. Poetry should aim to satisfy "taste," and not to instruct or exhort. Its object is the attainment of "Supernal Loveliness." Poe says further (in his essay on Longfellow) that the test for specious poetry is to ask the question: "Might not this matter be as well or better handled in prose?" He does not object to narrative or drama as such, and he adds that "it does not follow that the incitements of Passion, the precepts of Duty, or even the lessons of Truth, may not be introduced into a poem, and with advantage; for they may subserve, incidentally, in various ways the general purposes of the work."

In spite of a dash of estheticism, Poe's concern was to keep the ethical and intellectual elements of a poem in their due proportion, and to ensure that the poem be primarily a poem, and not a scientific treatise or a tract. The doctrine of *Poésie Pure* would go still further. According to it, poetry aspires to the "pure state," in which science, morality, and history (including story-telling?) should be ruled out altogether, and poetry becomes sheer word-music. Valéry, indeed, has only dallied with this notion; he has never, as many of his encomiasts would have us believe, held to it strictly. Such absolute poetry, as Valéry realizes, is at best an ideal limit: "Rien de si pur ne peut coexister avec les conditions de la vie." Consequently, he decided to admit an element of thought, and to allow his verse to please the intellect as well as the ear. He had long cherished, in any event, the hope of writing the Comedy of Intellect. Poetic immaculateness would receive fewer stains in the high altitude of metaphysics than in the smoky region of conflicts between man and man. He treated such abstruse subjects as time and change (*Le Cimitière Marin, Palme*). In *Ébauche d'un Serpent,* he sang the strange emergence of life, desire, existence—all symbolized by the snake—from the infinite nothingness of the realm of essence, where

> L'univers n'est qu'un défaut
> Dans le pureté du Non-Être.

But his principal theme was the old one of the mind awakening to self-consciousness (*La Jeune Parque, Air de Semiramis, Narcisse, La Pythie, La Fausse Morte,* etc.). This preoccupation led to the charge of Narcissism, although, of course, Valéry is far from making an idol of his own personality. His is rather an impersonal Narcissism of the intellect looking at its own conditions and workings. And the Narcissus of the poem died the moment he kissed the image of his own lips in the water. To a large extent, the poet has been concerned with the form of the mind's action—or rather, with the *fact* of its acting, and he has neglected its content.

IV

Just as Lucretius was the epic poet of Intellect, Valéry is the lyric. And this is no mean distinction. Criticism of a poet who has done well what he set out to do must always seem carping. Yet the critic in the long run has to ask: Why is this poet not the perfect poet? Although M. Valéry is, of course, much too modest ever to have claimed that he was trying to be the universal man, in his case the critic's question takes the form: What progress has he made toward that elusive ideal of his youth, universality?

His poetry has a wealth of music, a plenitude of ideas, poetically expressed. It has the rigor necessary to a true universality. Yet there is something lacking. As E. R. Curtius says: "Valéry's poetry oscillates between the icy region of a thought that is pure play with forms, and the dry fire of a sensibility that is pure impulsion and is directed toward no goal. It is the poetry of sensuous intellectuality. . . . The mean between intellect and sensation—the region of the soul and her beauty, in which we are accustomed to see the home of poetry and her beauty—is missing from Valéry. Here is, if you like, a void."[1] Those who would not use the word "soul" with the connotations that it has in the German language might prefer to rephrase Herr Curtius' criticism as follows: Is the universal poet to be a pure spirit or a rational animal? The pure spirit may spend his days intellectualizing his sensations; the rational animal, and the poet who is truly universal, would also take his themes from the wisdom of life. His model would be, not Leonardo, but another geometer-painter of the Renaissance, Piero della Francesca. With even greater purity of form than

---

[1] *Französischer Geist im Neuen Europa,* pp. 158-159.

Leonardo's, Piero seized that moment of delicate equilibrium when human life was in the flower of a pagan fullness which had not yet lost the restraint of the Middle Ages. And so skillful was the artist that his humanism does not detract from the formal beauty of the work but fuses with it and gives it meaning. But a humanist Valéry is not: he does not live in a world of men.

Before a final judgment can be hazarded as to Valéry's success thus far in his arduous undertaking, it is necessary to consider *La Crise de l'Esprit* and the extract from the lecture given at Zürich in 1922, both of which are included in the *Variété*. Shaken from his delvings into psychology and esthetics, our author looks at some of the questions that confront civilization after the World War. He sets out to discover why the Europe of the past has been more than its geographical position alone would have made it—a mere cape on the mainland of Asia. Its pre-eminence he finds to have been due to the characteristics of the European man: "eager activity, ardent and disinterested curiosity, a happy blend of imagination and logical rigor, a certain scepticism which is yet not pessimistic, a mysticism without resignation."

But whatever unity there was in the mind of Europe has dissolved. Valéry shows us the European Hamlet looking down on the mental disorder of a continent, which is attributed to "the free coexistence in all cultivated minds of the most dissimilar ideas and the most opposed principles of life and knowledge. That is what characterizes the modern epoch." T. S. Eliot has spoken of the need for the construction of a new spiritual unity of the Occident, which would consist in a unified view of the world such as the Thomistic system supplied for the Middle Ages. In this, what Valéry calls "principles of life" are probably more fundamental than the problems disputed at Geneva. Within his necessary limits, and in his concrete fashion, the poet too can contribute to this synthesis—perhaps a poet will be the first to sketch its outlines and to create its ritual and mythology. And thereby he may attain the sort of universality that is possible in our day.

V

For the last decade M. Valéry has relapsed into a poetic silence almost as complete as that which followed *Monsieur Teste*. He seems to have put his mind into some kind of order, and it may be that he is seeking an object worthy of its employment.

In his later poems the hymn of joy sung by the mind awakening becomes ever more triumphant. From the impure body of the Pythoness, writhing, panting, drunk, exhaling fumes from nostrils toughened by incense—

A la fumée, à la fureur! . . .

. . . comes at last the voice of the god bringing with it

Illumination, largesse!

We wait, expectantly, to learn if M. Valéry is addressing himself when the Dawn speaks to Semiramis:

EXISTE! . . . Sois enfin toi-même! dit l'Aurore,
O grande âme, il est temps que tu formes un corps!
Hâte-toi de choisir un jour digne d'éclore,
Parmi tant d'autres feux, tes immortels trésors!

Note—Although my opinion of M. Valéry's success in his intellectual quest has not been modified greatly in the seven years since this essay was published, subsequent developments call for these comments: 1. Immediately after the publication of this essay, M. Valéry became prolific, and his works were issued in popular editions. 2. His new writings were not such as to fulfill the sanguine expectations suggested in the conclusion of the essay. 3. Although T. S. Eliot's dream of a new synthesis still seems to me a worthy ideal, I should not like to be taken as seconding anything Mr. Eliot has said since then about the content of that synthesis, its social and economic foundation, or the method of its attainment.—P. B. R.

Part III

PROSPECTS AND DETERMINATIONS

KENNETH BURKE
Psychology and Form

It is not until the fourth scene of the first act that Hamlet confronts the ghost of his father. As soon as the situation has been made clear, the audience has been, consciously or unconsciously, waiting for this ghost to appear, while in the fourth scene this moment has been definitely promised. For earlier in the play Hamlet had arranged to come to the platform at night with Horatio to meet the ghost, and it is now night, he is with Horatio and Marcellus, and they are standing on the platform. Hamlet asks Horatio the hour.

> *Hor.* I think it lacks of twelve.
> *Mar.* No, it is struck.
> *Hor.* Indeed? I heard it not: then it draws near the season
>   Wherein the spirit held his wont to walk.

Promptly hereafter there is a sound off-stage. "A flourish of trumpets, and ordnance shot off within." Hamlet's friends have established the hour as twelve. It is time for the ghost. Sounds off-stage, and of course it is not the ghost. It is, rather, the sound of the king's carousal, for the king "keeps wassail." A tricky and useful detail. We have been waiting for a ghost, and get, startlingly, a blare of trumpets. And, once the trumpets are silent, we feel how desolate are these three men waiting for a ghost, on a bare "platform," feel it by this sudden juxtaposition of an imagined scene of lights and merriment. But the trumpets announcing a carousal have suggested a subject of conversation. In the darkness Hamlet discusses the excessive drinking of his countrymen. He points out that it tends to harm their reputation

From *Counter-Statement,* by Kenneth Burke. Pp. 38-56. Copyright, 1931. By permission of Harcourt, Brace and Co., Inc., and the author.

abroad, since, he argues, this one showy vice makes their virtues "in the general censure take corruption." And for this reason, although he himself is a native of this place, he does not approve of the custom. Indeed, there in the gloom he is talking very intelligently on these matters, and Horatio answers, "Look, my Lord, it comes." All this time we had been waiting for a ghost, and it comes at the one moment which was not pointing towards it. This ghost, so assiduously prepared for, is yet a surprise. And now that the ghost has come, we are waiting for something further. Program: a speech from Hamlet. Hamlet must confront the ghost. Here again Shakespeare can feed well upon the use of contrast for his effects. Hamlet has just been talking in a sober, rather argumentative manner—but now the flood-gates are unloosed:

> Angels and ministers of grace defend us!
> Be thou a spirit of health or goblin damn'd,
> Bring with thee airs from heaven or blasts from hell . . .

and the transition from the matter-of-fact to the grandiose, the full-throated and full-voweled, is a second burst of trumpets, perhaps more effective than the first, since it is the rich fulfillment of a promise. Yet this satisfaction in turn becomes an allurement, an itch for further developments. At first desiring solely to see Hamlet confront the ghost, we now want Hamlet to learn from the ghost the details of the murder—which are, however, with shrewdness and husbandry, reserved for "Scene V—Another part of the Platform."

I have gone into this scene at some length, since it illustrates so perfectly the relationship between psychology and form, and so aptly indicates how the one is to be defined in terms of the other. That is, the psychology here is not the psychology of the *hero,* but the psychology of the *audience.* And by that distinction, form would be the psychology of the audience. Or, seen from another angle, form is the creation of an appetite in the mind of the auditor, and the adequate satisfying of that appetite. This satisfaction—so complicated is the human mechanism—at times involves a temporary set of frustrations, but in the end these frustrations prove to be simply a more involved kind of satisfaction, and furthermore serve to make the satisfaction of fulfillment more intense. If, in a work of art, the poet says something, let us say, about a meeting, writes in such a way that we desire to observe that meeting, and then, if he places that meeting before us—that is form. While obviously, that is also the psychology of the audience, since it involves desires and their appeasements.

The seeming breach between form and subject-matter, between technique and psychology, which has taken place in the last century is the result, it seems to me, of scientific criteria being unconsciously introduced into matters of purely esthetic judgment. The flourishing of science has been so vigorous that we have not yet had time to make a spiritual readjustment adequate to the changes in our resources of material and knowledge. There are disorders of the social system which are caused solely by our undigested wealth (the basic disorder being, perhaps, the phenomenon of overproduction: to remedy this, instead of having all workers employed on half time, we have half working full time and the other half idle, so that whereas overproduction could be the greatest reward of applied science, it has been, up to now, the most menacing condition our modern civilization has had to face). It would be absurd to suppose that such social disorders would not be paralleled by disorders of culture and taste, especially since science is so pronouncedly a spiritual factor. So that we are, owing to the sudden wealth science has thrown upon us, all *nouveaux-riches* in matters of culture, and most poignantly in that field where lack of native firmness is most readily exposed, in matters of esthetic judgment.

One of the most striking derangements of taste which science has temporarily thrown upon us involves the understanding of psychology in art. Psychology has become a body of information (which is precisely what psychology in science should be, or must be). And similarly, in art, we tend to look for psychology as the purveying of information. Thus, a contemporary writer has objected to Joyce's *Ulysses* on the ground that there are more psychoanalytic data available in Freud. (How much more drastically he might, by the same system, have destroyed Homer's *Odysseus!*)

To his objection it was answered that one might, similarly, denounce Cézanne's trees in favor of state forestry bulletins. Yet are not Cézanne's landscapes themselves tainted with the psychology of information? Has he not, by perception, *pointed out* how one object lies against another, *indicated* what takes place between two colors (which is the psychology of science, and is less successful in the medium of art than in that of science, since in art such processes are at best implicit, whereas in science they are so readily made explicit)? Is Cézanne not, to that extent, a state forestry bulletin, except that he tells what goes on in the eye instead of on the tree? And do not the true values of his work lie elsewhere—and precisely in what I distinguish as the psychology of form?

Thus, the great influx of information has led the artist also to lay his emphasis on the giving of information—with the result that art tends more and more to substitute the psychology of the hero (the subject) for the psychology of the audience. Under such an attitude, when form is preserved it is preserved as an annex, a luxury, or, as some feel, a downright affectation. It remains, though sluggish, like the human appendix, for occasional demands are still made upon it; but its true vigor is gone, since it is no longer organically required. Proposition: The hypertrophy of the psychology of information is accompanied by the corresponding atrophy of the psychology of form.

In information, the matter is intrinsically interesting. And by intrinsically interesting I do not necessarily mean intrinsically valuable, as witness the intrinsic interest of backyard gossip or the most casual newspaper items. In art, at least the art of the great ages (Aeschylus, Shakespeare, Racine), the matter is interesting by means of an extrinsic use, a function. Consider, for instance, the speech of Mark Antony, the "Brutus is an honourable man." Imagine in the same place a very competently developed thesis on human conduct, with statistics, intelligence tests, definitions; imagine it as the finest thing of the sort ever written, and as really being at the roots of an understanding of Brutus. Obviously, the play would simply stop until Antony had finished. For in the case of Antony's speech, the value lies in the fact that his words are shaping the future of the audience's desires, not the desires of the Roman populace, but the desires of the pit. This is the psychology of form as distinguished from the psychology of information.

The distinction is, of course, absolutely true only in its non-existent extremes. Hamlet's advice to the players, for instance, has little of the quality which distinguishes Antony's speech. It is, rather, intrinsically interesting, although one could very easily prove how the play would benefit by some such delay at this point, and that anything which made this delay possible without violating the consistency of the subject would have, in this, its formal justification. It would, furthermore, be absurd to rule intrinsic interest out of literature. I wish simply to have it restored to its properly minor position, seen as merely one out of many possible elements of style. Goethe's prose, often poorly imagined or neutral in its line-for-line texture, especially in the treatment of romantic episode—perhaps he felt that the romantic episode in itself was enough? —is strengthened into a style possessing affirmative virtues by his rich use of aphorism. But this is, after all, but one of many possible facets of appeal. In some places, notably in *Wilhelm Meisters Lehrjahre* when Wilhelm's friends disclose the documents they have been collecting about his life unbeknown to him, the aphorisms are almost rousing in their efficacy, since they involve the story. But as a rule the appeal of aphorism is intrinsic: that is, it satisfies without being functionally related to the context.[1] Also, to return to the matter of Hamlet, it must be observed that the style in this passage is no mere "information-giving" style; in its alacrity, its development, it really makes this one fragment into a kind of miniature plot.

One reason why music can stand repetition so much more sturdily

---

[1] Similarly, the epigram of Racine is "pure art," because it usually serves to formulate or clarify some situation within the play itself. In Goethe the epigram is most often of independent validity, as in *Die Wahlverwandt-schaften*, where the ideas of Ottilie's diary are obviously carried over boldly from the author's notebook. In Shakespeare we have the union of extrinsic and intrinsic epigram, the epigram growing out of its context and yet valu-able independent of its context.

than correspondingly good prose is because music, of all the arts, is by its nature least suited to the psychology of information, and has remained closer to the psychology of form. Here form cannot atrophy. Every dissonant chord cries for its solution, and whether the musician resolves or refuses to resolve this dissonance into the chord which the body cries for, he is dealing in human appetites. Correspondingly good prose, however, more prone to the temptations of pure information, cannot so much bear repetition since the esthetic value of information is lost once that information is imparted. If one returns to such a work again it is purely because, in the chaos of modern life, he has been able to forget it. With a desire, on the other hand, its recovery is as agreeable as its discovery. One can memorize the dialogue between Hamlet and Guildenstern, where Hamlet gives Guildenstern the pipe to play on. For, once the speech is known, its repetition adds a new element to compensate for the loss of novelty. We cannot take a recurrent pleasure in the new (in information) but we can in the natural (in form). Already, at the moment when Hamlet is holding out the pipe to Guildenstern and asking him to play upon it, we "gloat over" Hamlet's triumphal descent upon Guildenstern, when, after Guildenstern has, under increasing embarrassment, protested three times that he cannot play the instrument, Hamlet launches the retort for which all this was preparation:

Why, look you now, how unworthy a thing you make of me. You would play upon me, you would seem to know my stops; you would pluck out the heart of my mystery; you would sound me from my lowest note to the top of my compass; and there is much music, excellent voice, in this little organ, yet cannot you make it speak. 'Sblood, do you think I am easier to be played on than a pipe? Call me what instrument you will, though you can fret me, you cannot play upon me.[1]

[1] One might indicate still further appropriateness here. As Hamlet finishes his speech, Polonius enters, and Hamlet turns to him, "God bless you, sir!" Thus, the plot is continued (for Polonius is always the promise of action) and a full stop is avoided: the embarrassment laid upon Rosencrantz and Guildenstern is not laid upon the audience.

In the opening lines we hear the promise of the close, and thus feel the emotional curve even more keenly than at first reading. Whereas in most modern art this element is underemphasized. It gives us the gossip of a plot, a plot which too often has for its value the mere fact that we do not know its outcome.[1]

Music, then, fitted less than any other art for imparting information, deals minutely in frustrations and fulfillments of desire,[2] and for that reason more often gives us those curves of emotion which, because they are natural, can bear repetition without loss. It is for this reason that music, like folk tales, is most capable of lulling us to sleep. A lullaby is a melody which comes quickly to rest, where the obstacles are easily overcome—and this is precisely the parallel to those waking dreams of struggle and conquest which (especially during childhood) we permit ourselves when falling asleep or when trying to induce sleep. Folk tales are just such waking dreams. Thus it is right that art should be called a "waking dream." The only difficulty with this definition (indicated by Charles Baudouin in his *Psychoanalysis and Aesthetics,* a very valuable study of Verhaeren) is that today we understand it to mean art as a waking dream for the artist. Modern criticism, and psychoanalysis in particular, is too prone to define the essence of art in terms of the artist's weaknesses. It is, rather, the audience which dreams, while the artist oversees the conditions which determine this dream. He is the manipulator of blood, brains, heart, and bowels which, while we sleep, dictate the mold of our desires. This is, of course, the real meaning of artistic felicity—an exaltation at the correctness of the procedure, so that we enjoy the steady march of doom in a Racinian tragedy with exactly the same equipment as that which

---

[1] Yet modern music has gone far in the attempt to renounce this aspect of itself. Its dissonances become static, demanding no particular resolution. And whereas an unfinished modulation by a classic musician occasions positive dissatisfaction, the refusal to resolve a dissonance in modern music does not dissatisfy us, but irritates or stimulates. Thus, "energy" takes the place of style.

[2] Suspense is the least complex kind of anticipation, as surprise is the least complex kind of fulfillment.

produces our delight with Benedick's "Peace! I'll stop your mouth. (*Kisses her*)" which terminates the imbroglio of *Much Ado About Nothing.*

The methods of maintaining interest which are most natural to the psychology of information (as it is applied to works of pure art) are surprise and suspense. The method most natural to the psychology of form is eloquence. For this reason the great ages of Aeschylus, Shakespeare, and Racine, dealing as they did with material which was more or less a matter of common knowledge so that the broad outlines of the plot were known in advance (while it is the broad outlines which are usually exploited to secure surprise and suspense) developed formal excellence, or eloquence, as the basis of appeal in their work.

Not that there is any difference in kind between the classic method and the method of the cheapest contemporary melodrama. The drama, more than any other form, must never lose sight of its audience: here the failure to satisfy the proper requirements is most disastrous. And since certain contemporary work is successful, it follows that rudimentary laws of composition are being complied with. The distinction is one of intensity rather than of kind. The contemporary audience hears the lines of a play or novel with the same equipment as it brings to reading the lines of its daily paper. It is content to have facts placed before it in some more or less adequate sequence. Eloquence is the minimizing of this interest in fact, *per se,* so that the "more or less adequate sequence" of their presentation must be relied on to a much greater extent. Thus, those elements of surprise and suspense are subtilized, carried down into the writing of a line or a sentence, until in all its smallest details the work bristles with disclosures, contrasts, restatements with a difference, ellipses, images, aphorism, volume, sound-values, in short all that complex wealth of minutiae which in their line-for-line aspect we call style and in their broader outlines we call form.

As a striking instance of a modern play with potentialities in which the intensity of eloquence is missing, I might cite a recent success, Capek's *R. U. R.* Here, in a melodrama which was often astonishing in the rightness of its technical procedure, when the author was finished he had written nothing but the scenario for a play by Shakespeare. It was a play in which the author produced time and again the opportunity, the demand, for eloquence, only to move on. (At other times, the most successful moments, he utilized the modern discovery of silence, writing moments wherein words could not possibly serve but to detract from the effect: this we might call the "flowering" of information.) The Adam and Eve scene of the last act, a "commission" which the Shakespeare of the comedies would have loved to fill, was in the verbal barrenness of Capek's play something shameless to the point of blushing. The Robot, turned human, prompted by the dawn of love to see his first sunrise, or hear the bird-call, and forced merely to say, "Oh, see the sunrise," or, "Hear the pretty birds"—here one could do nothing but wring his hands at the absence of that esthetic mold which produced the overslung "speeches" of Romeo and Juliet.

Suspense is the concern over the possible outcome of some specific detail of plot rather than for general qualities. Thus, "Will A marry B or C?" is suspense. In *Macbeth,* the turn from the murder scene to the porter scene is a much less literal channel of development. Here the presence of one quality calls forth the demand for another, rather than one tangible incident of plot awaking an interest in some other possible tangible incident of plot. To illustrate more fully, if an author managed over a certain number of his pages to produce a feeling of sultriness, or oppression, in the reader, this would unconsciously awaken in the reader the desire for a cold, fresh north wind—and thus some aspect of a north wind would be effective if called forth by some aspect of stuffiness. A good example of this is to be found in a contemporary poem, T. S. Eliot's *The Waste Land,* where the vulgar, oppressively trivial conversation in the public house calls forth in the poet a memory of a line from Shakespeare. These slobs in a public house, after a desolately low-visioned conversation, are now forced by closing time to leave the saloon. They say good-night. And suddenly the poet, feeling his release, drops into another good-night, a good-night with *désinvolture,* a good-night out of what was, within the conditions of the poem at least, a graceful and irrecoverable past.

"Well that Sunday Albert was home, they had a hot gammon,
    And they asked me in to dinner, to get the beauty of it hot"—
[at this point the bartender interrupts: it is closing time]
"Goodnight Bill. Goonight Lou. Goonight May. Goonight. Ta ta.
    Goonight. Goonight.
Good-night, ladies, good-night, sweet ladies, good-night, good-night."

There is much more to be said on these lines, which I have shortened somewhat in quotation to make my issue clearer. But I simply wish to point out here that this transition is a bold juxtaposition of one quality created by another, an association in ideas which, if not logical, is nevertheless emotionally natural. In the case of *Macbeth,* similarly, it would be absurd to say that the audience, after the murder scene, wants a porter scene. But the audience does want the quality which this porter particularizes. The dramatist might, conceivably, have introduced some entirely different character or event in this place, provided only that the event produced the same quality of relationship and contrast (grotesque seriousness followed by grotesque buffoonery). One of the most beautiful and satisfactory "forms" of this sort is to be found in Baudelaire's "Femmes Damnées," where the poet, after describing the business of a Lesbian seduction, turns to the full oratory of his apostrophe:

> *Descendez, descendez, lamentables victimes,*
> *Descendez le chemin de l'enfer éternel . . .*

while the stylistic efficacy of this transition contains a richness which transcends all moral (or unmoral) sophistication: the efficacy of appropriateness, of exactly the natural curve in treatment. Here is morality even for the godless, since it is a morality of art, being justified, if for no other reason, by its paralleling of that staleness, that disquieting loss of purpose, which must have followed the procedure of the two characters, the *femmes damnées* themselves, a remorse which, perhaps only physical in its origin, nevertheless becomes psychic.[1]

But to return, we have made three terms synonymous: form, psychology, and eloquence. And eloquence thereby becomes the essence of art, while pity, tragedy, sweetness, humor, in short all the emotions which we experience in life proper, as non-artists, are simply the material on which eloquence may feed. The arousing of pity, for instance, is not the central purpose of art, although it may be an adjunct of artistic effectiveness. One can feel pity much more keenly at the sight of some actual misfortune—and it would be a great mistake to see art merely as a weak representation of some actual experience.[2] That artists today are content to write under such an esthetic accounts in part for the inferior position which art holds in the community. Art, at least in the great periods when it has flowered, was the conversion, or transcendence, of emotion into eloquence, and was thus a factor added to life. I am reminded of St. Augustine's caricature of the theatre: that whereas we do not dare to wish people unhappy, we do want to feel sorry for them, and therefore turn to plays so that we can feel sorry although no real misery is involved. One might apply the parallel interpretation to the modern delight in happy endings, and say that we turn to art to indulge our humanitarianism in a well-wishing which we do not permit ourselves towards our actual neighbors. Surely the catharsis of art is more complicated than this, and more reputable.

Eloquence itself, as I hope to have established in the instance from *Hamlet* which I have analyzed, is no mere plaster added to a frame-

---

[1] As another aspect of the same subject, I could cite many examples from the fairy tale. Consider, for instance, when the hero is to spend the night in a bewitched castle. Obviously, as darkness descends, weird adventures must befall him. His bed rides him through the castle; two halves of a man challenge him to a game of nine-pins played with thigh bones and skulls. Or entirely different incidents may serve instead of these. The quality comes first, the particularization follows.

[2] Could not the Greek public's resistance to Euripides be accounted for in the fact that he, of the three great writers of Greek tragedy, betrayed his art, was guilty of esthetic impiety, in that he paid more attention to the arousing of emotion *per se* than to the sublimation of emotion into eloquence?

work of more stable qualities. Eloquence is simply the end of art, and is thus its essence. Even the poorest is eloquent, but in a poor way, with less intensity, until this aspect is obscured by others fattening upon its leanness. Eloquence is not showiness; it is, rather, the result of that desire in the artist to make a work perfect by adapting it in every minute detail to the racial appetites.

The distinction between the psychology of information and the psychology of form involves a definition of esthetic truth. It is here precisely, to combat the deflection which the strength of science has caused to our tastes, that we must examine the essential breach between scientific and artistic truth. Truth in art is not the discovery of facts, not an addition to human knowledge in the scientific sense of the word.[1] It is, rather, the exercise of human propriety, the formulation of symbols which rigidify our sense of poise and rhythm. Artistic truth is the externalization of taste.[2] I some-

---

[1] One of the most striking examples of the encroachment of scientific truth into art is the doctrine of "truth by distortion," whereby one aspect of an object is suppressed the better to emphasize some other aspect; this is, obviously, an attempt to *indicate* by art some fact of knowledge, to make some implicit aspect of an object as explicit as one can by means of the comparatively dumb method of art (dumb, that is, as compared to the perfect ease with which science can indicate its discoveries). Yet science has already made discoveries in the realm of this "factual truth," this "truth by distortion" which must put to shame any artist who relies on such matter for his effects. Consider, for instance, the motion-picture of a man vaulting. By photographing this process very rapidly, and running the reel very slowly, one has upon the screen the most striking set of factual truths to aid in our understanding of an athlete vaulting. Here, at our leisure, we can observe the contortions of four legs, a head, and a butt. This squirming thing we saw upon the screen showed us an infinity of factual truths anent the balances of an athlete vaulting. We can, from this, observe the marvelous system of balancing which the body provides for itself in the adjustments of moving. Yet, so far as the esthetic truth is concerned, this on the screen was not an athlete, but a squirming thing, a horror, displaying every fact of vaulting except the exhilaration of the act itself.

[2] The procedure of science involves the elimination of taste, employing as a substitute the corrective norm of the pragmatic test, the empirical experiment, which is entirely intellectual. Those who oppose the "intellectualism" of critics like Matthew Arnold are involved in an hilarious blunder, for Arnold's entire approach to the appreciation of art is through delicacies of taste intensified to the extent almost of squeamishness.

times wonder, for instance, whether the "artificial" speech of John Lyly might perhaps be "truer" than the revelations of Dostoevsky. Certainly at its best, in its feeling for a statement which returns upon itself, which attempts the systole to a diastole, it *could* be much truer than Dostoevsky.[1] And if it is not, it fails not through a mistake of Lyly's esthetic, but because Lyly was a man poor in character whereas Dostoevsky was rich and complex. When Swift, making the women of Brobdingnag enormous, deduces from this discrepancy between their size and Gulliver's that Gulliver could sit astride their nipples, he has written something which is esthetically true, which is, if I may be pardoned, profoundly "proper," as correct in its Euclidean deduction as any corollary in geometry. Given the companions of Ulysses in the cave of Polyphemus, it is true that they would escape clinging to the bellies of the herd let out to pasture. St. Ambrose, detailing the habits of God's creatures, and drawing from them moral maxims for the good of mankind, St. Ambrose in his limping natural history rich in scientific inaccuracies that are at the very heart of emotional rightness, St. Ambrose writes "Of night-birds, especially the nightingale which hatches her eggs by song; of the owl, the bat, and the cock at cockcrow; in what these may apply to the guidance of our habits," and in the sheer rightness of that program there is the truth of art. In introducing this talk of night-birds, after many pages devoted to other of God's creatures, he says:

What now! While we have been talking, you will notice how the birds of night have already started fluttering about you, and, in this same fact of warning us to leave off with our discussion, suggest thereby a further topic—

and this seems to me to contain the best wisdom of which the human frame is capable, an address, a discourse, which can make our material life seem blatant almost to the point of despair. And when the cock crows, and the thief abandons his traps, and the sun lights up, and we are in every way called back to God by the well-

---

[1] As for instance, the "conceit" of Endymion's awakening, when he forgets his own name, yet recalls that of his beloved.

meaning admonition of this bird, here the very blindnesses of religion become the deepest truths of art.

Thomas Mann and André Gide

W HEN Gustav von Aschenbach, the hero of Thomas Mann's *Death in Venice,* was about thirty-five years of age, he was taken ill in Vienna.   During the course of a conversation, one keen observer said of him: "You see, Aschenbach has always lived like this," and the speaker contracted the fingers of his left hand into a fist; "never like this," and he let his hand droop comfortably from the arm of a chair.   It is with such opening and closing of the hand that this essay is to deal.

In the early writings of both Mann and Gide the characters are exceptional, though always in keeping with our metaphor.   Mann's concern is with serious and lonely fellows, deviations from type, who are over-burdened with a feeling of divergency from their neighbors.   In stories like "Der Bajazzo" the deformations are more mental, but generally the subject is simplified by his imagining characters who are physically extravagant.   There is Tobias Mindernickel, whose ill-dressed, gaunt, ungainly figure excites the persecution of all healthy children.   He buys a little puppy, and names it Esau.   They become inseparable, but one day Esau leaps for food, is accidentally wounded by a knife which Tobias is holding, whereupon Tobias nurses his puppy with great tenderness.   After some days it is cured, it no longer lies gazing at him with bewildered, suffering eyes, it leaps down from its sick-bed, goes racing about with full delight in its puppyhood, with no thought that it is showing how it no longer needs Tobias's morbid tenderness.   It is a cheerful little mutt—and maddened at his loss, Tobias plunges his

From *Counter-Statement,* by Kenneth Burke.   Pp. 116-135.   Copyright, 1931. By permission of Harcourt, Brace and Co., Inc.

knife into it again, then forlornly gathers its dying body in his arms. Similarly, there is the little Herr Friedemann, who, humble as he is, can by the course of his story be still further humiliated and, in the very act of taking his life, grovels. Mann also writes of an abnormally fat man, who worships his adulterous wife abjectly, and falls dead of apoplexy at a particularly comical moment, topples like a collapsing building, when he feels the full weight of the indignities which have been heaped upon him. And Piepsam, Herr Gottlob Piepsam, a decayed alcoholic, a victim of life if there ever was one, is insulted as he goes to visit the grave of his wife. On the path to the cemetery he is passed by a boy on a bicycle, the merest child who is too happy to be anything but well-meaning, yet Piepsam resents him and works himself into a fatal rage—the story being told fancifully, even cheerfully. After Piepsam has been bundled off in an ambulance, one feels how brightly the sun is shining.

These outsiders (Mann later took over the word "outsider" from the English) appear under many guises. They watch, they compare themselves with others to their own detriment, they are earnest to the point of self-disgust, and they are weighted with vague responsibilities. In "Tonio Kröger" the concept has matured. Tonio's divergencies are subtler. As a writer, he observes the unliterary with nostalgia. Vacillating by temperament, one might almost say vacillating by profession, he seeks simple people, who form for him a kind of retrogressive ideal. He does not fraternize with them, he spies upon them. A Bohemian, he distrusts Bohemianism. He watches these others, awed by the healthiness, or the ease, of their satisfaction. It is a kind of inverted praising, since he envies them for qualities which he himself has outgrown. And it is melancholy.

Against this earnestness, this non-conforming mind's constant preoccupation with conformity, we find in the early writings of Gide much the same rotten elegance as characterizes Wilde's *The Picture of Dorian Gray*. Religious thinking is perverted to produce an atmosphere of decay and sinfulness. There is the Baudelairean tendency to invoke Satan as redeemer. Even in a work as late as *Les Nourritures terrestres,* we find a crooked evangelism, calling us to vague and unnatural revelations. These artificial prophecies, with a rhetorical, homiletic accent which Gide has since abandoned, suggest a kind of morbid Whitmanism. In place of expansion across an unpeopled continent, we have a pilgrimage through old, decaying cities, erotic excitations at the thought of anonymity and freedom among the ruins of other cultures. The hero who cries out to Nathaniel is seeking, not the vigor of health, but the intensity of corruption. The mood, if I understand it correctly, has by now lost much of its immediacy, but in his later works Gide has shown it capable of great readaptation; what we find earlier, in an archaistic terminology, is subsequently transformed into something wholly contemporary.

The most thorough contrast between these writers probably arises from the juxtaposition of Mann's *Death in Venice* and Gide's *The Immoralist*. Gustav von Aschenbach is nationally respected as a master of his calling. Parts of his works are even among the prescribed reading of school children. His austerity, his "morality of production," is emphasized. Aschenbach has clearly erected a structure of external dignity in keeping with the sobriety, the earnestness, which he has brought to the business of writing. But he is now undergoing a period of enervation. He finds that he cannot tackle his page with the necessary zest. As a purely therapeutic measure, he permits himself a trip to Venice, and here becomes fascinated by a young Polish boy, Tadzio, who is living at the same hotel. In his shy and troubled contemplation of this boy he finds an absorption which is painful, but imperious. Von Aschenbach remains outwardly the man of dignity honored by his nation—he does not, as I recall, ever exchange a word with this Tadzio, whose freshness, liquidity, immaturity, are the sinister counterpart of the desiccation of Aschenbach's declining years. But inwardly he is *notwendig liederlich und Abenteurer des Gefühls*. Necessarily dissolute—an adventurer of the emotions—the words are Mann's, when discussing this book in his *Betrachtungen eines Unpolitischen* years afterwards. We thus find again the notion that the artist faces *by profession* alternatives which are contrary to society. The theme of Aschenbach's gloomy infatuation coexists with the theme of the plague—and we observe the elderly man's erotic fevers metamorphose gradually into the fevers of incipient cholera. A poignant and inventive passage describing his cosmetic treatment at the hands of a barber is followed by Aschenbach's delirious remembrance of lines from the *Phaedrus,* wherein Socrates is speaking words of courtship and metaphysics indiscriminately, a merging which Aschenbach makes more pronounced by his own diseased reworking of the Platonic dialogue. A few pages later "a respectably shocked world" receives the news of his death.

The same themes, sickness and sexual vagary, underlie Gide's *The Immoralist.* Michel, after being at the verge of death and being nursed by his bride into vigorous health, subtly drives her to her own grave. Throughout the novel he is profuse in his tenderness, he is almost hysterically attentive to her, but at the same time he is steadily destroying her—and during the final march of her illness he takes her on that savage pilgrimage from city to city which inevitably results in her death. There has been a young Arab on the fringes of this plot, an insolent fellow who first charmed Michel by stealing from his wife. The reader places him unmistakably as a motive in this unpunishable murder. Despite the parallelism between *Death in Venice* and *The Immoralist,* the emphasis is very different. Whereas in Mann we feel most the sense of resistance, of resignation to the point of distress, and Aschenbach's dissolution is matched by a constant straining after self-discipline, in Gide we hear a narrator who relates with more than pride, with something akin to positive advocacy, the unclean details of his life. *"Je vais vous parler longuement de mon corps,"* he opens one chapter in a tone which I sometimes regret he has seen fit to drop from his later work; there is no mistaking its connotations; it is the accent of evangelism, of pleading.

Buddenbrooks and *Lafcadio's Adventure* do not fall in corresponding stages of their author's developments. *Buddenbrooks,* a remarkably comprehensive realistic novel of life in North Germany, comes much earlier. But the same contrast in attitude is apparent. We might interpret *Buddenbrooks* as having the theme of "Tonio Kröger" greatly subtilized and ramified. This "fall of a family" through four generations is also the "growth of an artist" through four generations. What is lost in health and moral certitude is gained in questioning and conscientiousness, in social and esthetic sensitiveness, until we arrive at little Hanno the musician, who, like Aschenbach, finally mingles inspiration with disease, as we watch his improvisations become the first symptoms of the typhoid fever that is to result in his death. In *Lafcadio's Adventure,* however, we meet with a brilliant type of villainy, an "esthetic criminal" who commits crimes for pure love of the art. The character of Lafcadio is perhaps Gide's most remarkable discovery. It suggests a merging of Stendhal's Julien Sorel with those criminals of Dostoevsky whose transgressions are inexplicable from the standpoint of utilitarian purpose.

In *Lafcadio's Adventure* Gide makes a notable change in nomenclature, recasting his "corruption" in more characteristically contemporary molds of thought. The transgressions have become "secular," advancing from sin to crime. If theology remains, it is relegated to a more superficial function; it becomes background, the story being built about a swindle whereby certain picturesque crooks fleece Catholic pietists. Lafcadio, who remembers five uncles but no father, has placed villainy on a distinguished and difficult plane. The author endows him with accomplishments somewhat lavishly, perhaps even a bit credulously; he seems eager that our sympathies be with this experimenter in crime, who can look upon kindly and vicious acts as almost interchangeable:

The old woman with the little white cloud above her head, who pointed to it and said: "It won't rain today!" that poor shrivelled old woman whose sack I carried on my shoulders (he had followed his fancy of travelling on foot for four days across the Apennines, between Bologna and Florence, and had slept a night at Covigliajo) and whom I kissed when we got to the top of the hill . . . one of what the *curé* of Covigliajo would have called my "good actions." I could just as easily have throttled her—my hand would have been as steady—when I felt her dirty wrinkled skin beneath my fingers . . . Ah! how caressingly she stroked and dusted my coat collar and said *"figlio mio! carino!"* . . . I wonder what made my joy so intense when afterwards—I was still in a sweat—I lay down on the moss—not smoking though—in the shade of that big chestnut-tree. I felt as though I could have clasped the whole of mankind to my heart in my single embrace—or strangled it, for that matter.

We shall not reconstruct here that gratuitous murder which recommends the hero particularly to our attention when poor Fleurissoire, attracted by this pleasant-seeming lad, chooses to seat himself in the same compartment with him and unknowingly excites Lafcadio to homicidal criticism. Gide exacts a very complex reception on the part of the reader. He asks us to observe a moral outrage committed by a charming scoundrel to whose well-being we are considerably pledged. Fleurissoire is the butt of much injustice in this book, but it is Lafcadio, insolent, despotic, with his mercurial slogan "what would happen if . . ." who earns our suffrage.

The war ends, the mythical post-war period begins, and Thomas Mann issues *The Magic Mountain,* Gide *The Counterfeiters.* Our contrast is by no means imperiled. Mann shows how for seven years, during his illness in the mountains, Hans Castorp has lain exposed to moral questionings. While each day observing his temperature and eating five enormous meals to combat the wastage of his phthisis, he is privileged to hear the grave problems of our culture aired by sparring critics, themselves diseased, who speak with much rhetorical and dialectic finish. In particular, a humanist and a Jesuit altercate for his benefit, until Mynheer Peeperkorn enters (a much grander version of Herr Kloterfahn in the story "Tristan") and routs them both by his inarticulate vitality. He is life, himself ailing, to be sure, but magnificent and overwhelming while he lasts—and Castorp's melancholy respect for him is, in a matured and complex form, Tonio Kröger's respect for the burghers whom he watched with aloof humility. Castorp has the attitude of a student. Under ordinary circumstances he would probably have been unthinking, but he is made sensitive by his illness and his seven years' elevation above the century. He amasses greater understanding chapter by chapter, or at least learns to play one statement against another—until once more we come to that bewildered fever which marks the close of both *Buddenbrooks* and *Death in Venice.*

At the last, as we see him on the battlefield, advancing to the aimless business of slaughter, simplified, regimented, unquestioning, we comprehend his evasion. For years he has been uncertain—he now embraces the arbitrary certainty of war. "Moralism, pessimism, humor"—these three qualities, whose interrelation Mann himself has stressed, are the dominant traits of this momentous novel, a summarization book, a comprehensive and symbolic work to be included in the world's literature of last wills and testaments.

To turn from *The Magic Mountain* to *The Counterfeiters* is to turn from brooding to shrewdness. Cruelty, malice, sensuality, intrigue—such elements are assiduously welded into an entertaining volume, of much subtle literary satisfaction. The reader of *The Magic Mountain* may have to deal with the fruits of complexity on the part of the author, but he receives them simply. The reader of *The Counterfeiters* finds complexity unresolved—he is not even at liberty to differentiate between the absurd and the beautiful. He is left fluctuant, in great tenuousness of moral values. The book contains Gide's development from sin to crime, and reaffirms his sympathy with deviations from the average ethical stock.

Returning to Aschenbach, ill at the age of thirty-five in Vienna, we find ourselves with correspondences for the closed and opened hand. It seems that Mann, who himself has situated the mainspring of his work in conscientiousness, is like his protagonist Aschenbach, with the hand contracted. And Gide, whose works could readily be taken by the immature or the trivial as invitations to the most unscrupulous kinds of living, who masters an air of suave corruption beyond any possible corrupt act, Gide can be the hand relaxed. *Gewissenhaftigkeit, Einsamkeit*—loneliness, the sense of responsibility—are Mann's words; but as the most distinctive device for Gide, I would quote from his Journal the triptych: *"nouveauté, vice, art."*

Our primary purpose, however, in establishing this distinction between the conscientious and the corrupt is to destroy it. One need not read far in the writings of Gide to discover the strong ethical trait which dominates his thinking. Perhaps no other modern writer has quoted the New Testament so frequently, or shown such readiness to settle secular issues by formulas drawn from religion. His critical work on Dostoevsky, with its theological distinction between the psychology of humility and the psychology of humiliation, is throughout an exercise in moral sensitiveness. And his Lafcadio is a mass of categorical imperatives. We learn from entries in his diary how, with the athleticism of an anchorite, he plunges a knife into his side for penance, one thrust "for having beaten Protos at chess," another thrust "for having answered before Protos," four thrusts "for having cried at hearing of Faby's death." Faby was one of his "uncles." Protos was his master in adventure, his accomplished rival, and Lafcadio punished himself, it seems, for not having been disdainful enough to let Protos win. Lafcadio's lamentable conduct might even be derived from an excess of scruples, though these scruples are peculiar to himself.

"I began to feel," Gide has written on his subject in his autobiography, *Si le Grain ne meurt,* "that perhaps all men's obligations were not the same, and that God himself might well abhor the uniformity which nature protests but towards which the Christian ideal seems to lead us in aiming to bring nature under control. I could concede none but an individual morality, its imperatives sometimes in conflict with those of other moralities. I was persuaded that each person, or at least each one of the elect, had to play a rôle on earth, which was wholly his own and did not resemble any other. And every attempt to submit to a general rule became treason in my eyes, yes, treason which I likened to that great unpardonable sin against the Holy Ghost, since the individual lost his precise, irreplaceable significance, his 'savor.'"

We should also consider Gide's *Strait is the Gate,* which constructs a sympathetic idyll out of the perverse rigors of chastity. As Alissa is courted by Jerome, the two progress into a difficult relationship, obscuring their sensual attraction in a state of pietistic exaltation. Jerome seeks her patiently and unerringly—and with the vocabulary of nobility she beckons to him while continually delaying the time of their union. At first she can offer logical pretexts for this delay, but as they are one by one removed she retreats behind the subterfuges of her faith, and with the assistance of Biblical quotations, morbidly chosen, she remains to the end difficult, pure, intact, a treasure, while loving Jerome with hysterical effusiveness. From the standpoint of its genesis the book is doubtless a companion piece to *The Immoralist*. Both are perverse studies in the frustration of heterosexual union, the one with the connotations of corruption, the other with connotations of great conscientiousness. When bringing them together, we see that Alissa's moral sensitiveness was no greater than that of Michel. Similarly we should recall in *The Counterfeiters* the brutal letter which the bastard Bernard Profitendieu writes to his nominal father, a dutifully vicious letter, and the first step, we might say, in the growth of Bernard's affection.

Has not Mann, on the other hand, spoken with fervor of a "sympathy with the abyss," an admitting of the morally chaotic, which he considers not merely the prerogative, but the duty, of the artist? Aschenbach is committed to conflict: whatever policy he decides upon for his conduct, he must continue to entertain disintegrating factors in contemplation. That practical "virtuous" procedure which silences the contrary is not allowed him. He must contain dissolution. In "the repellent, the diseased, the degenerate," Mann situates the ethical. Distinguishing between the moral and the virtuous, he finds that the moralist is "exposed to danger" and "resists no evil." As essential components of art he names "the forbidden, the adventurous, scrutiny, and self-abandonment." Defining sin as doubt, he pleads for sinfulness. His work might be called an epistemology of dignity, for he never relinquishes the love of dignity, and never ceases to make the possession of it difficult.

Mann has defined the problematical as the proper sphere of art ("art is the problematical sphere of the human"). In any event, the problematical is the sphere of his own art. Implicit in his work there is a cult of conflict, a deliberate entertaining of moral vacillation, which could not permit a rigid standard of judgments. He has said that the artist must contain his critic, must recognize the validity of contraries. This attitude could make such simple certainty as moral indignation impossible. It would imply exposure to mutually exclusive codes of conduct, diverse modes of behavior. Esthetically, as he himself has said, he finds the unification of this attitude in irony, which merges the sympathetic and antipathetic aspects of any subject. Unlike the satirist, the standpoint of the ironist is shifting—he cannot maintain a steady attack—by the standards of military morale he is treacherous; he belittles the things he lives for, and with melancholy praises what he abandons. He is equally tentative towards *Leben,* life, nature, and *Geist,* spirit, the intellectual order erected above life. The vigor of the pamphleteer is denied him. To the Rooseveltian mind he is corrosive— wherefore that "sympathy with the abyss" which anyone of rigid criteria, of sure distinctions between the admirable and the reprehensible, must feel as corrupting, and which Mann himself, approaching from the attitude of alien criticism, chose to designate as "dissolute." The ironist is essentially impure, even in the chemical sense of purity, since he is divided. He must deprecate his own enthusiasms, and distrust his own resentments. He will unite waveringly, as the components of his attitude, "dignity, repugnance, the problematical art."

To the slogan-minded, the ralliers about a flag, the marchers who convert a simple idea into a simple action, he is an "outsider." Yet he must observe them with nostalgia, he must feel a kind of awe for their fertile assurance, even while remaining on the alert to stifle it with irony each time he discovers it growing in unsuspected quarters within himself. It will continue to rise anew, for man has a tremendous fund of certainty—and one will find only too little of Mann's best ironic manner in his essays written during the war, or will find it without its counterpart of melancholy. Yet I grant that the slogans of his opponents were enough to infuriate any subtle man in his position; the temporary disorientation which turned him away from the ironist and towards the pamphleteer is readily understandable. In *The Magic Mountain,* however, the author has recovered from his citizenship to become again the artist. Castorp descends, not to a specific European war, but to regimentation, to the relief, even the suicidal relief, of the slogan-minded. He, the hero, represents the ultimate betrayal of his author's own most serious message. After years of vacillation he seeks the evasion of a monastery, though in these secular days, when the power of theology has dwindled, the dogmatic certainties for which people are burned will more often be those of patriotism, and the equivalent of churchly penance becomes the advance in numbers under arms.

What Mann does with irony, Gide parallels with experimentalism, with curiosity. He views any set code of values with distrust, because it implies the exclusion of other codes. He speculates as to "what would happen if . . . " He is on guard lest the possible be obscured by the real. In his autobiography we find him, characteristically, considering a whole civilization gratuitously different from our own:

"I thought of writing the imaginary history of a people, a nation, with wars, revolutions, changes of administration, typical happenings. . . . I wanted to invent heroes, sovereigns, statesmen, artists, an artistic tradition, an apocryphal literature, explaining and criticising movements, recounting the evolution of forms, quoting fragments of masterpieces. . . . And all to what purpose? To prove that the history of man could have been different—our habits, morals, customs, tastes, judgments, standards of beauty could have all been different—and yet the humanity of mankind would remain the same."

By recalling *Gulliver's Travels,* we see again how far removed we are from satire. Perhaps, in a much simpler and more lyrical form, Gide did write this book. I refer to *La Symphonie pastorale,* where he speculates upon a world foreign to him, an arbitrary world so far as this author is concerned, the world of blindness. He even contrives to forget his own knowledge, as when his blind heroine, trying to meditate her way into the world of sight, surmises that sunlight must be like the humming of a kettle.

Perhaps one may interpret Gide's "corruption" too literally. I do not believe that his work can be evaluated properly unless we go beyond the subject-matter to the underlying principles. His choice of material even implies a certain obscurantism, assuming a sophistication on the part of the reader whereby the reader would not attempt too slavishly to become the acting disciple of his author's speculations. Surely Gide would be the first to admit that we could not build a very convenient society out of Lafcadios, however admirable they are. I should take the specific events in Gide as hardly more than symbols: their parallel in life would not be the enacting of similar events, but the exercising of the complex state of mind which arises from the contemplation of such events with sympathy. To live a life like the life in Gide's books would be to commit under another form the very kind of exclusion which he abhors—Lafcadio is for the pious, he is not for poisoners and forgers. Nor must one, in placing this author's malice, forget his *Travels in the Congo,* with its protests against the systematic injustice meted out of the Negroes at the hands of the concessionaires.

Irony, novelty, experimentalism, vacillation, the cult of conflict—are not these men trying to make us at home in indecision, are they not trying to humanize the state of doubt? A philosopher has recently written of this new wilderness we now face, a wilderness not of nature, but of social forces. Perhaps there is an evasion, a shirking of responsibility, in becoming certain too quickly, particularly when our certainties involve reversions to an ideology which has the deceptive allurement of tradition. To seek the backing of the past may be as cowardly as to seek the backing of the many, and as flattering to our more trivial needs of conformity. Need people be in haste to rebel against the state of doubt, when doubt has not yet permeated the organs of our body, the processes of our metabolism, the desire for food and companionship, the gratification with sun and water? There is a large reserve of physical unquestioning, and until we find this reserve itself endangered by the humiliation of tentative living and unauthoritative thinking, are we compelled to reach out impetuously for set criteria? Since the body is dogmatic, a generator of belief, society might well be benefited by the corrective of a disintegrating art, which converts each simplicity into a complexity, which ruins the possibility of ready hierarchies, which concerns itself with the problematical, the experimental, and thus by implication works corrosively upon those expansionistic certainties preparing the way for our social cataclysms. An art may be of value purely through preventing a society from becoming too assertively, too hopelessly, itself.

MALCOLM COWLEY

John Dos Passos: The Poet and the World

JOHN DOS PASSOS [1] is in reality two novelists. One of them is a late-Romantic, an individualist, an esthete moving about the world in a portable ivory tower; the other is a collectivist, a radical historian of the class struggle. These two authors have collaborated in all his books, but the first had the larger share in *Three Soldiers* and *Manhattan Transfer*. The second, in his more convincing fashion, has written most of *The 42nd Parallel* and almost all of *1919*. The difference between the late-Romantic and the radical Dos Passos is important not only in his own career: it also helps to explain the recent course of American fiction.

The late-Romantic tendency in his novels goes back to his years in college. After graduating from a good preparatory school, Dos Passos entered Harvard in 1912, at the beginning of a period which was later known as that of the Harvard esthetes. I have described this period elsewhere, in reviewing the poems of E. E. Cummings, but I did not discuss the ideas which underlay its picturesque manifestations, its mixture of incense, patchouli and gin, its erudition displayed before barroom mirrors, its dreams in the Cambridge subway of laurel-crowned Thessalian dancers. The esthetes themselves were not philosophers; they did not seek to define their attitude; but most of them would have subscribed to the following propositions:

That the cultivation and expression of his own sensibility are the only justifiable ends for a poet.

That originality is his principal virtue.

---

[1] *1919*, by John Dos Passos. *The Big Money*, by John Dos Passos. New York: Harcourt, Brace and Company. 1932, 1936.

From *The New Republic*, LXX, pp. 303-305. April 27, 1932, and LXXXVIII, p. 34. September 9, 1936. Reprinted by permission.

That society is hostile, stupid and unmanageable: it is the world of the philistines, from which it is the poet's duty and privilege to remain aloof.

That the poet is always misunderstood by the world. He should, in fact, deliberately make himself misunderstandable, for the greater glory of art.

That he triumphs over the world, at moments, by mystically including it within himself: these are his moments of *ecstasy,* to be provoked by any means in his power—alcohol, drugs, madness or saintliness, venery, suicide.

That art, the undying expression of such moments, exists apart from the world; it is the poet's revenge on society.

That the past has more dignity than the present.

There are a dozen other propositions which might be added to this unwritten manifesto, but the ideas I have listed were those most generally held, and they are sufficient to explain the intellectual atmosphere of the young men who read *The Hill of Dreams,* and argued about St. Thomas in Boston bars, and contributed to *The Harvard Monthly.* The attitude was not confined to one college and one magazine. It was often embodied in *The Dial,* which for some years was almost a postgraduate edition of *The Monthly;* it existed in earlier publications like *The Yellow Book* and *La Revue Blanche;* it has a history, in fact, almost as long as that of the upper middle class under capitalism. For the last half-century it has furnished the intellectual background of poems and essays without number. It would seem to preclude, in its adherents, the objectivity that is generally associated with good fiction; yet the esthetes themselves sometimes wrote novels, as did their predecessors all over the world. Such novels, in fact, are still being published, and favorably criticised: "Mr. Zed has written the absorbing story of a talented musician tortured by the petty atmosphere of the society in which he is forced to live. His wife, whom the author portrays with witty malice, prevents him from breaking away. After an unhappy love affair and the failure of his artistic hopes, he commits suicide. . . ."

Such is the plot forever embroidered in the type of fiction that ought to be known as the art novel. There are two essential characters, two antagonists, the Poet and the World. The Poet— who may also be a painter, a violinist, an inventor, an architect or a Centaur—is generally to be identified with the author of the novel, or at least with the novelist's ideal picture of himself. He tries to assert his individuality in despite of the World, which is stupid, unmanageable and usually victorious. Sometimes the Poet triumphs, but the art novelists seem to realize, as a class, that the sort of hero they describe is likely to be defeated in the sort of society which he must face. This society is rarely presented in accurate terms. So little is it endowed with reality, so great is the author's solicitude for the Poet, that we are surprised to see him vanquished by such a shadowy opponent. It is as if we were watching motion pictures in the dark house of his mind. There are dream pictures, nightmare pictures; at last the walls crash in and the Poet disappears without ever knowing what it was all about; he dies by his own hand, leaving behind him the memory of his ecstatic moments and the bitter story of his failure, now published as a revenge on the world of the philistines.

The art novel has many variations. Often the World is embodied in the Poet's wife, whose social ambitions are the immediate cause of his defeat. Or the wife may be painted in attractive colors: she is married to a mediocre Poet who finally and reluctantly accepts her guidance, abandons his vain struggle for self-expression, and finds that mediocrity has its own consolations, its country clubs and business triumphs—this is the form in which the art novel is offered to readers of *The Saturday Evening Post*. Or again the Poet may be a woman who fights for the same ambitions, under the same difficulties, as her male prototypes. The scene of the struggle may be a town on the Minnesota prairies, an English rectory, an apartment on Washington Square or Beacon Hill; but always the characters are the same; the Poet and the World continue their fatal conflict; the Poet has all our sympathies. And the novelists who use this plot for the thousandth time are precisely those who believe that originality is a writer's chief virtue.

Many are unconscious of this dilemma. The story rises so immediately out of their lives, bursts upon them with such freshness, that they never recognize it as a family tale. Others deliberately face the problem and try to compensate for the staleness of the plot by the originality of their treatment. They experiment with new methods of story-telling—one of which, the stream of consciousness, seems peculiarly fitted to novels of this type. Perhaps they invest their characters with new significance, and rob them of any real significance, by making them symbolic. They adopt new manners, poetic, mystical, learned, witty, allusive or obfuscatory; and often, in token of their original talent, they invent new words and new ways of punctuating simple declarative sentences. Not all their ingenuity is wasted. Sometimes they make valuable discoveries; a few of the art novels, like *The Hill of Dreams,* are among the minor master-pieces of late-Romantic literature; and a very few, like *A Portrait of the Artist as a Young Man,* are masterpieces pure and simple.

Dos Passos' early books are neither masterpieces nor are they pure examples of the art novel. The world was always real to him, painfully real; it was never veiled with mysticism and his characters were rarely symbolic. Yet consider the plot of a novel like *Three Soldiers.* A talented young musician, during the War, finds that his sensibilities are being outraged, his aspirations crushed, by society as embodied in the American army. He deserts after the Armistice and begins to write a great orchestral poem. When the military police come to arrest him, the sheets of music flutter one by one into the spring breeze; and we are made to feel that the destruction of this symphony, this ecstatic song choked off and dispersed on the wind, is the real tragedy of the War. Some years later, in writing *Manhattan Transfer,* Dos Passos seemed to be undertaking a novel of a different type, one which tried to render the color and movement of a whole city; but the book, as it proceeds, becomes the story of Jimmy Herf (the Poet) and Ellen Thatcher (the Poet's wife), and the Poet is once again frustrated by the World: he leaves a Greenwich Village party after a last drink of gin and walks out alone, bareheaded, into the dawn. It is obvious, however, that a new conflict has been superimposed on the old one: the social ideas of the novelist are now at war with his personal emotions, which remain those of *The Dial* and *The Har-*

vard Monthly. Even in *1919,* this second conflict persists, but less acutely; the emotional values themselves are changing, to accord with the ideas; and the book as a whole belongs to a new category.

1919 is distinguished, first of all, by the very size of the project its author has undertaken. A long book in itself, containing 473 pages, it is merely the second chapter, as it were, of a novel which will compare in length with *Ulysses,* perhaps even with *Remembrance of Things Past.* Like the latter, it is a historical novel dealing with the yesterday that still exists in the author's memory. It might almost be called a news novel, since it uses newspaper headlines to suggest the flow of events, and tells the story of its characters in reportorial fashion. But its chief distinction lies in the author's emphasis. He is not recounting the tragedy of bewildered John Smith, the rise of ambitious Mary Jones, the efforts of sensitive Richard Robinson to maintain his ideals against the blundering malice of society. Such episodes recur in this novel, but they are seen in perspective. The real hero of *The 42nd Parallel* and *1919* is society itself, American society as embodied in forty or fifty representative characters who drift along with it, struggle to change its course, or merely to find a secure footing—perhaps they build a raft of wreckage, grow fat on the refuse floating about them; perhaps they go under in some obscure eddy—while always the current sweeps them onward toward new social horizons. In this sense, Dos Passos has written the first American collective novel.

The principal characters are brought forward one at a time; the story of each is told in bare, straightforward prose. Thus, J. Ward Moorehouse, born in Wilmington, Delaware, begins his business career in a real-estate office. He writes songs, marries and divorces a rich woman, works for a newspaper in Pittsburgh—at the end of fifty-seven pages he is a successful public-relations counselor embarked on a campaign to reconcile labor and capital at the expense of labor. Joe and Janey Williams are the children of a tugboat captain from Washington, D. C.; Janey studies shorthand; Joe plays baseball, enlists in the navy, deserts after a brawl and becomes a merchant seaman. Eleanor Stoddard is a poor Chicago girl who works at Marshall Field's; she learns how to speak French to her customers and order waiters about "with a crisp little refined mon-eyed voice." All these characters, first introduced in *The 42nd Parallel,* reappear in *1919,* where they are joined by others: Richard Ellsworth Savage, a Kent School boy who goes to Harvard and writes poetry; Daughter, a warm-hearted flapper from Dallas, Texas; Ben Compton, a spectacled Jew from Brooklyn who becomes a Wobbly. Gradually their careers draw closer together, till finally all of them are caught up in the War.

"This whole goddam war's a gold brick," says Joe Williams. "It ain't on the level, it's crooked from A to Z. No matter how it comes out, fellows like us get the s——y end of the stick, see? Well, what I say is all bets is off . . . every man go to hell in his own way . . . and three strikes is out, see?" Three strikes is out for Joe, when his skull is cracked in a saloon brawl at St. Nazaire, on Armistice night. Daughter is killed in an airplane accident; she provoked it herself in a fit of hysteria after being jilted by Dick Savage—who for his part survives as the shell of a man, all the best of him having died when he decided to join the army and make a career for himself and let his pacifist sentiments go hang. Benny Compton gets ten years in Atlanta prison as a conscientious ob-jector. Everybody in the novel suffers from the War and finds his own way of going to hell—everybody except the people without bowels, the empty people like Eleanor Stoddard and J. Ward Moorehouse, who stuff themselves with the proper sentiments and make the right contacts.

The great events that preceded and followed the Armistice are reflected in the lives of all these people; but Dos Passos has other methods, too, for rendering the sweep of history. In particular he has three technical devices which he uses both to broaden the scope of the novel and to give it a formal unity. The first of these con-sists of what he calls "Newsreels," a combination of newspaper headlines, stock-market reports, official communiqués and words from popular songs. The Newsreels effectively perform their func-tion in the book, that of giving dates and atmospheres, but in them-selves, judged as writing, they are not successful. The second device is a series of nine biographies interspersed through the text. Here are the lives, briefly told, of three middle-class rebels, Jack Reed, Randolph Bourne and Paxton Hibben; of three men of power, Roosevelt, Wilson and J. P. Morgan; and of three proletarian heroes. All these are successful both in themselves and in relation to the novel as a whole; and the passage dealing with the Wobbly martyr, Wesley Everest, is as powerful as anything Dos Passos has ever written.

The "Camera Eye," which is the third device, introduces more complicated standards of judgment. It consists in the memories of another character, presumably the author, who has adventures similar to those of his characters, but describes them in a different style, one which suggests Dos Passos' earlier books. The "Camera Eye" gives us photographs rich in emotional detail:

Ponte Decimo   in Ponte Decimo ambulances were parked in a moonlit square of bleak stone working-people's houses   hoarfrost covered everything   in the little bar the Successful Story Writer taught us to drink cognac and maraschino half and half
havanuzzerone
it turned out he was not writing what he felt he wanted to be writing   What can you tell them at home about the war?   it turned out he was not wanting what he wrote he wanted to be feeling cognac and maraschino   was no longer young   (It made us damn sore we greedy for what we felt we wanted tell 'em all they lied see new towns go to Genoa)   havanuzzerone?   it turned out that he wished he was a naked brown shepherd boy sitting on a hillside playing a flute in the sunlight

Exactly the same episode, so it happens, is described in Dos Passos' other manner, his prose manner, during the course of a chapter dealing with Dick Savage:

That night they parked the convoy in the main square of a godforsaken little burg on the outskirts of Genoa. They went with Sheldrake to have a drink in a bar and found themselves drinking with the Saturday Evening Post correspondent, who soon began to get tight and to say how he envied them their good looks and their sanguine youth and idealism. Steve picked him up about everything and argued bitterly that youth was the lousiest time in your life, and that he ought to be goddam glad he was forty years old and able to write about the war instead of fighting in it.

The relative merit of these two passages, as writing, is not an important question. The first is a good enough piece of impressionism, with undertones of E. E. Cummings and Gertrude Stein. The style of the second passage, except for a certain conversational quality, is almost colorless; it happens to be the most effective way of recording a particular series of words and actions; it aspires to no other virtue. The first passage might add something to a book in which, the plot being hackneyed or inconsequential, the emphasis had to be placed on the writing, but *1919* is not a novel of that sort. Again, the Camera Eye may justify itself in the next volume of this trilogy—or tetralogy—by assuming a closer relation to the story and binding together the different groups of characters; but in that case, I hope the style of it will change. So far it has been an element of disunity, a survival of the art novel in the midst of a different type of writing, and one in which Dos Passos excels.

He is, indeed, one of the few writers in whose case an equation can accurately and easily be drawn between social beliefs and artistic accomplishments. When he writes individualistically, with backward glances toward Imagism, Vorticism and the Insurrection of the Word, his prose is sentimental and without real distinction. When he writes as a social rebel, he writes not flawlessly by any means, but with conviction, power and a sense of depth, of striking through surfaces to the real forces beneath them. This last book, in which his political ideas have given shape to his emotions, and only the Camera Eye remains as a vestige of his earlier attitude, is not only the best of all his novels; it is, I believe, a landmark in American fiction.

II

Four years ago in reviewing *1919,* the second volume of John Dos Passos' trilogy, I tried to define two types of fiction that have been especially prominent since the War. An *art novel,* I said, was one that dealt with the opposition between a creatively gifted individual and the community surrounding him—in brief, between the Poet and the World. Usually in books of this type the Poet gets all the attention; he is described admiringly, tenderly, and yet we learn that he is nagged and broken and often, in the end, driven to suicide by an implacably stupid World. Dos Passos' earlier novels had applied this formula, but *The 42nd Parallel* and *1919* belonged to a second category: they were *collective novels,* whose real hero was American society at large, and this fact helped to explain their greater breadth and vigor. I added, however, that certain elements in these later books—and notably the autobiographical passages called the "Camera Eye"—suggested the art novel and therefore seemed out of place.

But after reviewing *The Big Money* and rereading the trilogy as a whole, it seems to me that this judgment has to be partly revised. I no longer believe that the art novel is a "bad" type of fiction (though the philosophy behind it is a bad philosophy for our times), nor do I believe that the collective novel is necessarily a "good" type (though it has advantages for writers trying to present our period of crisis). With more and more collective novels published every year, it is beginning to be obvious that the form in itself does not solve the writer's problems. Indeed, it raises new problems and creates new disadvantages. The collective novelist is tempted to overemphasize the blindness and impotence of individuals caught in the rip tides of history. He is obliged to devote less space to each of his characters, to relate their adventures more hastily, with the result that he always seems to be approaching them from the outside. I can see now that the Camera Eye is a device adopted by Dos Passos in order to supply the "inwardness" that is lacking in his general narrative.

I can see too that although the device is borrowed from the art novel—and indeed is a series of interior monologues resembling parts of Joyce's *Ulysses*—it is not in the least alien to the general plan of the trilogy. For the truth is that the art novel and the collective novel as conceived by Dos Passos are not in fundamental opposition: they are like the two sides of a coin. In the art novel, the emphasis is on the individual, in the collective novel it is on society as a whole; but in both we get the impression that society is stupid and all-powerful and fundamentally evil. Individuals ought to oppose it, but if they do so they are doomed. If, on the other hand, they reconcile themselves with society and try to get ahead in it, then they are damned forever, damned to be empty, shrill, destructive insects like Dick Savage and Eleanor Stoddard and J. Ward Moorehouse.

In an earlier novel, *Manhattan Transfer,* there is a paragraph that states one of Dos Passos' basic perceptions. Ellen Herf, having divorced the hero, decides to marry a rich politician whom she does not love:

Through dinner she felt a gradual icy coldness stealing through her like novocaine. She had made up her mind. It seemed as if she had set the photograph of herself in her own place, forever frozen into a single gesture. . . . Everything about her seemed to be growing hard and enameled, the air bluestreaked with cigarette smoke was turning to glass.

She had made up her mind. . . . Sometimes in reading Dos Passos it seems that not the nature of the decision but the mere fact of having reached it is the unforgivable offense. Dick Savage the ambulance driver decided not to be a pacifist, not to escape into neutral Spain, and from that moment he is forever frozen into a single gesture of selfishness and dissipation. Don Stevens the radical newspaper correspondent decides to be a good Communist, to obey party orders, and immediately he is stricken with the same paralysis of the heart. We have come a long way from the strong-willed heroes of the early nineteenth century—the English heroes, sons of Dick Whittington, who admired the world of their day and climbed to the top of it implacably; the French heroes like Julien Sorel and Rastignac and Monte Cristo who despised their world and yet learned how to press its buttons and pull its levers. To Dos Passos the world seems so vicious that any compromise with its standards turns a hero into a villain. The only characters he seems to like instinctively are those who know they are beaten, but still grit their teeth and try to hold on. That is the story of

Jimmy Herf in *Manhattan Transfer;* to some extent it is also the
story of Mary French and her father and Joe Askew, almost the
only admirable characters in *The Big Money*. And the same
lesson of dogged, courageous impotence is pointed by the Camera
Eye, especially in the admirable passage where the author remembers the execution of Sacco and Vanzetti:

America our nation has been beaten by strangers who have turned
our language inside out who have taken the clean words our fathers
spoke and made them slimy and foul
    their hired men sit on the judge's bench they sit back with their
feet on the tables under the dome of the State House they are ignorant
of our beliefs they have the dollars the guns the armed forces the
power-plants . . .
    all right we are two nations

"The hired men with guns stand ready to shoot," he says in
another passage, this one dealing with his visit to the striking
miners in Kentucky. "We have only words against POWER SUPER-
POWER." And these words that serve as our only weapons against
the machine guns and tear gas of the invaders, these words of
the vanquished nation are only that America in developing from
pioneer democracy into monopoly capitalism has followed a road
that leads toward sterility and slavery. Our world is evil, and yet
we are powerless to change or direct it. The sensitive individual
should cling to his own standards, and yet he is certain to go under.
Thus, the final message of Dos Passos' three collective novels is
similar to that of his earlier novels dealing with maladjusted artists.
Thus, for all the vigor of *1919* and *The Big Money*, they leave us
wondering whether the author hasn't overstated his case. For all
their scope and richness, they fail to express one side of contemporary life—the will to struggle ahead, the comradeship in struggle,
the consciousness of new men and new forces continually rising.
Although we may be for the moment a beaten nation, the fight
is not over.

Ernest Hemingway: *A Farewell to Spain*

JUST why did Ernest Hemingway [1] write a book on bull-fighting?
It is, make no mistake, a good book on bull-fighting, full of technical writing as accurate as anything printed in Spanish newspapers
like *El Sol* or *A.B.C.* and general information presented more
vividly and completely than ever before in Spanish or English.
Hemingway writes for those who have seen their first bull-fight,
or shortly intend to see it, or are wondering whether to do so if
they ever visit Spain. He tells them what, where, when, how—
the seats to buy, the buses or trains to take, the things to watch
for and which of them to applaud, which to salute with a volley
of oranges, empty bottles and dead fish. He tells how the bulls
are bred and tested, how the matadors are trained, glorified and,
in the end, killed off like bulls. He illustrates the text with dozens
of good photographs. In appendices, he gives further information, the dates of the principal *corridas* in Spain, Mexico and Peru,
the reactions of typical Anglo-Saxons and the achievements of
Sidney Franklin the one American matador. Everything is there,
even a store of pathetic or hilarious stories to read during dull moments of the fight, if there be any. In a word, he has written a
Baedeker of bulls, an admirable volume, but—

Being a good artist, he does a good job, never faking, skimping
or pretending. He often talks about himself, but meanwhile keeps
his eye on the thing outside, the object to be portrayed; by force
of prolonged attention, he makes the object larger than life, fills
it with all his knowledge and feeling, with himself. His book

[1] *Death in the Afternoon,* by Ernest Hemingway. New York: Charles
Scribner's Sons. 1932.

From *The New Republic,* LXXIII, pp. 76-7. November 30, 1932. Reprinted by permission.

about bull-fighting thus becomes something more, a book about sport in general and, since this particular sport is really an art, a book about artistic appreciation and literary criticism, yes, and the art of living, of drinking, of dying, of loving the Spanish land. But all this being said—

Like every good artist, Hemingway employs a double process of selection and diversification, of contraction and expansion. He says: "Let those who want to save the world if you can get to see it clear and as a whole." Writing in Anglo-Saxon words of one syllable he is sometimes more difficult than Whitehead or Paul Valéry, but what he means in this case is made clear enough by the addition of two more monosyllables and a comma. Let those who want to do so save the world, if *you* can get to see it clear and as a whole. Then, he continues, "Any part you make will represent the whole if it's made truly." This book, being truly made, represents in its own fashion the whole of life. But all this being said, one must add that the whole it represents is discolored and distorted by the point of view; that the book is full of self-conscious cruelty, bravado, pity and, especially when dying horses are concerned, a sort of uneasiness that ends by communicating itself to the reader. *Death in the Afternoon* is a less important book than *A Farewell to Arms;* its style is often labored and sometimes flowery (and isn't rendered any less so by Hemingway's apologies for fine writing; apologies never help); its best descriptions of bull-fights are less moving than the briefer description in *The Sun Also Rises.* For three years, in the midst of a world more tumultuous and exciting than any bull-fight, Hemingway has been writing and repolishing this book. Why did he choose this particular subject, this part to represent the whole?

The answer carries us back fifteen years. During the War, Hemingway served on the Italian front, first as an ambulance driver, later in the shock troops, the Arditi; he was seriously wounded and received two medals. The War, to judge from his books, has been the central experience in his career; he shows the effects of it more completely than any other American novelist. In an article recently printed in *The New Republic,* I tried to describe these effects in their relation to the writers of Hemingway's generation, which is also mine, reader, and possibly your own. I said that the War uprooted us, cut us off from our own class and country; that it taught us to assume what I called a spectatorial attitude toward life in general; that it encouraged us to write once more about old themes, simple themes like love and death; and, though I did not emphasize the point, that it gave us a sense of self-pity and self-esteem, a bitter aloofness in the midst of armies. The War, I said, "infected us with the slow poison of irresponsibility and unconcern for the future—the poison of travel, too . . . and the poison of danger, excitement, that made our old life intolerable. Then, as suddenly as it began for us, the War ended"—leaving behind it desires and habits which were difficult to satisfy in a world at peace.

Bull-fighting perhaps could serve as an emotional substitute for war. It provided everything, travel, excitement, crowds like armies watching the spectacle of danger. Hemingway says on the second page of his new book, "The only place where you could see life and death, *i.e.,* violent death now that the wars were over, was in the bull ring and I wanted very much to go to Spain where I could study it." His motives were not merely emotional; he was "trying to learn to write, commencing with the simplest things," and bull-fighting was an ideal subject; it dealt with fundamentals; apparently it was independent of morality, of social implications, of any connection with politics. "So I went to Spain to see bull-fights and try to write about them for myself. . . . It might be good to have a book about bull-fighting in English and a serious book on such an unmoral subject may have some value."

But the book when he came to write it ten years later disproved a good many of the ideas which he carried with him into Spain. There are contradictions between Hemingway's ideas and the ideas suggested to readers by his narrative. To give an obvious example, *Death in the Afternoon* is not at all an unmoral book, nor does it treat bull-fighting as an unmoral subject. If Hemingway praises the performance of a great matador, almost all his adjectives are rich in moral connotations: they are words like true, emotional, not tricked, pure, brave, honest, noble, candid, honorable, sincere. Other matadors are not merely inartistic: they are low, false, vulgar, cowardly; they are even "cynical."

A second contradiction is more important. "All art," he says, "is only done by the individual. The individual is all you ever have." But almost from beginning to end, *Death in the Afternoon* is a refutation of this idea. It is true that the art of the matador, the great individual, provides the "moment of truth" which is the climax of a good bull-fight, but Hemingway makes it clear that the matador's performance would be impossible without the collaboration of nameless people, dozens of them, hundreds, thousands, in circles gradually widening till they include almost a whole nation and a culture extending for centuries into the past. The matador, to begin with, must depend on the work of his own team, his *cuadrilla,* which is charged with the function of conducting the bull through the first two stages of the fight, of regulating his speed and carriage, of preparing him for the "moment of truth" when the sword goes in between the shoulder blades and bull and matador are for the moment one. But the bull, too, must play his part; he must be a brave, "candid" bull of a type that can be raised only by breeders of knowledge and integrity, encouraged by audiences which howl at the sight of inferior animals. The audience, moreover, must appreciate the finer points of the art, must know when to throw small dead animals of all sorts, including fish; it must hold a certain attitude toward bravery and death; it must, in short, be the sort of audience that exists only in Castille, Navarre, Andalusia and perhaps in Mexico City. The government, finally, must grant at the very least an intelligent toleration if the art of bull-fighting is to survive. The government might easily abolish it, not by jailing the matadors, but simply by seizing the ranches where bulls are raised and sending the animals to the slaughterhouse. As for the bull-fighters themselves, they grow up unencouraged, "having a natural talent as acrobats or jockeys or even writers have, and none of them are irreplaceable . . ." And so the author has described a complete circle. He began by saying that the individual, in art, is all you ever have; he ends by deciding that the individual, even the greatest matador, is replaceable and nonessential.

Hemingway is a master at not drawing implications. In this respect as in others, it is interesting to compare *Death in the Afternoon* with *Les Bestiaires,* a novel about bull-fighting written by a Frenchman of the same age. Henry de Montherlant sees implications everywhere. The modern *corrida de toros* implies the ancient sacrifice of a white bull to Mithra, which in turn leads him to consider the beauties of ritual, the mysteries of sacrifice, the glories of tradition, Royalism, Catholicism, patriotic ecstasy, till shortly the bulls, the author and his readers together are lost in a haze of emotion. Montherlant is inferior to Hemingway in hardness, honesty, freshness, keen perception, and yet in a sense I think he is justified. Bull-fighting really does imply a certain attitude toward life, a willingness to accept things as they are, bad as they are, and to recompense oneself by regarding them as a picturesque tragedy. Bull-fighting does, I think, imply an aristocracy, an established Church, a proletariat resigned to suffering pain in return for the privilege of seeing pain inflicted on others, and a rabble of gladiators, bootlickers and whores; but I am just as glad that Hemingway does not consciously draw these implications.

I don't mean to say that the book is without political meanings or contradictions. Hemingway detested the dictator Primo de Rivera—for many reasons, probably, but he mentions only one: Primo insisted on protecting the horses with belly-pads and thereby spoiled one part of the *corrida.* Hemingway hates policemen. Hemingway had many friends among the republican politicians when they were being hunted through the Pyrenees, but now they have come into power he is beginning to detest them also: he suspects them of wishing to abolish bull-fights "so that they will have no intellectual embarrassments at being different from their European colleagues when they meet at the League of Nations." Hemingway is disturbed by the peasant jacquerie in Andalusia, which is threatening the bull-breeding ranches, but at the same time he feels an instinctive friendship toward the peasants. I think he realizes the possibility that the Spanish people themselves, and not their government, might put an end to the bull-fight, replacing it by sports and arts more appropriate to a revolutionary society. On this matter, however, he takes no stand. To do so would force him to think about the present and the future, and he has fallen into the habit of writing with his eyes turned backwards.

This habit, revealed engagingly in all his books, is now becoming a vice. During the War, he dreamed about his boyhood in Michigan, where trout lay thickly in the cool streams in July. "One year they had cut the hemlock woods . . . You could not go back"—but you could write about it nostalgically; and later, in Paris and Spain, you could write about the brave days of the War; and still later, in Key West, you could write about Madrid and Pamplona and the bull-fights, always with an elegiac note, a tenderness for things past and never to be recaptured. All through the present book, but especially in the last chapter, one finds this note repeated, this regret for "the one year everyone drank so much and no one was nasty. There really was such a year." "Make all that come true again," he cries. But, "Pamplona is changed . . . Rafael says things are very changed and he won't go to Pamplona any more . . . Pamplona is changed, of course, but not so much as we are older." Always there is this grief for something that has died within us, for a state of security or felicity existing in youth or in the mind. "We will never ride back from Toledo in the dark, washing the dust out with Fundador, nor will there be that week of what happened in the night of that July in Madrid." It is all very brave, hard-boiled and wistful, but there are other chords for Hemingway to strike.

In a sense, every book he has written has been an elegy. He has given us his farewell to Michigan, to Montparnasse, his *Farewell to Arms;* his new book is a sort of elegy to Spain and vanished youth and the brave days of Belmonte and Maera. Hemingway's talent is great enough to justify us in making demands on it. Will he ever give us, I wonder, his farewell to farewells?

HORACE GREGORY

D. H. Lawrence: The Posthumous Reputation

I SHALL live just as blithely, unbought and unsold," wrote D. H. Lawrence in 1925. And in this remark there is a note of warning that describes the curious nature of his survival during the half dozen years following his death. Perhaps none of the earlier objections to his work has been removed since 1930, yet his influence has endured in the kind of fame that Matthew Arnold perceived in Shelley's reputation which was both legend and literature and both "ideal" and "ridiculous." Much of his ardent pamphleteering which gave his latter years the semblance of vivid, inexhaustible energy is now outmoded. And nothing seems to have grown so clearly out of fashion in a few short years than Lawrence's specific lectures on sex and obscenity. Today they seem to have gone to the same place reserved in memory for the events of early postwar Europe and America. Yet even in Lawrence's most perishable writing the character of his influence remains.

However, where Lawrence is reread, whether in scattered posthumous papers, or in the poems, short stories, or in the novels, it is the speaking voice that is heard clearest and remembered. We then recall Lawrence's letters, which seem always to renew at each date line a briefly interrupted conversation and with them we remember Mr. David Garnett's little sketches of how he worked: writing as he cooked his meals or sat in one corner of a room while others talked, writing as he unpacked boxes and suitcases, writing almost as he moved and breathed, as though the traveling of his hand across paper were the very reflex of his being. Surely this prodigality was "art for my sake" and was the visible power of the thing he called his "demon," which is to say that much of

From an essay to appear in the forthcoming volume *Makers and Ancestors* (Covici, Friede. 1937). Printed by permission.

it was scarcely art at all. Artfulness was sometimes deftly concealed within the larger rhythm of conversation; and sometimes his "demon" was called upon to gratify an urgently explicit demand of form: these moments are identified with the writing of *Sons and Lovers* as well as the writing of a half dozen poems and three or four short stories, but in the rest of everything he wrote the more flexible rule of "art for my sake" was applied and satisfied.

Lawrence, of course, was by no means unaware of what was happening; he had read his critics and matched his wit with theirs:

For me, give me a little splendour, and I'll leave perfection to the small fry . . . Ugh, Mr. Muir, think how horrible for us all, if I were perfect! or even if I had "perfect" gifts! Isn't splendour enough for you, Mr. Muir? Or do you find the peacock more "perfect" when he is moulting and has lost his tail, and therefore isn't so exaggerated, but is more "down to normal"?—For "perfection" is only one of "the normal" and the "average" in modern thought.

How well he knew that the image of the peacock's tail would fill the reader's eye; and there in the image itself, he had uncovered a fragment of the "splendor" he had sought, and with an eloquent gesture, passed it over to the reader. It was as though he had been saying: Mr. Muir has given me bread and I give you cake. My transformation of Mr. Muir's gift, dear reader, is your reward for reading me. This answer was always Lawrence's reply to authority, whether the authority was the Evangelist, preaching from a Nottinghamshire pulpit, or Roman law concealed within the new laws of the Fascisti, whether it was the British censor or Mr. Muir. But he was always least fortunate whenever he attempted to answer that authority directly: his ingenuity lay in the art of improvised distraction. And in distracted argument he was never more successful than in his reply to Mr. Muir.

With Lawrence's rejection of the average man came his distrust of the society around him: "Only the people we don't meet are the 'real' people," he wrote in "Jimmy and the Desperate Woman" —and his "real" people were "the simple, genuine, direct, spontaneous, unspoilt souls," which, of course, were not to be found among the people Lawrence saw on city streets, not in "London, New York, Paris," for "in the bursten cities, the dead tread heavily through the muddy air," and in each face he saw the same stigmata Blake had witnessed, "marks of weakness, marks of woe." These were his average, "normal" people, branded by service in the World War like Captain Herbertson in *Aaron's Rod,* mutilated by war and sanctified by bourgeois wealth like Chatterley, malformed by ignorance and poverty like the Nottinghamshire miner, or tricked and defeated like the American Indian, "Born with a caul, a black membrane over the face." And as Lawrence traveled he saw the same disease spread over half the earth—and he was not to be identified with any of that kind, the meek or humble or the dead. Though the physical resemblance to Lawrence's speaking voice may be traced throughout his novels, through Paul Morel, Lilly of *Aaron's Rod* or Mellors of *Lady Chatterley's Lover,* he was happiest in another kind of personality; the image of the bird was best: the mythical phoenix, the peacock, or the Tuscan nightingale. To defend the nightingale (as well as himself) against the "plaintive anthem" of John Keats' ode, he wrote:

How astonished the nightingale would be if he could be made to realize what sort of answer the poet was answering his song. He would fall off the bough with amazement.

Because a nightingale, when you answer him back, only shouts and sings louder. Suppose a few other nightingales pipe up in the neighboring bushes—as they always do. Then the blue-white sparks of sound go dazzling up to heaven. And suppose you, mere mortal, happen to be sitting on the shady bank having an altercation with the mistress of your heart, hammer and tongs, then the chief nightingale swells and goes at it like Caruso in the Third Act—simply a brilliant, bursting frenzy of music, singing you down, till you simply can't hear yourself speak to quarrel.

Of course the nightingale was the very thing Lawrence wished himself to be, the thing apart from the quarreling couple on the shady bank and his "art for my sake" had for its model the work of a creature who

. . . sings with a ringing, pinching vividness and a pristine asser-
tiveness that makes a mere man stand still. A kind of brilliant calling and interweaving of glittering exclamation such as must have been
heard on the first day of creation.

This was the splendor that was Lawrence's great concern, the
"bursting frenzy of music" that emanated from a source within
the body, and was itself the body, the physical being of a living
creature. The lack of that physical force was his definition of
modern tragedy, and it was the same emptiness he had witnessed
in the lives of the civilized people who surrounded him. In that
self-pitying, sad, silent company he had seen the image of Paul
Morel, his early self of *Sons and Lovers*.

. . . left in the end naked of everything, with the drift toward death
. . . It's the tragedy of thousands of young men in England.

But Lawrence's instructions to live the splendid life always had
the tendency to oversimplify the cure for complex (and human)
silences and fears. They were all too much like telling friends
and neighbors to be natural, to go be a *man*. His work had all
the skill and all the confident lack of knowledge of a man who
had carefully trained himself to conduct an orchestra by ear.
Throughout Lawrence's verse and prose a dominant rhythm persists above loose phrasing and verbal monotony; his ear had been
trained to catch the idiomatic inflection of English speech, avoiding always the outmoded rhythms of literary usage. In this respect his work shares the vitality of Whitman's verse and Melville's prose, and like them it contains the same self-taught art that
controlled its imagery.

Even the most casual reader of Lawrence will soon become aware
of how deliberately he avoided the urban image and how through
prose and verse there is a literal predominance of "birds, beast and
flowers." And as their number increases, how tropical they seem,
and we remember that his need for physical well-being followed
the hot course of the sun. But it is characteristic of Lawrence's
imagery that its action remains suspended in utter darkness or
in the full flood light of noon; and though it is frequently breath-

ing and alive, it seldom extends its force to an actual climax. How many of his images start bravely and end in helplessness, as though they could not carry the burden of their swelling heat and color to move elsewhere. And this same helplessness enters the majority of his many poems, all incomplete, all lacking in the distinction of a verb to give them motion and finality. How many of his novels end with the promise of a life beyond them yet to be fulfilled in the next novel, perhaps, but for the moment still unwritten. Only in *Sons and Lovers,* and in a few of the short stories do we find a definite space of time and action brought to an ultimate conclusion—only in these and in three or four of the *Last Poems.* The rest of his work leans heavily into the future, as though the next page .o be written would complete the large design of which his fragments were pencil sketches from the living model.

I suspect that this very characteristic of incompleted action is responsible for the air of expectancy which welcomed the publication of each posthumous volume of letters, stories, poems, essays or incidental papers. Lawrence in death seemed still in flight around the globe and it has been difficult to think of him as a middle-aged writer dying nerveless and exhausted in a sun-lit room in Southern France. The biographies of Lawrence, his self-imposed exile from England, the disorder among camp-followers of the Lawrence household may be used as sources for a facile parallel to Shelley's death and the legends which grew out of it. But how eagerly Lawrence would have hated Shelley and would have cheerfully denied all he had written, and did in fact answer his "Skylark" in the same language in which he replied to Keats' nightingale:

"Hail to thee, blithe Spirit!—bird thou never wert." Why should he insist on the bodilessness of beauty when we cannot know of any save embodied beauty? Who would' wish that the skylark were not a bird, but a spirit? If the whistling skylark were a spirit, then we should all wish to be spirits. Which were impious and flippant.

We need not stop to consider the flaws in Lawrence's heavy-footed questioning, but in this reply there is implied an entire century's increased distrust of Platonic reasoning. Between Shelley and Lawrence arose the shadow of Nietzsche's Zarathustra, who said as he descended from the mountain:

To blaspheme the earth is now the dreadfulest sin. . . . Man is a rope stretched between the animal and the Superman. . . . Aye, for the game of creating, my brethren, there is needed a holy Yea unto Life. . . .

Lawrence's great error, of course, was to echo the sound of Zarathustra's warning without clear knowledge of the myth from which Nietzsche's hero sprang, and lacking this knowledge he could not stride into another world that lay beyond good and evil. The literary heritage of the early nineteenth century had come down to him by way of Herman Melville and Walt Whitman. As he entered the latter phases of his career, traces of Whitman's eloquence spread throughout his writing, yet he was always to reject Whitman's democracy with uneasy violence. Whatever was to remain revolutionary in Lawrence's thinking was something that resembled philosophic anarchy. In a recently discovered paper, "Democracy" in the posthumous volume *Phoenix,* written in 1923, he used Whitman as text, in praise and blame, to reiterate his distrust of a bourgeois democracy and its possession of property. His rejection of authority included a consistent denial of Marx as well as Plato, of Aquinas as well as Judaism and all law of church and state.

Yet in this wide negation of authority lies one secret of his influence with a younger generation of post-War writers. To deny bourgeois authority and to leave England was to break down the barriers of class and national prejudice that had seemed impassable before 1918, or rather, had remained unbroken for nearly a hundred years. He had survived many forms of British bourgeois hostility which brought with them the lack of a large reading public, persecution from the War office, and the action of the British censor as well as charges of religious heresy. And there was ample evidence to convict him on any or all of these charges of public disfavor. His reply was that he alone remained alive in a dead world, a world in which the memory of its millions killed in a World War had spread the shadow of mass murder as well as lonely suicide over the furthest reaches of Anglo-Saxon civilization. And when his own death came, he made his own choice in preparation for it, convincing himself and those who read him that he had chosen the path of stilled and dark waters into oblivion.

Almost with his last breath he was to write, "For man the vast marvel is to be alive. For man, as for flower, and beast and bird . . ." and this reassurance in the goodness of physical being from someone whose self-taught and imperfect gifts alone sustained his eloquence, created a hero for a generation that feared the stillness of its own despair. It is not without perception that T. S. Eliot as well as others have read the warning of disease in Lawrence's heresies of behavior and craftsmanship. We know only too well his many failures, and among them we learn his refusal to abide by the truth of his observation in writing a brilliant analysis of Baron Corvo's *Hadrian the Seventh:* "A man must keep his earnestness nimble to escape ridicule." Yet his insight was never more profound nor more direct than when he associated Whitman with his own name, for it is through the work of Lawrence that the younger men in the present generation of British writers have learned the actual significance of Whitman's enduring reputation. Like Whitman, Lawrence left behind him no model of technique that would serve to crystallize the style of prose or poetry in those who followed him; like Whitman Lawrence's influence as a teacher was irrevocably bad; surely his literal imitators, like Horace Traubel's discipleship of Whitman, illustrate the master's flaws until their burlesque becomes so clear that pity or contempt deflects all criticism. Such imitation is the pathetic attempt to reproduce the absence of form, as though the devoted student had amputated his arm to stimulate the sensation of his master's missing hand. Lawrence's real strength, like his invisible presence living "blithely, unbought and unsold," is explicit only in the combined force of his legend with a small selection from his prolific work of less than twenty years, and from these fragments we learn again how vividly he revived the memory of the maker in English literature, restoring the moment of vision and insight as a mark of genius in English prose and poetry.

The Proletarian Poet

Curiosity," says Day Lewis,[1] "is, I suppose, the most dangerous and the most vital of all human virtues." Perhaps Day Lewis is not far wrong; perhaps for the moment we can agree that he is right, that curiosity is a good if not too serious human motive, and that he has braced himself upright to answer questions. Granting this, I prefer to think that he has animated his prose and verse by the creation of a character, a composite portrait of himself and others—the new English poet, a young man who has assumed the duty of re-instructing a bitter, faithless, rotting social organism, a post-War world. The character is, of course, still incomplete; he is a "Work In Progress," fated, like all of us, to grow old, perhaps to die in the next war, or worst of all, to exist within a kind of living death that too often surrounds the poet as he enters middle age—the fate of excellent talkers like Coleridge—or a fate in which the obsession of grandeur covered Wordsworth like a pall.

Given such a poet who is not speaking for himself alone, but for himself as well as others, the present book is further proof of generous intentions. The essay, "Revolution in Writing," is a sequel to the earlier prose, "A Hope for Poetry"; the poem, "A Time to Dance," extends the purpose of "The Magnetic Mountain," and the play, a choral ballet not intended for the stage, follows the precedent of Auden's "Paid on Both Sides," which was an experiment in dramatic form, neither play nor poem, but a charade.

[1] *A Time to Dance,* by C. Day Lewis. Random House. 1935.

From *The Partisan Review*, III, pp. 27-28. May, 1936. Reprinted by permission.

If we agree that we are listening to the voice of a spokesman for Day Lewis (rather than Day Lewis himself, or Spender, or Auden) we can then hear what he has to say with reasonable detachment. His ultimate desires are well in view: in the near future rises the hope of a new poetic myth, a myth which includes the use of machine imagery (tractor and automobile, radio and airplane) and at the end of its progress there is a vision of a classless-society. Toward this end the poet is drawn as surely as though he were attracted by the invisible forces of electromagnetism. Among his desires (though these may be retarded by indecision, by his physical existence within a hostile society) is the hope of retaining a sound body and clean mind. He is conscious of writing revolutionary literature, yet he seems to force his will toward communism; and though the germ of his revolutionary desire is genuine, its hothouse growth is less actual than the germ itself.

Because the spokesman is near the center of controversy in contemporary literature, we have much to learn from him. His merits, his personal sacrifices are so obvious that his gestures are scarcely short of the heroic; but such a poet is not likely to know his limitations: he is likely to mistake the future as accomplished fact, to prove, against his will, that his intellect has a swifter pace than his emotions. That is why, I think, Day Lewis' abilities remain potentials of a poetic imagination (read the shorter lyrics in the present volume); that is why I believe his haste endangers his more ambitious poems, which at their worst, are merely thin and repetitious.

"The Revolution in Literature" originated as a speech by radio; and it was written to be heard by the English middle-class professionals: the college instructor, the young writer who has not read Marx, young advertising men, young journalists—and even young businessmen who have wearied of the pose of seeming cynical. To the American communist, this speech may seem naïve or dangerously Platonic. He is likely to forget that Day Lewis' spokesman has the kind of Liberal heritage that permits free speech in Hyde Park on Sunday afternoons. It is a heritage that can allow for contradictions, like "His Majesty's Communist Government," a phrase that must sound strange to all Americans. It explains, I think, Day Lewis' happy definition of politics (one that seems unreal on this side of the Atlantic); it is so simple, so plausible: "the science of living together." It seems to come directly from a dictionary of eighteenth-century rationalism; and from that phrase we see a roomful of men talking *reasonably* with one another. When we read: "Where living together has become difficult and painful, the writer turns to the science of living together," the room in which the discussion is taking place seems filled with fresh air and morning light. I wonder what a New York or Chicago politician would think of it, and I wonder how a civil war Dubliner would respond to any definition of that kind. Day Lewis' essay recalls the atmosphere of Shelley's notes and letters; its last statement, "Evolution is the dance, revolutions are the steps," might well have been written by Shelley, had he read Darwin and then studied with his usual diligence *Das Kapital*.

It so happens that Day Lewis is not unwise in stressing the evolutionary elements in dialectical materialism. His English audience will recall almost subconsciously the name of Marx as Darwin's contemporary; they will remember that Marx walked the streets of London and that today one may visit his grave in Hampstead, that sober, not unpleasant Victorian neighborhood of stone-front houses and green back gardens.

The essay, however, tends to over-simplify the entire problem of revolutionary writing; and here one reads such truisms as: "Any good poem, simply because every good poem is a true statement of the poet's feelings, is bound to be of value: it gives us insight into the state of mind of a larger or smaller group of people." One has the unquiet conviction that the spokesman is *talking down* to his audience, assuming as he does so, that all poetry is so widely unread that no one remembers its primary definitions.

I would say that the rôle of spokesman has not been completely fortunate for Day Lewis' welfare, particularly in America, where his prose and verse have been bound together in two single volumes. It makes him appear a shade too eager to explain away difficult passages in his own verse; he is made to seem always on the defensive, hastily writing both prose and verse against the speed of time and change. "Noah and the Waters" is the least successful poem Day Lewis has written in five years. To see the masses of people as a flood rising to wipe clean the ruins of a dead civilization is symbolism with a vengeance—vengeance that is inanimate and inexact to the very edges of pathetic fallacy. One knows only too well what is about to happen, and when the voices from the flood call out, "Waters of the world unite," the worst has happened even beyond our usual expectations. The trouble with the poem is its irrefutable logic, a logic of a kind that entered Victorian poetry and destroyed it; it is too good (and I suspect too simple) to be true.

"A Time to Dance" is a far better poem (though best of all are those short lyrics, "The Conflict" and "In Two Worlds"); here there is airplane flight and satire of the world below; it is not until the latter half of the poem that the lines sag into inept parody and false jazz rhythms. And here at last I am reminded again of Shelley. I am not saying this in dispraise of Shelley's best work or in dispraise of all his political poems, some of which will remain among the best in revolutionary literature. Shelley at his worst, however, stepped out into the thin mid-air of prophecy; his logic was correct, yet the poetry itself had become intangible, unreal. Something of the same defeat seems to endanger Day Lewis's longer poems. It is not enough to say that some of the passages within them are carelessly written, and other passages adequately phrased; the danger lies deeper than that. Poetic logic is the logic of human emotion; should the poet travel too far beyond the range of his experience, his way is lost, his images lose force and his vitality is dissipated. It is better for Day Lewis to remember that he inhabits (as he knows well) two worlds. Let the confidence that he has gained extend his courage in making a further record of:

> The priest asking for silence the soldier asking for trouble:
> the politician for ten per cent; the traitor for a kiss;
> the lover for a steel whip; the teacher for instructions.

NEWTON ARVIN

ndividualism and the American Writer

THE artist, it cannot be too clearly understood," says Arthur Symons in his book on the symbolist movement, "has no more part in society than a monk in domestic life." The dogma of literary individualism has never been phrased more simply or more grotesquely; and, as Mr. Symons belongs to a generation now pretty completely superseded, it is no longer fashionable to say the thing in just these terms, or to appeal to such authority as his for support. But the spirit behind his epigram is a spirit that still operates not only in British but in American letters. Even sentimental estheticism, though the cut of its clothes is no longer in the mode of the nineties, has by no means disappeared; and, on a less fatuous level, the doctrine of irresponsibility—in more forms than one, of course—is virtually the prevailing gospel. The breach between our writers and our society could hardly be wider: one gets a measure of it by trying to imagine a contemporary poet or novelist of distinction occupying the kind of official post—an ambassadorship, a professorship, the editorship of a prosperous magazine or newspaper—which, fifty and sixty years ago, was one of the natural rewards of literary celebrity. This sort of thing is now a joke, and a stale joke at that. Yet there is intrinsically nothing funny in the conception of a writer's rôle in society as responsible to the point of officialdom; and many things are more unlikely than that we shall return to it in the course of events. Meanwhile, and for excellent reasons, the literary life in America is the scene of a sweeping separatism: the typical American writer is as tightly shut up in his own domain, and as jealous of his prerogatives, as one

From *The Nation*, CXXXIII, pp. 391-393. October 14, 1931. By permission of the editors and the author.

of the Free Cities of the late Middle Ages. Is this in the very nature of things, or is it a passing circumstance?

To ask such a question is to go, at once, below or beyond the purely literary terrain. It is to pose the whole problem of individuality and its life history. But it is to pose the problem in a form to which writers neither *as* writers nor as human beings can afford to be indifferent. There is really no more acute, no more concrete, no more pressingly personal a problem, at the moment, than this. Is our familiar individualism, our conception of ourselves as "simple, separate persons," equivalent any longer to the achievement of a sound individuality? "Trust thyself": does every heart still vibrate to that "iron string"? Specifically, can American writers hope to develop fully as individuals while divorcing themselves not only from society as a whole but from any class or group within society? With what group or class, indeed, *can* they ally themselves? Is the alternative to literary individualism the surrender to a merely political movement, or, worse still, to some form of repressive standardization? Are there now no supra-personal purposes with which a writer can affiliate himself?

Our answers to such questions will be really satisfactory only if, in giving them, we are able to look back upon the road we have come on. For the story of American letters is the story of the blossoming, the fruition, and the corruption of exactly the individualism that is now on trial. It is far from being a new thing: it is a many times more than twice-told tale. In its origins it was a fruitful principle because it corresponded to a historical reality, to a historical reality that is now part of our past. In short, American writers have always belonged to the middle class, and not only in the literal sense of being born in it: they have belonged to the middle class spiritually, and their self-reliance, their self-expression, their self-consciousness have expressed the sociological individualism of their class heritage. It is no accident that, emblematically at least, at the very gateway of American literature should stand two autobiographies: no accident that Jonathan Edwards should have written his "Personal Narrative" or Franklin the story of his life.

Nothing was more natural than that Edwards and Franklin should have taken themselves as subjects; between them, they span the whole reach, upward and downward, of the individualist principle; they are the sacred and profane extremes of one spirit— Edwards, with his Calvinistic particularism, his intense introspectiveness, his spiritual egoism; Franklin, with his complete system of self-help, his enlightened careerism, his pragmatic worship of frugality and diligence. Neither man can be imagined in a precapitalist order. Only one essential note in our national chorus remained to be struck, and that was the secessionist note of the frontier; when Fenimore Cooper created the character of Leatherstocking, the embodiment of backwoods resourcefulness, independence, and idiosyncrasy, the ensemble was complete.

Complete, that is, psychologically. In a literary sense, American individualism was not to reach its apogee until the generation which filled in the twenty or thirty years before the Civil War. These years witnessed, from a cultural point of view, the historic culmination of the principle of self-reliance: during these years that principle, because it rationalized the true needs of society, had a genuine spiritual authority. It was a period, in short, when our special form of individualism could really be reconciled with the deeper-lying claims of individuality; when a man could achieve distinction as a person without going much beyond the limits of self-reliance. This is, of course, what accounts for the literary pre-eminence, in the age, of Emerson ("Accept your genius and say what you think"), of Thoreau ("I would rather sit on a pumpkin and have it all to myself than be crowded on a velvet cushion"), and of Whitman ("I will effuse egotism"). In these three men our individualism, on its brighter side, attained its classic meridian. There was of course, even then, a darker side; there were men for whom the gospel of self-help—or the habit of estrangement, which is a form it may always take—proved to be the path toward confusion, morbidity, and a kind of impotence; and Poe, Hawthorne, and Melville, men of the richest endowments, paid a tragic price for sitting on pumpkins and effusing egotism. Their careers suggest that the principle, from the artist's point of view, is at best a precarious one; and that its spiritual fruitfulness is exhausted almost before it is realized.

The sequel of the Civil War demonstrated the exhaustion at least of its youthful energies. The triumph of economic irresponsibility, in the feverish burgeoning of big business after the war, coincided with the corruption of individualism as a cultural motive. Two things happened: on the one hand, the writers of secondary talents watered down and deodorized the old contumacy until it became reconcilable with the mildest heresies and even with a conformity in which neither self-reliance nor self-expression had breathing-space; on the other hand, the writers of genius, incapable of such surrender, went still farther along the path taken by Poe, Hawthorne, and Melville. To turn from Emerson to G. W. Curtis, from Thoreau to John Muir, from Whitman to Burroughs, is to turn, as if in a single life-span, from Moses to Zedekiah. The contrast is instructive enough, yet it is less eloquent than the spectacle offered by the higher careers of Henry James, Mark Twain, and Henry Adams. Hawthorne's theme of estrangement, the Ishmaelite theme that obsessed Melville were driven by Henry James to a formulation still more extreme; and expatriation, the frankest form of desertion, became both his literary munition and his personal fate. With Mark Twain the Fenimore Cooper wheel came full circle: the old, heroic anarchism of the backwoods is travestied, in its decay, by Mark Twain's vacillation between a servile conformity and the puerile philosophy of self-interest outlined in "What Is Man?" ("From his cradle to his grave a man never does a single thing which has any *first and foremost* object but one—to secure peace of mind, spiritual comfort *for himself.*") For Mark Twain the outcome was, not Emerson's and Whitman's "fatalistic optimism," but an equally fatalistic pessimism; and Henry Adams, who had a truer sense of the limits of self-interest, but whose social impotence and personal isolation were still more thoroughgoing, stands very close to Mark Twain as our first consistent preacher of futility.

II

By the turn of the century the old class basis of American literature was rapidly entering upon the cycle of erosion, subsidence, and re-emergence. It was still true that American writers belonged personally to the middle classes, but the old bond between literary expression and 'the middle-class philosophy had been broken once for all; and henceforth there seemed to be only the choice between a loyalism that was the negation of individuality and a repudiation that too generally left its heresiarchs high and dry. For a fresh alignment of a positive sort the time was not yet ripe; and by the second decade of the century we found ourselves in the midst of an individualistic revolt which superficially seemed to appeal to the authority of Emerson, Thoreau, and Whitman, but which, unlike theirs, was radically personal and anti-social. It had been anticipated, a few years before, by the Nietzschean egoism of Jack London and the antinomianism of Dreiser; and it was to mingle the elements of misanthropy, transcendentalism, anarchism, and high aspiration in bewildering proportions. The new individualism ran the whole gamut from the Menckenian-Cabellian praise of aristocracy to Anderson's primitivism and O'Neill's romantic affirmations, from Lewis' exposure of the standardized bourgeois to Van Wyck Brooks' subtle studies in frustration. In the perspective of history, the high colors in which this generation dealt will doubtless show like the hues in the clouds that surround a setting sun. It was the last chapter of one volume, not the first of a new one; and of this essential belatedness the patriarchal gravity, the chilly sagacity of such poets as Robinson and Frost are but convenient measures.

The vitality of that movement was naturally still shorter-lived than the "Emersonian June" itself had been. The hopeless sterility of a pure individualism at this moment in history could hardly be more dramatically demonstrated than by the collapse of the Menckenian boom in our own "reconstruction" after the war. The men who led it, of course, still survive, but they have subsided either into silence or into a bewilderment that masks itself variously; and their juniors, for the most part, have drawn the moral from their experience in either one of two disastrous but natural ways. One group, the heirs of Poe, Hawthorne, and Melville, have retreated, in their despair of finding solid ground on which to build a personal life, to an explicit philosophy of negation; and pitched here and there on the sands of the Waste Land one descries the tents, black as Tamburlaine's on the third day of a siege, of Jeffers and MacLeish, of Krutch and Aiken, of Hemingway and Faulkner. The other group, less honest emotionally, but intellectually more impressive, has taken refuge from the high winds of individualism in the shelter of some archaic code, religious, authoritarian, or sociological: humanism, neo-Thomism, Alexandrianism, royalism, or agrarianism. Both the negativists and the authoritarians betray all the symptoms of corruption: both shine with the phosphorescence of decay; but the latter have at least the logic that goes with positive loyalties.

For the necessary answers to the questions we began with are becoming clearer and clearer to middle-class intellectuals; they have long been clear to our handful of working-class writers. That it is not possible for a writer to develop a rich individuality and remain loyal to an individualist society in its later stages—this was the discovery of the Menckenian generation. All questions of humanitarian sentiment aside, that generation discovered that to cooperate with an inhumane system is to be personally corrupted and demoralized. The experience of the last decade has shown, though the proof was hardly needed, that mere nonconformity leads nowhere but to barrenness. If individuality means anything, as distinguished from individualism, it means the achievement, personally, of a many-sided unity, a rich and complicated integration; and in an individualistic economy it is not possible for anyone, certainly not for a writer, either to develop freely on all sides or to unify his personal life in the only fruitful way—that is, by organizing it with reference to a significant purpose. It is the paradox of individuality that it is meaningless without its social pole: neither the variety nor the centrality that go to make it up can be described except with constant (though of course not exclusive) reference to a group. Now that American writers, consciously or unconsciously, have made their final break with the middle class, it should be obvious that, unless they prefer a bleak or an elegant futility, they can turn in but one direction, to the proletariat. By identifying their interests with the life and needs of that class they can at once enrich and unify their own lives in the one way now historically open to them. Far from being a merely political or sociological affiliation, this joining of forces with the working class is chiefly important, even now, and certainly in the long run, on psychological and cultural grounds. It is a question, for the writer, not of sentiment or quixotism, but of self-preservation. Our literary history is the true argument, and this it would be idle to labor further.

How many things this may mean as time goes on, there is no space to say here; and indeed it would be both presumptuous and irrelevant, in this connection, to undertake to say them. One must grant that the case for a proletarian literature is not always cogently stated or wisely defended—any more than the case against it. One must insist that to adopt the proletarian point of view does not mean, for a novelist, to deal solely with economic conflicts, or, for a poet, to be a voice only for protest, momentous as both things are and *implicit* as they are bound to be. That a truly proletarian literature, for us in America at least, would mean a break with the mood of self-pity, with the cult of romantic separatism, with sickly subjectivism and melodramatic misanthropy—this much is almost too clear to deserve stating. But the duty of the critic is certainly not to file an order for a particular sort of fiction or poetry before the event; his duty is to clarify, as best he can, the circumstances in which fiction and poetry must take shape, and to rationalize their manifestations when they arrive. For the moment the important thing is that American criticism should define its position: in the midst of so much confusion, so much wasted effort, so much hesitation, this will itself be an advance.

ROBERT CANTWELL

No Landmarks

I⊤ is remarkable that of all of Henry James' critical writing, the most widely quoted should be a brief paragraph from the essay on Hawthorne; an incidental observation in a book which was written almost at the beginning of his career and in the first enthusiasm of his exile. When James made a catalogue of the inadequacies of American life, and included in the catalogue such diverse items as a court, a sporting class and personal loyalties, he made a statement which has gotten under the skin of a whole generation of critics, and one which, for that reason, has received a disproportionate attention from his biographers. It has been cited as evidence of his lack of penetration and of that snobbishness so very frequently attributed to him; it has, I think, contributed a good deal to the contemporary popular impression of James, most fully and frankly expressed by Burton Rascoe:

Henry James, a fat, wistful remittance man with a passion for elegance to obscure the affront to his delicacy that was borne in on him by the fact that his grandfather was a highly successful merchant (or man of trade) in Syracuse, New York, and by the hauteur of Boston Back Bay society too flagrantly contemptuous of his origins, shook the dust from a "vulgar" America and removed himself to England, where through a long period he braced English aristocratic society and, in novels, gave a profound psychological significance to the manner in which a duchess accepted a cup of tea from a younger, remote cousin of a son of a man with whom she had had, in the remote past, an irregular affair.

There is a note of impatience in this characterization which suggests that it has other sources than James' writing, and proceeds

From *The Symposium*, IV, pp. 70-84. January, 1933. Reprinted by permission.

from another determination than that of giving an unbiased portrait. I can imagine an individual such as Mr. Rascoe pictures condemning New England for having no court; I cannot, however, by any strain of the imagination, picture him writing *The Aspern Papers* or *The Wings of the Dove*. But in his reference to the significance James gave to the manner in which a cup of tea was passed around, Mr. Rascoe has stated a popular misconception of James' novels, one that seems to be firmly established on a lack of understanding of them and of the circumstances that gave them their peculiar form. The error is a common one. Even Van Wyck Brooks, whose objection and preferences are generally formulated on a higher level, has recently hinted in *The American Spectator* that people who enjoy reading the novels do so because they wish to enter the society pictured in them—which is somewhat like saying that a secret urge to hunt for whales is involved in an appreciation of *Moby Dick*. A heartless confusion of means and ends is apparent in these two views: for both critics emphasize James' symbols rather than the use he put them to.

The paragraph from the essay on Hawthorne is in one respect unusual in the great body of James' critical writing. It is a list of specific social institutions. Except for the inclusion of "personal loyalties" among the absent graces, it is literally true. New England in Hawthorne's time had no court and no sporting class nor any of the other institutions James listed. None had been developed by the time James wrote. The society had, in fact, produced no institutions which were in any sense permanent and which might have provided the novelist with a convenient method of identifying his characters and relating them to their environment. There was nothing like "that vast nursery" of which he later wrote, "that vast nursery of sharp appeals and concrete images which calls itself, *for blest convenience,* London." There were no social symbols generally accepted or widely agreed upon in America as those he mentioned were accepted and agreed upon in England; the institutions that had been developed were, or seemed to James, so unstable, so involved in controversy, as to be useless as points of reference. The process of social change was so accelerated in James' time that to identify individuals in terms of existing institutions seemed as valid as taking bearings by spotting a cloud being borne along in a storm. When he wrote the essay on Hawthorne he had lived through a prolonged economic crisis and through a period of intense social antagonisms—antagonisms which took the form of sectional disputes, uprisings and insurrections, and which reached their climax in a violent and protracted revolution. The way of living, the accepted customs, the economic foundations of a whole social order had been forcibly destroyed in the South, while in the North industrialism was rapidly changing the character of the country and the way of living of most of its inhabitants. In his own lifetime, New York had been so expanded and enlarged, under the pressure of competitive business, as to be almost unrecognizable from year to year.

With this general background, it is not surprising that he expressed his envy of Balzac's monarchical and ecclesiastical order. He could see a kind of order in that society, as he could see a kind of order in the society of Victorian England. But in the America of his time the change was proceeding more rapidly than elsewhere; business was reaching more directly into more kinds of activity, and possessed more power over the community, for the business men who were the agents of change were unrestrained by tradition—or, to phrase it differently, the opposition to them was less securely established.

If he found, in England, the sort of institutions he had pointed out America didn't have, they at least seldom appeared in his fiction. An awareness of social change was too deeply a part of him; it made him hesitate about bringing any reference to anything so perishable as an entrenched belief, or a national custom, or a system of government, or a hierarchy of social values, into anything so precious as his art. Even the material characteristics of the environment weren't solid or substantial enough to have an important place in his writing. He had seen the physical landmarks of a society changing too rapidly in the riot of speculative "growth." So the very buildings, the rooms, the furniture surrounding his characters gradually disappeared after *Washington Square,* and when it became necessary to refer to physical objects, they were characterized, not by the mention of specific features they possessed, but by the mention of intangibles—the glint of light on something, an atmosphere determined by the emotional state of the character through whose eyes the objects were observed. Rooms became timeless, featureless places of meeting, blank Elizabethan stages for indefinite agitations, triumphs and embarrassments. Even more remarkably, the house around which the conflict revolves, in *The Spoils of Poynton,* is described elaborately, with conviction and almost exclusively in terms of its desirability, its beauty, rather than in terms of the features which make it beautiful or desirable.

The material characteristics of the scene were only one aspect of it. Codified beliefs underwent a rapid transformation in time of sweeping social changes. "One had seen, in fiction," he wrote in the preface to *The Turn of the Screw,* "some grand wrong doing, or better still wrong being, imputed, seen it promised and announced as by the hot breath of the Pit—and then, all lamentably, sink to the compass of some particular brutality, some particular immorality, some particular infamy, portrayed: with the result, alas, of the demonstration's falling sadly short." As a prudent artist he attempted to take out a reasonable insurance to protect his own demonstrations from such failure, and it was against the time when other conditions, other matters of "appreciation, speculation, imagination" would influence the reader's judgments, that his works must be insured. For his art was again too precious in his scheme of values to permit his regarding it complacently as having a future value of simple historical interest, its drives and catastrophes reduced to the level of "some particular immorality." There remained a kind of solution, and in working it out James became, in a very special sense, a master of the ambiguous statement, of the elastic definition, of the broad, hospitable abstraction. You could bring to the "perfectly independent and irresponsible little fiction" whatever body of traditional beliefs you happened to possess; it could absorb them; it was equipped, like some wonderfully alert witness on the stand, with "a conscious provision of prompt retort to the sharpest question that may be addressed to it." In *The Turn of the Screw* the method is obvious. "Only make the reader's general vision of evil intense enough, I said to myself . . . and his own experience, his own imagination, his own sympathy . . . and horror . . . will supply him quite sufficiently with all the particulars. Make him *think* the evil, make him think it for himself, and you are released from weak specifications."

There are other indications that James identified the specific with the weak. Both in his fiction and in his critical writing the terms he habitually employed were remarkably broad—words such as life, intensity, experience, form, drama, so inclusive the reader might find in them almost any meaning he desired, precisely as in *The Turn of the Screw* the form of the outrage is dependent upon the reader's prior knowledge rather than upon specific information James gives. He became, more than any other novelist, the analyst and dramatist of the *general*. If the method most clearly stated in the preface to *The Turn of the Screw* is followed through his work, if that story of the "horrific" is compared with *Master Eustace,* *The American* with *The Golden Bowl,* or, in criticism, if the essay on Hawthorne is compared with his prefaces to his own work, there will be noted a steady decline in the margin of specific information presented, and a progressive increase in the abstractions and the generalized observations. He seems to have been conscious of this development in his writing. At least he spoke of "the charm of the dramatic struggle" which (in this case a definition of "propriety" is involved) became "the struggle somehow to fit propriety into a smooth general case which is really all the while bristling and crumbling into fierce particular ones." It may be that on precisely this point such readers as Mr. Rascoe and Mr. Brooks falter and fail, for because of the broad inclusiveness of James' language, his reliance on generalities in both his analysis and his description, the rare specific act darts out of his page with an unnatural vigor.

Similarly, in comment on his own work James employed generalities to the extent that particular reference is sometimes difficult to establish. When he says, for example, of *The Awkward Age,* that it is "precisely a study of one of these curtailed or extended periods of tension and apprehension, an account of the manner in which the resented interference with ancient liberties came in a particular instance to be dealt with," the description adequately characterizes *The Awkward Age,* but it is also applicable, in one sense or another, to almost every novel that has ever been written.

II

The awareness of social change I have attributed to James led him to avoid placing his reliance on a particular system of morality, and led him to identify his characters in other ways than by relating them directly to their environment. "I revelled in the notion," he said, "of the occasion as a thing in itself." If the individual could be located clearly by reference to a social system that was changing rapidly he could be located with reference to those individuals around him, to his immediate situation, in which the fluctuant social order need figure only indirectly, or, to use a Jamesian term, to his "predicament." James described this process of location in terms that suggest another kind of effort:

I remember that . . . I drew on a sheet of paper . . . the neat figure of a circle consisting of a number of small round objects deposed at equal distance about a central object. The central object was my situation, my subject in itself, to which the thing would owe its title, and the small rounds represented so many distinct lamps, as I liked to call them, the function of each of which would be to light, with all due intensity, one of its aspects . . . each of my "lamps" would be the light of a single "social occasion" in the history and intercourse of the characters concerned, and would bring out to the full the latent colour of the scene in question and cause it to illustrate, to the last drop, its bearing on my theme.

The relation of the individual to his predicament was complex. The self-consciousness of James' characters has been frequently noted, and their scrupulous examination of their own motives and conduct, their constant curiosity as to the motives and emotions of those around them, has been variously interpreted. There is however another aspect of this self-consciousness, its *use* in the story as a whole. For as long as the individual—this is more applicable to the middle and later novels than to the early work—remains conscious of himself, he is to that extent *unconscious* of his predicament, unconscious, that is, both of the implications of his acts and of their influence on those about him. The progress within each novel is toward the individual's greater understanding of the predicament and, simultaneously toward a loss of self-consciousness, a progress James himself likened significantly to a game of blind man's buff, with the characters growing "warm" as they approached this moment of realization and "cold" as they drew away from it. The climax is at the moment of awareness or of discovery, when the individual recognizes his predicament and sees his own blindness in relation to it—for the self-analysis is, most frequently, self-deception. Examined in this way, the analysis and the complicated probings into questions of deportment assume a different importance in the novels; they become little more than formal or dramatic delay, hastening or retarding the forthcoming tragic or comic effect by leading the character away from a knowledge of his predicament while steadily enlightening the spectator as to the nature of it.

Identifying the individual in terms other than those of "current actualities" led James to develop an involved technique for relating his characters to each other. The swift, the sweeping alterations of social habits in America, the lack of points of reference in even the material characteristics of the scene, led him to find an exceptional importance in the relatively more permanent landmarks of Europe. The following quotation from the preface to *Portrait of a Lady* is only incidentally connected with this essay, but it has an independent beauty, and it may give some insight into the peculiar importance of the scene itself in James' mind:

. . . the waterside life, the wondrous lagoon spread before me, and the ceaseless human chatter of Venice came in at my windows, to which I seem to myself to have been constantly driven, in the fruitless fidget of composition, as if to see whether, out in the blue channel, the ship of some right suggestion, of some better phrase, of the next happy twist of my subject, the next true touch for my canvas, mightn't come into sight. But I recall vividly enough that the response most elicited, in general, was the rather grim admonition that romantic and historic sites, such as Italy abounds in, offer the artist a questionable aid to concentration when they themselves are not to be the subject of it. They are too rich in their own life and too charged with their own meanings merely to help him out with a lame phrase; they draw him away from his small questions to their greater ones; so that, after a little, he feels while thus yearning toward them in his difficulty, as if he were asking an army of glorious veterans to help him to arrest a peddler who has given him the wrong change.

Finally, the little story of *Julia Bride* expresses more clearly what James meant by his list of the inadequacies of American life, and throws an incidental light on his belief in the connection between the social structure of a society and the sort of art produced in it. *Julia Bride* was written after his visit to America in 1904. In that visit he was overwhelmed by the material changes that had taken place in the scene; New York was no "vast nursery of sharp appeals and concrete images" for him, but rather left him dazed and bewildered, lost, in a very real sense, among the anonymous buildings and the traditionous places. In his absence his resistance to middle-class commercial enterprise had grown less stubborn; after his visit he could envision "the great adventure of a society reaching out into the apparent void for consummations, after having earnestly gathered in so many of the preparations and necessities." *Julia Bride* I interpret as a specific illustration of his meaning, pertinent to this discussion by revealing what James meant by landmarks, and with the added value of demonstrating the disproportion between James' symbols and what he tried to make them convey.

Julia Bride is a minor comedy in the hierarchy of James fiction, yet it is like his best work in its indirection and the studied avoidance of the direct statement. The story revolves around Julia, who is planning to marry; she is in love with the young man she intends to marry, but recognized the special advantage to herself in the fact that he is rich. Her reputation, however, has been clouded by several past engagements, all innocent in character as James' heroines are invariably and ambiguously innocent, and it is necessary for her somehow to establish this innocence. She appeals first to one of her step-fathers for aid; but her step-father is in a predicament similar to her own; he too hopes to marry a woman of wealth, as he also is in need of money. His reputation, in turn, is clouded because he has permitted Julia's mother to accuse him in getting her divorce. Julia clears his name, in this instance, and appeals to one of her former lovers. The lover agrees to help her; he too needs money badly, and in a moment of awareness Julia perceives that he recognizes the financial advantage to himself of an association with her potential husband. He too intends to marry because of his need for money, and his reputation in turn has been disturbed by his past association with Julia. The story is laid in Central Park and in the Museum, and its point consists in the implicit contrast between the feverish scramble of the characters for money and the serenity of the two small "consummations"—the park and the museum—that a society founded on the scramble for money permits to exist. The very extravagance and artificiality of the situation thus becomes a direct comment on the society. As a social critic, James reached this point—although to us now the idea of corporations reaching out into the void for further consummations like the park and the museum must arouse a certain fatigue, if not more emphatic responses.

III

To turn from *Julia Bride* to Grace Lumpkin's *To Make My Bread* involves a certain strain on the imagination; *Julia Bride* is among the last works of an artist whose long career and experience in fiction were behind him, *To Make My Bread* is a first novel. It is also a step toward a proletarian literature; that is, a literature about propertyless workers, embodying their point of view, illustrating their position in the contemporary society and advocating a revolutionary correction of it. It has another distinction, as Grace Lumpkin is among the few proletarian writers who do not begin with an assumption that a strong belief in a cause excuses any amount of careless writing about it. Moreover, as an example of proletarian literature, her book has a special application to this essay, for the points of reference in it are not what is fixed and rigid in society, but what is in the process of change. Social changes are defined as mass movements, and the characters are identified by their relation to them. There are two such movements in the story, the first the transformation of the characters from farmers to mill hands, and the second their intellectual and emotional development into class-conscious workers. The moment of realization for them, when they recognize the nature of their rôle in the society, and the implications of it, has for them a significance analogous to that which James gives his characters when they lose their consciousness of self and become conscious of their predicament—although the difference is great, for in James this moment of awareness has a sort of final value, it is an end in itself, while to the characters of *To Make My Bread* it is a more vital experience, a step in the movement in which the book itself, the reader's response to it, is thought of as part of the larger, continuous process of social change.

I do not intend to establish a comparison between the work of Henry James and that of Grace Lumpkin, but to think of these two novels in connection with each other may give clearer meaning to the term proletarian literature and suggest somewhat the possible development of it. *To Make My Bread* revolves around a specific historical event, of importance to the movement of which it is a part, and of affirmative emotional value *only* in terms of this movement. It is based on a prolonged series of strikes that took place a few years ago around Gastonia, North Carolina. Treating of this event, and celebrating the heroes of it, the novel increases the importance of the happening by strengthening its tradition: there are, to this point of view, no "historic sites" so charged with their own meaning as to distract the artist from his task; the function of art is rather to charge these sites and events with meaning, so that they become a part of the consciousness of class and a point of reference in it. Thus, as farmers the characters are presented as not recognizing their status in the society as it is organized. Physical hardships and partial starvation prepare them for the first great movement, the transfer to the factory, when their land has been absorbed by a lumber company. In the factory, their emotional and intellectual development to the point where they are conscious of the class struggle is presented by the multiplication of incidents: the oppression they live under, the increasing demand on the part of their employers for greater effort with fewer rewards, the increasing gap between the claims of their employers and the actuality as they know it.

So, too, the form of the novel is not rigid, but responds to the development of the characters. In the early sections the prose is slow in tempo and rich in sensuous impressions; the personal responses of the individuals to what happens and what they see are analyzed with attention to the unique importance such responses have for those directly involved. As the process of change becomes more rapid the prose changes as well, and these personal responses lose their value. Disappointments, humiliations, these minor crises in the lives of individuals form the substance of the early part of the story; but as the antagonisms of the society grow more intense, when a strike is on and the opposed forces are openly in conflict, the personal crises give way in the full tide of happenings, and their importance disappears when the greater hazards are involved; a murder or a savage attack become episodes in a struggle which is only beginning. The prose changes from slow detailed analysis and the elaboration of incident to simple, factual statements.

There are also disappointments in the book: the factory, for example, is never clearly presented, and its importance in the life of the characters is only remotely suggested; the terms used to communicate impressions of it are markedly careless and general, as though the author felt a lack of familiarity with it, and no need to develop the unique sensations and experiences directly connected with it. For a century industry has been the most conspicuous item on the American social landscape, and in avoiding it writers have avoided the very features of contemporary life that have been forced most emphatically on their attention. Except for whale-fishing, there has been almost no writing about a specific industry, with the particular conditions and dangers of that industry made the central matter of the fiction, and it may be that *Moby Dick,* the mystical digressions rejected, gives additional insight into the sort of literature that may be expected when the proletarian tradition becomes more firmly established. But at the present moment the conclusion may be stated as a question: How much of the forthrightness, the assurance of *To Make My Bread,* and of what it implies in the way of future development, comes out of a definite knowledge of the place of literature in the social order? How much of the complexities, the indecisions and indirections of James' art came out of his knowledge that it was an orphan-literature, its values sharply at variance with those of the dominant class of his time? Surely his sense of the high importance of art was directly connected with his sense of the precarious position of art in an exploitive society, a society in which the heritages and landmarks of culture were sacrificed for personal acquisition. Thus he searched, in a progressively smaller field, for traditions which seemed to have dignity enough to entitle them to a place in his art, and could not envision a literature so closely allied with the culture of a class as to be occupied with creating traditions rather than using them. *To Make My Bread,* in turn, with its weaknesses, gives a new meaning to the term, "beginning of a tradition," while the works of Henry James so richly and fully illustrate what is meant by the end of one.

Sinclair Lewis

W ITH some fifteen novels to his credit at the age of fifty, together with enough short stories to fill several more volumes, Sinclair Lewis stands out as the most prolific author of his genera-

From *The New Republic,* LXXXVIII, pp. 298-301. October 21, 1936. Reprinted by permission.

tion, with the mournful exception of Upton Sinclair. It is almost the worst thing you can say about him. For although Lewis has written at least two first-rate novels, and created a dozen powerful characters, and produced half-a-hundred masterly satirical sketches scattered throughout these books—as well as added new words to the language and popularized, more than anybody else, a new and skeptical slant on American life—he has also turned out as much journalistic rubbish as any good novelist has signed his name to, and he has written novels so shallow and dull they would have wrecked any reputation except his own.

He has, in fact, been one of the most plunging and erratic writers in our literary history; unpredictability, waywardness, unevenness are his distinguishing characteristics, as a brooding inconclusiveness is the mark of Sherwood Anderson. He has written the best novel of American business in *Babbitt,* only to make up for it by writing the worst in *Work of Art* and adding half-a-dozen wretched *Saturday Evening Post* stories on the same subject to the bargain. He has written the sharpest parodies of the lush, rococo, euphemistic sales-talk of American business life that we have, but he has also weighed down his novels with a heavy burden of unreal and exaggerated jargon, palmed off as common speech, with unfunny topical jokes, passed on as native humor, and the weight of that dated mockery grows heavier every year.

But Lewis has not only been the most uneven of American novelists; he has also been one of the most ambitious. There is an architectural symmetry in the order of the books that followed *Main Street.* Unlike his contemporaries, who seem always to have been improvising in the sequence of their work, Lewis apparently recognized a conscious program for his writing simultaneously with his recognition of his power, and seems to have driven toward its realization with something of the high-pressure intensity he has satirized so often. Where Dreiser gives the impression of having brooded, with a sort of ponderous aimlessness, over whatever lay close at hand, forever turning aside, distracted by every incidental issue, and where Anderson and Vachel Lindsay, more than any of the others, were blown about in the cross-currents of American life until they were saturated with its apparently patternless variety, Lewis visualized on the strength of *Main Street* a cycle of novels comparable at least in scope to those of Zola and Balzac.

It was a spacious and inclusive project, bolder than anything an American novelist had tried to do, signalizing a final break with that narrowness of outlook which, exemplified in a thousand old swimming-hole sentimentalities, pathetic regionalisms and phony family dilemmas, had become almost the sole driving force of American fiction. And even now, when the limitations and short-comings of that imaginative exploration are more apparent than its freshness and originality, it is still a little breath-taking to con-sider the broad outlines of the work that Lewis laid out for him-self, to see that he planned nothing less than a catalogue of the interwoven worlds of American society, the small towns and cities, the worlds of business, of science, of religion, of education, and eventually the worlds of labor and professional politics, working it out at a time when the shabby, optimistic, patriotic smugness of the American literary tradition—the tradition of Henry Van Dyke that, significantly, he attacked in his Nobel Prize address—still im-prisoned the imaginations of so many of his contemporaries.

Lewis had a line on American society, and tenacity, if not much flexibility and resourcefulness, in following it. But more than that he had a sense of the physical variety and the cultural monotony of the country, an easy familiarity with the small towns and square cities, the real-estate developments and restricted residential areas, the small business men, the country doctors, the religious fakers, the clubwomen, the county officeholders, the village atheists and single-taxers, the schoolteachers, librarians, the windbags of the lower income groups, the crazy professors and the maddened, hyperthyroid, high-pressure salesmen—the main types of middle-class and lower-middle-class provincial society, conspicuous now be-cause he has identified them so thoroughly. He had a grasp of these people and their environments, together with a sense of the country as a whole, where so many of his generation had nothing but an oppressed conviction of its emptiness or a dread of its rawness.

Only Vachel Lindsay and Upton Sinclair had seen so much of the country, in the elementary geographical sense of the term. Lewis had never taken any of the wild and pathetic zigzag journeys of Lindsay, dropping in on miners and hill-billies and reading poems for his supper, nor had he spent a season in the hell of the stockyards, as did Upton Sinclair, his first guide, at the beginning of a career no less extraordinary. But he had knocked around at an impressive variety of jobs after he left Yale in 1904— he had been a janitor in Upton Sinclair's Helicon Hall, a soda jerk, a reporter on *The San Francisco Bulletin*—which was probably, under Fremont Older in the days before his capitulation, the best paper in the country to be a reporter on—a ghost writer for Jack London and an editor, in Washington, of a magazine for the deaf; he had taken the grand cruise of his generation on a cattle boat to England and had hitchhiked through the Middle West. He had traveled over the face of the country and, although within pretty narrow limits, up and down through its social strata. And although his first four books were hack jobs, the native experiences he had packed away were too powerful to be satisfied with evocations of the joys of a stenographer's work, or of the wisdom of picturesque and homely old folks, or of an aristocratic Eastern girl made wholesome by contact with the great West—the substance of *The Job, The Innocents* and *Free Air*. Even as hack work those books are bad. They seem to tremble with some internal explosive disgust; in a way they are like the bad jokes and stale opinions that Babbitt and his friends take refuge in at their parties, when they dare not express even a little of what is going on in their minds, lest they betray their hatred of their environments, their boredom, their thwarted desire for change.

Apparently Lewis thought at the beginning of his career that the muse could be embraced and laid aside at will, and that she would not take her revenge by addling the wits of her ravisher— at least his first books prove nothing except that he did not believe the writing of fiction demanded a writer's full energy and his deepest understanding. That implicit irresponsibility has been his greatest limitation as a novelist and the source of much of the unevenness of his work. Even the broad project mentioned above— the cycle of novels following *Main Street*—is a vision of an imaginative survey of American life such as a glorified and super-competent hack writer might conceive: a writer, that is, who thought of his writing, not in terms of its momentary inspirations and the pressure of living that played through him and upon him, but in terms of the accomplishment of a foreknown task; who thought of a novel of business, of religion, of science, as if he believed he could turn his art to any subject, regardless of how much it meant to him and how close to his heart it lay; who felt that it lay within his power to "collect material" without becoming emotionally entangled in it or acting in response to what it implied. T. K. Whipple, who has written the only searching study of Lewis that we have, has compared his attitude in studying American society with that of a Red Indian stalking through the land of his enemies—it is a good description, for it suggests his wariness and vigilance, the surface accuracy of his observation, what can be called the heartlessness of his approach, and above all his enforced detachment from the scene he viewed and the solitary and personal basis of his satire.

Now that the scandals that attended the publications of Lewis' books have been forgotten, the outlines of the world he created are clearer. On re-examination that world seems in a more advanced state of decay and disintegration than Lewis' first critics·were willing to admit—it is, as Whipple has said, a city of the dead, in which the dead are above all determined that no one shall live. After *Main Street* his characters were still the long-winded, provincial, narrow-visioned old folks, the dreamy and timid job-holders, the clerks and salesmen and doctors—with here and there a workman from the semi-independent crafts—who figured in his first books and were all dominated by those strange, self-satisfied, self-possessed, jovially witless bankers and business men who loom so large in Lewis' world. But where such characters had been harm-

less and happy in the early novels, they were now vindictive, spiteful, vaguely threatening in their inertia and immobility. Before
the War Lewis had written of their provincialism as if it were a
source of serenity, however its expression might rasp on the sensibilities of the cultivated; for the provincials and the innocents
themselves, it was an insulation against the cares of the world and
not without its own homely poetry and wisdom.

But with *Main Street* that provincialism was identified as an evil
force, destructive not only to the Carol Kennicotts and Eric Val-
borgs, to Martin Arrowsmith and Paul Reisling—it was also poison-
ing the lives of those who clung to it and triumphed and, when
their guards were down for a moment, were seen to be bewildered,
distressed, clinging desperately to their appearance of smugness because they had nothing else to cling to. The problem of *Main
Street* might have been "how much of Gopher Prairie's eleven
miles of cement walk" was "made out of the tombstones of John
Keatses"—but the message of *Babbitt, Arrowsmith, Elmer Gantry,*
however Lewis might deny that it was his intention to preach it,
was simply that American society was death to any disinterested
effort, to any human tolerance, almost to any human sympathy;
that it was regimented within an inch of its intellectual life; that
any deviation from its norm of self-seeking, money-grubbing,
career-making, throat-cutting, treachery, slander, blackmailing, was
instantly punished with exile and disgrace; that spontaneity or
generous emotions or a freedom from calculation, among the cal-
culating wolves of business, amounted to suicide of a long-drawn-
out and painful kind. Lewis drew a revolutionary picture of
American middle-class life without coming to revolutionary conclusions about it, unlike Upton Sinclair, who leaped to revolutionary conclusions and then filled in the picture; he recognized the
mechanics of capitalist control, and satirized them, without challenging the ends to which they were applied or visualizing any
alternative except an escape—for those sensitive souls enlightened
enough to be aware of their horror—into reverie and day-dreaming.

The moral atmosphere, with exceptions that will be noted, grew
thicker and more poisonous with each succeeding book. Carol

Kennicott's sensibilities were outraged by Gopher Prairie, and she was revolted by the hypocrisy and narrowness she found there, but the enemies she faced were largely passive—inertia, sluggishness and sullenness, the dominance of petrified prejudice. In comparison with *Babbitt* and the books that followed it, this is an almost pastoral view of life. The difference is not only in the greater violence of the later books, the general strike that interrupts *Babbitt* midway, the flare of melodrama in Reisling's attempt to murder his wife, the corruption and blackmail that accompany Babbitt's business career. It is rather in the cagey watchfulness with which Babbitt's friends of the service clubs bear down on each other for every deviation from their class line, and it is nowhere better dramatized than in the sequence that follows Reisling's tragedy—when Babbitt, shaken by it, develops an intermittent sort of tolerance, the others, particularly the sinister Virgil Gunch, get their knives ready for him at once, and the high point of the book, perhaps the highest point of Lewis' writing, is the realization that they are ready to spring, like the stronger wolves on a crippled member of the pack, at the first sign of Babbitt's confusion and dismay.

Yet even Babbitt's sacrifices for the good opinion of such prosperous thugs is nothing compared with the desperation of Angus Duer, in *Arrowsmith,* who tries to cut the throat of a watchman who has inadvertently threatened his career, and the indifference that Carol Kennicott faced in Gopher Prairie is nothing compared with the sustained enmity and malice that Arrowsmith faces in Wheatsylvania. The enemy—the provincial, conforming, suspicious enemy—is no longer merely passive and mocking; it has become aggressive, strident, criminal; it turns to blackmail and violence; it is ready to frame and destroy anyone who even raises questions that it cannot answer. And by the time *It Can't Happen Here* was written, Lewis' picture of the world was such that the violence with which the book is filled had become obsessive and perverse, divorced from any purpose and uncontrolled by any aim, an eruption of cruelty and horror and little more.

Spaced unevenly between the works in which this panorama

of social damnation is drawn are those books of Lewis' that even his acquiescent critics usually overlook: *Mantrap, The Trail of the Hawk, Work of Art, Ann Vickers, Dodsworth,* the grotesque short stories that he wrote for *The Saturday Evening Post* and that seem particularly bad because there is so much evidence that Lewis knew so much better when he wrote them. He has never been a fastidious writer—he has a gift for slogans, a talent for mimicry, a kind of tormented delight in some of the cruder commonplaces of American speech, but he has always manipulated his people awkwardly to make them demonstrate what he wanted them to reveal about society, and his works have always been weakened, even in their moments of gravity, by a tumultuous and slapstick humor that seems less an expression of emotion than of a desire to escape it. As his career has developed he has relied more and more on his ability to capture the perishable local color of American life, the blaring and raucous Babbittry that surrounds his people, the pep-talks, the idiot drooling of advertisers and go-getters, instead of the indefinite but still sustained and consequential conflicts of Carol and her husband, of Babbitt and his friends—but this material, which was used in *Main Street* to show what a character who could not stomach it was up against, began to be used in the novels that followed almost for its own sake, until with *The Man Who Knew Coolidge* there was scarcely anything else in the book.

But precisely because Lewis has attached so little fundamental importance to such outpourings as Dr. Pickerbaugh's health sermons, or Chum Frinkley's poems, his increasing insistence on material of this sort is all the more clearly a sign of imaginative indecision and doubt. And how, after having so clearly shown the mechanics of American business control in *Babbitt,* and the psychological ravages of it, could he have drawn so unrealistic a figure of a millionaire as Dodsworth, or so romantic a business man as the Ora Weagle of *Work of Art?* In his best books Lewis had told us that the pursuit of wealth—or even a career in a business-dominated society—was a fierce and scrambling affair that killed its victims and crippled its victors; now he presented an industrialist whose unaccountable naïveté persisted (although he collected secret reports on the dissipations of his employees), and a starry-eyed, well-meaning hotel manager whose poetic dreams revolved around the creation of more elaborate comforts for the exhausted Babbitts who could afford them—presented without art, without irony, at best with a kind of curdled romanticism that gave an impression of spleen and exasperation on the part of their author. With these books Lewis' explorations into American society stopped. His characters had become idealizations of the Babbitts he had previously condemned; his satire had degenerated to a kind of stylized mockery, closer in spirit to George Ade's *Fables in Slang* or to some of Mencken's less purposeful buffoonery than to the realities of American life—or it had become so broad and farcical that it had lost its point, just as, in his antifascist novel, his fascists were presented as so weird and unearthly that no practicing strikebreakers, vigilantes, lynchers, anti-Semites, jingoes or acquiescent journalists need feel an instant's identification with them.

But with all this acknowledged, the positive contribution of Lewis' novels remains—and, in one sense, if books like *Dodsworth, Work of Art,* or *Ann Vickers* seem so shallow, it is in large part because Lewis himself has made us conscious in his best work of the native realities that are absent in them. In his best books he has caught, better than anybody else, the desultory, inhibited, half-sad and half-contented middle-class life of the Middle West, a life of spiritless conflicts and drives in the country, of social gatherings as nerve-racking and exhausting as final examinations, of interminable business plots and fears of ruin, of frightened infidelities, limitless ambitions, of forced enthusiasms and false simplicities—a life hedged in behind social barriers set by the least enlightened members of the community and existing under a dictatorship that is no less powerful for being masked and unadmitted by those who bow to it. And even in his worst books Lewis has always been able to summon up some neglected, recognizable corner of the country—the run-down, red-leather hotel lobbies of

Work of Art, the formaldehyde, oiled-floor, civil-service stench of public buildings in *Ann Vickers*—with such graphic power that he has always seemed to be setting the stage for some more momentous drama than he has ever shown taking place.

That effect may be the result of his inability clearly to imagine any antagonist capable of sustained struggle with the rulers of his city of the dead. He is more aware of the monstrous extent of the stables that must be cleaned than he is of the possibility of any Hercules ever cleaning them; and when he pictures people who are pitted against their environments he usually shows them struggling without much hope of victory, without allies, and often with ingrown doubts as to whether or not they are on the right side. And most often, when their feeble feints establish the strength of the enemy, they merely subside into that outward acquiescence and inward rebellion that is the death of drama—so Carol Kennicott, defeated in Gopher Prairie, dreams of a grass hut over some tropical river bank; Babbitt hungers for some wild woodland spirit as he awakens into the steel world of Zenith; Ora Weagle plans gigantic and flawless super-hotels as he fires the help of a run-down Florida boarding house, and these vague aspirations to escape their own environments are presented by Lewis as conferring some secret distinction on the people who hold them.

In denying that he is a satirist Lewis has said that he is a romantic, in much the same sense that these characters of his are romantics, and that he has rebelled against American society because it has none of the picturesque feudal remains that he associated with a rich and stable culture. But his characters are not romantic rebels committed to struggle. They are self-dramatists whose imaginations flower from their evasions of conflict—they are always posing before themselves and others, not in order to fulfill a consistent Byronic rôle, and to take the responsibility for it, but in order to conceal their true reactions and to hide the concerns that oppress them. They are always in the camp of their enemies; they cannot forget themselves for a moment, lest they reveal the depths of their revulsion. They dramatize themselves in order to endure the demands of a society that they have no hope of bettering and whose reality they cannot face, and they imagine themselves in all kinds of rôles—except the ones they actually occupy—because they cannot get through their days without the help of such fantasy.

So the final testimony of Lewis' novels always seems a little grimmer than he apparently intended it to be, and never so grim as when he envisions the rebels and aspiring spirits who front the resolute conformists. He never comes so close to giving a clinical description of psychic breakdown as when he shows his characters making their peace with the world. It was a mistake of his critics to see in these novels evidence of that intellectual awakening and skeptical self-criticism which has become known as America's coming-of-age. For Lewis is the historian of America's catastrophic going-to-pieces—or at least of the going-to-pieces of her middle class —with no remedy to offer for the decline that he records; and he has dramatized the process of disintegration, as well as his own dilemma, in the outlines of his novels, in the progress of his characters, and sometimes, and most painfully, in the lapses of taste and precision that periodically weaken the structure of his prose.

WILLIAM PHILLIPS and PHILIP RAHV
Private Experience and Public Philosophy

THAT "free individual interpretation" and "private experience" are essential to poetry is one postulate that few critics have cared to question. Also, for the most part they agree that the greatness of a poem is in some way related to the outlook or public philosophy of the poet. But here the argument begins. For what is "private" to one group is "public" to another, and frequently it is claimed that a harmonious marriage of the two is impossible because ultimately they are incompatible. Thus compartmentalized, experience and philosophy are pitted against each other. T. S. Eliot, who embodies the contradictions as well as the achievements of his period, sees the necessity for both elements while contending they are incompatible. The two quotations are from "Poetry and Propaganda," written in 1930:

Yet we can hardly doubt that the "truest" philosophy is the best material for the greatest poet; so that the poet must be rated in the end both by the philosophy he realizes in his poetry and by the fullness and adequacy of the realization.

There is a gulf, and I think an impassable one, between the intuitions of the poets as such, and any particular philosophy, or even any philosophical direction rather than any other.

The position Eliot takes in this essay and his eclectic conclusions betray a rudderless philosophy of value; that is, a notion that no one philosophy is true and that any "profound" philosophy may be held and used by poets. Sharing this notion, poets during the last few decades felt relieved of responsibility for their ideas. Experience—personal, ever more unique experience—became the

From *Poetry: A Magazine of Verse*, XLVIII, pp. 98-105. May, 1936. Reprinted by permission.

touchstone of poetry. Today the problem looms again: as poets pass from one intellectual climate into another public philosophy and private experience are put up as the horns of a poetic dilemma. Suspension among a variety of beliefs, with the consequent gyrations into formal experiments, is no longer acceptable to those who have taken a definite attitude toward the world we live in. How to communicate this attitude, even while maintaining the integrity of personal experience, is one of the major problems of the poet in this age.

We are convinced that behind many of the attacks on revolutionary poetry lurks the notion of the contradiction we have just discussed. What else will account for the charge that the philosophy of social revolution strait-jackets the poet's experience, leaving no room for the play of his imagination and the unique quality of his personal emotions? We are led to believe that the revolutionary poet is a mere puppet pulled by the strings of sociology and politics, and that his talent is spent on the linguistic decoration of a closed order of beliefs. Naturally, such poetry is regarded as a violent break with tradition—a noble medium reduced to the service of menial utilitarian ends.

If, however, theory is at bottom no more than history generalizing about itself, then let us check the indictment against the poetic objects involved. You could easily fit this theory to a body of anonymous poetry, inasmuch as all the poems, expressing an impersonal public philosophy, would prove to be essentially identical. But except for ideological direction, what is there in common between Fearing and Schneider, either in method, intention, or feeling? And though both Gregory and Aragon move within the Marxian orbit, in his actual verse-texture Gregory is as far away from Aragon as he is from Allen Tate. The fact is that revolutionary poetry teems with personal tonalities, and is composed of many strains and tendencies. It is true, of course, that the work of a small scattered group of "leftists," poaching on the fringes of revolutionary poetry, does illustrate in several ways the charges of impersonality and barren publicism. But it is just as dishonest to identify this group with revolutionary poetry in its representative aspects as it would be for a Marxist to identify the criticism of T. S. Eliot with that of William Lyon Phelps for the sole reason that from a strictly political point of view both are anti-communist. Caught in the wiles of literalism, the infantile "left-ists" have equated the weapon of art with the art of weapons, with the result that they are not writing poetry but clichéd slogans and stale manifestoes. Yet the critics of the right hardly excel in this respect, for in their own field they too have accepted this monstrous equation. Fundamentally it involves the same faulty understanding of Marxism, though one group accepts it and the other rejects it.

If we were to explore all the corners of the creative problem implied in this controversy, we should hear its echoes in the philosophic question concerning the relation of the ego to the objective world. Or, granting that poetry is an objective body of poems, having continuity and a social status, what is the relation of poetry to the individual poet? Assume a contradiction between a public philosophy and the private experience of the poet and what you get is poetic solipsism, whereby the history and tradition of poetry are dissolved in the acid of uniqueness. A contradiction arises between the poet and the objective meanings of the poetry that has been written, and the only reality remaining to him is his own work. French poetry of post-symbolist days and the writing of the *transition* school actually approached this state. In Paul Valéry's essay, "A Foreword," we observe the process of ideas by means of which any given poetry purges itself of all else, even of other poetry:

. . . One can say that the greatest . . . of the versified works which have come down to us belong to the didactic or historical order.

Finally, toward the middle of the nineteenth century, French literature saw the birth of a remarkable ambition—that of isolating poetry from every essence other than its own.

I mean to say that our tendency . . . toward a beauty always more independent of all *subjects,* and free from sentimental vulgar interest . . . was leading to an almost inhuman state.

This inhuman state was the dead end, though much important poetry steered clear of it.

It would be almost gratuitous to recall that Shakespeare was soaked in prevailing "Elizabethan" attitudes, and that Dante did not seek poetic pastures fenced off from Catholic philosophy. It is only in times like the present, when opposing philosophies battle for power and art is compelled to choose between several public viewpoints, that the presence of social thought in poetry is questioned. The choice before him makes the writer aware of the implications of his work in other fields of discourse and action; it shows him how his private experience illustrates and confirms one public philosophy rather than another. He does not choose between freedom and bondage, but between freedom within one frame and freedom within another. Homer was not free to write from the outlook of Goethe, and many poets today reject the "freedom" to see through the eyes of Robinson Jeffers, for example. Whether a poet has consciously or unconsciously taken to a set of beliefs is irrelevant if we are concerned with objective social effects. In facing the task of creation, however, the distinction may be crucial. In this decade many of our most important poets are pitching their writing in a revolutionary key. But since this is in defiance of habitual attitudes, the poet must consciously adjust his medium to his philosophy. At this point a host of creative questions take on new meaning, because the way the adjustment is made has much to do with the quality of the poem.

Consider the question of theme. Unfortunately many misguided enthusiasts of revolution, effacing their own experience, take for their subject-matter the public philosophy as such, or attempt to adorn with rhetorical language conventionalized patterns of feeling and action. What they don't see is that these patterns are, in the final analysis, just as impersonal as the philosophy itself. Hence we get poems that are really editorial write-ups, a kind of "reality" on parade from which the deeper spiritual and emotional insights are necessarily banished. If there is to be an ever-fresh balance between the accent of the poet and the attitude he shares with other people, he must understand the connection between what is *real* to him as an individual and what is *real* to him as a partisan of some given philosophy.

Too often reality is thought of as a pictorial essence, or invoked as a platonic idea. Both the kind of poetry which is a series of snapshots and the kind which is pure generalization fail to convey the full human meaning of the subject. Experience as such, abstracted from the social situation that bore and reared it, is merely a fake short-cut to a desperate originality; and philosophy divested of the *genius loci,* no matter how nobly declaimed, is like a pedant preaching in meter. To see oneself truly is to see oneself in relation to the larger social issue, and to see the larger social issue truly is to see oneself in it.

Of course, to talk about a philosophy without considering its validity would be like talking about international diplomacy without reference to the concrete interests of nations. We have argued that there is no contradiction between philosophy and experience, but patently such a contradiction is inevitable if the philosophy is false. It was necessary for Eliot to pervert the testimony of his early poems before he could enter credibly into the sanctum of theology. On the other hand, poets like Verlaine, Rimbaud, and Crane accepted no philosophies within their reach, for their experience denied its validity. But today poets are being drawn to an interpretation of the world which is but a broader generalization of the evidence inherent in their own material. No honest and typical experience of our age can exclude a sense of the organized vulgarity and corruption of modern society. The movement of history has again made possible the much desired integration of the poet's conception with the leading ideas of his time.

This necessary integration is being achieved by those revolutionary poets who have been most aware that their revolt is esthetic as well as social, and that as such it is a revolt within the tradition of poetry rather than against it. In the work of Horace Gregory, Kenneth Fearing, and a number of younger poets—who make up the representative school of revolutionary poetry in this country—we observe the emergence of a basic symbolism of rejection and aspiration marking the development of the medium to articulate in its own terms a new hope and a valiant effort. On this ground they have come in conflict with a counter-symbolism of barricades and flag-waving lifted from the surface of events. Those following the line of least resistance grasp these precipitant and standardized emblems as substitutes for the living tissue of the thing itself. In their own right such emblems may exercise a certain appeal for naïve readers, yet they remain a means of evading poetic endeavor. No matter what color it runs to, centrally heated rhetoric stifles the spirit. It is only when the poet, sustained by an objective world-view, tempers his symbols in the fires of his own imagination, that he is able to achieve that intensity and truth which is poetry.

R. P. BLACKMUR

Notes on E. E. Cummings' Language

In his four books of verse, his play, and the autobiographical *Enormous Room*,[1] Mr. Cummings has amassed a special vocabulary and has developed from it a special use of language which these notes are intended to analyze and make explicit. Critics have commonly said, when they understood Mr. Cummings' vocabulary at all, that he has enriched the language with a new idiom; had they been further interested in the uses of language, they would no doubt have said that he had added to the general sensibility of his time. Certainly his work has had many imitators. Young poets have found it easy to adopt the attitudes from which Mr. Cummings has written, just as they often adopt the superficial attitudes of Swinburne and Keats. The curious thing about Mr. Cummings' influence is that his imitators have been able to emulate as well as ape him; which is not so frequently the case with the influence of Swinburne and Keats. Mr. Cummings is a school of writing in himself; so that it is necessary to state the underlying assumptions of his mind, and of the school which he teaches, before dealing with the specific results in poetry of those assumptions.

It is possible to say that Mr. Cummings belongs to the anti-culture group; what has been called at various times vorticism, futurism, dadaism, surrealism, and so on.[2] Part of the general dogma of this group is a sentimental denial of the intelligence

---

[1] As of 1930. There would seem little modification of these notes necessary because of *Eimi* or the subsequent volumes of verse.

[2] The reader is referred to the late numbers *Transition* for a serial and collaborative expression of the latest form which this group has assumed: the Battle of the Word.

From *The Double Agent. Essays in Craft and Elucidation.* Pp. 1-29. Arrow Editions, New York. Copyright, 1935, by R. P. Blackmur. By permission of the author.

and the deliberate assertion that the unintelligible is the only object of significant experience. These dogmas have been defended with considerable dialectical skill, in the very practical premise that only by presenting the unintelligible as viable and actual *per se* can the culture of the *dead intelligence* (Brattle Street, the Colleges, and the Reviews) be shocked into sentience. It is argued that only by denying to the intelligence its function of discerning quality and order, can the failures of the intelligence be overcome; that if we take things as they come without remembering what has gone before or guessing what may come next, and if we accept these things at their face value, we shall know life, at least in the arts, as it really is. Nothing could be more arrogant, and more deceptively persuasive to the childish spirit, than such an attitude when held as fundamental. It appeals to the intellect which wishes to work swiftly and is in love with immediate certainty. A mind based on it accepts every fragment of experience as final and every notion as definite, yet never suffers from the delusion that it has learned anything. By an astonishing accident, enough unanimity exists among these people to permit them to agree among themselves; to permit them, even, to seem spiritually indistinguishable as they appear in public.

The central attitude of this group has developed, in its sectaries, a logical and thoroughgoing set of principles and habits. In America, for example, the cause of lively arts has been advanced against the ancient seven; because the lively arts are necessarily immediate in appeal and utterly transitory. Thus we find in Mr. Cummings' recent verse and in his play *Him* the side show and the cabaret set up as "inevitable" frames for experience. Jazz effects, tough dialects, tough guys, slim hot queens, barkers, fairies, and so on, are made into the media and symbols of poetry. Which is proper enough in Shakespeare where such effects are used ornamentally or for pure play. But in Cummings such effects are employed as substance, as the very mainstay of the poetry. There is a continuous effort to escape the realism of the intelligence in favor of the realism of the obvious. What might be stodgy or dull because not properly worked up into poetry is replaced by the tawdry and by the fiction of the immediate.

It is no great advantage to get rid of one set of flabby generalities if the result is merely the immersion of the sensibility in another set only superficially less flabby. The hardness of the tough guy is mostly in the novelty of the language. There is no hardness in the emotion. The poet is as far from the concrete as before. By denying the dead intelligence and putting on the heresy of unintelligence, the poet only succeeds in substituting one set of unnourished conventions for another. What survives, with a deceptive air of reality, is a surface. That the deception is often intentional hardly excuses it. The surface is meant to clothe and illuminate a real substance, but in fact it is impenetrable. We are left, after experiencing this sort of art, with the certainty that there was nothing to penetrate. The surface was perfect; the deceit was childish; and the conception was incorrigibly sentimental: all because of the dogma which made them possible.

If Mr. Cummings' tough-guy poems are excellent examples of this sentimentality, it is only natural that his other poems—those clothed in the more familiar language of the lyric—should betray even more obviously, even more perfectly, the same fault. There, in the lyric, there is no pretense at hardness of surface. We are admitted at once to the bare emotion. What is most striking, in every instance, about this emotion is the fact that, in so far as it exists at all, it is Mr. Cummings' emotion, so that our best knowledge of it must be, finally, our best guess. It is not an emotion resulting from the poem; it existed before the poem began and is a result of the poet's private life. Besides its inspiration, every element in the poem, and its final meaning as well, must be taken at face value or not at all. This is the extreme form, in poetry, of romantic egoism: whatever I experience is real and final, and whatever I say represents what I experience. Such a dogma is the natural counterpart of the denial of the intelligence.

Our interest is not in the abstract principle, but in the results of its application in poetry. Assuming that a poem should in some sense be understood, should have a meaning apart from the poet's private life, either one of two things will be true about any poem written from such an attitude as we have ascribed to Mr. Cummings. Either the poem will appear in terms so conventional that everybody will understand it—when it will be flat and no poem at all; or it will appear in language so far distorted from convention as to be inapprehensible except by lucky guess. In neither instance will the poem be genuinely complete. It will be the notes for a poem, from which might flow an infinite number of possible poems, but from which no particular poem can be certainly deduced. It is the purpose of this paper to examine a few of the more obvious types of distortion which Mr. Cummings has practiced upon language.

The question central to such a discussion will be what kind of meaning does Mr. Cummings' poetry have; what is the kind of equivalence between the language and its object? The pursuit of such a question involves us immediately in the relations between words and feelings, and the relations between the intelligence and its field in experience—all relations which are precise only in terms themselves essentially poetic—in the feeling for an image, the sense of an idiom. Such relations may only be asserted, may be judged only tentatively, only instinctively, by what seems to be the disciplined experience, but what amounts, perhaps, only to the formed taste. Here criticism is appreciation. But appreciation, even, can take measures to be certain of its grounds, and to be full should betray the constant apprehension of an end which is the necessary consequence, the proper rounding off, of just those grounds. In the examination of Mr. Cummings' writings the grounds will be the facts about the words he uses, and the end will be apprehended in the quality of the meaning his use of these words permits.

There is one attitude towards Mr. Cummings' language which has deceived those who hold it. The typographical peculiarities of his verse have caught and irritated public attention. Excessive hyphenation of single words, the use of lower case "i," the breaking of lines, the insertion of punctuation between the letters of a word, and so on, will have a possible critical importance to the textual scholarship of the future; but extensive consideration of these peculiarities today has very little importance, carries almost no reference to the meaning of the poems. Mr. Cummings' experiments in typography merely extend the theory of notation by adding to the number, *not* to the *kind,* of conventions the reader must bear in mind, and are dangerous only because since their uses cannot readily be defined, they often obscure rather than clarify the exact meaning. No doubt the continued practice of such notation would produce a set of well-ordered conventions susceptible of general use. At present the practice can only be "allowed for," recognized in the particular instance, felt, and forgotten: as the diacritical marks in the dictionary are forgotten once the sound of the word has been learned. The poem, after all, only takes wing on the page. It persists in the ear.

Considering typographical peculiarities for our present purposes as either irrelevant or unaccountable, there remain the much more important peculiarities of Mr. Cummings' vocabulary itself; of the poem after it has been read, as it is in the mind's ear, as it is on the page only for reassurance and correction.[1]

If a reader, sufficiently familiar with these poems not to be caught on the snag of novelty, inspects carefully any score of them no matter how widely scattered, he will be in two sorts—a vagueness of image and a constant recurrence of words. Since the one depends considerably upon the other, a short list of some of Mr. Cummings' favorite words will be a good preliminary to the examination of his images. In *Tulips and Chimneys* words such as these occur frequently: thrilling, flowers, serious, absolute, sweet, unspeaking, utter, gradual, ultimate, final, serene, frail, grave, tremendous, slender, fragile, skillful, carefully, musical, intent, young, gay, untimid, incorrigible, groping, dim, slow, certain, diliberate, strong, chiselled, subtle, tremulous, perpetual, crisp, perfect, sudden, faint, strenuous, minute, superlative, keen, ecstatic,

---

[1] It is not meant to disparage Mr. Cummings' inventions, which are often excellent, but to minimize an exaggerated contemporary interest. *A Survey of Modernist Poetry* by Laura Riding and Robert Graves, is a study in original punctuation and spelling. Their point is made by printing sonnet 129 in its original notation beside a modern version; the point being that Shakespeare knew what he was doing and that his editors did not.

fleet, delicious stars, enthusiastic, capable, dull, bright. In listing these as favorite words, it is meant that these words do the greater part of the work in the poems where they occur; these are the words which qualify the subject-matter of the poems, and are sometimes even the subjects themselves. Observe that none of them, taken alone, are very concrete words; and observe that many of them are the rather abstract, which is to say typical, names for precise qualities, but are not, and cannot be, as originally important words in a poem, very precise or very concrete or very abstract: they are middling words, not in themselves very much one thing or the other and should be useful only with respect to something concrete in itself.

If we take Mr. Cummings' most favored word "flower" and inspect the uses to which he puts it, we should have some sort of key to the kind of poetry he writes. In *Tulips and Chimneys* the word "flower" turns up, to a casual count, forty-eight times, and in *&*, a much smaller volume, twenty-one times. We have among others the following: smile like a flower; riverly as a flower; steeped in burning flowers; last flower; lipping flowers; more silently than a flower; snow flower; world flower; softer than flower; forehead a flight of flowers; feet are flowers in vases; air is deep with flower; slow supple flower of beauty; flower-terrible; flower of thy mouth stars and flowers; mouth a new flower; flower of silence; god's flowers; flowers of reminding; dissonant flowers; flower-stricken air; Sunday flower; tremendous flower; speaking flower; flower of kiss; futile flowers, etc., etc. Besides the general term there is a quantity of lilies and roses, and a good assortment of daisies, pansies, buttercups, violets and chrysanthemums. There are also many examples of such associated words as "petals" and "blooms" and "blossoms," which, since they are similarly used, may be taken as alternative to flowers.

Now it is evident that this word must attract Mr. Cummings' mind very much; it must contain for him an almost unlimited variety and extent of meaning; as the mystic says God, or at least as the incomplete mystic repeats the name of God to every occasion of his soul, Mr. Cummings in some of his poems says flower.

The question is, whether or not the reader can possibly have shared the experience which Mr. Cummings has had of the word; whether or not it is possible to discern, after any amount of effort, the precise impact which Mr. Cummings undoubtedly feels upon his whole experience when he uses the word. "Flower" like every other word not specifically the expression of a logical relation, began life as a metaphor, as a leap from feeling to feeling, as a bridge in the imagination to give meaning to both those feelings. Presumably, the amount of meaning possible to the word is increased with each use, but only the meaning *possible*. Actually, in practice, a very different process goes on. Since people are occupied mostly with communication and argument and conversation, with the erection of discursive relationships, words are commonly spoken and written with the least possible meaning preserved, instead of the most. History is taken for granted, ignored or denied. Only the outsides of words, so to speak, are used; and doubtless the outsides of words are all that the discursive intellect needs. But when a word is used in a poem it should be the sum of all its appropriate history made concrete and particular in the individual context; and in poetry all words act *as if* they were so used, because the only kind of meaning poetry can have requires that all its words resume their full life: the full life being modified and made unique by the *qualifications* the words perform one upon the other in the poem. Thus even a very bad poem may seem good to its author, when the author is not an acute critic and believes that there is life in his words merely because there was life (and a very different sort of life, truly) in the feelings which they represent. An author should remember, with the Indians, that the reality of a word is anterior to, and greater than, his use of it can ever be; that there is a perfection to the feelings in words to which his cannot hope to attain, but that his chief labor will be toward the approximation of that perfection.

We sometimes speak of a poet as a master of his words, and we sometimes say that a man's poetry has been run away with by words—meaning that he has not mastered his words but has been overpowered by his peculiar experience of certain among them.

Both these notions are commonly improper, because they represent misconceptions of the nature of poetry in so far as they lay any stress upon originality, or lack of it, in the poet's use of words. The only mastery possible to the poet consists in that entire submission to his words which is perfect knowledge. The only originality of which the poet is properly capable will be in the choice of order, and even this choice is largely a process of discovery rather than of origination. As for words running away with a poet or a poem, it would be more accurate to say that the poet's *ideas* had run away with him than his words.

This is precisely what has occurred to Mr. Cummings in his use of the word "flower" as a maid of all work. The word has become an idea, and in the process has been deprived of its history, its qualities, and its meaning. An idea, the intellectual pin upon which a thought is hung, is not transmissible in poetry as an important element in the poem and ought only to be employed to pass over, with the greatest possible velocity, the area of the uninteresting (what the poet was not interested in). That is, in a poem whose chief intent was the notation of character and yet required a descriptive setting might well use for the description such vague words as space and time, but could not use such words as goodness or nobleness without the risk of flatness. In Mr. Cummings' poetry we find the contrary; the word "flower," because of the originality with which he conceives it, becomes an idea and is used to represent the most interesting and most important aspect of his poem. Hence the center of the poem is permanently abstract and unknowable for the reader, and remains altogether without qualifications and concreteness. It is not the mere frequency of use that deadens the word flower into an idea; it is the kind of thought which each use illustrates in common. By seldom saying *what* flower, by seldom relating immitigably the abstract word to the specific experience, the content of the word vanishes; it has no inner mystery, only an impenetrable surface.

This is the defect, the essential deceit, we were trying to define. Without questioning Mr. Cummings, or any poet, as to sincerity (which is a personal attitude, irrelevant to the poetry considered) it is possible to say that when in any poem the important words are forced by their use to remain impenetrable, when they can be made to surrender nothing actually to the senses—then the poem is defective and the poet's words have so far deceived him as to become ideas merely.[1] Mr. Cummings is not so much writing poetry, as he is dreaming, idly ringing the changes of his reveries.

Perhaps a small divagation may make clearer the relation of these remarks to Mr. Cummings' poems. Any poetry which does not consider itself as much of an art and having the same responsibilities to the consumer as the arts of silversmithing or cobbling shoes—any such poetry is likely to do little more than rehearse a waking dream. Dreams are everywhere ominous and full of meaning; and why should they not be? They hold the images of the secret self, and to the initiate dreamer betray the nerve of life at every turn, not through any effort to do so, or because of any inherited regimen, but simply because they cannot help it. Dreams are like that—to the dreamer the maximal limit of experience. As it happens, dreams employ words and pictorial images to fill out their flux with a veil of substance. Pictures are natural to everyone, and words, because they are prevalent, seem common and inherently sensible. Hence, both picture and word, and then with a little stretching of the fancy the substance of the dream itself, seem expressible just as they occur—as things created, as the very flux of life. Mr. Cummings' poems are often nothing more than the report of just such dreams. He believes he knows what he knows, and no doubt he does. But he also believes apparently, that the words which he encourages most vividly to mind are those most precisely fitted to put his poem on paper. He transfers

---

[1] It should be confessed that for all those persons who regard poetry only as a medium of communication, these remarks are quite vitiated. What is communicated had best remain as abstract as possible, dealing with concrete as typical only; then "meaning" will be found to reside most clearly in the realm of ideas, and everything will be given as of equal import. But here poetry is regarded not at all as communication but as expression, as statement, as presentation of experience, and the emphasis will be on what is made known concretely. The question is not what one shares with the poet, but what one knows in the poem.

the indubitable magic of his private musings from the cell of his mind, where it is honest incantation, to the realm of poetry. Here he forgets that poetry, so far as it takes a permanent form, is written and is meant to be read, and that it cannot be a mere private musing. Merely because his private fancy furnishes his liveliest images, is the worst reason for assuming that this private fancy will be approximately experienced by the reader or even indicated on the printed page.

But it is unfair to limit this description to Mr. Cummings; indeed, so limited, it is not even a description of Mr. Cummings. Take the *Oxford Book of English Verse,* or any anthology of poems equally well known, and turn from the poems printed therein of such widely separated poets as Surrey, Crashaw, Marvell, Burns, Wordsworth, Shelley, and Swinburne, to the collected works of these poets respectively. Does not the description of Mr. Cummings' mind at work given above apply nearly as well to the bulk of this poetry as to that of Mr. Cummings, at least on the senses' first immersion? The anthology poems being well known are conceived to be understood, to be definitely intelligible, and to have, without inspection, a precise meaning. The descent upon the collected poems of all or of any one of these authors is by and large a descent into tenuity. Most of their work, most of any poet's work, with half a dozen exceptions, is tenuous and vague, private exercises or public playthings of a soul inverse. So far as he is able, the reader struggles to reach the concrete, the solid, the definite; he must have these qualities, or their counterparts among the realm of the spirit, before he can understand what he reads. To translate such qualities from the realm of his private experience to the conventional forms of poetry is the problem of the poet; and the problem of the reader, likewise, is to come well equipped with the talent and the taste for discerning the meaning of those conventions as they particularly occur. Neither the poet's casual language nor the reader's casual interlocution is likely to be much help. There must be a ground common but exterior to each: that is the poem. The best poems take the best but not always the hardest reading; and no doubt it is so with the writing. Certainly, in neither case are dreams or simple reveries enough. Dreams are natural and are minatory or portentous; but except when by accident they fall into forms that fit the intelligence, they never negotiate the miracle of meaning between the poet and the poem, the poem and the reader.

Most poetry fails of this negotiation, and it is sometimes assumed that the negotiation was never meant, by the poet, to be made. For the poet, private expression is said to be enough; for the reader, the agitation of the senses, the perception of verbal beauty, the mere sense of stirring life in the words, are supposed sufficient. If this defense had a true premise—if the poet did express himself to his private satisfaction—it would be unanswerable; and to many it is so. But I think the case is different, and this is the real charge against Mr. Cummings: the poet does not ever express himself privately. The mind cannot understand, cannot properly know its own musings until those musings take some sort of conventional form. Properly speaking, a poet, or any man, cannot be adequate to himself in terms of himself. True consciousness and true expression of consciousness must be external to the blind seat of consciousness—man as sensorium. Even a simple image must be fitted among other images, and conned with them, before it is understood. That is, it must take a form in language which is highly traditional and conventional. The genius of the poet is to make the convention apparently disappear into the use to which he puts it.

Mr. Cummings and the group with which he is here roughly associated, the anti-culture or anti-intelligence group, persists to the contrary. Because experience is fragmentary as it strikes the consciousness it is thought to be essentially discontinuous and therefore essentially unintelligible except in the fragmentary form in which it occurred. They credit the words they use with immaculate conception and there hold them unquestionable. A poem, because it happens, must mean something and mean it without relation to anything but the private experience which inspired it. Certainly it means something, but not a poem; it means that something exciting happened to the writer and that a mystery is happening to the reader. The fallacy is double; they believe in the inexorable significance of the unique experience; and they have discarded the only method of making the unique experience into a poem—the conventions of the intelligence. As a matter of fact they do not write without conventions, but being ignorant of what they use, they resort most commonly to their own inefficient or superficial conventions—such as Mr. Cummings' flower and doll. The effect is convention without substance; the unique experience becomes a rhetorical assurance.

If we examine next, for the sake of the greatest possible contrast, one of the "tough" poems in *Is 5*, we will find a similar breach with the concrete. The use of vague words like "flower" in the lyrical poems as unexpanded similes, is no more an example of sentimental egoism than the use of vague conventions about villains. The distortion differs in terms but is essentially identical.

Sometimes the surface of the poem is so well constructed that the distortion is hard to discover. Intensity of process occasionally triumphs over the subject. Less frequently the subject itself is conceived directly and takes naturally the terms which the language supplies. The poem numbered "One XII" in *Is 5* is an example in so far as the sentimental frame does not obscure the process.

> now dis "daughter" uv eve (who aint precisely slim) sim
> ply don't know duh meanin uv duh woid sin in
> not disagreeable contras tuh dat not exactly fat
> "father" (adjustin his robe) who now puts on his flat hat.

It is to be noted in this epigram, that there is no inexorable reason for either the dialect or the lapses from it into straight English. No one in particular is speaking, unless it be Mr. Cummings slumming in morals along with he-men and lady social workers, and taking it for granted that the dialect and the really refined language which the dialect exercises together give a setting. There are many other poems in *Is 5*, more sentimental and less successful, where the realism is of a more obvious sort; not having reference to an ideal so much as to a kind of scientific reality. That is, there is an effort to ground an emotion, or the facts which make the emotion, in the style of the character to whom the emotion happens. It is the reporter, the man with the good ear for spoken rhythms, who writes out of memory. The war poems and the poem about Bill and his chip ("One XVI") are examples. Style in this sense (something laid on) is only an attribute; is not the character, it is likely to be sentimental and melodramatic. That is, the emotion which is named in the poem (by one of its attributes) is in excess of its established source (that same attribute). There is a certain immediate protection afforded to this insufficiency by the surface toughness, by the convention of burlesque; as if by mocking one-self one made sure there was something to mock. It is a kind of trickery resulting from eager but lazy senses; where the sensation itself is an excess, and appears to have done all the work of intuition and intelligence; where sensation, so far as poetry goes, without being attached to some central body of experience, genuinely understood and *formed* in the mind.

The intrusion of science into art always results in a sentimental realism and always obfuscates form when that science is not kept subordinate to the qualitative experience of the senses—as witness the run of sociological novels. The analogues of science, where conventions are made to do the work of feeling instead of crowning it, are even more dangerous. Mr. Cummings' tough guy and his hard-boiled dialects are such analogues.

Mr. Cummings has a fine talent for using familiar, even almost dead words, in such a context as to make them suddenly impervious to every ordinary sense; they become unable to speak, but with a great air of being, bursting with something very important and precise to say. "The bigness of cannon is *skilful* . . . enormous rhythm of *absurdity* . . . *slimness* of *evenslicing* eyes are chisels . . . electric Distinct face haughtily vital *clinched* in a swoon of *synopsis* . . . my friend's being continually whittles *keen* careful futile *flowers,*" etc. With the possible exception of the compound *evenslicing* the italicized words are all ordinary words; all in nor-mal contexts have a variety of meaning both connotative and de-notative; the particular context being such as to indicate a particular meaning, to establish precisely a feeling, a sensation or a relation.

Mr. Cummings' contexts are employed to an opposite purpose in so far as they wipe out altogether the history of the word, its past associations and general character. To seize Mr. Cummings' meaning there is only the free and *uninstructed* intuition. Something precise is no doubt intended; the warrant for the belief is in the almost violent isolation into which the words are thrown; but that precision can seldom, by this method, become any more than just that "something precise." The reality, the event, the feeling, which we will allow Mr. Cummings has in mind, is not sensibly in the word. It is one thing for meaning to be difficult, or abstruse—hidden in its heart, that is. "Absent thee from *felicity* a while," Blake's "Time is the mercy of eternity" are reasonable examples; there the mystery is inside the words. In Mr. Cummings' words the mystery flies in the face, is on the surface; because there is no inside, no realm of possibility, of essence.

The general movement of Mr. Cummings' language is away from communicable precision. If it be argued that the particular use of one of the italicized words above merely makes the word unique, the retort is that such uniqueness is too perfect, is sterile. If by removing the general sense of a word the special sense is apotheosized, it is only so at the expense of the general sense itself. The destruction of the general sense of a word results in the loss of that word's individuality; for in practice the character of a word (which is its sense) is manifest only in good society, and meaning is distinguished only by conventional association. Mr. Cummings' use of words results in a large number of conventions, but these conventions do not permeate the words themselves, do not modify their souls or change their fates; they cannot be adopted by the reader because they cannot be essentially understood. They should rather be called inventions.

If we take a paragraph from the poem beginning on page thirty in *Is 5*, we will discover another terminus of the emotional habit of mind which produced the emphasis on the word "flower" in *Tulips and Chimneys*.

the Bar, tinking luscious jugs dint of ripe silver with warmlyish
wetflat splurging smells waltz the glush of squirting taps plus slush
of foam knocked off and a faint piddle-of-drops she says I ploc spittle
what the lands thaz me kin in no sir hopping sawdust you kiddo he's
a palping wreaths of badly Yep cigars who jim hin why gluey grins
topple together eyes pout gestures stickily point made glints squinting
who's a wink bum-nothing and money fizzily mouth take big wobbly
foot-steps every goggle cent of it get our ears dribbles sofe right old
feller belch the chap hic summore eh chuckles skulch.

Now the point is that effect of this whole paragraph has much in
common with the effect of the word "flower." It is a flower disintegrated, and the parts are not component; so that by presenting an analysis of his image Mr. Cummings has not let us into
its secret; the analysis is not a true analysis, because it exhibits,
finally, what are still only the results, not the grounds, of his private
conventions, his personal emotions. It is indubitable that the words
are alive; they jostle, even overturn, the reader in the assurance
of their vitality; but the notion of what their true vitality is remains Mr. Cummings' very own. The words remain emotive.
They have a gusty air of being something, but they defeat themselves in the effort to say what, and come at last to a bad end, all
fallen in a heap.

The easiest *explanation* of the passage would be to say that each
separate little collection of words in it is a note for an image; an
abstraction, very keen and lively in Mr. Cummings' mind, of something very precise and concrete. Some of the words seem like a
painter's notes, some a philologist's. But they are all, as they
are presented, notes, abstractions, ideas—with their concrete objects unknown—except to the most arbitrary guess. The guess must
be arbitrary because of the quantity, not the quality, of the words
employed. Mr. Cummings is not here overworking the individual
words, but by heaping so many of them together he destroys their
individuality. Meaning really residual in the word is not exhausted, is not even touched; it must remain abstract and only an
emotional substitute for it can be caught. The interesting fact

about emotional substitutes in poetry, as elsewhere, is their thinness, and the inadequacy resulting from the thinness. The thinness is compulsory because they can, so far as the poem is concerned, exist only as a surface; they cannot possess tentacular roots reaching into, and feeding on, feelings, because the feelings do not exist, are only present by legerdemain. Genuine emotion in poetry perhaps does not *exist* at all; though it is none the less real for that, because a genuine emotion does not need the warrant of existence: it is the necessary result, in the mind, of a convention of feelings: like the notion of divine grace.

In *Tulips and Chimneys* (p. 109) there is a poem whose first and last lines supply an excellent opposition of proper and improper distortion of language.

> the Cambridge ladies who live in furnished souls . . .
>
>   the
>
> moon rattles like a fragment of angry candy.

In the context the word "soul" has the element of surprise which is surprise at *justness;* at *aptness;* it fits in and finishes off the notion of the line. "Furnished souls" is a good, if slight, conceit; and there is no trouble for the reader who wishes to know what the line means: he has merely to *extend* his knowledge slightly, just as Mr. Cummings merely extended the sense of his language slightly by releasing his particular words in this particular order. The whole work that the poet here demands of his reader is pretty well defined. The reader does not have to *guess;* he is enabled to *know.* The reader is not collecting data, he is aware of a meaning.

It would be unfair not to quote the context of the second line.

> . . . the Cambridge ladies do not care, above
> Cambridge if sometimes in its box of
> sky lavender and cornerless, the
> moon rattles like a fragment of angry candy.

We can say that Mr. Cummings is putting beauty next to the tawdry; juxtaposing the dead with the live; or that he is being sentimentally philosophical in verse—that is, releasing from inadequate sources something intended to be an emotion.[1]

We can go on illustrating Mr. Cummings' probable intentions almost infinitely. What Mr. Cummings likes or admires, what he holds dear in life, he very commonly calls flowers, or dolls, or candy —terms with which he is astonishingly generous; as if he thought by making his terms general enough their vagueness could not matter, and never noticed that the words so used enervate themselves in a kind of hardened instinct. We can understand what Mr. Cummings intended by "moon" and "candy" but in the process of understanding, the meaning of the words themselves disappears. The thrill of the association of "rattles" with "moon" and "angry" with "candy" becomes useless as a guide. "Rattles" and "angry" can only be continued in the meaning of the line if the reader supplies them with a force, a definiteness of suggestion, with which Mr. Cummings has not endowed them.

The distortion is here not a release of observation so keen that commonplace language would not hold it; it is not the presentation of a vision so complete that words must lose their normal meanings in order to suggest it. It is, on the contrary, the distortion of the commonplace itself; and the difficulty about a commonplace is that it cannot be known, it has no character, no fate, and no essence. It is a substitute for these.

True meaning (which is here to say knowledge) can only exist where some contact, however remote, is preserved between the language, forms, or symbols in which it is given and something concrete, individual, or sensual which inspired it; and the degree in which the meaning is seized will depend on the degree in which the particular concreteness is realized. Thus the technique of "meaning" will employ distortion only in so far as the sense of this concreteness is promoted by it. When contrast and contradic-

---

[1] That is, as the most common form of sentimentality is the use of emotion in *excess* of its impetus in the feelings, here we have an example of emotion which fails by a great deal to *come up* to its impetus. It is a very different thing from understatement, where the implications are always definite and where successful disarming.

tion disturb the ultimate precision of the senses the distortion involved is inappropriate and destructive. Mr. Cummings' line about the moon and candy does not weld a contradiction, does not identify a substance by a thrill of novel association. It leaves the reader at a loss: where it is impossible to *know,* after any amount of effort and good will, what the words mean. If it be argued that Mr. Cummings was not interested in meaning then Mr. Cummings is not a serious poet, is a mere collector of sensations, and can be of very little value to us. And to defend Mr. Cummings on the ground that he is in the pretty good company of Swinburne, Crashaw, and Victor Hugo, is partly to ignore the fact that by the same argument all four also enjoy the companionship of Edgar Guest. Such defense would show a very poor knowledge of the verses of Mr. Cummings, who is nothing if not serious in the attempt to exhibit precise knowledge. His interest in words and in their real meaning is probably greater than that of most poets of similar dimensions. He has consciously stretched syntax, word order, and meaning in just the effort to expand knowledge in poetry; and his failure is because he has gone too far, has lost sight of meaning altogether—and because, perhaps, the experience which he attempts to translate into poetry remained always personal to him and was never known objectively as itself. By his eagerness Mr. Cummings' relation to language has become confused; he has put down what has meant much to him and can mean little to us, because for us it is not put down—is only indicated, only possibly there. The freshness and depth of his private experience is not denied; but it is certain that, so far as its meaning goes, in the poetry into which he translated it, sentimentality, empty convention, and commonplace rule. In short, Mr. Cummings' poetry ends in ideas *about* things.

When Mr. Cummings resorts of language for the *thrill* that words may be made to give, when he allows his thrill to appear as an equivalent for concrete meaning, he is often more successful than when he is engaged more ambitiously. This is true of poets like Swinburne and Poe, Shelley and the early Marlowe: where the first pair depended almost as much upon *thrill* as Mr. Cummings in those poems where they made use of it at all, and where the second pair, particularly Marlowe, used their thrills more appropriately as ornament: where all four were most successful in their less ambitious works, though perhaps not as interesting. Likewise, today, there is the example of Archibald MacLeish, whose best lines are those that thrill and do nothing more. So that at least in general opinion Mr. Cummings is in this respect not in bad company. But if an examination of thrill be made, whether in Mr. Cummings' verse or in that of others, it will be shown that the use of thrill has at heart the same sentimental impenetrability that defeats the possibility of meaning elsewhere. Only here, in the realm of thrill, the practice is comparatively less illegitimate. Thrill, by itself, or in its proper place, is an exceedingly important element in any poem: it is the circulation of its blood, the *quickness* of life, by which we know it, when there is anything in it to know, most intimately. To use a word for its thrill is to resurrect it from the dead; it is the incarnation of life in consciousness; it is movement.[1]

But what Mr. Cummings does, when he is using language as thrill, is not to resurrect a word from the dead: he more often produces an apparition, in itself startling and even ominous, but still only a ghost: it is all a thrill, and what it is that thrilled us cannot be determined. For example, in *XLI Poems,* the following phrases depend considerably for their effect upon the thrill that is in them: "Prisms of sharp *mind;* where strange birds *purr;* into

---

[1] Cf. Owen Barfield's *Poetic Diction* (London, Faber and Gwyer, 1928), page 202. "For what is absolutely necessary to the present existence of poetry? Movement. The wisdom which she has imparted may remain for a time at rest, but she herself will always be found to have gone forward to where there is life, and therefore movement, *now*. And we have seen that the experience of aesthetic pleasure betrays the real presence of movement. . . . But without the continued existence of poetry, without a steady influx of new meaning into language, even the knowledge and wisdom which poetry herself has given in the past must wither away into a species of mechanical calculation. Great poetry is the progressive incarnation of life in consciousness." That is, we must know what thrills us; else being merely thrilled we are left gasping and aghast, like the little girl on the roller-coaster.

the *smiling* sky *tense* with *blending,* ways cloaked with *renewal;* sinuous riot; *steeped* with burning flowers; little kittens who are called *spring;* electric Distinct face haughtily vital clinched in a *swoon* of synopsis; unreal *precise* intrinsic fragment of actuality; an orchid whose *velocity* is *sculptural;* scythe takes *crisply* the *whim* of thy *smoothness;* perpendicular taste; wet stars, etc., etc." (The italics are mine.)

Take especially the phrase, "scythe takes *crisply* the *whim* of thy *smoothness.*" We know in the poem that it is the scythe of death and that it is youth and beauty (in connection with love) that is to be cut off. So much is familiar, is very conventional; and so the conventional or dead emotion is placed before us; the educated reader receives it and reacts to it without a whimper. But Mr. Cummings must not have been content with presenting the conventional emotion in its conventional form; he felt bound to enliven it with metaphor, with overtones of the senses and the spirit: so that he substituted for the direct statement a rather indirect image combining three unusually sensed words for the sake of the *thrill* the special combination might afford. As the phrase stands there is no precision in it. There is a great suggestion of precision about it—like men going off to war; but precisely *what* is left for the reader to guess, to supply from his own heart. By themselves *whim* and *smoothness* are abstract quality words; and in order for them to escape the tensity, the firm disposition, of concrete meaning, they should demand a particular reference.

Smoothness is probably the smoothness of the body and is used here as a kind of metonomy; but it may be pure metaphor and represent what is really to die—the spirit—taken in its physical terms; or it may be that all that is to be understood is a pure tautology. And so on. Even with this possible variety of reference, *smoothness* would not be very objectionable, were it the only word in the phrase used in this way, or were the other words used to clarify the *smoothness.* But we have also the noun *whim* bearing directly on *smoothness* and the adverb *crisply* which while it directly modifies *takes,* really controls the entire phrase. Taken seriously, *whim,* with reference to the smoothness of either the body or the spirit or the love it inspires, is to say the least a light word; one might almost say a "metrical" word, introduced to stretch the measure, or because the author liked the sound of it, or enjoyed whimsy. It diminishes without limiting the possibilities of *smoothness*. Because it is here, in the phrase, it is inseparable from the phrase's notion of smoothness; yet instead of assisting, tends to prevent what that notion of smoothness is from being divulged.

Crisply is even more difficult to account for; associated with a scythe it perhaps brings to mind the sound of a scythe in a hay-field, which is surely not the reference here intended; it would be very difficult for such a crispness to associate itself with death, which the scythe represents, or *whim,* or *smoothness* in either the spiritual or fleshly sense. If it implies merely a cleanness, a swift-ness of motion in the apparition of death, some other word would have seemed better chosen. If this analysis be correct, the three words are unalterably combined by the force of *crisply* in such a way as to defeat the only possible sense their *thrilling* use would have had. They are, so to speak, only the notions of themselves and those selves must remain forever unknown. All we are left with in such a phrase as this is the strangeness which struck us on our first encounter; and the only difference is that the strange-ness is the more intensified the more we prolong the examination. This is another test of poetry: whether we understand the *strange-ness* of a poem or not.[1]

As it happens there is an exquisite example of the proper use of this strangeness, this thrill, in another poem of Mr. Cummings'; where he speaks of a cathedral before whose face "the streets turn

---

[1] *Poetic Diction, op. cit.,* pp. 197-8: "It (strangeness) is not synonymous with wonder; for wonder is our reaction to things which we are conscious of not quite understanding, or at any rate of understanding less than we had thought. The element of strangeness in beauty has the contrary effect. It arises from contact with a different kind of *consciousness* from our own, different, yet not so remote that we cannot partly share it, as indeed, in such a connexion, the mere word 'contact' implies. Strangeness, in fact, arouses wonder when we do not understand; aesthetic imagination when we do."

young with rain." While there might be some question as to whether the use of *young* presents the only adequate image, there is certainly no question at all that the phrase is entirely successful: that is, the suggestive feeling in *young* makes the juncture, the emotional conjugation, of streets and rain transparent and perfect. This may be so because there is no element of essential contradiction, in the terms of feeling, between the emotional word *young* and the factual word *streets* and *rain;* or because, positively, what happens to the context by the insertion of *young* is, by a necessary leap of the imagination, something qualified. *Young* may be as abstract a word by itself, as purely relative and notional a word, as any other; but here it is brought into the concrete, is fixed there in a proper habitation. Just because reference is not commonly made either to young streets or young rain, the combination here effected is the more appropriate. The surprise, the contrast, which lend force to the phrase, do not exist in the poem; but exist, if at all, rather in the mind of the reader who did not foresee the slight stretch of his sensibility that the phrase requires—which the phrase not only requires but necessitates. This then is a *strangeness* understood by its own viableness. No preliminary agreement of taste, or contract of symbols, was necessary.

The point is that Mr. Cummings did not here attempt the impossible, he merely stretched the probable. The business of the poet who deals largely with tactual and visual images, as Mr. Cummings does for the meat of his work, is to escape the prison of his private mind; to use in his poem as little as possible of the experience that happened to him personally, and on the other hand to employ as much as possible of that experience as it is data.

It is idle for a critic to make the familiar statement that the mind of the writer is his work, or that "the style is the man," when by mind and man is meant the private experience of the author. So far as, in this sense, the mind *is* the work, or the style *is* the man, we can understand the work or the style only through an accidental unanimity; and what we understand is likely to be very thin—perhaps only the terms of understanding. For the author himself, in such circumstances, can have understood very little more. He has been pursuing the impossible, when the probable was right at hand; he has been transcending his experience instead of submitting to it. And this is just what Mr. Cummings does in the phrases quoted above.

It would be ungracious to suppose that as a poet "a swoon of synopsis" did not represent to Mr. Cummings a very definite and very suggestive image. But to assent to that image would be a kind of *tour de force;* the application of such assent would imply that because the words appear, and being words contain notions, they must in this particular instance exhibit the undeniable sign of interior feeling. The proper process of poetry designs exactly what the reader will perceive; that is what is meant when a word is said to be inevitable or *juste*. But this exactness of perception can only come about when there is an extreme fidelity on the part of the poet to his words as living things; which he can discover and control—which he must learn, and nourish, and stretch; but which he cannot invent. The unanimity in our possible experience of words implies that the only unanimity which the reader can feel in what the poet represents must be likewise exterior to the poet; must be somehow both anterior and posterior to the poet's own experience. The poet's mind, perhaps, is what he is outside himself with; is what he has learned; is what he knows; it is also what the reader knows. So long as he is content to remain in his private mind, he is unknowable, impenetrable, and sentimental. All his words perhaps must thrill us, because we cannot know them in the very degree that we sympathize with them. But the best thrills are those we have without knowing it.

This essay has proceeded so far on the explicit assumption that the poems of Mr. Cummings are unintelligible, and that no amount of effort on the part of the reader can make them less so. We began by connecting Mr. Cummings to two schools, or groups, which are much the same essentially—the anti-culture group which denies the intelligence, and the group, not limited to writers of which the essential attitude is most easily defined as sentimental egoism or romantic idealism. Where these schools are most obviously identical is in the poetry they nourish; the avowed interest is the relentless pursuit of the actual in terms of the immediate as the immediate is given, without overt criticism, to the ego. Unintelligibility is a necessary consequence of such a pursuit, if by the intelligible we mean something concrete, qualified, permanent, and public. Poetry, if we understand it, is not in immediacy at all. It is not given to the senses or to the free intuition. Thus, when poetry is written as if its substance were immediate and given, we have as a result a distorted sensibility and a violent inner confusion. We have, if the poet follows his principles, something abstract, vague, impermanent, and essentially private. When every sensation and every word is taken as final and perfect, the substance which sensations report and for which words must stand remains inexplicable. We can understand only by accident.

Of course there is another side to the matter. In a sense anyone can understand Mr. Cummings and his kind by the mere assertion that he does understand. Nothing else is needed but a little natural sympathy and a certain aptness for the resumption of a childish sensibility. In much the same way we understand a stranger's grief—by setting up a private and less painful simulacrum. If we take the most sentimental and romantic writers as they come, there will be always about their works an excited freshness, the rush of sensation and intuition, all the ominous glow of immediacy. They will be eagerly at home in the mystery of life. Adroitness, expertness, readiness for any experience, will enlighten their activities even where they most miserably fail. They are all actors, ready to take any part, for they put themselves, and nothing else, into every part they play. Commonly their real success will depend on the familiarity of the moments into which they sink themselves; they will depend on convention more than others, because they have nothing else to depend on.

So with the poetry of Mr. Cummings we might be altogether contented and pleased, were he himself content with the measure of his actual performance. But no poetry is so pretentious. No poetry ever claimed to mean more; and in making this claim it cannot avoid submitting itself, disastrously, to the criticism of the intelligence. So soon as we take it seriously, trying to discover what it really says about human destiny and the terms of love and death, we see how little material there is in this poetry except the assurance, made with continuous gusto, that the material exists. We look at the poetry. Sometimes one word, in itself vague and cloudy, is made to take on the work of an entire philosophy—like flower. Sometimes words pile themselves up blindly, each defeating the purport of the others. No feeling is ever defined. No emotion betrays a structure. Experience is its own phantoms, and flows willy-nilly. With the reality of experience the reality of language is lost. No metaphor crosses the bridge of tautology, and every simile is unexpanded. All the *thought* is metonymy, yet the substance is never assigned; so in the end we have only the thrill of substance.

Such an art when it pretends to measure life is essentially vicarious; it is a substitute for something that never was—like a tin soldier, or Peter Pan. It has all the flourish of life and every sentimental sincerity. Taken for what it is, it is charming and even instructive. Taken solemnly, as it is meant to be, the distortion by which it exists is too much for it, and it seems a kind of baby-talk.

A Critic's Job of Work

CRITICISM, I take it, is the formal discourse of an amateur. When there is enough love and enough knowledge represented in the discourse it is a self-sufficient but by no means an isolated art. It witnesses constantly in its own life its interdependence with the

From *The Double Agent. Essays in Craft and Elucidation,* by R. P. Blackmur. Pp. 269-302. Arrow Editions, New York. Copyright, 1935, by R. P. Blackmur. By permission of the author.

other arts. It lays out the terms and parallels of appreciation from the outside in order to convict itself of internal intimacy; it names and arranges what it knows and loves, and searches endlessly with every fresh impulse or impression for better names and more orderly arrangements. It is only in this sense that poetry (or some other art) is a criticism of life; poetry names and arranges, and thus arrests and transfixes its subject in a form which has a life of its own forever separate but springing from the life which confronts it. Poetry is life at the remove of form and meaning; not life lived but life framed and identified. So the criticism of poetry is bound to be occupied at once with the terms and modes by which the remove was made and with the relation between—in the ambiguous stock phrase—content and form; which is to say with the establishment and appreciation of human or moral value. It will be the underlying effort of this essay to indicate approaches to criticism wherein these two problems—of form and value—will appear inextricable but not confused—like the stones in an arch or the timbers in a building.

These approaches—these we wish to eulogize—are not the only ones, nor the only good ones, nor are they complete. No approach opens on anything except from its own point of view and in terms of its own prepossessions. Let us set against each other for a time the facts of various approaches to see whether there is a residue, not of fact but of principle.

The approaches to—or the escapes from—the central work of criticism are as various as the heresies of the Christian church, and like them testify to occasional needs, fanatic emphasis, special interest, or intellectual pride, all flowing from and even the worst of them enlightening the same body of insight. Every critic like every theologian and every philosopher is a casuist in spite of himself. To escape or surmount the discontinuity of knowledge, each resorts to a particular heresy and makes it predominant and even omnivorous.[1]

---

[1] The rashest heresy of our day and climate is that exemplified by T. S. Eliot when he postulates an orthodoxy which exists whether anyone knows it or not.

For most minds, once doctrine is sighted and is held to be the completion of insight, the doctrinal mode of thinking seems the only one possible. When doctrine totters it seems it can fall only into the gulf of bewilderment; few minds risk the fall; most seize the remnants and swear the edifice remains, when doctrine becomes intolerable dogma.[1] All fall notwithstanding; for as knowledge itself is a fall from the paradise of undifferentiated sensation, so equally every formula of knowledge must fall the moment too much weight is laid upon it—the moment it becomes omnivorous and pretends to be omnipotent—the moment, in short, it is taken literally. Literal knowledge is dead knowledge; and the worst bewilderment—which is always only comparative—is better than death. Yet no form, no formula, of knowledge ought to be surrendered merely because it runs the risk in bad or desperate hands of being used literally; and similarly, in our own thinking, whether it is carried to the point of formal discourse or not, we cannot only afford, we ought scrupulously to risk the use of any concept that seems propitious or helpful in getting over gaps. Only the use should be consciously provisional, speculative, and dramatic. The end-virtue of humility comes only after a long train of humiliations; and the chief labor of humbling is the constant, resourceful restoration of ignorance.

The classic contemporary example of use and misuse is attached to the name of Freud. Freud himself has constantly emphasized the provisional, dramatic character of his speculations: they are employed as imaginative illumination, to be relied on no more and no less than the sailor relies upon his buoys and beacons.[2] But the impetus of Freud was so great that a school of literalists arose with all the mad consequence of schism and heresy and fundamentalism which have no more honorable place in the scientific

[1] Baudelaire's sonnet "Le Gouffre" dramatizes this sentiment at once as he saw it surmounted in Pascal and as it occurred insurmountably in himself.

[2] Santayana's essay "A Long Way Round to Nirvana" (in *Some Turns of Thought in Modern Philosophy*) illustrates the poetic-philosophic character of Freud's insight into death by setting up its analogue in Indian philosophy; and by his comparison only adds to the stimulus of Freud.

than the artistic imagination. Elsewhere, from one point of view, Caesarism in Rome and Berlin is only the literalist conception of the need for a positive state. So, too, the economic insights of Marxism, merely by being taken literally in their own field, are held to affect the subject and value of the arts, where actually they offer only a limited field of interest and enliven an irrelevant purpose. It is an amusing exercise—as it refreshes the terms of bewilderment and provides a common clue to the secrets of all the modes of thinking—to restore the insights of Freud and Fascism and Marxism to the terms of the Church; when the sexual drama in Freud becomes the drama of original sin, and the politics of Hitler and Lenin becomes the politics of the City of God in the sense that theology provides both the sanctions of economics and the values of culture. Controversy is in terms absolutely held, when the problems argued are falsely conceived because necessarily abstracted from "real" experience. The vital or fatal nexus is in interest and emotion and is established when the terms can be represented dramatically, almost, as it were, for their own sakes alone and with only a pious or ritualistic regard for the doctrines in which they are clothed. The simple, and fatal, example is in the glory men attach to war; the vital, but precarious example, is in the intermittent conception of free institutions and the persistent reformulation of the myth of reason. Then the doctrines do not matter, since they are taken only for what they are worth (whatever rhetorical pretensions to the contrary) as guides and props, as aids to navigation. What does matter is the experience, the life represented and the value discovered, and both dramatized or enacted under the banner of doctrine. All banners are wrong-headed, but they make rallying points, free the impulse to cry out, and give meaning to the cry itself simply by making it seem appropriate.

It is on some analogue or parallel to these remarks alone that we understand and use the thought and art of those whose doctrines differ from our own. We either discount, absorb, or dominate the doctrine for the sake of the life that goes with it, for the sake of what is *formed* in the progressive act of thinking. When

we do more—when we refine or elaborate the abstracted notion
of form—we play a different game, which has merit of its own
like chess, but which applied to the world we live in produces
false dilemmas like solipsism and infant damnation. There is,
taking solipsism for example, a fundamental distinction. Because
of the logical doctrine prepared to support it, technical philosophers
employ years [1] to get around the impasse in which it leaves them;
whereas men of poetic imagination merely use it for the dramatic
insight it contains—as Eliot uses it in the last section of *The Waste
Land;* or as, say, everyone uses the residual mythology of the Greek
religion—which its priests nevertheless used as literal sanction for
blood and power.

Fortunately, there exists archetypes of unindoctrinated thinking.
Let us incline our minds like reflectors to catch the light of the
early Plato and the whole Montaigne. Is not the inexhaustible
stimulus and fertility of the *Dialogues* and the *Essays* due as much
as anything to the absence of positive doctrine? Is it not that the
early Plato always holds conflicting ideas in shifting balance, presenting them in contest and evolution, with victory only the last
shift? Is it not that Montaigne is always making room for another idea, and implying always a third for provisional adjudicat-
ing irony? Are not the forms of both men themselves ironic,
betraying in its most intimate recesses the duplicity of every
thought pointing out, so to speak, in the act of self-incrimination,
and showing it not paled on a pin but in the buff life? . . . Such
an approach, such an attempt at vivid questing, borrowed and no
doubt adulterated by our own needs, is the only rational approach
to the multiplication of doctrine and arrogant technologies which
fills out the body of critical thinking. Anything else is a succumb-
ing, not an approach; and it is surely the commonest of ironies to
observe a man altogether out of his depth do his cause fatal harm
merely because, having once succumbed to an idea, he thinks it

---

[1] Santayana found it necessary to resort to his only sustained labor of
dialectic, *Scepticism and Animal Faith,* which, though a beautiful monument
of intellectual play, is ultimately valuable for its *incidental* moral wisdom.

necessary to stick to it. Thought is a beacon not a life-raft, and to confuse the functions is tragic. The tragic character of thought —as any perspective will show—is that it takes a rigid mold too soon; chooses destiny like a Calvinist, in infancy, instead of waiting slowly for old age, and hence for the most part works against the world, good sense, and its own object: as anyone may see by taking a perspective of any given idea of democracy, of justice, or the nature of the creative act.

Imaginative skepticism and dramatic irony—the modes of Montaigne and Plato—keep the mind athletic and the spirit on the stretch. Hence the juvenescence of *The Tempest* and hence, too, perhaps, the air almost of precocity in *Back to Methuselah*. Hence, at any rate, the sustaining power of such varied works as *The Brothers Karamazoff, Cousine Bette,* and *The Magic Mountain*. Dante, whom the faithful might take to the contrary, is yet "the chief imagination of Christendom"; he took his doctrine once and for all from the Church and from St. Thomas and used it as a foil (in the painter's sense) to give recessiveness, background, and contrast. Virgil and Aristotle, Beatrice and Bertrans de Born have in their way as much importance as St. Thomas and the Church. It was this security of reference that made Dante so much more a free spirit than were, say, Swift and Laurence Sterne. Dante had a habit (not a theory) of imagination which enabled him to dramatize with equal ardor and effect what his doctrine blessed, what it assailed, and what, at heart, it was indifferent to. Doctrine was the seed and structure of vision, and for his poems (at least to us) never more. *The Divine Comedy* no less than the *Dialogues* and the *Essays* is a true *Speculum Mentis*.

With lesser thinkers and lesser artists—and in the defective works of the greater—we have in reading, in criticising, to supply the skepticism and the irony, or, as may be, the imagination and the drama, to the degree, which cannot be complete since then we should have had no prompts, that they are lacking. We have to rub the looking-glass clear. With Hamlet, for example, we have to struggle and guess to bring the motive out of obscurity: a struggle which, aiming at the wrong end, the psychoanalysts have darkened with counsel. With Shelley we have to flesh out the Platonic Ideas, as with Blake we have to cut away, since it cannot be dramatized, all the excrescence of doctrine. With Baudelaire we have sometimes to struggle with and sometimes to suppress the problem of belief, working out the irony implicit in either attitude. Similarly, with a writer like Pascal, in order to get the most out of him, in order to compose an artistic judgment, we must consider such an idea as that of the necessity of the wager, not solemnly as Pascal took it, but as a dramatized possibility, a savage, but provisional irony; and we need to show that the skepticisms of Montaigne and Pascal are not at all the same thing—that where one produced serenity the other produced excruciation.

Again, speaking of André Gide, we should remind ourselves not that he has been the apologist of homosexuality, not that he has become a communist, but that he is *par excellence* the French puritan chastened by the wisdom of the body, and that he has thus an acutely scrupulous ethical sensibility. It is by acknowledging the sensibility that we feel the impact of the apologetics and the political conversion. Another necessity in the apprehension of Gide might be put as the recognition of similarity in difference of the precocious small boys in Dostoevsky and Gide, *e.g.*, Kolya in *Karamazoff* and young George in *The Counterfeiters:* they are small, cruel engines, all naked sensibility and no scruple, demoniacally possessed, and used to keep things going. And these in turn for presenting the *terrible* quality of the young intelligence: of Henry James, of the children in *The Turn of the Screw,* of *Maisie,* and all the rest, all beautifully efficient agents of dramatic judgment and action, in that they take all things seriously for themselves, with the least prejudice of preparation, candidly, with an intelligence life has not yet violated.

Such feats of agility and attention as these remarks illustrate seem facile and even commonplace, and from facile points of view there is no need to take them otherwise. Taken superficially they provide escape from the whole labor of specific understanding; or, worse, they provide an easy vault from casual interpretation to an omnivorous world-view. We might take solemnly and as of universal application the two notions of demonic possession and inviolate intelligence of Gide, Dostoievski, and James, and on that frail nexus build an unassailable theory of the sources of art, wisdom, and value; unassailable because affording only a stereotyped vision, like that of conservative capitalism, without reference in the real world. The maturity of Shakespeare and of Gertrude Stein would then be found on the same childish level.

But we need not go so far in order to draw back. The modes of Montaigne and Plato contain their own safety. Any single insight is good only at and up to a certain point of development and not beyond, which is to say that it is a provisional and tentative and highly selective approach to its field. Furthermore, no observation, no collection of observations, ever tells the whole story; there is always room for more, and at the hypothetical limit of attention and interest there will always remain, quite untouched, the thing itself. Thus the complex character—I say nothing of the value—of the remarks above reveals itself. They flow from a dramatic combination of all the skills and conventions of the thinking mind. They are commonplace only as a criticism—as an end-product or function. Like walking, criticism is a pretty nearly universal art; both require a constant intricate shifting and catching of balance; neither can be questioned much in process; and few perform either really well. For either a new terrain is fatiguing and awkward, and in our day most men prefer paved walks or some form of rapid transit—some easy theory or outmastering dogma. A good critic keeps his criticism from becoming either instinctive or vicarious, and the labor of his understanding is always specific, like the art which he examines; and he knows that the sum of his best work comes only to the pedagogy of elucidation and appreciation. He observes facts and he delights in discriminations. The object remains, and should remain, itself, only made more available and seen in a clearer light. The imagination of Dante is for us only equal to what we can know of it at a given time.

Which brings us to what, as T. S. Eliot would say,[1] I have been leading up to all the time, and what has indeed been said several times by the way. Any rational approach is valid to literature and may be properly called critical which fastens at any point upon the work itself. The utility of a given approach depends partly upon the strength of the mind making it and partly upon the recognition of the limits appropriate to it. Limits may be of scope, degree, or relevance, and may be either plainly laid out by the critic himself, or may be determined by his readers; and it is, by our argument, the latter case that commonly falls, since an active mind tends to overestimate the scope of its tools and to take as necessary those doctrinal considerations which habit has made seem instinctive. No critic is required to limit himself to a single approach, nor is he likely to be able to do so; facts cannot be exhibited without comment, and comment involves the generality of the mind. Furthermore, a consciously complex approach like that of Kenneth Burke or T. S. Eliot, by setting up parallels of reference, affords a more flexible, more available, more stimulating standard of judgment—though of course at a greater risk of prejudice—than a single approach. What produces the evil of stultification and the malice of controversy is the confused approach, when the limits are not seen because they tend to cancel each other out, and the driving power becomes emotional.

The worse evil of fanatic falsification—of arrogant irrationality and barbarism in all its forms—arises when a body of criticism is governed by an *idée fixe,* a really exaggerated heresy, when a notion of genuine but small scope is taken literally as of universal application. This is the body of tendentious criticism where, since something is assumed proved before the evidence is in, distortion,

[1] . . . that when "morals cease to be a matter of tradition and orthodoxy —that is, of the habits of the community formulated, corrected, and elevated by the continuous thought and direction of the Church—and when each man is to elaborate his own, then *personality* becomes a thing of alarming importance." (*After Strange Gods.*) Thus Mr. Eliot becomes one of those viewers-with-alarm whose next step is the very hysteria of disorder they wish to escape. The hysteria of institutions is more dreadful than that of individuals.

vitiation, and absolute assertion become supreme virtues. I cannot help feeling that such writers as Maritain and Massis—no less than Nordau before them—are tendentious in this sense. But even here, in this worst order of criticism, there is a taint of legitimacy. Once we reduce, in a man like Irving Babbitt, the magnitude of application of such notions as the inner check and the higher will, which were for Babbitt paramount—that is, when we determine the limits within which he really worked—then the massive erudition and acute observation with which his work is packed become permanently available.

And there is no good to be got in objecting to and disallowing those orders of criticism which have an ulterior purpose. *Ulterior* is not in itself a pejorative, but only so when applied to an enemy. Since criticism is not autonomous—not a light but a process of elucidation—it cannot avoid discovering constantly within itself a purpose or purposes ulterior in the good sense. The danger is in not knowing what is ulterior and what is not, which is much the same as the cognate danger in the arts themselves. The arts serve purposes beyond themselves; the purposes of what they dramatize or represent at that remove from the flux which gives them order and meaning and value; and to deny those purposes is like asserting that the function of a handsaw is to hang above a bench and that to cut wood is to belittle it. But the purposes are varied and so bound in his subject that the artist cannot always design for them. The critic, if that is his bent, may concern himself with those purposes or with some one among them which obsess him; but he must be certain to distinguish between what is genuinely ulterior to the works he examines and what is merely irrelevant; and he must further not assume except within the realm of his special argument that other purposes either do not exist or are negligible or that the works may not be profitably discussed apart from ulterior purposes and as examples of dramatic possibility alone.

II

Three examples of contemporary criticism primarily concerned with the ulterior purposes of literature should, set side by side, exhibit both the defects and the unchastened virtues of that approach; though they must do so only tentatively and somewhat invidiously—with an exaggeration for effect. Each work is assumed to be a representative ornament of its kind, carrying within it the seeds of its own death and multiplication. Let us take then, with an eye sharpened by the dangers involved, Santayana's essay on Lucretius (in *Three Philosophical Poets*), Van Wyck Brooks' *Pilgrimage of Henry James,* and Granville Hicks' *The Great Tradition*. Though that of the third is more obvious in our predicament, the urgency in the approach is equal in all three.

Santayana's essay represents a conversion or transvaluation of an actually poetic ordering of nature to the terms of a moral philosophy which, whatever its own responsibilities, is free of the special responsibility of poetry. So ably and so persuasively is it composed, his picture seems complete and to contain so much of what was important in Lucretius that *De Rerum Natura* itself can be left behind. The philosophical nature of the insight, its moral scope and defect, the influence upon it of the Democritan atom, once grasped intellectually as Santayana shows us how to grasp them, seem a good substitute for the poem and far more available. But, what Santayana remembers but does not here emphasize since it was beyond his immediate interest, there is no vicar for poetry on earth. Poetry is idiom, a special and fresh saying, and cannot for its life be said otherwise; and there is, finally, as much difference between words used about a poem and the poem as there is between words used about a painting and the painting. The gap is absolute. Yet I do not mean to suggest that Santayana's essay—that any philosophical criticism—is beside the point. It is true that the essay may be taken as a venture in philosophy for its own sake, but it is also true that it reveals a body of facts about an ulterior purpose in Lucretius' poem—doubtless the very purpose Lucretius himself would have chosen to see enhanced. If we return to the poem it will be warmer as the facts come alive in the verse. The re-conversion comes naturally in this instance in that, through idioms differently construed but equally imaginative, philosophy and poetry both buttress and express moral value. The one enacts or represents in the flesh what the other reduces to principle or raises to the ideal. The only precaution the critic of poetry need take is negative: that neither poetry nor philosophy can ever fully satisfy the other's purposes, though each may seem to do so if taken in an ulterior fashion. The relationship is mutual but not equivalent.

When we turn deliberately from Santayana on Lucretius to Van Wyck Brooks on Henry James, we turn from the consideration of the rational ulterior purposes of art to the consideration of the irrational underlying predicament of the artist himself, not only as it predicts his art and is reflected in it, but also, and in effect predominantly, as it represents the conditioning of nineteenth-century American culture. The consideration is sociological, the method of approach that of literary psychology, and the burden obsessive. The conversion is from literary to biographical values. Art is taken not as the objectification or mirroring of social experience but as a personal expression and escape-fantasy of the artist's personal life in dramatic extension. The point for emphasis is that the cultural situation of Henry James' America stultified the expression and made every escape ineffectual—even that of Europe. This theme—the private tragedy of the unsuccessful artist—was one of Henry James' own; but James saw it as typical or universal—as a characteristic tragedy of the human spirit—illustrated, as it happened for him, against the Anglo-American background. Brooks, taking the same theme, raises it to an obsession, an omnivorous concept, under which all other themes can be subsumed. Applied to American cultural history, such obsessive thinking is suggestive in the very exaggeration of its terms, and applied to the private predicament of Henry James the man it dramatically emphasizes—uses for all and more than it is worth— an obvious conflict that tormented him. As history or as biography the book is a persuasive imaginative picture, although clearly not the only one to be seen. Used as a nexus between James the man and the novels themselves, the book has only possible relevance and cannot be held as material. *Hamlet,* by a similar argument, could be shown to be an unsuccessful expression of Shakespeare's personality. To remain useful in the field of literary criticism, Brooks' notions ought to be kept parallel to James' novels but never allowed to merge with them. The corrective, the proof of the gap, is perhaps in the great air of freedom and sway of mastery that pervades the "Prefaces" James wrote to his collected edition. For James art was enough because it molded and mirrored and valued all the life he knew. What Brooks' parallel strictures can do is to help us decide from another point of view whether to choose the values James dramatized. They cannot affect or elucidate but rather—if the gap is closed by will—obfuscate the values themselves.

In short, the order of criticism of which Brooks is a masterly exponent, and which we may call the psycho-sociological order, is primarily and in the end concerned less with the purposes, ulterior or not, of the arts than with some of the ulterior *uses* to which the arts can be appropriately put. Only what is said in the meantime, by the way—and does not depend upon the essence of argument but only accompanies it—can be applied to the arts themselves. There is nothing, it should be added, in Brooks' writings to show that he believes otherwise or would claim more; he is content with that scope and degree of value to which his method and the strength of his mind limit him; and his value is the greater and more urgent for that.

Such tacit humility, such implicit admission of contingency, are not immediate characteristics of Granville Hicks' *The Great Tradition,* though they may, so serious is his purpose, be merely virtues of which he deliberately, for the time being and in order to gain his point, deprives himself of the benefit. If this is so, however expedient his tactics may seem on the short view they will defeat him on the long. But let us examine the book on the ground of our present concern alone. Like Brooks, Hicks presents

an interpretation of American literature since the Civil War, dealing with the whole body rather than single figures. Like Brooks
he has a touchstone in an obsessive idea, but where we may say
that Brooks *uses* his idea—as we think for more than it is worth—
we must say that Hicks is victimized by his idea to the point where
the travail of judgment is suspended and becomes the mere reiteration of formula. He judges literature as it expressed or failed to
express the economic conflict of classes sharpened by the industrial
revolution, and he judges individual writers as they used or did
not use an ideology resembling the Marxist analysis as prime clue
to the clear representation of social drama. Thus Howells comes
off better than Henry James, and Frank Norris better than Mark
Twain, and, in our own day, Dos Passos is stuck on a thin eminence that must alarm him.

Controversy is not here a profitable exercise, but it may be said
for the sake of the record that although every period of history
presents a class struggle, some far more acute than our own, the
themes of great art have seldom lent themselves to propaganda
for an economic insight, finding, as it happened, religious, moral
or psychological—that is to say, interpretative—insights more appropriate impulses. If *Piers Plowman* dealt with the class struggle, *The Canterbury Tales* did not, and Hicks would be hard put,
if he looked sharp, to make out a better case of social implication
in Dostoievski than in Henry James.

What vitiates *The Great Tradition* is its tendentiousness. Nothing could be more exciting, nothing more vital, than a book by
Hicks which discovered and examined the facts of a literature
whose major theme hung on an honest dramatic view of the class
struggle—and there is indeed such a literature now emerging from
the depression. And on the other hand it would be worth while
to have Hicks sharpen his teeth on all the fraudulent or pseudo-
art which actually slanders the terms of the class and every other
struggle.

The book with which he presents us performs a very different
operation. There is an initial hortatory assumption that American
literature ought to represent the class struggle from a Marxist view-

point, and that it ought thus to be the spur and guide to political action. Proceeding, the point is either proved or the literature dismissed and its authors slandered. Hicks is not disengaging for emphasis and contemporary need an ulterior purpose; he is not writing criticism at all; he is writing a fanatic's history and a casuist's polemic, with the probable result—which is what was meant by suggesting above that he had misconceived his tactics—that he will convert no one who retains the least love of literature or the least knowledge of the themes which engage the most of life. It should be emphasized that there is no more quarrel with Hicks' economic insight as such than there was with the insights of Santayana and Van Wyck Brooks. The quarrel is deeper. While it is true and good that the arts may be used to illustrate social propaganda—though it is not a great use—you can no more use an economic insight as your chief critical tool than you can make much out of the Mass by submitting the doctrine of transubstantiation to chemical analysis.

These three writers have one great formal fact in common, which they illustrate as differently as may be. They are concerned with the separable content of literature, with what may be said without consideration of its specific setting and apparition in a form; which is why, perhaps, all three leave literature so soon behind. The quantity of what can be said directly about the content alone of a given work of art is seldom great, but the least saying may be the innervation of an infinite intellectual structure, which, however valuable in itself, has for the most part only an asserted relation with the works from which it springs. The sense of continuous relationship, of sustained contact, with the works nominally in hand is rare and when found uncommonly exhilarating; it is the fine object of criticism; as it seems to put us in direct possession of the principles whereby the works move without injuring or disintegrating the body of the works themselyes. This sense of intimacy by inner contact cannot arise from methods of approach which hinge on seized separable content. We have constantly—if our interest is really in literature—to prod ourselves back, to remind ourselves that there was a poem, a play, or a novel of some initial and we hope terminal concern, or we have to falsify and set up fictions [1] to the effect that no matter what we are saying we are really talking about art after all. The question must often be whether the prodding and reminding is worth the labor, whether we might not better assign the works that require it to a different category than that of criticism.

III

Similar strictures and identical precautions are necessary in thinking of other, quite different approaches to criticism, where if there are no ulterior purposes to allow for there are other no less limiting features—there are certainly such, for example, for me in thinking of my own. The ulterior motive, or the limiting feature, whichever it is, is a variable constant. One does not always know what it is, nor what nor how much work it does; but one always knows it is there—for strength or weakness. It may be only the strength of emphasis—which is necessarily distortion; or it may be the worse strength of a simplifying formula, which skeletonizes and transforms what we want to recognize in the flesh. It may be only the weakness of what is unfinished, undeveloped, or unseen—the weakness that follows on emphasis; or it may be the weakness that shows when pertinent things are deliberately dismissed or ignored, which is the corresponding weakness of the mind strong in formula. No mind can avoid distortion and formula altogether, nor would wish to; but minds rush to the defense of qualities they think cannot be avoided, and that, in itself, is an ulterior motive, a limiting feature of the mind that rushes. I say nothing of one's

[1] Such a fiction, if not consciously so contrived, is the fiction of the organic continuity of all literature as expounded by T. S. Eliot in his essay, "Tradition and the Individual Talent." The locus is famous and represents that each new work of art slightly alters the relationships among the whole order of existing works. The notion has truth, but it is a mathematical truth and has little relevance to the arts. Used as Eliot uses it, it is an experimental conceit and pushes the mind forward. Taken seriously it is bad constitutional law, in the sense that it would provoke numberless artificial and insoluble problems.

personal prepossessions, of the damage of one's personal prepossessions, of the damage of one's private experience, of the malice
and false tolerance they inculcate into judgment. I know that my
own essays suffer variously, but I cannot bring myself to specify
the indulgences I would ask; mostly, I hope, that general indulgence which consists in the task of bringing my distortions and
emphases and opinions into balance with other distortions, other
emphases and better opinions.

But rather than myself, let us examine briefly, because of their
differences from each other and from the three critics already
handled, the modes of approach to the act of criticism and habits
of critical work of I. A. Richards, Kenneth Burke, and S. Foster
Damon. It is to characterize them and to judge the *character* of
their work—its typical scope and value—that we want to examine
them. With the objective validity of their varying theories we are
not much here concerned. Objective standards of criticism, as we
hope them to exist at all, must have an existence anterior and superior to the practice of particular critics. The personal element
in a given critic—what he happens to know and happens to be
able to understand—is strong or obstinate enough to reach into
his esthetic theories; and as most critics do not have the coherence
of philosophers it seems doubtful if any outsider could ever reach
the same conclusions as the critic did by adopting his esthetics.
Esthetics sometimes seems only as implicit in the practice of criticism as the atomic physics is present in sunlight when you feel it.

But some critics deliberately expand the theoretic phase of every
practical problem. There is a tendency to urge the scientific principle and the statistical method, and in doing so to bring in the
whole assorted world of thought. That Mr. Richards, who is an
admirable critic and whose love and knowledge of poetry are in-
contestable, is a victim of the expansiveness of his mind in these
directions, is what characterizes, and reduces, the scope of his work
as literary criticism. It is possible that he ought not to be called
a literary critic at all. If we list the titles of his books we are in
a quandary: *The Foundations of Aesthetics, The Meaning of
Meaning* (these with C. K. Ogden), *The Principles of Literary*

Criticism, Science and Poetry, Practical Criticism, Mencius on the Mind, and *Coleridge on Imagination.* The apparatus is so vast, so labyrinthine, so inclusive—and the amount of actual literary criticism is so small that it seems almost a by-product instead of the central target. The slightest volume, physically, *Science and Poetry,* contains proportionally the most literary criticism, and contains, curiously, his one obvious failure in appreciation—since amply redressed—his misjudgment of the nature of Yeats' poetry. His work is for the most part *about* a department of the mind which includes the pedagogy of sensibility and the practice of literary criticism. The matters he investigates are the problems of belief, of meaning, of communication, of the nature of controversy, and of poetic language as the supreme mode of imagination. The discussion of these problems is made to focus for the most part on poetry because poetry provides the only great monuments of imagination available to verbal imagination. His bottom contention might, I think, be put as this: that words have a synergical power, in the realms of feeling, emotions, and value, to create a reality, or the sense of it, not contained in the words separately; and that the power and the reality as experienced in great poetry make the chief source of meaning and value for the life we live. This contention I share; except that I should wish to put on the same level, as sources of meaning and value, modes of imagination that have no medium in words—though words may call on them—and are not susceptible of verbal reformulation: the modes of great acting, architecture, music and painting. Thus I can assent to Mr. Richards' positive statement of the task of criticism, because I can add to it positive tasks in analogous fields: "To recall that poetry is the supreme use of language, man's chief co-ordinating instrument, in the service of the most integral purposes of life; and to explore, with thoroughness, the intricacies of the modes of language as working modes of the mind." But I want this criticism, engaged in this task, constantly to be confronted with examples of poetry, and I want it so for the very practical purpose of assisting in pretty immediate appreciation of the use, meaning, and value of the language in that particular poetry. I want it to assist in doing for me what it actually assists Mr. Richards in doing, whatever that is, when he is reading poetry for its own sake.

Mr. Richards wants it to do that, too, but he wants it to do a great deal else first. Before it gets to actual poetry (from which it is said to spring) he wants literary criticism to become something else and much more: he wants it to become, indeed, the master department of the mind. As we become aware of the scope of poetry, we see, according to Mr. Richards that the

study of the modes of language becomes, as it attempts to be thorough, the most fundamental and extensive of all inquiries. It is no preliminary or preparation for other profounder studies. . . . The very formation of the objects which these studies propose to examine takes place through the processes (of which imagination and fancy are modes) by which the words they use acquire their meanings. Criticism is the science of these meanings. . . . Critics in the future must have a theoretical equipment which has not been felt to be necessary in the past. . . . But the critical equipment will not be *primarily* philosophical. It will be rather a command *of the methods of general linguistic analysis*.[1]

I think we may take it that *Mencius on the Mind* is an example of the kind of excursion on which Mr. Richards would lead us. It is an excursion into multiple definition, and it is a good one if that is where you want to go and are in no hurry to come back: you learn the enormous variety and complexity of the operations possible in the process of verbally describing and defining brief passages of imaginative language and the equal variety and complexity of the result; you learn the practical impossibility of verbally ascertaining what an author means—and you hear nothing of the other ways of apprehending meaning at all. The instance is in the translation of Mencius, because Mr. Richards happens to be interested in Mencius, and because it is easy to see the difficulties of translating Chinese; but the principles and method of applica-

[1] All quoted material is from the last four pages of *Coleridge on Imagination*.

tion would work as well on passages from Milton or Rudyard Kipling. The real point of Mr. Richards' book is the impossibility of understanding, short of a lifetime's analysis and compensation, the mechanism of meaning in even a small body of work. There is no question of the exemplary value and stimulus of Mr. Richards' work; but there is no question either that few would care to emulate him for any purpose of literary criticism. In the first place it would take too long, and in the second he does not answer the questions literary criticism would put. The literal adoption of Mr. Richards' approach to literary criticism would stultify the very power it was aimed to enhance—the power of imaginative apprehension, of imaginative co-ordination of varied and separate elements. Mr. Richards' work is something to be aware of, but deep awareness is the limit of use. It is notable that in his admirable incidental criticism of such poets as Eliot, Lawrence, Yeats and Hopkins, Mr. Richards does not himself find it necessary to be more than aware of his own doctrines of linguistic analysis. As philosophy from Descartes to Bradley transformed itself into a study of the modes of knowing, Mr. Richards would transform literary criticism into the science of linguistics. Epistemology is a great subject, and so is linguistics; but they come neither in first nor final places; the one is only a fragment of wisdom and the other only a fraction of the means of understanding. Literary criticism is not a science—though it may be the object of one; and to try to make it one is to turn it upside down. Right side up, Mr. Richards' contribution shrinks in weight and dominion but remains intact and preserves its importance. We may conclude that it was the newness of his view that led him to exaggerate it, and we ought to add the probability that had he not exaggerated it we should never have seen either that it was new or valuable at all.

From another point of view than that of literary criticism, and as a contribution to a psychological theory of knowledge, Mr. Richards' work is not heretical, but is integral and integrating, and especially when it incorporates poetry into its procedure; but from our point of view the heresy is profound—and is far more distorting than the heresies of Santayana, Brooks, and Hicks, which carry with them obviously the impetus for their correction. Because it is possible to apply scientific methods to the language of poetry, and because scientific methods engross their subject matter, Mr. Richards places the whole burden of criticism in the application of a scientific approach, and asserts it to be an implement for the judgment of poetry. Actually, it can handle only the language and its words and cannot touch—except by assertion—the imaginative product of the words which is poetry: which is the object revealed or elucidated by criticism. Criticism must be concerned, first and last—whatever comes between—with the poem as it is read and as what it represents is felt. As no amount of physics and physiology can explain the *feeling* of things seen as green or even certify their existence, so no amount of linguistic analysis can explain the *feeling* or existence of a poem. Yet the physics in the one case and the linguistics in the other may be useful both to the poet and the reader. It may be useful, for example, in extracting facts of meaning from a poem, to show that, whether the poet was aware of it or not, the semantic history of a word was so and so; but only if the semantics can be resolved into the ambiguities and precisions created by the poem. Similarly with any branch of linguistics; and similarly with the applications of psychology—Mr. Richards' other emphasis. No statistical description can either explain or demean a poem unless the description is translated back to the imaginative apprehension or feeling which must have taken place without it. The light of science is parallel or in the background where feeling or meaning is concerned. The Oedipus complex does not explain *Oedipus Rex;* not that Mr. Richards would think it did. Otherwise he could not believe that "poetry is the supreme use of language" and more, could not convey in his comments on T. S. Eliot's *Ash Wednesday* the actuality of his belief that poetry is the supreme use.

It is the interest and fascination of Mr. Richards' work in reference to different levels of sensibility, including the poetic, that has given him both a wide and a penetrating influence. No literary critic can escape his influence; an influence that stimulates the mind as much as anything by showing the sheer excitement as well as profundity of the problems of language—many of which he has himself made genuine problems, at least for the readers of poetry: an influence, obviously, worth deliberately incorporating by reducing it to one's own size and needs. In T. S. Eliot the influence is conspicuous if slight. Mr. Kenneth Burke is considerably indebted, partly directly to Mr. Richards, partly to the influences which acted upon Mr. Richards (as Bentham's theory of Fictions) and partly to the frame of mind which helped mold them both. But Mr. Burke is clearly a different person—and different from anyone writing today; and the virtues, the defects, and the élan of his criticism are his own.

Some years ago, when Mr. Burke was an animating influence on the staff of *The Dial,* Miss Marianne Moore published a poem in that magazine called "Picking and Choosing" which contained the following lines:

> and Burke is a
> psychologist—of acute and racoon-
> like curiosity. *Summa diligentia*
> to the humbug, whose name is so amusing—very young
> and ve-
> ry rushed, Caesar crossed the Alps on the 'top of a
> *diligence.'* We are not daft about the meaning but this
> familiarity
> with wrong meanings puzzles one.

In the index of Miss Moore's *Observations,* we find under Burke that the reference is to Edmund, but it is really to Kenneth just the same. There is no acuter curiosity than Mr. Burke's engaged in associating the meanings, right and wrong, of the business of literature with the business of life and vice versa. No one has a greater awareness—not even Mr. Richards—of the important part wrong meanings play in establishing the consistency of right ones. The writer of whom he reminds us, for buoyancy and sheer remarkableness of his speculations, is Charles Santiago Saunders Peirce; one is enlivened by them without any *necessary* reference to their truth; hence they have truth for their own purposes, that is, for their own uses. Into what these purposes or uses are it is our present business to inquire.

As Mr. Richards in fact uses literature as a springboard or source for scientific method of a philosophy of value, Mr. Burke uses literature, not only as a springboard but also as a resort or home, for philosophy or psychology of moral possibility. Literature is the hold-all and the persuasive form for the patterns of possibility. In literature we see unique possibilities enacted, actualized, and in the moral and psychological philosophies we see the types of possibility generalized, see their abstracted, convertible forms. In some literature, and in some aspects of most literature, and in some aspects of most literature of either great magnitude or great possibility, we see, so to speak, the enactment or dramatic representation of the type or patterns. Thus Mr. Burke can make a thrilling intellectual pursuit of the subintelligent writing of Erskine Caldwell: where he shows that Caldwell gains a great effect of humanity by putting in *none himself,* appealing to the reader's common stock: *i.e.,* what is called for so desperately by the pattern of the story must needs be generously supplied. Exactly as thrilling is his demonstration of the great emotional rôle of the outsider as played in the supremely intelligent works of Thomas Mann and André Gide. His common illustrations of the pervasive spread of symbolic pattern are drawn from Shakespeare and from the type of the popular or pulp press. I think that on the whole his method could be applied with equal fruitfulness to Shakespeare, Dashiell Hammett, or Marie Corelli; as indeed he does apply it with equal force both to the field of anarchic private morals and to the outline of a secular conversion to Communism—as in, respectively, *Toward a Better Life* and *Permanence and Change.*

The real harvest that we barn from Mr. Burke's writings is his presentation of the types of ways the mind works in the written word. He is more interested in the psychological means of the meaning, and how it might mean (and often really does) something else, than in the meaning itself. Like Mr. Richards, but for another purpose, he is engaged largely in the meaning of meaning, and is therefore much bound up with considerations of language, but on the plane of emotional and intellectual patterns rather than on the emotional plane; which is why his essays deal with literature (or other writings) as it dramatizes or unfolds character (a character is a pattern of emotions and notions) rather than with lyric or meditative poetry which is Mr. Richards' field. So we find language containing felt character as well as felt co-ordination. The representation of character, and of aspiration and symbol, must always be rhetorical; and therefore we find that for Mr. Burke the rightly rhetorical is the profoundly hortatory. Thus literature may be seen as an inexhaustible reservoir of moral or character philosophies in action.

It is the technique of such philosophies that Mr. Burke explores, as he pursues it through curiosities of development and conversion and duplicity; it is the technique of the notions that may be put into or taken out of literature, but it is only a part of the technique of literature itself. The final reference is to the psychological and moral possibilities of the mind, and these certainly do not exhaust the technique or the reality of literature. The reality in literature is an object of contemplation and of feeling, like the reality of a picture or a cathedral, not a route of speculation. If we remember this and make the appropriate reductions here as elsewhere, Mr. Burke's essays become as pertinent to literary criticism as they are to the general ethical play of the mind. Otherwise they become too much a methodology for its own sake on the one hand, and too much a philosophy at one remove on the other. A man writes as he can; but those who use his writings have the further responsibility of redefining their scope, an operation (of which Mr. Burke is a master) which alone uses them to the full.

It is in relation to these examples which I have so unjustly held up of the philosophical, the sociological, or psychological approaches to criticism that I wish to examine an example of what composes, after all, the great bulk of serious writings about literature: a work of literary scholarship. Upon scholarship all other forms of literary criticism depend, so long as they are criticism, in much the same way that architecture depends on engineering. The great editors of the last century—men such as Dyce and Skeat and Gifford and

Furness—performed work as valuable to the use of literature, and with far less complement of harm, as men like Hazlitt and Arnold and Pater. Scholarship, being bent on the collection, arrangement, and scrutiny of facts, has the positive advantage over other forms of criticism that it is a co-operative labor, and may be completed and corrected by subsequent scholars; and it has the negative advantage that it is not bound to investigate the mysteries of meaning or to connect literature with other departments of life—it has only to furnish the factual materials for such investigations and connections. It is not surprising to find that the great scholars are sometimes good critics, though usually in restricted fields; and it is a fact, on the other hand, that the great critics are themselves either good scholars or know how to take great advantage of scholarship. Perhaps we may put it that for the most part dead critics remain alive in us to the extent that they form part of our scholarship. It is Dr. Johnson's statements of fact that we preserve of him as a critic; his opinions have long since become a part of that imaginative structure, his personality. A last fact about scholarship is this, that so far as its conclusions are sound they are subject to use and digestion not debate by those outside the fold. And of bad scholarship as of bad criticism we have only to find means to minimize what we cannot destroy.

It is difficult to find an example of scholarship pure and simple, of high character, which can be made to seem relevant to the discussion in hand. What I want is to bring into the discussion the omnipresence of scholarship as a background and its immediate and necessary availability to every other mode of approach. What I want is almost anonymous. Failing that, I choose S. Foster Damon's *William Blake* (as I might have taken J. L. Lowes' *Road to Xanadu*) which, because of its special subject matter, brings its scholarship a little nearer the terms of discussion than a Shakespeare commentary would have done. The scholar's major problem with Blake happened to be one which many scholars could not handle, some refused to see, and some fumbled. A great part of Blake's meaning is not open to ordinarily well-instructed readers, but must be brought out by the detailed solution of something very like an enormous and enormously complicated acrostic puzzle. Not only earnest scrutiny of the poems as printed, but also a study of Blake's reading, a reconstruction of habits of thought, and an industrious piecing together into a consistent key of thousands of clues throughout the work, were necessary before many even of the simplest appearing poems could be explained. It is one thing to explain a mystical poet, like Crashaw, who was attached to a recognized church, and difficult enough; but it is a far more difficult thing to explain a mystical poet like Blake, who was so much an eclectic in his sources that his mystery as well as his apprehension of it was practically his own. All Mr. Damon had to go on besides the texts, and the small body of previous scholarship that was pertinent, were the general outlines of insight to which all mystics apparently adhere. The only explanation would be in the facts of what Blake meant to mean when he habitually said one thing in order to hide and enhance another; and in order to be convincing —poetry being what it is—the facts adduced had to be self-evident. It is not a question here whether the mystery enlightened was worth it. The result for emphasis is that Mr. Damon made Blake exactly what he seemed least to be, perhaps the most intellectually consistent of the greater poets in English. Since the chief weapons used are the extended facts of scholarship, the picture Mr. Damon produced cannot be destroyed even though later and other scholarship modifies, re-arranges, or adds to it with different or other facts. The only suspicion that might attach is that the picture is too consistent and that the facts are made to tell too much, and direct, but instructed, apprehension not enough.

My point about Mr. Damon's work is typical and double. First, that the same sort of work, the adduction of ultimately self-evident facts, can be done and must be done in other kinds of poetry than Blake's. Blake is merely an extreme and obvious example of an unusually difficult poet who hid his facts on purpose. The work must be done to the appropriate degree of digging out the facts in all orders of poetry—and especially perhaps in contemporary poetry, where we tend to let the work go either because it seems too easy or because it seems supererogatory. Self-evident facts are paradoxically the hardest to come by; they are not evident till they are seen; yet the meaning of a poem—the part of it which is intellectually formulable—must invariably depend on this order of facts, the facts about the meanings of the elements aside from their final meaning in combination. The rest of the poem, what it is, what it shows, its final value as a created emotion, its meanings, if you like, *as* a poem, cannot in the more serious orders of poetry develop itself to the full without this factual or intellectual meaning to show the way. The other point is already made, and has been made before in this essay, but it may still be emphasized. Although the scholarly account is indispensable it does not tell the whole story. It is only the basis and perhaps ultimately the residue of all the other stories. But it must be seen to first.

My own approach, such as it is, and if it can be named, does not tell the whole story either; the reader is conscientiously left with the poem, with the real work yet to do; and I wish to advance it—as indeed I have been advancing it *seriatim*—only in connection with the reduced and compensated approaches I have laid out; and I expect, too, that if my approach is used at all it will require its own reduction as well as its compensations. Which is why this essay has taken its present form, preferring for once, in the realm of theory and apologetics, the implicit to the explicit statement. It is, I suppose, an approach to literary criticism—to the discourse of an amateur—primarily through the technique, in the widest sense of that word, of the examples handled; technique on the plane of words and even of linguistics in Mr. Richards' sense, but also technique on the plane of intellectual and emotional patterns in Mr. Burke's sense, and technique, too, in that there is a technique of securing and arranging and representing a fundamental view of life. The advantage of the technical approach is I think double. It readily admits other approaches and is anxious to be complemented by them. Furthermore, in a sense, it is able to incorporate the technical aspect, which always exists, of what is secured by other approaches—as I have argued elsewhere that so unpromising a matter as T. S. Eliot's religious convictions may be profitable considered as a dominant element in his technique of revealing the actual. The second advantage of the technical approach is a consequence of the first; it treats of nothing in literature except in its capacity of reduction to literary fact, which is where it resembles scholarship, only passing beyond it in that its facts are usually further into the heart of the literature than the facts of most scholarship. Aristotle, curiously, is here the type and master; as the *Poetics* is nothing but a collection and explanation of the facts of Greek poetry, it is the factual aspect that is invariably produced. The rest of the labor is in the effort to find understandable terms to fit the composition of the facts. After all, it is only the facts about a poem, a play, a novel, that can be reduced to tractable form, talked about, and examined; the rest is the product of the facts, from the technical point of view, and not a product but the thing itself from its own point of view. The rest, whatever it is, can only be known, not talked about.

But facts are not simple or easy to come at; not all the facts will appear to one mind, and the same facts appear differently in the light of different minds. No attention is undivided, no single approach sufficient, no predilection guaranteed, when facts of what their arrangements create are in question. In short, for the arts, *mere* technical scrutiny of any order is not enough without the direct apprehension—which may come first or last—to which all scrutinies that show facts contribute.

It may be that there are principles that cover both the direct apprehension and the labor of providing modes for the understanding of the expressive arts. If so, they are Socratic and found within, and subject to the fundamental skepticism as in Montaigne. There must be seeds, let us say—seeds, germs, beginning forms upon which I can rely and to which I resort. When I use a word, an image, a notion, there must be in its small nodular apparent form, as in the peas I am testing on my desk, at least prophetically, the whole future growth, the whole harvested life; and not rhetorically, not in a formula, but stubbornly, pervasively, heart-hidden, materially, in both the anterior and the eventual prospect as well as in the small handled form of the nub. What is it, what are they, these seeds of understanding? And if I know, are they logical? Do they take the processional form of the words I use? Or do they take a form like that of the silver backing a glass, a dark that enholds all brightness? Is every metaphor—and the assertion of understanding is our great metaphor—mixed by the necessity of its intention? What is the mixture of a word, an image, a notion?

The mixture, if I may start a hare so late, the mixture, even in the fresh use of an old word, is made in the pre-conscious, and is by hypothesis unascertainable. But let us not use hypotheses, let us not desire to ascertain. By intuition we adventure in the preconscious; and there, where the adventure is, there is no need or suspicion of certainty or meaning; there is the living, expanding, *prescient* substance without the tags and handles of conscious form. Art is the looking-glass of the pre-conscious, and when it is deepest seems to participate in it sensibly. Or, better, for purposes of criticism, our sensibility resumes the division of the senses and faculties at the same time that it preens itself into conscious form. Criticism may have as an object the establishment and evaluation (comparison and analysis) of the modes of making the pre-conscious *consciously* available.

But this emphasis upon the pre-conscious need not be insisted on; once recognized it may be tacitly assumed, and the effort of the mind will be, as it were, restored to its own plane—only a little sensitive to the tap-roots below. On its own plane—that is, the plane where almost everything is taken for granted in order to assume adequate implementation in handling what is taken for granted by others; where because you can list the items of your bewilderment and can move from one to another you assert that the achievement of motion is the experience of order; where, therefore, you must adopt always an attitude of provisional skepticism; where, imperatively, you must scrutinize and scrutinize until you have revealed, if it is there, the inscrutable divination, or, if it is not, the void of personal ambition; where, finally, you must stop short only when you have, with all the facts you can muster, indicated, surrounded, detached, somehow found the way demonstrably to get at, in pretty conscious terms which others may use, the substance of your chosen case.

APPENDIX I

Recent Works of American Criticism

(This list is selective. It includes some books on the background of American criticism, some of literary biography, some on critical theory, and some of more specific analysis of form and style. Those of the last two types will be found of special value in supplementing the essays in this book. Titles marked with the asterisk are especially recommended in extending the study of the foregoing essays. Works by the critics discussed in the "Foreword" and "Introduction" are also listed.)

Adler, Mortimer J. *Art and Prudence: A Study in Practical Philosophy.** 1937.

Aiken, Conrad. *Skepticisms: Notes on Contemporary Poetry.* 1919.

Arvin, Newton. *Hawthorne.** 1929.

Babbitt, Irving. *Literature and the American College.** 1908.
> *The New Laokoön.* 1910.
> *Masters of Modern French Criticism.** 1912.
> *Rousseau and Romanticism.** 1919.
> *On Being Creative, and Other Essays.** 1932.

Beach, Joseph Warren. *The Method of Henry James.** 1918.
> *The Technique of Thomas Hardy.* 1922.
> *The Outlook of American Prose.* 1926.
> *The Twentieth Century Novel.** 1932.

Beer, Thomas. *Stephen Crane: A Study in American Letters.* 1923.

Blackmur, R. P. *The Double Agent: Essays in Craft and Elucidation.** 1935.

Boas, George. *A Primer for Critics.* 1937.

Bourne, Randolph S. *The History of a Literary Radical, and Other Essays.* 1920.

Boynton, Percy H. *Some Contemporary Americans.* 1924.
> *More Contemporary Americans.* 1927.
> *The Challenge of American Criticism.* 1931.
> *Literature and American Life.* 1936.

Brooks, Van Wyck. *The Wine of the Puritans.** 1909.
> *America's Coming of Age.** 1915.
> *Letters and Leadership.* 1918.
> *The Ordeal of Mark Twain.* 1920.

Brooks, Van Wyck. *The Pilgrimage of Henry James.** 1925.
    Emerson and Others. 1927.
    Sketches in Criticism. 1932.
    *The Flowering of New England.** 1936.
Brownell, William Crary. *American Prose Masters.* 1909.
    *Criticism.** 1914.
    *Standards.** 1917.
    The Genius of Style. 1924.
    Democratic Distinction in America. 1927.
    The Spirit of Society. 1927.
Buermeyer, Laurence. *The Aesthetic Experience.** 1929.
    and others. *Art and Education.* 1929.
Burke, Kenneth. *Counter-Statement.** 1931.
    Permanence and Change: An Anatomy of Purpose. 1935.
Calverton, V. F. *The Newer Spirit.* 1925.
    The New Ground of Criticism. 1930.
    The Liberation of American Literature. 1931.
    American Literature. 1931.
Canby, Henry Seidel. *Definitions.* First Series, 1922. Second Series, 1924.
    American Estimates. 1929.
    Classic Americans. 1931.
Chamberlain, John. *Farewell to Reform.* 1932.
Cheney, Sheldon. *The New Movement in the Theatre.* 1914.
    Expressionism in Art. 1934.
Collins, Seward. "Criticism in America" in *The Bookman,* LXXI (1930), 241-56, 400-15; LXXII (1930), 145-64, 209-28.
Cowley, Malcolm. *Exile's Return: A Narrative of Ideas.* 1934.
Crane, R. S. "History versus Criticism in the University Study of Literature" in *The English Journal,* College Edition, XXIV (1935), 645-67.
Deutsch, Babette. *This Modern Poetry.* 1935.
De Voto, Bernard. *Mark Twain's America.* 1932.
Dickinson, Thomas H. *The Case of the American Drama.* 1915.
    Playwrights of the New American Theatre. 1925.
Dudley, Dorothy. *Forgotten Frontiers: Dreiser and the Land of the Free.* 1932.
Eastman, Max. *The Literary Mind: Its Place in an Age of Science.* 1931.
    Artists in Uniform: A Study of Literature and Bureaucratism. 1934.
    Art and the Life of Action. 1934.

Emerson, Ralph Waldo. *Complete Works.* 1903-4. (Vol. II and III: *Essays;* IV: *Representative Men.*)

Eliot, T. S. *The Sacred Wood.** 1920.
Homage to John Dryden. 1924.
*For Launcelot Andrewes.** 1928.
Dante. 1929.
*Selected Essays, 1917-32.** 1932.
*The Use of Poetry and the Use of Criticism.** 1933.
After Strange Gods. 1933.
*Essays Ancient and Modern.** 1936.

Farrell, James T. *A Note on Literary Criticism.** 1936.

Foerster, Norman. *American Criticism: A Study in Literary Theory from Poe to the Present.* 1928.
Toward Standards: A Study of the Present Critical Movement in American Letters. 1930.

Follett, Wilson. *The Modern Novel.* 1923.

Frank, Waldo. *Salvos: An Informal Book about Books and Plays.* 1924.
The Re-Discovery of America. 1928.

Freeman, Joseph. *An American Testament: A Narrative of Rebels and Romantics.* 1936.

Frye, Prosser Hall. *Romance and Tragedy.* 1922.
Visions and Chimeras. 1929.

Gates, Lewis E. *Studies and Appreciations.* 1900.

Goodman, Paul. "Neo-Classicism, Platonism, and Romanticism," in *The Journal of Philosophy,* XXXI (1934), 148-63.

Greenlaw, Edwin. *The Province of Literary History.* 1931.

Gregory, Horace. *Pilgrim of the Apocalypse: A Critical Study of D. H. Lawrence.* 1933.
*Makers and Ancestors.** 1937.

Grudin, Louis. *A Primer of Aesthetics: Logical Approaches to a Philosophy of Art.* 1930.

Guerard, Albert. *Literature and Society.** 1935.
Art for Art's Sake. 1936.

Hackett, Francis. *Horizons: A Book of Criticism.* 1918.

Hazlitt, Henry. *The Anatomy of Criticism.* 1933.

Hearn, Lafcadio. *Appreciations of Poetry.* 1916.
Complete Lectures on Art, Literature, and Philosophy. 1932.

Hicks, Granville. *The Great Tradition: An Interpretation of American Literature since the Civil War.** 1933. Revised edition, 1935.
and John Stuart. *John Reed: The Making of a Revolutionary.* 1936.

Horton, Philip. *Hart Crane: The Life of an American Poet.* 1937.

Howells, William Dean. *Criticism and Fiction.** 1902.
    Literature and Life. 1902.
Huneker, James Gibbons. *Iconoclasts.* 1905.
    Visionaries. 1905.
    Egoists. 1909.
    Promenades of an Impressionist. 1910.
    Unicorns. 1917.
    Bedouins. 1920.
James, Henry. *French Poets and Novelists.** 1878.
    *Hawthorne.** 1879.
    *Partial Portraits.** 1888.
    *Essays in London.** 1893.
    *Notes on Novelists, and Some Other Notes.** 1916.
    Prefaces to his *Novels and Tales.** New York Edition. 1907-17.
    Notes and Reviews. 1921.
    Views and Reviews. 1908.
    *The Art of the Novel.** 1934.
Josephson, Matthew. *Portrait of the Artist as an American.** 1930.
Krutch, Joseph Wood. *Edgar Allan Poe: A Study in Genius.* 1926.
    *The Modern Temper.** 1929.
    Experience and Art: Some Aspects of the Esthetics of Literature.
        1932.
Lewisohn, Ludwig. *The Drama and the Stage.* 1922.
    The Creative Life. 1924.
    Expression in America. 1932.
Littell, Robert. *Read America First.* 1926.
Lovett, Robert Morss. *Edith Wharton.* 1925.
Lowell, James Russell. *My Study Windows.* 1871.
    Latest Literary Essays and Addresses. 1892.
    Lectures on the English Poets. 1897.
Lowes, John Livingston. *Convention and Revolt in Poetry.* 1919.
    *The Road to Xanadu: A Study in the Ways of the Imagination.**
        1927.
    Essays in Appreciation. 1936.
Macy, John. *The Spirit of American Literature.* 1913.
    The Critical Game. 1922.
Masters, Edgar Lee. *Vachel Lindsay: A Poet in America.* 1935.
    Whitman. 1937.
Matthiessen, F. O. *Sarah Orne Jewett.* 1929.
    The Achievement of T. S. Eliot: An Essay on the Nature of
        *Poetry.** 1935.
McKeon, Richard P. "Literary Criticism and the Concept of Imitation
    in Antiquity" in *Modern Philology,* XXXIV (1936), 1-35.

Mencken, H. L. *A Book of Prefaces.** 1917.

    Prejudices: Six series. 1919-27.

Mercier, Louis J. A. *The Challenge of Humanism: An Essay in Comparative Criticism.* 1933.

Mims, Edwin. *Adventurous America.* 1929.

Monroe, Harriet. *Poets and Their Art.* 1926.

More, Paul Elmer. *Shelburne Essays:* Eleven volumes. 1904-21.

    The Demon of the Absolute. 1928.

    *On Being Human.** 1936.

    *Selected Shelburne Essays.** 1935.

Mumford, Lewis. *The Story of Utopias.* 1922.

    Sticks and Stones. 1924.

    *The Golden Day.** 1926.

    Herman Melville. 1929.

    American Taste. 1929.

    The Brown Decades. 1931.

Munson, Gorham B. *Destinations: A Canvass of American Literature since 1900.* 1928.

    Style and Form in American Prose. 1929.

    *The Dilemma of the Liberated.** 1930.

Nathan, George Jean. *The Critic and the Drama.* 1922.

    Materia Critica. 1924.

    Since Ibsen. 1933.

Parker, Dewitt H. *The Analysis of Beauty.* 1926.

Parrington, Vernon Louis. *Main Currents in American Thought: An Interpretation of American Literature from the Beginnings to 1920.* Completed to 1900 only. 1927-30.

Poe, Edgar Allan. *Works,* edited by Edmund Clarence Stedman and George Edward Woodberry. 1894-5. *Literary Criticism.** Vols. VI-VIII.

Pound, Ezra. *Pavannes and Divisions.** 1918.

    *Instigations.** 1920.

    *How to Read.** 1933.

    *Make It New.** 1935.

Roberts, Morris. *Henry James' Criticism.* 1929.

Rosenfeld, Paul. *Port of New York: Essays on Fourteen American Moderns.* 1924.

    Men Seen. 1925.

Santayana, George. *The Sense of Beauty.* 1896.

    *Three Philosophical Poets: Lucretius, Dante, Goethe.** 1910.

    *Character and Opinion in the United States.** 1920.

    *The Genteel Tradition at Bay.** 1931.

    Obiter Scripta: Lectures, Essays, and Reviews. 1936.

Shafer, Robert. *Paul Elmer More and American Criticism.* 1935.

Sherman, Stuart Pratt. *Americans.* 1922.

    The Genius of America: Studies on Behalf of the Younger Generation. 1923.

    The Main Stream. 1927.

Shipley, Joseph T. *The Quest for Literature: A Survey of Literary Criticism and the Theories of the Literary Forms.* 1931.

Shuster, George N. *The Catholic Spirit in Modern English Literature.* 1922.

    The Catholic Church and Current Literature. 1929.

Sinclair, Upton. *Mammonart.* 1925.

Spencer, Theodore. *Death and Elizabethan Tragedy.* 1936.

Spingarn, J. E. *The New Criticism.* 1911.

    *Creative Criticism.** 1917. New edition, 1931.

Stearns, Harold E. *America and the Young Intellectual.** 1921.

Stein, Leo. *The A.B.C. of Aesthetics.* 1927.

Tate, Allen. *Reactionary Essays on Poetry and Ideas.** 1936.

Untermeyer, Louis. *American Poetry since 1900.* 1923.

Van Doren, Carl. *The American Novel.* 1921.

    Contemporary American Novelists. 1922.

    Many Minds. 1923.

Van Doren, Mark. *The Poetry of John Dryden.* 1920.

    Edwin Arlington Robinson. 1927.

Wharton, Edith. *The Writing of Fiction.* 1925.

Whipple, T. K. *Spokesmen: Modern Writers and American Life.** 1928.

Whitman, Walt. *Democratic Vistas.* 1871.

    Complete Writings. 1902.

    Criticism, An Essay. 1913.

Wickham, Harvey. *The Impuritans.* 1929.

Williamson, George. *The Donne Tradition.* 1930.

Wilson, Edmund. *Axel's Castle: A Study in the Imaginative Literature of 1870-1930.** 1931.

Winters, Yvor. *Primitivism and Decadence: A Study of American Experimental Poetry.** 1937.

Woodberry, George Edward. *The Torch.* 1905.

    The Appreciation of Literature. 1907.

    Two Phases of Criticism. 1914.

    Collected Essays. 1920-21.

Young, Stark. *The Flower in Drama.** 1923.

    *Glamor.** 1926.

    The Theatre. 1927.

APPENDIX II

Collections of Contemporary American Criticism

A Modern Book of Criticism, edited by Ludwig Lewisohn. 1919.
Essays defining and illustrating the impressionist and liberal view-points by French critics (Anatole France, Jules Lemaître, Remy de Gourmont), German (Friedrich Hebbel, Wilhelm Dilthey, Johannes Volkelt, Richard Moritz Meyer, Hugo von Hofmannsthal, Richard Mueller-Freienfels, Alfred Kerr), English and Irish (George Moore, George Bernard Shaw, Arthur Symons, John Galsworthy, Arnold Bennett, W. L. George, Thomas MacDonagh, John Cooper Powys), and American (James Gibbons Huneker, J. E. Spingarn, H. L. Mencken, Ludwig Lewisohn, Francis Hackett, Van Wyck Brooks, Randolph Bourne).

Criticism in America, Its Function and Status, edited by J. E. Spingarn. 1924.
Essays by Irving Babbitt, Van Wyck Brooks, William Crary Brownell, Ernest Boyd, T. S. Eliot, H. L. Mencken, Stuart Pratt Sherman, J. E. Spingarn, George Edward Woodberry.

Contemporary American Criticism, edited by James Cloyd Bowman. 1926.
Essays by James Russell Lowell, Walt Whitman, J. E. Spingarn, H. L. Mencken, William Crary Brownell, Irving Babbitt, Grant Showerman, Stuart Pratt Sherman, Percy H. Boynton, Van Wyck Brooks, Sherwood Anderson, Robert Morss Lovett, Carl van Doren, Irwin Edman, Llewellyn Jones, Theodore Maynard, William McFee, John Macy, Henry Seidel Canby, Amy Lowell, Conrad Aiken, Fred Lewis Pattee, George Edward Woodberry.

American Criticism: 1926, edited by William A. Drake. 1926.
Essays and reviews covering the year from July 1925 to July 1926 by Henry Seidel Canby, Samuel C. Chew, Mary M. Colum, Robert L. Duffus, Waldo Frank, Zona Gale, Herbert S. Gorman, Alyse Gregory, Albert Guerard, Joseph Wood Krutch, Sinclair Lewis, Archibald MacLeish, Edgar Lee Masters, H. L. Mencken, W. B. Pressey, Agnes Repplier, Edith Rickert, Cameron Rogers, Anne Douglas Sedgwick, Gilbert Seldes, Stuart Pratt Sherman, Harrison Smith, Logan Pearsall Smith, C. B. Tinker, Charles K. Trueblood, Carl van Doren, Arnold Whitredge, Edmund Wilson, P. W. Wilson.

The New Criticism, edited by Edwin Berry Burgum. 1930.
  Essays, chiefly in esthetic theory, by J. E. Spingarn, Benedetto
  Croce, Bernard Bosanquet, George Santayana, E. F. Carritt, I. A.
  Richards, Laurence Buermeyer, J. B. S. Haldane, J. W. N. Sullivan,
  Roger Fry, Ramon Fernandez, Dewitt H. Parker, T. S. Eliot,
  Oswald Spengler, Elie Faure, Edwin Muir.
American Critical Essays, edited by Norman Foerster. 1930.
  Essays illustrating the development of criticism in America by
  Edgar Allan Poe, Ralph Waldo Emerson, James Russell Lowell,
  Walt Whitman, William Dean Howells, Henry James, Lewis E.
  Gates, George Edward Woodberry, William Crary Brownell, Ir-
  ving Babbitt, Paul Elmer More, Prosser Hall Frye, J. E. Spingarn,
  Stuart Pratt Sherman, Van Wyck Brooks.
*Humanism and America: Essays on the Outlook of Modern Civiliza-
  tion,* edited by Norman Foerster. 1930.
  Essays defending the Humanist position by Lewis Trenchard More,
  Irving Babbitt, Paul Elmer More, G. R. Elliott, T. S. Eliot, Frank
  Jewett Mather, Jr., Alan Reynolds Thompson, Robert Shafer,
  Harry Hayden Clark, Stanley P. Chase, Gorham B. Munson,
  Bernard Bandler II, Sherlock Bronson Gass, Richard Lindley
  Brown.
The Critique of Humanism: A Symposium, edited by C. Hartley
  Grattan. 1930.
  Essays in opposition to Humanism by C. Hartley Grattan, Edmund
  Wilson, Malcolm Cowley, Henry Hazlitt, Burton Rascoe, Allen
  Tate, Kenneth Burke, Henry-Russell Hitchcock, Jr., R. P. Black-
  mur, John Chamberlain, Bernard Bandler II, Yvor Winters, Lewis
  Mumford.
Proletarian Literature in the United States: An Anthology, edited by
  Granville Hicks, Michael Gold, Isidor Schneider, Joseph North,
  Paul Peters, Alan Calmer. 1935.
  Includes essays defining the proletarian doctrine in literature by
  Obed Brooks, Edwin Berry Burgum, Alan Calmer, Malcolm Cow-
  ley, Michael Gold, Granville Hicks, Joshua Kunitz, William
  Phillips and Philip Rahv, Bernard Smith.
After the Genteel Tradition. American Writers since 1910, edited by
  Malcolm Cowley. 1937.
  Essays, chiefly on post-War American writers, by John Chamberlain,
  Robert Cantwell, Lionel Trilling, Bernard Smith, Newton Arvin,
  Robert Morss Lovett, Louis Kronenberger, Peter Monro Jack,
  Hildegarde Flanner, Malcolm Cowley, John Peale Bishop, Hamilton
  Basso.

APPENDIX III

American Magazines Publishing Criticism

(This check-list includes the most important journals that have published the work of American critics since 1900. A number of standard magazines are included, but an effort has been made to include the best of the independent journals that have encouraged critical activity and literary experiment. The dates and personnel of these have been described as closely as their irregular careers permit. Magazines published in foreign countries are included when they have been edited or contributed to by American writers. Those of special interest in supplementing this volume are indicated by the asterisk.)

American Literature: A Journal of Literary History, Criticism, and Bibliography. Founded in 1929. Durham, N. C. Published quarterly.

The American Mercury. Founded in 1924 by H. L. Mencken and George Jean Nathan. Edited by H. L. Mencken alone, 1925-33. Since then edited by Henry Hazlitt, Charles Angoff, Paul Palmer. New York City. Published monthly.*

The American Review. Founded in 1933 and edited by Seward Collins. New York City. Published ten months of the year.*

The American Spectator. Founded in 1932 and edited for its first three years by George Jean Nathan, Ernest Boyd, Van Wyck Brooks, Theodore Dreiser, Eugene O'Neill. New York City. Published monthly, but during the past two ·years less regularly.

Blast: An Anglo-American Quarterly. A Review of the Great English Vortex. Founded in 1914 by Ezra Pound and Wyndham Lewis. London. Discontinued in 1915.*

Blues: A Magazine of New Rhythms. Founded in 1929 and edited by Charles Henri Ford. Columbus, Miss., later New York. Bimonthly. Discontinued in 1933.

The Bookman. Edited by John Farrar from 1921 to 1928; by Seward Collins and Burton Rascoe, 1928-9; by Seward Collins, 1930-3. New York City. Published monthly. Discontinued in 1933 with the founding of *The American Review.*

Books Abroad: A Quarterly Publication Devoted to Comment on Foreign Books. Founded in 1928 and edited by Roy Temple House, recently with the assistance of an editorial board. University of Oklahoma, Norman, Okla. Published quarterly.

Broom: An International Magazine of the Arts. Founded in 1921. Edited by Harold A. Loeb, Alfred Kreymborg, Malcolm Cowley, Slater Brown. Rome, Berlin, New York. Published monthly. Discontinued in 1924.*

The Catholic World: A Monthly Magazine of General Literature and Science. Founded in 1865. New York. Published monthly.

The Chicago Literary Times. Founded in 1923 and edited by Ben Hecht. Chicago. Published bi-weekly. Discontinued in 1924.

The Commonweal: A Weekly Review of Literature, the Arts, and Public Affairs. Founded in 1924 and edited by Michael Williams and George Shuster. New York. Published weekly.

Contact. Founded in 1921 and edited by Robert McAlmon and William Carlos Williams. New York. Discontinued in 1921 after five monthly issues. Resumed in 1932 as *Contact: An American Quarterly* and edited by William Carlos Williams. Discontinued in 1933.

The Criterion. Founded in 1922 and edited by T. S. Eliot. London. Published quarterly except during 1927-8 when it was called *The Monthly Criterion;* still running.*

The Dial. Founded in New York as a monthly in 1920 after an earlier career as a weekly in Chicago. Edited by Scofield Thayer, 1920-5; by Marianne Moore, 1925-9. New York. Published monthly. Discontinued in 1929.*

The Double Dealer. Founded in 1921. Edited by Julius Weis Friend and Basil Thompson. New Orleans. Published monthly. Discontinued in 1926.

The Exile. Founded in 1927 and edited by Ezra Pound. Paris and Rapallo, Italy. Published quarterly. Discontinued in 1928.*

The Figure in the Carpet: A Magazine of Prose. Founded in 1927 and edited by Hansell Baugh. Known later as *The Salient.* New York. Discontinued in 1928.

The Forum and Century. Founded in 1886; combined with *The Century Magazine,* 1931. Edited by Henry Goddard Leach. New York. Published monthly.

The Freeman. Founded in 1920 and edited by Francis Neilson and Albert Jay Nock; associate editor, Van Wyck Brooks. New York. Published weekly. Discontinued in 1924.*

Front: A Radical Tri-Lingual Magazine. Being an International Review of Literature. Founded in 1930. American Editor: Norman Macleod. The Hague, Holland. Discontinued in 1932.*

The Frontier: A Regional Literary Quarterly. Founded in 1920 but re-organized as a regional magazine in 1927. Edited by H. G. Merriam. Missoula, Montana. Published quarterly.

The Fugitive. Founded in 1922 and edited by John Crowe Ransom, Donald Davidson, Allen Tate, and others. Nashville, Tenn. Published monthly. Discontinued in 1925.*

The Guardian: A Monthly Journal of Life, Art, and Letters. Founded in 1925. Board of Editors: Abraham N. Gerbovoy, Madeline Leof, Abe Grosner, Herman Silverman, Harry A. Potamkin. Philadelphia. Published monthly. Discontinued in 1925.

The Gyroscope. Founded in 1929 and edited by Yvor Winters, Janet Lewis, Howard Baker. Issued irregularly. Palo Alto, Cal. Discontinued in 1931.*

The Hound and Horn. Founded in 1927. First editors: Lincoln Kirstein, Bernard Bandler II, Varian Fry, R. P. Blackmur; editor after 1931, Lincoln Kirstein, with Allen Tate and Yvor Winters as regional editors. Cambridge, Mass., and New York. Published quarterly. Discontinued in 1934.*

Larus. Founded in 1927 and edited by Sherry Mangan. Later combined with *Tempo.* Editor for France: Virgil Thompson. Lynn, Mass. Published monthly. Discontinued in 1928.

The Laughing Horse. Founded in 1923. Edited by Willard Johnson and others. Santa Fe, N. M. Published quarterly; later irregularly. Discontinued in 1931.

Left: A Quarterly Review of Radical and Experimental Art. Founded in 1931. Editors: George Redfield, Jay du Von, Marvin Klein, R. C. Lorenz, W. K. Jordan. Davenport, Iowa. Published quarterly. Discontinued in 1932.

The Liberator. Founded in 1918 as successor to *The Masses.* Edited by Robert Minor. New York. Published monthly. Merged with *Workers' Monthly, Labor Herald,* and *Soviet Russia.* Later became *The Communist.* Discontinued in 1924.

The Little Review: A Monthly Devoted to Literature, Drama, Music, and Art. Founded in 1914 and edited by Margaret C. Anderson and Jane Heap. Chicago, New York, Paris. Published monthly at first, later irregularly. Discontinued in 1929.*

Manuscripts. Founded in 1922 and edited co-operatively by Sherwood Anderson, Paul Rosenfeld, William Carlos Williams, Waldo Frank, and others. New York. Issued irregularly. Discontinued in 1923.

The Masses: A Monthly Devoted to the Interests of the Working People. Founded in 1911. Edited by Max Eastman and Floyd

Dell. New York. Published monthly. Discontinued in 1917. Continued as *The Liberator* and later as *The New Masses.*

The Measure: A Journal of Poetry. Founded in 1921. Editorial Board: Maxwell Anderson, Padraic Colum, David Morton, George O'Neil, Genevieve Taggard, and others. New York. Issued irregularly. Discontinued in 1926.

The Modern Quarterly. Founded in 1923 and edited by V. F. Calverton and S. D. Schmalhausen. Baltimore, Md. Published quarterly and continued as monthly in New York.

Modern Philology: A Journal Devoted to Research in Medieval and Modern Literature. Founded in 1905 by John Matthews Manly; present editor, R. S. Crane. Chicago. Published quarterly.

The Modern Review: A Quarterly. Founded in 1922 and edited by Fiskwoode Tarleton. Winchester, Mass. Published quarterly. Discontinued in 1924.

Morada: A Tri-lingual Advance Guard Quarterly. Founded in 1929 and edited by Norman Macleod. Cagnes sur Mer, France, and Albuquerque, N. M. Published quarterly. Discontinued in 1932.

The Nation. Founded in 1865. Edited by Paul Elmer More, 1909-14. Reorganized by Oswald Garrison Villard in 1918 and edited by him and others until 1932. Edited since 1935 by Joseph Wood Krutch, Max Lerner, and Freda Kirchwey. New York. Published weekly.*

Nativity: An American Quarterly. Founded in 1930 and edited by Boris J. Israel. Delaware, Ohio. Published quarterly. Discontinued in 1932.

The New Freeman. Founded in 1930 and edited by Suzanne La Follette. New York. Published weekly. Discontinued in 1931.

The New Masses. Founded in 1926, continuing *The Masses* and *The Liberator.* Editors: Egmont Arens, Joseph Freeman, Hugo Gellert, Michael Gold, James Rorty, John Sloan, and others. New York. Published monthly, later as weekly.

The New Republic. Founded in 1914 and edited by Herbert Croly, Walter Lippmann, Francis Hackett, Philip Littell, and others; at present by Bruce Bliven, Robert Morss Lovett, Stark Young, Malcolm Cowley, George Soule. New York. Published weekly.*

The New Review: An International Note Book for the Arts. Founded in 1931. Editors: Samuel Putnam, Ezra Pound, Maxwell Bodenheim, Richard Thoma. Paris. Published bi-monthly. Discontinued in 1932.

Pagany: A Native Quarterly. Founded in 1930 and edited by Richard

Johns. Boston and New York. Published quarterly. Discontinued in 1933.

The Partisan Review. Founded in 1935. Editors: Alan Calmer, Jack Conroy, Ben Field, William Phillips, Philip Rahv, Clinton Simpson. New York. Published monthly. Suspended in 1937.*

The Playboy: A Portfolio of Art and Satire. Founded in 1919 and edited by Egmont Arens. New York. Published irregularly. Discontinued in 1924.

The Ploughshare: A Magazine of the Literature, Arts, and Life Evolving in Woodstock. Founded in 1912. Editors: Hervey White, Carl Eric Lindin, Allan Updegraff. Woodstock, N. Y. Discontinued in 1920.

Poetry: A Magazine of Verse. Founded in 1912 and edited from 1912 to 1936 by Harriet Monroe. Since 1936 by Morton Dauwen Zabel. Associate Editors: Ezra Pound, Alice Corbin Henderson, Eunice Tietjens, Helen Hoyt, Emanuel Carnevali, Marion Strobel, George Dillon, Jessica Nelson North, M. D. Zabel. Chicago. Published monthly.*

Reedy's Mirror: A Weekly Dealing in Politics and Literature. Founded in 1891 as *The Mirror;* bought in 1913 and edited by William Marion Reedy. St. Louis, Mo. Published weekly. Discontinued in 1920.

S4N. Publication of the S4N Society to Promote Open-minded Consideration of Theories and Practices of Art. Founded in 1919 and edited by Norman Fitts. Northampton, Mass., and New Haven, Conn. Issued irregularly. Discontinued in 1925 and merged with *The Modern Review.**

The Saturday Review of Literature. Founded in 1924 and edited by Henry Seidel Canby until 1936; since 1936 by Bernard De Voto. New York. Published weekly.

Secession: A Quarterly. An Independent Magazine of Modern Letters. Founded in 1922. Editors: Gorham B. Munson, Kenneth Burke, Matthew Josephson. Vienna, Berlin, Reutte (Tirol), New York. Issued quarterly at first, then irregularly. Discontinued in 1924.*

The Seven Arts: A Monthly. Founded in 1916 and edited by James Oppenheim and others. Published monthly. Discontinued in 1917 and later merged with *The Dial.**

The Sewanee Review: A Quarterly of Life and Letters. Founded in 1892. Now edited by William Knickerbocker. University of the South, Sewanee, Tenn. Published quarterly.

The Southern Review. Founded in 1935. Editor: Charles Pipkin;

Managing Editors: Cleanth Brooks and Robert Penn Warren. Baton Rouge, Louisiana. Published quarterly.*

The Symposium: A Critical Review. Founded in 1930. Editors: James Burnham and Philip E. Wheelwright. New York City. Published quarterly. Discontinued in 1934.*

Tambour: A Monthly Magazine. Founded in 1929 and edited by Harold J. Salemson. Paris. Published monthly, later irregularly. Discontinued in 1932.

This Quarter: An International Quarterly Review of Arts and Letters. Founded in 1925 and edited by Ernest Walsh and Ethel Moorhead. Milan, Italy, and Cannes, France. Discontinued in 1926. Resumed as new series and edited by Edward W. Titus in 1929. Paris. Published quarterly. Discontinued in 1934.

Transition: An International Magazine for Creative Experiment. Founded in 1927. Editors: Eugene Jolas, Elliott Paul, and others. Paris. Published monthly, 1927-8, quarterly 1928-30. Discontinued in 1930. Resumed publication as quarterly in The Hague, 1932-6, and in New York from 1936, still under Eugene Jolas.*

The Virginia Quarterly Review. Founded in 1925 and edited by James Southall Wilson and others. University of Virginia, Charlottesville. Published quarterly.

The Wave: A Bi-monthly Journal of Art and Letters. Founded in 1922 and edited by Vincent Starrett. Chicago. Issued irregularly. Discontinued in 1924.

The Westminster Magazine. Founded in 1916 at Oglethorpe University, Georgia. Issued quarterly. Last editor, Robert England. Discontinued in 1935.

The Yale Review: A National Quarterly. Founded in 1892; reorganized in 1911. Edited by Wilbur Cross. New Haven, Conn. Published quarterly.

APPENDIX IV
Notes on Contributors

(These notes are chiefly bibliographical in character. Titles marked with the asterisk will be found of special value in supplementing the material included in this volume. In the case of some contributors who have not published books, several titles of essays in periodicals are appended; others may be found by consulting *The Reader's Guide to Periodical Literature* and *The International Index to Periodicals*.)

ARVIN, NEWTON. Born: Valparaiso, Ind., 1900. Educated: Harvard University (B.A., 1921). Member of the Department of English, Smith College, since 1922; associate professor since 1935. Contributor to *The New Republic, The Nation, The New Freeman, The Bookman, The Partisan Review, The Saturday Review of Literature.* Author: * *Hawthorne* (1929). Editor: *The Heart of Hawthorne's Journals* (1929). Has in preparation a critical study of Walt Whitman.

BABBITT, IRVING. Born: Dayton, Ohio, 1865. Educated: Harvard University (B.A., 1889; M.A., 1893); Sorbonne (1891-2). Instructor of French, Williams College, 1893-4; instructor of French, Harvard, 1894-1902; assistant professor, 1902-12; professor, 1912-32. Lecturer at Sorbonne, 1923. Died in 1932. Author: * *Literature and the American College* (1908), * *The New Laokoön* (1910), * *The Masters of Modern French Criticism* (1912), * *Rousseau and Romanticism* (1919), *Democracy and Leadership* (1924), * *On Being Creative* (1932); contributor to scholarly and critical journals, and to *Humanism and America* (1930); editor of Taine's *Introduction à l'Histoire de la Littérature Anglaise* (1898), Renan's *Souvenirs de l'Enfance* (1902), Voltaire's *Zadig* (1905), Racine's *Phèdre* (1910); translator and editor of *The Dhammapada* (1936).

BLACKMUR, RICHARD P. Born: Springfield, Mass., 1904. Contributor to *The Hound and Horn, The New Republic, Poetry, The Virginia Quarterly Review, The Nation, The Southern Review.* Member of the editorial staff of *The Hound and Horn,* 1928-9. Author: * *The Double Agent: Essays in Craft and Elucidation* (1935) and *From Jordan's Delight* (poems, 1937). Has in preparation a critical biography of Henry Adams. Awarded Guggenheim Fellowship, 1937. *Cf.* * "The Expense of Greatness," *Virginia Quarterly Re-*

view, July 1936; * "The Later Poetry of W. B. Yeats," *Southern Review,* October 1936; "The Composition in Nine Poets," *Southern Review,* January 1937. Many reviews in *The Hound and Horn* and *Poetry.*

BOGAN, LOUISE. Born: Livermore Falls, Maine, 1897. Educated: New England schools and the Girls' Latin School, Boston. Contributor of criticism to *The New Republic, The Saturday Review of Literature, Poetry, The Measure.* Author of books of verse: *Body of This Death* (1923), *Dark Summer* (1929), *The Sleeping Fury* (1937).

BROOKS, VAN WYCK. Born: Plainfield, N. J., 1886. Educated: Harvard University (B.A., 1907). On the editorial staff of Doubleday, Page and Co., 1907-9; lecturer at Leland Stanford University, 1911-3; editor for the Century Company, 1915-8; assistant editor of *The Seven Arts,* 1917; assistant editor of *The Freeman,* 1920-4; founder and editor, with Alfred Kreymborg, Paul Rosenfeld, and Lewis Mumford, of *The First American Caravan* (1927). Granted the Dial Award, 1923; Pulitzer Prize in History, 1937. Author: * *The Wine of the Puritans* (1909), *The Malady of the Ideal* (1913), *John Addington Symonds* (1914), *The World of H. G. Wells* (1915), * *America's Coming of Age* (1915), * *Letters and Leadership* (1918), * *The Ordeal of Mark Twain* (1920), * *The Pilgrimage of Henry James* (1925), *Emerson and Others* (1927), * *Sketches in Criticism* (1932), *Life of Emerson* (1932), * *Three Essays on America* (1934), * *The Flowering of New England* (1936). Translator of works by Amiel, André Chamson, George Duhamel, Paul Gauguin, René Bazalgette, Romain Rolland. Editor of *The History of a Literary Radical and Other Essays* by Randolph Bourne (1920), *Journal of the First Voyage to America* by Christopher Columbus (1924).

BURKE, KENNETH. Born: Pittsburgh, 1897. Educated: Ohio State University. Research worker, Laura Spelman Rockefeller Memorial Foundation, 1926-7. Music critic of *The Dial,* 1927-9. Editor for the Bureau of Social Hygiene, 1928-9. Music critic of *The Nation,* 1933-5. Contributor to *The Dial, The New Republic, Secession, Broom, The Nation, Poetry, The Symposium, The Southern Review,* and other journals. Granted the Dial Award, 1928. Awarded a Guggenheim Fellowship, 1932. Author of books of literary and philosophic criticism: * *Counter-Statement* (1931), *Permanence and Change: Anatomy of Purpose* (1935), *Attitudes Toward History* (1937); and of books of narrative: *The White Oxen* (1924) and *Towards a Better Life* (1932).

CANTWELL, ROBERT EMMETT. Born: Little Falls, Wash., 1908. Educated: University of Washington. Worked as factory hand, section hand, common laborer, welder's assistant. Contributor to *The New Republic, The Nation, The Hound and Horn, The Symposium, The New Outlook, Time.* On editorial staff of *The New Republic,* 1933-5; literary critic of *The New Outlook,* 1932-5; on editorial staff of *Time* since 1935. Author of two novels: *Laugh and Lie Down* (1931) and *The Land of Plenty* (1934).

COWLEY, MALCOLM. Born: Belsano, Pa., 1898. Educated: Harvard University (B.A., 1920), University of Montpellier on American Field Service Fellowship, 1921-3. War service in the American Ambulance Service, 1917-8. Free lance writer in New York, 1923-9. Contributor to *The Dial, The New Republic, New York Herald-Tribune Books, The New Freeman,* and other journals. Translated many books from the French: Paul Valéry, Maurice Barrès, Raymond Radiguet, Pierre Mac Orlan, Princess Bibesco, *et al.* Awarded Guarantors Prize by *Poetry* in 1928. Author of book of poems: *Blue Juniata* (1929), and of * *Exile's Return: A Narrative of Ideas* (1934). An editor of *The New Republic* since 1930.

ELIOT, THOMAS STEARNS. Born: St. Louis, Mo., 1888. Educated: Smith Academy, St. Louis; Harvard University (B.A., 1909; M.A., 1910); Sorbonne (1911-2); Merton College, Oxford (1912-4). Worked in London as teacher, editor, bank clerk, and as assistant editor of *The Egoist,* 1917-9. Founder and editor of *The Criterion* since 1922. Member of the editorial board of Faber and Faber, London. Granted the Dial Award, 1922. Became a British subject in 1927. Held the Charles Eliot Norton Professorship of Poetry, Harvard University, 1932-3. Delivered the Page-Barbour Lectures, University of Virginia, 1933. Author of books of verse: *Prufrock and Other Observations* (1917), *Poems* (1919), *Ara Vos Prec* (1919), *Poems* (1920), *The Waste Land* (1922), *Poems, 1909-25* (1925), *The Journey of the Magi* (1927), *A Song for Simeon* (1928), *Animula* (1929), *Ash Wednesday* (1930), *Marina* (1930), *Triumphal March* (1931), *Poems, 1909-35* (1936); poetic drama: *Sweeney Agonistes* (1932), *The Rock* (co-author, 1934), *Murder in the Cathedral* (1935); books of criticism: * *The Sacred Wood* (1920), * *Homage to John Dryden* (1924), * *For Launcelot Andrewes* (1928), *Shakespeare and the Stoicism of Seneca* (1928), *Dante* (1929), *Thoughts after Lambeth* (1931), *Charles Whibley: A Memoir* (1931), * *Selected Essays, 1917-32* (1932), *John Dryden* (1932), * *The Use of Poetry and the Use of Criticism* (1933), * *After Strange Gods* (1934), * *Elizabethan Essays* (1935), * *Essays*

Ancient and Modern (1936); translator, with introduction, of *Anabasis* by St.-J. Perse (1930); editor, with introductions, of *Seneca: His Tenne Tragedies* (1927), John Dryden's *Of Dramatick Poesie* (1928), *Selected Poems* by Ezra Pound (1928), Samuel Johnson's *London: A Poem and The Vanity of Human Wishes* (1930), Baudelaire's *Intimate Journals* (1930), *Selected Poems* by Marianne Moore (1935), *Nightwood* by Djuna Barnes (1937).

FERGUSSON, FRANCIS. Educated: Harvard University. Teacher of dramatic literature and production at Bennington College, Vermont, since 1935. Dramatic critic of *The Bookman*, 1930-2. Contributor to *The Hound and Horn, The Bookman, Poetry, The American Review*.

GREGORY, HORACE. Born: Milwaukee, Wis., 1898. Educated: German-English Academy, Milwaukee School of Fine Arts, University of Wisconsin (B.A., 1923). On Faculty of English Department, Sarah Lawrence College, since 1934. Contributor of essays and reviews to *The Nation, The New Republic, Poetry, New York Herald-Tribune Books, The New Freeman, The American Caravan, The New Masses, The Partisan Review, New Verse, The New York Sun, The Symposium*. Awarded the Lyric Prize by *Poetry* in 1928 and the Helen Haire Levinson Prize in 1934. Author of books of criticism: *Pilgrim of the Apocalypse: A Critical Study of D. H. Lawrence* (1933) and * *Makers and Ancestors* (1937). Books of verse: *Chelsea Rooming House* (1930), *No Retreat* (1933), *Chorus for Survival* (1934). Translator: *The Poems of Catullus* (1931). Editor: *New Letters in America* (1937-).

KRUTCH, JOSEPH WOOD. Born: Knoxville, Tenn., 1893. Educated: University of Tennessee (B.A., 1915), Columbia University (M.A., 1916; Ph.D., 1923). Member of the Psychological Corps of the U. S. Army during the War. Assistant Professor of English, Brooklyn Polytechnic Institute, 1920-3; professor of English, Vassar College, 1924-5; assistant professor, School of Journalism, Columbia University, 1925-37; professor in 1937. Joined staff of *The Nation* as critic of drama, 1924; became an editor in 1935. Member of editorial board of the Literary Guild, 1925-35. Awarded a Guggenheim Fellowship, 1930. Author: *Comedy and Conscience after the Restoration* (1924), *Edgar Allan Poe: A Study in Genius* (1926), * *The Modern Temper* (1929), *Five Masters* (1930), * *Experience and Art* (1932), *Was Europe a Success?* (1934).

LOVETT, ROBERT MORSS. Born: Boston, 1870. Educated: Boston Latin School, Harvard University (B.A., 1892). Assistant and instructor in English at Harvard, 1892-3; instructor of English at University of Chicago, 1893-6; assistant professor, 1896-1904; associate professor, 1904-9; professor, 1909-36. Member of the editorial staff of *The Dial,* 1917-9; of the editorial board of *The New Republic,* since 1921. Contributor of reviews and essays to *The New Republic, The Dial, The Nation, The Bookman,* and other journals. Author: *A History of English Literature* (with William Vaughn Moody, 1902), *A First View of English Literature* (with Moody, 1905), * *Edith Wharton* (1925), *A Preface to Fiction* (1930), *A History of the Novel in England* (with Helen Sard Hughes, 1932); and of fiction: *Richard Gresham* (1904), *A Winged Victory* (1907); play: *Cowards* (1914).

MENCKEN, HENRY LOUIS. Born: Baltimore, 1880. Educated: Private schools in Baltimore and the Baltimore Polytechnic (graduated 1896). On staff of *The Baltimore Herald* (1903-6), *Baltimore Sun* (1906-10), *Baltimore Evening Sun* since 1910. Literary critic of *The Smart Set,* 1908-14; co-editor with George Jean Nathan, 1914-23. Founder and editor of *The American Mercury,* 1924-33. Author of critical essays: *George Bernard Shaw* (1905), *The Philosophy of Friedrich Nietzsche* (1908), *A Book of Burlesques* (1916), * *A Book of Prefaces* (1917), *Damn! A Book of Calumny* (1918), *In Defense of Women* (1918), *The American Language* (1918; fourth and revised edition, 1936), * *Prejudices* (six series, 1919-27), * *Selected Prejudices* (1927), *James Branch Cabell* (1927); books of speculative prose: *Treatise on the Gods* (1930), *Treatise on Right and Wrong* (1934); of plays: *The Artist* (1912), *Heliogabalus* (with George Jean Nathan) (1920); of verse: *Ventures into Verse* (1903); co-author of *Men vs. the Man* (1910), *Europe after 8:15* (1914), *A Little Book in C Major* (1916), *The American Credo* (1920), *Americana* (1925, 1926), *Notes on Democracy* (1926); editor: *We Moderns* by Edwin Muir (1920), *Essays* by J. G. Huneker (1929), *The American Democrat* by James Fenimore Cooper (1931).

MOORE, MARIANNE. Born: St. Louis, Mo., 1887. Educated: Bryn Mawr College (B.A., 1909). Teacher at the United States Indian School, Carlisle, Pa., 1911-5; assistant at the Hudson Park Branch, New York Public Library, 1919-25; editor of *The Dial,* 1925-9. Granted the Dial Award, 1924; the Helen Haire Levinson Prize by *Poetry,* 1932. Contributor of criticism to *Broom, The Dial, Poetry, The Criterion, Life and Letters Today, The Westminster Magazine, Books, Close-Up,* and other journals. Author of books of verse: *Poems* (1920), *Observations* (1924), *Selected Poems* (1935), *The Pangolin and Other Verse* (1936).

MORE, PAUL ELMER. Born: St. Louis, Mo., 1864. Educated: Washington University (B.A., 1887; M.A., 1892), Harvard University (M.A., 1893). Taught Sanscrit at Harvard, 1894-5; assistant professor of Sanscrit, Bryn Mawr College, 1895-7. Literary editor of *The Independent*, 1901; literary editor of *The New York Evening Post*, 1903; editor of *The Nation*, 1909-14; retired to Princeton in 1914; lecturer on Plato in the Department of Classics, Princeton University. Died, 1937. Author of literary essays: * *Shelburne Essays* (eleven volumes, 1904-21, the last four of which bore individual titles: *The Drift of Romanticism* [1913], *Aristocracy and Justice* [1915], *With the Wits* [1919], *A New England Group and Others* [1921]), * *The New Shelburne Essays: The Demon of the Absolute* (1928), *The Skeptical Approach to Religion* (1934), * *On Being Human* (1936); books of philosophical and religious discussion: *Nietzsche* (1912), *Platonism* (1917), *The Religion of Plato* (1921), *Hellenistic Philosophies* (1923), *The Christ of the New Testament* (1924), *Christ the Word* (1927), *The Catholic Faith* (1931); poems: *Helena* (1890); novel: *The Jessica Letters* (with Corra May Harris, 1904); biography; *Benjamin Franklin* (1900); selections: * *Selected Shelburne Essays* (1935).

PHILLIPS, WILLIAM. Born: New York City, 1907. Educated: College of the City of New York (B.A., 1928); New York University (M.A., 1930). Taught English at New York University, 1929-32. Editor of *The Partisan Review* since 1934. Contributor to *The Symposium, Dynamo, The Nation, The New Masses*. Cf. * "Categories for Criticism," *Symposium*, January 1933; "Sensibility in Modern Poetry," *Dynamo*, April 1934; "The Anatomy of Liberalism," *Partisan Review*, February 1934; * "Form and Content," *Partisan Review*, January 1935; "The Humanism of André Malraux," *Partisan Review*, June 1936. Co-author with Philip Rahv: "Recent Problems in Revolutionary Literature," in *Proletarian Literature in the United States* (1935); * "Functions of Criticism," *Partisan Review*, April 1935; * "Some Aspects of Literary Criticism," *Science and Society*, Winter 1937.

RAHV, PHILIP. Born: Kupin, Ukraine, 1908. Came to America, 1922. Educated: elementary and high school, Providence, R. I. Editor of *The Partisan Review* since 1934. Contributor to *International Literature, The New Masses, Fantasy, The Little Magazine, Poetry*. Cf. * "The Literary Class War," *New Masses*, 1932; "Henry Hazlitt and Marxist Criticism," *International Literature*, June 1934; "T. S. Eliot," *Fantasy*, Winter 1934; "Valedictory to the Propaganda Issue," *Little Magazine*, September 1934; "The Esthetic of

Migration," *Partisan Review*, April 1936. For joint writings with William Phillips, see PHILLIPS above.

RANSOM, JOHN CROWE. Born: Pulaski, Tenn., 1888. Educated: Vanderbilt University (B.A., 1909); Christ Church, Oxford (Rhodes Scholar, B.A., 1913). Member of the English faculty at Vanderbilt University since 1914; professor since 1924. Awarded a Guggenheim Fellowship in 1931. One of the founders and editors of *The Fugitive* (1922-5). Author of books of verse: *Poems about God* (1919), *Grace After Meat* (1924), *Chills and Fever* (1924), *Two Gentlemen in Bonds* (1927); and of a volume of critical prose: *God Without Thunder* (1930). Contributor to *The Virginia Quarterly Review, The Southern Review, The New Republic, The Saturday Review of Literature, The Bookman, The American Review*, and *I'll Take My Stand* (1930).

RICE, PHILIP BLAIR. Born: Martinsville, Indiana, 1904. Educated: Universities of Illinois and Indiana; Balliol College, Oxford (Rhodes Scholar). Employed in newspaper work in Paris and Cincinnati, 1928-30. Member of the Department of Philosophy, University of Cincinnati, since 1930. Contributor to *The Symposium, The Nation, Poetry*. Cf. "A Modern Poet's Technique: Guillaume Apollinaire," *Symposium*, October 1931; * "Out of the Waste Land," *Symposium*, October 1932; "Poets and the Wars," *Nation*, February 13, 1935.

SANTAYANA, GEORGE. Born: Madrid, 1863. Came to the United States in 1872. Educated: Harvard University (B.A., 1886), University of Berlin (1886-8), King's College, Cambridge University (1896-7). Teacher of philosophy at Harvard University, 1889-1912. Hyde Lecturer at the Sorbonne, 1905-6. Returned to Europe to live (England, France, Italy) in 1914. Author of books of philosophic enquiry and criticism: * *The Sense of Beauty* (1896), *Interpretations of Poetry and Religion* (1900), *The Life of Reason: Reason and Common Sense* (1905), *Reason in Society* (1905), *Reason in Religion* (1905), *Reason in Art* (1905), *Reason in Science* (1906), * *Three Philosophical Poets: Lucretius, Dante, Goethe* (1910), *Winds of Doctrine* (1913), *Egoism in German Philosophy* (1916), *Philosophical Opinion in America* (1918), * *Character and Opinion in the United States* (1920), *Soliloquies in England, and Later Soliloquies* (1922), *Skepticism and Animal Faith* (1923), *Dialogues in Limbo* (1925), *Platonism and the Spiritual Life* (1927), *The Realm of Essence* (1927), *The Realm of Matter* (1930), * *The Genteel Tradition at Bay* (1931), *Some Turns of Thought in Modern Philosophy* (1933), * *Obiter Dicta: Lectures, Essays, and Reviews* (1936); of poems:

Sonnets and Poems (1894), *Lucifer, or The Heavenly Truce* (1898; new edition, 1924), *Poems* (1922); and a novel: *The Last Puritan* (1935). Selections: *Little Essays Drawn from the Writings of George Santayana,* by Logan Pearsall Smith (1920).

SHUSTER, GEORGE N. Born: Lancaster, Wis., 1894. Educated: University of Notre Dame (B.A., 1915; M.A., 1920); University of Poitiers (1918-9); Columbia University (1924-5). Professor and Head of the Department of English, Notre Dame, 1920-4; instructor, Brooklyn Polytechnic Institute, 1924-5; Professor of English, St. Joseph's College for Women, Brooklyn, since 1924. Associate editor of *The Commonweal,* 1925-6; managing editor since 1929. War service in the Intelligence section, U. S. Army. Oberlaender Trust Fellow in Germany, 1932. Contributor to *The Bookman, The Saturday Review of Literature, The Commonweal,* and other journals. Author of *The Catholic Spirit in Modern English Literature* (1922), *Newman: Prose and Poetry* (1925), *English Literature* (1926), *The Catholic Spirit in America* (1929), *The Catholic Church and Current Literature* (1929). Other books: *The Hill of Happiness* (1926), *The Eternal Magnet* (1929), *The Germans* (1932), *Strong Man Rules* (1934), *Like a Mighty Army* (1935).

SPENCER, THEODORE. Born, 1902. Educated: Princeton University (B.A., 1923), Cambridge University, England (B.A., 1925), Harvard University (Ph.D., 1928). At present Assistant Professor of English, Harvard University. Author: *Death and Elizabethan Tragedy* (1936); poems in *Ten Introductions,* edited by Genevieve Taggard and Dudley Fitts (1935); editor: *A Garland for John Donne* (1931). Contributor to *The New Republic, The Atlantic Monthly, The Saturday Review of Literature, The Criterion.* Cf. * "The Poetry of T. S. Eliot," *Atlantic Monthly,* January 1933; "John Marston," *Criterion,* July 1934; "A Commentary on Shakespeare's *Troilus and Cressida,*" *Studies in English Literature* (Tokyo, Japan, 1936).

SPINGARN, JOEL ELIAS. Born: New York City, 1875. Educated: Columbia University (B.A., Ph.D., 1899), Harvard University (1895-6). Assistant and tutor in Comparative Literature at Columbia University, 1899-1909; professor, 1909-11. Engaged in political, military, and journalistic activities, 1911-23; a founder and adviser of Harcourt, Brace and Co., 1919-32. Author of histories and essays in criticism: *A History of Literary Criticism in the Renaissance* (1899; new edition, 1908), * *The New Criticism* (1911), * *Creative Criticism* (1917; revised and enlarged edition, 1931); of books of verse: *The New Hesperides* (1911), *Poems* (1924), *Poetry* *and Religion* (1924); of controversial pamphlets: *A Question of Academic Freedom* (1911) and *A Spingarn Enchiridion* (1929). Editor of *Critical Essays of the Seventeenth Century* (1908-9), *Temple's Essays* (1909), *A Renaissance Courtesy Book: The Galateo of Della Casa* (1914), *Goethe's Literary Essays* (1921), *Civilization in the United States* (1923), *Criticism in America* (1924), *The European Library* (1920-5).

TATE (JOHN ORLEY) ALLEN. Born: Fairfax County, Virginia, 1899. Educated: schools in Louisville and Nashville, Georgetown University, University of Virginia, Vanderbilt University (B.A., 1922). Was one of the founders and editors of *The Fugitive* (1922-5). Lecturer on English Literature, Southwestern University, Memphis, 1934-6. Southern editor of *The Hound and Horn*, 1932-4. Guggenheim Fellowship, 1928-30. Author of books of verse: *Mr. Pope and Other Poems* (1928), *Three Poems* (1930), *Poems, 1928-31* (1932), *The Mediterranean and Other Poems* (1936); of biographies: *Stonewall Jackson, The Good Soldier* (1928), *Jefferson Davis, His Rise and Fall* (1929); and of a volume of critical essays: * *Reactionary Essays on Poetry and Ideas* (1936). Contributor to *The New Republic, The Nation, The Hound and Horn, The Criterion, The Symposium, The Southern Review, The Virginia Quarterly Review, Poetry, Purpose, This Quarter, Transition, The Critique of Humanism* (1930), *I'll Take My Stand* (1930); co-editor of *Who Owns America?* (1936).

TROY, WILLIAM. Born: Chicago, 1903. Educated: Yale University (B.A., 1925), Columbia University, University of Grenoble, Sorbonne. Held an American Field Service Fellowship in France, 1929-30. Taught at University of New Hampshire and New York University; at present a member of the Department of English, Bennington College. Contributor to *The Symposium, The Nation, The New Republic, The Bookman, The New York Times Book Review*. Cf. * "Proust in Retrospect," *Symposium*, July 1931; "A Note on Gertrude Stein," *Nation*, Sept. 6, 1933; "The Romantic Agony," *Nation*, Oct. 11, 1933; "T. S. Eliot," *Nation*, April 25, 1934; "James Joyce," *Nation*, Feb. 14, 1934; * "The Critic's Job," *Nation*, Dec. 4, 1935; "On Being Contemporary," *Nation*, April 22, 1936; "The Poetry of Doom," *Nation*, October 31, 1936.

TRUEBLOOD, CHARLES K. Born: 1893. Educated: Earlham College (B.S., 1913); Haverford College (B.S., 1914); Harvard University (M.A., 1915; Ph.D., 1931). Assistant Professor of Psychology, Brown University, 1932-5. Associate, American Psychological Association. Writer on psychological subjects. Contributor of literary essays and

reviews to *The Dial* and *Poetry. Cf.* "Emily Dickinson," *The Dial,*
April 1926; "Poetic Biography," *Dial,* October 1926; "The Poetry
of Thomas Hardy," *Dial,* June 1927; * "Biography," *Dial,* August
1927; "The Education of William James," *Dial,* October 1927;
* "Criticism of Biography," *Dial,* December 1927; "The Poetry of
Concentration," *Dial,* January 1928; "A Rhetoric of Intuition," *Dial,*
May 1928; "The Art of Mr. Strachey," *Dial,* April 1929; * "Realis-
tic Biography," *Dial,* June 1929; "Edith Sitwell," *Poetry,* June 1937.
* "The Esthetics of Gerard Hopkins," *Poetry,* August 1937.

WARREN, ROBERT PENN. Born: Todd County, Kentucky, 1905. Educated:
Vanderbilt University, University of California, Yale University,
Oxford University (Rhodes Scholar). Taught English at South-
western College and Vanderbilt University; at present at Louisiana
State University. Managing Editor of *The Southern Review* since
its founding in 1935. Author: *John Brown* (1928), *Thirty-six
Poems* (1936). Contributor to the symposium *I'll Take My Stand*
(1930) and to *Who Owns America?* (1936). Contributor of re-
views and essays to *The New Republic, Virginia Quarterly Review,
The Southern Review, Poetry, The American Review.*

WILSON, EDMUND. Born: Red Bank, N. J., 1895. Educated: Hill School,
Pottstown, Pa., Princeton University (B.A., 1916). War service in
France, 1917-9. On staff of *The New York Sun,* 1919-20; managing
editor of *Vanity Fair,* 1920-1; member of the editorial board and
literary editor of *The New Republic,* 1926-31. Awarded a Guggenheim Fellowship, 1935. Contributor of criticism to *The Dial, The
New Republic, The Nation, The Atlantic Monthly, The Hound
and Horn.* Author of two books of imaginative prose: *The Under-
taker's Garland* (with John Peale Bishop, 1922) and *Discordant
Encounters* (1927); of a novel: *I Thought of Daisy* (1929); book
of verse: *Poets, Farewell!* (1929); a book of literary criticism,
* *Axel's Castle* (1931); two books of social reporting: *The American Jitters: A Year of the Slump* (1932) and *Travels in Two
Democracies* (1936); and a book of plays, *This Room and This
Gin and These Sandwiches* (1937).

WINTERS, (ARTHUR) YVOR. Born: Chicago, 1900. Educated: University
of Chicago, University of Colorado (B.A., M.A.), and Stanford University (Ph.D.). Has lived and taught school in Colorado, New
Mexico, Idaho; now member of the Department of English of
Stanford University. Contributor of criticism to *Poetry, The Hound
and Horn, The New Republic, The Dial, The American Caravan,
This Quarter.* Founded and was one of the editors of *The Gyroscope* (1929-31). Author of books of verse: *The Immobile Wind*

(1921), *The Magpie's Shadow* (1922), *The Bare Hills* (1928), *The Proof* (1930), *The Journey* (1931), *Before Disaster* (1934) and of a critical study: * *Primitivism and Decadence: A Study of American Experimental Poetry* (1937).

YOUNG, STARK. Born: Como, Miss., 1881. Educated: University of Mississippi, at the University of Mississippi (1904-7), University of Texas (1907-15), and Amherst College (1915-21). Joined staff of *The New Republic* as dramatic critic in 1921. Dramatic critic of *The New York Times,* 1924-5; associate editor of *The Theatre Arts Magazine* since 1925; an editor of *The New Republic* since 1925. Lecturer in Italy on the George Westinghouse Foundation, 1931. Author of books of critical essays: * *The Flower in Drama* (1923), *The Three Fountains* (1924), * *Glamour* (1925), *The Theatre* (1927); fiction: *Heaven Trees* (1926), *The Torches Flare* (1927), *River House* (1929), *The Street of the Islands* (1930), *So Red the Rose* (1934), *Feliciana* (1935); plays: *The Saint* (1924), *The Colonnade* (1926).